Computers and Data Processing

COMPUTERS

DATA

AND

PROCESSING

HARVEY M. DEITEL
Boston College
BARBARA DEITEL

ACADEMIC PRESS, INC.
(Harcourt Brace Jovanovich, Publishers)
Orlando San Diego San Francisco
New York London Toronto Montreal
Sydney Tokyo São Paulo

Illustration credits appear on page 623.
Trademarks appear on page 622.

Academic Press, Inc.
Orlando, Florida 32887

United Kingdom Edition Published by Academic Press, Inc.
(London) Ltd., 24/28 Oval Road, London NW1 7DX

ISBN: 0-12-209020-9
Library of Congress Catalog Card Number: 83-71919
Printed in the United States of America

Dedicated with love to
Julius and Miriam Zigman,
our children Paul and Abbey,
And in loving memory of Morris and Lena Deitel

Brief Contents

Detailed Contents

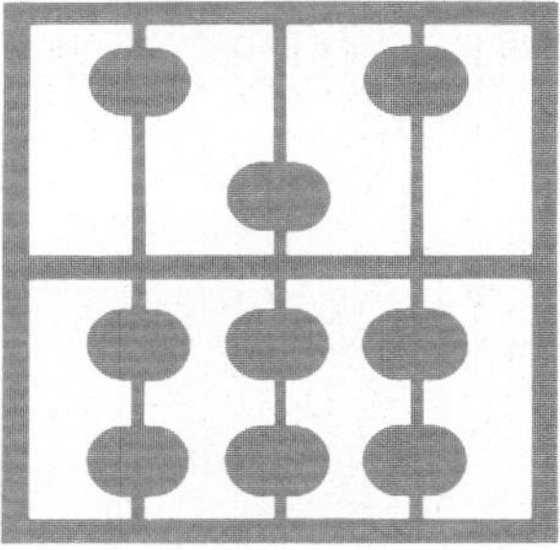

Part Two Hardware 45

3 The Processor 47

4 Input: Gateway to the Computer 73

5 Output: Getting Results from Computers 101

Enrichment Pieces

6 Secondary Storage 133

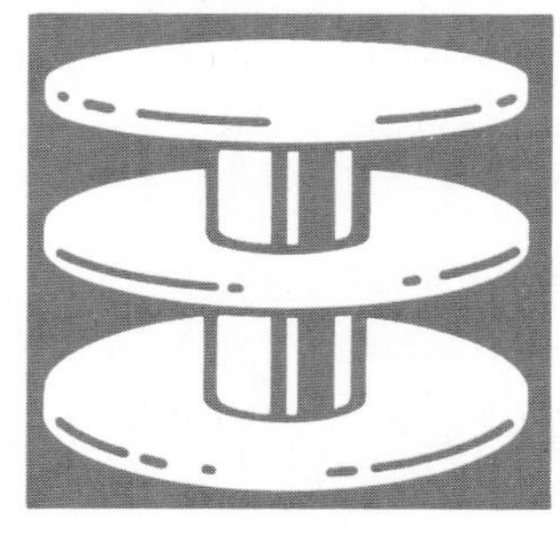

7 Data Communications 155

Part Three Software 183

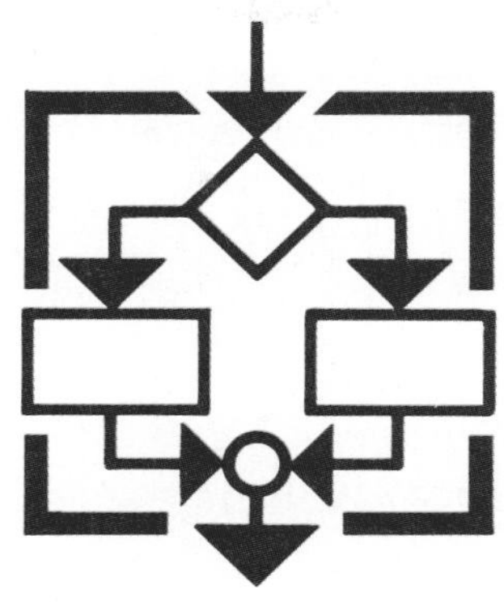

8 Structured Programming 185

9 Programming Languages 219

Enrichment Pieces

10 Structured Systems Analysis and Design; Systems Acquisition 245

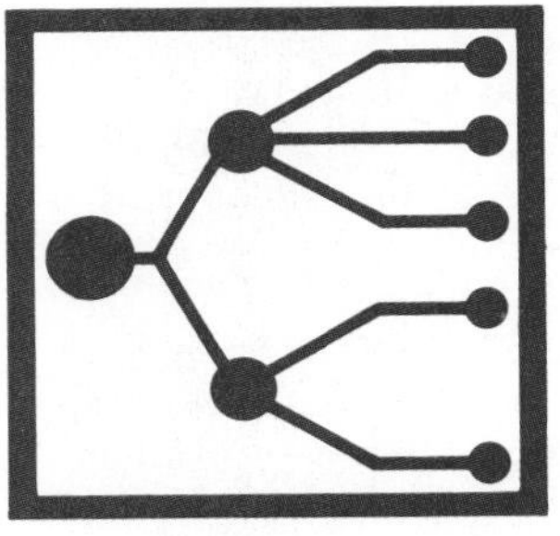

12 Operating Systems 307

Part Four Computers in Business 331

13 Personal Computing 333

Enrichment Pieces

14 Office Automation 369

Enrichment Piece

15 Electronic Funds Transfer Systems, Security, Privacy, and Computer Crime 397

Part Five Computers in Society 421

16 Robotics and Artificial Intelligence 423

Enrichment Pieces

17 Computers and Medicine 449

Enrichment Pieces

18 Computers and the Handicapped 465

Enrichment Pieces

19 Computers and Transportation 489

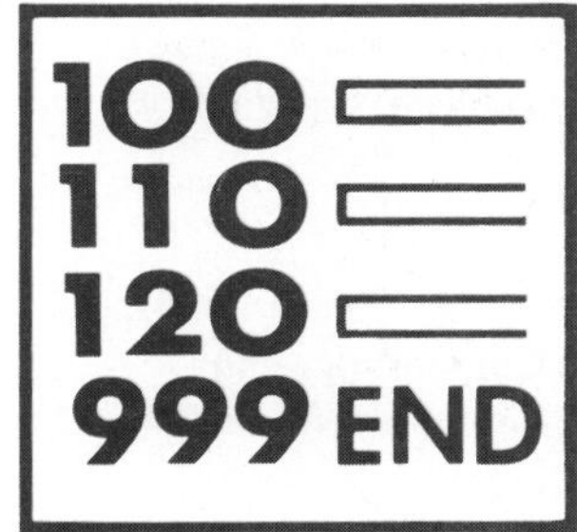
100
110
120
999 END

Appendix B Number Systems 569

Appendix C The Computing Profession 583

Preface

Computers and Data Processing is the product of one of the most ambitious research, writing, and production efforts ever undertaken in computer science publishing. Our goals were clear: make the book exciting, complete, up-to-the-minute, innovative, and visually smashing; deal with controversial issues head on, and include humor and anecdotal asides for the reader's enjoyment. The book contains one of the most dramatic and comprehensive graphics packages that has appeared in an introductory computer text.

The average person who will read this text is already well aware of the enormous impact computers are having on our personal lives and business enterprises. A familiarity with computers, how they work, and the kinds of applications they are used for is essential for living in today's increasingly complex world. This text is designed for use in a one-semester college course that introduces the basic principles of computers; it meets or exceeds the guidelines of the major professional organizations for computer literacy courses taught by departments of computer science, management, data processing, information sciences, and others.

We enjoyed writing the text; it gave us an opportunity to immerse ourselves in the most current information available in the computer field. We have read thousands of articles and communicated with hundreds of companies, organizations, and government agencies. We have met hundreds of interesting people at computer trade shows and professional conferences throughout the country, and we have had the opportunity to work with some of the leading professionals in the publishing industry. We sincerely hope you'll enjoy reading the text as well.

Features of the Text

We have loaded *Computers and Data Processing* with innovative materials in addition to presenting traditional basic computing concepts. We probe the reader's mind with challenging questions. We attack controversial issues directly.

The pictures in the text were acquired from hundreds of companies, publishers, and photographers who gave us their enthusiastic cooperation. These photographs and illustrations bring the reader right into the environments where computers are being used; the vast majority of these pictures are supplied as transparencies and color slides for projection in the classroom.

We have included a number of carefully chosen cartoons and anecdotes; our goal is not so much to get fast laughs, but rather to draw the reader's attention to important issues these pieces raise. Consider them carefully; there is much food for thought here.

We have included numerous enrichment pieces that are highlighted against color backdrops. They supplement the text, but we strongly recommend their inclusion in the required readings for the course. The material in these pieces is included in the exercises.

At this point, the reader should turn to the section titled "A Tour of the Text" on pages 8 through 17 for an overview of the book and a discussion of its unique features. This section is especially important to instructors considering the book for adoption.

For those courses that include a programming component, we have provided Chapter 8, "Structured Programming," and Appendix A, "BASIC Programming." Chapter 8 covers the general principles of developing good programs; it is written in a language-independent manner and should be covered in all courses regardless of the particular programming language being used. For courses that use BASIC, Appendix A includes a substantial treatment of the language. The Appendix is carefully divided into four modules. Module 1 presents an introduction to the language. Module 2 introduces the elements of structured programming in BASIC with six case studies covering decision making, looping, counting, totaling, averaging, and finding the largest of a series of numbers; the case studies parallel Case Studies 1 through 6 of Chapter 8. Module 3 presents the more substantial topics of single-subscripted arrays, subroutines, and program development with stubs and drivers; its three case studies parallel Cases 7 through 9 of Chapter 8. Module 4 presents a series of advanced case studies that examine the important topics of fancy print formatting, sorting, double-subscripted arrays, and using randomness to develop simulation programs.

For the Student

We have included several features to help the student master the material. Each chapter begins with an attention-getting illustration, a statement of learning objectives, a chapter outline, and one or more thought-provoking quotations. Each chapter ends with a summary and an alphabetized list of important terms. Twenty self-review exercises—10 matching and 10 fill-in-the-blanks—are included; answers for these are provided to help the student evaluate his or her progress. Ten discussion questions are included to create material for homework and class discussions. Each chapter also includes one or more suggested projects. Many of these encourage the students to perform work outside the classroom—to investigate and experience the applications and implications of computers in the society around them.

A comprehensive **Glossary** includes definitions of the 570 terms that are highlighted in the **Important Terms** sections throughout the text. An especially thorough **Index** includes page references for the approximately 1200 terms that are highlighted in boldface type in the chapters.

The student *Study Guide* is the ideal supplement for the student who wishes to reinforce his or her knowledge of the material and prepare for course examinations. For each chapter of the text the study guide states the learning objectives, includes a section titled "Taking Notes" that provides a detailed outline of the text material, and includes 60 short answer questions with answers—15 true/false, 15 multiple choice, 15 matching, and 15 fill-in-the-blanks. The student who reads the text, reads the notes, does the 20 self-review exercises in the text, and does the 60 self-review exercises in the *Study Guide* should certainly master the material.

Appendix C provides a wealth of information for people considering careers in the computer field or in closely related fields. It discusses many of the popular positions held by computing professionals, describes available educational programs, and lists the key professional organizations and certification programs. Perhaps the most valuable feature of the appendix is its presentation on how to go about searching for a job; the appendix describes how to prepare a résumé and cover letter and provides the names and addresses of more than 100 of the leading employers in the computer industry throughout the United States. College seniors should write to the personnel directors of these and other companies in the fall; many of them will send literature about careers they offer, their salary scales and benefits, and how to apply for jobs they offer.

For the Instructor

We have worked very hard to provide the instructor with valuable teaching materials to help make the classes interesting and enjoyable. We believe strongly in the value of graphics and illustrations, so we have assembled the largest support package of slides and transparencies ever used with an introductory computer science text. We have selected 100 illustrations from the text for the *Transparencies Package*, and we have chosen 270 pictures from the text for inclusion in the *Color*

Slides Package. Thus, most of the art from the text is available for projection in the classroom.

We have prepared a *Test Bank* containing examination questions and answers for each of the nineteen chapters of the text. A *Computerized Testing Service* and *Test Generation Software* are available from the publisher. The *Instructor's Manual* contains numerous teaching hints and provides answers to each of the discussion questions from the main text.

Acknowledgments

One of the pleasures of authorship is acknowledging the many people whose names may not appear on the cover but without whose efforts, cooperation, and encouragement a work of this scope could never have been completed.

We are fortunate to have been able to work with the extraordinary team of publishing professionals at Academic Press. These people had to work under the strain of tight deadlines and demanding authors to make this project happen; they did it with vigor, determination, and dedication.

Steve Dowling, President of Academic Press College Publishers, committed substantial resources to the development and production of the text and bent the rules to ensure that we received the publishing effort we wanted. Karen Bierstedt managed every phase of a complex production effort; her extraordinary management and diplomacy skills are very much responsible for making this text a reality. Lenn Holland handled the myriad of details of interfacing with the compositor, the color separator, the printer, and the binder. Janet Lowenstein skillfully edited the manuscript. Chris Martin painstakingly cleared publication permissions on the book's huge art package. Frank Soley designed the entire text, developed the art styles, and resolved the complex array of technical problems associated with producing a full-color textbook. Sandy Pouliot dummied the book; she fit the pieces of the text and illustrations puzzle together to create a visually pleasing and pedagogically sound presentation. We are grateful to John Parker, Academic Press's ever present representative in the Boston area, for making the contact that initiated this publishing effort.

Dale Brown, our computer science editor, provided many valuable suggestions that helped shape the final product, and he recruited and supervised a demanding and insightful team of reviewers. These people scrutinized every word, every illustration, and every aspect of the pedagogy of the text. They provided innumerable suggestions that helped refine the manuscript in ways we could never have achieved on our own. We are very pleased to acknowledge their efforts:

Darrell Abney, Nashville Technical Institute
Julian Andersen, Shoreline Community College
Russell Blankenfeld, Rochester Community College
Kolman Brand, Nassau Community College
Michael Capsuto, Cypress College
John Carroll, San Diego State University
Laura Cooper, College of Mainland
Van Cunningham, American Technical University
Wil Dershimer, Seminole Community College
Joe Evans, Southwest Missouri State College
Judie Gammage, El Centro College
Homer Gerber, University of Central Florida
Gilbert Ghez, Roosevelt University
Carla Hall, Florissant Valley Community College
Don Henderson, Western Kentucky University
Robert Lacey, Valencia Community College
Joseph McMenamin, Grossmont Community College
Stephen Mansfield, McHenry Community College
J. Hayden Mathews, Murray State College
Amanda Meredith, Florida Junior College
Cathie Norris, North Texas State University
Curtis Rawson, Kirkwood Community College
Paul Ross, Millersville State University
Alan Schwartz, University of Missouri-St. Louis
Earl Talbert, Central Piedmont Community College
E. M. Teagarden, Dakota State College
James R. Walters, Pikes Peak Community College
Judith Wilson, University of Cincinnati
David Whitney, San Francisco State University

We would also like to thank Fr. J. Donald Monan, S. J., President of Boston College;

Fr. Joseph Fahey, S. J., Academic Vice President; Dean John Neuhauser of the School of Management; and Professors Peter Kugel, James Gips, Peter Olivieri, and Richard Maffei for their friendship and encouragement, and for creating an environment in which this writing effort could thrive.

We hope you'll enjoy reading our text. We would greatly appreciate your comments and criticisms addressed to:

Harvey and Barbara Deitel
c/o Computer Science Editor
Academic Press, Inc.
Orlando, FL 32887

We will respond to all correspondence immediately.

Computers and Data Processing

Chapter 1. The Information Revolution

Chapter 2. The Evolution of Computers

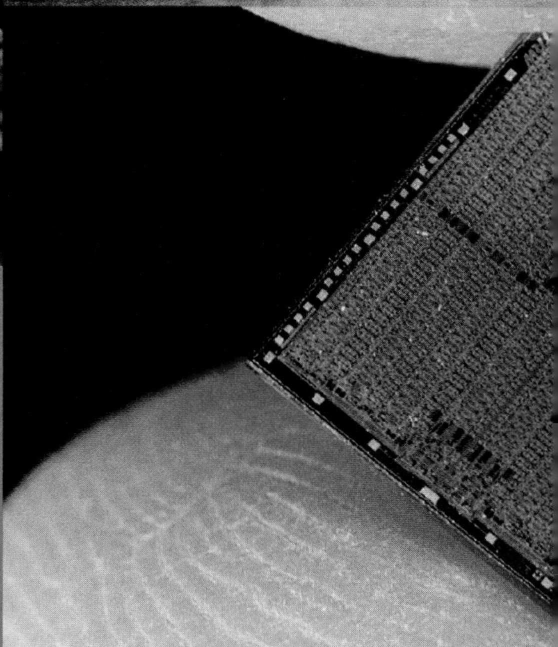

Part One

Introduction

Today, thousands of humans desperately lie waiting for tissue-matched organs to become available for life-saving organ transplants; tomorrow economical computerized artificial organs may be manufactured in minutes to a patient's specifications. Our ancestors worked 80- to 100-hour weeks under generally poor working conditions; with tireless computerized robots providing food, clothing, and shelter, it may become possible for future generations to work one- or two-day work weeks or not to have to work at all. With the application of computers to medicine, a person born a few hundred years from now might conceivably expect to live twice as long as someone born today. Thirty years ago computers could play chess about as well as human novices; within the next several decades, a computer is almost certain to capture the world chess championship. Today, if we want a fact we might have to spend hours or days tracking it down; in a few decades the vast majority of facts known to humankind may be accessible to us in seconds from our personal computers. All these developments may come about because of computers—machines that process huge amounts of information at staggering speeds. Part One of this book introduces some fundamental computer concepts, overviews the text, and gives a concise account of the evolution of the modern computer.

Chapter 1

The Information Revolution

After reading this chapter you will understand:

1. What the Information Revolution is and how it is affecting our lives
2. Why it is important to study computers
3. Some of the key benefits of using computers
4. Some of the dangers of increasing our dependency on computers
5. How this text is organized

Left: The New York Stock Exchange makes extensive use of computers to keep up with today's huge trading volumes that sometimes reach 40 million shares per hour.

Outline

What networks of railroads, highways and canals were in another age, networks of telecommunications, information and computerization . . . are today.

Bruno Kreisky, Austrian Chancellor

We are reaching the stage where the problems we must solve are going to become insoluble without computers. I do not fear computers. I fear the lack of them.

Isaac Asimov

Introducing the Computer

We are in the midst of what is commonly called the **Information Revolution**, a period of change that may prove as significant to our lives as the Industrial Revolution was to our ancestors. Computer technology is at the root of this change, and continuing advancements in that technology seem to ensure that this revolution will touch all our lives. We can only begin to guess the effects of the Information Revolution, but we can be certain that living through the revolution in the 1980s and 1990s will be exciting and challenging.

The machines of the 1800s, which triggered the Industrial Revolution, helped workers extend their muscle power. Most machines assist us in this way. Cars, for example, let us travel farther in less time than we can by foot or horse; typewriters enable us to write with less strain than we can by hand. Computers, however, are unique machines in that they help us extend our brain power. Their capabilities make it possible for us to do in hours what might otherwise take days (such as projecting sales or balancing a budget) and to work other problems we probably could not otherwise handle. We can now manage our personal lives and business enterprises with the useful information computers generate, and we can have that information sooner than if we were to try to create it ourselves. Computers help us tackle difficult personal and business decisions with greater assurance that the consequences of the decisions have been carefully anticipated.

At the beginning of this century the most common occupation in the United States was farming; today it is information handling. Ours has become an information-based society, and we depend on computers to help us handle this information. Computers, unknown to the masses as recently as a decade ago, have now become a common fixture in many homes, classrooms, and small businesses. In the 1940s computers were scarce. In the late 1980s computers will be in most homes and businesses, in automobiles, toys, and appliances.

Businesses are becoming so dependent on computers that in a few years it may be difficult to get a job as an office clerk without having some computer expertise. Computerized robots are already replacing blue-collar workers on assembly lines (Figure 1–1); eventually they may be able to replace white-collar workers as well. Students are being prepared for these changes. But what about people already in industry? Will they be able to adapt as their environments become more heavily computerized? As you will see throughout this book, the impact computers have and will have

Figure 1–1 These computer-controlled robots weld car bodies ten times faster than humans and with much greater accuracy.

on society provokes many serious questions. You will be frequently asked to consider carefully the consequences of computer technology.

Within the next decade computers could become the world's largest industry, displacing both the automobile and oil industries. It has been forecast that International Business Machines Corporation (IBM), one of the foremost manufacturers of computers, could become the world's largest company by the year 2000.

Why are computers becoming so popular? Simply put, they are becoming financially accessible and both useful and attractive to more people. As recently as the late 1950s most computers filled entire rooms and cost hundreds of thousands, even millions, of dollars. Today **microprocessors** (Figure 1–2), tiny computers etched onto thin slivers of silicon called **silicon chips**, may be purchased for a few dollars apiece. There is every reason to believe that in a few years the cost of these microprocessors will be so negligible that computing will be almost free. Certainly this will dramatically change our lives.

People are coming into contact with computers daily. These machines, once thought mysterious, are now being used routinely as more and more people are beginning to realize that computers are merely devices that follow sets of instructions, called **computer programs** or **software**, that have been written by **computer programmers**.

People are finding that the instructions computers follow help to simplify their own lives. Programs may instruct a computer to perform such functions as totaling a store's cash receipts or preparing a company's payroll, customer statements, or tax returns. They may instruct a computer to perform such varied tasks as computing missile trajectories or controlling a robot arm to weld car bodies. They may instruct a traffic control computer when to change traffic lights or an air traffic control computer how to determine whether two planes are on a collision course.

"The computer is down! Everybody think!"

©Creative Computing

Many people would be surprised to discover that they already own several computers, most likely in the form of microprocessor chips embedded in digital clocks, digital watches, TV sets, home video games, microwave ovens, and automobiles. Home appliances already contain talking computers that warn if the washing machine is overloaded or the dishwasher needs more soap.

The power of the prohibitively expensive "giant brains" of a few years ago is now available

Figure 1–2 The microprocessor chip shown here is as powerful as the room-size computers of a few decades ago.

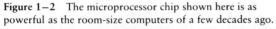

Figure 1–3 The IBM Personal Computer is one of the best-selling personal computer systems in the world.

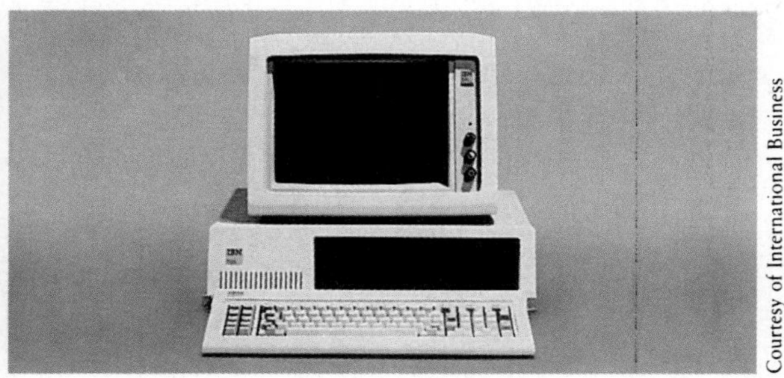

Courtesy of International Business Machines Corporation

in desktop **personal computers** (Figure 1–3) that cost only from a few hundred to a few thousand dollars. School systems are under tremendous pressure from parents and students alike to increase the use of personal computers and offer more computer courses. Small businesses are already finding it difficult to remain competitive without using computers to assist in such office procedures as preparing payroll, taking inventory, billing customers, and budgeting.

Computers may also be instructed to assist in creating new products. The production and distribution of this textbook was itself highly computerized. The text was written on a word processor (see Chapter 14; see "A Tour of the Text" for more detailed information on this book), and later typeset on a computerized photocomposition system. The photographs and color in the diagrams were processed and prepared with computerized laser-scanning systems (see Chapter 5). In marketing research for this book, computers were used to compile the results of a detailed survey of more than a thousand professors teaching introductory computer courses. Computers scanned lists of faculty members to determine which instructors might be interested in receiving examination copies of the text.

Computers have become so useful in so many areas of life that they have become indispensable to many people. Computers have become a part of our lives.

The Benefits

You may agree that computers are becoming a more important part of our lives but still wonder: Why invest a great deal of time and effort to consider this technology? Part of the answer is that computers are everywhere around us in our personal lives and in our business enterprises. They are one of the most significant technologies that will influence our future.

More importantly, studying how computers work will help you learn how they can help you extend your thought processes. If you want to reap the benefits of most other machines, you need only know how to operate them. You can benefit from a car by driving one, even if you don't understand how it works. Computers operate differently, however. They are problem-solving tools. To benefit from a computer, you must be able to ask the right question about the problem and to manipulate the information correctly to reach an answer. To do that, you must understand the technology.

Once understood and programmed correctly, computers can be used to make life more convenient, more enjoyable, and more rewarding. They can enrich every facet of life. They are fun to use and can help reduce tedious work. They can be used to improve the lives of disadvantaged and handicapped people, facilitate major breakthroughs in medicine, increase leisure time, speed the pace of education, help make businesses more profitable, improve communication, make transportation smoother, safer, and faster, help save energy and conserve other valuable natural resources, help reduce crime, control the cost of government, and extend explorations in outer space. Surely any technology that offers such significant benefits is worth studying!

The Dangers

Although computers can help us improve the quality of our lives, many people consider them potentially dangerous. They fear that computers could be the greatest boon to those who would invade our privacy or wage war against us. Others wonder if computers will relegate us to pushing buttons, thus destroying the incentive to achieve. Some people fear that massive unemployment will result as machines displace workers. They wonder if our computer-controlled weapons of destruction will become so complex that we might lose control of them and cause an accidental nuclear war. Might a poorly designed computer system cause the life support system of an intensive care patient to fail? Will the personal touch disappear? Will society be divided into the "computer-haves" and the "computer-have-nots"? An understanding of computer logic will help to dispel many of these fears.

"They'll never replace Thorndike, there, with a computer . . . because nobody knows what he does."

Figure 1–4 The "help" key is one of the most important keys on today's computer keyboards. The user may press it at any time to receive useful information about how to proceed. Providing assistance in this manner makes computers more user-friendly.

Looking to the Future

Despite the fear of computers some people have, most people are somehow involved in the Information Revolution and, therefore, with computers. Although the inflation of the 1970s and early 1980s hit many industries, the costs of computing have been decreasing rather than increasing—in fact, decreasing dramatically. Many people even delay purchasing computers because they hope that the prices will decline even further. Computing costs can be expected to decline to the point that we may soon be able to afford all the computer power we could possibly use, so that almost any imaginable application of computers may be attempted. Similarly, the costs of data communications will also continue declining as transmission capacities increase. Therefore, we will be able to transmit huge amounts of information between computers at great speed and nominal cost.

We can also expect the base of potential computer users and applications to continue to broaden, creating new computing careers and new benefits from computers. This extension of computer use is already evident in the growing interest in purchasing home computers. In fact, as people use computers successfully, they continue to give computers more to do. If computers malfunctioned regularly or if their costs were too high, people would avoid using them. But the experience with computers has been a positive one. It seems as though there is an "applications spiral," with an ever-increasing range of applications being attempted.

Perhaps this growth in the number of users is a result of the important trend toward creating systems that are **user-friendly** (Figure 1–4), that is, systems that can be easily used by untrained people. The really big breakthroughs in this area will not come until the late 1980s and early 1990s. For example, personal computers may already be economical enough for many people to own, but they are still very unfriendly devices. Speech synthesis and speech recognition may help solve this problem as computers converse with their users in everyday English.

Lastly, laser technology will greatly affect the course of computing over the next several decades. A **laser** is a device that creates an intense beam of monochromatic (one-color) light (Figure 1–5). The text contains many in-depth explanations of how the special properties of laser beams are used in today's computers and data communications systems. It has been forecast that by the year 2000 today's electronic computers will be replaced by laser-driven "optical computers."

Will the world be a better place as a result of the Information Revolution, or just a different place? Certainly it will be different. We can help ensure that it becomes a better place by carefully studying computers, examining the many controversial issues raised about them, and devoting careful thought to planning computer applications.

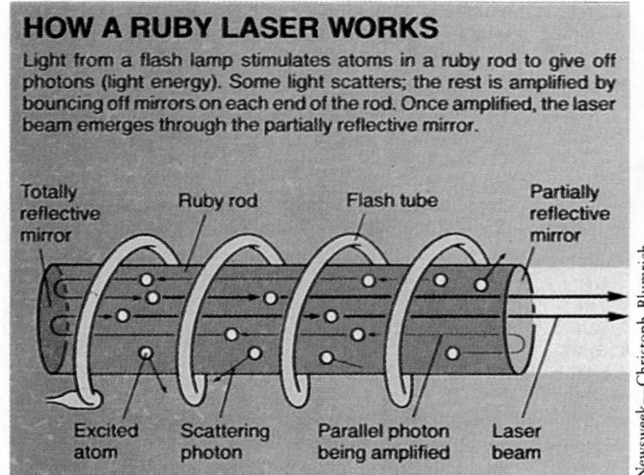
HOW A RUBY LASER WORKS
Light from a flash lamp stimulates atoms in a ruby rod to give off photons (light energy). Some light scatters; the rest is amplified by bouncing off mirrors on each end of the rod. Once amplified, the laser beam emerges through the partially reflective mirror.
Totally reflective mirror
Ruby rod
Flash tube
Partially reflective mirror
Excited atom
Scattering photon
Parallel photon being amplified
Laser beam
Newsweek—Christoph Blumrich

Figure 1–5 How a laser works.

"I still miss the days when we just read the letters and made a list."

A Tour of the Text

Computers and Data Processing is divided into five major sections and three appendices (Figure 1). Each section consists of several related chapters.

Part I of the text provides an informal introduction to the computer field. Chapter 1 introduces some basic computing concepts and overviews the text. Chapter 2 traces the evolution of modern computing systems from the earliest mechanical calculating devices to today's microchips. The history of the field is divided into four distinct "generations," each defined by major innovations in electronics technology. The fifth generation, expected to appear about 1990, is discussed.

Part II of the text introduces computer **hardware**, the actual computing equipment. Chapter 3, "The Processor," discusses the so-called brain of the computer. The chapter contains two special sections, one describing the manufacture of microprocessor computers and the other the physical operation of computers. It concludes with a discussion of biochips and how they make "living computers" possible.

The many ways in which data may be entered into computers is considered in Chapter 4, "Input: Gateway to the Computer." Today we enter most information into computers on typewriterlike keyboards (Figure 2), but more user-friendly input methods are becoming popular, including **touch sensing**, in which the user simply touches a symbol on a display screen (Figure 3), and **speech recognition**, in which the computer recognizes spoken commands. Various input devices that automatically read markings on paper are also discussed (Figure 4).

Chapter 5, "Output: Getting Results from the Computer" examines how computers present their results, or **outputs**. The chapter considers the more popular types of printers that produce output on paper and focuses on **laser printing**, the printing technology of the future, in which intense beams of light are used to draw letters, digits, and even pictures. Also included is an explanation of how computer-controlled lasers may be used to realize three-dimensional television by a technique called **laser holography**. The operation of display screen terminals is discussed. Computerized speech generation, called **speech synthesis**, is explained in detail, with an in-depth treatment of phoneme coding. The operation of computer output microfilm devices is considered, as is **computer graphics**, the computerized preparation and processing of pictures. The use of computers in the Shroud of Turin controversy is examined—bringing together the ancient and the modern.

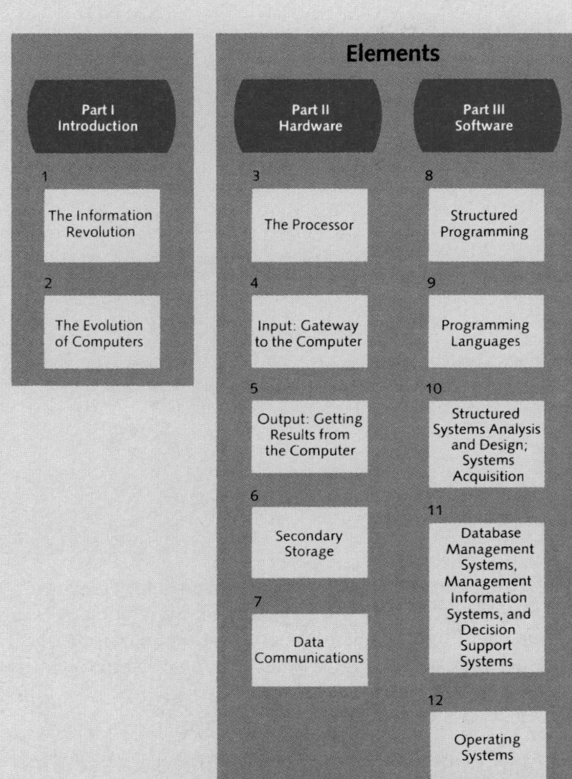

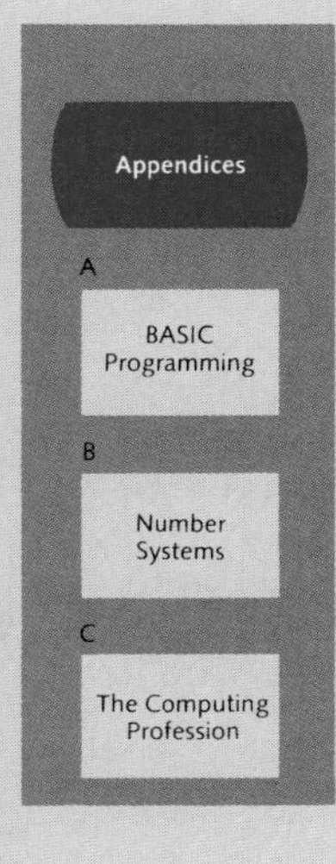

Figure 1 *Above*: The structure of this text.

Figure 2 *Right*: In addition to the normal keys on conventional typewriter keyboards, computer keyboards often contain many special-purpose keys.

Figure 3 *Below*: With touch sensing the user enters data into the computer by touching a word or a symbol on the display screen.

Figure 4 *Below right*: The bar-coded information on this package identifies the manufacturer and the product. This information is read by using laser beams that form the "netting" of red light in the picture.

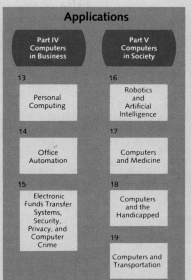

Courtesy of International Business Machines Corporation

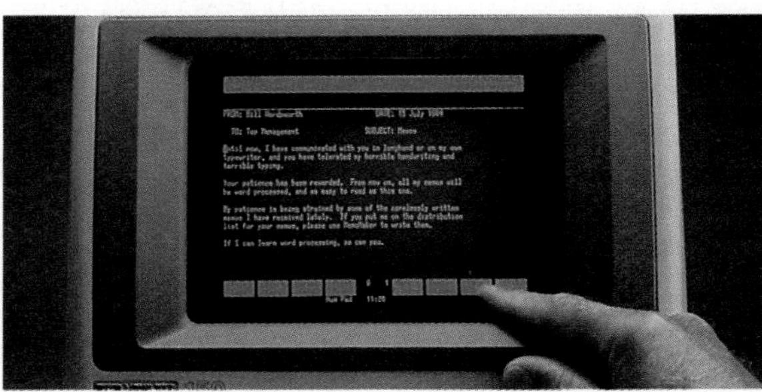

Courtesy of International Business Machines Corporation

RON MORGAN
"OK, OK, I believe you."

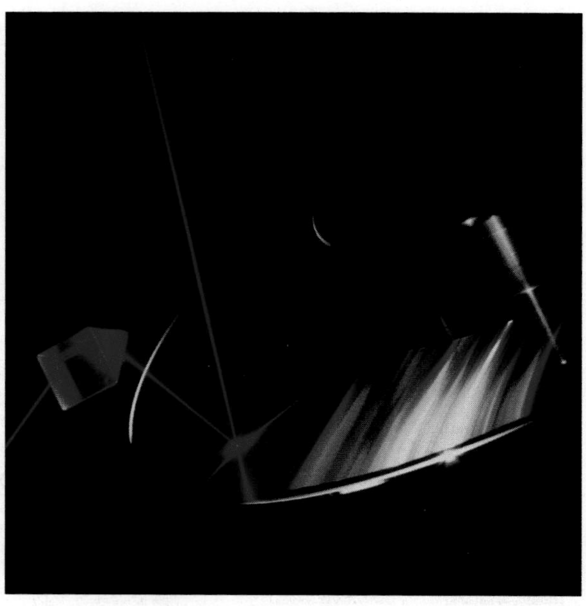

Figure 5 Today's optical disks are designed for permanent, nonerasable storage of huge amounts of information. A laser beam literally burns the information into the surface of the disk forming microscopic pits in the surface. The pits are then read by another laser beam.

Chapter 6, "Secondary Storage," considers the storage and retrieval of massive amounts of computer-accessible information from **secondary storage** devices such as magnetic tape and magnetic disks. The operation of floppy disks and large-capacity Winchester disks, now so popular on personal computers, is discussed, and the relative speeds and capacities of these devices are compared. The chapter concludes with a discussion of the use of lasers with optical disks, one of the newer secondary storage technologies (Figure 5).

The movement of data between computer systems is examined in Chapter 7, "Data Communications." The chapter covers the components and operation of typical **data communications** systems, the various types of communications networks, and communications via space satellites (Figure 6). It examines issues of security and privacy and discusses problems raised by **transborder data flow**, the transmission of information across international borders. Once again the focus is on lasers in an in-depth discussion of **fiber optics**, the communications cable technology of the future in which beams of laser light are transmitted over glass "wires" (Figure 7).

Part III of the text deals with software, or computer programs, the sets of instructions that programmers write to inform the computer how to solve particular problems. Chapter 8, "Structured Programming," presents a general discussion of program design principles. The discussion is independent of any particular programming language. **Structured flowcharting** and **pseudocode**, state-of-the-practice techniques that foster the development of high-quality computer programs, are explored. The chapter presents a detailed discussion of the chief programmer team concept that has proved so successful in the development of small- and medium-size software systems. Nine case studies are included to illustrate the use of structured flowcharting and pseudocode in structured program development.

Chapter 9, "Programming Languages," considers the various important **programming languages** that are commonly used. The chapter traces the evolution of programming languages from the tedious machine languages of the 1940s to the convenient English-like query languages of the 1980s. A survey of the most important and popular programming languages is presented, including BASIC (discussed in detail in Appendix A), FORTRAN, COBOL, PL/1, RPG, APL, Pascal, C, Ada, Forth, LISP, and LOGO.

Figure 6 Huge antennas like these transmit information to and receive information from space satellites in stationary orbit 22,300 miles above the earth. They make around-the-world communications as convenient as telephoning someone in a nearby town.

Figure 7 Fiber optic cable made from extremely pure glass can actually bend beams of laser light.

Chapter 10, "Structured Systems Analysis and Design" discusses the development, installation, evaluation, and control of computer systems. The chapter is particularly relevant for people who are likely to develop their own computer-based systems or who work in organizations in which computer systems development is an ongoing activity. For others, several popular means for acquiring systems from various types of systems suppliers are discussed. The chapter ends with a detailed case study using the state-of-the-practice techniques of structured systems analysis and structured systems design to develop a computerized reservations system for a car rental agency.

Certain computer applications systems are particularly useful to businesses and organizations. Chapter 11, "Database Management Systems, Decision Support Systems, and Management Information Systems," discusses these systems. **Database management systems** (DBMS) control the secure storage and accessing of the large amounts of information that businesses must process. The chapter discusses the major types of database management systems and includes a case study on the type receiving the most attention today—the relational DBMS. It also discusses **management information systems** (MIS), computerized systems that on a regular schedule provide managers with the information they need to perform their key tasks of planning, organizing, directing, and controlling. A detailed case study considers nine of the key computer systems that constitute a major portion of most management information systems. The chapter proceeds with a discussion of **decision support systems** (DSS), "interactive" computer-based systems that support management decision-making activities. They are especially useful in support of the planning function. Two particularly valuable case studies on DSS are included. The first introduces the notion of "electronic worksheets" — the most successful software products of all time and the ones that brought DSS systems to the attention of personal computer users (Figure 8). The second case study provides a detailed look at decision support in a typical business planning situation. A mathematical model of a business is created and solved in several interesting ways to yield useful information to support management decision making.

Operating systems are the software systems that manage the computer's hardware and make it more "friendly" and usable to computer users. Chapter 12, "Operating Systems," considers the functions and capabilities of such systems. It illustrates why multiuser operating systems are so much more complex than single-user systems. It briefly introduces some of today's most popular personal computer operating systems, including the UNIX system developed by Bell Laboratories and the XENIX and MS-DOS systems developed by Microsoft. MS-DOS is supplied as PC-DOS with the IBM Personal Computer (often called simply the PC). A detailed case study on CP/M, a widely used personal computer operating system, is provided.

Parts IV and V of the text contain seven major

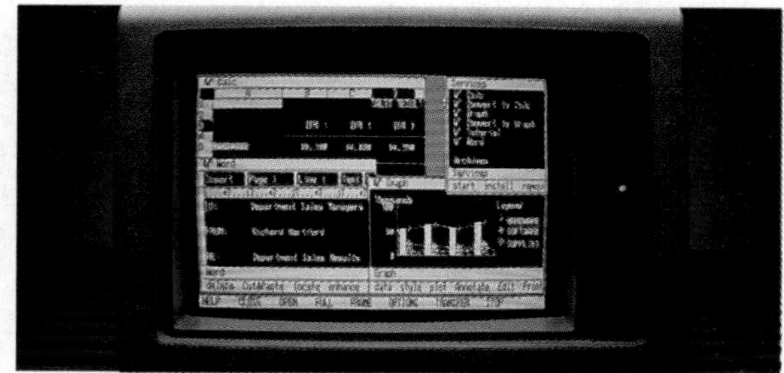

Figure 8 VisiOn Calc (Trademark of VisiCorp) converts the screen of a personal computer into an "electronic worksheet." With this particular version, the user may place information in as many as 63 columns across and 254 rows down. VisiOn Calc is especially useful in financial planning and budgeting applications.

Figure 9 This "credit card calculator" contains a microprocessor chip, a keyboard, and a display screen. It doesn't even need a battery; it runs on solar power.

applications chapters that describe exciting computer applications. Part IV considers the use of computers in business.

The personal computer, made possible by the tiny and economical microprocessor, is reshaping the computer industry and our society as well. The microprocessor is so economical that it has become possible to build powerful personal computers for less than a hundred dollars and extremely powerful systems that rival the capabilities of the million-dollar systems of a few years ago for only a few thousand dollars. Even "credit card" computers have become available (Figure 9). Now small businesses and individuals may have their own computers at their disposal 24 hours a day.

Chapter 13, "Personal Computing," traces the evolution of personal computing and includes detailed case studies on two of the most important personal computers for the 1980s—the IBM Personal Computer and Apple's Macintosh. The capabilities and services of a typical computer retail store and how to buy or lease a personal computer are considered. The use of home computers in our daily lives is discussed: how they can help to save energy, plan nutritious meals, balance checkbooks, maintain home budgets, and remind us about important appointments. A case study on the Viewtron videotex service is presented—we'll see how Viewtron combines computers and communications to bring a world of information into people's homes. The chapter also looks at portable computers, transportables, and so-called notebook computers (Figure 10).

Figure 10 This "notebook" computer weighs only 3 pounds and is small enough to slip into a briefcase with plenty of room to spare.

Chapter 14, "Office Automation," discusses the use of computers and communications in automating information-processing functions in offices. Today's automated offices feature computer work stations at every desk (Figure 11); these are tied together with local communications networks within the office and "long haul" networks between cities. The chapter examines **word processing** (computerized text manipulation), a leading technology in **office automation**, and other key office automation technologies, including electronic mail, facsimile (picture) transmission, voice mail, teleconferencing, and the electronic blackboard. An extremely detailed case study on word processing with Apple's Macintosh personal computer is presented. The chapter concludes with a forecast of future directions in office automation.

Figure 11 Computer work stations at every desk are common fixtures in today's automated offices.

The possible uses of computer technology present us with critical issues of security, privacy, and crime. Chapter 15, "Electronic Funds Transfer Systems, Security, Privacy, and Computer Crime," begins to examine some of these intriguing social issues. The chapter looks into **electronic funds transfer** (EFT), the storage and movement of our money as electronic signals (Figure 12). Privacy and social issues raised by EFT are examined, and the chapter summarizes important legislation and regulations for protecting our rights. The chapter discusses computer crimes and measures that can be taken to prevent them.

Part V deals with computers in society. Chapter 16, "Robotics and Artificial Intelligence," consid-

Figure 12 Automated teller machines like this are already handling huge volumes of transactions that used to require human tellers. These computerized machines have greatly reduced the cost per transaction, and they are available to customers 24 hours a day.

Figure 13 The Grand Master™ chess computer made by Milton Bradley can play at any of 12 skill levels, tell you which is your best move, and even play against itself. It uses a hidden magnetic system to move the pieces.

ers the intriguing and highly controversial areas of **artificial intelligence** and **robotics**. Can computers think? Can they reason effectively in unfamiliar situations? Can they make value judgments and plot strategies? The notion of **intelligent computers** is one that many people absolutely refuse to accept, but we can and are building computers that *appear* to exhibit intelligent behavior. This in itself is highly controversial, and the chapter raises many of the controversial issues. Chess-playing computers (Figure 13), which are on the brink of beating the world's best human chess players, are examined.

Expert systems computer systems that function at the levels of human experts in various fields, are investigated. Expert systems are designed to contain the cumulative knowledge and even the rules of thumb of a given field. Researchers have already produced expert medical diagnosis systems and expert prospecting systems that pinpoint valuable mineral deposits.

Robots, known as steel-collar workers, are considered, including their programming and operation, and important advances in the development of robot senses. Researchers are creating robots that will have some senses that humans lack, such as infrared vision for seeing in the dark. Scientists are also on the verge of creating the intelligent anthropomorphic (humanlike) robots we have been reading about for so many years in science fiction (Figure 14). Fears some people have about this technology are discussed. Will these robots cause massive unemployment and destroy our economy? Will they be so productive that the human work ethic will disappear as robots provide abundant food and material wealth, and people focus their attention on other issues? Is it possible that robots may eventually dominate humankind? This chapter distinguishes science from science fiction.

Chapter 17, "Computers and Medicine," discusses the many exciting ways in which computers are now being used and will be used in the future in medical applications (Figure 15), such as computerized diagnosis expert systems that are already "outperforming" doctors, computerized scanning systems that can "see" inside a patient without the need for exploratory surgery, and tiny microprocessors that control implantable devices

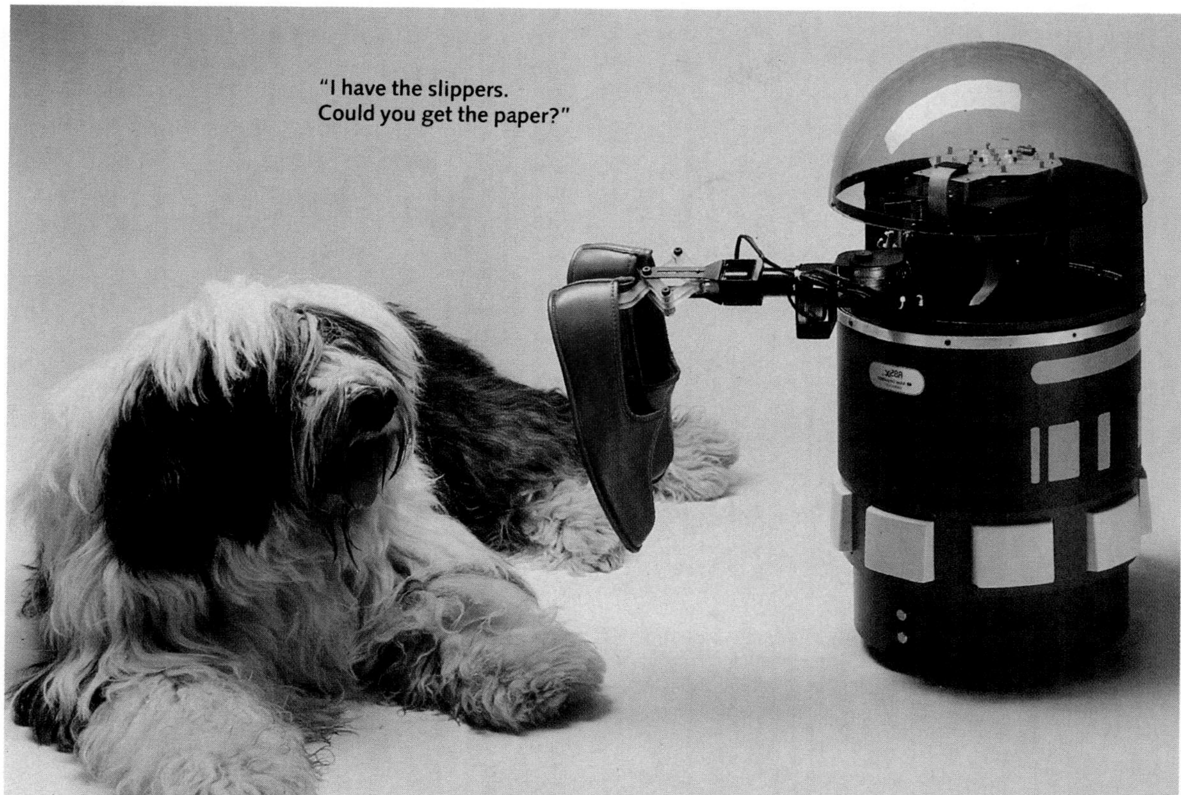

"I have the slippers.
Could you get the paper?"

Figure 14 *Above*: The RB5X Intelligent Robot™ comes with sonar and tactile sensors that enable it to detect and avoid obstacles. It can be programmed to vacuum around the house, lift small objects, carry messages, and even sense and extinguish small fires.

Figure 15 *Below*: This composite portrait was made by angiography, an exciting medical diagnosis tool in which a fluid that is opaque to X rays is injected into the bloodstream.

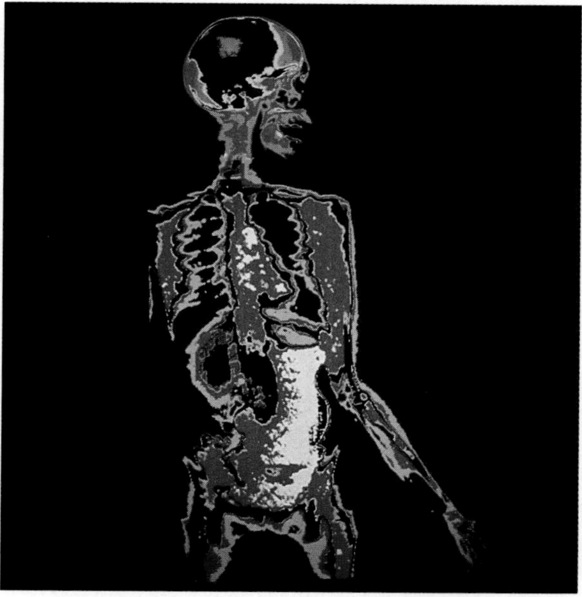

such as heart pacemakers and insulin dispensers for diabetes patients.

Chapter 18, "Computers and the Handicapped," discusses the ways in which computers can be used to assist people with physical handicaps. In this regard, the microprocessor may well be the most important technological breakthrough of the twentieth century. How will computers help solve the many problems faced by handicapped people in their personal lives and business careers? Will computers help eliminate certain handicaps completely? Might they actually create new ones? The chapter considers how computers are being used to help the blind, the deaf, the nonvocal, and the paralyzed. The chapter mentions dozens of de-

Figure 16 Professor Jerrold Petrofsky of Wright State University in Dayton, Ohio, uses computer-controlled stimulation of leg muscles to help this paralyzed patient move her legs. This research may make it possible for people with certain types of paralysis to walk comfortably. Commercial products based upon these techniques could become available in the 1990s if all goes well.

vices and techniques and focuses on the exciting Kurzweil Reading Machine for the blind, a computerized device that uses optical-scanning techniques to input text directly from a book and then reads the book aloud using computer-generated synthetic speech. Computerized "bionic" arms, legs, and hands are helping amputees lead more normal lives. But perhaps most exciting are the discussions of how researchers are using computers in efforts to restore sight to the blind, hearing to the deaf, and mobility to the paralyzed (Figure 16).

Chapter 19, "Computers and Transportation," discusses the use of computers in today's transportation systems and the ways in which they make possible future innovations in transportation (Figure 17). Computers are becoming more and more important to transportation, improving fuel efficiency, reducing dangerous exhaust emissions, detecting and reporting malfunctions, enforcing secure entry to vehicles, helping commuters arrange car pools, synchronizing traffic lights to en-

Figure 17 The Personal Rapid Transit System, designed by J. Edward Anderson of the University of Minnesota, could soon become reality. The computer-controlled cars automatically guide riders to destinations the riders specify when they pay their fare. The system automatically sends empty cars to the stations most likely to need them.

sure smooth traffic flow, helping to dispatch road service vehicles, and controlling driving simulators used in driver education courses. They are also used in air, rail, and ocean travel.

The text includes three appendices. Appendix A is a complete minicourse on the **BASIC programming language**. The discussion is carefully keyed to the case studies on structured programming in Chapter 8. After studying this appendix, the reader should be able to write and understand useful BASIC programs quickly and easily. To take maximum advantage of this portion of the text, the reader should have access to a computer system. All programs should be entered and tested on the computer.

Appendix B explains the principles of the various number systems that are useful in the study of computers, the most important of which is the **binary number system**, also called the **base two number system**, in which all numbers are expressed as combinations of zeros and ones (Figure 18).

Appendix C on the computing profession has been included for the reader considering a career in the field.

Decimal Number	Binary Number
0	0
1	1
2	10
3	11
4	100
5	101
6	110
7	111
8	1000
9	1001
10	1010
100	1100100
1000	1111101000

Figure 18 Selected decimal numbers and their binary equivalents.

Summary 

1. The most common occupation today is information handling.
2. By the late 1980s computers will be found in most homes, classrooms, and businesses, as well as in automobiles, and appliances.
3. In the late 1950s computers cost hundreds of thousands, or even millions, of dollars. Today, tiny microprocessor computers cost a few dollars apiece.
4. Computerized robots are already replacing blue-collar workers; they may soon be replacing white-collar workers as well.
5. Personal computers are allowing more people to come in contact with computers.
6. Computers may soon become the world's largest industry.
7. The microprocessor "computer on a chip" is placing computing power at our fingertips.
8. Data communications is the movement of data between computer systems.
9. Computers can reduce tedious work, hasten major breakthroughs in medicine, give people more leisure time, speed education, make businesses more profitable, improve communications, help transport people faster and more safely, help reduce crime, and help control the cost of government.
10. Computers are helping the handicapped to become more self-sufficient and compete effectively in the job marketplace.

11. The fields of robotics and artificial intelligence have combined to create robots that walk, talk, and understand humans. Many people fear there may soon be robots that are smarter than humans.

12. As computers become more user-friendly, many more people will take advantage of the benefits they have to offer.

13. Computerized speech synthesis and speech recognition enable computers to carry on conversations with humans.

14. Laser technology will greatly affect computing in the next several decades.

15. Communications networks are opening up a world of information to people with personal computers.

Important Terms 

artificial intelligence
BASIC programming language
base two number system
binary number system
computer program
computer programmer
data communications
expert systems
fiber optics
hardware
Information Revolution
intelligent computer
laser
management information systems (MIS)
microprocessor
office automation
operating systems
output
personal computer
programming language
pseudocode
robotics
secondary storage
silicon chip
software
speech recognition
speech synthesis
touch sensing
user-friendly
word processing

Self-Review Exercises 

Matching

Next to the term in column A, place the letter of the statement in column B that best describes it.

Column A

1. Hardware
2. Secondary storage
3. Touch sensing
4. VisiOn Calc
5. Robot
6. Processor
7. Laser holography
8. Relational
9. Biochip
10. Word processing

Column B

A. The "brain" of the computer
B. Three-dimensional television
C. Database management system
D. A leading office automation technology
E. "Living computer"
F. Electronic worksheet
G. A user-friendly input method
H. Magnetic tape and magnetic disk
I. Steel-collar worker
J. The actual computing equipment

Fill-in-the-Blanks

Fill in the blanks in each of the following:

1. It is believed that ______ could become the world's largest company by the year 2000.

2. ______ are tiny computers etched onto thin slivers of silicon.

3. People who write the instructions that computers follow are called ______.

4. In general, the costs of computing have been ______ (increasing/decreasing) dramatically.

5. Computers that can be easily used by untrained people are said to be ______.

6. A ______ is a device that creates an intense beam of monochromatic light.

7. The transmission of information across international borders is called ______.

8. ______ control the secure storage and accessing of the large amounts of information that businesses must process.

9. Interactive computer-based systems that support management decision-making activities are called ______.

10. The software systems that manage the computer's hardware and make it more friendly and usable to computer users are called ______.

Answers to Self-Review Exercises

Matching: 1 J, 2 H, 3 G, 4 F, 5 I, 6 A, 7 B, 8 C, 9 E, 10 D

Fill-in-the-Blanks:

1. IBM
2. Microprocessors
3. computer programmers
4. decreasing
5. user-friendly
6. laser
7. transborder data flow
8. Database management systems
9. decision support systems
10. operating systems

Discussion Questions 

1. What is meant by the Information Revolution?

2. Do you believe that machines can be intelligent? Defend your position.

3. Suppose that genuinely intelligent machines really did exist. How might these be used to improve our businesses and personal lives? What dangers can you foresee?

4. What are the major trends that will affect the future development of computers?

5. Give several reasons why it is important for people to study computers today.

6. In what sense are computers different from other machines that also help us extend our capabilities?

7. Now that you have some idea of the kinds of applications for which computers are being used, propose several innovative new applications.

8. What are the key aspects of computers that make them useful for such a broad range of applications?

9. What do you think it would be like to carry on a conversation with a talking computer?

10. What does it mean for a computer system to be user-friendly?

Projects 

1. As you read this book, develop a computer applications scrapbook. Include in your scrapbook articles from newspapers and magazines. Summarize the content of any television programs you watch that discuss computer applications.

2. As you read this text, make a list of the various controversial issues that are raised. Include other controversial issues. Discuss these issues and how you feel they should be handled. Ask the opinions of several friends and relatives.

UNIVAC

Chapter 2

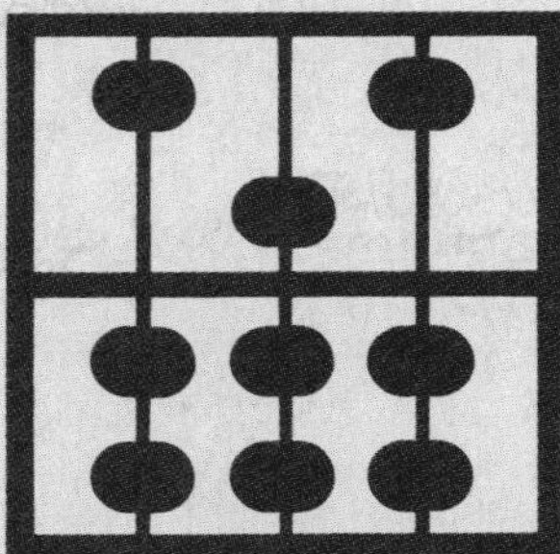

The Evolution of Computers

After reading this chapter you will understand:

1. How early mechanical calculating devices led to modern computers
2. The importance of punched-card control
3. The important contributions made to the computer field by Aiken, Atanasoff, Babbage, Boole, Eckert, Hollerith, Lady Lovelace, Mauchly, von Neumann, Wilkes, and others
4. What the four generations of computing are and the important developments that signaled each, and how the fifth generation is likely to evolve
5. How some of the leading companies in the computer field evolved

Left: Computers have evolved from the calculating devices of several hundred years ago to the room-size machines of the 1950s (*top*) to the tiny microprocessors (*bottom*) of the 1980s.

Outline

Early Computing Devices
- The Abacus
- Napier's Bones
- Pascal's Arithmetic Machine
- Leibniz and the Stepped Reckoner
- Jacquard's Loom
- Babbage's Analytical Engine
- Lady Lovelace: The World's First Computer Programmer
- Boolean Logic
- Hollerith's Punched-Card Tabulating Machines
- Powers and the Simultaneous Punching Machine

The Dawn of the Modern Computer Age
- Aiken and the Harvard Mark I
- Atanasoff and the ABC
- Mauchly, Eckert, and the ENIAC
- Von Neumann and the Stored Program Concept
- Wilkes and the EDSAC
- UNIVAC: The First Commercial Computer
- IBM: The Giant Awakens

Generations of Computers
- The First Generation: 1951–1959
- The Second Generation: 1959–1964
- The Third Generation: 1964–1970
- The Fourth Generation: 1970-Present
- The Fifth Generation: 1990?

Suppose for the moment that the automobile industry had developed at the same rate as computers and over the same period: how much cheaper and more efficient would the current models be? If you have not already heard the analogy, the answer is shattering. Today you would be able to buy a Rolls-Royce for $2.75, it would do three million miles to the gallon, and it would deliver enough power to drive the *Queen Elizabeth II*. And if you were interested in miniaturization, you could place half a dozen of them on a pinhead.

Christopher Evans
The Micro Millennium

For as long as people have needed to keep records and calculate, they have worked to create an accurate computing tool that is simple to use. For centuries two devices were used worldwide: the abacus and the slide rule. Their near extinction came quickly—with the computer revolution of the 1970s.

Early Computing Devices

The Abacus

The history of the evolution of computers begins thousands of years ago with the **abacus**, the world's oldest known computing device. It was used by the Chinese as early as 600 B.C. and is still in use today.

The abacus is an instrument that uses beads, or counters, which represent the numerical unit of notation (units, tens, hundreds, thousands), attached to wires or grooves on a frame. One popular version of the abacus is shown in Figure 2–1. Beads are strung in columns on several wires supported by a wood frame. Each column has an upper wire and a lower wire. The upper wire contains two beads worth five units each, and the lower wire contains five beads worth one unit each. Numbers are formed by moving beads so that they are positioned against either the center bar or the outer part of the frame. Beads positioned at the center bar are calculated in determining the number, but beads positioned at the outer frame are not. If a bead on the top wire is positioned at the center bar, then it represents five units; otherwise it represents zero. A bead on the bottom wire positioned at the center bar represents one unit; otherwise it represents zero. The rightmost wire is in what is called the ones position, the next wire is in the tens position, the next is in the hundreds position, and so on, just as in the decimal number system we use today. Each column of beads is then counted and totaled. For example, the abacus in the figure illustrates the number 7,230,189.

In 1946 a Japanese clerk named Masturaki and an American serviceman, Private Wood, were given several arithmetic calculations to perform. Wood used an electronic desk calculator, and Masturaki an abacus. Masturaki easily outperformed Wood.

Napier's Bones

In 1615 the Scottish mathematician John Napier invented a computing device that facilitated the operations of multiplication and division. A series of sticks, which became known as **Napier's Bones**,

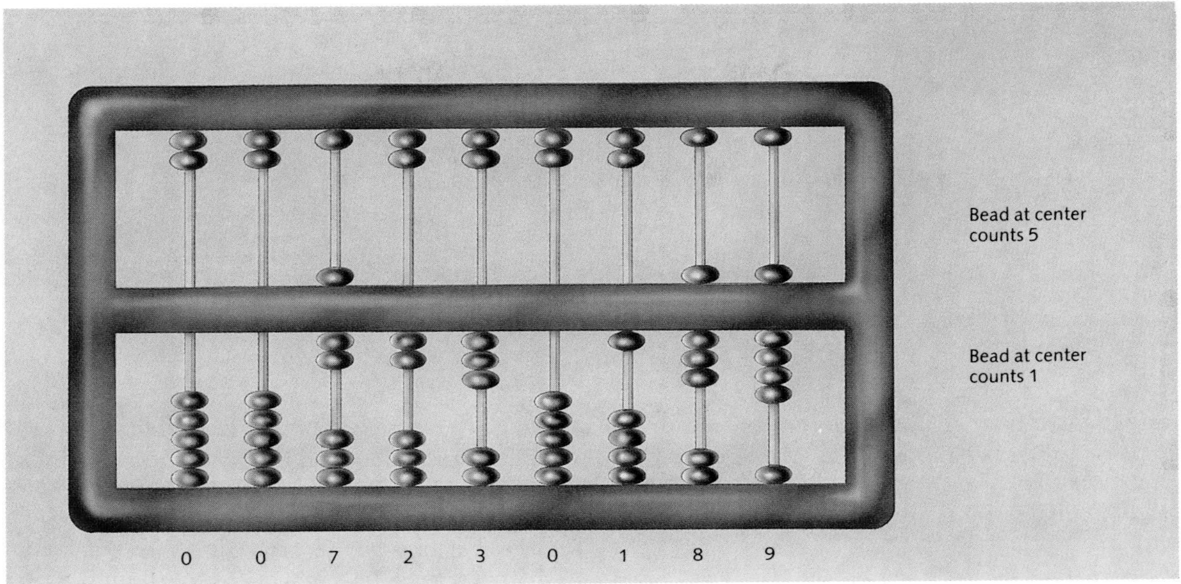

Figure 2–1 An abacus, the world's oldest known computing device. Here the number 7,230,189 is represented.

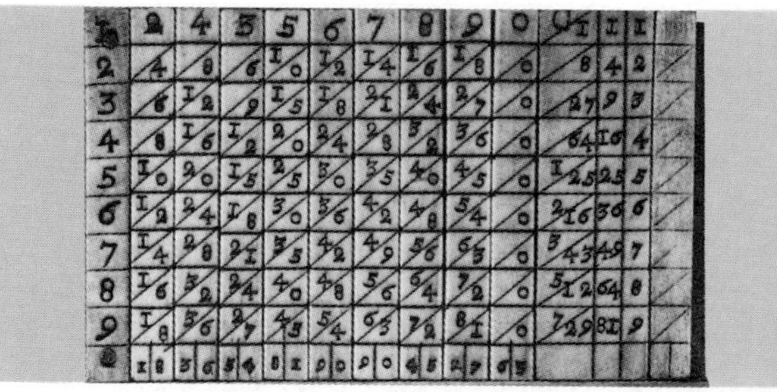

Figure 2–2 Napier's Bones. Napier used these sticks to simplify the operations of multiplication and division. This led to the development of the slide rule.

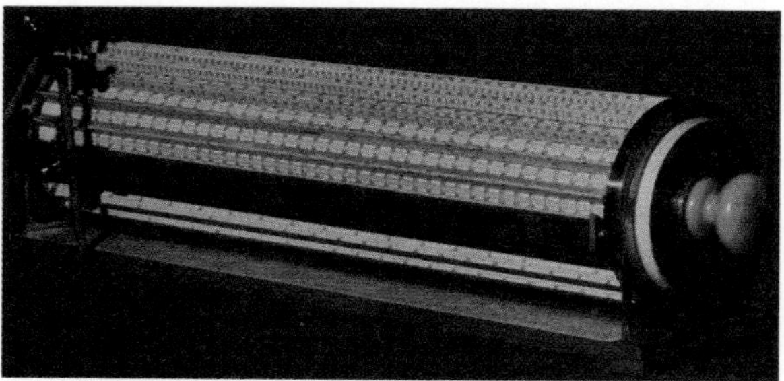

Figure 2–3 An early slide rule.

were marked in a manner similar to the multiplication tables used today. This apparatus reduced multiplication and division into simpler calculations of addition and subtraction (Figure 2–2).

In 1620, using the principles of Napier's Bones, Edmund Gunter developed the first **slide rule** (Figure 2–3). Since then the slide rule has been widely used by scientists, mathematicians, and businesspeople for performing rapid calculations. After 350 years of reliable service, the slide rule was made extinct almost overnight by the introduction of the electronic pocket calculator in the early 1970s.

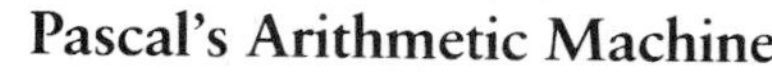

Pascal's Arithmetic Machine

In 1642 the French mathematician and philosopher Blaise Pascal, then only 19 years of age, designed a calculating machine (Figure 2–4) for performing tedious arithmetic. **Pascal's arithmetic machine** was constructed of a series of cleverly connected wheels, each of which contained the digits 0 through 9. Toothed gears were used so that when a given wheel rotated through a complete turn, the wheel to its left would rotate through one-tenth of a turn. Ten rotations of a wheel caused the wheel to its left to rotate through one complete turn. This is exactly how the odometers on automobiles work as they record mileage.

Pascal revealed his machine to the public in 1645, but it was not very successful. The machine was expensive, required considerable skill to operate, and could only be serviced by a small group of Pascal's workers.

Leibniz and the Stepped Reckoner

It is unworthy of excellent men to lose hours like slaves in the labor of calculations which could safely be relegated to anyone else if machines were used.

Gottfried Wilhelm Leibniz

Pascal's machine was capable of performing addition and subtraction, but it required considerable manual effort for performing multiplication and division. In 1673 the German philosopher

Figure 2–4 Pascal's arithmetic machine. The circular dials contain the digits 0 through 9. Numbers are entered by dialing them in a manner similar to dialing a telephone number. The answers to calculations appear in the windows located above the dials.

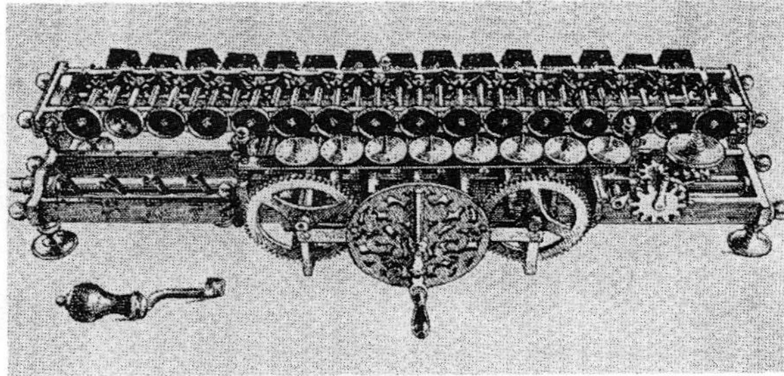

Figure 2–5 Leibniz's Stepped Reckoner.

and mathematician Gottfried Leibniz modified Pascal's machine so that it could perform multiplication and division directly. Leibniz's machine represented a great stride forward in the development of automatic calculators.

Leibniz's Stepped Reckoner (Figure 2–5) used a movable carriage operating on wheels. Multiplication was implemented as a series of additions performed automatically by the machine, and division was performed through subtraction. The machine thus turned the more complex arithmetic operations into a series of steps involving simpler operations, which is exactly how today's computer systems work.

The demand for Leibniz's machines was largely for its help in calculating tables of common mathematical functions. In the seventeenth century producing one of these tables might have been a life's work. Today machines can perform these calculations in seconds at the touch of a few buttons.

Jacquard's Loom

A major contribution to computing methods came from an unlikely source—the weaving industry. In 1801 Joseph Marie Jacquard developed an attachment for weaving looms (Figure 2–6) that used punched cards to "program" a loom to create a specific pattern. The same pattern could be repeated many times, and exact copies of rugs and tapestries could be made.

Jacquard's invention was made available in France in 1805. Seven years later 11,000 looms were operating with the Jacquard attachment. A portrait of Jacquard woven on one of his looms appears in Figure 2–7.

Courtesy of International Business Machines Corporation

Figure 2–6 Jacquard's loom. Notice the punched-card attachment on top.

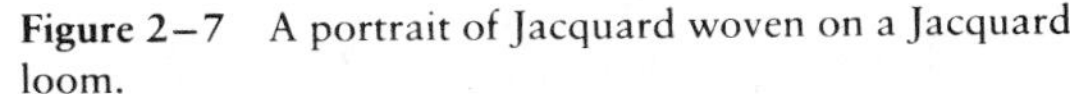

Figure 2–7 A portrait of Jacquard woven on a Jacquard loom.

During the nineteeth century many of the important developments in computing machines, which are still in evidence in today's computers, were inspired by the success of the **punched-card control** in the **Jacquard loom.**

Babbage's Analytical Engine

I am thinking that all these tables might be calculated by machinery.

Charles Babbage

Charles Babbage (Figure 2–8) was born in England in 1791. Educated in mathematics at the University of Cambridge, he eventually became Lucasian Professor there, a position held years before by Isaac Newton.

While a student, Babbage proposed the construction of the **Difference Engine** (Figure 2–9), a machine for automatically calculating and printing mathematical tables. In 1830, with a grant from the British government, he began construction of the machine.

Figure 2–8 Charles Babbage. In the nineteenth century Babbage devoted his life to the construction of calculating machines, which strongly resemble modern computer systems.

Figure 2–9 A model of a portion of Babbage's Difference Engine.

As Babbage worked on the Difference Engine, he developed the idea for an even more ambitious calculating machine, which he called the **Analytical Engine.** He abandoned the Difference Engine project in 1834 to begin work on his new idea (Figure 2–10). As envisioned by Babbage, the Analytical Engine was to have a storage of 1000 numbers of 50 decimal digits each. Numbers were to be stored on wheels of 10 positions each. Punched cards similar to those used by Jacquard were to hold the sequences of instructions to be performed and the data to be entered into the machine.

The Analytical Engine was to have four units:

1. The *store* was to hold data and the results of calculations.
2. The *mill* was to be a central mechanism for performing mathematical operations.
3. A system of gears and levers was to transfer data back and forth between the store and the mill.
4. The *input/output unit* was to read data from outside the Analytical Engine into its store and display the results of its calculations.

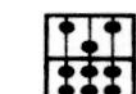

Figure 2–10 A portion of Babbage's Analytical Engine. The organization of this machine was remarkably similar to that of modern digital computers.

It is remarkable that this description of the Analytical Engine corresponds so closely to the organization of present-day computer systems. Babbage truly was a hundred years ahead of his time in proposing this machine!

Unfortunately, Babbage never completed the Analytical Engine. The technology of the time was inadequate for producing the necessary mechanical components to the required precision. Also, there was no real need for such a powerful machine—the calculating devices already available were more than capable of meeting the computing needs of the mid- to late 1800s. As a result, the British government stopped supporting Babbage's projects in 1842, and he was left without funds to continue his research.

Because of the Analytical Engine, Babbage is remembered as the father of the computer; had he finished it, it would have been the first completely automatic, general-purpose computer. Other people, however, continued his work. In 1855 George Scheutz, a Swedish printer, built a working Difference Engine, and in 1889 Babbage's son, Henry, built a working model of the mill portion of the Analytical Engine. Both of Babbage's machines greatly influenced future researchers and eventually led to the development of the modern digital computer.

Lady Lovelace: The World's First Computer Programmer

We may say most aptly that the Analytical Engine weaves algebraical patterns just as the Jacquard loom weaves flowers and leaves.

Ada Lovelace

In 1842 Augusta Ada Byron, Countess of Lovelace (Figure 2–11), daughter of the poet Lord Byron, translated a paper on Babbage's Analytical Engine from French to English. During her work on the translation she made abundant notes, and at one point included a detailed sequence of instructions for the Analytical Engine to perform certain complex calculations. This is generally considered the first computer program and gives Lady Lovelace the distinction of being regarded by many as the world's first computer programmer. One of the latest programming languages, Ada (see Chapter 9 for a discussion of programming languages), was named after Lady Lovelace.

Figure 2–11 Lady Ada Lovelace, considered by many the world's first computer programmer.

Boolean Logic

The calculating machines of the nineteenth century used decimal numbers. **Binary**, or **base two**, numbers were not adopted in the design of computer systems until the twentieth century. (Number systems are discussed in Appendix B.)

The application of the binary system to computers was facilitated by work performed in the mid-1800s by the British mathematician George Boole. In 1854 he published the principles of **Boolean logic**, the mathematics of variables with values that can be only "true" or "false." Almost a century passed before the usefulness of his work in computer systems design became apparent.

Researchers in the twentieth century found that it was difficult to build an electrical element for representing a decimal digit (zero through nine) but that it was much easier to build reliable electronics for representing **binary digits** (ones and zeros). Boole's logic was a perfect match for such a system. It completely described the operations needed for implementing and controlling two-valued circuit elements. The match also helped spawn one of the most significant developments of the twentieth century—the **digital computer**.

Hollerith's Punched-Card Tabulating Machines

The U.S. Constitution requires that a census be taken every 10 years to provide the population counts for determining congressional districts. The census was originally supposed to be a simple head count, but over the years it has grown to include the tabulation of social, ethnic, and economic data as well.

The census of 1880 was analyzed manually and took seven and a half years to complete. It was estimated then that if the census of 1890 were also performed manually, it would not be completed until 1902—two years after the census of 1900!

In 1879 John Billings, an employee of the Census Bureau, suggested the use of punched cards for recording the facts about the population. Billings also suggested the use of mechanical card-processing equipment. Billings's associate Herman Hollerith was intrigued and immediately began designing such equipment.

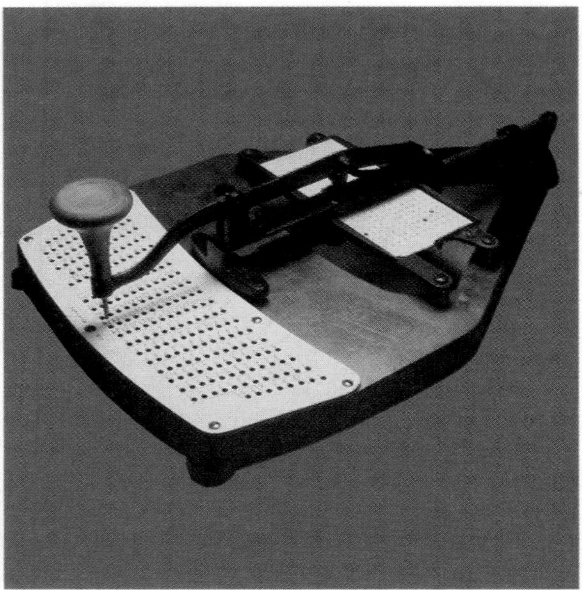

Figure 2–12 A card-punch machine used in the census of 1890. Each hole corresponded to particular data to be recorded. Machine operators moved the handle above the appropriate hole and pressed down, causing the machine to punch a hole in the card at the top right of the machine.

Hollerith left the Census Bureau in 1882 to become an instructor at the Massachusetts Institute of Technology (MIT). He continued working on his machines and a year later went to work for the U.S. Patent Office, which on March 31, 1884, issued him the first patent for a data processing machine.

By 1889 Hollerith's machines had been thoroughly proved and were chosen by the government for the 1890 census. That census took only two and a half years to complete. A punching device (Figure 2–12) was used to record facts about individuals by punching holes in specific locations on the cards. The tabulating machine (Figure 2–13) then pressed pins against the cards. When a pin passed through a hole, the pin went into a jar of mercury. This completed an electrical circuit that caused a simple mechanical counter to be increased by one.

Figure 2–13 *Right*: Hollerith's punched-card tabulating machine. Devices like this were used in the census of 1890.

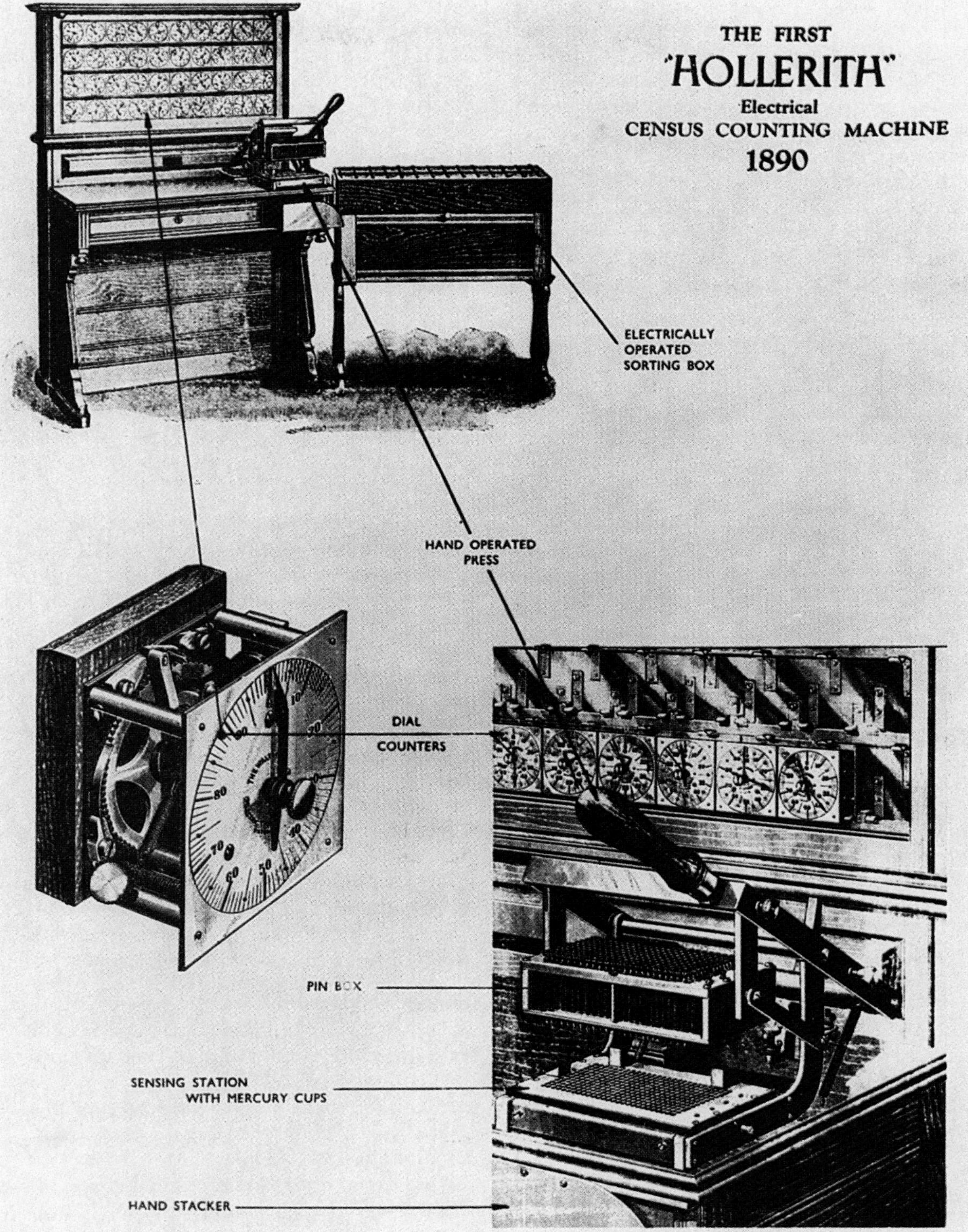
THE FIRST
"HOLLERITH"
Electrical
CENSUS COUNTING MACHINE
1890
ELECTRICALLY
OPERATED
SORTING BOX
HAND OPERATED
PRESS
DIAL
COUNTERS
PIN BOX
SENSING STATION
WITH MERCURY CUPS
HAND STACKER

Hollerith started the Tabulating Machine Company in 1896. After a series of mergers it became the Computing-Tabulating-Recording Company. In 1924, under the leadership of Thomas J. Watson, Sr., the company was renamed International Business Machines Corporation (IBM). IBM has since grown to become the world's largest computer company.

Powers and the Simultaneous Punching Machine

Hollerith's successor at the Census Bureau was James Powers. As Powers worked on improving Hollerith's equipment and developing new machines, he kept the rights for all the patents he received.

> **Largest Bookkeeping Job**
>
> During the 1920s and 1930s punched-card data processing became the accepted means for handling large-scale information-tabulating tasks. In 1935 the largest bookkeeping job ever was mandated by the U.S. government. The Social Security Act of 1935 required that the government keep detailed employment records on 26 million people. The massive task was handled by a production line of people and card-processing machines that punched, sorted, checked, and filed half a million cards per day.

PHOTO: COURTESY OF THE NEW YORK NEWS

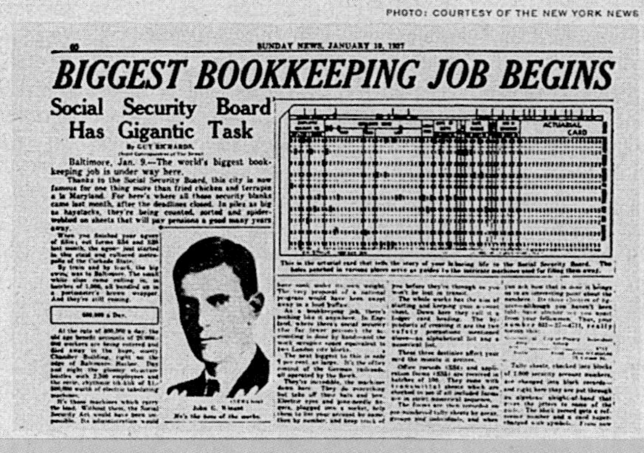

SUNDAY NEWS

BIGGEST BOOKKEEPING JOB BEGINS

Social Security Board Has Gigantic Task

Baltimore, Jan. 9.—The world's biggest bookkeeping job is under way here.

Thanks to the Social Security Board, this city is now famous for one thing more than fried chicken and terrapin a la Maryland. For here's where all those security blanks came last month, after the deadlines closed. In piles as big as haystacks, they're being counted, sorted and spider-webbed on sheets that will pay pensions a good many years away.

Powers's contribution was the **simultaneous punching machine**. This device allowed an operator, after typing in data, to check and correct the data before it was actually punched onto cards. With earlier card-punching equipment, if an error was made the entire card had to be repunched—a costly and time-consuming procedure. The Census Bureau ordered 300 of Powers's machines for the 1910 census.

Powers left the Census Bureau in 1911 to form the Powers Accounting Machine Company. His company also followed the merger route and eventually became Sperry Rand, the manufacturer of UNIVAC computers, which remains a formidable competitor in the computer industry.

The Dawn of the Modern Computer Age

The punched-card equipment developed in the late 1800s and early 1900s had proved its value in both government and business, but these machines were not true computers. Not until the late 1930s did work begin on the development of what are considered modern computers; this work was speeded by the pressures of World War II. The government saw the potential of these new computing devices in the war effort and funded their development handsomely.

Aiken and the Harvard Mark I

If Babbage had lived 75 years later, I would have been out of a job.

Howard Aiken

The punched-card equipment of the 1930s was simply too slow to perform the massive computations in many mathematical and scientific problems. In 1939 Howard Aiken of Harvard University began work on a machine to perform these calculations faster. IBM provided Aiken with substantial support, and the Harvard Mark I was completed in 1944, the date historians generally call the dawn of the modern computer age.

The Mark I performed faithfully for 10 years. It represented the first working realization of

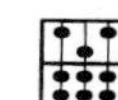

The Mark I

The Mark I was a huge machine, 51 feet long, 8 feet high, and 3 feet deep, and weighed many tons. The machine contained 3000 mechanical switches, 750,000 electronic components, and 500 miles of wiring. It was controlled by punched-paper tape, and it stored its numbers in mechanical switches. The Mark I used decimal numbers instead of the binary numbers of today's systems, and its calculations were accurate to 23 digits. It could perform three additions per second, one multiplication in 6 seconds, and one division in 12 seconds. These capabilities made the Mark I much faster than any other machine previously built.

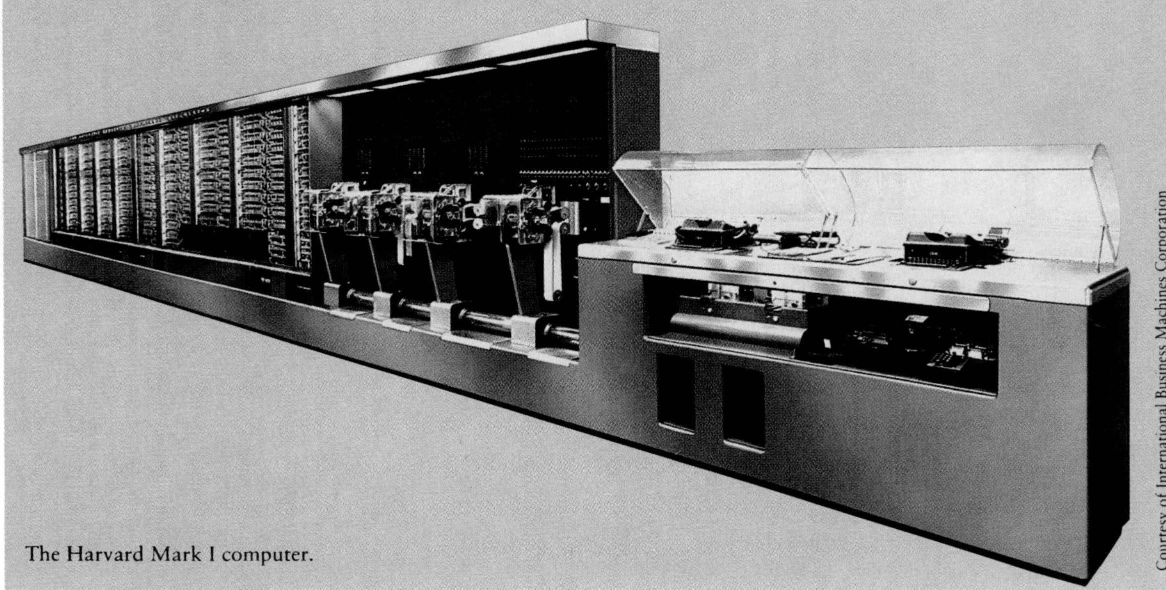

The Harvard Mark I computer.

Courtesy of International Business Machines Corporation

Babbage's Analytical Engine—a century after Babbage conceived of it. The Mark I was the first successful **general-purpose digital computer** and the first **electromechanical computer**.

Atanasoff and the ABC

In 1942 John Vincent Atanasoff of Iowa State College and Clifford Berry, his graduate student, completed work on an electronic vacuum tube computer. The *ABC* (for Atanasoff-Berry Computer) is recognized today as the first true **electronic digital computer**. (Although many people regard the ENIAC, which is described in the next section, as the first such computer, a 1973 court decision found in favor of Atanasoff and the ABC that it was the first.) The machine (Figure 2–14) was also the first to use the binary system for representing numbers. It was designed specifically for solving simultaneous equations. Atanasoff is credited by many historians as being the father of the electronic computer.

Mauchly, Eckert, and the ENIAC

While Atanasoff was working on the ABC, he met and discussed his project with John W. Mauchly of the University of Pennsylvania. From their discussions Mauchly devised his own ideas on how to build a better computer. He teamed up with J. Presper Eckert, Jr., a graduate student, and together they built the first **electronic general-purpose computer**, the *ENIAC* (for Electronic Numerical Integrator and Computer). The ENIAC was funded by the U.S. Army as the need for computing accurate ballistics tables increased

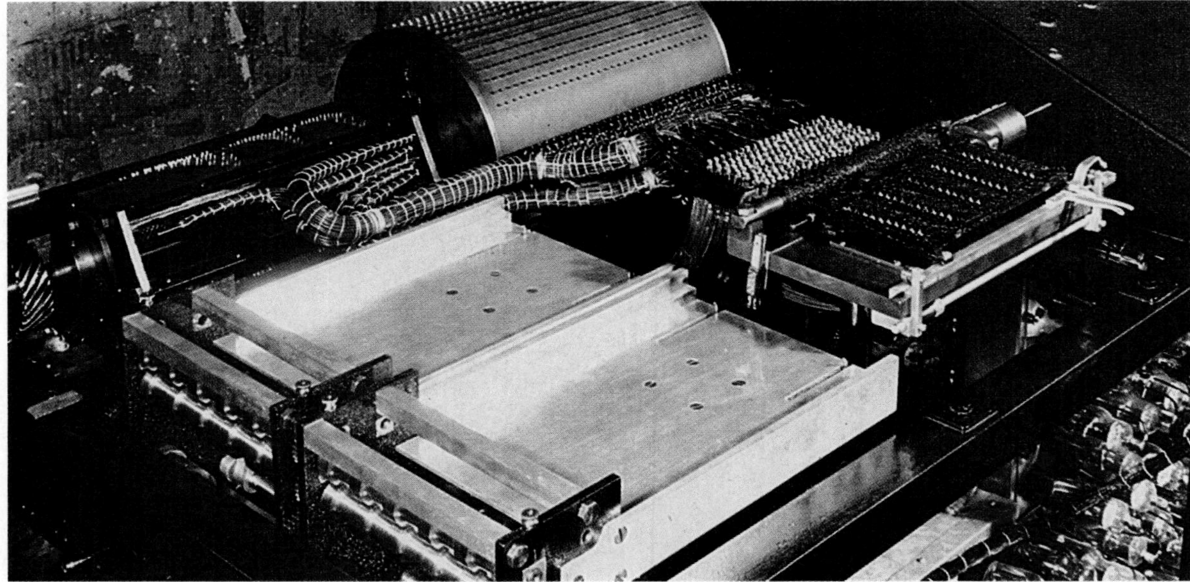

Figure 2–14 The Atanasoff-Berry Computer.

during World War II. (Unfortunately, it was not completed until 1945, several months after the war ended. The government had, instead, used the Mark I.)

The ENIAC was a far more important machine than the ABC—the ABC was really just a laboratory curiosity—and was used for many years to perform substantial computing tasks.

Von Neumann and the Stored Program Concept

In 1946 the mathematician John von Neumann joined the Mauchly and Eckert team and began working on an improved version of the ENIAC called the **EDVAC** (for Electronic Discrete Variable Automatic Computer). Von Neumann proposed that the program as well as the data it operated on should be stored in the computer's memory. The computer could then perform the program at electronic speeds rather than at the slow mechanical speeds of reading programs from punched cards. Many historians consider this **stored program concept** among the most important developments in the computer field in the twentieth century.

Wilkes and the EDSAC

While the EDVAC was being developed, a team headed by Maurice Wilkes at the University of Cambridge in England developed the *EDSAC* (for Electronic Delay Storage Automatic Calculator). EDSAC also incorporated the stored program concept. Because the EDSAC began operating in 1949 (before EDVAC), it is given the distinction of being the world's first **stored program computer**. At the opening of the Digital Computer Museum in Marlboro, Massachusetts (now in Boston), in 1979, Wilkes commented:

> As soon as we started programming, we found to our surprise that it wasn't as easy to get programs right as we had thought. Debugging had to be discovered. I can remember the exact instant when I realized that a large part of my life from then on was going to be spent in finding mistakes in my own programs.

UNIVAC: The First Commercial Computer

In 1946 Eckert and Mauchly left the University of Pennsylvania to form the Eckert-Mauchly Com-

The ENIAC

The ENIAC occupied 1500 square feet of floor space and weighed 30 tons. It consumed so much electricity that it actually dimmed the lights of the city of Philadelphia (it was kept at the University of Pennsylvania there) when it was turned on. The machine was completely electronic, consisting of 19,000 vacuum tubes and tens of thousands of other electronic components. It had 500,000 soldered joints and no moving parts.

Unlike the ABC and today's binary computers, the ENIAC used decimal arithmetic. Every digit in the machine could contain any of the decimal digits from zero to nine. Counting proceeded from 0, 1, 2, 3, 4, 5, 6, 7, 8, 9 and then to "0 carry the 1" to form the number 10. In binary, only the digits zero and one are used, and numbers are carried on every second count. Binary is awkward for humans but convenient for computers. A binary digit (or **bit**, as it is called) can be built out of one switch that may be open or closed (off or on). Binary numbers inside the computers must be converted back and forth to decimal for the convenience of human users.

Because the ENIAC was completely electronic, it performed calculations much faster than the electromechanical computers of the time, such as the Mark I. ENIAC could perform 5000 additions or 300 multiplications of 10-digit numbers per second, making it more than a thousand times faster than the Mark I. (It is interesting to note that many of today's home computers are more than a hundred times faster than the ENIAC, weigh less than 30 pounds, consume about one-thousandth the power, cost about one-thousandth as much, and can store thousands of times as much information.)

At a recent computer convention, J. Presper Eckert, Jr., told an interesting story about debugging. Because the vacuum tubes used in the ENIAC were relatively short-lived, backups for every panel of tubes were kept handy. One particular bug was traced to a certain panel of these tubes. The engineers were sure that this bug was the cause of the trouble and replaced the defective panel with the backup panel, but the same problem surfaced again almost immediately. The engineers were bewildered and spent days checking the entire ENIAC top to bottom. As a last resort, the replacement panel was checked, and it had exactly the same hardware bug as the original panel—an incredible coincidence. This experience demonstrated how difficult it was going to be to keep these giant machines running. Today's computers are designed with self-checking features that continuously examine the computers for problems.

puter Corporation. Three years later Remington Rand acquired the company and the patents Eckert and Mauchly had retained for the ENIAC. The company intended to develop commercial data processing systems. In 1951 Remington Rand installed the first of these systems at the Bureau of the Census. The computer, called *UNIVAC I*, was used reliably around the clock through 1963. The UNIVAC received a great deal of publicity when it was used by the Columbia Broadcasting System (CBS) to forecast the election of Dwight Eisenhower as president of the United States in 1952 (Figure 2–15). The computer was able to predict the Eisenhower win with only about 3 percent of the popular vote counted.

Figure 2–15 The UNIVAC computer projecting Eisenhower the winner in the 1952 presidential election. Notice Walter Cronkite on the right and J. Presper Eckert, Jr., in the center.

IBM: The Giant Awakens

You have to put your heart in the business and the business in your heart.

Thomas J. Watson, Sr.

In the early 1950s IBM was already a large company specializing in typewriters, adding machines, and punched-card processing machines. The company had been dominated by Thomas J. Watson, Sr., for the previous three decades and had been tremendously successful. Thomas J. Watson, Jr., convinced his father that the time was right for IBM to enter the computer field. In 1953 the company introduced its model 701

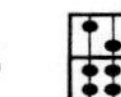

computer system for business, but not until the model 650 was introduced in 1954 did IBM achieve prominence in the field. The 650 was the world's most popular business computer during the 1950s; it gave IBM the lead in the computer field, a lead it firmly holds to this day.

Figure 2–16 These vacuum tubes on the bottom are several inches tall. On the top is an integrated circuit board used in today's computers. It contains the equivalent of many thousands of vacuum tubes.

Generations of Computers

Since the early 1950s computer capabilities have been increasing steadily as costs have continued to decline. This evolution has been driven by a continuing series of major advances in electronics. The groups of computer systems associated with each of these significant advances have been categorized as **generations of computers**. To date, the computer field has evolved through four generations.

The First Generation: 1951–1959

The commercial computer industry began with the introduction of the UNIVAC I in 1951. **Vacuum tubes** (Figure 2–16) were the key electronic components used in the computers of that time. Completely electronic vacuum tube computers operated much faster than electromechanical computers with moving parts such as the Harvard Mark I, but they had some drawbacks. Vacuum tubes were bulky, consumed a great deal of electricity, gave off an enormous amount of heat, and were prone to failure. Tube failures were so common that these computers had difficulty operating reliably for more than a few hours at a time.

First generation computers typically processed a few thousand instructions per second and could store 10,000 to 20,000 characters—very little by today's standards. Many different types of memory were tried, but the most important was **magnetic core memory**, developed in 1950 by Jay W. Forrester for the **Whirlwind I** computer at MIT (Figure 2–17). Magnetic cores (Figure 2–18) are tiny donut-shaped pieces of metal that can be magnetized in one of two directions (corresponding to the binary "0" or "1").

The most successful first generation computer was IBM's 650. IBM originally estimated the market at perhaps 40 or 50 systems; several thousand 650s were eventually installed! Perhaps the chief reason for the 650's success was its powerful punched-card input and output capabilities.

The Second Generation: 1959–1964

With the invention of the **transistor** at Bell Laboratories in 1948 (Figure 2–19), it became clear that transistors would quickly replace vacuum tubes. They were smaller, more reliable, used less energy, and gave off very little heat. In addition, computers with transistors operated much faster than those with vacuum tubes. By 1959 computer systems were delivered featuring the complete replacement of vacuum tubes with transistors.

First generation computers were **dedicated systems**, that is, only one person at a time could use the machine. Designers of second generation systems realized that much better utilization could be achieved by allowing several users to share the machine jointly. This concept, called **multiprogramming**, proved to be tremendously successful. In the early 1960s several groups in industry and at universities pioneered the concept of **timesharing**, a method of sharing a computer in which tens or hundreds of users access the central computer through typewriterlike **terminals**.

Control Data Corporation (CDC) was the most significant new company to appear on the scene during the second generation. Today, CDC is one

Figure 2–17 The Whirlwind I computer. Jay W. Forrester (center, in light suit) developed magnetic core memory for this computer, which was completed at MIT in 1950.

Figure 2–18 Magnetic core memory. Each donut-shaped magnetic core has three wires running through it. By adjusting the currents running through the wires, a computer can read the value in a core ("0" or "1"), set a core to a specific value, or flip a core's value to the opposite value ("0" becomes "1" and "1" becomes "0").

Figure 2–19 The first transistor.

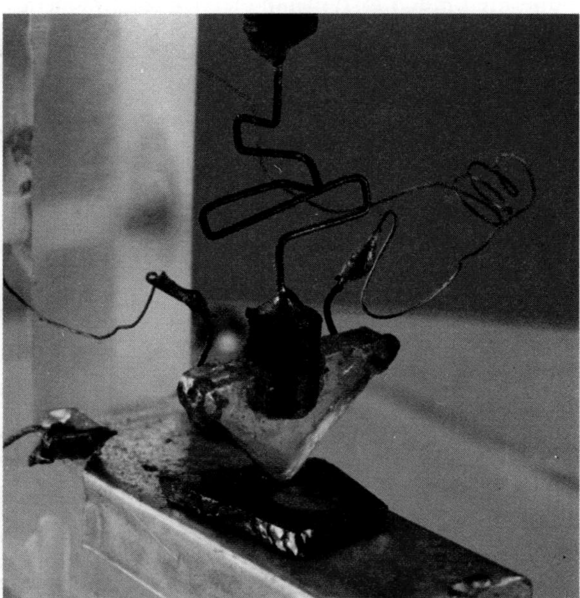

of the world's leading manufacturers of **supercomputers**, the enormously powerful machines used to perform the most complex mathematical and scientific calculations.

During the second generation the importance of computers in business data processing became established. The most successful second generation computer was the **IBM 1401.** By 1964 IBM had installed more 1401 computers than all other computer systems in the world combined.

The Third Generation: 1964–1970

The third generation was triggered by the introduction of **integrated circuits**, in which the equivalent of hundreds and even thousands of transistors could be placed on a small silicon chip (Figure 2–20). The use of these tiny chips in third generation computers dramatically reduced costs, size, and power requirements for electronic circuits. (See Chapter 3 for a detailed discussion of how these silicon chips are manufactured.)

On April 7, 1964, IBM made one of the most important announcements in the history of the computer field. It had developed the **System/360** (Figure 2–21), a complete family of computers designed to replace all previous IBM computers. The 360 series had several models, ranging from a small data processing computer for business applications to a large-scale supercomputer for scientific applications. The models were **upwards compatible**, that is, programs that would run on a small model would also run on the larger models. A growth-oriented organization could begin with a small 360 to meet its current and near-term needs and then install a larger model as its needs grew. The concept was brilliant, and the 360 series became the best-selling computers of the 1960s.

Figure 2–20 The first commercially available integrated circuit, greatly enlarged. This chip, developed by Fairchild Semiconductor, is a flip-flop—a device capable of representing a single "bit" of information (either a "0" or a "1").

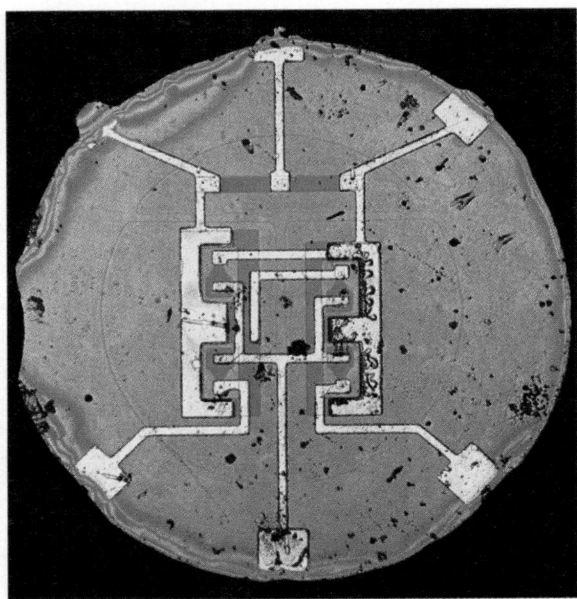

Courtesy of International Business Machines Corporation

Figure 2–21 The IBM System/360. This model, the 360/30, was one of the smaller computers in the 360 family.

During the third generation Control Data Corporation strengthened its position in the supercomputer field with the delivery of the CDC 6600 in 1964. This machine, able to perform 3 million instructions per second, was the most powerful computer available for the next several years. In 1969 CDC introduced the even faster 7600 that could perform a staggering 36 million operations per second!

The integrated-circuit technology of the third generation made possible the production of small but powerful **minicomputers.** The most important entry in this field was the PDP-8 (Figure 2–22), first delivered by Digital Equipment Corporation (DEC) in 1965. The PDP-8's design made it extremely useful as a **process control computer**—thousands of PDP-8s were used to control production lines, laboratories, petroleum refineries, and even small businesses. The machine established DEC as the leading manufacturer of minicomputers. Today DEC is the second largest computer company in the United States.

Figure 2–22 The PDP-8 minicomputer, introduced by Digital Equipment Corporation in 1965, was the first computer to sell for less than $20,000.

The Fourth Generation: 1970–Present

The advent of **large-scale integrated circuitry** (LSI) with many thousands of transistors on a single silicon chip signaled the beginning of the fourth generation. In 1970 IBM announced its **System/370** to replace the 360s. The 370s used LSI technology, ran existing 360 programs, and replaced core memory with faster and cheaper **metal oxide semiconductor** (MOS) memories. At about this time the industry was "generation conscious" and was being primed to expect the announcement of the fourth generation. When IBM's announcement finally came industry reaction was mixed, because the 370s did not appear to be enough of a breakthrough to represent an entirely new generation. Industry experts labeled the 370 "evolutionary" rather than "revolutionary" and generally refused to acknowledge that the fourth generation had arrived. Only in the mid- to late 1970s did it become socially acceptable to call a computer a fourth generation machine.

A series of court decisions at this time dramatically changed the industry. IBM was told tha it had to make its computer software (the programs, programming systems, and related docu-

Figure 2–23 The PDP-11 series of minicomputers produced by Digital Equipment Corporation helped propel DEC to the rank of second largest computer company in the United States.

ments) available for a price to anyone who wanted it. This created an intensely competitive environment, friendly to the development of companies building IBM-compatible **hardware** (the computer and its equipment). These companies, called the PCMs (for **plug compatible mainframers**), were able to build hardware to compete with the IBM systems and obtain IBM software for use by PCM clients.

One of the most important PCM enterprises was founded by Gene Amdahl, who had been a designer of the IBM 360. In 1970 he left IBM and started Amdahl Corporation. In 1975 Amdahl Corporation installed its first 470 V/6 system. The machine sold for less than one of the larger IBM 370s, was considerably more powerful, and used existing IBM software.

During the fourth generation the minicomputer industry has enjoyed explosive growth. Digital Equipment Corporation used large-scale integration in the development of its very successful PDP-11 series of minicomputers introduced in 1970 (Figure 2–23).

The supercomputer field has also grown. Seymour Cray, Control Data Corporation's chief designer, left CDC in 1972 to form Cray Research Inc. In 1976 the company introduced the *CRAY-1*, which performs 80 million instructions per second, and in 1982 the CRAY X-MP (Figure 2–24), which performs 1 billion instructions per second.

One of the most important developments of the fourth generation was the introduction of the **microcomputer.** The complete "computer on a chip" has become commonplace. Computer power that might have cost hundreds of thousands of dollars 20 years ago now costs only a few dollars. The microcomputer has profoundly changed the computer industry and society as a whole, as we will see throughout this text.

The next several generations of computers will probably be accompanied by increases in the **scale of integration**—how many transistors can be placed on a small silicon chip. Current research is in the areas of **very-large-scale integration** (VLSI) and **ultra-large-scale integration** (ULSI). As these efforts come to fruition, they may well signal new generations of computer electronics.

The Fifth Generation: 1990?

Each of the first four generations was signaled by a major advance in hardware component technology. It is widely believed that the fifth generation will arrive when breakthroughs in software make it possible to produce truly intelligent machines. (The current state of the art in this field, artificial intelligence, is discussed in Chapter 16, along with the closely related field of robotics.)

The Japanese have made the realization of the fifth generation of computers by the year 1990 a national priority. Government and industry are expected to spend $1 billion on research and development. American computer companies are studying the Japanese effort but have not as yet made a similar commitment.

Figure 2–24 *Left*: The CRAY X-MP supercomputer, introduced in 1982, can perform 1 billion instructions per second.

Supercomputers: A Special Breed

Control Data Corporation has maintained its reputation as an industry leader in the field of supercomputers since the second generation. When the CDC 6600 was first announced, its rated speed of approximately 3 million operations per second was astonishing. Then the 6600 was replaced by the 7600, which could perform 36 million operations per second, a number thought incredible at the time. During the fourth generation, CDC announced the STAR-100, which could perform approximately 100 million operations per second! Then came the CDC CYBER 205, which can perform 800 million operations per second. By the late 1980s it is expected that computers capable of performing 5 billion instructions per second will be available. Technology in the 1990s may make it possible for computers to perform 100 billion instructions per second!

Why the interest in such power? Quite simply, there are many problems that cannot be solved without it. Take the weather, for example. When a computer is built that can analyze temperature, humidity, pressure, and other readings from millions or even billions of points around the globe, and that can do this thousands of times a day, it may become possible to forecast climatic conditions months in advance. With accurate weather projections available, farmers could get the maximum number of crops per growing season by planting the best crops for the forecasted weather conditions. People could be warned well in advance of impending floods and severe storms. Smoother, safer routes could be chosen for planes and ships.

Computing devices are no longer just a tool for record keeping, as they were in the early days of the abacus. Since then changes have taken place not only in the ways people compute but also in the reasons they compute.

Control Data Corporation and Cray Research Inc. remain the two most important manufacturers of supercomputers. This Control Data CYBER 205 can perform 800 million instructions per second.

Summary

1. The abacus is the oldest known computing device. It was developed by the Chinese about 600 B.C.

2. In the early 1600s John Napier invented a device called Napier's Bones for facilitating multiplication and division. Using the principles of Napier's Bones, Edmund Gunter invented the first slide rule in 1620.

3. In 1642 Blaise Pascal invented a computing device for performing tedious arithmetic. It used a system of toothed gears similar to that used in today's automobile odometers. In 1673 a modification of Pascal's machine, Gottfried Leibniz's Stepped Reckoner, was introduced. It could perform multiplications and divisions directly.

4. One of the most important developments in computing machines was introduced in 1801 by Joseph Marie Jacquard. He invented an attachment for weaving looms that used punched cards to program the loom to produce a specific pattern.

5. In 1830 Charles Babbage started working on the Difference Engine, a machine for calculating and printing mathematical tables. He abandoned the project in 1834 in favor of the more ambitious Analytical Engine. If the Analytical Engine had been completed, it would have been the first completely automatic, general-purpose computer. For his design of the Analytical Engine, Babbage is remembered as the father of the computer.

6. Ada, Countess of Lovelace, is recognized by many as the world's first computer programmer for her detailed instructions for the Analytical Engine, noted while working on a translation of a paper on the Analytical Engine.

7. In 1854 George Boole published the principles of Boolean logic. Almost a century later these principles became the basis of the design of modern computers.

8. Using card tabulating equipment developed by Herman Hollerith, the Census Bureau completed the census of 1890 in one-third the time it took for the census of 1880. Hollerith formed the Tabulating Machine Company in 1896, which eventually became International Business Machines Corporation (IBM) in 1924.

9. James Powers designed a simultaneous punching machine that allowed an operator to correct errors before typed data was actually punched onto cards. His computing company eventually became Sperry Rand, the manufacturer of UNIVAC computers.

10. The Harvard Mark I, completed in 1944, signaled the beginning of the modern computer age.

11. In 1942 John Vincent Atanasoff and Clifford Berry completed work on the ABC—the first true electronic digital computer and the first computer to use the binary system for representing numbers. In 1945 Mauchly and Eckert completed the ENIAC—the first electronic general-purpose computer.

12. One of the most important developments in the computer field in the twentieth century was the stored program concept, proposed by John von Neumann in 1946. The EDSAC was the first stored program computer, completed by Maurice Wilkes in 1949.

13. Jay W. Forrester developed magnetic core memory in 1950.

14. The first commercial computer system was the UNIVAC I, installed at the Census Bureau in 1951.

15. Significant advances in computer systems have been categorized by generations. First generation computer systems used vacuum tubes, which were bulky, used a great deal of energy, and were prone to failure. Second generation computers used transistors instead of vacuum tubes. Transistors were smaller, more reliable, and used less energy. Third generation computers, like the IBM/360 series, used integrated circuits. The 360 introduced the family concept of computers, by which an organization could start with a small computer and then upgrade to larger systems as it grew. During the fourth generation, the microcomputer was introduced, signaling a revolution in the computer industry. The Japanese are attempting to develop fifth generation computers by 1990. They believe the key to the fifth generation will be software breakthroughs that make it possible to build truly intelligent machines.

Important Terms 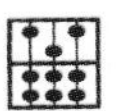

abacus
Babbage's Analytical Engine
Babbage's Difference Engine
binary digit
bit
Boolean logic
family of computers
generations of computers
integrated circuits
Jacquard loom
large-scale integrated circuitry (LSI)
Leibniz's Stepped Reckoner
magnetic core memory
microcomputer
minicomputer
multiprogramming
Napier's Bones
Pascal's arithmetic machine
plug compatible mainframers (PCMs)
process control computer
punched-card control
stored program concept
supercomputer
terminal
timesharing
transistor
ultra-large-scale integration (ULSI)
upwards compatible
vacuum tube
very-large-scale integration (VLSI)

Self-Review Exercises 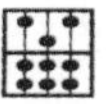

Matching

Next to each of the person's names mentioned in column A, place the letter of the item in column B with which that person is most closely identified.

Column A	Column B
1. Howard Aiken	A. First punched card tabulating machines
2. John Vincent Atanasoff	B. Magnetic core memory
3. Charles Babbage	C. Mathematics of true/false variables
4. George Boole	D. First computer programmer
5. Mauchly and Eckert	E. Founded IBM
6. Jay W. Forrester	F. Stored program concept
7. Herman Hollerith	G. ABC
8. Ada Lovelace	H. Harvard Mark I
9. John von Neumann	I. ENIAC
10. Thomas J. Watson, Sr.	J. Analytical Engine

Fill-in-the-Blanks

Fill in the blanks in each of the following:

1. The slide rule was made extinct by the ______.

2. Many important nineteenth-century computing developments were inspired by the success of ______ in the Jacquard loom.

3. The design of Babbage's ______ corresponds closely to the organization of present-day computer systems.

4. ______ developed the simultaneous punching machine.

5. The ______ was similar to the ABC in concept, but it was a working general-purpose computer rather than just a laboratory curiosity.

6. The method of sharing a computer in which tens or hundreds of users access the computer through typewriterlike terminals is called ______.

7. The ______ was supposed to be the first stored program computer.

8. The ______ was the first stored program computer.

9. The first commercial data processing system was the ______.

10. Control Data Corporation and Cray Research Inc. are best known for the production of ______.

Answers to Self-Review Exercises

Matching: 1 H, 2 G, 3 J, 4 C, 5 I, 6 B, 7 A, 8 D, 9 F, 10 E

Fill-in-the-Blanks:
1. electronic pocket calculator
2. punched-card control
3. Analytical Engine
4. James Powers
5. ENIAC
6. timesharing
7. EDVAC
8. EDSAC
9. UNIVAC I
10. supercomputers

Discussion Questions

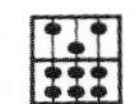

1. What is the oldest known computing device and how does it pertain to modern-day computers?

2. How did Pascal's arithmetic machine operate? What contemporary device is it similar to?

3. List the key sections of Babbage's Analytical Engine and discuss their functions.

4. How is Herman Hollerith's work important to the evolution of computers?

5. Why is Boolean logic important to modern computing?

6. Compare the capabilities of the ENIAC and the Mark I.

7. What is meant by generations of computers?

8. What does upwards compatible mean?

9. What do the Japanese believe is the key to the development of fifth generation computers?

10. How might history have changed if Babbage had been able to complete his Analytical Engine in 1840, thus giving the world a general-purpose computer a hundred years sooner?

Project

A visit to the Computer Museum can provide more information about the evolution of computers. You may also write for a brochure:

The Computer Museum
Museum Wharf
Boston, MA 02210

Part Two

Hardware

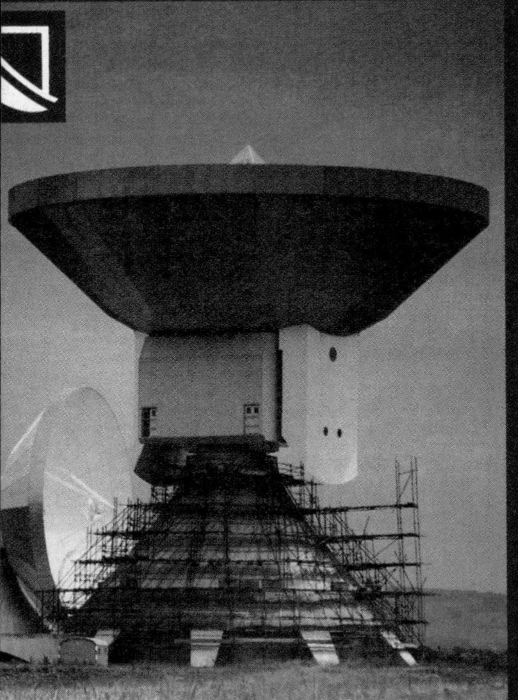

What are computers? How do they work? How do they process, store, and transmit information? Is the operation of computers so complex that only electronic geniuses can understand them, or are they simple enough for most of us to appreciate and understand? How fast do computers work? How much information can they store? How quickly can they exchange information among themselves? Why is storing computer data considered "the pits?" How have space satellites changed the picture of communications? Can computers take a poll? Can they concentrate? What are those marvelous devices called microchips? How are they made? Why are so many of them thrown away rather than fixed? What are "computers on ice?" Can we build living computers (fleshware)? Do computers like bars? Can they process garbage? Can they load bullets? How are lasers changing the world of computers and communications? What is touch sensing? Can computers see? Can they hear? Can they speak? Can they create magnificent pictures? Can they process three-dimensional information? Do computers ever make mistakes?

All these questions are answered in Part Two of this book. The next five chapters introduce computer hardware—the actual devices of computer systems. Studying hardware will help us to understand the capabilities of computers. In Part Three we will study software, which enables us to tell computers what tasks they are to perform.

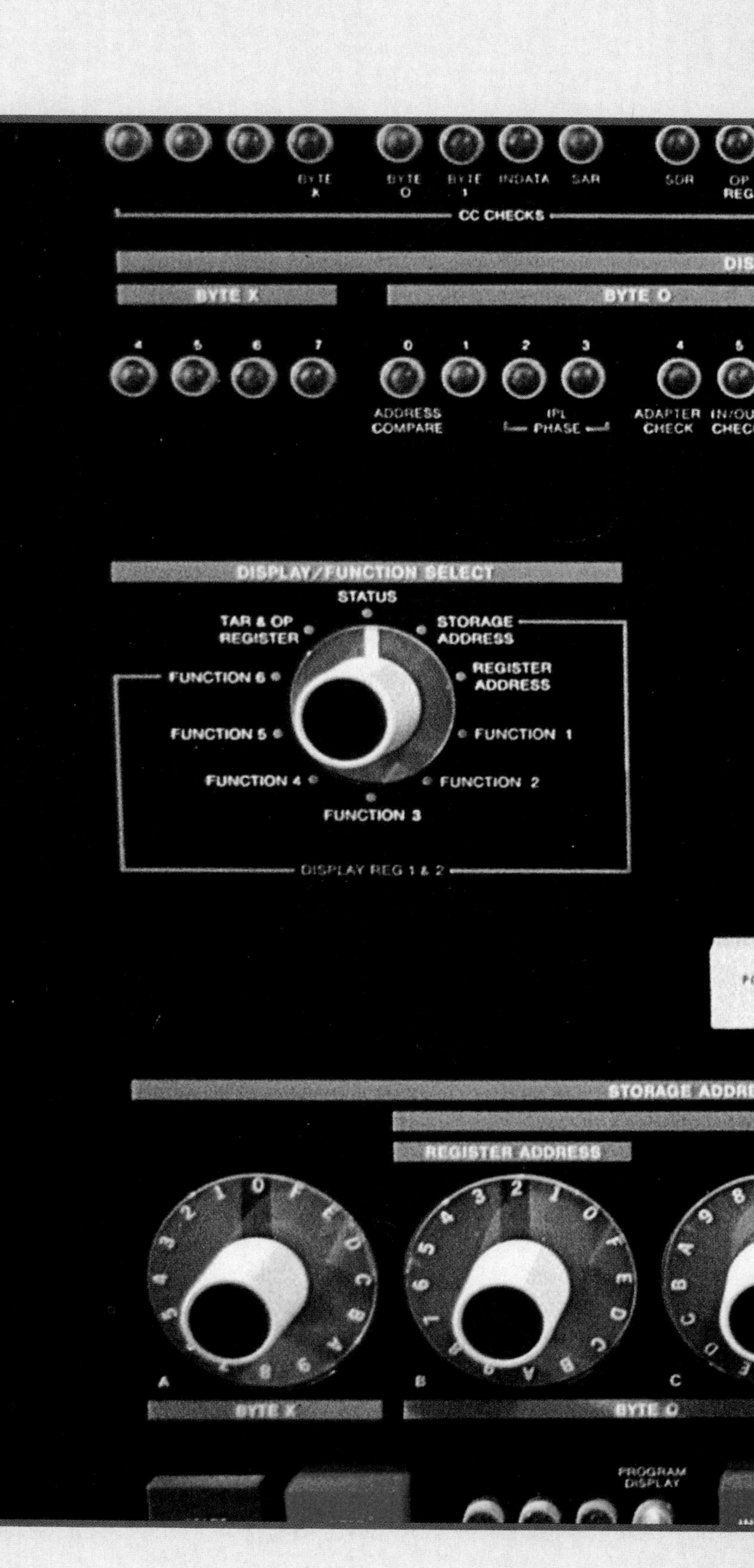
BYTE X
BYTE 0
BYTE 1
INDATA
SAR
SDR
OP REG
CC CHECKS
BYTE X
BYTE 0
ADDRESS COMPARE
IPL PHASE
ADAPTER CHECK
IN/OUT CHECK
INSTRUCTION STEP
DISPLAY/FUNCTION SELECT
STATUS
TAR & OP REGISTER
STORAGE ADDRESS
REGISTER ADDRESS
FUNCTION 6
FUNCTION 5
FUNCTION 4
FUNCTION 3
FUNCTION 2
FUNCTION 1
DISPLAY REG 1 & 2
STORE
CMPR
LOAD
CC CHECK
LAMP TEST
CC CHECK RESET
STORAGE ADDRESS
REGISTER ADDRESS
BYTE X
BYTE 0
PROGRAM DISPLAY

Chapter 3

The Processor

After reading this chapter you will understand:

1. What the major units and electronic components of the computer are and what they do
2. How data is organized and processed inside the computer
3. How computers make decisions
4. What a computer's instruction set is and what the major types of computer instructions are
5. What a microchip is and how microchips are manufactured

Left: The processor of the computer controls its operations, much as the brain controls the human body. This illustration shows the console of a large computer system. The knobs, buttons, toggles, and lights all help a person to monitor and control the operation of the computer.

Outline

In the future, you're going to get computers as prizes in breakfast cereals. You'll throw them out because your house will be littered with them.
Robert Lucky

Throughout this text, we will be focusing on **digital computers**, devices that perform calculations by *counting* numbers precisely. The abacus is a digital device that facilitates counting "whole numbers" of beads. Until recently, another type of computer, the **analog computer**, was also popular. Analog computers solve problems by **measuring**. For example, in a simple thermometer, liquid expands as the temperature rises. The thermometer is marked with temperatures to correspond to the height of a column of liquid; the height is used to measure a person's temperature.

Digital computers count precisely; analog computers can only measure to a certain level of accuracy. When a person reads a thermometer, for example, the person may say the temperature is 98.6, when in fact the exact temperature may be 98.59821643.

Analog computers were popular throughout the 1950s and 1960s when the cost of digital computers was still very high. Digital electronics has recently become so inexpensive that the world is "going digital," and analog computers are rarely used today. Even the common thermometer is being replaced by its digital counterpart.

Every digital computer system contains a **central processing unit** (CPU), or **processor**, that guides the computer through the various steps it takes to solve problems. The processor is the "brain" of the computer, controlling it in much the same way that the human brain controls the body. Most people don't believe that the computer's "brain" has any real intelligence, but researchers in the growing field of **artificial intelligence** are developing machines that do exhibit intelligent behavior. We will discuss artificial intelligence in Chapter 16, but now we will look at how the processor works.

The Basic Computer Processing Cycle

Computers perform only simple operations, but they do so with great speed and accuracy. Figure 3–1 shows the basic computer processing cycle. Information is entered into the computer through an **input unit**, such as the keyboard of a computer terminal. The computer then performs various calculations in its processing unit and presents the results of these calculations to the user via an **output unit**, such as a printer or video screen. The example in the figure shows a simple payroll application. The user types in an employee's name and hourly salary and then enters the number of hours the employee worked each day. The computer then calculates the sum of these daily fig-

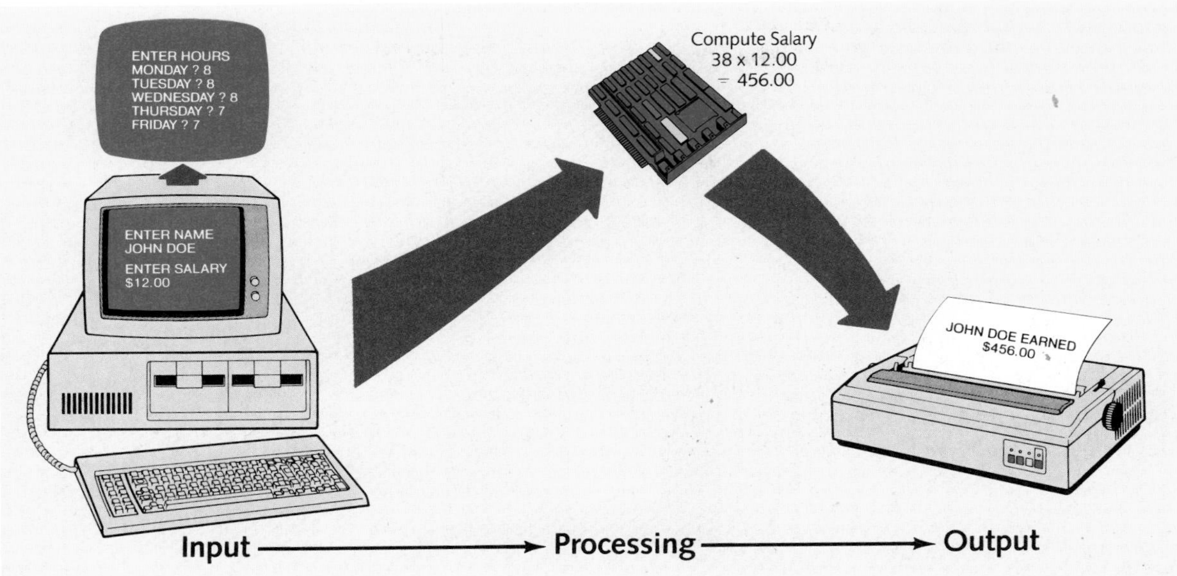

Figure 3–1 The basic computer processing cycle.

ures to determine that the employee worked a total of 38 hours. It multiplies this figure by the employee's hourly salary of $12 to determine that the employee earned a total of $456 for the week. The computer then prints this information for the user.

This simplified view of the functions the computer performs is called a **logical view** of the computer. A **physical view** of the computer reveals how the computer's actual knobs, buttons, bells, and whistles all work together to perform these functions. We focus on this view next.

The Central Processing Unit

Figure 3–2 shows the basic components of the computer system: the CPU, the input unit, and the output unit. (Chapters 4 and 5 discuss the input and output units in detail.) The CPU actually consists of three logical units: the **arithmetic and logic unit** (ALU), **main storage** (or the storage unit), and the **control unit**.

The ALU performs the arithmetic operations of addition, subtraction, multiplication, and division. It also makes such logical decisions as determining if this year's sales total is greater than last year's. Main storage stores information that arrives via the input unit so that this information is available to the ALU when actual calculations are to be performed. The storage unit also retains the results of the ALU's calculations until they can be presented to the user via the output unit. The control unit coordinates the operations of the other two units. In today's computer systems, all these functions take place on the surface of a microchip that is smaller than a paper clip (see Fig. 3–3 and the special section "How Microchips Are Made" on pages 52–57).

Main storage is used to retain active information, but because it is relatively expensive, most information is kept in the less costly **secondary storage**, or **auxiliary storage**. The most common secondary storage devices are tapes and disks (see Chapter 6, "Secondary Storage"). When information is to be processed, the computer transfers the information from secondary storage to main storage. After processing, the modified information is returned to secondary storage so that main storage may be reused (Figure 3–4). One of the jobs of the **operating system** of a computer is to make sure that the most active information is in main storage (see Chapter 12).

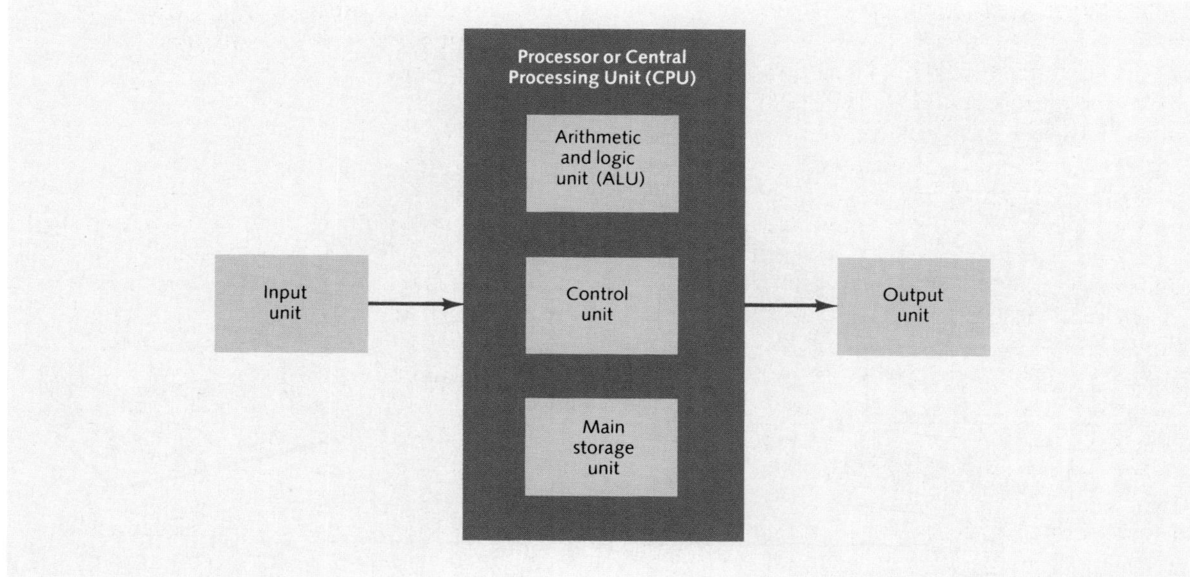

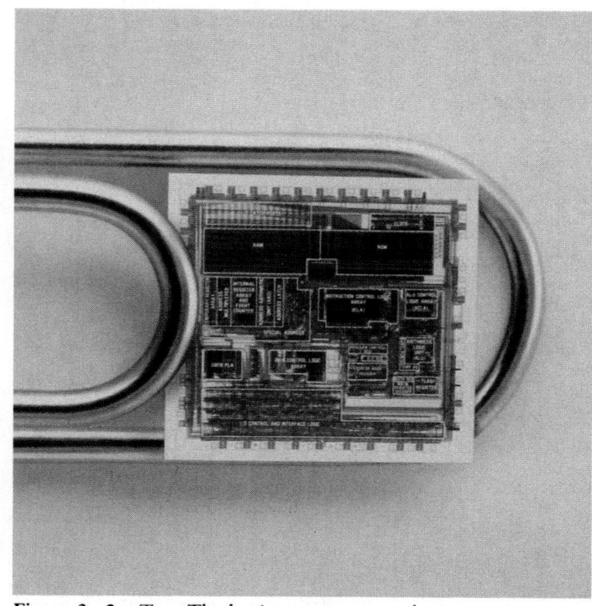

Figure 3–2 *Top:* The basic components of a computer system.

Figure 3–3 *Above:* Today's computers can be placed on a silicon chip smaller than a paper clip. The major components of the chip are labeled. The main memory is the wide dark area along the top of the chip. The ALU is at the right of the chip just below center. The other components are parts of the control unit.

Figure 3–4 *Left:* Shuttling information between main storage and secondary storage.

Arithmetic and Logic Unit

The ALU can actually make decisions. It does so by comparing pieces of information to one another. Based on the results of a comparison, the computer is able to select alternative actions to perform. The capabilities for comparison operations are "built in" to the computer; they do not have to be programmed by the user. A computer's built-in operations are called **machine language instructions**, **instructions**, or **machine instructions**. The set of all of a computer's built-in operations is called an **instruction set**. A computer may have as many as 100 or more instructions in its instruction set.

The three common comparison operations are:

1. **Equal to**. The computer determines if two pieces of information are identical. For instance, a highway patrol officer chasing a speeding car radios in the license number of the car. The computer compares the license number to a stored list of license numbers for stolen cars. If the computer detects an "equal to" comparison, the officer is notified that the car is stolen and that extra help will be sent to aid in apprehending the criminal.
2. **Greater than**. The computer determines if one quantity is larger than another. In credit card applications, for example, a store clerk will check with the central computer to see if a buyer should be allowed to charge a purchase. The computer has the buyer's account number, credit limit, and current balance on file. If the sum of the current balance plus the price of the new purchase is greater than the allowed credit limit, the purchase cannot be charged.
3. **Less than**. The computer determines if one quantity is smaller than another. Many banks offer free checking to customers who maintain a certain minimum balance, for example. The bank's computer, when preparing a customer's monthly statement, checks to see if the current balance is less than the minimum balance. If it is, the computer may charge the customer a penalty.

Combinations of these basic comparisons are used to form three other popular comparison operations: **not equal to**, **less than or equal to**, and **greater than or equal to**.

Main Storage

The sequences of instructions that tell the computer how to process data are called **computer programs**. These instruction sequences are prepared by computer programmers. A computer program must be in main storage for the computer to be able to perform, or **execute**, the program's instructions. Data must also be in main storage in order to be processed by an executing program.

Main storage is divided into a series of **locations**, each of which may contain either a data item or an instruction. Every location has an **address** and a **value** (Figure 3–5). The location address is used by the computer to refer to a particular location, just as a street address is used to refer to a particular house. The value is what is stored in that location, just as a certain person lives in a house at a particular address.

Figure 3–5 The computer's main storage is a series of locations (the rectangles). Each location has a location address (0, 1, 2, and so on) and contains a value (37, 42, 0, and so on).

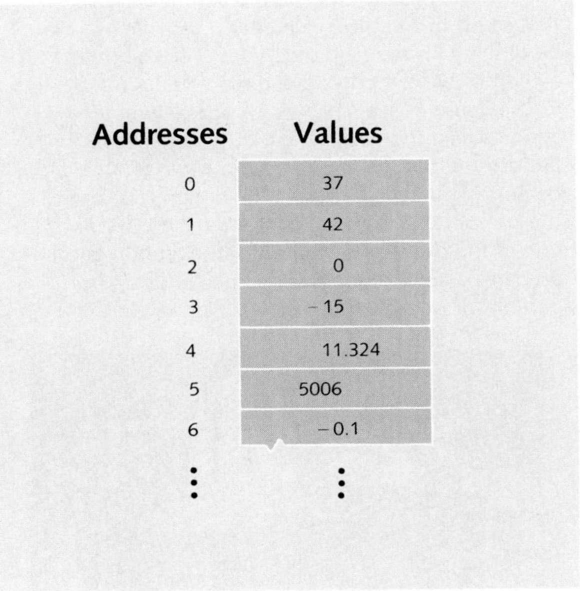

Addresses	Values
0	37
1	42
2	0
3	−15
4	11.324
5	5006
6	−0.1
⋮	⋮

How Microchips Are Made

Microchips—the heart of today's computer systems—begin with one of the most abundant materials on earth: common sand. The sand is heated to an extremely high temperature, about 1420° C, at which point it melts and forms liquid silicon, the material from which microchips are made. Silicon is used because it can be made either to conduct electricity or not, depending on special impurities "doped" into it. A proper combination of conducting and nonconducting regions makes an area of a chip behave just like a transistor, the electrical element from which computer circuits are built.

The process by which microchips are produced is similar in its first step to making rock candy. A "seed crystal" of silicon is dipped into a vat of liquid silicon, rotated, and withdrawn. Eventually, a large cylindrical crystal forms, about 3 or 4 inches wide and several feet long. This crystal is processed by machine into a smooth cylinder and sliced with a diamond saw into thin circular wafers of silicon (Figure 1). Each wafer is smoothed on both sides and then finely polished on one side. The wafer is heated in either oxygen or steam at about 1200° C (Figure 2) until a layer of silicon dioxide forms on it, much like oxygen makes iron rust. The wafer is then coated with a special light-sensitive material called **photoresist** (Figure 3).

The circuits to be placed on the silicon chips are extremely complex; many contain hundreds of thousands of electrical elements. These circuits are designed with the help of CAD/CAM (computer-aided design/computer-aided manufacturing) devices (Figure 4; see Chapter 5). These computer systems help the designer produce complex circuit patterns more quickly and accurately than would be possible manually. When the design is complete, the computer system contains a detailed description of the circuit. The computer then automatically prepares a large **photomask** containing the circuit pattern for one layer of the chip (Figure 5). The

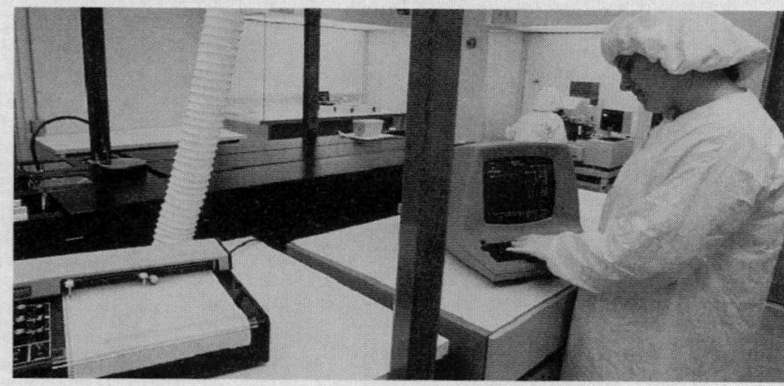

Figure 1 *Above top:* Each of these silicon wafers will eventually hold several hundred copies of a computer chip.

Figure 2 *Above middle:* Inserting a canister full of silicon wafers into a high temperature steam bath that will coat the wafers with a thin layer of silicon dioxide.

Figure 3 *Above bottom:* The application of photoresist is a highly automated step in the silicon wafer fabrication process. This person is programming the microprocessor that controls the photoresist process.

Figure 4 *Left:* CAD/CAM systems like this are used to design the large and complex drawings that represent the circuit patterns to be inscribed on chips. An operator at a display console types instructions that are interpreted by the computer. The design is displayed on the screen. The device in the background allows the designer to obtain a paper copy of the pattern. The finished design is transferred to a computer tape, which is used to control the device that produces a master photographic plate.

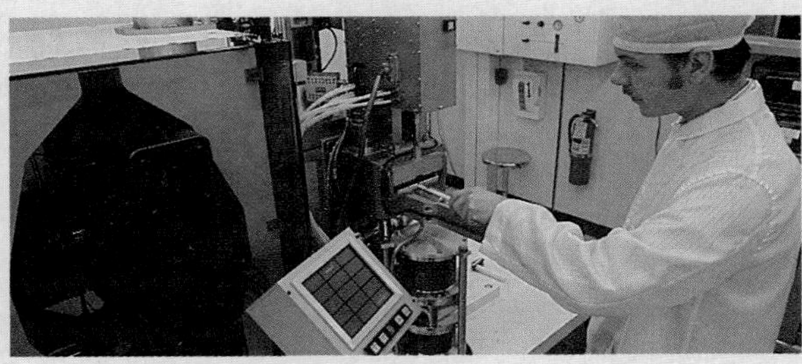

Figure 5 This computer-controlled electron-beam machine is used to produce the photomasks.

mask is carefully checked for flaws. Then the large mask is photoreduced to produce a master plate about 5 inches square. This master plate is used to place hundreds of tiny copies of the circuit pattern on a photomask the size of the silicon wafer.

The wafer is then exposed to ultraviolet light through the photomask containing the repeated circuit pattern. It is then dipped into a developer solution that washes away any unexposed portions of the photoresist. Then it is dipped into an acid bath that washes away the exposed areas of the silicon dioxide layer. Another wash removes the top layer of photoresist. This leaves the circuit pattern etched in the silicon dioxide layer. Some systems etch the circuit patterns with ionized gases called **plasmas** (Figure 6). This completes the etching of one layer; the entire process is then repeated many more times, once for each additional layer of the chip. Some chips have as many as a dozen or more

Figure 6 Plasma etching equipment is used here to etch silicon wafers with a mixture of gases.

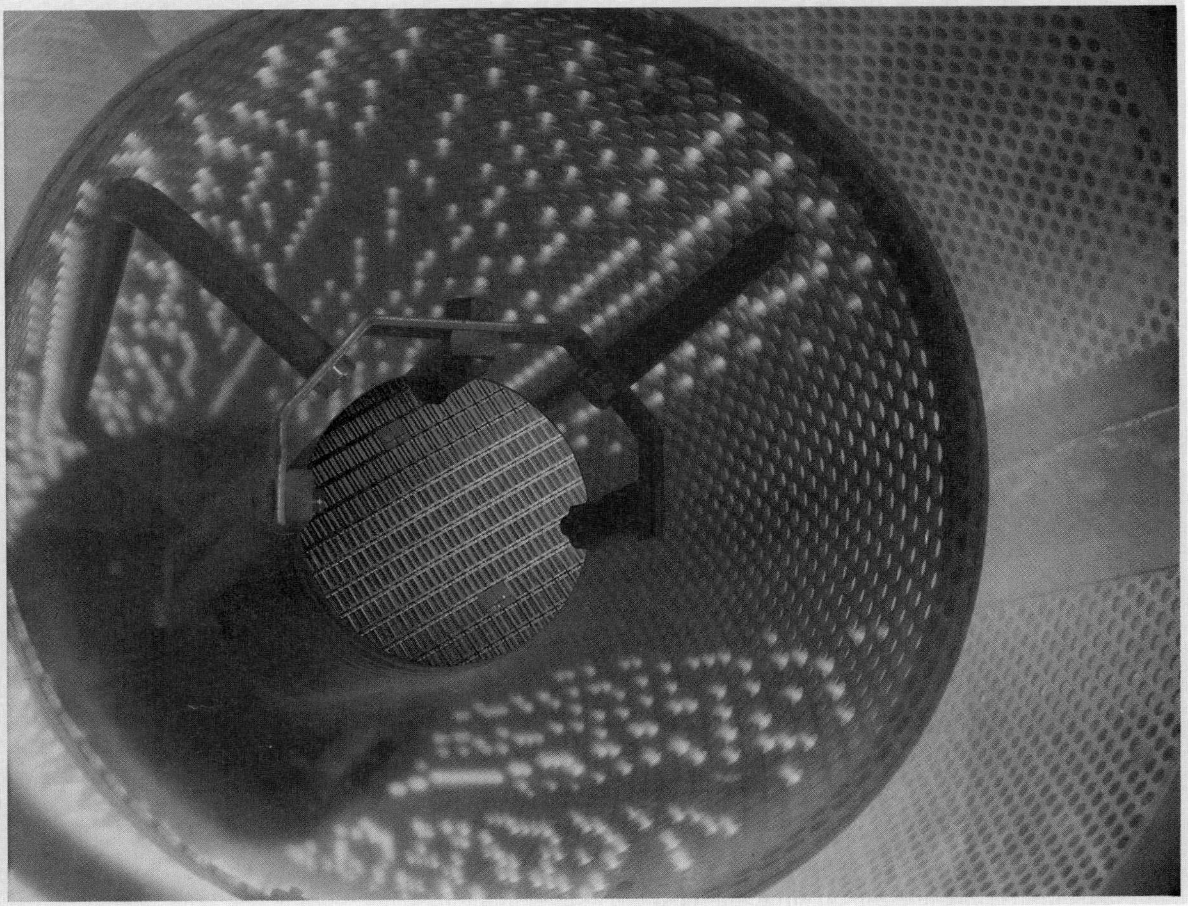

layers, and each new layer must be precisely aligned over the previous one (Figures 7 and 8). The multilayered chip is then soaked in a doping chemical and baked again (Figure 9), causing the desired impurities to seep into the silicon.

Of the hundreds of chips now etched into the wafer (Figure 10), as many as 80 percent may be defective. A computerized testing device probes each chip to determine which ones are flawless and which are flawed (Figure 11). The flawed chips are marked with an ink spot. The individual chips are then sliced from the wafer, and any flawed chips are discarded (it's cheaper to throw them away than to try to repair them).

For protection each chip is bonded to a **chip carrier** (a chip will crumble like a cookie if dropped). The chip is connected to the electrodes of the carrier by gold wires (Figure 12). These electrodes are the carrier's connection (Figures 13 and 14) to other circuit elements with which the chip will be combined to form a more complex electronic device. The chip is sealed in a protective plastic coating and is subjected to exhaustive testing by more automated equipment. Only flawless chips are shipped to customers.

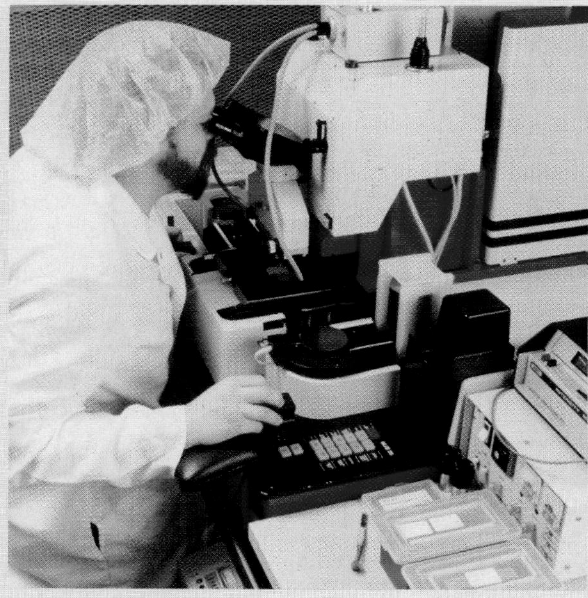

Figure 7 *Above:* A technician is aligning a photomask with a pattern previously etched into a silicon wafer.

Figure 8 *Below left:* Optical alignment of the logic pattern.

Figure 9 *Below:* A technician inserts silicon wafers into a high temperature oven for "doping" the chips.

Figure 10 *Bottom:* This finished silicon wafer has been etched with more than 7 million transistors.

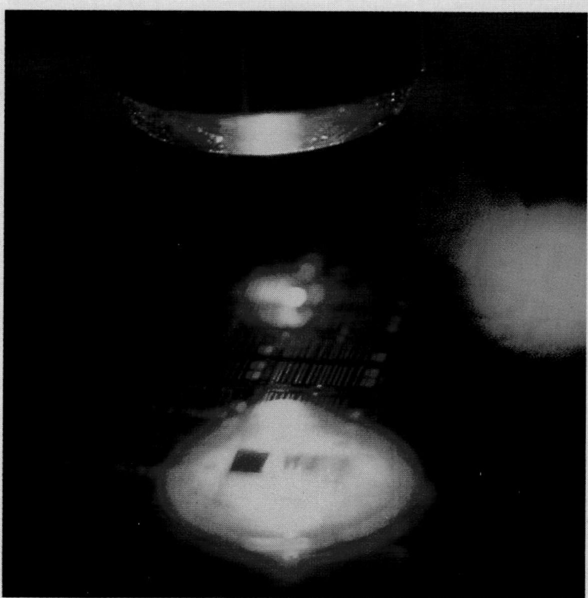

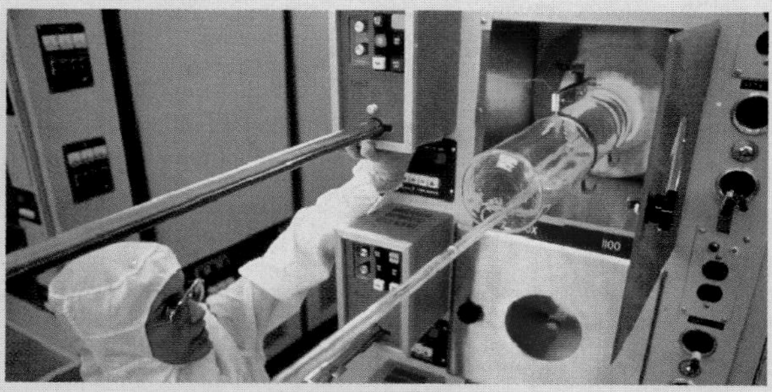

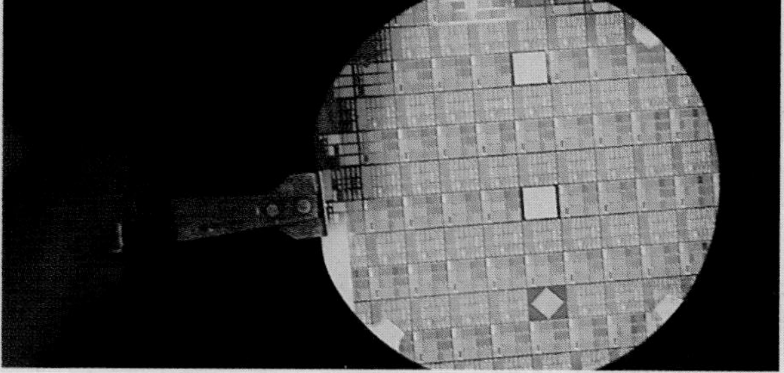

Figure 11 As part of the quality control process, each semiconductor chip is electronically probed to ensure that it works properly and performs well.

Figure 12 Here automated equipment is shown wiring a silicon chip to its carrier with gold filaments only one-third as thick as a human hair.

Figure 13 The silicon chips are sealed in protective carriers. The chip to the left and below the person's thumb is in place on a carrier with many legs—these are the electrodes that connect the chip to the outside world.

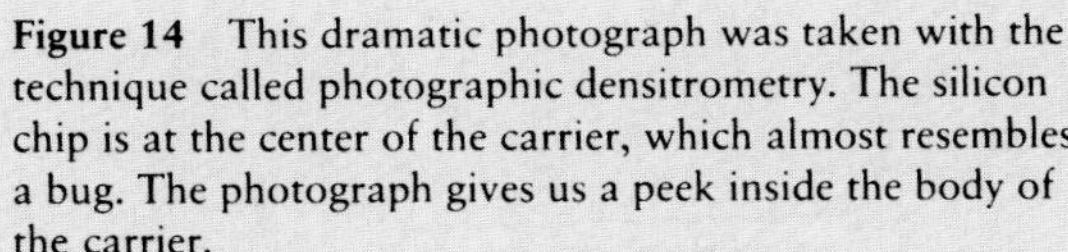

Figure 14 This dramatic photograph was taken with the technique called photographic densitometry. The silicon chip is at the center of the carrier, which almost resembles a bug. The photograph gives us a peek inside the body of the carrier.

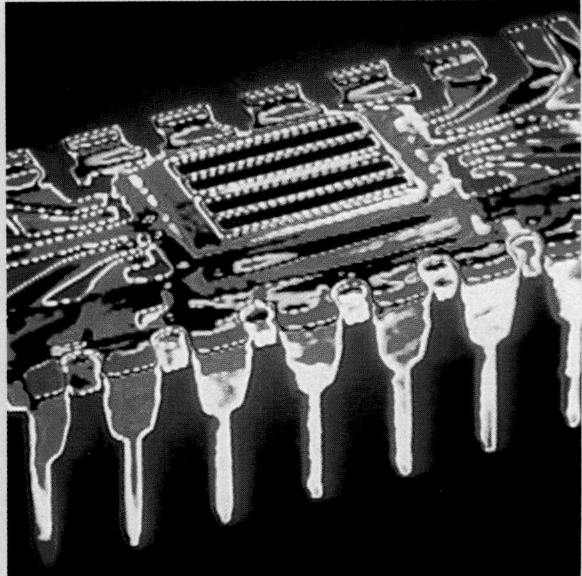

All this processing occurs in so-called clean rooms with special air purification systems (Figure 15). Scrupulous cleanliness is absolutely essential in processing microchips. In fact, a hospital operating room may have a hundred times as much dust as a chip factory.

Most of the finished chips are purchased by companies that combine them to form large complex electronic systems. As many as several hundred chips may be plugged into a single **printed circuit board**, which has also been designed by a computer (Figures 16, 17, 18).

Most of the U.S. firms that make and use microchips are located south of San Francisco in the Santa Clara Valley, otherwise known as Silicon Valley (Figure 19). Since 1957, when Fairchild Semiconductor was founded, there has been constant growth in the area. Companies such as Intel, Siliconix, Synertek, and Advanced Micro Devices were started by people from Fairchild. Some of the newer inhabitants are Apple and Atari, leading manufacturers of personal computers. During the early 1980s competition for qualified engineers has been fierce. Companies have offered very high salaries and extensive benefits packages to entice employees.

Figure 15 Scrupulous cleanliness is absolutely essential in semiconductor processing. This person operates a cleaning station that prepares the silicon wafers for the next step in their manufacture.

Figure 16 A finished printed circuit board. Dozens of chip carriers will be plugged into this empty board to complete a complex electronic component.

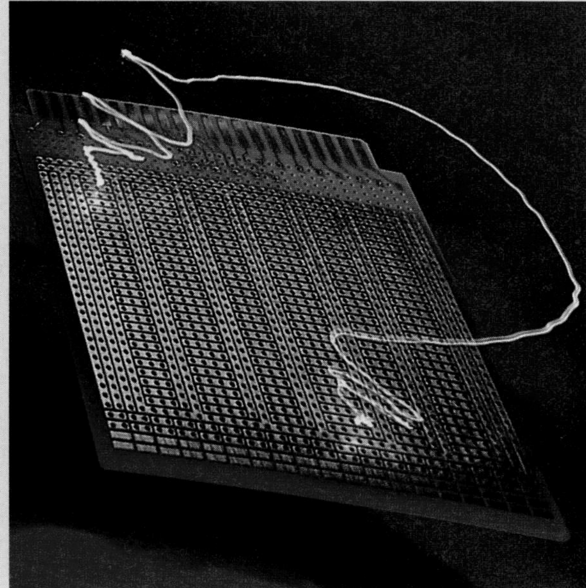

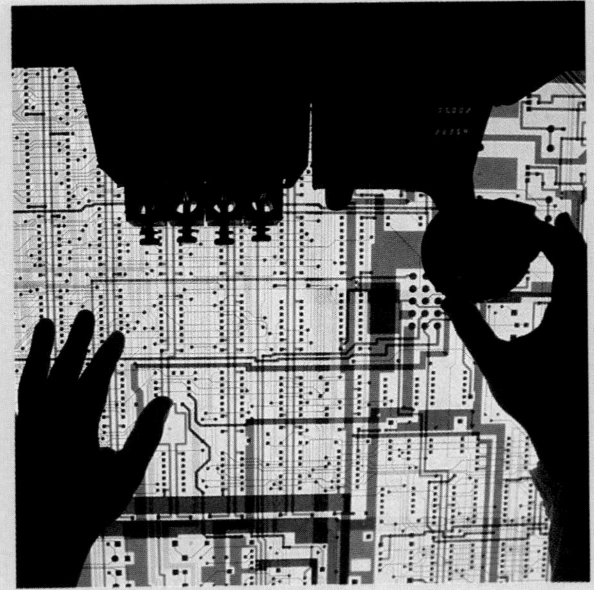

Figure 17 Computerized equipment is used to produce the photographic negatives for printed circuit boards that hold the chip carriers.

Figure 18 The finished product! Hundreds of chips enclosed in chip carriers are plugged into a printed circuit board to form a complex circuit that is part of a large-scale computer system.

Figure 19 An aerial view of a small section of Silicon Valley.

The Binary Number System

As we saw in Chapter 2, some early computers performed through use of the **decimal number system**, with electronic components representing digits from zero through nine. It is much easier and less costly to build electronic components that use the **binary number system**, with components representing only a zero or a one. (Appendix B of the text contains a detailed discussion on number systems.)

The bit—the unit on which computer storage is based—may contain either a zero, for off, or a one, for on, but nothing else. Computer electronics is capable of determining if a particular bit is "0" (that is, off) or "1" (that is, on). The computer may also "flip" a bit from "0" to "1" or vice versa, so bits are often called **flip-flops**, operating very much like "on/off" toggle switches (Figure 3–6).

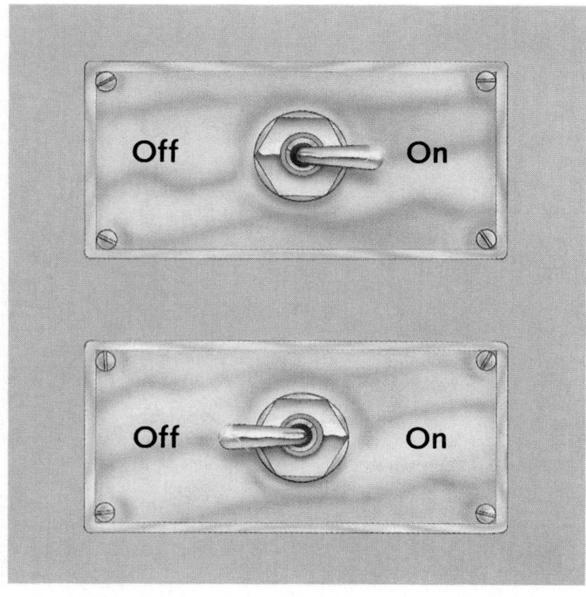

Figure 3–6 An "on/off" toggle switch is like a bit. It can be "on" (a binary 1) or "off" (a binary 0), and it can be flipped from one position to the other.

All the amazing things computers do involve the processing of only zeros and ones (see "How a Computer Really Works"). Of course, the key to the computer's success is that this processing occurs at millions of operations per second (billions on the world's fastest computers) and with incredible accuracy. This is because computers function electronically—the speed of electricity through a circuit is approximately 100,000 miles per second! Computers that process 1 trillion operations per second may be common in the next century.

Data Organization

Now let's consider how data is organized in computers. A bit can be used to represent two different things, such as "day" and "night." To represent more than two things, a series of bits is needed.

Computers process bits quite naturally, but bits are too small for people to handle conveniently. The smallest unit of data that people normally handle is a **character** (also called a **byte**), such as a letter (*A*), a digit (7), or a dollar sign ($). Ordinarily, users enter characters into computers by typing them at a keyboard. Some computers actually recognize human speech (see Chapter 4, "Input: Gateway to the Computer"), so users don't have to type information.

Numeric characters are the digits 0 through 9. **Alphabetic characters** are the letters of the alphabet, either the uppercase letters *A* through *Z* or the lowercase letters *a* through *z*. Blanks are generally treated as alphabetic characters. Other characters that users may type at a keyboard, such as symbols and punctuation marks, are called **special characters**.

When a user types a character, a pattern of bits is transferred electronically from the keyboard to the main storage in the processing unit. With one bit, only two different characters can be represented; 0 might correspond to one of the characters, for example, and 1 might correspond to the other. With two bits, four different characters can be represented because there are four different patterns:

00 (binary 0)
01 (binary 1)
10 (binary 2)
11 (binary 3)

How a Computer Really Works

How does the computer manipulate zeros and ones to perform its wonders? It's really quite simple.

Computer circuits are built from three fundamental circuit components—AND, OR, and NOT—whose operations are explained in Figure 1. These components are then combined to form more complex circuits.

One of the most common circuits used in today's computers is the **half-adder** (Figure 2). The half-adder adds two binary digits and produces a sum. Half-adders may be combined to add two binary numbers, each consisting of several digits.

The half-adder operates as follows. The two binary digits input at the left are simultaneously routed to the OR and the bottom AND. The output of the OR is routed to the top AND. The output of the bottom AND becomes the left digit of the sum; this output is also routed to the NOT. The output of the NOT enters the top AND. The output of the top AND becomes the rightmost digit of the sum.

The figure shows how the half-adder adds 1 + 1 to produce 10 (or binary 2). Verify that the half-adder correctly produces each of these four possible sums:

0 + 0 = 00 (binary 0)
0 + 1 = 01 (binary 1)
1 + 0 = 01 (binary 1)
1 + 1 = 10 (binary 2)

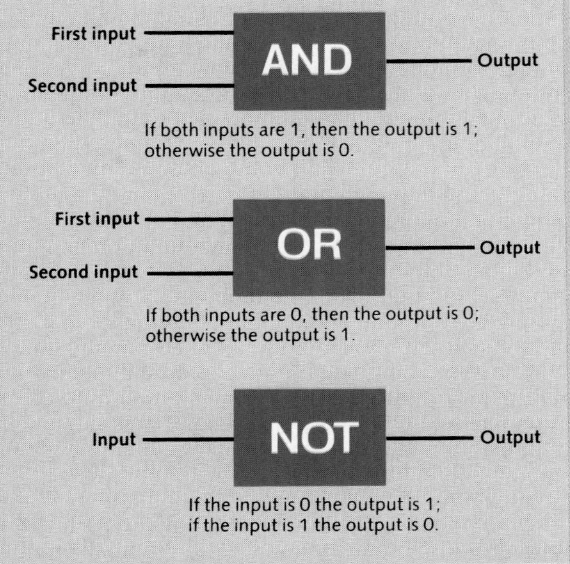

Figure 1 The three fundamental circuit operations, AND, OR, and NOT. All of the computer's more complex capabilities are provided by combining these fundamental operations.

Figure 2 This box represents a half-adder circuit that adds two binary numbers and produces the binary sum. The half-adder is one of the most common circuits used in computers.

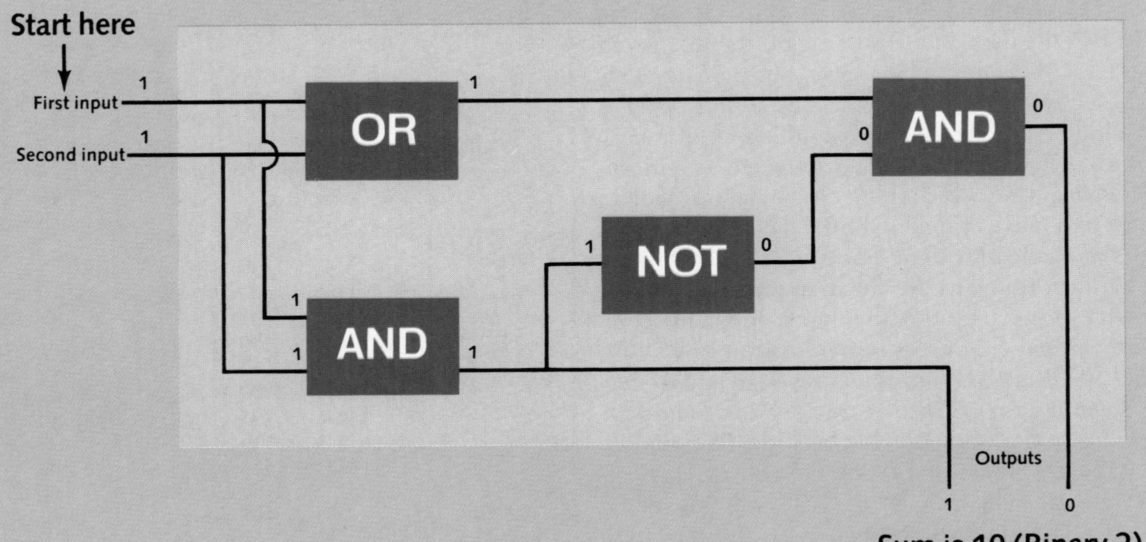

With three bits, eight patterns are possible:

000 (binary 0)
001 (binary 1)
010 (binary 2)
011 (binary 3)
100 (binary 4)
101 (binary 5)
110 (binary 6)
111 (binary 7)

And so on. If you wanted to represent 26 lowercase letters, 26 uppercase letters, 10 digits, and perhaps 30 or 40 special characters, enough bits would be needed to represent 26 + 26 + 10 + 40 = 102 characters. Because six bits can represent 64 characters and seven bits 128 characters, at least seven bits would be needed for the patterns. With eight bits, 256 different characters can be represented, many more than most keyboards allow.

A list of all the characters that can be used with a particular computer and the bit patterns that correspond to each of those characters is called a **character set.** Two character sets have become widely standardized: **EBCDIC** (for Extended Binary Coded Decimal Interchange Code), used mostly on large IBM computers, and **ASCII** (for American Standard Code for Information Interchange), used on most personal computers and for data communications.

EBCDIC uses patterns of eight bits per character; ASCII generally uses seven bits per character. These standards are so widely used that many computers are designed to handle both of them. In EBCDIC, all characters are treated as patterns of eight bits. Each character, or byte, is divided into two halves called **nybbles**: The leftmost four bits are called the **zone** portion of the byte; the rightmost four bits are the **digit** portion. The letters of the alphabet, the digits, and some common special characters represented in EBCDIC and ASCII are shown in Figures 3–7 and 3–8.

Computers organize characters into logical groups of data called fields, records, files, and databases. A group of related characters is a **field.** A **numeric field** such as "12689" contains only digits. An **alphabetic field** such as "Shirley Smith" contains letters and blanks. An **alphanumeric field** such as "1017 Windsor Drive" contains digits, letters, and blanks. Any field that contains at least one special character such as "$42,315.82" is simply called a **character field.** A **field** is a single piece of information. For example, "Mary

Figure 3–7 The uppercase letters and the digits in the EBCDIC and ASCII character sets.

	EBCDIC bit pattern		ASCII bit pattern
Uppercase letters			
A	1100	0001	1 0 0 0 0 0 1
B	1100	0010	1 0 0 0 0 1 0
C	1100	0011	1 0 0 0 0 1 1
D	1100	0100	1 0 0 0 1 0 0
E	1100	0101	1 0 0 0 1 0 1
F	1100	0110	1 0 0 0 1 1 0
G	1100	0111	1 0 0 0 1 1 1
H	1100	1000	1 0 0 1 0 0 0
I	1100	1001	1 0 0 1 0 0 1
J	1101	0001	1 0 0 1 0 1 0
K	1101	0010	1 0 0 1 0 1 1
L	1101	0011	1 0 0 1 1 0 0
M	1101	0100	1 0 0 1 1 0 1
N	1101	0101	1 0 0 1 1 1 0
O	1101	0110	1 0 0 1 1 1 1
P	1101	0111	1 0 1 0 0 0 0
Q	1101	1000	1 0 1 0 0 0 1
R	1101	1001	1 0 1 0 0 1 0
S	1110	0010	1 0 1 0 0 1 1
T	1110	0011	1 0 1 0 1 0 0
U	1110	0100	1 0 1 0 1 0 1
V	1110	0101	1 0 1 0 1 1 0
W	1110	0110	1 0 1 0 1 1 1
X	1110	0111	1 0 1 1 0 0 0
Y	1110	1000	1 0 1 1 0 0 1
Z	1110	1001	1 0 1 1 0 1 0
Digits			
0	1111	0000	0 1 1 0 0 0 0
1	1111	0001	0 1 1 0 0 0 1
2	1111	0010	0 1 1 0 0 1 0
3	1111	0011	0 1 1 0 0 1 1
4	1111	0100	0 1 1 0 1 0 0
5	1111	0101	0 1 1 0 1 0 1
6	1111	0110	0 1 1 0 1 1 0
7	1111	0111	0 1 1 0 1 1 1
8	1111	1000	0 1 1 1 0 0 0
9	1111	1001	0 1 1 1 0 0 1

Doe" might appear in a name field, "37 Watkins Road" might appear in a street address field, "Boston" might appear in a city field, and "(617) 555-1212" might appear in a telephone number field.

A **record** is a group of related fields. A student record in a university might contain various fields about that student, such as name, address, student identification number, year of graduation, grades, and club memberships.

A **file** is a group of related records. An inventory file, for example, might contain one record for each type of item carried by a department store. Each record might consist of several fields, such as the item number, item description, item price, quantity on hand, reorder point, and minimum number to reorder.

A **database** may be viewed as a collection of related files. A business might have a database consisting of files of employee information, customer accounts, suppliers, inventory, shipping and receiving, payroll, accounts payable, and so on.

Figure 3–8 Some lower case letters and special characters in the EBCDIC and ASCII character sets.

	EBCDIC bit pattern	ASCII bit pattern
Lowercase letters		
a	1000 0001	1100001
b	1000 0010	1100010
c	1000 0011	1100011
d	1000 0100	1100100
e	1000 0101	1100101
f	1000 0110	1100110
g	1000 0111	1100111
Special characters		
Blank	0100 0000	0100000
?	0110 1111	0111111
$	0101 1011	0100100
*	0101 1100	0101010
#	0111 1011	0100011
:	0111 1010	0111010

"Name, date of demise and denomination in nine characters per field or less."

Main Storage Size and Addressing

Each computer has its own main storage size. The larger the main storage, the more powerful the computer, because larger programs and more data can be kept available for rapid execution and access.

Main storage is measured in units of K bytes. Although K is ordinarily used to equal 1000, in computer applications K equals 1024 (2 raised to the 10th power). Personal computers generally have main storage sizes of 4K to 512K bytes or more. Each year typical main storage sizes increase and the price of storage tends to decrease. Some large mainframe computers have main storage sizes as large as 16KK bytes or more, that is, 16 x 1024 x 1024, or more than 16 million bytes of storage. The capital letter **M** is used to indicate 1024 x 1024, or approximately 1 million positions of memory. The quantity 16Mb is read as "sixteen **megabytes**."

Every byte in a computer's main storage has a unique address. The processor stores information into a particular byte and retrieves information from it by referring to the byte's address. Main storage addresses are generally numbered 0, 1, 2, up to some maximum number that is one less than the main storage size. For example, a 4K computer would have addresses ranging from 0 to 4095 (4K minus 1).

If a field that is several characters long is to be stored at location 1000, the first character is stored in 1000, the second character is stored in 1001, the third character is stored in 1002, and so forth. If a field that is several characters long is to be retrieved from main storage address 2000, then the first character is retrieved from 2000, the second character from 2001, and so on. So instructions that manipulate information in the computer's main storage must include: (1) the address of the start of the data field; (2) the length of the data field in bytes; and (3) the operation to be performed upon the data.

Editing

Data placed in main storage is processed at very high speeds by following the instructions in a computer program. The data may be used in various calculations to produce results. These results are then "prettied up" before they are presented to the user through the computer's output unit (see Chapter 5). For example, a payroll program might read the hours an employee worked each day and then sum these figures to determine that the employee worked 40 hours in one week. Other input data might include the employee's hourly salary and various deduction rates. The computer would perform the calculations to determine the gross pay and then subtract the deductions. It might determine that this employee should be paid 412.1 dollars. It would then "pretty this up" by preceding it with a dollar sign and appending a zero to the end so that "$412.10" would appear on the employee's paycheck. Such reorganization or rearrangement operations are called **editing**.

Destructive Read-In and Nondestructive Read-Out

When the processor stores data in a main storage location, it does not check to see if that location already contains information; it simply puts the new information in the location, destroying any information that was already there. This process, called **destructive read-in**, is comparable to making a new recording over an existing one on a tape recorder.

When the processor reads information from a storage location, it doesn't actually remove that data. Rather, it makes a copy of the data, leaving the original data intact. The process of reading data out of a storage location is often called **nondestructive read-out**. Using the tape recorder analogy again, when a recording is played back, the material is not erased and may be replayed many times.

Machine Language Instructions

The various operations a computer can interpret and perform are called its machine language instructions. Most computers have instructions that can input data from outside the computer into the computer's main storage, output data from main storage, perform simple arithmetic calculations, move data between main storage locations, edit data, perform comparisons, and handle many other functions.

The processor reads the instructions in a computer program and performs these instructions one at a time in the proper sequence. Machine language instruction formats vary widely among the different types of computers. For example, large-scale scientific computers, such as those used by the National Aeronautics and Space Administration (NASA) in the space shuttle program, generally have instructions that perform precise mathematical calculations at great speed. Data processing computers used by businesses generally have instructions that can manipulate and edit large amounts of information efficiently.

Some computers have instructions that reference only a single piece of data; these are called **single operand instructions**. Other computers have instructions that specify two or more data items; these are called **multiple operand instructions**. The more operands per instruction, the more powerful the instruction.

For example, to calculate the sum of two numbers, one stored at location 1000 and four bytes long and another stored at location 2000 and three bytes long, a machine language instruc-

tion like

ADD 1000 4 2000 3

might be used. By convention, such machines generally add the two numbers together and place the result in the first field (in this case, addresses 1000 through 1003). This, of course, destroys the value that was there initially. For readability we will use an English word to represent the operation and decimal numbers to represent the operands; genuine machine languages use binary ones and zeros.

A machine that has only single operand instructions would perform the same addition by a sequence of instructions that might look like

```
LOAD    1000 4
ADD     2000 3
STORE   1000 4
```

The LOAD instruction loads a special **register** (a temporary storage device in the ALU, often called an **accumulator**) with the 4-byte number starting at location 1000. The ADD instruction adds to the contents of the accumulator the 3-byte number beginning at location 2000. Finally, the STORE instruction stores the results of the previous calculation from the accumulator into the 4-byte field beginning at location 1000. Thus, computers with single operand instructions generally require many more instructions to accomplish the same tasks than would be required by computers with multiple operand instructions. As the price of computers continues to decline, their machine languages are tending toward multiple operand instruction sets.

Machine language programming is tedious and susceptible to error. As we will see in our discussion of programming languages in Chapter 9, most programming today is actually done in high-level languages that use English words and common mathematical notations.

The Instruction Execution Cycle

Now let's consider the execution of a typical machine language instruction in more detail. The computer must always know which location in main storage contains the next instruction to be executed. For this purpose, there is a special register in the CPU called the **instruction counter.** After each instruction is performed, the CPU automatically updates the instruction counter with the address of the next instruction to be performed.

Suppose the instruction counter contains address 5000. The computer **fetches** the instruction from location 5000 and places it into another special register in the CPU called the **instruction register.** The electronic components of the computer are designed in such a way that the computer can determine what type of instruction is in the instruction register—an addition, a subtraction, an input operation, an output operation, an edit operation, a comparison, and so on. If a computer's instruction register contains a multiplication instruction such as

MUL 6000 4 7500 3

the instruction is to multiply the 4-byte number starting in location 6000 by the 3-byte number starting in location 7500 and deposit the result in the 4-byte field at 6000.

The CPU proceeds as follows. First it fetches the 4-byte number from locations 6000 to 6003 and loads it into a register in the ALU. Then it fetches the 3-byte number from locations 7500 to 7502 and loads it into another register in the ALU. The product of the two values in the ALU registers is then calculated and deposited into a third ALU register. The CPU then stores this result back into the 4-byte field beginning at location 6000. (If the multiplication results in a number larger than four bytes, an **overflow error**

Drawing by Richter; © 1983 The New Yorker Magazine, Inc.

has been made. Most computers will terminate a program when such a serious error occurs. For this reason, overflow is called a **fatal error**).

In short, most computers use the following scheme:

1. Fetch the next instruction from the address indicated in the instruction counter and place it in the instruction register.
2. Fetch the data to be operated upon and place it in registers in the ALU.
3. Perform the indicated operation.
4. Store the result of the operation back into main storage.

Why all this shuttling of instructions and data? Why not simply perform the calculations directly in the computer's main storage?

It is useful here to compare the operation of a computer system to that of a hospital with hundreds of rooms for patients and only a single operating room. A patient who requires surgery is moved from his or her own room and taken to the operating room. After the operation the patient is returned to his or her room, and the next patient is taken to the operating room. It would be too costly to provide each of the several hundred patient rooms with the expensive equipment required in an operating room.

Similarly, operations on data can only be performed in the CPU, so data is brought from main storage to the CPU. It remains there while it is being operated on and is returned to main storage when the operation is completed. The electronics required to perform operations is kept busy in much the same way that the hospital's operating room is kept busy.

Variable Word-Length and Fixed Word-Length Machines

The examples we have considered so far are for computers that are **variable word length machines**. These machines allow fields to occupy as many bytes as needed, within certain limits. For example, the name "John Doe" can be stored in an 8-byte field (remembering that the blank is also treated as a byte); the name "George Washington" requires a 17-byte field. Variable word-length machines are more convenient for processing text, where words of different lengths are manipulated.

Fixed word-length machines process all information as fixed-size groups of bytes. These machines are less flexible, but they can perform certain operations much faster, particularly mathematical calculations. Fixed word-length machines perform their operations in terms of *words* rather than individual bytes. A word may be several bytes long, but every word on the machine is exactly the same size, and all manipulations involve words rather than individual bytes. The programming examples in the next two sections are for fixed word-length machines.

Some computers can perform both fixed-length operations and variable-length operations while executing a single program. This makes it possible to generate the most efficient programs for a given application.

Machine Language Programming

Every computer can understand a limited set of machine language instructions. A sequence of these instructions as well as data items forms a computer program that tells the computer how to solve a particular problem. The computer does not come equipped to solve specific problems. Rather, it is a general-purpose instrument that is capable of performing the instructions in computer programs supplied by people. In this sense, the computer is very much like a phonograph, and computer programs are like phonograph records.

How are computers programmed? A computer programmer writes a program that solves a given problem. The program is placed into the computer's main storage through an input device. The computer then performs each instruction, one at a time. Normally, instructions are performed sequentially, but it is possible for the computer to **jump**, or **branch**, to another instruction in the program. We'll soon see why this is important.

Figure 3–9 shows a simple machine language program that has been placed into a computer's main storage at locations 00 through 12. Locations 00 through 08 each contain a machine language instruction. Locations 09 through 12 are reserved for data to be used by the instructions. Our sample computer always begins with the instruction in location 00. Each instruction has two parts—an operation such as READ, LOAD, ADD, STORE, PRINT, or STOP—and an operand, which is the address of the storage location containing the data referenced in the instruction.

Now let's see exactly how our computer performs the program in the figure. The first instruction, READ 09, causes the computer to read a value into storage location 09. The user types in a value of 4001, and location 09 changes from its starting value of +0 to a new value of +4001. Because the value in this location can change as the program runs, location 09 is called a **variable**. A location that contains a fixed value is called a **constant**.

The next two instructions, READ 10 and READ 11, obtain two more values. Let's assume the user types 2000 and then 6005, so that after the READs, the storage locations contain

09: +4001
10: +2000
11: +6005

The instruction LOAD 09 causes the value +4001 to be loaded into the accumulator in the ALU; that is where information must be placed to be used in calculations. The next instructions, ADD 10 and ADD 11, each cause a value to be added into the one already in the accumulator. After these instructions are executed, the accumulator contains the sum +12006. The instruction STORE 12 takes the value in the accumulator and places it back into storage at location 12. This frees the accumulator for further calculations. The instruction PRINT 12 then prints or displays the sum +12006 on an output device. The instruction STOP causes the computer to terminate this program.

Looping: The Real Power of the Computer

Now that we've written a program to sum 3 numbers, we could easily write one to sum 100 numbers. If we use the same approach as in Figure 3–9, our program would be very long: It would contain 100 READ instructions, a LOAD, 99 ADDS, a PRINT, a STOP, 100 storage locations for the numbers, and a storage location for the sum. The program in Figure 3–10 adds 100 numbers, but it is much shorter than the several

Figure 3–9 A machine language program that reads three numbers and prints their sum.

Main Storage

	Addresses	Location Contents	
Instructions	00	READ 09	Read first number into location 09
	01	READ 10	Read second number into location 10
	02	READ 11	Read third number into location 11
	03	LOAD 09	Place first number into accumulator
	04	ADD 10	Add second number into accumulator
	05	ADD 11	Add third number into accumulator
	06	STORE 12	Store sum of the three numbers into location 12
	07	PRINT 12	Print sum of three numbers from location 12
	08	STOP	End of program
Data Items	09	+0	Storage area for first number
	10	+0	Storage area for second number
	11	+0	Storage area for third number
	12	+0	Storage area for sum of three numbers

hundred locations we would need with the first approach. That's because this program uses the technique of **looping**. Looping allows the computer to reuse certain instructions many times, greatly reducing the number of instructions the programmer must write.

The program in Figure 3–10 essentially consists of the following steps:

1. Read the next number.
2. Add the number into the running total.
3. Add 1 to the count of numbers processed.
4. If this count is not yet 100, go back to step 1.
5. Print the total.
6. Stop.

In step 4 the program makes a decision. If all 100 numbers have not yet been processed, the program goes back to step 1, thus forming a **loop** of the first four steps. This loop is repeated 100 times. After the 100th number is processed, the program continues to step 5, where it prints the sum, and then to step 6, where it stops. You can compare this series of steps to the machine language program in the figure to see how they are actually programmed. Note that

Step 1	corresponds to	READ 11
Step 2	corresponds to	LOAD 12 ADD 11 STORE 12
Step 3	corresponds to	LOAD 13 ADD 14 STORE 13
Step 4	corresponds to	COMPARE 15 IF NOT EQUAL GO TO 00
Step 5	corresponds to	PRINT 12
Step 6	corresponds to	STOP

The program uses three variables:

Location 11, storage area for next number
Location 12, storage area for total of numbers
Location 13, storage area for counting the numbers

and two constants:

Location 14, constant of +1 used for counting
Location 15, constant of +100 used for comparing

Figure 3–10 A machine language program that uses looping to read 100 numbers and print their sum.

		Addresses	Location contents	
	Instructions	00	READ 11	Read next number into location 11
		01	LOAD 12	Load total of all numbers into accumulator
		02	ADD 11	Add next number to total in accumulator
		03	STORE 12	Store total back into storage location 12
		04	LOAD 13	Load count of numbers into accumulator
		05	ADD 14	Add 1 to indicate another number has been processed
		06	STORE 13	Store count back into storage location 13
		07	COMPARE 15	Compare count in accumulator to constant of + 100 in location 15
		08	IF NOT EQUAL GO TO 00	If the count is not as yet 100 then go read and process next number
		09	PRINT 12	Print the total of the numbers
		10	STOP	End of program
Data	Variables	11	+0	Storage area for next number
		12	+0	Storage area for total of numbers
		13	+0	Storage area for counting the numbers
	Constants	14	+1	Constant value of + 1 for counting
		15	+100	Constant value of + 100 for comparing

Figure 3–11 The Josephson junction.

Thus, the technique of looping is a powerful one that saves the programmer a great deal of time. In fact, most computer programs contain at least one loop, and large programs usually contain many.

The Josephson Junction: The "Computer on Ice"

An exciting storage technology now under development is the **Josephson junction**, a data processing switch designed to operate at low temperatures (Figure 3–11). The principle behind its operation is that at temperatures within a few degrees of absolute zero, −273° C, some metals become superconductive, that is, offer no resistance to an electric current. Once started, an electric current can flow indefinitely in a superconductive circuit. Because of their microscopic size, high speed, and minimal energy consumption, Josephson junctions can be used to build ultra-high capacity, ultra-fast computers. Today's supercomputers are pushing the one-**BIPS** (billion instructions per second) range. It is believed that computers using Josephson junction switches may operate in the 100-BIPS range. This means that in their first year of operation Josephson computers could perform more calculations than all computer calculations made since the dawn of civilization.

Consequences of Technology

The revolutionary changes that have occurred in computer technology have allowed programmers to process vast amounts of material with great speed. Such capabilities provide the potential for great power in many areas. In information retrieval applications we could ask questions of our supercomputer, and it might be able to search the sum total of humankind's knowledge in just a few moments. Should such awesome power be made freely available to anyone who wants it? Would it put a Big Brother in our lives, or would it help us guard our privacy in a manner not possible today? These questions remain to be answered.

Biochips (Fleshware?)

As the quest for ever smaller yet more powerful microcircuits pushes the limits of current technologies, a new type of computer chip made from proteins—the **biochip**—is being developed. Computer scientists, genetic engineers, and microelectronic engineers are working to create "living" computers that will be able to grow and reproduce.

The biocomputer would be structured like the human brain, with billions of bioprocessors processing information simultaneously. (Today's computers generally use one or perhaps a few processors.) It is conceivable that biochips could carry a signal a million times faster than human nerves, that **biobits** could operate a hundred million times faster than human nerve junctions, and that the "circuitry" of a biochip could be packaged a million times more densely than that of the human brain. These observations point to the possibility of developing computers of enormous "intellectual" capacity. A biochip the size of a thimble might be able to contain as much computer storage as has been manufactured for all computers ever built!

A biochip implanted in the human body would require so little energy that it could be powered indefinitely by body heat. Biochip technology may make possible the development of artificial nerves or replacements for any other body part. (Do you suppose this technology might enable development of an artificial brain?) **Bioprocessors** could be the key to restoring sight to the blind and hearing to the deaf. Inserted in the body, biochips could act as chemical laboratories monitoring the intake of dangerous chemicals and issuing warnings sufficiently in advance to prevent serious health problems. These startling capabilities may become available by the turn of the century.

Computers facilitate biochip research. In particular, computer graphics techniques (see Chapter 5) help genetic engineers design the proteins needed for biochips on a computer screen before attempting to grow them in a laboratory.

Biochips could present a savings in cost which is of great importance as the cost of building the superchips of the future is becoming a real concern. Biochips would literally grow themselves, and at nominal cost.

Biochips may also be of importance because of their ability to withstand radiation. The Department of Defense is concerned about a phenomenon called EMP (electromagnetic pulse). After a nuclear explosion, EMP would generate currents that would cause electronic instrumentation to malfunction. It is believed that biocircuits would be less susceptible to EMP problems. Even everyday exposure to cosmic radiation is a concern. Certain types of cosmic rays can cause a silicon chip to "flip a bit" accidentally. Again, it is believed that biochips would be more resistant to such problems.

Offshoots of such technology present many intriguing possibilities. For example, implanting preprogrammed chips could supply humans with specialized capabilities. In Chapter 16 we discuss the field of artificial intelligence and the notion of "expert systems." "Expert biochips" could conceivably be implanted in the human brain so that a person could be "given" the knowledge and reasoning capabilities of an expert in any field. Perhaps there could be a "doctor chip" or a "professor chip." How about an "SAT chip," containing definitions of all those obscure vocabulary words needed to score high on Scholastic Aptitude Tests for college admissions? For that matter, how about an "encyclopedia chip," or even a "sum-total-of-human-knowledge chip"?

Perhaps it would be possible to implant a "learning biochip" in the brain of a great sur-

geon. The chip would absorb the knowledge contained in this person's brain. It would then be removed, and duplicated in the laboratory. These "cloned" chips could then be implanted in the brains of aspiring doctors.

These many possibilities are at once horrifying and intriguing. Such capabilities generate an unending stream of philosophical, ethical, and theological questions. Technology is, and always has been, a double-edged sword.

Summary

1. The central processing unit (CPU, or processor) guides the computer through the various steps of solving a problem.
2. Data enters the computer through an input unit, is processed by the central processing unit, and is then made available to the user through an output unit.
3. A logical view of a computer shows what functions the computer performs. A physical view of a computer shows how the mechanisms of the computer actually perform these functions.
4. The three logical units that make up the central processing unit are the arithmetic and logic unit (ALU), main storage (or storage unit), and the control unit.
5. The ALU performs arithmetic operations and makes logical decisions by comparing pieces of information. Main storage stores data that arrives from an input unit so the data is available to the ALU when it performs calculations. The results of the ALU's calculations are also stored in main storage until they are presented to a user via an output unit. The control unit coordinates the operations of main storage and the ALU.
6. Main storage retains active programs and data. It is relatively expensive, so secondary storage is used to store programs and data until they are needed in main storage.
7. The set of a computer's built-in operations is called its instruction set. A computer program is a set of instructions that tells a computer how to solve a particular problem.
8. A computer program must be in main storage in order for a computer to be able to perform its instructions. Main storage is divided into locations. Each location has an address and a value. The value in a particular location may be either an instruction or a piece of data.
9. The basic unit of computer storage is called a bit (binary digit). A bit may contain only a zero or a one.
10. A numeric character is any digit 0 to 9. An alphabetic character is any letter of the alphabet or a blank. Special characters are any characters other than digits, letters, or blanks.
11. The set of all characters that can be used with a particular computer as well as the bit patterns that correspond to those characters is called a character set. The two most widely used character sets are EBCDIC (Extended Binary Coded Decimal Interchange Code), and ASCII (American Standard Code for Information Interchange).
12. A group of related characters is called a field. A numeric field contains only digits. An alphabetic field contains only letters and blanks. An alphanumeric field contains letters, blanks, and digits. Any field that contains a special character is called a character field. A field is a single piece of information. A record is a group of related fields. A file is a group of related records. A database is a collection of related files.
13. When the processor stores data in a main storage location, it destroys any information that was already there. This is called destructive read-in. When the processor reads information from a storage location, it makes a copy of the data while leaving the original data intact. This is called nondestructive read-out.

14. The processor reads instructions from a computer program in main storage and performs these instructions one at a time in the proper order. The instruction counter contains the address of the next instruction to be performed.

15. Fixed word-length machines treat all fields as being the same size. Variable word-length machines allow fields to be as long or as short as they need to be (within certain limits).

Important Terms 

accumulator
address
arithmetic and logic unit (ALU)
biochip
byte
central processing unit (CPU)
character
computer program
control unit
database
destructive read-in
execute a program
field
file
fixed word-length machine
flip-flop
half-adder
input unit
Josephson junction
location
looping
machine language instruction
main storage
nondestructive read-out
nybble
output unit
record
register
secondary storage
variable word-length machine

Self-Review Exercises 

Matching

Next to the term in column A, place the letter of the statement in column B that best describes it.

Column A

1. Processor
2. An input unit
3. Josephson junction
4. Auxiliary storage
5. ALU
6. Left nybble
7. An output unit
8. Looping
9. Built-in operation
10. Biochip

Column B

A. Machine language instruction
B. Video screen
C. Makes logical decisions
D. Zone
E. "Brain" of the computer
F. Reusing instructions
G. Keyboard of a computer terminal
H. "Living" computer
I. Tapes and disks
J. "Frozen" computer

Fill-in-the-Blanks

Fill in the blanks in each of the following:

1. Digital computers perform calculations by ______ numbers precisely.

2. The CPU consists of three logical units: the ______ , ______ , and ______ .

3. A computer program must be in ______ storage for the computer to perform or execute the program's instructions.

4. The smallest unit of data that people normally handle is a ______ .

5. The two character sets that have become widely standardized are ______ and ______ .

6. A group of related characters is a ______ .

7. Main storage is measured in units of ______ .

8. The various operations a computer can interpret and perform are called ______ .

9. After each instruction is performed, the CPU automatically updates the ______ with the address of the next instruction to be performed.

10. Computers with ______ allow fields to occupy as many bytes as needed.

Answers to Self-Review Exercises

Matching: 1 E, 2 G, 3 J, 4 I, 5 C, 6 D, 7 B, 8 F, 9 A, 10 H

Fill-in-the-Blanks:
1. counting
2. arithmetic and logic unit, storage unit, control unit
3. main
4. character
5. EBCDIC, ASCII
6. field
7. K bytes
8. machine language instructions
9. instruction counter
10. variable word length

Discussion Questions 

1. What are some of the differences between main storage and secondary storage?

2. List the three common built-in comparison operations. Give your own examples of how each might be used.

3. What is an instruction set?

4. Explain the concept of a computer program.

5. Distinguish between a location's address and its value.

6. List the various levels of data from bit to database. Give an example of each.

7. Explain the concepts of destructive read-in and nondestructive read-out.

8. Explain how the computer performs its instruction execution cycle. Use a division instruction as an example.

9. Show how to modify the machine language program of Figure 3–10 so that it will calculate the sum of 1000 numbers. What feature of this program makes it so easy to modify?

10. What is a biochip? Give some possible applications of biochips.

Project 

Building and using biochips raises many ethical questions. Should we attempt to construct a "living" computer? What if it could reproduce itself? Suppose it were "smart" enough to improve upon its own design—what might it evolve into? Discuss these questions with several people, and write a report summarizing the issues raised and the points made.

BATCH DATE
HOURS
RATE
POSTING PERIOD
GROSS
DEPARTMENT
COMPLETION CODE
CYCLES PAID
JOB STEP
STATUS
QUANTITY COMPLETE
EMPLOYEE NUMBER
HOURS CODE
RATE CODE
SHIFT CODE
LABOR EXPENSE CCN
LABOR EXPENSE ACCOUNT
PREMIUM EXPENSE CCN
WORK ORDER NUMBER
FUNCTION
MACHINE CENTER
PERCENT COMPLETE
XEROX 1330
XEROX 1330

Chapter 4

Input: Gateway to the Computer

After reading this chapter you will understand:

1. What is meant by computer input
2. How punched cards operate and the reasons for the decline in their use
3. What is meant by on-line and off-line computer usage
4. Various user-friendly input methods including touch sensing and voice recognition
5. The source data automation techniques of optical character recognition, magnetic ink character recognition, and bar code reading

Left: The most common computer input mechanism in use today is the conventional typewriter keyboard. Many computer input devices also use a "10-key numeric pad" like that shown at the right of this keyboard. This grouping of numeric keys makes it possible to enter numbers into the computer very quickly.

Outline

Enter to grow in wisdom.

Inscription on the 1890 gate to Harvard Yard

Since the early days of the abacus, computation devices have been used and sought to make record keeping simpler, to speed computation, and to make our lives easier in general. Developers of computer input equipment are aware of these needs, and their latest equipment is evidence of their user consciousness.

Computers process data at incredible speeds, but the data must already be in the main storage of the computer for processing to occur. Getting data into the computer is called **input**. It is a slow operation compared to the internal processing speed of the computer. In this chapter we consider the various input devices. We will look at **output** techniques in the next chapter.

A wide variety of input, output, and storage

Figure 4–1 Some of the common peripheral devices used with large computers.

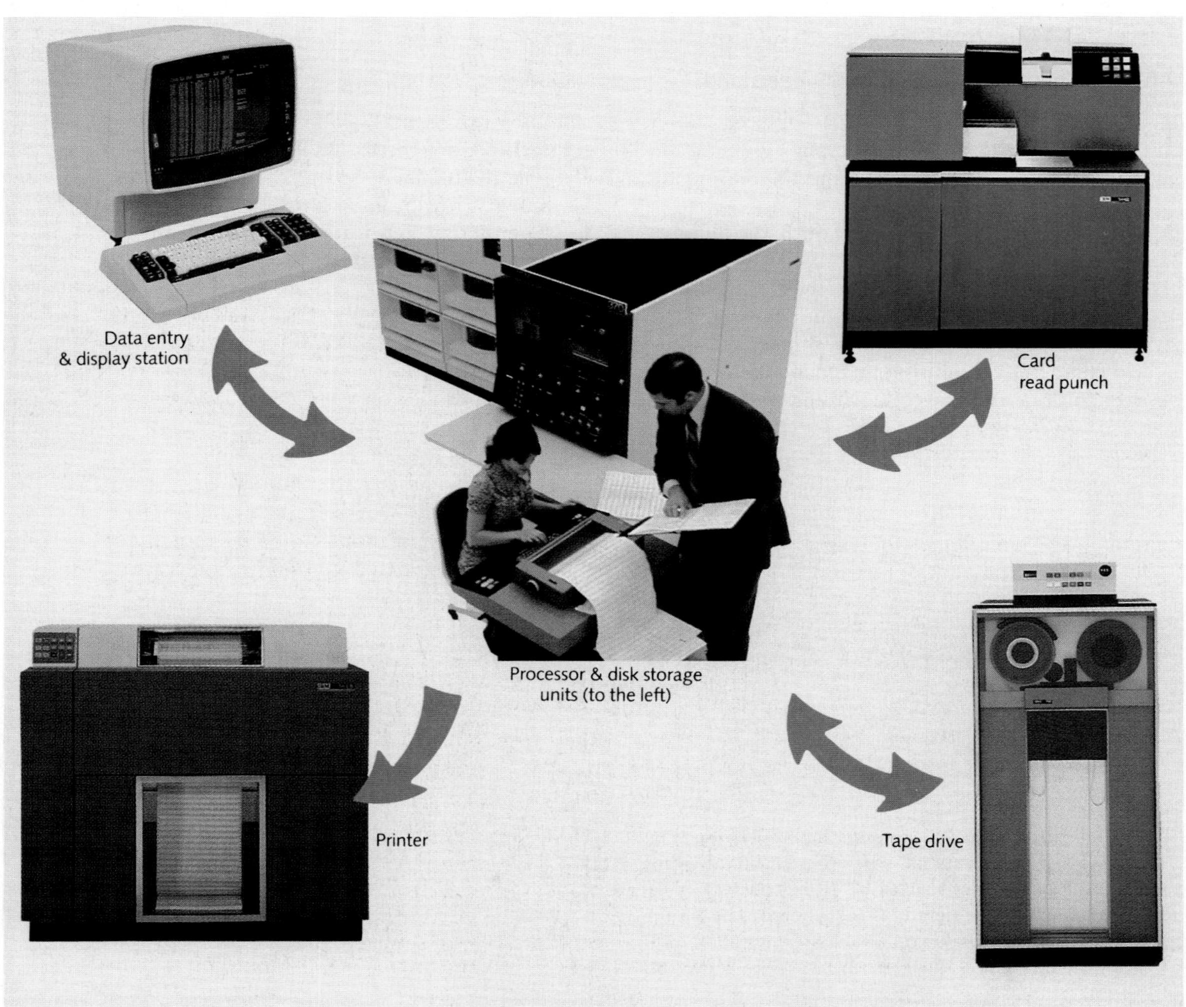

Courtesy of International Business Machines Corporation

devices are available. In fact, so many different devices exist that each computer system uses only those few that are appropriate for its applications. These devices are built separately from the processing unit and main storage of the computer, so they are called **peripheral devices.** Figure 4–1 shows some of the input, output, and storage peripheral devices commonly used on larger computer systems.

Punched Cards

The concept of recording data on cards as a pattern of holes dates from Jacquard's loom of the early 1800s and Hollerith's tabulating machines of the 1880s and is still in use today. Although computer **punched cards** are somewhat outmoded, the phrase, "Do not bend, fold, spindle, or mutilate," which is associated with them, has become a part of our culture.

The most common card format is the 80-column card with rectangular holes introduced by IBM in 1928 (Figure 4–2). Each column of the card contains a pattern of holes to represent one

Garbage-In-Garbage-Out

If you don't put correct information into the computer, you can't produce correct results. *GIGO, garbage-in-garbage-out,* summarizes the rule. A famous anecdote about GIGO dates from the early space program days of the 1960s. One of the Gemini (two-person) capsules was due to land at a specific point in the ocean, and all the rescue ships were in place. The capsule's retro-rockets were fired at the exact moment indicated by the computer controlling the flight. Everyone in the rescue fleet looked skyward in great anticipation. TV cameras were set to record the historic moment when the capsule was to appear—but there was no capsule. Great concern followed. When radio contact was reestablished with the astronauts and radar tracking picked up the capsule, it appeared more than 100 miles off target! The astronauts landed in the ocean and bobbed around in the waves for several hours, getting quite seasick.

NASA checked the computer equipment and found that it was functioning perfectly. But when the computer program that ordered the retro-rockets to fire was examined, it was found that a piece of bad data had been input. The program had required the number of hours in the day to make its calculations. The programmer had naively entered 24 hours, but a day is not exactly 24 hours in length (that's why we have leap years). The difference accounted precisely for the 100-mile error in the landing. A testament to GIGO!

Figure 4–2 A typical 80-column card showing how digits, letters, and special characters are represented by combinations of holes.

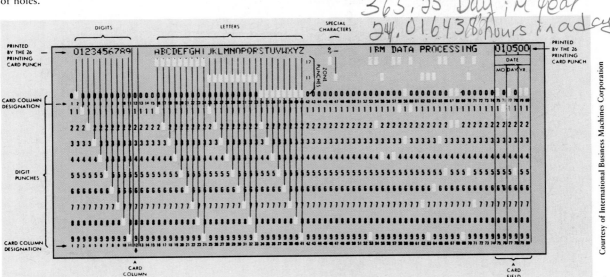

Courtesy of International Business Machines Corporation

character, so up to 80 characters of data may be punched in an 80-column card. The card has 12 rows. The various letters, digits, and special symbols are represented by punching one, two, or three holes in a particular column (Figure 4–3).

The large size of the 80-column format worried many users because of the occasional paper shortages and projected increases in consumption. In 1970 IBM announced its System/3 computer system, and with it a new smaller card format. The new cards (Figure 4–4) have space for punching 96 characters in three rows, or tiers, of 32 characters each. They have a number of advantages over the 80-column cards, including being smaller, cheaper, easier to handle, and less costly to store. Nevertheless, the 96-column card has, for the most part, disappeared, for reasons that will soon become clear.

Figure 4–3 The hole punches that correspond to the digits, letters, and special symbols most commonly used with punched card inputs.

Digits	Holes Punched	Letters	Holes Punched	Symbols	Holes Punched
0	0	A	12–1	&	12
1	1	B	12–2	¢	12–2–8
2	2	C	12–3	.	12–3–8
3	3	D	12–4	<	12–4–8
4	4	E	12–5	(	12–5–8
5	5	F	12–6	+	12–6–8
6	6	G	12–7	|	12–7–8
7	7	H	12–8	–	11
8	8	I	12–9	!	11–2–8
9	9	J	11–1	$	11–3–8
		K	11–2	*	11–4–8
		L	11–3	)	11–5–8
		M	11–4	;	11–6–8
		N	11–5	□	11–7–8
		O	11–6	/	0–1
		P	11–7	,	0–3–8
		Q	11–8	%	0–4–8
		R	11–9	_	0–5–8
		S	0–2	>	0–6–8
		T	0–3	?	0–7–8
		U	0–4	:	2–8
		V	0–5	#	3–8
		W	0–6	@	4–8
		X	0–7	'	5–8
		Y	0–8	=	6–8
		Z	0–9	"	7–8
				(Blank)	

The Keypunch Machine

Data from a **source document** is punched onto cards by a **keypunch** machine (Figure 4–5). The machine has a typewriterlike keyboard, a hole-punching mechanism, and a card transport mechanism for moving cards through the machine. A stack of blank cards is placed in the machine. One card at a time is moved to the *punching station*. An operator then types the data to appear on the card.

Figure 4–4 A 96-column card.

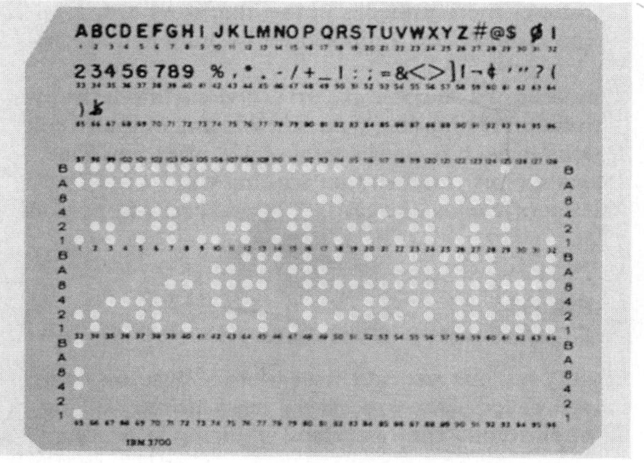

Courtesy of International Business Machines Corporation

"Murder, huh? I'm in for bending, folding and mutilating computer cards."

Figure 4–5 The keypunch machine has been one of the most popular data entry devices of all time.

Card Verification

To ensure that the keypunched data is correct before it enters the computer, a **card verifier** may be used. A verifying operator feeds in the cards punched by the keypunch operator and retypes all the information. The card verifying machine does not punch holes; it merely checks that the holes already punched in the card are the same as the characters being retyped by the card verifying operator. If they are, the card is considered correct, and it may be entered into the computer. If they are not, the verifier flashes a warning, the card is marked for repunching, and a corrected card is punched and inserted in the card deck to replace the bad card.

Verification is an expensive and time-consuming process. It ensures high reliability, but it does not guarantee perfection. The verifying operator should not be the same person as the keypunch operator, or the same mistakes might be made in verification as were made in keypunching. Verification is expensive, but it is often cheaper than correcting errors after they have entered the computer system.

Eliminating Verification

The risk of errors with manual keystroking is great. Techniques have been developed, however, to eliminate verification without increasing input error rates. Most of these methods use the computer system itself to scan incoming cards for certain common errors. By using the following techniques, many organizations have eliminated the need for verification.

1. **Edit checks** ensure that digits are not entered where letters are required, and vice versa. If the edit program discovers such an error, the card is listed on a printed report with an indication of the error. A person may then correct and resubmit the card.
2. **Range checks** ensure that a data item has a value within a specific range. For example, a date should contain a month number from 1 to 12, but months of 0 or 14 would be considered errors.
3. **Reasonableness checks** ensure that a data item is reasonable. Data items that fail reasonableness checks are not always incorrect. For example, a reasonableness check on a person's age could be "less than 150," but it is possible, although unlikely, that a person would live to that age.

Reading Cards into the Computer

Once cards have been punched and verified, they are entered into the main computer system through a device called a **card reader**. The computer operator places the deck of cards in the **input hopper**. Cards are then read one at a time as they pass a **read station** and are then stacked in an **output hopper**. One popular reading technique is to shine intense light at the card. Where a hole is punched, the light shines through; where there is no hole, the light is blocked. Photosensors detect light passing through the holes and the computer reads the photosensors, converting the hole patterns into corresponding bit patterns. Some high-speed card readers can process more than 1000 cards per minute.

The card reader is "affectionately" called the card chewer by many frustrated operators. Handling paper at high speeds is a difficult task, and occasionally an operator has helplessly stood by watching a malfunctioning card reader maul a deck.

An Assessment

Punched cards were the primary data entry medium through the early 1970s when, in the United

States alone, about half a million keypunch machines were in use, and most computer systems had one or more high-speed card readers. Their use is declining rapidly now because of their many disadvantages. Cards are bulky to handle and expensive to produce, process, and store. They cannot be reused and can file only as much information as can be stored in 80 characters (the more popular tapes and disks can store thousands of times as much information in the same amount of space). **File integrity** problems are possible with cards; they can be removed from files, replaced with other cards with altered data, and easily lost or stolen. Because of the availability of improved input methods, the vast majority of computer systems built today do not even have card readers.

Key-to-Tape and Key-to-Disk Systems

Because of the many disadvantages of punched cards and the continuing decline in the price of computer power, it became economical in the early 1970s for larger data entry installations to replace keypunch machines with **key-to-tape** (Figure 4–6) and **key-to-disk** (Figure 4–7) machines. These are sometimes called **intelligent data entry devices** because they have their own built-in computers to control the data entry process. Instead of punching holes in nonreusable cards, operators type on a keyboard to enter computerized data directly onto reusable magnetic tapes and disks.

Figure 4–6 Key-to-tape devices generally have only a single data entry station.

Although the systems are more complex than keypunching, they are more economical.

Terminal-Oriented Systems

A large portion of users now operate **on-line** to computers, that is, through terminals or keyboards directly connected to computers or data communications networks. Timesharing (see Chapter 12 for a discussion of timesharing) has made it possible for hundreds and even thousands of users to be on-line to a single computer system

"I guess our customer training wasn't too good. The company wants to install a keyboard-to-wastebasket system."

Figure 4–7 Key-to-disk devices generally handle many data entry stations simultaneously.

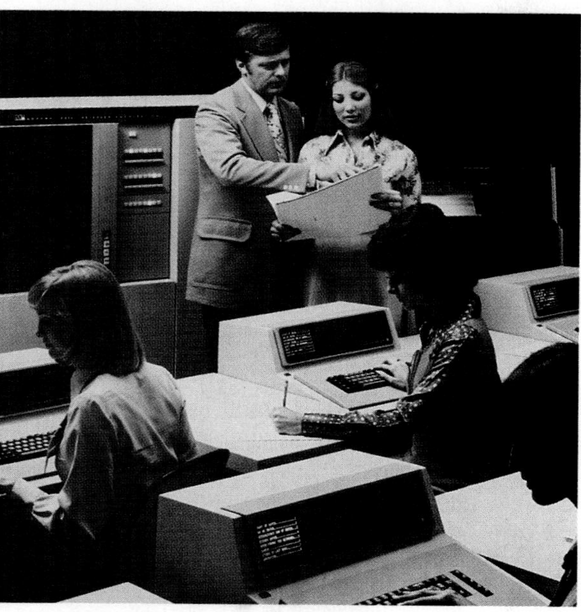

at once. Personal computers generally accept their inputs directly from attached keyboards.

This on-line operation is another improvement over punched cards. With punched cards users operate **off-line** from their computers. They submit work and receive results through devices not directly connected to the computers. This method of operation is often called **batch processing**, in which data is collected, entered into the computer, and processed in groups called **batches**. Results may be returned hours later.

On-line, terminal-oriented systems are often called **transaction-processing systems**. Individual data items are entered into the computer and processed immediately—each of these items is called a transaction.

Touch Sensing

Over the years many people have viewed computers as rather unfriendly devices and have been reluctant to work with them. One way the industry is making the user/computer interface more user-friendly to the general public is through the technology of **touch sensing**. An operator does not need to be an expert typist and does not have to be intimately familiar with the often messy details of running a computer. Instead, the operator merely points to drawings, diagrams, symbols, or words on a screen (Figure 4–8). The computer senses that a particular area of the screen is being touched and responds accordingly. People seem to enjoy pointing to what they want. In fact, one study estimates that 95 percent of the population could competently and easily operate a touch sensitive device without prior training.

Figure 4–8 The touch control screen of the Xerox 5700 Electronic Printing System gives the operator control over all system operations. The screen replaces the usual operator control panel found on similar devices. The screen displays pictures of buttons; the operator touches the screen where a button is displayed to tell the machine to perform the function indicated by the button.

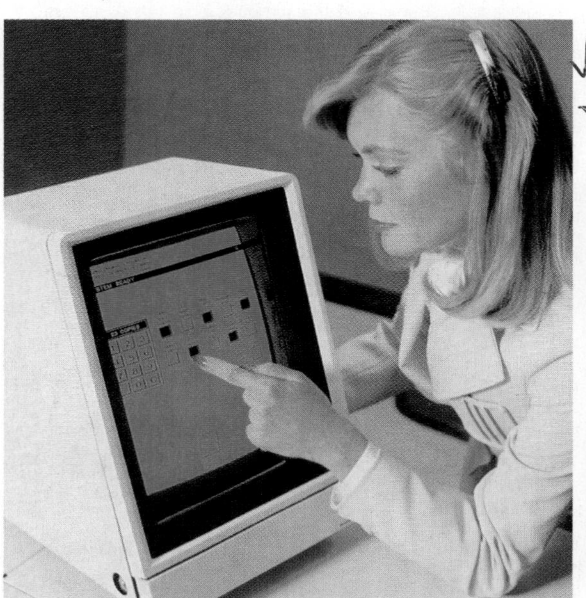

For touch sensing to be effective, the number of choices displayed on the screen at one time should be small, perhaps 10 or fewer. Having too many choices may lead to confusion. Because human fingers are large compared to individual characters on a screen, it is impractical to display a large number of choices anyway.

With touch sensing, any symbol, picture, or customized set of buttons useful for a particular application may be displayed. When a regular typewriter keyboard is appropriate, a conventional keyboard may be displayed. When a numeric keyboard is appropriate, a 10-key numeric pad can be shown.

The display can be tailored to the needs of the application and to the educational level of the users. For example, a computer-assisted instruction (CAI) system for kindergarten children might contain simple pictures, whereas one for older

Touch Tour

The concept of touch-sensing terminals has been adopted by the developers of Walt Disney's EPCOT (Experimental Prototype Community of Tomorrow) located near Orlando, Florida. Scattered throughout EPCOT are information stations that use touch sensing. Once a visitor indicates the main topic, the computer displays a **menu**, or list of subtopics. By pressing numbers or letters, visitors are guided along until the information they want appears on the screen. Besides being informative, the system is fun to use, even for people with no computer training.

students might use a substantial vocabulary of words and phrases. Engineers could use a system with symbols for electrical components, and football coaches could use one with symbols for each of the key players.

Figure 4–9 shows many ways of inputting touch-sensitive data on a **cathode ray tube** (CRT), a display unit attached to a computer terminal. In diagram (a), the user touches the screen directly (also see Figures 4–11 and 4–13). In Figure 4–9, diagram (b), the user "writes" on the screen with a device called a **light pen** (also see Figures 4–10 and 4–14). The light pen detects light from the characters on the screen and then sends a message to the computer indicating the position the user is pointing to. In diagram (c) of Figure 4–9, the user writes on a data tablet, which senses the

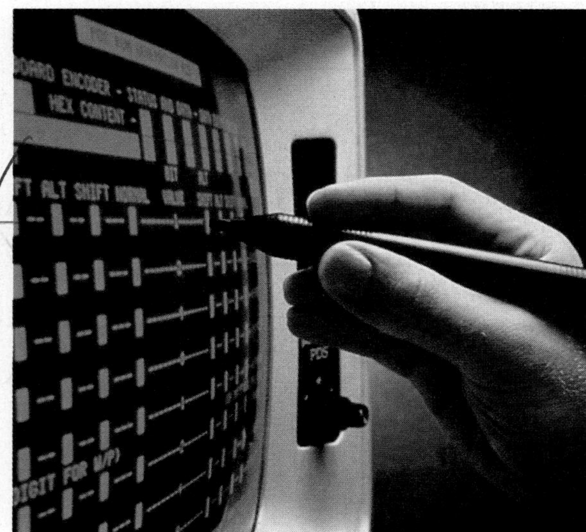

Figure 4–10 A light pen.

Figure 4–9 Inputting touch-sensitive data.

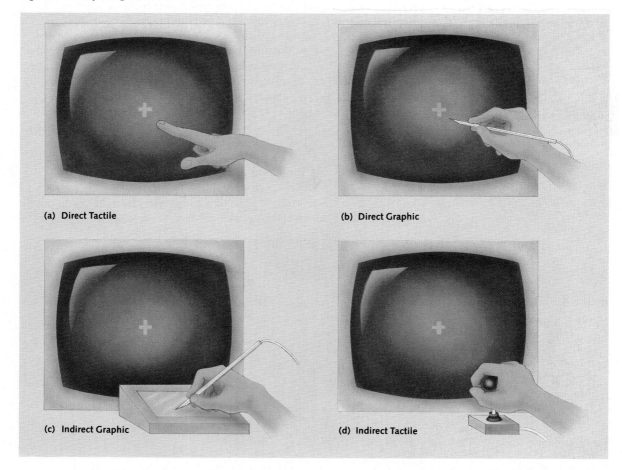

(a) Direct Tactile

(b) Direct Graphic

(c) Indirect Graphic

(d) Indirect Tactile

Frame 1: The passenger presses the screen to select DENVER as the destination city.

Frame 2: The computer displays today's flights to Denver. The person Touches the screen on the desired flight number, and then touches either the word COACH or the phrase FIRST CLASS.

Frame 3: For seat selection, the passenger then presses WINDOW, CENTER or AISLE. The section is then selected — either SMOKING or NON-SMOKING.

Frame 4: The computer then displays all of the ticket information so that the customer may review it to see if it is correct. The customer presses YES or NO.

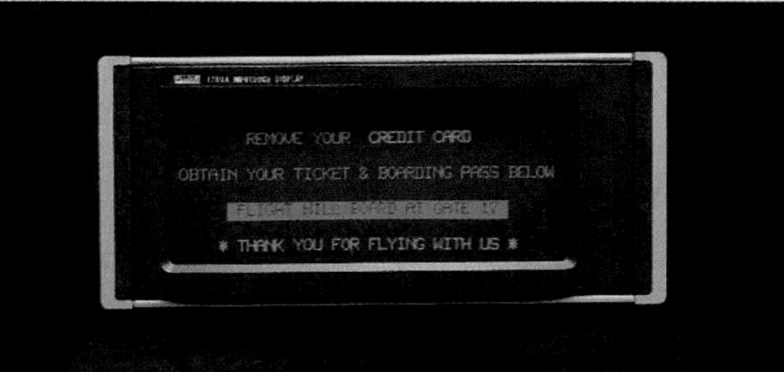

Frame 5: The computer prints the ticket and thanks the customer.

Figure 4–11 Here a touch sensitive screen is used in a system designed for airline passengers to help them make their own reservations and write their own air tickets automatically.

position of the pen and causes the figure being drawn by the user to appear simultaneously on the screen (also see Figure 4–12). In Figure 4–9, diagram (d), the user manipulates a **joystick** like that used with video games; as the joystick is moved, the cursor moves in the corresponding direction on the screen. (Figure 4–15 shows an input device called a **cursor.**)

CRTs are called **soft copy** devices because they do not produce a paper copy (**hard copy**) of the displayed data. Hard copy can be produced when the CRT is connected to a printer and when the user specifically requests it.

Figure 4–12 Small digitizer tablets are available for use with personal computers.

Other Input Devices

Another type of user-friendly system is the computerized **speech recognition** device. This input device analyzes spoken commands and converts them to computer-stored data. A surgeon can issue commands to control devices in the operating room. A handicapped person can use voice commands to control the movement of a wheelchair. Security systems use speech recognition devices to identify people.

A TV camera (Figure 4–16) can also work as an input device. It can be designed to convert a picture into digital data, that is, to digitize the picture. The picture may then be printed on a computer printer.

Other input devices use so-called membrane keyboards. The membrane (Figure 4–17) has no movable keys. Instead it is a flat surface imprinted with pictures of the keys. When the picture of a key is pressed, it causes the flat surface to come in contact with another flat "membrane" behind it. An electrical signal is generated to indicate that the key in that position has been pressed. Membrane keyboards cost less than those with moving parts and resist damage by cigarette ashes, spilled liquids, and dust.

Another innovative device is the three-dimensional digitizer (Figure 4–18). The user moves the hand-held stylus around a three-dimensional object (in this case a plane model). Information about the shape of the object is conveyed to the computer, which can then display the object from any angle. Figures 4–19 and 4–20 on page 84 show other interesting input devices.

Figure 4–13 In this inventory control application, the user may call up one of eight different inventory control functions by pressing the appropriate rectangle on the touch sensitive screen. The bottom rectangle allows the user to "EXIT" from the inventory application; this causes a fresh screen to be displayed with other options.

Figure 4–14 This person is designing a truck body with the assistance of a CAD (Computer Assisted Design) system. He may modify the design by pointing to the appropriate lines or shapes on the screen with a light pen and then pressing one of the control buttons at the left.

Figure 4–15 This small hand-held device is called a cursor. The user positions it above a word, phrase, or diagram on a digitizing tablet. The user then presses one of the buttons to transmit the cursor position to the computer, thus telling the computer what is being selected by the user.

Figure 4–16 *Above left:* A TV camera may also be used as a computer input device. This system uses a TV camera to record a person's picture. The computer "digitizes" the picture into a series of lighter and darker colored areas, and prints the picture on a computer printer.

Figure 4–17 *Above right:* A membrane keyboard.

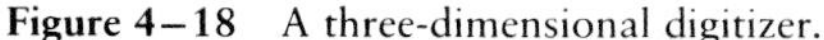

Figure 4–18 A three-dimensional digitizer.

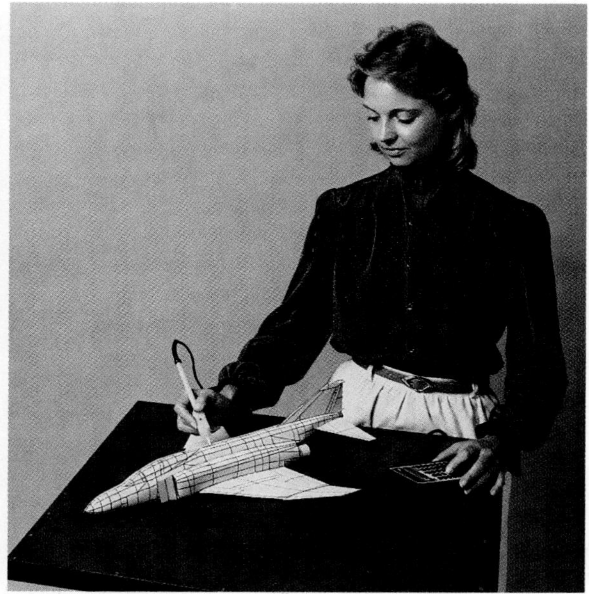

Source Data Automation

Data processing has traditionally begun with the conversion of data documents to computer-readable form by manual data entry techniques such as keypunching. As we have seen, this process is slow, labor intensive, expensive, and prone to error.

Bypassing manual data entry is called **source data automation** (SDA). The goal of SDA is to capture data automatically and in computer-readable form where it originates. The advantages are obvious—reduced cost, elimination of duplicate effort, reduced need for skilled data entry operators, fast and accurate data entry, and faster results because of the reduced input times.

Several techniques for source data automation are widely used, including: (1) **magnetic ink character recognition** (MICR), used mostly in automated check processing; (2) **optical character recognition** (OCR), used in applications where the computer reads human-readable symbols directly; (3) **optical mark recognition** (OMR), used in exam scoring, survey taking, and utility meter

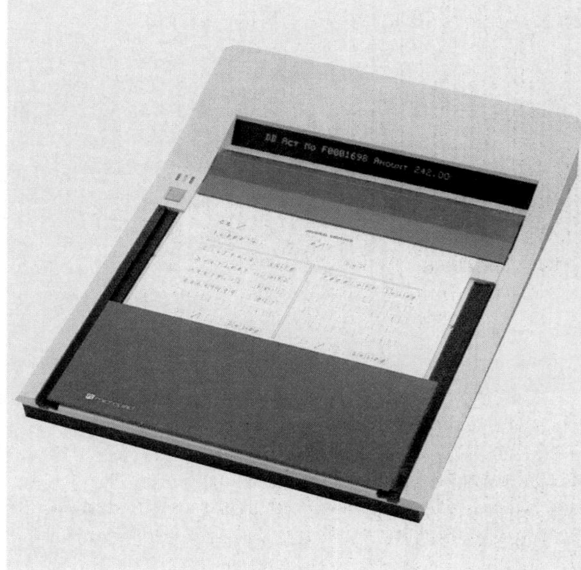

Figure 4–19 This input device uses a pressure-sensitive writing surface to capture handwritten data at the time of writing. Anyone who can write can use this simple device to enter information into a computer.

Figure 4–20 This input device is called a mouse. The mouse sits on a flat surface next to a computer terminal, and the person using it moves it in a given direction. Roller bearings on the bottom of the mouse detect motion. This information is transmitted to the computer, and a blip displayed on the screen moves in the same direction as the mouse. So the mouse may be used to point to items on the screen.

Figure 4–21 *Below:* Data may be entered directly into the computer through computer terminals like the one shown here.

Figure 4–22 *Bottom:* The grid pattern used by an MICR reader to help recognize characters.

Courtesy of International Business Machines Corporation

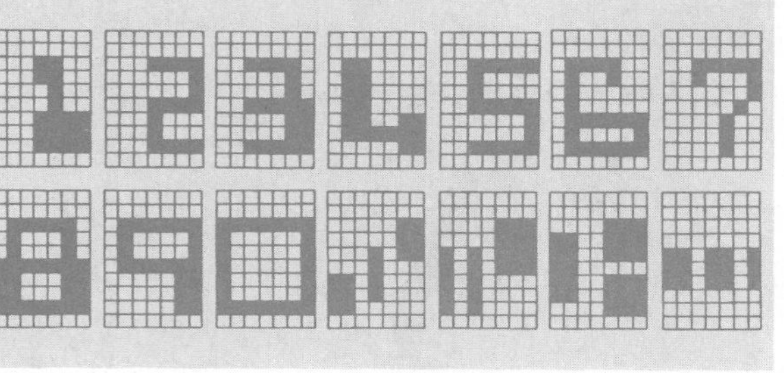

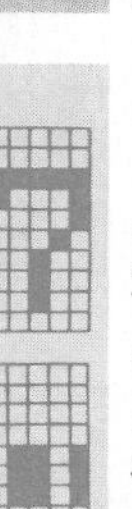

Courtesy of International Business Machines Corporation

reading applications; and (4) **bar code reading,** used in inventory systems and in automated supermarket checkout systems.

The trend is moving away from even these popular techniques. In fact, most input will eventually be performed by **direct data entry,** where the data is captured at its source and entered directly into the computer with no paper documents being produced (Figure 4–21). Direct data entry is now used, for example, when an airline reservationist types information about a flight into the computer while speaking with a customer on the telephone.

Figure 4–23 (a) A sample check using MICR characters. (b) The commonly used MICR characters and special symbols.

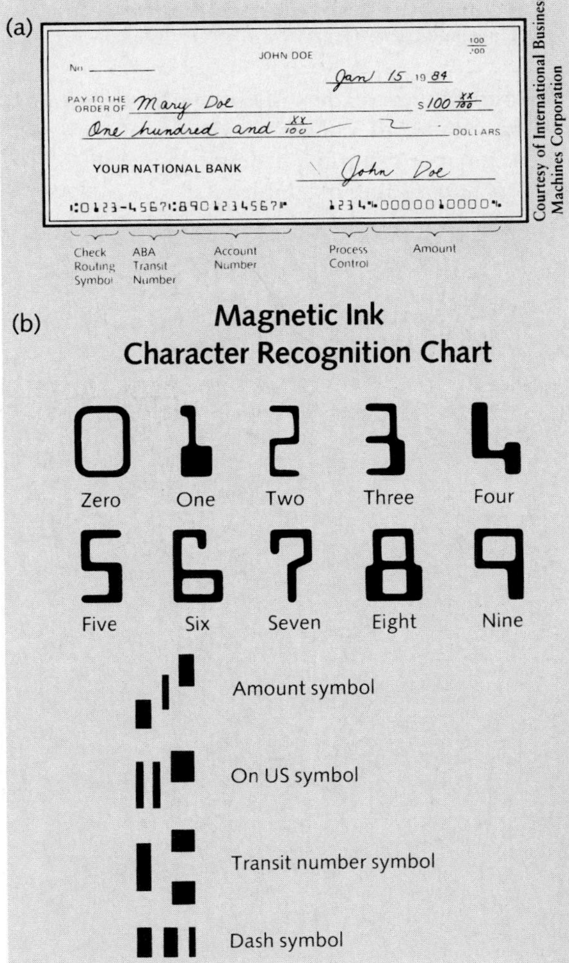

Courtesy of International Business Machines Corporation

Magnetic Ink Character Recognition

Magnetic ink character recognition is a technique developed by the banking industry to speed check processing. The ink used in MICR characters is magnetic, and MICR readers are sensitive to the magnetized ink. The sensors in an MICR reader recognize each character by comparing it to a grid pattern (Figure 4–22). Figure 4–23 shows a sample check with MICR characters encoded across the bottom. The numbers at the bottom left of the check identify the bank and the account number. The amount of the check at the bottom right is typed manually in the process of clearing the check. Many checks also contain the check number printed in MICR characters along the bottom, which makes it possible to identify checks by number on a customer's computer-prepared bank statement. The MICR character set contains the digits 0 to 9 and four special-purpose symbols used to separate and identify the pieces of information on the bottom of a check.

Many large banks process millions of checks each day. To handle such volumes, they use high-speed MICR readers, each capable of processing 50,000 to 100,000 checks per hour. This means that the reading mechanisms (Figure 4–24) have to handle as many as 20 or 30 checks per second accurately and without damaging them. If that doesn't sound impressive enough, consider that both sides of a check are microfilmed as it passes through an MICR reader.

Figure 4–24 A check passing through an MICR reader. During processing the paper moves so quickly through this device that it can't be seen.

Courtesy of International Business Machines Corporation

Optical Character Recognition

Optical character recognition devices read handwritten or typewritten characters and symbols and convert them directly into computer codes faster than people can type and at far less cost.

OCRs can be classified according to their reading capabilities. These capabilities are described in terms of a font, that is, the complete assortment of letters, digits, and special characters of one style and size. **Hand-print readers** can read hand-printed characters. The characters must be printed very carefully in order to be readable (Figure 4–25).

Printed-font readers read typewritten and typeset characters. They are classified according to the variety of fonts they read:

1. **Single-font readers** are normally used in special-purpose applications such as reading gasoline purchase slips with credit card impressions.
2. **Multifont readers** are used in data-processing operations that must service many different types of OCR applications.
3. **Omnifont readers** are the most versatile and most expensive devices on the market today. They can read most printed fonts and are often equipped with complex programs that help them learn new fonts. The premier machine of this type is the Kurzweil OCR reader (see the box on page 89).

Some of the more popular OCR fonts are shown in Figure 4–26. The most widely used OCR font in the United States is **OCR-A**. Many organizations are pressing to change to **OCR-B**, which is used internationally because most people find it easier to read, but studies have shown that OCR-A is recognized by reading machines far more reliably than OCR-B.

OCR devices have been built to read a variety of documents. These readers fall into the following classes:

1. **Journal tape readers** are designed primarily for the retail trades. These devices read the narrow paper printouts produced by cash registers and adding machines.

Figure 4–25 Rules for correct printing of hand-printed characters in OCR applications.

Rule	Right	Wrong
Characters should be in boxes	2 5 7	2 5 7
Character should almost fill the box	8 3 1	8 3 1
Loops should be closed	8 6 9	8 6 9
Characters should not connect	1 0 0	1 0 0
Adjacent lines should connect	E T 4	E T 4
Shapes should be simple	0 3 7	0 3 7
Block-style characters should be used	A X 2	A X 2

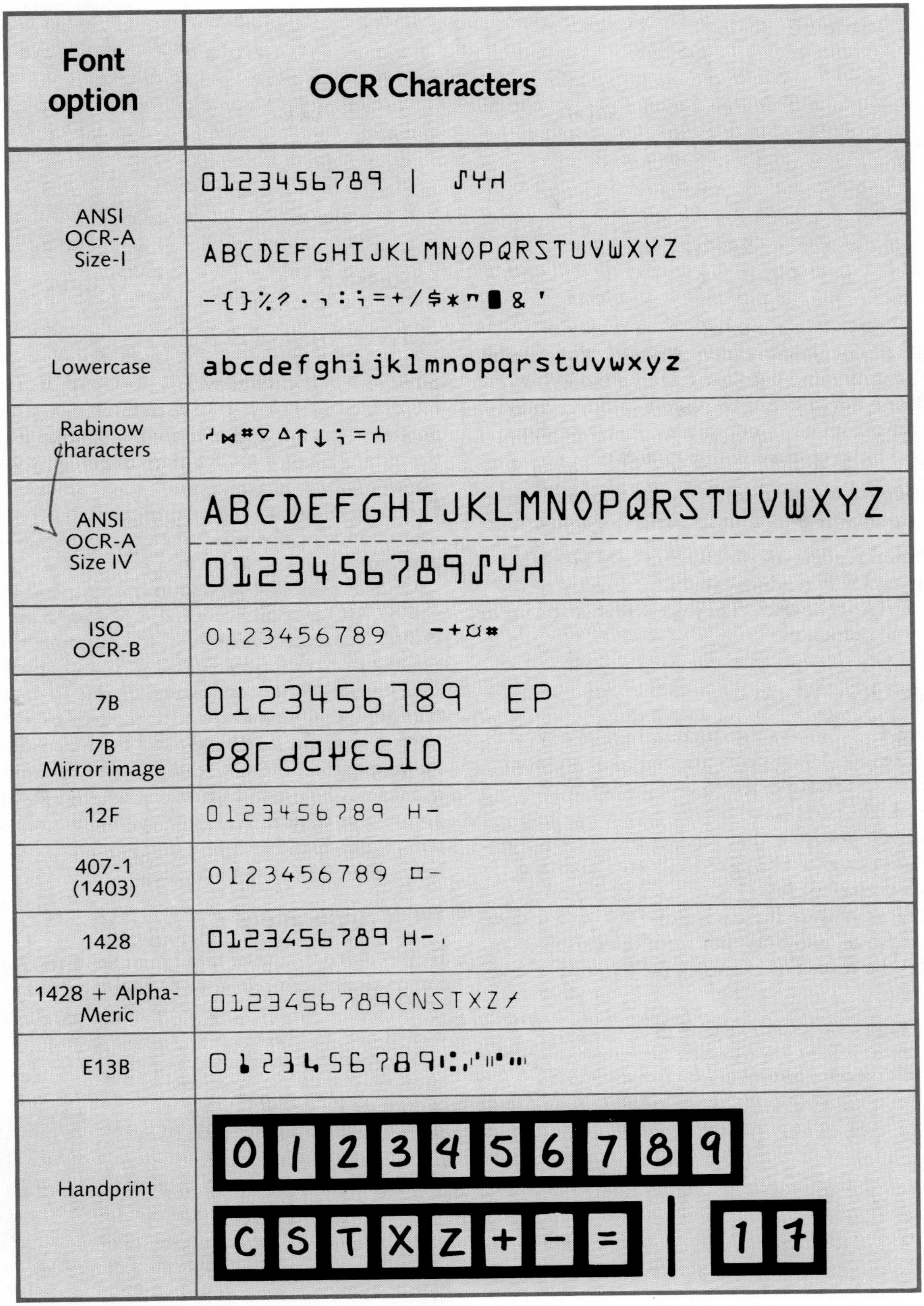

Font option	OCR Characters
ANSI OCR-A Size-I	0123456789 | ⑁⑂⑃ ABCDEFGHIJKLMNOPQRSTUVWXYZ -{}%?.,:;=+/$*"█&'
Lowercase	abcdefghijklmnopqrstuvwxyz
Rabinow characters	⑁⋈#▽△↑↓;=⑃
ANSI OCR-A Size IV	ABCDEFGHIJKLMNOPQRSTUVWXYZ 0123456789⑁⑂⑃
ISO OCR-B	0123456789 -+¤⁕
7B	0123456789 EP
7B Mirror image	P8765432I0
12F	0123456789 H-
407-1 (1403)	0123456789 ⌑-
1428	0123456789 H-,
1428 + Alpha-Meric	0123456789CNSTXZ/
E13B	0123456789⑆⑇⑈⑉
Handprint	0 1 2 3 4 5 6 7 8 9 C S T X Z + - = | 1 7

Figure 4–26 Some of the more popular OCR readable fonts.

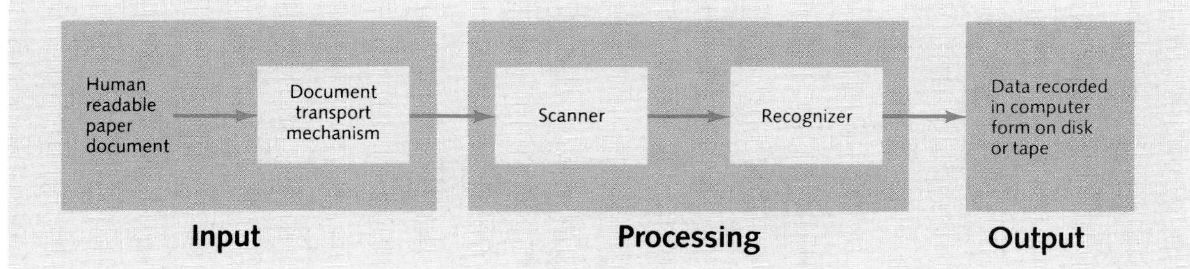

Figure 4–27 Organization of a typical OCR reader.

2. **Small document readers** are used primarily by the utility and gasoline retailing industries. These devices read the credit card imprinted stubs from gasoline stations, meter readings, and bills returned with payments.
3. **Page readers** read full pages of text, and some are capable of reading a variety of fonts.
4. **Wand readers** are small hand-held units that bring OCR reading capability directly to the source of the data. They are widely used in the retail trades.

How OCR Works

Figure 4–27 shows the organization of a typical OCR reader. Documents are placed in an input stacker and transported to a scanning mechanism. Light is reflected off the page onto light-sensitive photocells that register the presence or absence of light. The photocells are "digitized" into a pattern of bits (Figure 4–28). Computer programs analyze these patterns looking for the lines, curves, and dots that form the various symbols to be read. For example, the letter *i* is recognized as a vertical line with a dot above it; *O* is recognized as a closed curve without any straight portions that might, for example, confuse it with the letter *D*. Some OCRs place documents with unrecognizable characters in a reject stacker. Others display unrecognizable characters on a screen, and the operator reenters them at a keyboard.

Optical character recognition is not, and never can be, 100 percent accurate in reading hand-printed characters. Consider, for example, the reading of hand-printed catalog codes known to contain both letters and digits. People frequently confuse the numeric zero with the letter *O*, the letter *S* with the number *5*, and the letter *Z* with the number 2. So OCR reading of hand printing should not be used in situations where very high accuracy is critical. Nevertheless, many OCR systems today read hand-printed characters with better than 99 percent accuracy.

OCR Applications

To speed processing of retail merchandise, many companies place preprinted OCR readable tags

Figure 4–28 The scanner reads the "5" by converting it to a bit pattern. The recognizer compares the bit pattern to a set of prestored patterns to see if there is a match.

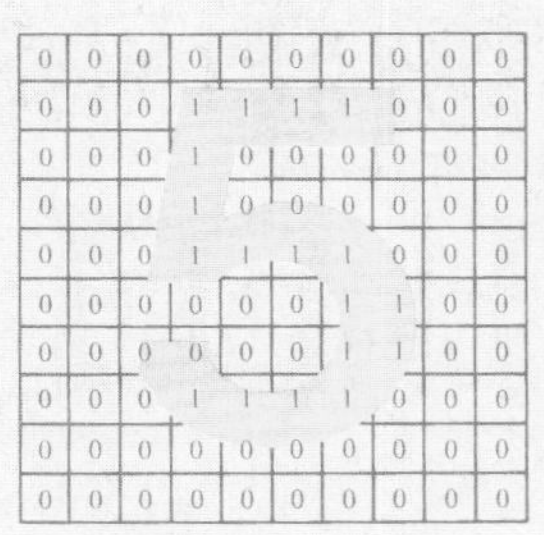

Figure 4–29 This device is widely used in the retail clothing industry. It prints price tags with OCR readable characters, and pins the tags to garments.

The Kurzweil OCR Reader

One of the most versatile OCR readers on the market today is made by Kurzweil Computer Products of Cambridge, Massachusetts. The company, a division of the Xerox Corporation, pioneered the development of omnifont devices capable of reading a large variety of typewritten, printed, and hand-printed characters.

A recent version of the machine can recognize up to 75 characters per second. Complex software is the key to providing the omnifont capability, and a high-speed CPU capable of executing 6 to 7 million instructions per second makes possible the 75 character per second recognition rate. (With the trend in computer hardware toward faster CPUs, we can expect that future Kurzweil machines will read much faster than this.) To proceed at this rate means the machine executes approximately 80,000 instructions to recognize a single character! (We can only wonder how many "instructions" the human mind requires to perform the same task.)

The machine has a number of unique features, including a built-in 40,000-word dictionary to allow the checking of words with unrecognizable characters. This reduces the need for operator identification of unreadable characters by 80 to 90 percent.

Another unique feature is the machine's ability to learn new type fonts. Figure 2 shows the screen as it appears when learning a new font. Whenever the machine can't recognize a character, it displays a large version of the character for the operator to examine. The operator types in the character at the keyboard, and the machine associates the typed character with the displayed character, thus "learning" the character for future reference.

Raymond Kurzweil, president of the company, distinguished himself as a young man by using his OCR concepts in concert with speech synthesis techniques to develop a reading machine for the blind. The Kurzweil reading machine is discussed further in Chapter 18.

Figure 1 The Kurzweil OCR reader.

Figure 2 The screen of the Kurzweil OCR reader displaying an unrecognized character.

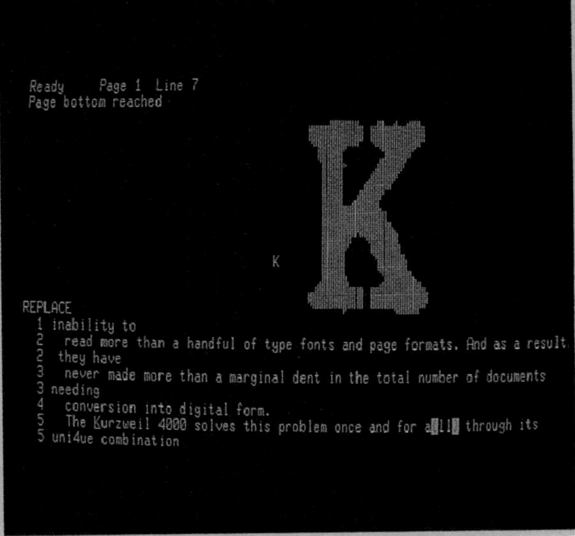

on all items. At the checkout counter a clerk removes the tag and either places it in a bin for later processing or reads it with a wand reader as part of the checkout procedure. The tag contains the price, product code, and often a description of the item. As the tag is scanned, this information is read and the register automatically prints it on the customer's receipt, while also transmitting it to the store's computer to keep inventory and sales figures current. Figure 4–29 shows a device used to print the OCR readable tags and pin them to garments.

In some OCR applications the computer prints a document on which people may record additional figures or make changes. This form, called a **turnaround document**, is then resubmitted to the computer with the computer-printed and hand-printed data both being read back in. This system is especially effective in taking inventories. The computer prints the part number in an OCR-readable format, and the inventory taker records the quantity on hand manually. The part number and the quantity are then both read back into the computer system by an OCR device to update the inventory information.

Some OCR devices can read as many as 1000 characters per second in applications like these and make as few as one or two errors per 100,000 characters read. These speeds will undoubtedly increase and error rates will decrease as OCR equipment improves.

Optical Mark Recognition

Optical mark recognition is a form of OCR in which pencil marks are recognized in particular positions on a specially designed form. Figure 4–30 shows an OMR document commonly used for recording answers to multiple-choice exams. Both numeric and alphabetic data may be recorded by blackening the appropriate circles with a pencil. Answers must be recorded with some care on OMR forms, as is shown in Figure 4–31. The circles must be completely blackened with pencil, and no stray marks should appear on the paper. The document is read by an OMR reader that converts the data in the blackened circles to computer-readable form and stores it on tape or disk. The information is then processed by a computer that compares an individual's answers to the correct ones prestored in the computer, grades the exam, and prints the results.

Figure 4–31 The correct ways to make pencil marks on an OMR document.

EXAMPLES	IMPORTANT DIRECTIONS FOR MARKING ANSWERS
WRONG 1 ① ⊗ ③ ④ ⑤ WRONG 2 ① ② ✓ ④ ⑤ WRONG 3 ① ② ③ ● ⑤ RIGHT 4 ① ② ③ ● ⑤	• Use #2 pencil only. • Do NOT use ink or ballpoint pens. • Make heavy black marks that fill the circle completely. • Erase cleanly any answer you wish to change • Make no stray marks on the answer sheet.

Figure 4–30 An OMR document used for recording answers to multiple choice exams.

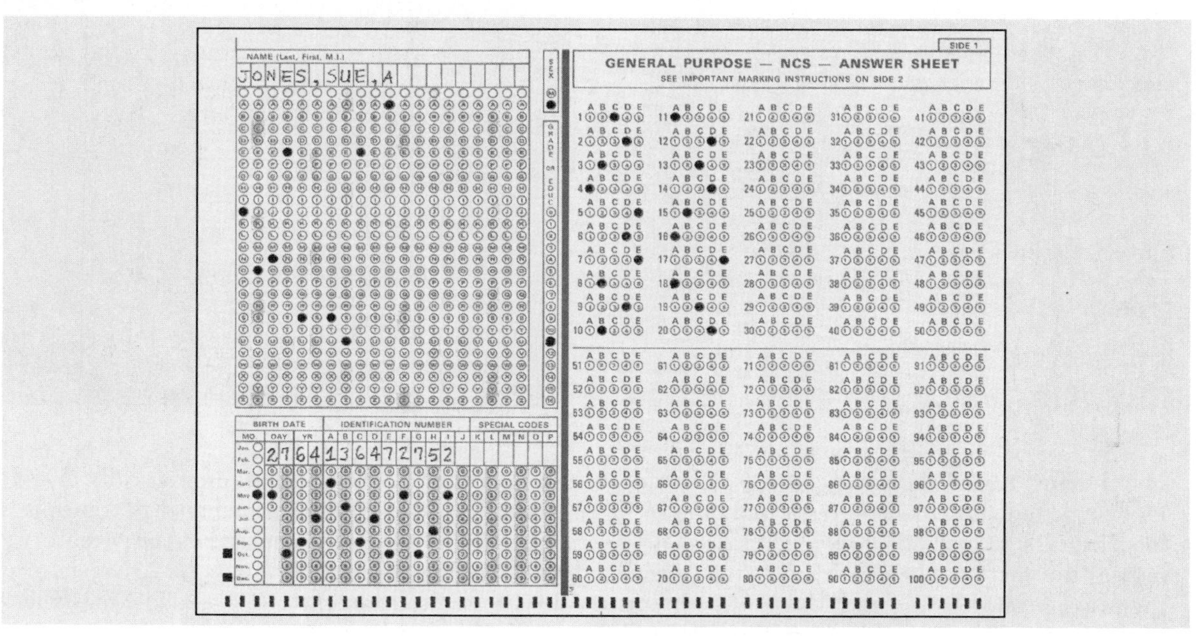
SIDE 1

NAME (Last, First, M.I.)

JONES, SUE, A

GENERAL PURPOSE — NCS — ANSWER SHEET

SEE IMPORTANT MARKING INSTRUCTIONS ON SIDE 2

BIRTH DATE | IDENTIFICATION NUMBER | SPECIAL CODES

MO. DAY YR | A B C D E F G H I J | K L M N O P

2 7 6 4 1 3 6 4 7 2 7 5 2

Combining OCR and OMR

In the earlier years of business data processing, when a customer sent in a bill with a payment, the information was keypunched. Today many large utility companies use source data automation to speed the processing of paid bills. One type of utility billing system combines OCR and OMR. The bills are printed on a high-speed computer printer using an OCR readable font. When the customer sends in the bill and payment, an employee matches the check amount with the amount due. If the customer pays a different amount, this amount is pencil marked on the OMR portion of the bill; otherwise the OMR portion is left blank. Now the bills are stacked in a high-speed OCR/OMR reader and converted to computer-readable form. The customer account numbers are read automatically by the OCR reader, thus eliminating the need for manual keying. In most cases, customers pay the correct amount, and the OMR portion of the form is left empty, thus completely automating the input of the transaction.

Enter partial payment below

MUNICIPAL WATER WORKS

Account Number	Gross Amount	Net Amount	Last Day To Pay Net
RL45332	56 01	45 98	4 30 8-

DISCOUNT TERMS 10 DAYS

Present Reading	Previous Reading	Consumption Gals.
3255886	2369014	887

E D JONES
745 CHESTNUT ST
ANYTOWN USA

PLEASE RETURN THIS WITH YOUR PAYMENT

A turnaround document using both OCR and OMR.

Courtesy of International Business Machines Corporation

Bar Code Reading

Bar code reading is one of the most rapidly growing areas in the field of source data automation. Bar code readers recognize coded information from a series of wide and narrow bars, such as those on the merchandise label in Figure 4–32. A bar-coded label is either scanned, that is, checked for data, with a hand-held wand reader, such as that in Figure 4–33, or the article with the bar coded information is passed over a reading station, such as those found in supermarkets. The tip of the wand contains photocells that are sensitive to the presence or absence of light. Scanning should be done at an even pace so that wide and narrow black bars are properly recognized (Figure 4–34).

Labeling articles with bar-coded data is a time-consuming process, but it greatly speeds inputting that information into computers, such as in supermarket check-out and inventory control applications. Bar code printers (Figure 4–35) can produce tags and labels with letters, digits, and special characters.

Figure 4–32 A typical bar-coded label containing a product description, a product code, and the actual bar-coded information.

Figure 4–33 A bar code reader for wand-reading applications.

Bar Code Applications

Bar codes are known most commonly from their use in supermarket check-out counters, but their applicability is more far reaching. For instance, in book circulation systems bar codes are speeding the check-in and check-out of books as well as keeping track of overdue books and fines at many libraries.

When a library card holder brings books to the check-out desk, a clerk passes a wand reader over the library card. The person's identification number is bar encoded on the card. As the number is read, the central computer system displays the borrower's record on a screen. If any overdue books or fines

Figure 1 Orders may be entered quickly by scanning bar codes.

are outstanding, the person is asked to take care of these obligations before being allowed to take out more books.

If the borrower's record is clear, the clerk passes the wand reader over the bar-coded information that identifies the book. The computer system records this information in its files and calculates the due date. When a book is checked in, the process is reversed and the "book out" information is removed from the person's file, and any fines are automatically assessed. Overdue notices are automatically produced by the computer system.

Some companies use bar codes for processing sales. A company may supply its salespeople with portable computer terminals equipped with bar code wand readers that can communicate over standard telephone lines to a central ordering facility. A salesperson at the customer's site works with order forms containing bar-coded item numbers (Figure 1). If the customer needs a case of a particular type and size of shampoo, for example, the salesperson scans the bar-coded product code and then types in the quantity on the portable terminal. The order is entered quickly and is transmitted directly to the computer for immediate processing, eliminating delays in mailing and keying in the data.

Many businesses speed up such time-consuming and costly chores as inventory taking by effective use of bar codes. In one method, bar code labels are placed on all items. Portable bar code readers, like the one shown in Figure 2, are used to enter the coded information into a computer system mounted on a belt loop. Notice that the woman in the figure is also wearing what appears to be a large wristwatch on her left hand. It is nothing more than a paper keyboard with the various digits and a few special symbols printed on it. As the woman takes inventory, she first scans the bar-coded identification on the item itself and then counts the items. She could then key in the exact count of items on the portable computer; instead she uses the wand reader to scan the correct digits on the paper keyboard indicating the count. When the inventory is complete, all the data is eventually loaded into a larger computer system for processing.

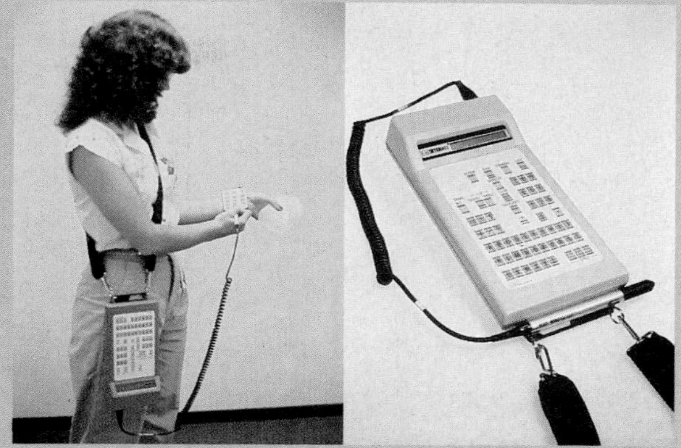

Figure 2 *Above left:* Taking inventory with a portable bar code reader.

Figure 3 *Above right:* This portable computer terminal has no keys as such. Instead, the user passes the attached wand reader over the appropriate bar-coded symbol. The user may enter digits, letters, spaces, and certain "control" characters.

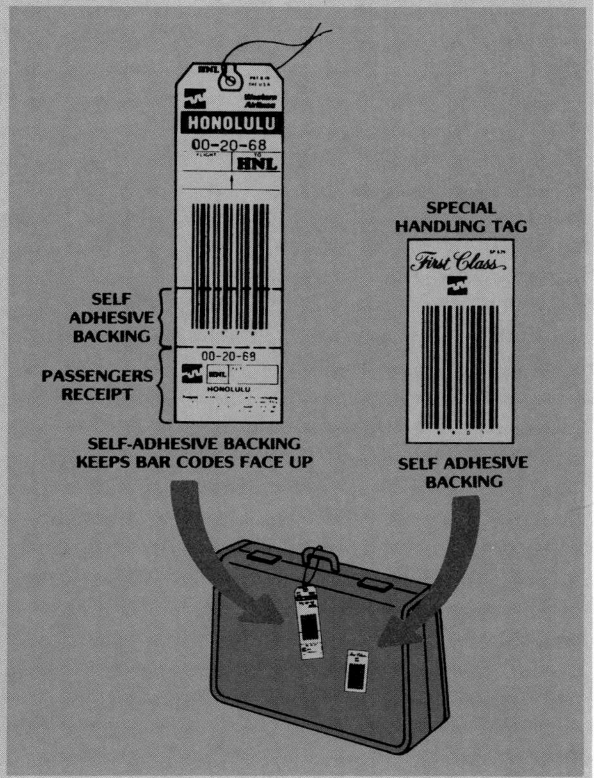

Figure 4 Bar-coded luggage tags are used to automate the luggage handling process. Laser beam scanners read the tags as the luggage passes on a conveyor belt. A computer controlled system then automatically routes the luggage to the correct flight for loading.

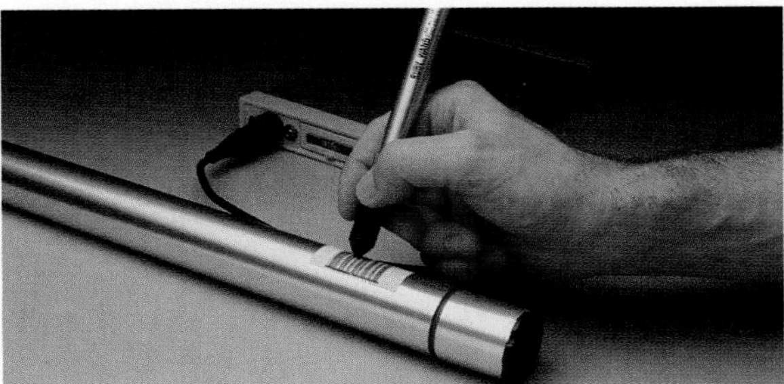

Figure 4–34 Using a hand-held wand reader to read a bar-coded tag.

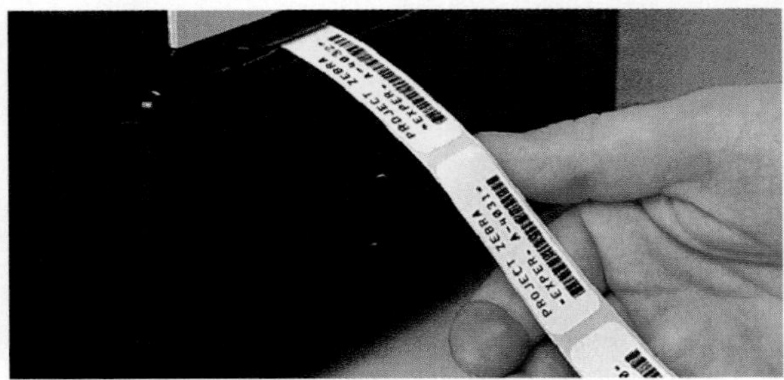

Figure 4–35 A bar code label printer.

Figure 4–36 A supermarket check-out clerk passes the UPC-coded portion of a package over the scanner built into the check-out counter.

Universal Product Code

Since 1973 supermarkets around the country have been using bar code scanners to speed the check-out process (Figure 4–36). The scanners, usually built into the check-out counters, read the product codes on the food packages as the clerk passes each package over the scanner's "eye." Food manufacturers have adopted a special bar code convention, called the **Universal Product Code** (UPC), that is now placed on almost all prepackaged items normally sold in supermarkets and other retail stores.

The UPC is a bar code scheme consisting of 10 digits. The leftmost five digits identify the manufacturer of the item, and the rightmost five digits identify the particular item (Figure 4–37). Each digit is formed by blackening different combinations of seven possible bars. The coding scheme uses **even parity**, that is, all the representations of the digits have an even number of ones (or an even number of bars). This helps determine if the machine has read the code properly. If the machine reads a code that appears to be composed of an odd number of ones, it sounds a beeper to ask the clerk to rescan the item or enter the information manually. Mistakes do occur, but experiments have shown that the chance is less than one error in several million digits—far greater accuracy than that of a check-out clerk manually keying in product codes and prices.

Many supermarkets fared poorly with UPC scanning in the mid- to late 1970s, but now the bugs seem to have been worked out and consumers are becoming accustomed to the new technology. By the late 1980s most supermarkets will be using some form of scanning. Some systems even have a computerized speech synthesizer that describes each item and states its price as the item passes over the scanner. (Speech synthesizers are

0
51000 02141
DIRECTIONS: Stir soup in pan. Gradually stir one can of water into soup. Heat to boiling, stirring occasionally. Makes about 2½ cups. Promptly refrigerate unused portions.
MUSHROOM SAUCE: Stir contents well. Stir in ⅓ cup of milk. Heat to boil, simmer two minutes. Makes about 1½ cups. Serve on meat or fish.
Satisfaction guaranteed or money back. Store unopened can at room temperature. Recommend use by month and year on top line of can end.
Golden Mushroom
WITH SLICED MUSHROOMS
NET WT. 10¾ OZ.
SOUP
(305 GRAMS)
0
51000 01021
DIRECTIONS
Empty soup into pan. Stir in 1 can of water. Heat to full boil, stirring occasionally. Makes about 2½ cups of soup. Promptly refrigerate unused portions.
Satisfaction guaranteed or money back. Store unopened can at room temperature. Recommend use by month and year on top line of can end.
ABC Vegetable
MADE WITH BEEF STOCK
NET WT. 10½ OZ.
SOUP
(298 GRAMS)

Figure 4–37 The Universal Product Code uses both a manufacturer code (leftmost five digits) and a product code (rightmost five digits). On these two different Campbell's soup products the manufacturer's code is the same (51000), but the Golden Mushroom soup has code 02141 and the ABC Vegetable soup has code 01021.

discussed in Chapter 5.) The UPC scanners even handle "specials" like two cans of sauce for 79 cents. When the first can passes, the scanner charges 40 cents; whenever the second can passes, the scanner "remembers" to charge 39 cents.

Benefits of UPC Scanning

Both supermarkets and customers share in the benefits of UPC scanning. From the customer's standpoint, check-out is faster and more accurate. The customer receives a neatly itemized register tape containing the description, quantity, and price of each item purchased. The supermarket benefits by faster check-out; it needs fewer check-out lanes and fewer employees. Time-consuming hand stamping of item prices is replaced, where allowed, with shelf labels, check-out errors are reduced, and bookkeeping chores are speeded.

UPC scanning can also benefit management by providing it with valuable information. For example, one supermarket chain used a back-room computer to analyze information supplied by its scanners. The chain was able to identify more than a thousand items that were only marginally profitable. It stopped carrying those items, causing an immediate improvement in profitability.

UPC scanning and computers can also be used

by supermarket management to analyze the effectiveness of advertising campaigns by keeping track of the purchases of store specials. They can enable supermarkets to maintain current inventory information, prevent lost sales due to "stock-outs," monitor sales of perishable items, determine how to allocate precious shelf space, and measure customers' responses to in-store merchandising tests. Data from the scanners can also help a store schedule its employee hours to serve customers better during peak periods.

Controversial Issues in UPC Scanning

Reception to UPC scanning has not, however, always been good. In January 1983 *Better Homes and Gardens* reported a frustrated consumer saying, "What with refunds, rebates, cents-off coupons, and the Universal Product Code, I wonder if anybody really knows what a box of detergent costs nowadays" (p. 114).

Item pricing is perhaps the most controversial issue surrounding UPC scanning. Supermarkets stand to save hundreds of millions of dollars per year if they do not have to stamp prices on individual items, but consumer groups feel that item pricing is essential to help consumers make cost-conscious buying decisions. They insist that item pricing facilitates comparison shopping, meal planning, budgeting, and verification by the consumer that the correct price is being charged for each item. Supermarkets argue that many of the price-stamped items are difficult to read and that the consumer often loses time at the check-out counter while a clerk calls for a price check. Several states have passed laws requiring individual item pricing.

The possibilities for rapid price hikes with UPC scanning concern many consumer advocates. One supermarket chain raised the price of a popular item in a few of its stores and used the scanner inputs to monitor the effects on volume. When it determined that sales volume did not change significantly, it immediately raised the price at all stores in the chain.

Scanning makes it possible to change prices several times a day so that prices could be set higher during peak periods. While that may not necessarily be an unethical practice, many people would consider it a misuse of scanning technology.

Directions in UPC Scanning

One manufacturer is developing a system that will take items as they are received at the loading docks, scan them, and automatically imprint them with unit prices. Others are using **laser holography**, a technique for creating three-dimensional pictures, to produce scanners that can read the UPC code off an item no matter how the item is positioned. This speeds checkout even more because clerks do not have to position each item carefully over the scanner eye. We can expect to see increasingly creative uses for UPC scanning. Resistance to it will certainly diminish as its contributions to efficiency become more evident.

Summary 

1. Computers input information from a wide variety of input devices.
2. Punched cards are declining in use because cards are bulky, expensive, occasionally in short supply, not reusable, have a small capacity, and have file integrity problems.
3. Verification is the "repunching" of cards to be sure they were punched correctly. It is an expensive and time-consuming process that is being replaced by editing and checking programs.
4. Key-to-tape and key-to-disk systems facilitate high-speed and accurate data entry onto reusable magnetic tapes and disks.
5. Terminal-oriented systems allow users to access the computer on-line (through devices directly connected to the computer). With

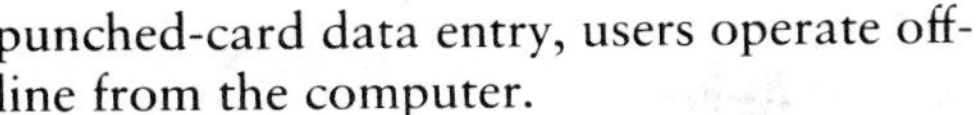

punched-card data entry, users operate off-line from the computer.

6. Touch sensing allows users to point to characters, words, or symbols on the screen of a CRT to initiate the actions they wish to take. It is one of the most user-friendly interfaces.

7. Source data automation techniques capture data automatically from source documents in computer-readable form so that manual data entry is eliminated.

8. In direct data entry, data is captured at its source and entered directly into a computer with no paper being produced.

9. Magnetic ink character recognition (MICR) is used primarily by the banking industry for check processing. Optical character recognition (OCR) devices read handwritten, typewritten, or typeset characters and symbols and convert them directly into computer codes.

10. Different types of optical readers can read journal tapes from cash registers and adding machines, small documents, and full pages of text. Current OCR devices read up to 1000 characters per second with as few as one or two errors per 100,000 characters read. Future OCR readers are expected to be even faster and more reliable.

11. Optical mark recognition (OMR) devices read pencil marks placed in fixed positions on specially designed forms and convert this information directly to computer codes.

12. Bar code readers use optical-scanning techniques to read a series of wide and narrow bars designed to represent letters, numbers, and symbols.

13. The Universal Product Code (UPC) is a specially designed bar code for use in supermarkets and retail stores, which identifies items by manufacturer and product type.

14. Advantages of UPC scanning include reductions in the number of check-out clerks needed, faster and more accurate check-out for the consumer, a neat itemized list of all purchases, and generation of useful management information.

15. Item pricing is perhaps the most controversial issue surrounding UPC scanning. Supermarkets can save hundreds of millions of dollars per year by not stamping prices on each item, but consumer groups insist that item pricing is essential for comparison shopping. The item pricing controversy may eventually be resolved by new equipment for scanning items as they arrive at the supermarket and automatically stamping them with the current prices.

Important Terms 

bar code reading
batch processing
card reader
card verifier
direct data entry
edit check
even parity
file integrity
hard copy
keypunch
key-to-disk
key-to-tape
light pen
magnetic ink character recognition (MICR)
off-line
omnifont reader
on-line
optical character recognition (OCR)
optical mark recognition (OMR)
peripheral device
punched card
range check
reasonableness check
soft copy
source data automation (SDA)
touch sensing
transaction-processing system
turnaround document
Universal Product Code (UPC)
wand reader

Self-Review Exercises 

Matching

Next to the term in column A, place the letter of the statement in column B that best describes it.

Column A	Column B
1. Range check	A. Most versatile OCR device
2. Hard copy	B. Keyboard with nonmovable keys
3. OCR-A	C. OCR font which is best for machines
4. OMR	D. OCR font which is best for people
5. Membrane	E. Paper image
6. OCR-B	F. Bar code used in supermarkets
7. UPC	G. Screen image
8. Omnifont reader	H. Age less than 150
9. Soft copy	I. Month should be 1 to 12
10. Reasonableness check	J. Useful in exam scoring applications

Fill-in-the-Blanks

Fill in the blanks in each of the following:

1. ______ ensure that digits are not entered where letters are required, and vice versa.

2. Because individual cards can easily be removed from files or replaced by cards with altered data, cards are said to have ______ problems.

3. In ______ systems, individual data items are entered into the computer and processed immediately.

4. With the user-friendly technique of ______ , the user enters information into the computer by placing his or her finger on the surface of a display screen.

5. With ______ , data is captured at its source and entered directly into the computer with no paper documents being produced.

6. Most check processing today involves the source data automation technique of ______ .

7. ______ devices read handwritten or typewritten characters and symbols and convert them directly into computer codes.

8. A computer-printed document on which people record additional information and which is resubmitted to the computer to be read back in (usually on an OCR/OMR device) is called a ______ .

9. ______ is perhaps the most controversial issue surrounding UPC scanning.

10. The technique of ______ is used in scanners that can read the UPC code off an item no matter how the item is positioned.

Answers to Self-Review Exercises

Matching: 1 I, 2 E, 3 C, 4 J, 5 B, 6 D, 7 F, 8 A, 9 G, 10 H

Fill-in-the-Blanks:

1. Edit checks
2. file integrity
3. transaction-processing
4. touch sensing
5. direct data entry
6. magnetic ink character recognition (MICR)
7. Optical character recognition (OCR)
8. turnaround document
9. Item pricing
10. laser holography

Discussion Questions 

1. Why is it critical to prevent wrong data from entering the computer?

2. What techniques are used to help eliminate the need for card verification?

3. Compare off-line and on-line computer usage.

4. Give several reasons why touch sensing is becoming an increasingly popular data entry method and suggest several applications for which touch-sensing terminals would be useful.

5. What are some of the most widely used techniques for source data automation?

6. How does direct data entry differ from source data automation?

7. Explain briefly how an OCR reader works.

8. What is a turnaround document? Discuss several applications of turnaround documents.

9. Explain the structure of the Universal Product Code.

10. Discuss the advantages and disadvantages of item pricing.

Projects 

1. Visit a supermarket that uses UPC scanning. Talk with the store manager, clerks, and several customers about the system. Ask to see the "back-room" computer. What management information is obtained from the system? Report on your visit.

2. Write to several manufacturers of supermarket scanning systems and request literature on their UPC scanning systems. Prepare a report on the current state of supermarket scanning systems. A list of some of the major manufacturers of supermarket scanning systems follows.

Data Terminal Systems Inc.
124 Acton Street
Maynard, MA 01754

International Business Machines Corporation
1133 Westchester Avenue
White Plains, NY 10604

Sweda International Inc.
34 Maple Avenue
Pine Brook, NJ 07058

TEC America Inc.
TEC Supermarket Systems
19250 Van Ness Avenue
Torrance, CA 90501

Vidac
1054 Shary Circle
Concord, CA 94518

3. One of the best overviews on supermarket scanning systems is the Food Marketing Institute's *Guide to Scanning*, prepared by the consulting firm of Booz, Allen & Hamilton. Copies are available for a small fee from:

Research Division
Food Marketing Institute
1750 K Street, N.W.
Washington, DC 20006

Write for this publication and present a report summarizing its contents.

Chapter 5

Output: Getting Results from Computers

After reading this chapter you will understand:

1. The major types of computer output devices, how they operate, what features they offer, and why they are so important in today's computer systems
2. The reasons for the popularity of portable terminals
3. What ergonomics is and why it is increasing in importance
4. How computers can be made to speak their outputs
5. How computer graphics are generated and why graphics are an important form of computer output

Left: The most popular computer output devices are the printer and the CRT display.

Outline

In the short term you're making more copies. In the long term you'll call it up on the screen.

Mary Jo Merrifield

As we have seen, computers are becoming more and more important in our lives and are generating an increasing portion of the information we use. This information from computers is known as **output**. Output can appear in various forms. It may be in readable form on paper or computer terminal screens, or in secondary storage such as tape and disk, for later use. In this chapter we consider these and many other popular means of generating computer outputs. Secondary storage is discussed in Chapter 6.

Printed Reports

Among the most common forms of computer output are printed reports, which are normally divided into three categories: **detail reports**, which list every item being processed; **summary reports**, which provide a concise overview of the information; and **exception reports**, which highlight individual items requiring human attention. For example, in an inventory control application for a department store, a detail report might list every item carried, a summary report might show total sales by department, and an exception report might highlight only best-selling items and weak sellers. Detail reports tend to be used by company personnel in their day-to-day responsibilities. Summary and exception reports are particularly useful to busy managers.

Reports may also be classified by how often they are produced. **Periodic reports** appear on a regular schedule, such as weekly, monthly, quarterly, or annually. They generally represent the bulk of an organization's reporting. **Demand reports** are produced as needed. **Ad hoc reports** are designed and produced in response to special requests and are essential in decision support systems, as we will see in Chapter 11.

Internal reports are generated for use within an organization; **external reports** are sent to customers or other companies. Internal reports usually contain substantial amounts of information and can appear cluttered (Figure 5–1); external reports (Figure 5–2) are designed to be readable and easy to understand. They must often be preprinted on special forms as required by law, such as tax forms and other government reporting documents.

Stock forms are generally blank or lined forms on which any report can be printed (Figure 5–3). **Preprinted forms** (Figure 5–4) may be of various designs. Some contain headings and ruled lines to minimize the amount of information that must be printed by the computer and to make the information more readable. Preprinted forms can be attractively designed to help a company convey a good impression to its clients, but they consume valuable storage space and may be expensive and time-consuming to produce. If a company runs out of certain key forms, the operation of its business could be affected.

Types of Printers

One of the most common computer output devices for producing reports on paper (hard copy) is the printer. Printers are of two basic types: impact or nonimpact. They operate either as **character printers** (printing only one character at a time), **line printers** (printing an entire line at once), or **page printers** (forming one line at a time, but actually printing an entire page at a time).

Impact Printers

Impact printers function like typewriters: They strike a mechanical hammer against a ribbon to

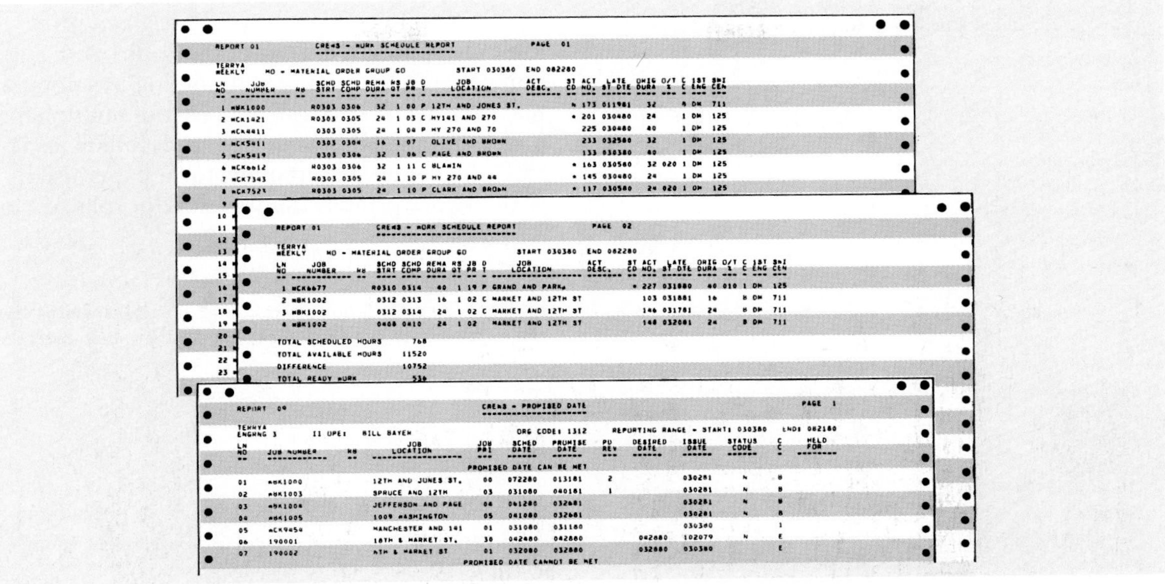

Figure 5–1 Internal reports are generally packed with information. They use abbreviations and codes to save space.

Figure 5–2 Samples of external reports provided to customers by an investment brokerage firm.

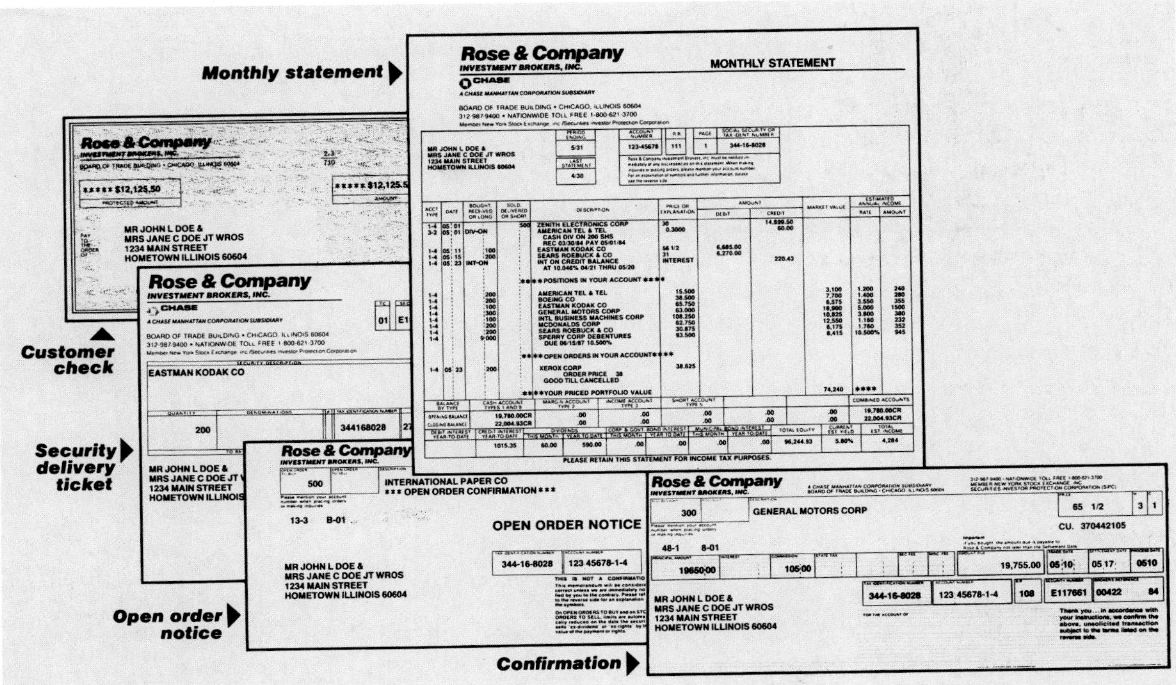

Product 9902
Product 9901
Product 9900

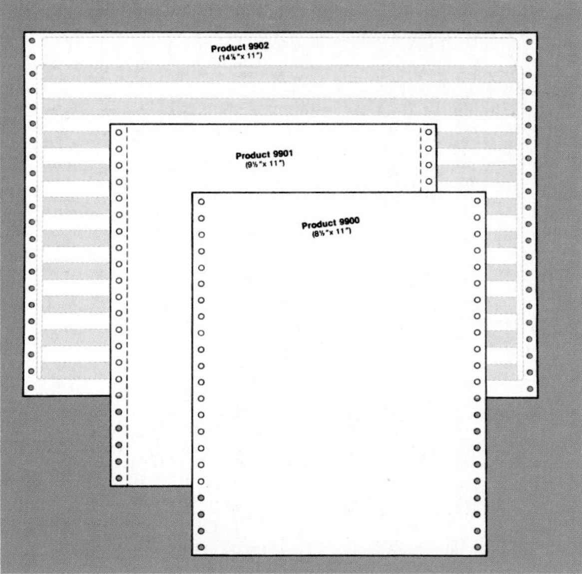

leave an impression on paper. They can print **multiple copies** by using special forms with carbon paper. This feature is becoming less popular, however, because of the high cost of multiple-part paper and the labor required to **decollate** (separate) the copies. **Continuous form paper** used with impact printers comes either in rolls or,

Figure 5–3 *Left:* Stock paper comes in various widths either completely blank or with light-colored bars to help users read printed data.

Figure 5–4 *Below:* A preprinted form used in a customer billing system (accounts receivable).

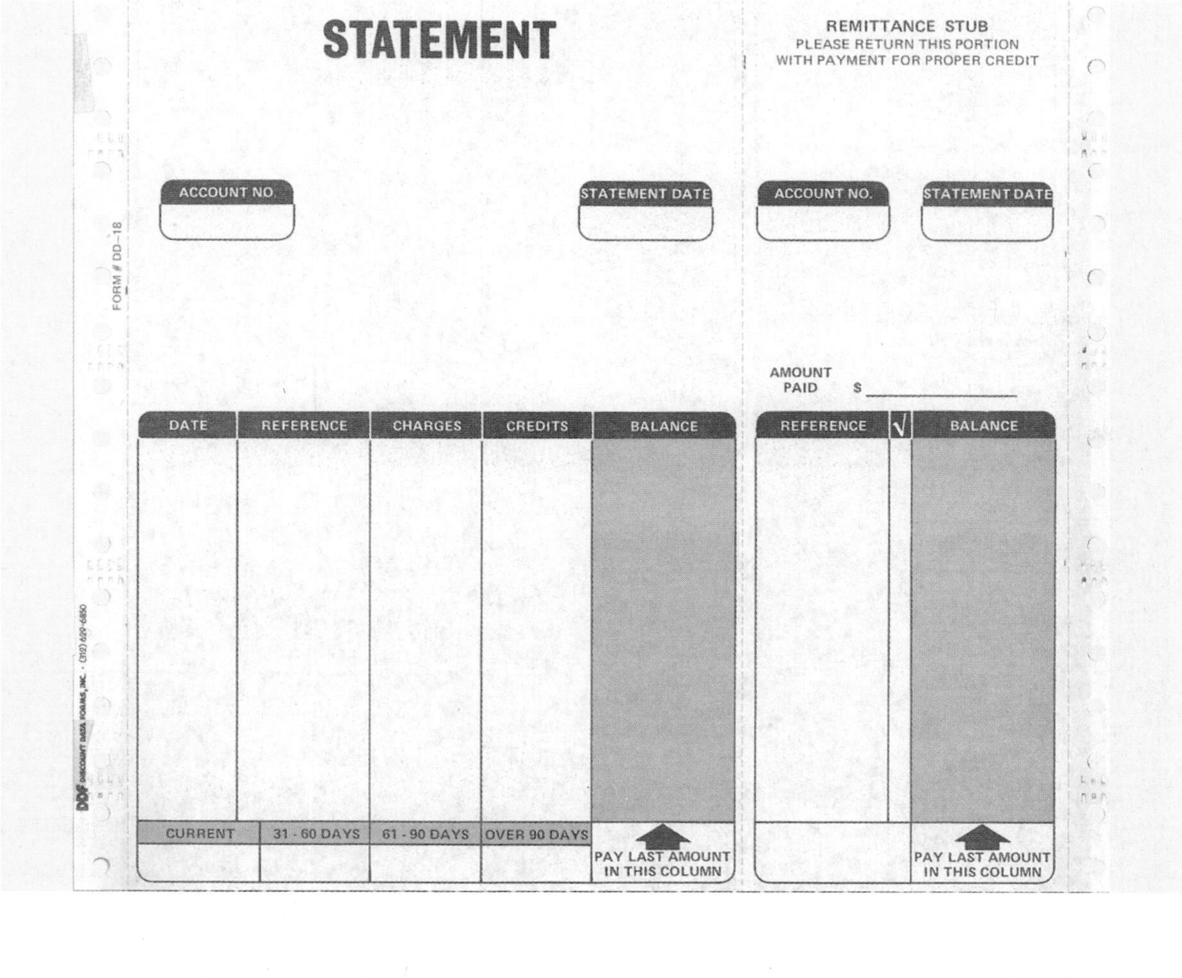

STATEMENT
REMITTANCE STUB
PLEASE RETURN THIS PORTION
WITH PAYMENT FOR PROPER CREDIT
ACCOUNT NO.
STATEMENT DATE
ACCOUNT NO.
STATEMENT DATE
FORM # DD-18
AMOUNT PAID $
DATE
REFERENCE
CHARGES
CREDITS
BALANCE
REFERENCE
√
BALANCE
CURRENT
31 - 60 DAYS
61 - 90 DAYS
OVER 90 DAYS
PAY LAST AMOUNT IN THIS COLUMN
PAY LAST AMOUNT IN THIS COLUMN

more commonly, as fanfolded, perforated pages. The paper may be advanced by **friction feed,** in which a roller mechanism forces it to move through the machine, or a **pin-feed** mechanism, which advances the paper on pins that fit in equally spaced holes on both sides.

Printers used with computer systems fall into several categories.

Dot-matrix printers (Figures 5–5 and 5–6) are character printers that create an image on paper by driving a series of small pins against a ribbon. They form letters, numbers, symbols, and even graphics out of dots (Figures 5–7 and 5–8) and work in print speeds ranging from 30 cps (characters per second) to 300 or more cps. These printers are compact and economical and can print a wide variety of character styles (Figure 5–9). The quality of print is not generally acceptable for "finished" copy such as business letters. Figures 5–10 through 5–14 show many interesting applications of dot-matrix printing.

Figure 5–6 This dot matrix printer is a KSR (for keyboard send/receive) device. It can receive information from the central computer, and it can transmit information entered at its keyboard to the central computer.

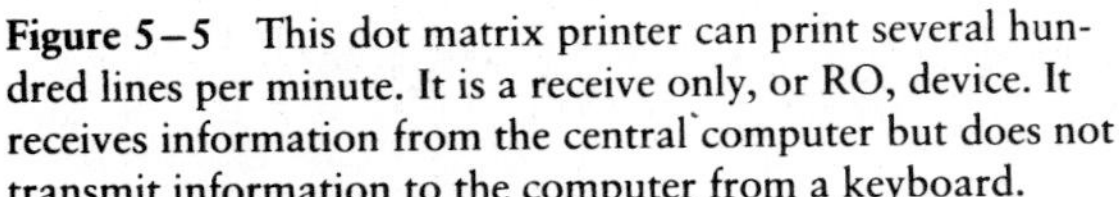

Figure 5–5 This dot matrix printer can print several hundred lines per minute. It is a receive only, or RO, device. It receives information from the central computer but does not transmit information to the computer from a keyboard.

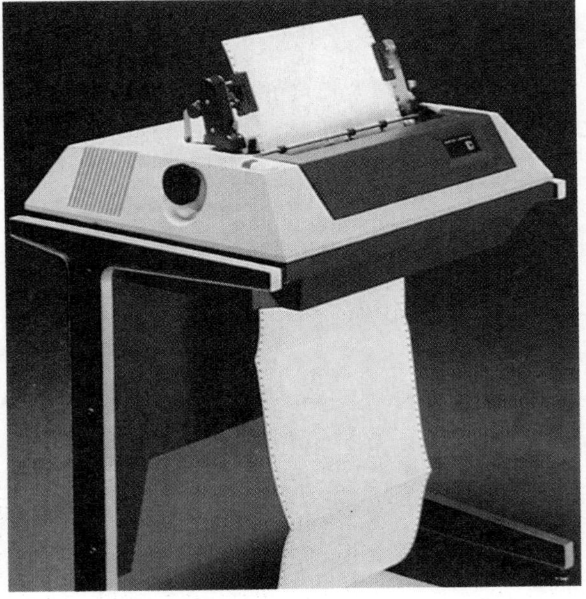

Figure 5–7 A 5 × 7 dot matrix representation of the letter *B*.

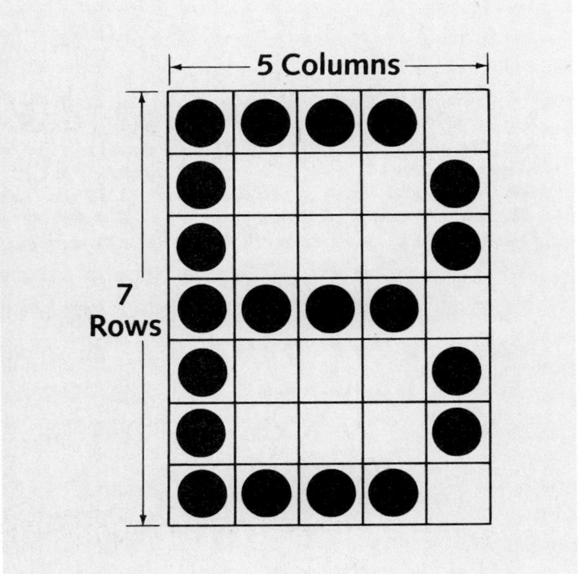

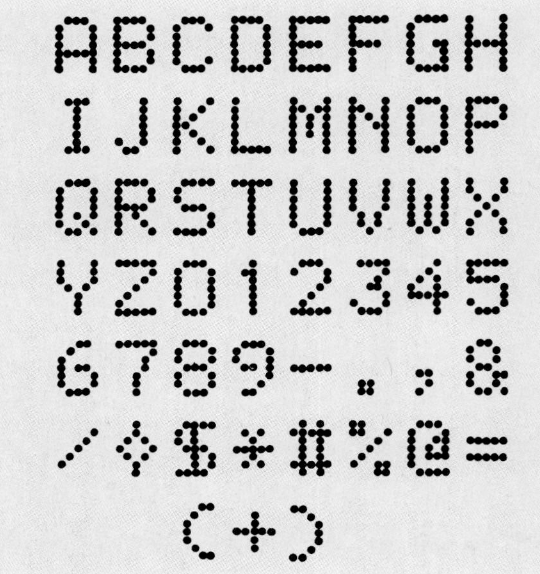

Figure 5–8 A character set composed of 5 × 7 dot matrix characters.

Figure 5–10 Dot matrix printers can print bar coded information as well as characters in OCR fonts.

Figure 5–9 The range of type styles available on dot matrix printers is limited only by the programmer's imagination.

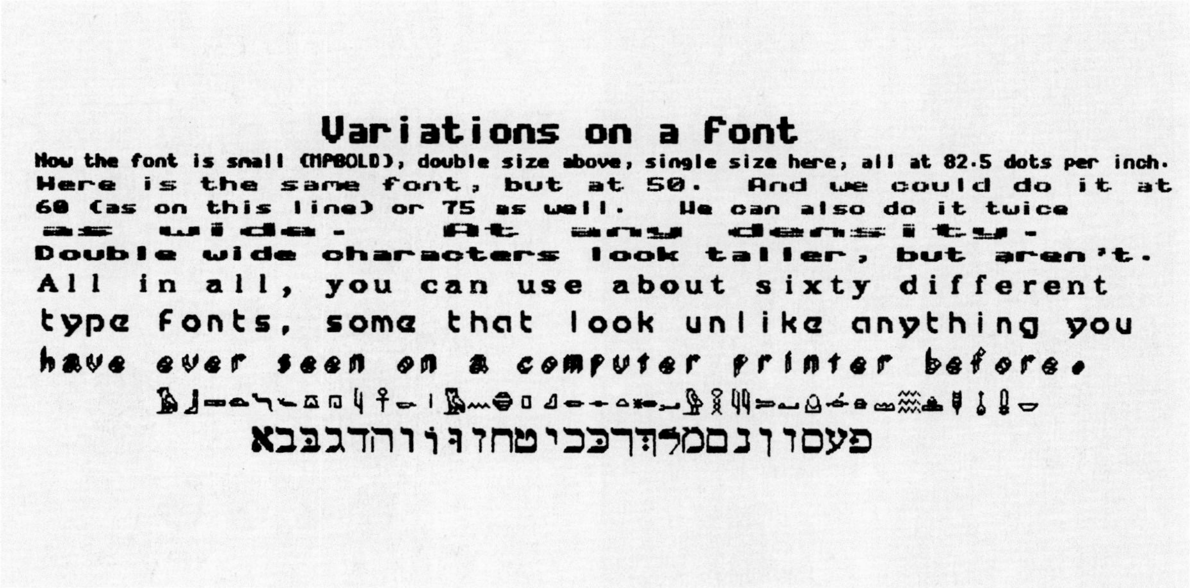

Variations on a Font

Now the font is small (MPBOLD), double size above, single size here, all at 82.5 dots per inch. Here is the same font, but at 50. And we could do it at 60 (as on this line) or 75 as well. We can also do it twice as wide. At any density. Double wide characters look taller, but aren't. All in all, you can use about sixty different type fonts, some that look unlike anything you have ever seen on a computer printer before.

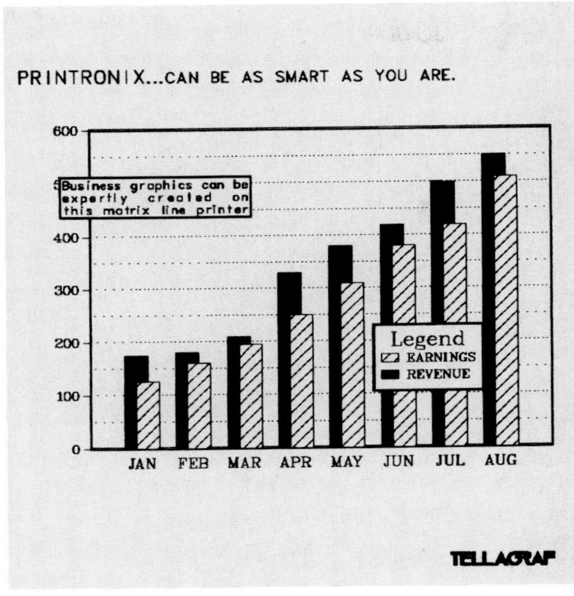

Figure 5–11 Business graphics like this bar chart can be printed on a dot matrix printer.

Figure 5–12 A pie chart produced by a dot matrix printer.

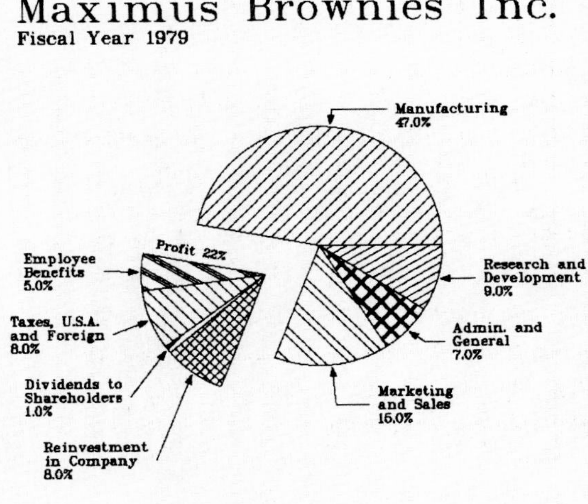

Figure 5–13 Even photographs may be printed with a dot matrix printer. This photograph was first entered into the computer with a digitizer that scanned the photograph and coded it as a series of light and dark areas. The darker areas have dots close together; the lighter areas have dots farther apart.

Figure 5–14 Even three-dimensional effects can be achieved with dot matrix printers. The software that forms these graphics can be very complex.

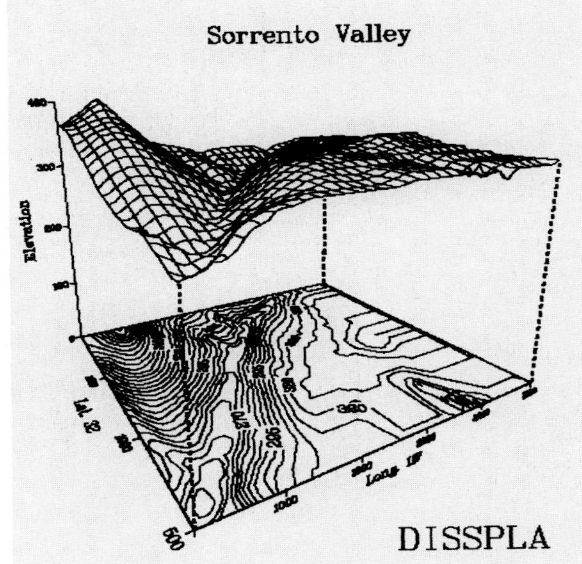

Daisy-wheel and thimble printers are character printers that get their names from the shapes of their printing elements. A **daisy-wheel printer** has characters on long fingers connected to a central pin, giving the appearance of a daisy (Figure 5–15). The **thimble printer** element has projections, called fingers, connected to a circular carrier and looks like a thimble used in sewing (Figure 5–16). Both printers spin the print element at high speed until the finger with the appropriate symbol is located above the print position on the paper. The finger is then struck by a hammer that drives it against a ribbon that in turn strikes the paper. These printers are ordinarily slower than dot-matrix printers, but their output is of better quality. They are often called **letter-quality printers** because their print quality is as good as that of an office typewriter. They are also called **formed character printers** because each print finger contains a fully formed character rather than a pattern of dots (Figures 5–17 and 5–18). These printers operate at about 10 to 50 cps and are widely used in word-processing systems (see Chapter 14).

Figure 5–16 The printing element of the thimble printer.

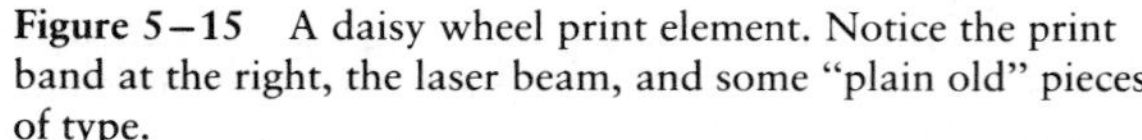

Figure 5–15 A daisy wheel print element. Notice the print band at the right, the laser beam, and some "plain old" pieces of type.

Figure 5–17 A close-up of the fingers of a daisy wheel printer. Notice the fully formed characters.

Band printers (Figures 5–19, 5–20 and 5–21) are line printers that print at speeds of several hundred to as many as 3000 lines per minute. They arrange the symbols on a continuous loop that spins at very high speeds. Every print position on the printer has a hammer that can strike a symbol as it "flies" by on the loop. When the symbol to be printed is above the correct print position, the hammer strikes the band against a ribbon, leaving an impression on paper.

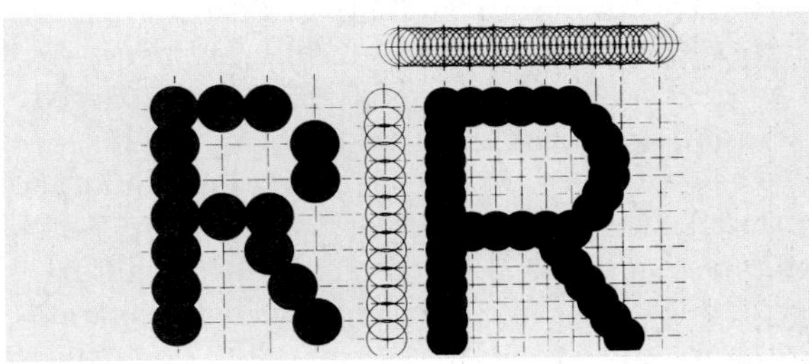

Figure 5–18 By overlapping dots, it is possible for correspondence quality printers to produce letters that are almost as crisp as those produced by letter quality printers. This letter *R* was formed by making two passes. On the second pass the print head was lowered down the page by the width of half a dot.

Figure 5–20 One of the fastest impact printers available, this band printer runs at 3000 lines per minute. At 132/150/160 characters per line, that's up to 8000 characters per second (cps).

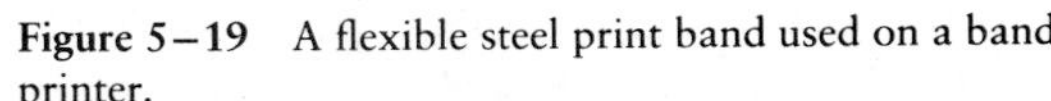

Figure 5–19 A flexible steel print band used on a band printer.

Figure 5–21 An inside view of a large band printer showing some of its key components.

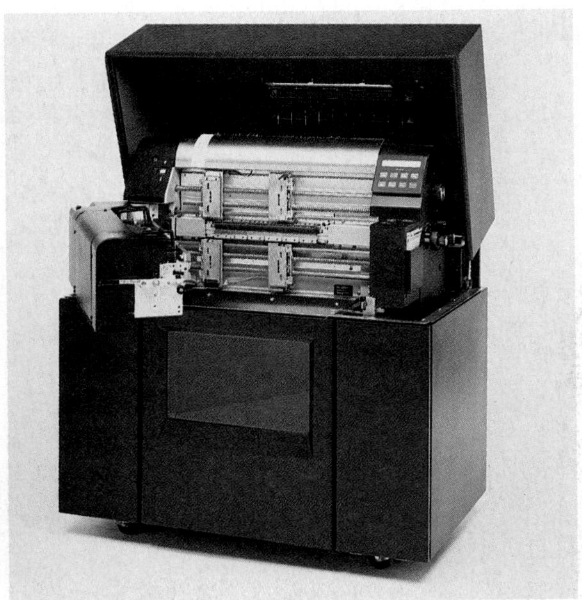

Drum printers (Figure 5–22) are line printers with characters arranged in circles around a cylindrical drum. Each circular band consists of all the printable characters, with one band corresponding to each possible print position on a line. The drum spins at a steady speed, positioning each character above the desired print position within the time it takes for one revolution of the drum. As the desired characters rotate by, hammers at each of the print positions strike at the right moment, forcing the ribbon and paper against the drum. Drum printers operate at speeds comparable to high-speed band printers, but the print lines may appear wavy.

Impact printers, in contrast to nonimpact printers, generally produce letter-quality copies. They do, however, have some disadvantages over nonimpact printers. Because of their many moving parts, impact printers tend to be noisy and to generate a great deal of heat. They may also be expensive to build and repair.

Nonimpact Printers

Nonimpact printers use electronic or photographic techniques to produce reports at high speeds. These printers use thermal, electrostatic, laser, and other methods to create their images. One form of nonimpact printer is the page printer, which can produce an entire page, or pages, of copy at one time. In general, nonimpact printers are quieter, faster, have fewer moving parts, and are less likely to break down than impact printers.

Thermal printers are dot-matrix printers that operate by driving heated pins against special heat-sensitive paper to "burn" the image onto the paper. They are quiet, but many people don't like the feel of thermal paper, and the images tend to fade.

Electrostatic printers are page printers that use light beams or laser beams to induce electric charges on paper or a metal drum. The charged areas attract toner chemical to form images.

Laser printers are the fastest type of nonimpact printers. The precise light of lasers (Figure 5–23) makes it possible to guide crisp dots of light to exact locations on a page. This principle is used in laser printers like the Xerox 9700. Each square inch of a page is treated as a grid of 300 by 300 dots. Each of the 90,000 possible dots per square inch is either left blank or darkened. The dots may be arranged to make characters, symbols, graphics, or patterns of very fine quality and almost unlimited variety. The versatility of the laser printing concept is demonstrated by the sample printouts shown in Figure 5–24.

Most laser printers can print on standard-size sheets of plain paper at rates of about two pages per second or about 18,000 lines of text per minute. Some printers can print on both sides of a

Figure 5–22 A character drum used on a drum printer.

Figure 5–23 A pinpoint laser beam passing through the eye of a needle. To emphasize the precision of laser light, suppose 1000 needles were placed in a line each one foot apart from the next. The scattering of the laser beam is so minimal that the beam would pass through the eyes of all the needles without touching the edge of a single one!

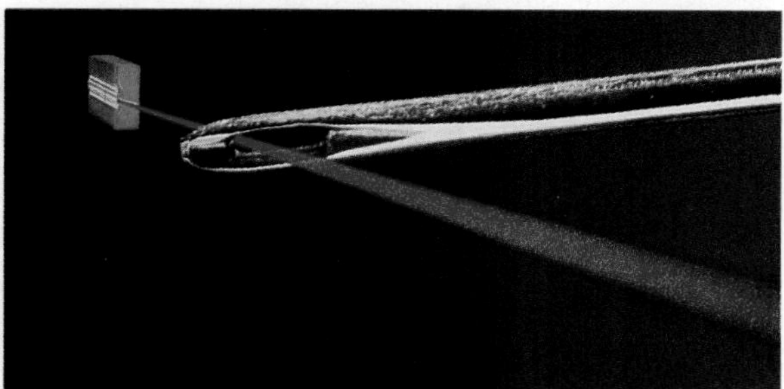

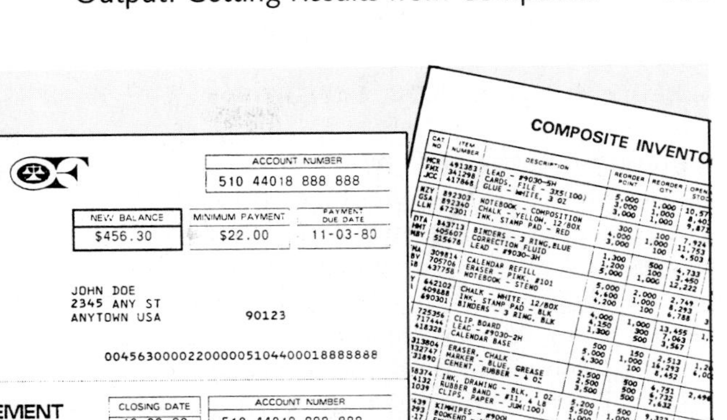

FIDELITY BANK
OKLAHOMA CITY OK

ACCOUNT NUMBER
510 44018 888 888

MasterCard
MASTERCARD SVCE 44
FIDELITY BANK
P O BOX 220000
DALLAS TX 75396

NEW BALANCE	MINIMUM PAYMENT	PAYMENT DUE DATE
$456.30	$22.00	11-03-80

RETAIN YOUR SALES COPY
TO VERIFY CHARGES

JOHN DOE
2345 ANY ST
ANYTOWN USA 90123

IMPORTANT

00456300002200000510440001888888 8

345

YOUR REVOLVING CREDIT LINE FOR PURCHASES AND CASH ADVANCES	
$5000.00	$4543.70

STATEMENT

CLOSING DATE	ACCOUNT NUMBER
10-09-80	510 44018 888 888

POSTING DATE	REFERENCE NUMBER	DATE AND DESCRIPTION OF TRANSACTION	$ AMOUNT
0916	73404580	0909 BURSAR'S OFFICE OU NORMAN OK	307.00
0918	29707110114	0912 NATIONAL SHIRT SHOPS OKLAHOMA CITY OK	29.10
0919	76311807	0912 RECORD TOWN 13 OKLAHOMA CITY OK	16.30
0922	22693584175	0912 RICHMAN BORTHERS 2354 OKLAHOMA CITY OK	48.88
1003	27703112053	PAYMENT - THANK YOU	650.15CR
1007	16026815259	0912 TG&Y FAMILY CTR 70 NORMAN OK	15.61
1007	15000010342	0927 H J WILSON JEWELER 39 NORMAN OK	39.41

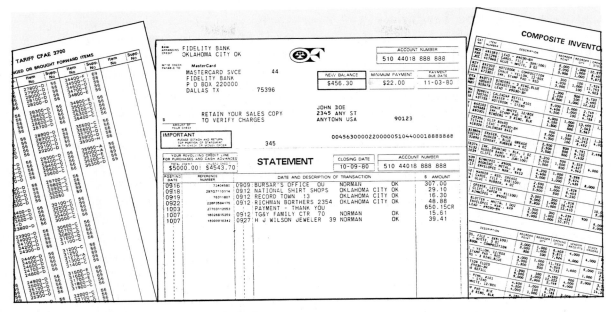

Figure 5–24 All of the information on these sample pages was printed by a laser printer.

page (this is called **duplexing**). Although only one copy can be printed at a time, laser printers operate so quickly that multiple copies can be produced by simply running a report as many times as necessary. This means that each copy is an original, a great improvement over using multiple-part paper. Another feature is that background forms and data can be printed at the same time.

Another advantage of laser printers is the many innovative computer output applications they have made possible. The Pennsylvania Power & Light Company, for example, uses its laser printer to print on each customer's monthly bill a bar chart depicting that customer's average daily electricity usage for the last 13 months. Customers can see the effects of any conservation measures they use.

Terminal-Oriented Systems

In addition to hard copy, output may be presented to the user as a soft copy visual display. Some terminals have the capability both to display on a screen and to print on paper. When a printed copy is needed, the user types a command instructing the printer to produce hard copy. It is common to have a single printer shared by many terminals.

As we saw in Chapter 4, terminals are on-line, that is, directly attached to the computer. As information is entered, it is processed by the computer, and output is provided in seconds. This type of interaction is needed in banking and airline reservation systems, where immediate answers are necessary.

With these on-line terminal systems, the user essentially carries on a dialogue with the computer. This type of interaction is often called **conversational computing.** The computer types a message to the user, called a **prompt**, to which the user responds, usually in an abbreviated code. When a user makes a request that will require some time for the computer to process, the computer prints a confirmation message indicating that it is working on the request. These considerations can greatly affect the usability, user-friendliness, and performance of a conversational computing system.

Homework 6/16

Cathode Ray Tube Terminals

Cathode ray tube (CRT) terminals (Figure 5–25) are one of the most popular types of terminals. They are often used as time sharing terminals and as console input/output devices for small computers. CRTs operate in the same manner as TV picture tubes. A heater coil heats up a cathode, causing it to emit a beam of electrons (Figure 5–26). The beam is accelerated and focused so that it is sharp. A deflection structure aims the beam so that it strikes a special coating (called a **phosphor**) on the front of the screen at a precise dot location. As electrons strike the coating it glows, and the intended characters or graphics are displayed as patterns of illuminated dots.

Features of CRT Terminals

A wide range of features are available for CRTs. These include the following.

Scrolling is available on most CRTs. As each new line of data is added to a display, the data already displayed moves up one line to make room for the new data. The line of data that was

Figure 5–25 A CRT terminal. The detached keyboard may be positioned for the user's maximum comfort.

How a Laser Printer Works

The figure at right shows the internal operation of an IBM laser printer. Information to be printed arrives and is held in a temporary storage area called an **input/output buffer**. The processor formats a complete page at a time and passes the page image to another storage area called a **page buffer**. The page buffer sends a copy of the page to internal storage and another copy to the character generator. The copy is maintained in internal storage so that a single page may be reprinted many times. The internal storage copy is also useful for restarting the system in case of a paper jam. The **character generator** forms the actual print image of each character as a pattern of "on" and "off" bits. The actual type style to be used has been selected by the user and specified to the laser printer via various control commands.

At this point, the printer "knows" exactly what the finished page is going to look like. All characters, graphics, and background business forms to be printed are "in place." The page is then transmitted to the **scan assembly,** where an electronic image of the page is created as a pattern of "on" and "off" bits in precisely the right order for printing.

The scan assembly sends the "on" and "off" bits to the **laser printhead assembly**. It actually sends only one bit at a time, transmitting the bits corresponding to one complete "slice" of the page image. If a given bit is supposed to be "off," the laser shoots a beam of light; if the bit is supposed to be "on," the light is suppressed. The laser beam corresponding to an "off" bit is directed to exactly the right position on a rotating drum by a rotating mirror. The laser beam strikes the electrically charged drum and discharges the drum's surface at that point. After the laser has scanned the drum and discharged all the appropriate "off" bits for the entire page, toner is applied to the drum, and it sticks to the remaining charged portions. A sheet of paper is then rolled against the drum, transferring the image to the paper. The drum is then recharged and is ready to receive information for the next page to be printed.

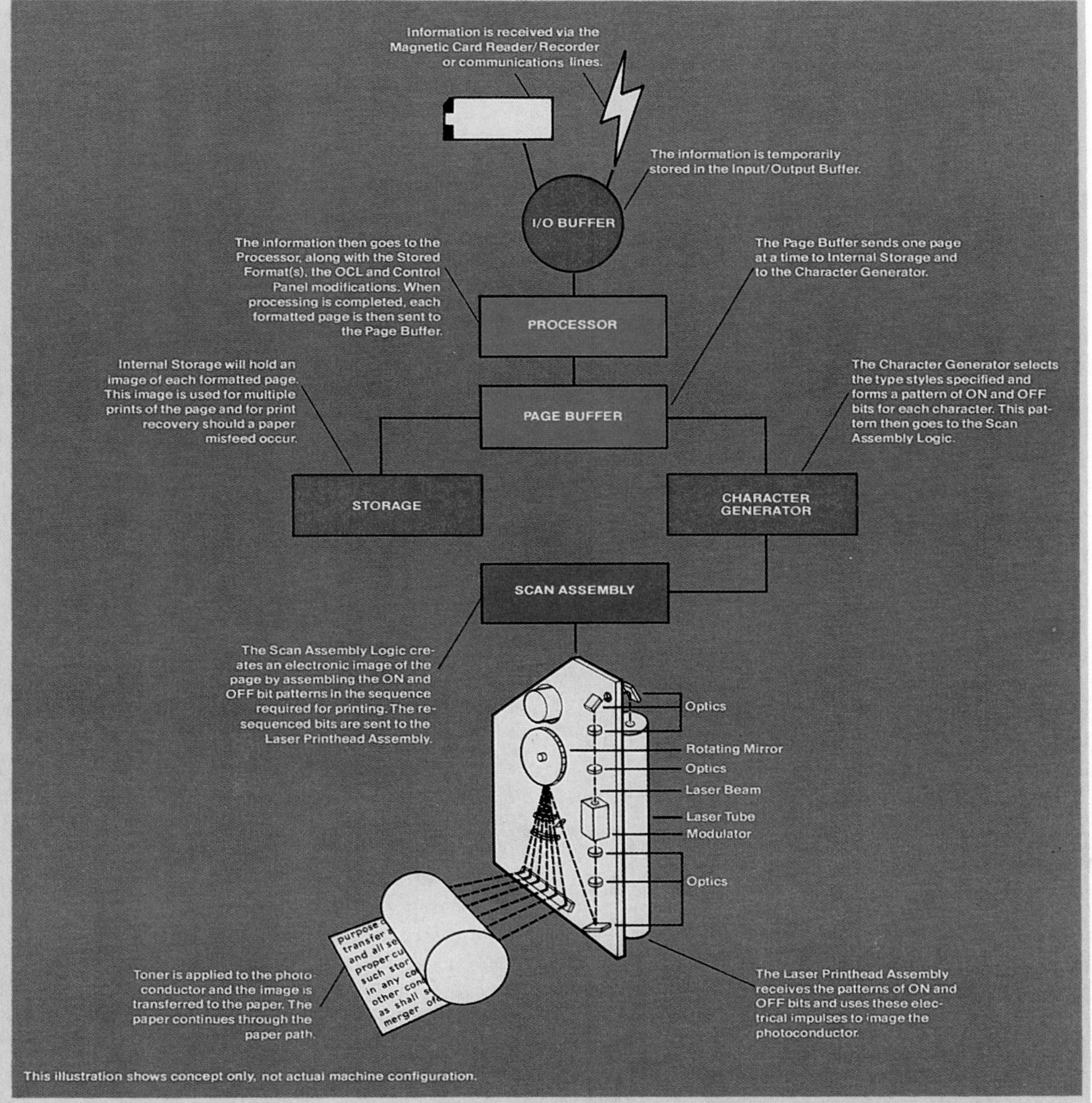

Courtesy of International Business Machines Corporation

The internal operation of an IBM laser printer.

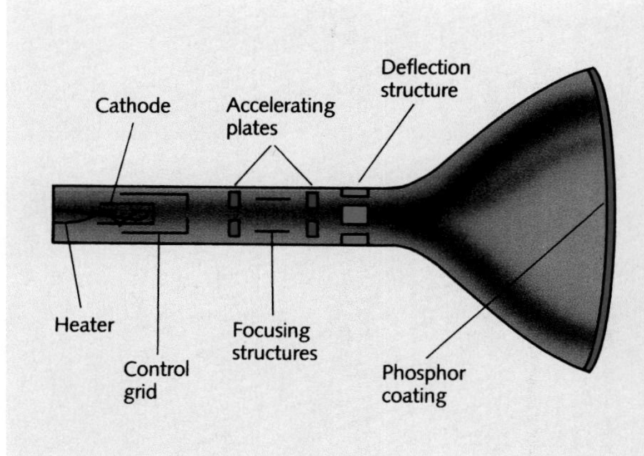

Figure 5–26 The components of a cathode ray tube.

at the top moves off the display screen. A screen that displays 24 lines would always show the most recent 24 lines, with the current line displayed at the bottom of the screen. Some systems allow both forward and backward scrolling (Figure 5–27).

Paging is available on those CRTs that can store one or more full screen images (either in a local memory at the terminal or at the central computer). Paging allows a terminal user to redisplay prior screen images or to "skip ahead" a full page at a time.

Split screen allows the screen to be divided into several separate areas. Some of these areas can be scrolled, while others remain fixed.

THE FAMILY
CIRCUS
By Bil Keane
Copyright 1982
The Register and Tribune
Syndicate, Inc.
"Wow! You mean you get to play video games
all day, Daddy?"

Figure 5–27 Scrolling.

Reversed fields is a particularly useful feature for highlighting information. Normally, information displayed on CRTs shows as light characters against a dark background. Reversed fields show dark characters against a light background. By combining regular and reversed fields, an applications designer can make screen images more interesting and can emphasize important information (Figure 5–28).

Character or line blinking is a feature by which a character, a group of characters, or an entire line can be made to blink repeatedly to call the user's attention to important information.

Protected fields are fields of information that cannot be changed. In data entry applications, it is common to display certain words, phrases, and lines to guide the operator. As information is typed, it fills in the blank areas on the screen but does not disturb protected areas.

Partial screen transmit is a feature that works with the protected fields feature. A user who finishes entering data can transmit that data from the screen to the CPU for processing without also transmitting the protected information from the screen.

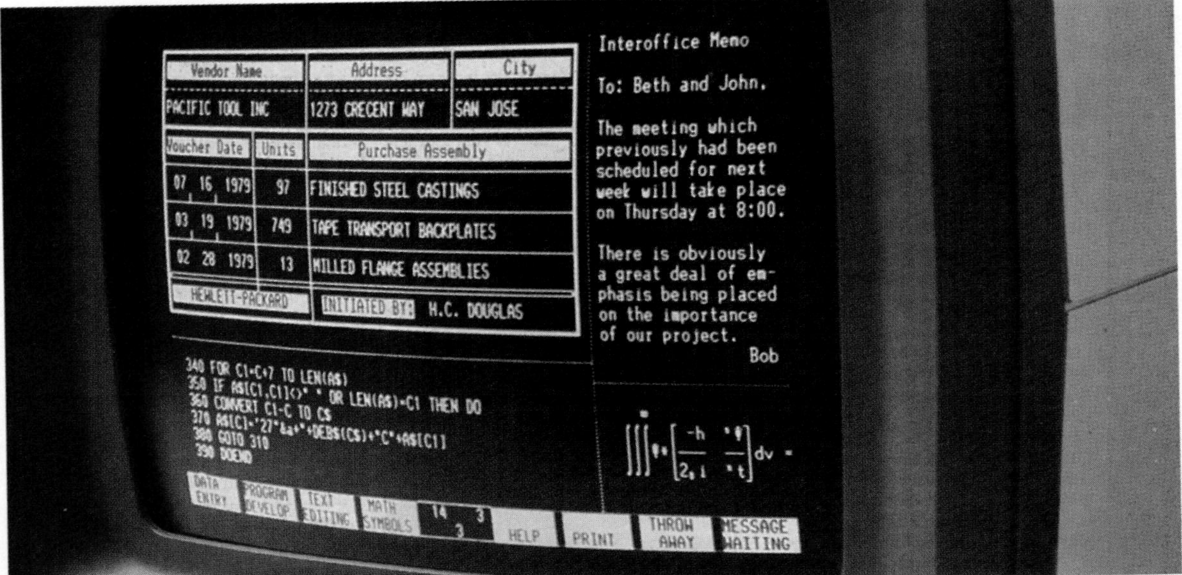

Figure 5–28 This CRT screen display uses many advanced features such as reversed fields, line drawing, split screen, and mathematical symbols.

Character or line brightness control is a feature that lets certain characters or lines be displayed more brightly than others on the screen.

Underscoring allows certain information to be underlined.

Cursor control is one of the most useful features on a CRT. The **cursor** is a blip of light that may be moved to any position on the screen to call attention to that location. The most common cursor control functions allow the user or program to move the cursor left, right, up, or down on the screen. A **cursor home** function is often

THE IMPORTANT THING IS NOT TO BE INTIMIDATED BY THE HARDWARE.

Ergonomics

Ergonomics, sometimes called human engineering, is the study of the relationship of people and machines. People work with and depend on machines to a greater extent now than ever before, and this dependency will surely increase. Improving the person-machine relationship is one of the most important goals of ergonomics.

For example, in recent years much controversy has surrounded the possibility that CRTs are health hazards. Many people who work with them regularly complain of headaches, eyestrain, fatigue, and various skin disorders. Users have expressed concern about exposure to radiation. To date little evidence exists to support the contention that CRTs are indeed dangerous to users' health. Nevertheless, some unions have negotiated contracts requiring that exposure to them be limited and that pregnant women be given the option to switch to other jobs. Many offices have improved their lighting, installed shades to cut down on glare, scheduled more breaks, and taken other measures to ensure that employees using CRTs are made more comfortable.

provided to return the cursor to the starting position on the screen, normally near the top left corner. Many systems allow the user to select either a blinking or a nonblinking cursor.

Self-test allows the user, by flipping a switch, to cause the CRT to display a test pattern and run an internal program to check that the CRT is functioning properly.

Another popular feature is color CRTs. These systems can display both text and graphics (Figure 5–29) and convey much more information in a more pleasing format than conventional light-on-dark images.

Portable Terminals

It is common today to see people conducting business outside their offices with **portable computer terminals** (Figure 5–30). These terminals may be connected to standard telephone lines to place orders, check delivery times, analyze customer needs, and handle other business needs.

Many portable terminals have built-in printers and **acoustic couplers** (Figure 5–31), devices that enable the terminal to communicate with a computer over standard telephone lines.

CRTs can even come in briefcase-size portables. Some portable terminals include a CRT, a printer, a tape cassette for storage, and a built-in acoustic coupler for data communications.

Figure 5–29 These IBM CRTs contain many features that help generate business graphics quickly and conveniently. The color graphics printer at the right is used to get a hard copy of a screen presentation (soft copy) when needed.

Figure 5–30 Portable computer terminals make it possible to access company computers even while on a business trip.

Figure 5–31 A portable thermal printing computer terminal with a built-in acoustic coupler to accommodate a telephone handset.

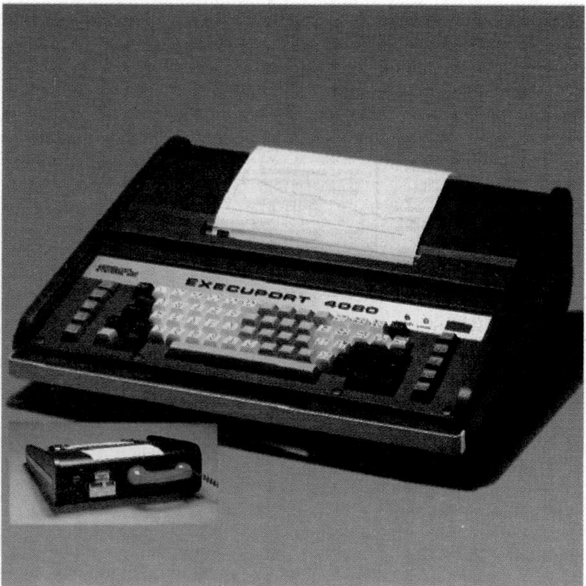

The World of Computer Graphics

Computer graphics is the creation and manipulation of pictures by computers. A picture may be input to a computer by a digitizer, so that the computer may store and manipulate it. A variety of output devices present computer-generated pictures to users. These include dot-matrix impact printers, ink-jet printers, CRTs, plotters (see Figure 6 for a description), and devices that create an image on color film. The illustrations in this section will familiarize you with the wide range of computer graphics capabilities of today's computers.

Graphic CRTs

Figure 1 *Right:* A "green on dark" graphics CRT.

Figure 2 *Below:* This color CRT can display up to 4,913 color shades.

Color Dot-Matrix Impact Printers

Figure 3 Each of these graphics was prepared on a dot matrix printer. The top was printed with a black ribbon; the bottom was printed with a multicolor ribbon. Which do you prefer?

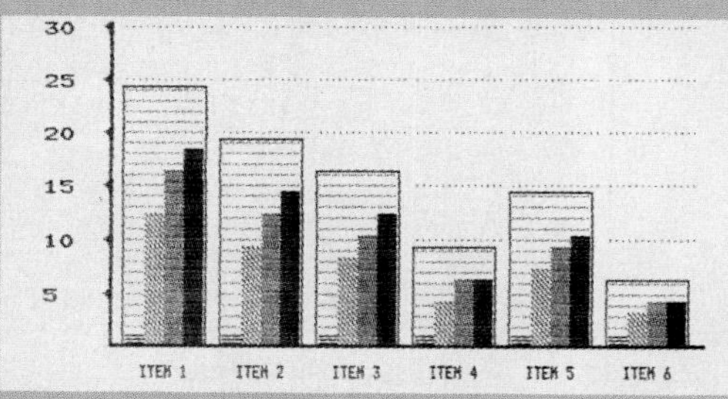

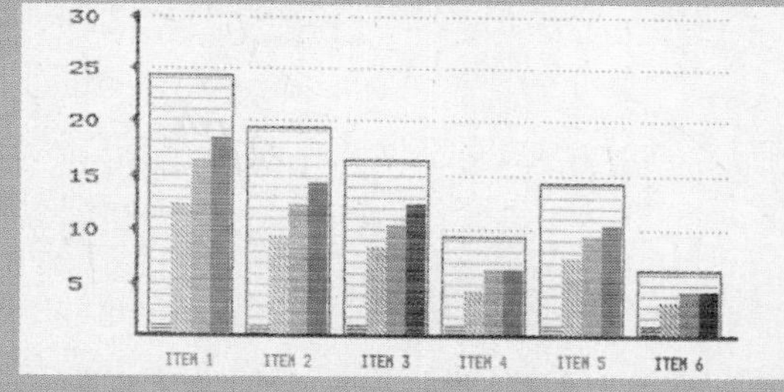

Color Ink-Jet Printers

Figure 4 *Below:* This diagram shows the operation of an ink-jet printer. Three reservoirs hold ink received from large ink cartridges. Yellow, magenta, and cyan inks are used. When a drop of ink of a certain color is desired, the crystal on the appropriate channel generates a pulse of pressure that forces a droplet of ink to shoot out of the nozzle and strike the paper. This diagram was prepared on an ink-jet printer that operates in this manner.

Figure 5 *Bottom:* Graphics produced with a color ink-jet printer.

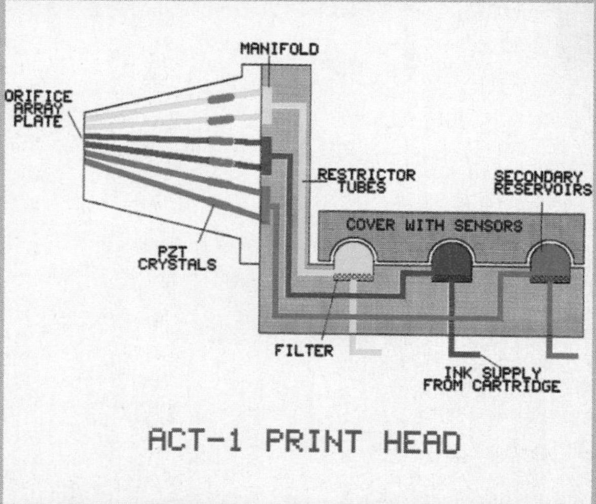

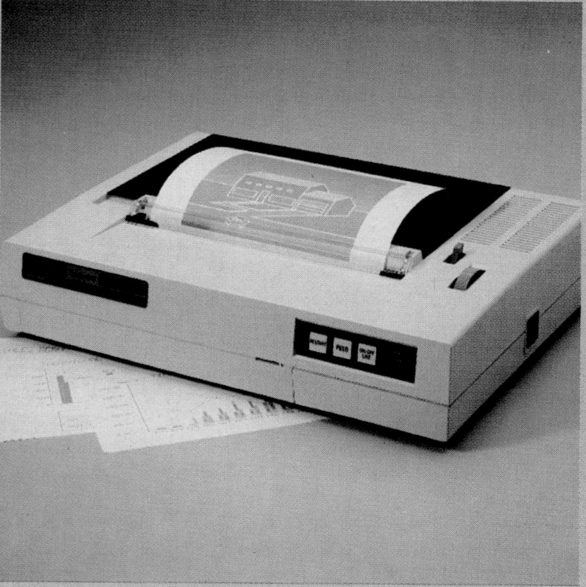

Drum Plotters

Figure 6 *Below:* A drum plotter. The pen (seen here at the center of its track) can only move left or right. The paper is rolled back and forth across the drum so that the pen may reach any point on the page.

Figure 7 *Right:* Computer art prepared on a drum plotter.

Other Graphic Output Devices

Figure 8 *Right:* As the head of this four-pen plotter moves across the page it traces out a contour map.

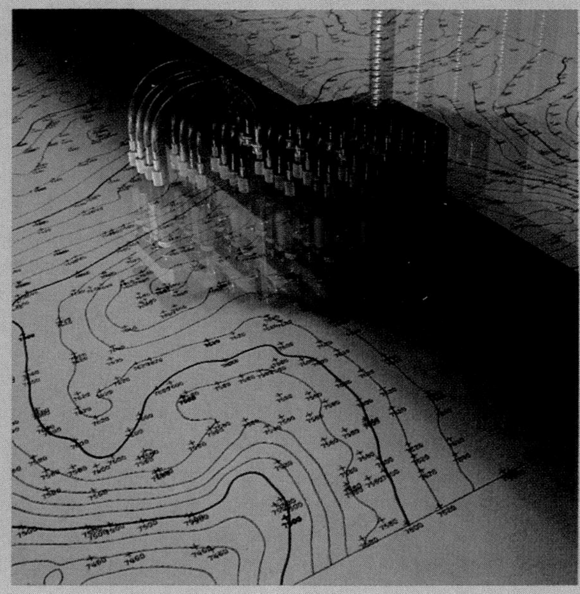

Other Graphic Output Devices (*continued*)

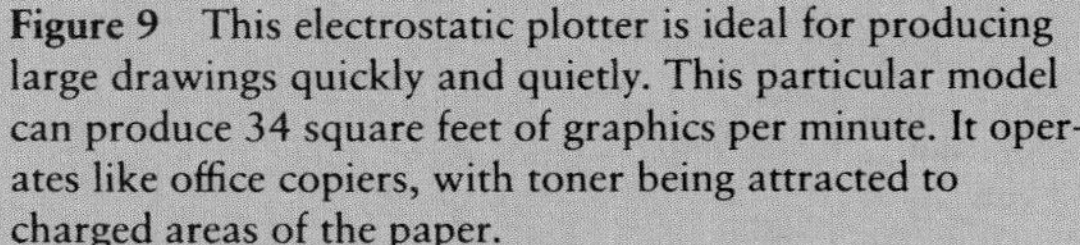

Figure 9 This electrostatic plotter is ideal for producing large drawings quickly and quietly. This particular model can produce 34 square feet of graphics per minute. It operates like office copiers, with toner being attracted to charged areas of the paper.

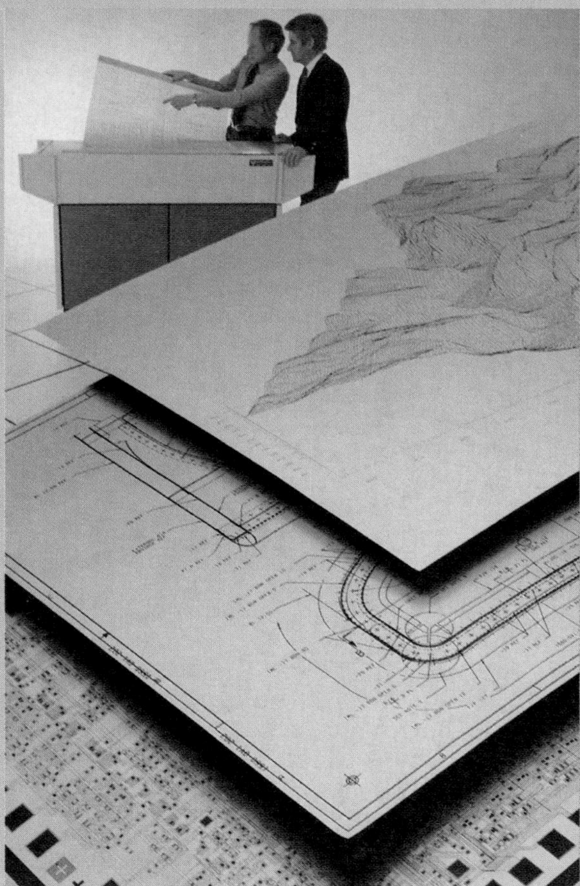

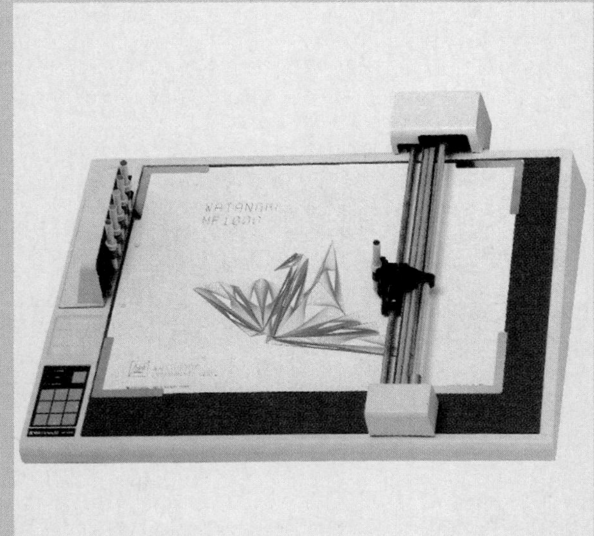

Figure 10 Multipen plotters. To change pen colors, the mechanism moves to the pen rack, replaces the current pen in its slot, moves over to the new pen, and pulls it from its slot. Plotters like these use static electricity to hold the paper down while plotting.

Figure 11 With a desktop plotter handy, it is easy to get a precise copy of a graphic appearing on a color CRT.

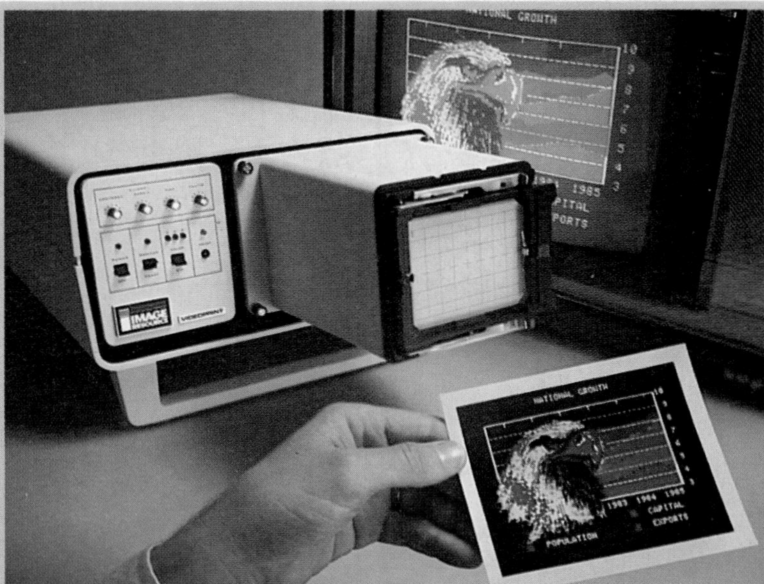

Figure 12 The Videoprint is an output device that produces distortion-free color photographs directly from the computer's video output signal. The quality of the photography is much better than is possible with simple off-the-screen photography.

Computer-Aided Design (CAD)

Figure 13 Using a CAD system for city planning.

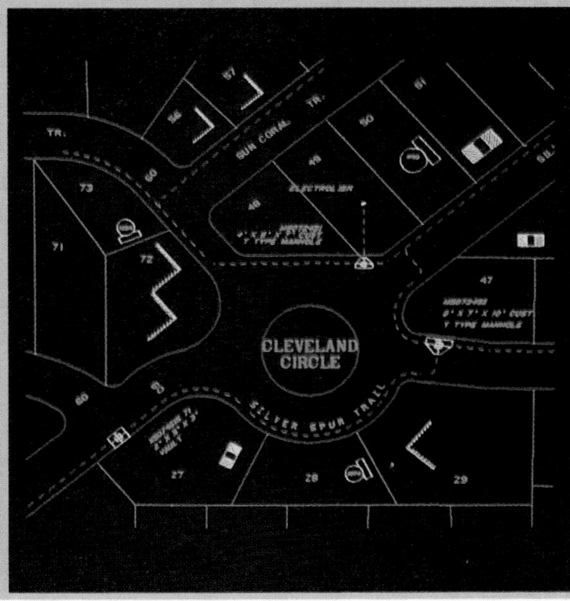

COMPUTERS
cartoons by JOHNS
"WAIT'LL I GET CONTROL OF MYSELF AND I'LL TELL YOU WHAT THE COMPUTER THOUGHT OF YOUR DESIGN SPECIFICATIONS!"

Computer-Aided Design (CAD) (*continued*)

Figure 14 Applicon's CAD/CAM system, BRAVO, features integrated 3D design, drafting, and documentation.

Figure 15 Using an automated drafting system, the designer enters a sketch freehand. The computer system then neatly redraws the circuit. Modifications can be made easily. The designer simply draws the changes and the computer updates and redraws the entire diagram. The computer then automatically produces the complete parts list needed to build the circuit.

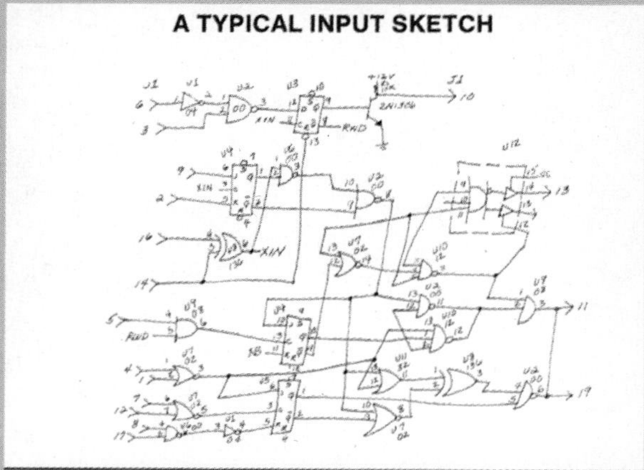

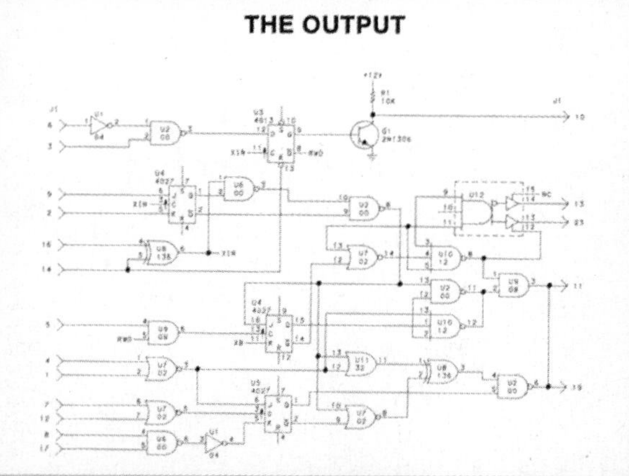

Image Enhancement

Figure 16 Cronus Industries of Dallas, Texas, has developed a CAD software package for use in designing new buildings. Once the user's specifications are entered into the computer, the system automatically designs the complete building in less than three minutes.

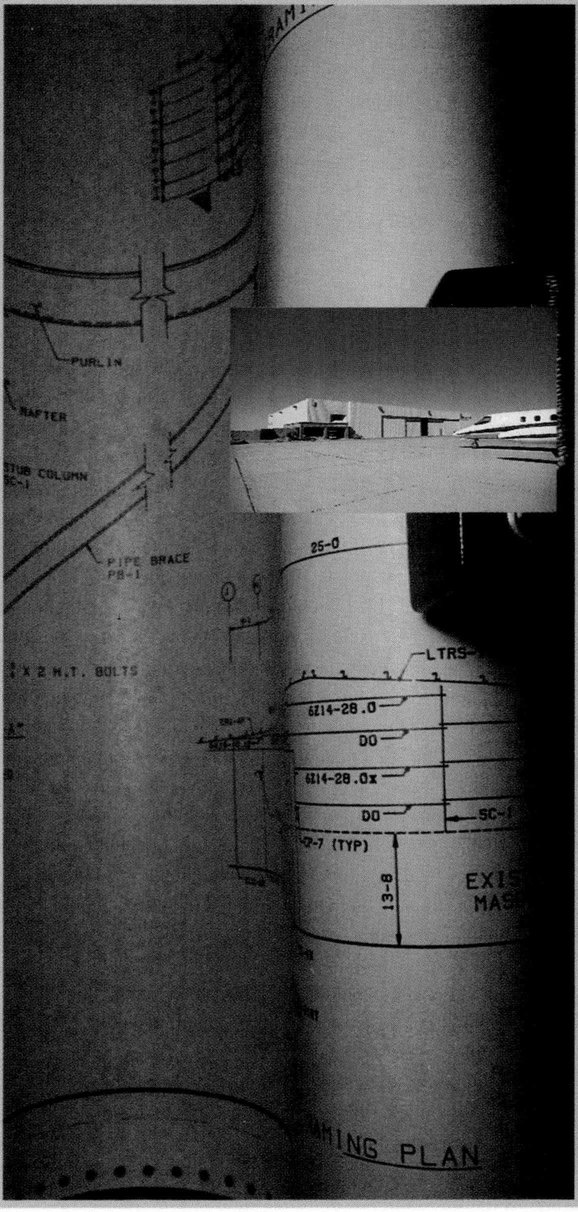

Figure 17 The top photo of the Grand Canyon was taken by satellite and then enhanced by computer processing to sharpen surface features. Further computer processing produced the bottom photo showing areas composed of similar materials in similar colors.

Other Types of Computer Output

Computer Output Microfilm

Microfilm has long been a popular means for storing information in less space than is taken up by paper documents. Today **computer output microfilm** (COM) has become a popular method of obtaining and storing computer output.

COM recorders produce outputs much faster than large impact printers; speeds of 20,000 lines or more per minute are common. **Dry-silver film processing,** neater than the old wet-chemical film processing, makes the use of COM appealing.

Organizations that use COM often have millions of pages of information on microfilm. With **computer-assisted image processing** (see Figure 5–32 for a description), any one of these images can be located and displayed in seconds.

Most COM systems output information onto **microfiche,** 4-inch by 6-inch film cards that can hold hundreds of pages of computer output (Figure 5–33). Information on fiche can only be read with special magnifying devices; hand-held microfiche readers, desktop readers, and reader-printers are all popular.

Microfilm has many advantages. Computer outputs can be produced much faster than with impact printers and can be made available sooner to users. Fiche can be duplicated quickly and economically to produce multiple copies of reports. Fiche require far less storage space than paper reports, and they can be mailed for a small fraction of the cost.

There are also disadvantages. Fiche can only be read with the assistance of magnifying devices. The user cannot make marks or comments on the film, and fiche cannot be modified. If a file of information changes frequently and needs to be kept current, new fiche must be produced, which may be expensive. Also, a file of fiche cards lacks file integrity; it is easy to remove or replace one card, so the fiche file may not represent the corresponding computer file at any moment. Security, too, can be a problem. It is much easier to conceal a few fiche than to conceal several thousand pages of computer printout.

Figure 5–32 A computer-assisted image processing station. The microfilm images are stored on continuous rolls inside the film magazines in the rack at the left. The computer contains an index to all of the information stored on the film. Any one image can be located and displayed in seconds. Hard copy is obtained at the push of a button.

Speech Synthesis

Some of the most user-friendly computer systems actually speak their outputs through a **speech synthesizer.** Perhaps the earliest widely marketed product using speech synthesis was Texas Instruments' Speak and Spell toy marketed in 1978. Today talking toys are common, as are talking microwave ovens, watches, automobiles, elevators—the list goes on and on. Such devices are enormously helpful to the handicapped (see Chapter 18). Computerized language translators that recognize speech in one language and use speech synthesis to speak it back in another are becoming available.

Voice response systems, using the concept of speech synthesis, have been used for years by the telephone company (who isn't familiar with the message, "The number you have called, . . . has been changed to . . .") and are already used in

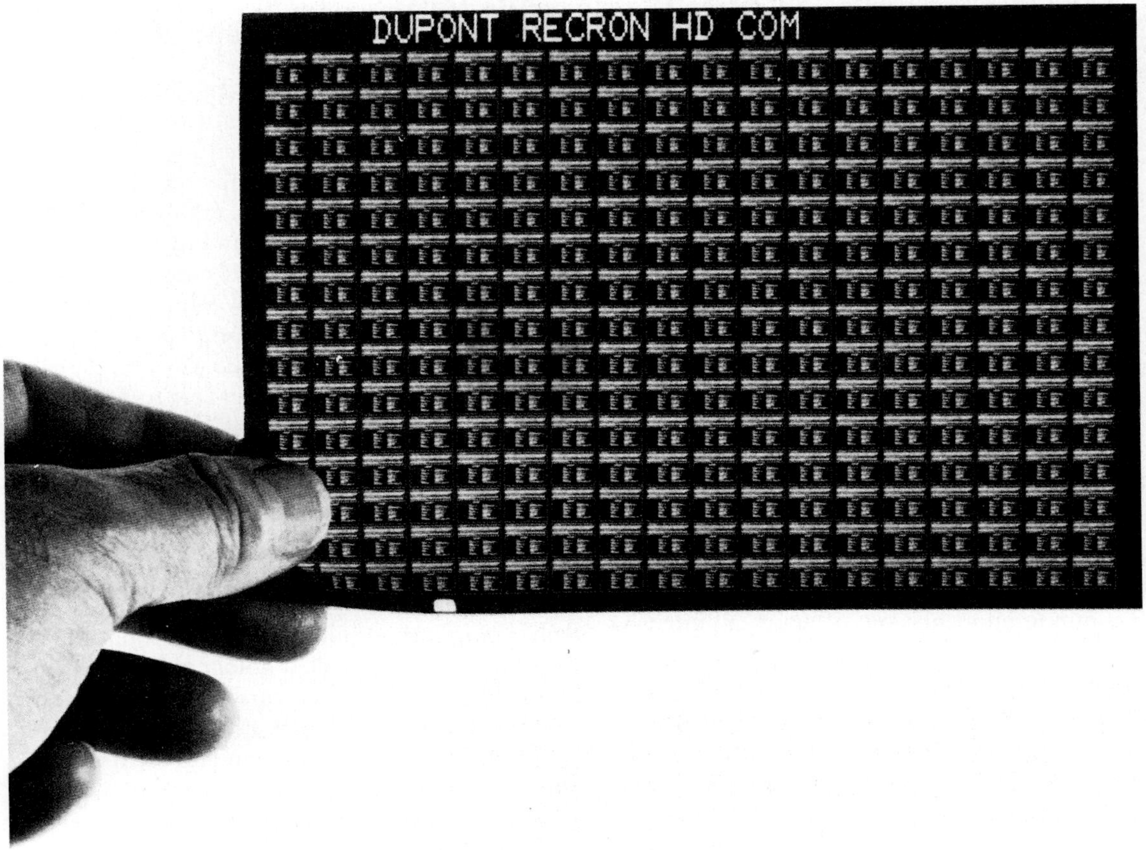

Figure 5–33 A 4 × 6-inch microfiche card containing 15 rows and 18 columns, for a total of 270 pages of data.

many computer applications. When a salesperson telephones to inquire about the status of an order, the computer answers through a voice response unit. Today the inquiries are made with portable computer terminals hooked to the telephone; tomorrow they will be handled by computerized voice recognition systems so the salesperson won't have to carry a portable terminal.

Speech synthesis may be used with full-word pronunciation or with letter-by-letter pronunciation. The latter option is helpful when the computer is pronouncing chemical formulas like H_2SO_4 (sulfuric acid) and other technical jargon. It's especially useful for people who are still trying to get accustomed to computerized speech.

State-of-the-art speech synthesizers generate high-quality speech, but these systems are expensive. The quality of speech available in most commercial products still sounds rather mechanical. (A talking soft-drink machine at a pizza parlor became so popular that it had to be restocked twice as often as the nontalking ones. Unfortunately, the proprietors were so annoyed by the mechanical voice that they disabled it to get some peace and quiet!) The problems of making a mechanical voice sound human are enormously complex. Another problem is the limited vocabulary of today's synthesizers. Many researchers believe that these problems can be solved and that extremely high quality and economical speech synthesizers will be available within 5 to 10 years.

Speech Synthesis Techniques

Speech engineers use devices like sound spectrographs (Figure 5–34) to "visualize" speech. Once they understand what speech "looks like," they attempt to build devices that generate similar patterns. Several techniques for generating synthesized speech have become popular. **Waveform digitization** works by studying the human voice on an oscilloscope. The voice appears as a series of waveforms. To store these waveforms for playback would require too much expensive storage, so the voice is sampled periodically and only the condensed information is then played back later. Because information is lost in this process, the played back voice is never as "rich" as the original.

Phoneme coding uses the common sounds of the English language, called **phonemes**, to enable the computer to speak (Figure 5–35). About 40 to 70 common phonemes out of which all English words may be formed are prestored in the computer. The speech synthesizer speaks a given word by successively pronouncing its component phonemes. For example, the word **intruder** can be formed in either of the following ways (you should pronounce each one and see which you like best).

I N T R U D E R
I1 I3 N T R IU U1 D ER R

Many other variations are possible. Thus, the real skill in using phoneme coding to develop speech is the clever combination of the phonemes to form smoothly pronounced words. The SC-01 speech synthesizer chip manufactured by Votrax allows the user to control other aspects of the speech as well, including volume, intonation, and inflection. The chip can even produce special sound effects.

Linear predictive coding takes a mathematical approach. A series of mathematical formulas is used to describe the way human speech is produced. This technique essentially models the process of forming human sounds, taking into account the effects of the vocal cords and the shape of the mouth, lips, and tongue. Sounds are coded in terms of these relationships. When particular sounds are needed, the appropriate mathematical equations are solved to produce waveforms that are then "played" through speakers to produce the sounds.

Three-Dimensional Computer Output

Some computer output devices can produce three-dimensional effects, called **holograms**. The most promising technology appears to be computer-controlled laser holography. A person may actually walk around the hologram and see it from any position when in fact the object isn't even there. Holograms contain an enormous amount of descriptive information.

With the production of increasingly powerful

Figure 5–34 This sound spectrogram helps speech engineers see what speech "looks like" by displaying the frequencies that make up each sound. In fact, most sounds are made up of a combination of frequencies—some high (screechy sounding) and some low (like those produced by a deep voice). The chart shows the frequencies that make up each of the sounds in the phrase *SYNTHETIC SPEECH*.

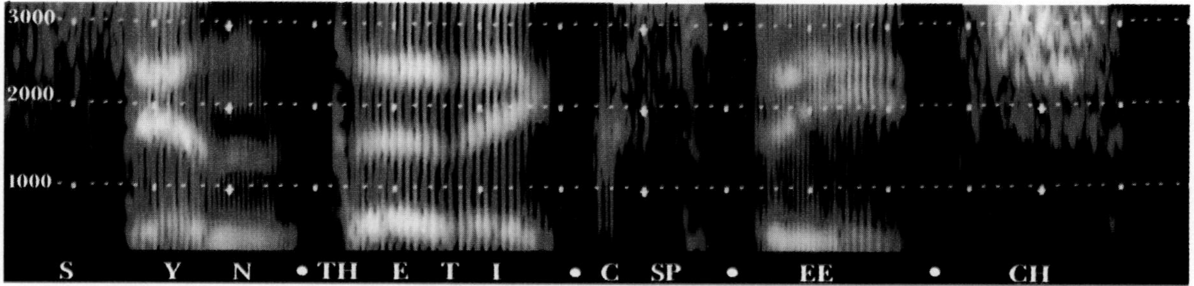

Phoneme Symbol	Example Word	Phoneme Symbol	Example Word	Phoneme Symbol	Example Word
EH3	jackEt	EH2	Enlist	EH1	hEAv
PAO	(no sound)	DT	buTTer	A2	mAde
A1[1]	mAde	ZH	aZure	AH2	hOnest
I3	inhibIt	I2	Inhibit	I1	inhIbit
M	Mat	N	suN	B	Bag
V	Van	CH[2]	CHip	SH	SHop
Z	Zoo	AW1	lAWful	NG	thiNG
AH1	fAther	OO1	lOOking	OO	bOOk
L	Land	K	triCK	J[3]	Judge
H	Hello	G	Get	F	Fast
D	paiD	S	paSS	A	dAY
AY[4]	dAY	Y1	Yard	UH3	missIOn
AH	mOp	P	Past	O	cOld
I	pIn	U	mOve	Y	anY
T	Tap	R	Red	E	mEEt
W	Win	AE	dAd	AE1	After
AW2	sAlty	UH2	About	UH1	Uncle
UH	cUp	O2	fOr	O3	abOArd
IU	yOU	U1[5]	yOU	THV	THe
TH	THin	ER	bIrd	EH	gEt
E1	bE	AW	cAll	PA1[6]	(no sound)
STOP[7]	(no sound)				

[1] Longer duration than A2 phoneme
[2] T phoneme must precede CH phoneme to produce correct CH sound
[3] D phoneme must precede J phoneme to produce correct J sound
[4] Shorter duration than A phoneme
[5] Longer duration than IU phoneme
[6] Longer duration than PAO
[7] Indicates the end of the phoneme sequence for a word

Figure 5–35 The phonemes used in the Votrax SC-01 speech synthesizer chip. The sound of each phoneme symbol is indicated by the capitalized letters in the example word.

computers, it will become possible to create three-dimensional motion pictures because the computer will be able to regenerate the hologram at 30 frames per second, fast enough so that the human eye perceives continuous motion. How such technology would change our lives can't be predicted, but certainly it would affect it in many ways, providing three-dimensional education and entertainment.

The Shroud of Turin: An Ancient Mystery

We have been talking about computers as a key to the future, but can the computer help us unravel our past? Computers are being used by historians and archaeologists to examine ancient artifacts to determine their authenticity. One of the most fascinating of these efforts is the ongoing investigation of the Shroud of Turin, believed to be the burial cloth of Jesus of Nazareth, which is imprinted with the image of a man with arms crossed. The 14-foot cloth has been stored in the tightest security in a cathedral in Turin, Italy, since 1578, but its history can be traced even further.

The picture at the left in Figure 1 shows the shroud as it appears to the human eye. When the first photograph of the shroud was taken in the late 19th century, it revealed an incredible fact: The photographic negative showed a positive image, and thus the image on the shroud itself is a perfect negative! This is strong evidence that the image on the shroud couldn't have been painted by a person, as has been suggested. The forger would have had to have done this hundreds (thousands?) of years before photography was invented and negative imaging was understood. Some researchers claim that the image was formed by an extraordinary burst of energy, not explainable by any known phenomenon of nature. Many other explanations have also been offered, but none has been satisfactory.

One of the most startling discoveries about the shroud was evidenced before millions of TV viewers on ABC's "20/20" program. Using a computerized image analyzer (manufactured by LogE/Interpretation Systems Inc.), scientists made a three-dimensional relief image of the face on the shroud appear (Figure 2). This seemed to demonstrate that the shroud contained three-dimensional information, making it even more unlikely that the image was hand-painted by a forger.

As of this writing the controversy continues. Whether or not the shroud is authentic, it has held up to the scrutiny of the same sophisticated computer techniques that sent humans to the moon and brought back incredible pictures of the planets. If the image on the shroud is a forgery, it may well be the most masterful forgery of all time!

Figure 1 At left is a photograph of the 14-foot Shroud of Turin. At right is a photographic negative of the picture showing that the shroud itself is a negative image.

Figure 2 A three-dimensional relief image of the face on the Shroud of Turin.

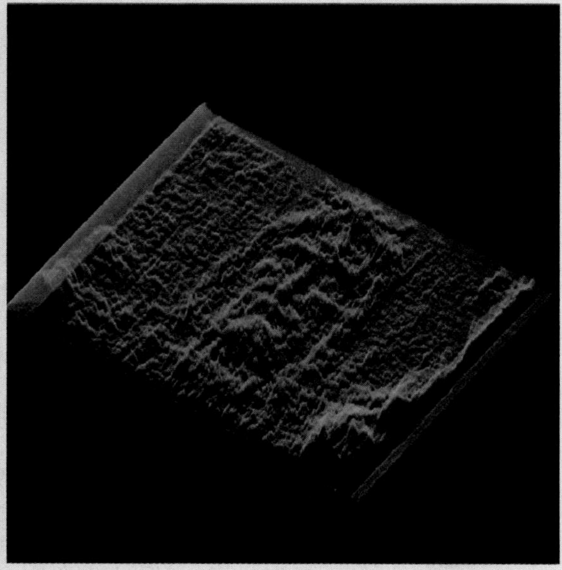

Applications for the Future

As computers begin to enter our lives in a more human way, some interesting practical and psychological benefits may result. An airline pilot who must watch literally hundreds of dials at one time could be instructed by a talking computer to "turn left now" to avoid a collision, and talking fire alarms could direct people to the safest exits. Three-dimensional flight simulators may help pilots learn how to fly airplanes while still on the ground, and surgeons may be able to practice complex operations before attempting them on patients. The computer, which has generally been viewed as a "number cruncher," may, in fact, cause humankind to develop an entire psychology of human-machine interaction.

Summary 

1. Printed reports are the most common form of computer output. These may appear as detail, summary, or exception reports.
2. Internal reports are for use within a company, and external reports are distributed outside the company.
3. Preprinted forms contain headings and lines to aid in readability and to minimize the amount of information that must be printed by the computer. Stock forms are either blank or horizontally ruled.
4. Impact printers operate by striking a mechanical hammer against a ribbon to leave an impression on paper. Printers that operate on that principle include dot-matrix printers, daisy-wheel and thimble printers, band printers, and drum printers.
5. Impact printers can produce multiple copies at one time and are capable of printing speeds up to thousands of lines per minute.
6. Continuous form paper is guided through printers by friction-feed or pin-feed mechanisms.
7. Nonimpact printers use electronic or photographic techniques to produce reports. These printers include thermal, electrostatic, and laser methods.
8. Nonimpact printers are quieter, faster, and often produce finer quality output than impact printers.
9. Printers are called hard copy output devices because they produce paper copies; computer terminals, such as CRTs, are soft copy devices that display output on screens.
10. Computer graphics is the creation and manipulation of pictures by computer.
11. Portable terminals enable businesspeople to access company computers from the field by telephone.
12. Ergonomics, or human engineering, is the study of the relationship between people and machines.
13. Computer output microfilm (COM) recorders produce computer output directly onto microfilm, especially microfiche. Microfiche are small and inexpensive to duplicate and mail, and may be produced much faster than impact printer outputs.
14. Using speech synthesis, computers actually speak their outputs. The three most common forms of speech synthesis are waveform digitization, phoneme coding, and linear predictive coding.
15. With computer-controlled laser holography, computers are be able to produce three-dimensional images.

Important Terms 

band printer
cathode ray tube (CRT)
character printer
computer-assisted image processing
computer graphics
computer output microfilm (COM)
cursor
daisy-wheel printer
dot-matrix printer
drum printer
dry-silver film processing
electrostatic printer
ergonomics
hologram
impact printer
laser printer
line printer
linear predictive coding
microfiche
nonimpact printer
page printer
phoneme
phoneme coding
plotter
portable terminal
scrolling
thermal printer
thimble printer
voice response system
waveform digitization

Self-Review Exercises 

Matching

Next to the term in column A, place the letter of the statement in column B that best describes it.

Column A

1. Soft copy
2. Prompt
3. Ergonomics
4. Output
5. Speech synthesis
6. Microfiche
7. Holography
8. Laser printer
9. Cursor
10. External report

Column B

A. Nonimpact device
B. User-friendly computer output
C. Sent to a company's customer
D. Three-dimensional picture
E. Blip of light
F. Information that comes from computers
G. Relationship between people and machines
H. Visual display output
I. Film cards
J. A cue to an interactive user

Fill-in-the-Blanks

Fill in the blanks in each of the following:

1. The three categories of printed reports are exception reports, ______ , and ______ .

2. ______ reports are used within an organization.

3. ______ reports are produced in response to special requests.

4. ______ reports highlight individual items that require human attention.

5. Fields of information displayed on a CRT and that cannot be changed are called ______ .

6. The creation and manipulation of pictures by computers is called ______ .

7. ______ are the common sounds out of which all English words can be formed.

8. With the technique of ______ , information normally displayed as light on dark may be displayed as dark on light for emphasis.

9. ______ is a speech synthesis technique that uses mathematical models to describe the process of forming human sounds.

10. Letter-quality printers generally use ______ characters instead of patterns of dots.

Answers to Self-Review Exercises

Matching: 1 H, 2 J, 3 G, 4 F, 5 B, 6 I, 7 D, 8 A, 9 E, 10 C

Fill-in-the-Blanks:

1. detail reports, summary reports
2. Internal
3. Ad hoc
4. Exception
5. protected fields
6. computer graphics
7. Phonemes
8. reversed fields
9. Linear predictive coding
10. fully formed

Discussion Questions 

1. Distinguish between detail, summary, and exception reports. Give an example of how each might be used in a classroom attendance record keeping system.

2. Give some advantages and disadvantages of using preprinted forms.

3. Distinguish between character printers, line printers, and page printers.

4. What does it mean for printed output to be of letter-quality? What kinds of printers produce letter-quality output?

5. Explain briefly how a laser printer works.

6. List and briefly describe several features commonly available on CRT terminals.

7. What is ergonomics? Why is it increasing in importance?

8. Give several advantages and disadvantages of using computer output microfilm (COM) instead of generating paper reports.

9. Suggest several applications for three-dimensional computer output not mentioned in the text.

10. What are the major types of color graphics hard copy devices? Describe briefly how each operates.

Projects 

1. Prepare a report listing as many different types of computer outputs as you can that are not mentioned in this chapter (for example, computer-generated music).

2. Visit a local computer store or a trade show at which computer equipment is exhibited. Report on the types of output devices you observed. Include pictures of these devices and sample outputs in your report.

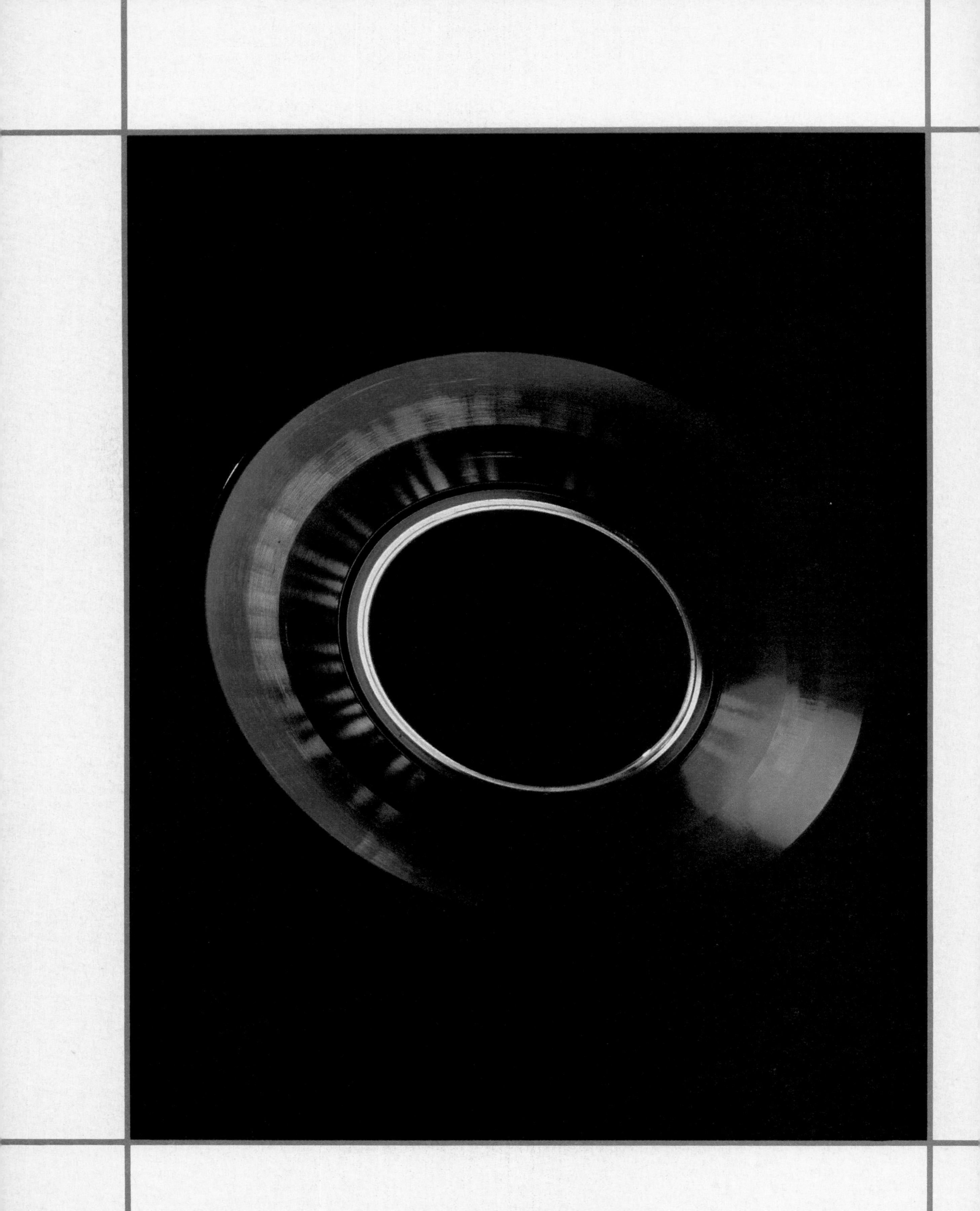

Chapter 6

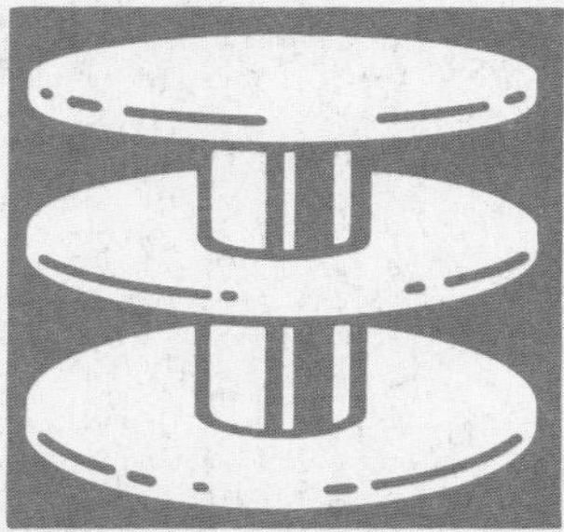

Secondary Storage

After reading this chapter you will understand:

1. How secondary storage differs from main storage
2. What types of secondary storage devices are available
3. How various secondary storage devices work
4. How information is stored on and accessed from secondary storage devices
5. The most popular file organization methods

Left: This "optical disk" platter has been filled with data "burned" into its surface by a laser. This technology allows the recording of 25 times as much data in the same amount of space as is possible with magnetic disks. The platter will record the equivalent of 2 million pages of double spaced information.

Outline

Today, the average businessman working for 30 years consumes over one million sheets of letter-sized paper weighing 8,500 pounds. Scattered on the ground, that much paper would cover an area five times as large as Yankee Stadium. With the Laser Optical Memory Disc, however, you'll be able to store that same information in an area smaller than a hat box.

Matsushita Electric

Computers process massive amounts of information at incredibly fast speeds, as we saw in Chapter 5. At any given time, only a small part of that information must be immediately accessible. That information is kept in main storage. The other data, generally thousands of times more than can be placed in main storage, is kept in external storage devices known as **secondary storage**, or auxiliary storage. Secondary storage is less expensive and larger, but slower to access, than main storage. In this chapter we consider secondary storage devices, such as **tapes** and **disks**, how information is organized on them, and how information is transferred between them and main storage.

Figure 6–1 Paper tape has been a popular secondary storage medium for many years, but its use is declining rapidly. Holes punched in the tape define the various character codes.

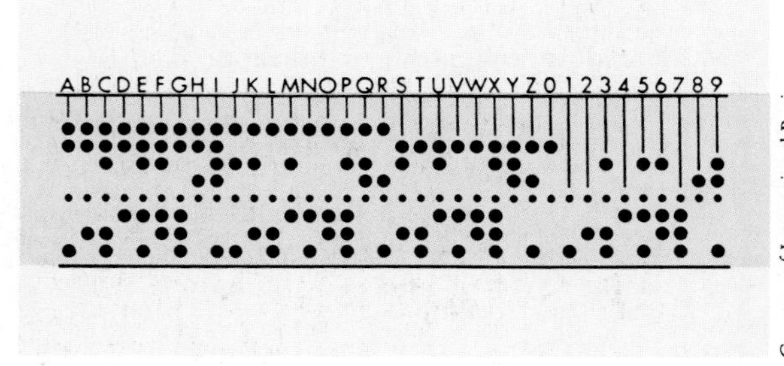

Courtesy of International Business Machines Corporation

Figure 6–2 Letters and digits are represented as combinations of holes in punched-paper tape.

Magnetic Tape Storage

Some computer systems still use **punched paper-tape** storage (Figures 6–1 and 6–2), but most of the tapes used on computer systems today are **magnetic tapes**, like those used on home tape recorders. The tape can receive information that is output from the computer or it can provide information to be input by the computer. Made from a strong yet lightweight plastic, the typically half-inch tape is most commonly wound on 10½-inch reels that hold 2400 feet of tape (Figures 6–3 and 6–4). Tape is also used for **batch-processing** applications in which large amounts of data are processed on each run. A good example of this is the Social Security Administration's printing of millions of benefit checks each month. It is commonly used for **backing up** (that is, making copies of) information recorded on disks for security purposes. The tape is passed

Figure 6–3 The various sizes of tape reels shown here hold 600 feet, 1200 feet, and 2400 feet of half-inch computer tape. Tapes also come in cassettes like those shown.

Figure 6–4 *Above:* A computer operator mounting a reel of tape onto a tape drive.

over a **read/write head** (an apparatus that can read or write data) at very high speeds; tape can move as quickly as 200 inches per second on expensive, high-capacity tape drives—the devices that read or record the data onto tape. The actual rate that characters can be read from or written onto tape depends on this speed as well as the number of characters per inch, or **density**, recorded on the tape. Densities of 1600 bpi (bytes per inch) are widely used. Tape drives that handle 6250 bpi are becoming more common (Figures 6–5 and 6–6). Certainly the trend will be toward increasing this density to meet the larger storage demands being placed on computers. Some indus-

Figure 6–5 *Below:* These tape drives can store 6250 characters of information in a single inch of computer tape and can process the tape at 200 inches per second. Thus, they can read or write 1,250,000 characters in one second! That's about as much information as a professional typist can type in a full week!

Figure 6–6 This close-up view of a tape drive shows the various buttons that control the functions of the drive. The buttons in the top row indicate the status of the drive; select, for example, means the drive is actually reading or writing information. The buttons in the bottom row may be pressed by the operator to control the tape; unload/rewind, for example, causes the tape to rewind to the beginning and then unload so that an operator may remove and store the tape.

try analysts believe that the next major step will be 25,000 bpi!

Characters are represented on magnetic tape as a series of spots, each representing one bit. One character is recorded across a section of tape as a series of bits. Usually nine bits are used; eight of them designate the character and one is a **parity bit,** that is, an error detection device to check for coding errors. Thus there are actually nine **tracks,** or **channels,** on the tape. The bit patterns that correspond to each character belong to a **character set.** The two most common character sets are EBCDIC (for Extended Binary Coded Decimal Interchange Code) and ASCII (for American Standard Code for Information Interchange).

Transfer Rate

Data is placed on tape so that it may be retrieved and placed in main storage as needed. Speed is often a major concern in accessibility of data. The **data transfer rate** is the number of characters per second (cps) that may be transferred between main storage and a particular secondary storage device. Transfer rates with tape depend on the density and speed in inches per second of the tape drive. Multiplying these figures together gives a transfer rate of 320,000 cps, for example, for a 1600-bpi drive running at 200 inches per second. For a 6250-bpi drive running at 200 inches per second, the transfer rate is 1,250,000 cps. Tape transfer rates of 5,000,000 cps are on the hori-

zon. To realize the enormity of this figure, consider the speed of a good typist—about 500 characters per minute. So one of these tape drives could transfer as much information in one second as a good typist could enter into the computer in about 10,000 minutes—roughly a month of typing! And the computer can transfer this information absolutely error-free!

Organizing Records on Tape

Records are written and retrieved from tape in order one after the other (Figure 6–7) in what is called **sequential access.** To obtain information from a tape, a computer issues a command to the tape drive that starts the tape moving. The drive must accelerate up to speed before the actual transfer of data begins. While the tape drive is accelerating, the read/write head simply passes over a section of tape called an **interblock gap** (Figure 6–8). This tape is kept empty to avoid the possibility that material may be skipped during acceleration. The tape drive passes the recorded information to the computer, and then it must stop. Stopping requires some time, too, so another interblock gap is needed. This starting and stopping motion could tear the tape to shreds, so high-speed tape drives are usually designed with vacuum columns to hold some extra lengths of the tape instead of keeping the tape stretched taut (Figure 6–9).

Interblock gaps can consume a large portion of the available tape, so, to minimize the number of interblock gaps needed, records are often recorded in groups or **blocks** (Figure 6–10). If, for example, 20 records are recorded together in one block, and each record requires 80 characters, the **blocksize** is 1600 (20 times 80). The **blocking factor** is said to be 20, the **logical record size** is 80, and the **physical record size** is 1600 (the same as the blocksize).

Limited storage space also necessitates the interblock gaps. The computer must transfer an entire block of data into main storage before that data may be processed. Because the capacity of main storage is limited, only a relatively small amount of storage is available to hold these blocks. After a block of data is read into main storage, the tape drive must stop transferring data and must stop moving.

Retrieval may be time-consuming in another way, too. If a tape is positioned at its start and the information stored at the end of the tape is

Figure 6–7 Records in sequential order on tape.

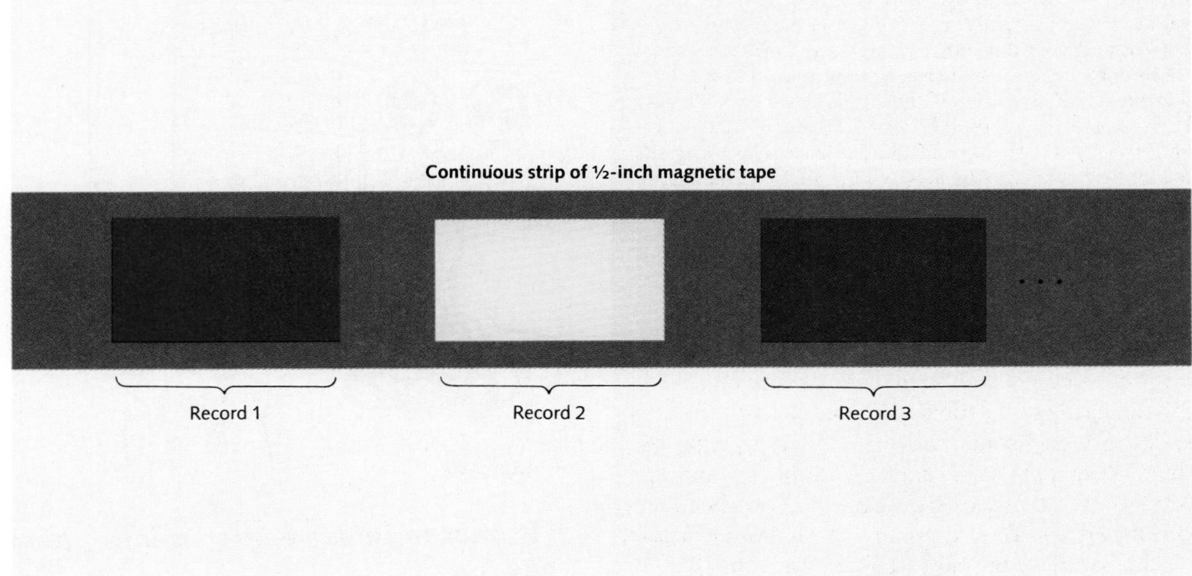

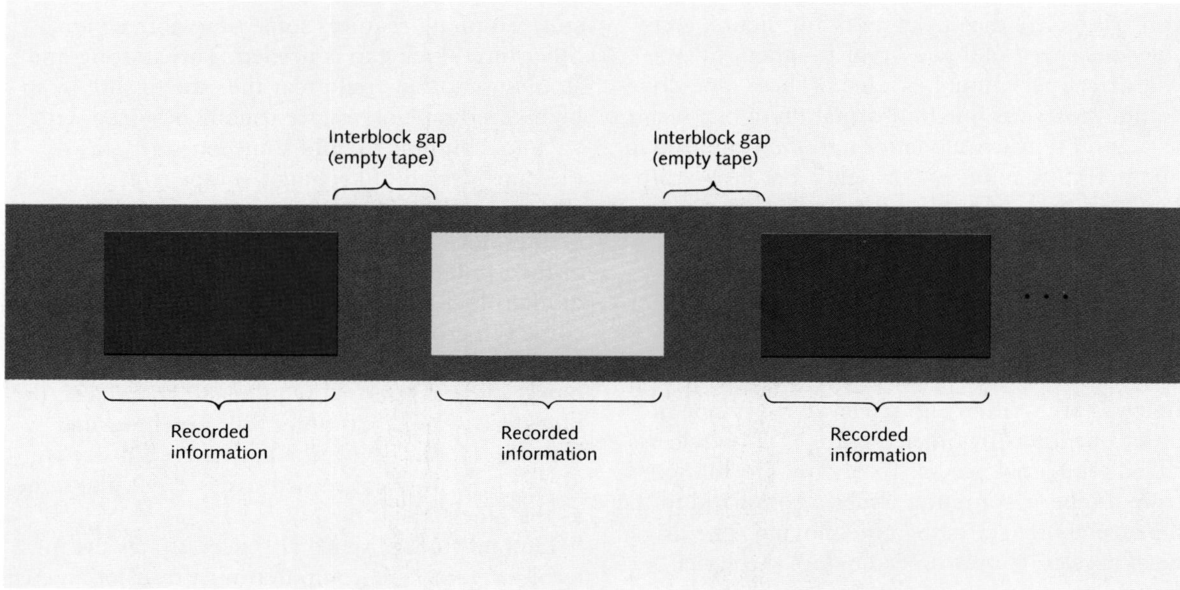

Figure 6–8 Interblock gaps.

Figure 6–9 This tape drive reads or writes data at 200 inches per second. To prevent the tape from being damaged, the tape is routed through two vacuum columns.

"It likes to unwind after a long, hard day."

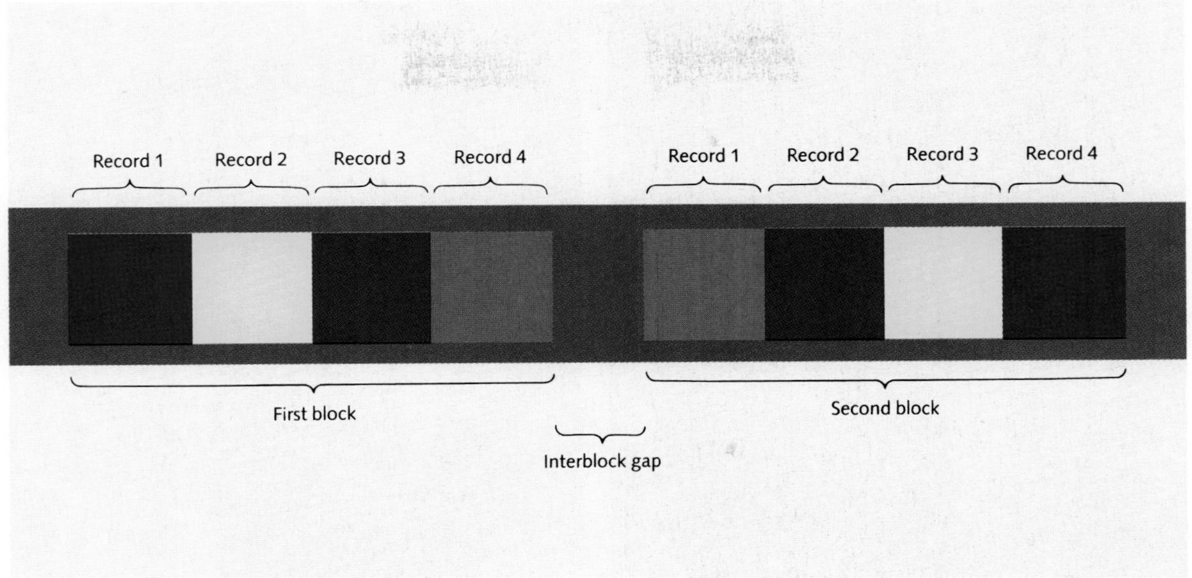

Figure 6–10 In this example, four records are recorded in each block.

needed, the computer must read the tape from beginning to end, a process that could require several minutes. Similarly, tape cannot provide the fast response needed in such operations as airline reservations and bank teller transactions. These require the ability to find a piece of information among millions or even billions of characters in a few seconds. For these applications, disk storage should be used (Figure 6–11).

Figure 6–11 Some large computer installations may have a hundred or more disk drives. Control Data Corporation's Cleveland Data Center is the heart of its time-sharing operations. The disk drives store customer data and programs for hundreds of thousands of CDC's time-sharing users.

Disk Storage

In today's **instant access** applications, disk is the most popular secondary storage medium. Disks consist of flat **platters** that look like phonograph records (Figure 6–12). Several are often stacked on top of each other and connected by a spindle forming a **disk pack** (Figures 6–13, 6–14, and 6–15). Disks rotate at very high fixed speeds, often at more than 3000 revolutions per minute—about a hundred times faster than an LP record!

The platters, usually 14 inches in diameter for large disk systems, are coated with a magnetizeable material. Information is recorded in circles

Figure 6–12 Disk platters must be manufactured under "clean room" conditions that are dust-free.

Figure 6–13 A disk pack is a series of platters connected by a common spindle.

Figure 6–15 A computer operator mounting a removable disk pack.

Figure 6–14 The key portions of a disk pack.

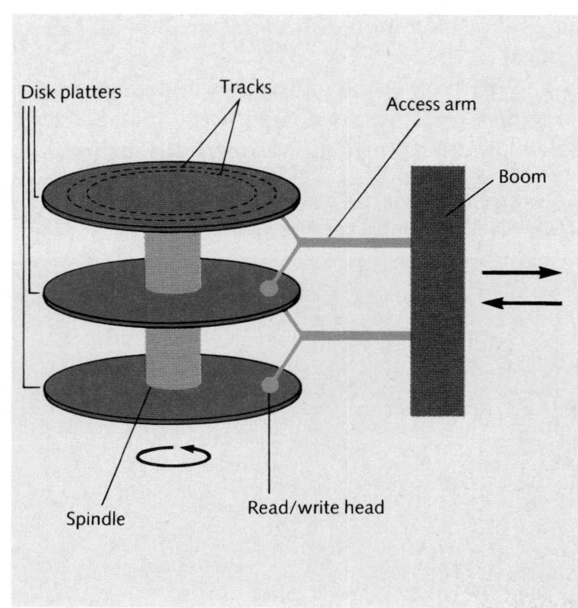

called **tracks** rather than in one continuous spiral as on a phonograph record. To change tracks, the read/write head must jump between tracks, in a process called a **seek** (Figure 6–16). The number of tracks on different types of disks can vary from a few hundred to many thousands per surface. The density of tracks on some disks is so great that they can store billions of bytes of data and make any of them available to the CPU in a fraction of a second.

Various types of disks are available. Two of the most popular types are floppy disks and Winchester disks.

Floppy Disks

Floppy disks, sometimes called **flexible disks** or **diskettes**, can store between a few hundred thousand and several million characters of information (Figures 6–17 and 6–18). It takes only about a tenth of a second for a floppy disk drive to retrieve any piece of data directly. The disk's

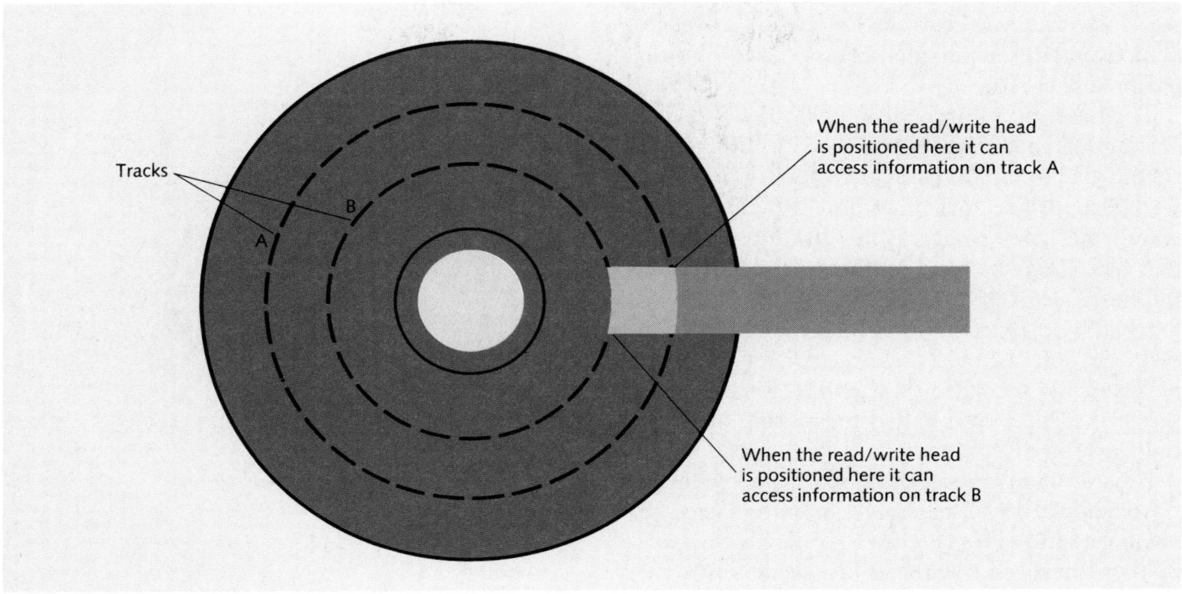
Tracks
A
B
When the read/write head is positioned here it can access information on track A
When the read/write head is positioned here it can access information on track B

Figure 6–16 The information on a disk is recorded in circular tracks. The process of moving the read/write head is called a seek.

Figure 6–17 Floppy disks are most commonly sold in the 5¼- and 8-inch sizes. Smaller floppies are also available.

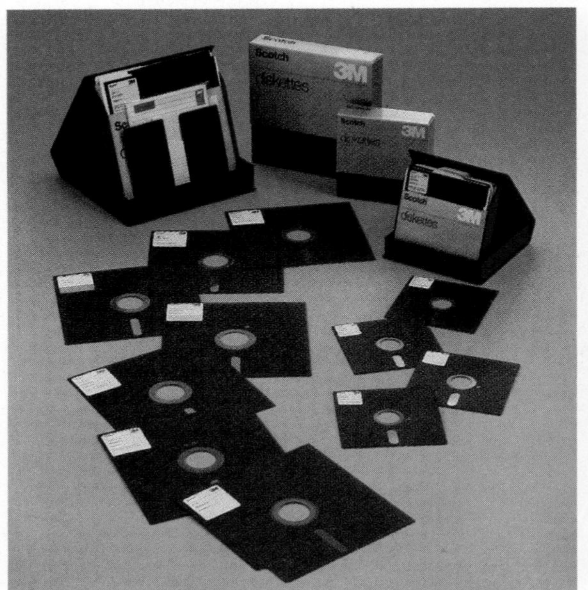
3M
diskettes

Figure 6–18 Inserting an 8-inch floppy disk into a floppy disk drive.

small size and low cost (only a few dollars each) helped spawn the personal computer revolution in the late 1970s.

The heart of a floppy disk, or floppy, is a circle of magnetic material (Figure 6–19). Information is recorded in circular tracks in turn divided into wedge-shaped **sectors** (Figure 6–20). The hardware is designed to access the disk by sector number. Disks may be **hard-sectored** or **soft-sectored.** On hard-sectored disks, sectors are physically marked by a series of holes near the center of the disk. On soft-sectored disks, sector locations are magnetically recorded on the disk. Recording this sector information is called **formatting** or **initializing** the disk.

Before the invention of floppy disks by Shugart Associates in 1972, personal computers used small **cassette tapes** (Figure 6–21), which have neither the speed nor reliability needed by computer systems. Floppies are so reliable that some manufacturers certify that their disks are error-free at time of purchase and will remain error-free for 10 million passes under a read/write head (See also Figures 6–22 and 6–23).

Figure 6–20 Here the data is recorded in equal-sized blocks, called sectors.

Figure 6–19 Inside the protector of a floppy disk is the circular disk itself and a special fabric that cushions and cleans the disk.

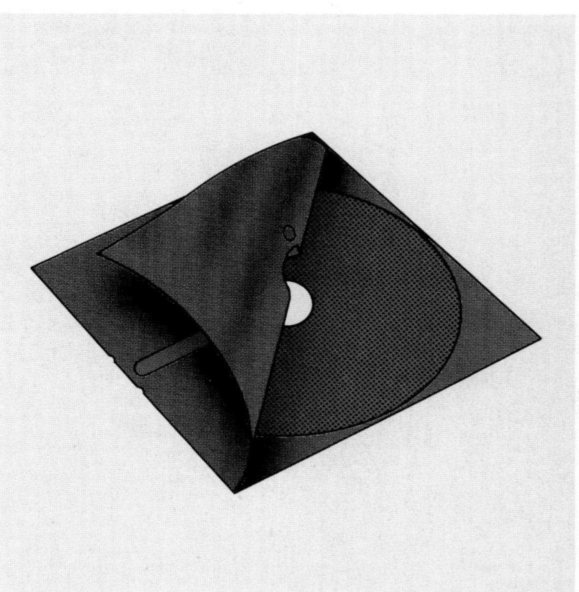

Figure 6–21 Tape cassettes and cartridges.

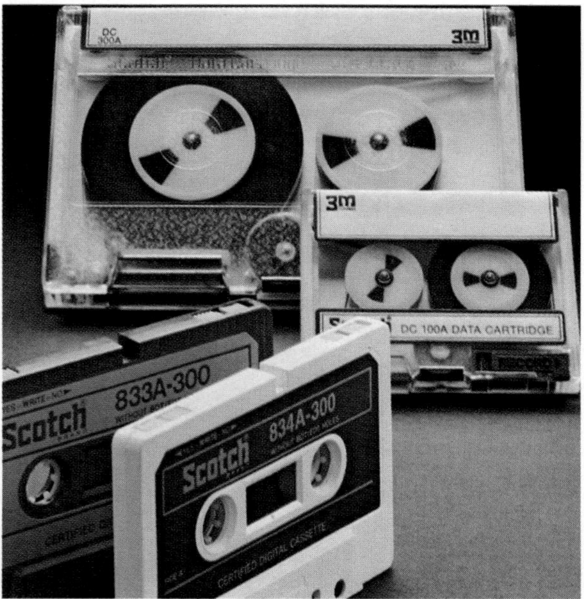

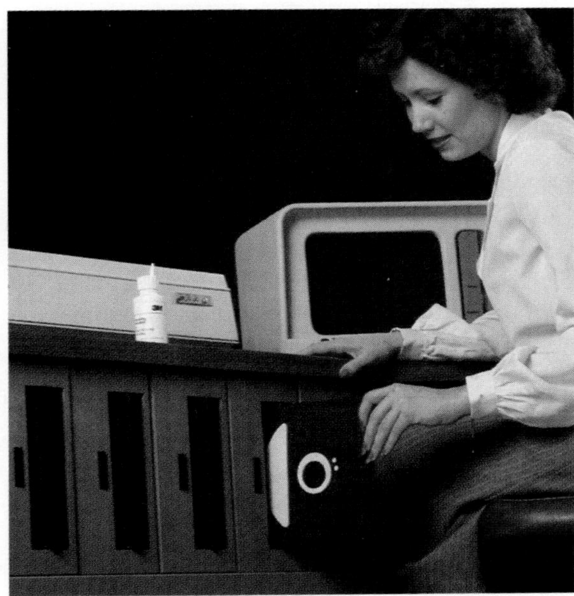

Figure 6–22 Floppy disk drives are reliable and require little maintenance. Here the operator is inserting a special cleaning diskette into the drive. The whole process requires only a few minutes about once a month.

Winchester Disks

The trends in secondary storage devices over the years have been toward increasing storage capacity and reliability and decreasing data access time and costs. In the 1970s **Winchester disks** were developed to improve removable disk technology (Figure 6–24).

Winchesters are manufactured under "clean room" conditions and are permanently sealed in plastic casings. This prevents impurities like smoke and dust particles from damaging the disk surfaces or read/write heads, and allows much more data to be recorded per surface than is possible with nonsealed disk packs (Figures 6–25 and 6–26).

Winchesters, affectionately called Winnies, are becoming extremely popular with personal computer users. The huge capacity of a single Winchester disk enables it to replace dozens of floppy disks on a home or small-business computer system.

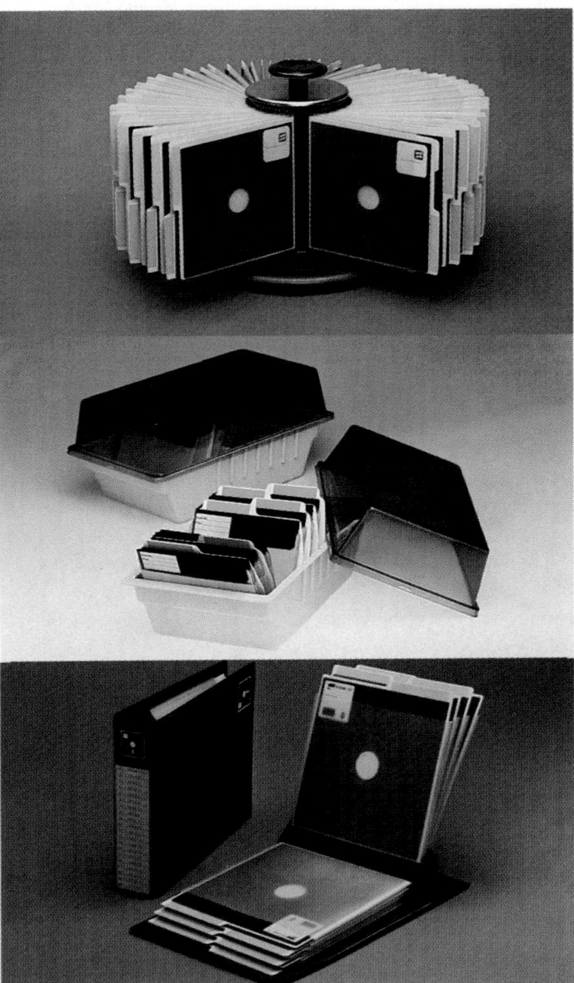

Figure 6–23 Many types of storage units are available for filing floppy disks.

Figure 6–24 A Winchester sealed disk module among several conventional disk packs. The other disk packs may be removed from their casings, but the Winchester is permanently sealed in its case.

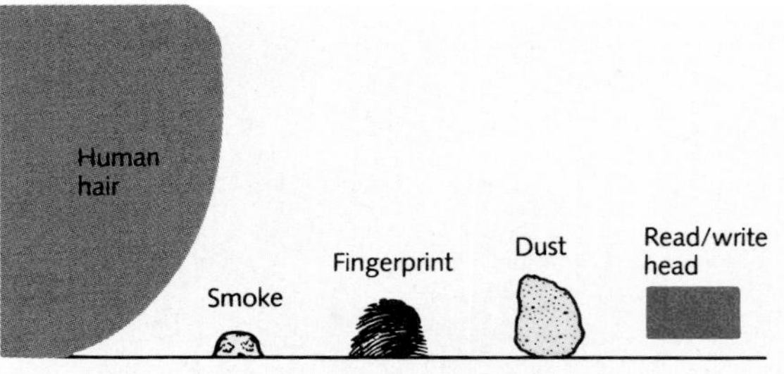

Figure 6–25 Disk read/write heads do not actually touch the surface of a disk. Rather, they fly above the surface only a few millionths of an inch away. The heads are so close to the surface that even a fingerprint would not fit between them.

Figure 6–26 This cutaway view gives us a look at the inside of a sealed Winchester disk drive. The read/write heads and the access arms are visible in the center of the drawing.

How Data Is Stored on Disk

The method of accessing data is similar for all disks. Large computer systems generally access data on disk by a method known as **cylinder-track-and-record.** When the supporting arm, called a boom, is set at a particular position, each of the read/write heads is positioned over a track. Together they form a "stack of tracks," which is called a **cylinder** (Figure 6–27). Each boom position defines a cylinder. Then a **recording surface** is specified to indicate which platter is to be accessed and whether the data is on the top or bottom of the platter. This defines the track to be referenced. At this point, it is merely necessary to specify which record (or sector) on that track is to be read.

The time it takes to access a particular record of information on a disk has three components:

seek time, latency time, and data transfer time (Figure 6–28). **Seek time** is the time it takes to position the boom to the appropriate cylinder. **Latency time,** or rotational delay, is the time it takes for the desired record to spin around to the read/write head. **Data transfer time** is the time it takes for the complete record to pass under the read/write head.

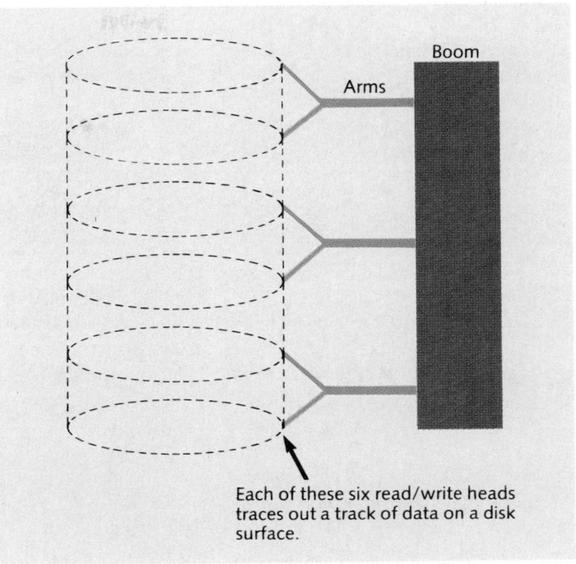
Boom
Arms
Each of these six read/write heads traces out a track of data on a disk surface.

Figure 6–27 The "stack of tracks" traced out by the read/write heads forms a cylinder.

Mass Storage Devices

Huge libraries of tapes are common in many companies (Figure 6–29). Organizing these libraries for rapid access is difficult and time-consuming, and the consequences of a misfile can be devastating.

Many systems have been developed for automating massive tape libraries. One of the most widely used is the IBM 3850 mass storage system (Figure 6–30). The 3850 can store as many as 472 billion (about half a trillion) characters of information, the equivalent of several thousand reels of tape or about 27 million newspaper pages!

Using a honeycombed wall storage unit, the 3850 stores data in 2-inch by 4-inch bullet-shaped cannisters (Figure 6–31) each containing about 50 million characters of data. When the data in a

Figure 6–28 The three components of a disk access. (1) Seek time, (2) latency time, (3) data transfer time.

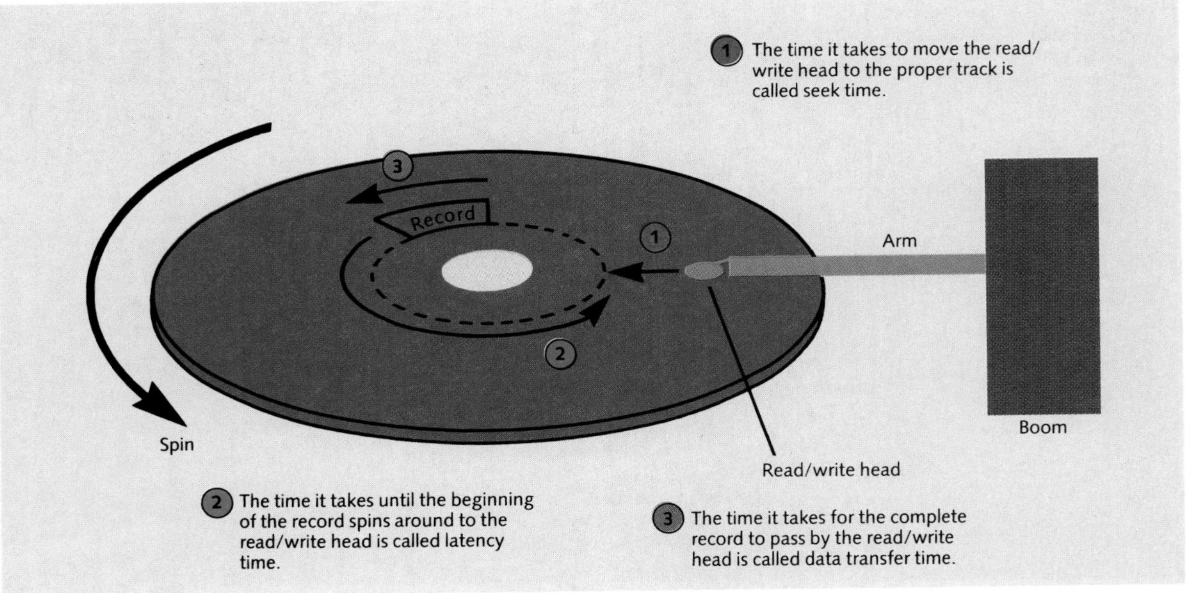
1 The time it takes to move the read/write head to the proper track is called seek time.
3
Record
1
Arm
2
Spin
Boom
Read/write head
2 The time it takes until the beginning of the record spins around to the read/write head is called latency time.
3 The time it takes for the complete record to pass by the read/write head is called data transfer time.

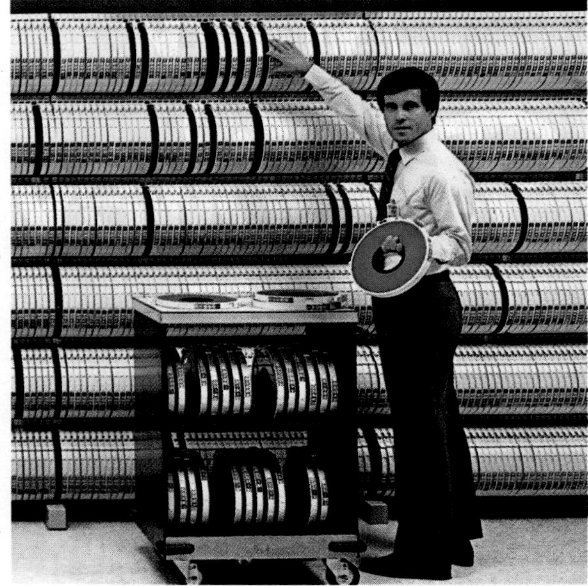

Courtesy of International Business Machines Corporation

Figure 6–29 Many large organizations have tens of thousands of tapes in their tape libraries.

Figure 6–30 An inside view of the honeycomb of storage slots in the IBM 3850 mass storage system.

Courtesy of International Business Machines Corporation

Courtesy of International Business Machines Corporation

Figure 6–31 Each of these cannisters can fit in the palm of a hand. Inside, each stores about 50 million characters on a long strip of tape.

Figure 6–32 Time-lapse photography showing a tape reel being mounted on a tape drive by an automated tape library system.

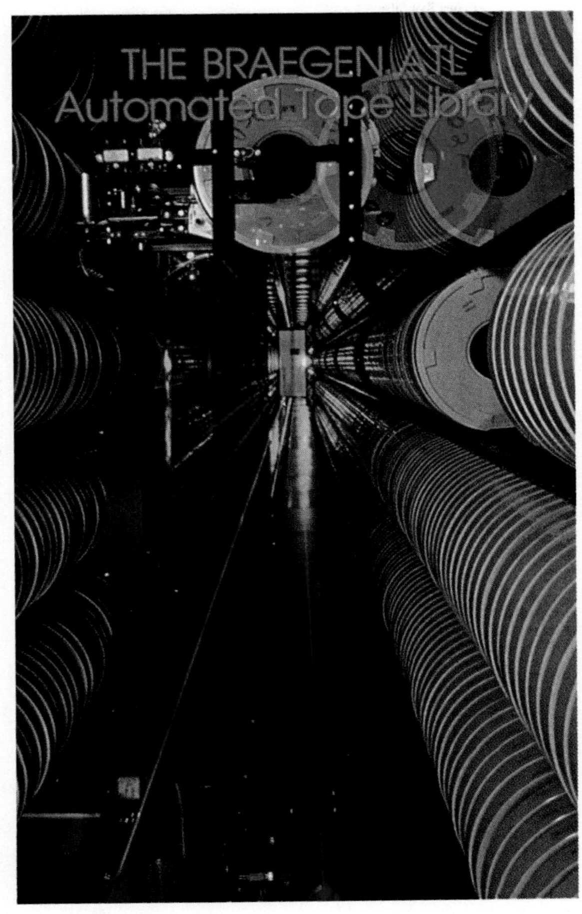

Figure 6–33 This picture, taken from inside the ATL cabinet, is another time-lapse photograph. It shows a tape being returned to the correct storage slot in the cabinet.

Figure 6–34 Here, a dozen tape drives are positioned along the ATL cabinet. Tapes may be mounted automatically by the ATL from any of these drives.

particular cannister is needed, a mechanical device selects the cannister and brings it to a mechanism that transfers the data to disk. This process can require about 30 seconds. The tape librarian's job is automated, misfiles are eliminated, and access is speeded.

The Braegen Corporation of Anaheim, California, produces the Automated Tape Library (ATL) system (Figures 6–32, 6–33, and 6–34). ATL completely automates the handling of tapes in a large tape library. It can locate and mount on a tape drive any of several thousand tapes in less than 20 seconds. After being used, the tape is returned to the correct slot automatically.

Bubble Memory

One of the most promising technologies for new secondary storage devices is the magnetic **bubble memory**, originally developed at Bell Laboratories in 1966. These devices store bits as the presence or absence of magnetic **bubbles** on a thin film of synthetic garnet (Figure 6–35). In the early 1980s the high production costs of bubble memory led to uncertainty among companies interested in the

Figure 6–35 A bubble memory device.

Courtesy of International Business Machines Corporation

technology. Nevertheless, it is believed that bubble memory might eventually replace disk storage.

Magnetic bubbles are tiny magnetized spots, about one-twentieth the diameter of a human hair. They are stored in a thin crystalline film and moved around the film by magnetic force. They can store more information in a given space than silicon chips and retrieve information faster than tapes and disks; they do not lose data if electrical power is turned off. A 32K byte bubble memory is about half the size of a package of cigarettes.

The bubbles are moved along tracks etched in a garnet film. Bubbles are read as they move past a fixed point in the track. The presence of a bubble indicates a one; the absence of a bubble indicates a zero. New bubbles are created by a bubble generator coil. When a current goes through the loop, it generates a bubble that rushes around the track. The bubbles are always in motion. Particular bits can only be read each time the bubbles make a complete revolution around the track.

Bubble memories are much slower than integrated circuits. A character stored in a bubble memory can be read in a few thousandths of a second; a character stored in a silicon chip can be read in a few billionths of a second. Over the next decade bubble memory may improve to become more attractive than magnetic disk memories for its reduced size, increased access speeds, reduced power consumption, greater reliability, and lower cost per byte of storage.

"NO WONDER HE NEVER FORGETS. HE HAS A BUBBLE MEMORY WITH A STORAGE CAPACITY OF 360 MEGABYTES"

Optical Disks

Most storage technologies use some form of magnetizable material. Reading and writing are accomplished by using electric currents and magnetic fields.

An innovative storage technology is the **optical disk**, which does not use magnetic materials. Rather, bits are stored on an optical disk by pinpoint laser beams that burn microscopic pits into the surface of the disk (Figure 6–36). The absence or presence of a pit determines whether a bit is zero or one. Current technology uses pits that are 1 micron (a millionth of a meter) across and 4 microns apart. This translates to about 5000 pits per inch on a straight line. The pits are read by another laser beam, one that is weak enough to avoid damaging the disk's surface.

Unfortunately, the pits are not erasable, so an optical disk can only be used to record information once. Thus they are comparable to books, record albums, or motion picture films—once recorded they may be read many times, but they may not be rerecorded.

The first laser disks commercially available

Library of Congress

The Library of Congress has replaced its card files with an optical disk system made by the Xerox Corporation. The catalog cards were previously stored in file cabinets that if placed side by side would form a line as long as a football field. The information previously contained in those cabinets is now stored on thirty 14-inch optical disks!

One use for optical disks is **facsimile storage**, on which documents are reproduced and stored electronically. For example, if you wanted to search through all back issues of the *New York Times*, an optical disk system would make it possible to locate and view any page within seconds. Optical disk is appropriate for this application because back issues, of course, will never change. Reusable optical disks are under development.

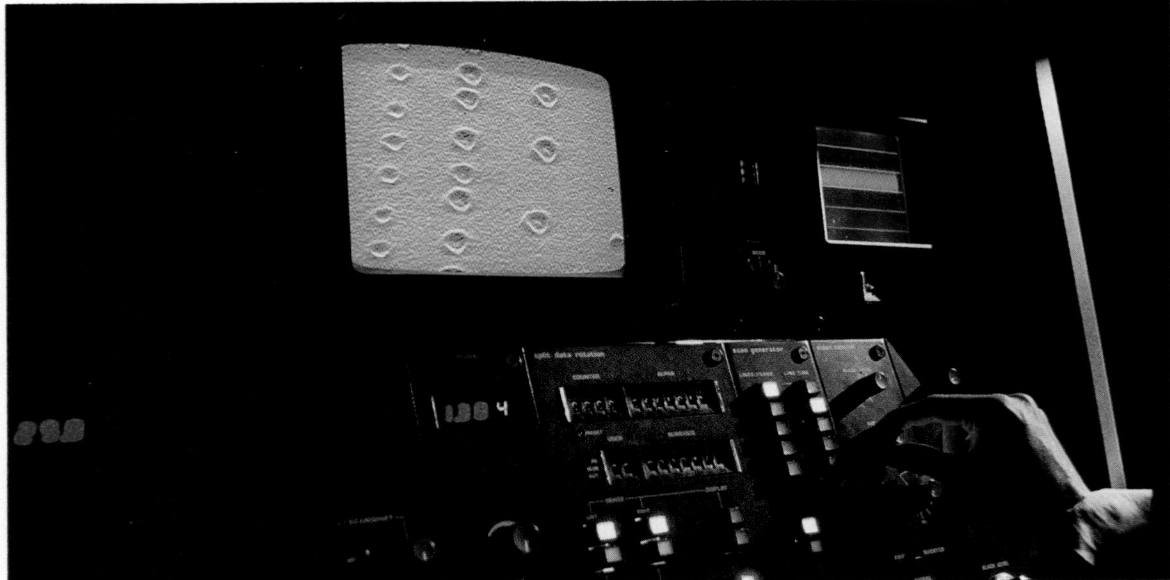

Figure 6–36 The picture being displayed on the monitor of a scanning electron microscope shows laser data as a series of pits (bits) burned into the surface of an optical disk. With current technology an optical disk is a "write only once" medium; it cannot be erased and reused.

were used on TV videodisk systems (Figure 6–37). Each side of a videodisk can hold 54,000 complete frames (still pictures) or about half an hour of a TV program or movie; a two-sided videodisk can hold an hour's worth of programming. The laser beam can easily jump ahead, review, scan, or play frames in any sequence under computer control. This makes it an ideal form of storage for interactive educational applications.

The Laser Card

Drexler Technology Corporation of Mountain View, California, has an interesting application for optical memory. They have taken a standard-size credit card and optically encoded a strip about the same size as the magnetic strips now used on credit cards. Magnetic strips can hold about 200 characters of information, enough for an account number, customer name and address, and a few useful facts. But the optical strip can hold about a million characters, enough to serve as a complete record of a customer's transactions with a bank (quite simply, a replacement for a savings passbook). The huge capacity of the card enables it to carry a color picture of the cardholder, a fingerprint, a voice sample, and, of course, a signature.

Figure 6–37 This type of videodisk is read by a low intensity laser beam. The laser beam reading method allows us to jump from one area of the disk to another quickly. This makes it useful in applications where the computer makes a decision and then plays back an appropriate portion of the disk.

File Organization Methods

Information may be organized in secondary storage in various ways, including **sequential organization,** in which records are organized one after the other; **direct organization**, in which records are organized so that any one may be referenced immediately; and **indexed sequential organization,** in which records are organized so that they may be read either sequentially or directly.

Sequential Files

In sequential files, records are placed in order by **key**, a code that identifies a record. For instance, an employee number might be used as a key in a payroll application, or a part number might be used as a key in an inventory application.

Let us consider a very simple inventory application. A **master file** might have one record for each type of part. This record might include a part number, a description of the part, and the quantity of the part on hand.

On a typical run, we might want to update the file to reflect sales of parts as well as the arrival of new parts. The master file contains all the records for all of the parts. A **transaction file**, or **detail file**, contains all the adjustments to the inventory including sales and arrivals.

Processing proceeds as follows. A record from the master file is read and a record from the transaction file is read. Whenever the part number or key field of a record appearing on the transaction file matches the part number on the master file, the appropriate update is made. When a record appears on the master file but shows no current transactions, it simply means that this part was "inactive" in this processing period. If a record appears on the transaction file but not on the master file, there is a problem because information about "nonexistent" parts is being processed. This kind of error can happen if a record has been added to the transaction file but not yet been added to the master file, or if someone has entered an invalid part number. One way or the other, such an error should be highlighted on a report for investigation.

Direct Files

In applications such as banking systems and airline reservation systems, information on secondary storage must be accessed very quickly, usually in a fraction of a second. Disk hardware, in theory, makes it possible to do this, but unfortunately the disk doesn't "know" about things like flight numbers or bank account numbers; it only knows about cylinders, tracks, records, and sectors. Thus, software must be used in any given application to translate, for example, a customer's account number into the location on a disk where the information about that customer is stored.

Direct access, or **random access** as it is sometimes called, allows access to a certain record on a disk without a sequential search of every record before the desired one in the file can be found.

One technique for facilitating direct access is called **hashing**. The address where the record is to be placed on disk is determined by a calculation involving the key field, and the record is placed at that address. To retrieve that record, the computer uses the same hashing calculation to determine where on the disk the record is stored.

Sometimes two different account numbers will hash into the same location on disk in what is called a **collision** or, more colorfully, a **hash crash**. The second record obviously can't be put in the same place as the first. So the computer system places the second record in the first available slot near the first record.

When retrieving this second record, the computer uses hashing to locate the record on the disk. When the customer account numbers are compared, they will be different. A record-by-record search may then be used to locate the correct record. This may seem costly, but with a good hashing method it is only occasionally necessary.

Indexed Sequential Files

Sequential access is ideal for applications in which massive amounts of data must be processed and a large portion of the file is processed on each run. Direct access is geared to applications in which an individual piece of information must be lo-

cated quickly, but only a small percentage of the file's records are processed in one session.

Indexed sequential files are organized so that their records may be accessed either sequentially or randomly. The key to performing this "magic" is that the computer maintains an **index** that lists the record key of every record and the location of the record. For large files this index can be large, so the index is often condensed somewhat to show only certain major areas of the file. For example, the index might show the disk locations where records begin for customers whose last names start with *A*, *B*, and so on. Such an index might only have 26 entries, but searching the file is still much faster than sequential access would be. If a customer's last name begins with *Z*, searching the index (a much faster operation than searching the file) reveals where the *Z*s begin. The search for this particular customer is then started in the file at that point. The *Z*s are then searched sequentially until that customer's record is found.

Applications for the Future

Computer storage is becoming smaller, cheaper, faster, and more energy efficient. Soon storages will be available that rival the human brain in capacity. What does all this mean?

Entire libraries of books will be stored on tiny chips. (A laser-encoded disk already exists that can store on one side the words contained in 200,000 books.) We will be able to reference any piece of information in seconds and get a hard copy by pressing a button. The massive capacities of these devices will allow the storage of sound and color motion pictures for instant retrieval. Encyclopedias will come alive. People might carry wallet-size cards containing their medical histories. In case of accident, a physician could rapidly determine any medications to which the victim might have an allergic reaction.

This wealth of information will be instantly available. How might it change our lives? Having information at our fingertips might help us make more informed decisions, but it could also have the opposite effect: We could be so flooded with information that we are unable to use it.

Computers will help us wade through this information to find exactly what we want, so they may well be our salvation. But aren't computers responsible for generating this information explosion in the first place? As always, technology can be a mixed blessing.

Summary

1. Compared to secondary storage, main storage is faster, but smaller and more costly.
2. The two most important forms of secondary storage are tape and disk.
3. Data is stored on tape and disk as tiny magnetized spots. The information is read or written as the tape or disk passes by a read/write head. Each spot represents one bit. On nine-track tape, eight bits designate the character and one bit is a parity bit for error detection.
4. The data transfer rate is the number of characters per second that may be transferred between main storage and a secondary storage device.
5. With sequential access, records are written or retrieved in order one after the other.
6. Interblock gaps are portions of blank tape that pass over the read/write head as the tape drive speeds up or slows down.
7. Tape is useful in batch processing applications in which large amounts of data are processed. It is also popular for backing up information recorded on disks for security purposes.

8. Disks are flat platters that look like phonograph records. They are coated with a magnetizable material. Information is recorded on the surface of a disk platter in circular tracks.
9. The time it takes to access information on a disk has three components—seek time, latency time, and data transfer time.
10. Because of their reliability, small size, and low cost, floppy disks are popular with users of personal computers.
11. Mass storage systems are used to automate large tape libraries.
12. Bubble memory devices store bits as the presence or absence of magnetic bubbles on a thin film of synthetic garnet. Bubble memories can store more information than semiconductor chips, can retrieve information faster than tapes and disks, and do not lose their data when power is turned off.
13. Direct access (or random access) allows immediate access to a record on a disk without a search through all the records that come before it. It is most valuable when speedy access is needed.
14. In sequential files, records are placed in order by key. Sequential file processing is ideal when large amounts of data must be processed and when a large portion of the file is processed on each run. With indexed sequential files, records may be accessed either sequentially or randomly.
15. Optical disks are currently used for permanent storage of massive amounts of information. Reusable optical disks are being developed.

Important Terms

backing up
block
bubble memory
channel
collision
cylinder
data transfer time
density
detail file
direct access
disk
floppy disk
formatting
hashing
indexed sequential organization
interblock gap
key
latency time
master file
optical disk
parity bit
platter
random access
read/write head
secondary storage
sector
seek
sequential access
track
Winchester disk

Self-Review Exercises 

Matching

Next to the term in column A, place the letter of the statement in column B that best describes it.

Column A

1. Density
2. Optical disk
3. Back up
4. Tape
5. Key
6. Parity bit
7. Block
8. Cylinder
9. Direct organization
10. Sector

Column B

A. Error detection aid
B. Code that identifies a record
C. Group of records
D. Magnetic storage
E. Make a copy for security
F. Stack of tracks
G. Number of characters per inch
H. Portion of a track
I. Records can be referenced immediately
J. Bits are burned in by a laser

Fill-in-the-Blanks

Fill in the blanks in each of the following:

1. The number of characters per second that may be transferred between main storage and a secondary storage device is called the ______ .

2. The ______ is the section of empty tape between successive blocks.

3. Records which are written and retrieved in order one after the other are said to be accessed ______ .

4. A ______ is the process by which the read/write head on a disk jumps between tracks.

5. ______ disks are permanently sealed in plastic casings.

6. The components of accessing information on a disk are ______ , ______ , and ______ time.

7. When two different account numbers hash into the same location we have a ______ .

8. Recording sector information on a disk is called initializing or ______ the disk.

9. A storage device that moves bits around a thin film of synthetic garnet is ______ .

10. Optical disks are read by ______ .

Answers to Self-Review Exercises

Matching: 1 G, 2 J, 3 E, 4 D, 5 B, 6 A, 7 C, 8 F, 9 I, 10 H

Fill-in-the-Blanks:
1. data transfer rate
2. interblock gap
3. sequentially
4. seek
5. Winchester
6. seek, latency, data transfer
7. collision or hash crash
8. formatting
9. magnetic bubble memory
10. laser beams

Discussion Questions

1. How is secondary storage different from main storage?

2. What are the two most important types of secondary storage? For what types of applications is each best?

3. How is data stored on tape?

4. What two factors determine the data transfer rate of a tape drive?

5. Why are records often recorded in groups or blocks?

6. List three different ways files can be organized on disk. Explain each briefly.

7. Why are mass storage devices useful?

8. What are bubble memories? What are the disadvantages of their use? Why are they expected to become popular?

9. Describe floppy disks and Winchester disks.

10. Discuss the advantages and disadvantages that may result from the wealth of information computers put at our fingertips.

Projects 

1. Visit several computer stores and prepare a report on the various secondary storage devices they sell. Compare and contrast each of these devices with regard to cost, storage capacity, and speed of accessing information.

2. Suppose technology advanced to the point that it would be possible for you to own a computer storage device containing all the information that has been published since the dawn of civilization. Prepare a report describing how you might take advantage of such an incredible abundance of information.

Chapter 7

Data Communications

After reading this chapter you will understand:

1. How the field of data communications evolved
2. How computers communicate with one another
3. The various arrangements of communication networks and their advantages and disadvantages
4. How data communications affects individual security and privacy
5. Why fiber optics is the communications cable technology of the future

Left: This antenna is part of the largest earth station in the world. Located at Raisting, Bavaria, West Germany, it is operated by the German Federal Post Office. It transmits data to and receives data from satellites orbiting 22,300 miles above the earth. Computers throughout the world may now communicate with one another as easily as if they were in adjacent rooms.

Outline

It took five months to get word back to Queen Isabella about the voyage of Columbus, two weeks for Europe to hear about Lincoln's assassination, and only 1.3 seconds to get the word from Neil Armstrong that man can walk on the moon.

Isaac Asimov, Isaac Asimov's Book of Facts

We have been discussing computers as a means of storing and retrieving information. Traditionally, computers have performed these operations independently of one another. But recent advances have permitted the transmission of information from one processing location to another. **Data communications** is the name given to the transmission of computer data between computer systems and terminals. The trend today is toward **networks** of cooperating computers that can share information.

History

In 1832 Samuel Morse learned that electricity could be sent instantly over wires. He observed, "If the presence of electricity can be made visible in any part of a circuit, I see no reason why intelligence may not be transmitted instantaneously by electricity." Twelve years later Morse produced a working telegraph that transmitted information through short and long tones, commonly known as dots and dashes. This code (Figure 7–1) was one of the earliest schemes for representing letters and numbers. Morse's first message, the now-famous "What hath God wrought," began the era of electronic communications.

The first patent for a telephone that could carry human voices was issued to Alexander Graham Bell on March 7, 1876. Three days later, in a Boston boardinghouse, Bell spilled battery acid over his clothes and by telephone called his friend and associate in another room: "Mr. Watson, come here. I want you." This was the first audible sentence ever spoken over an electronic communications line.

The age of computer communications began with a demonstration at Dartmouth College in New Hampshire in 1940. During a conference of the American Mathematical Society, a paper was presented by George Stibitz on the development of his relay calculator at Bell Laboratories in New York City. Afterward an operator sat down at a Teletype machine connected by telephone lines to the relay calculator in New York. The operator entered data, the New York computer performed the calculations, and the result was sent back to the Teletype at Dartmouth.

Since then data communications has advanced rapidly. **Timesharing**, in which a large central computer is shared by many users at once, began in the early 1960s. Some dramatic demonstra-

Figure 7–1 The International Morse Code is used to send messages via shortwave radio. Notice the special symbol consisting of three shorts, three longs, and three shorts—the famous SOS, or "save our ship," code used by ships in distress.

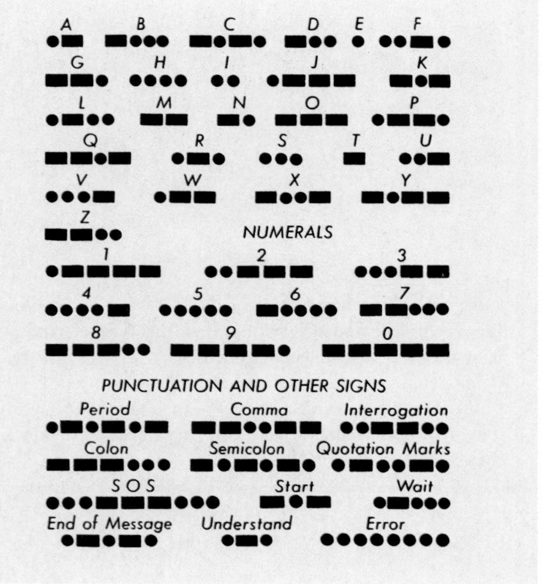

tions were performed as people in Europe dialed up (that is, connected with a system through a telephone capability) computers at American universities and used these computers to perform complex calculations. The focus shifted in the mid-1960s from timesharing a single large computer among many users to **networking**, in which many computers are interconnected. Other developments in data communications have been affected by the Federal Communications Commission (FCC), whose rulings have made the communications industry more competitive.

As we evaluate computer and communications technologies, we see that both have had and will continue to have enormous impact on our lives. Both are improving constantly.

How Data Communications Systems Work

Figure 7–2 shows the major components of a simple data communications system. A user sitting at a terminal wishes to communicate with a computer system over conventional telephone lines. Computers transmit bits of **digital** data, and telephone lines transmit **analog** data, or continuous waveforms. The digital data typed by a computer user must be transformed into analog data for transmission over a phone line. This is the function of a **modem** (for **mo**dulator/**dem**odulator). The converted data is then transmitted in analog form over the telephone network to the main

Figure 7–2 The components of a simple data communications system.

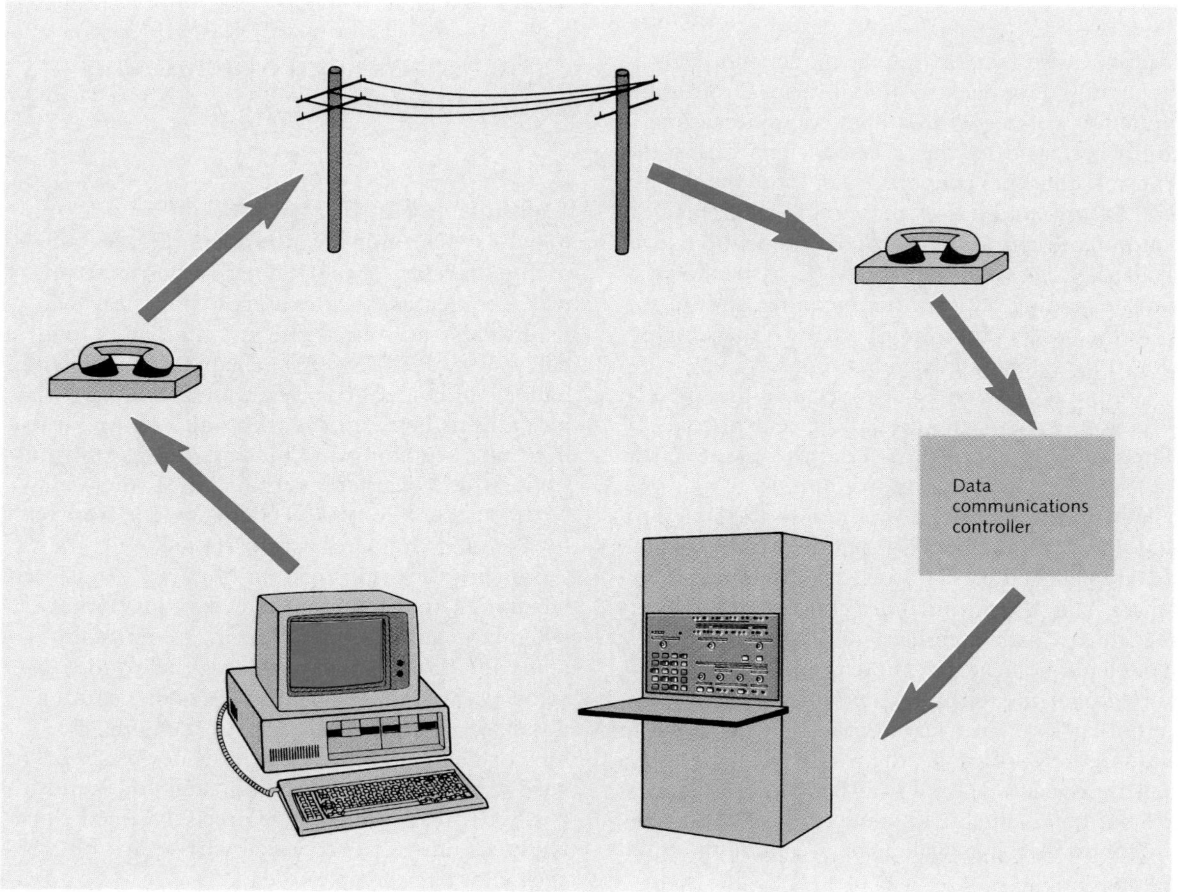

Lincoln's Logic

One of our favorite stories (the source of which we have yet to determine) tells of Abraham Lincoln's response to the telegraph and its use during the American Civil War. One of Lincoln's young lieutenants informed the President that a telegraph network had been installed for communicating information to and from the battlefields. The young man excitedly said, "Mr. President, do you know what this means?"

Lincoln responded, "No, son, what does it mean?"

"It means we'll be able to make decisions with the speed of light!"

After deliberating, the older and wiser Lincoln quietly responded, "Yes, lieutenant, that is true. But we'll also be able to make *wrong* decisions with the speed of light!"

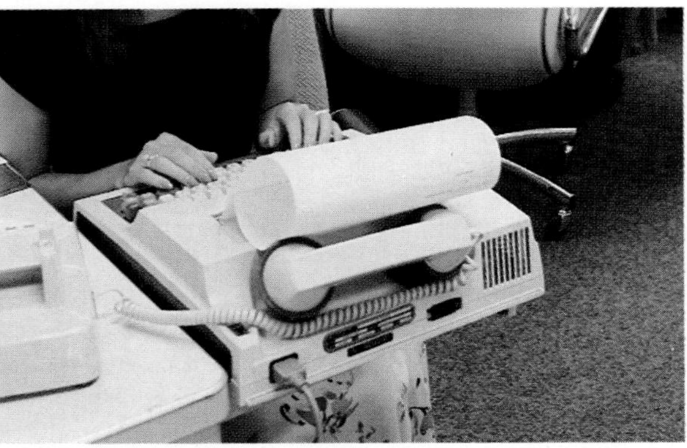

Figure 7–3 A telephone handset in an acoustic coupler modem.

computer site, where another modem converts the analog data back to digital form. Ordinarily a modem is connected to a **data communications controller**, a device that receives signals from the transmission line, converts them into computerized form, and passes them on to the central computer system. The data communications controller handles many of the chores associated with managing data communications and thus frees the central computer system so that it may work on performing useful computations.

Communication may also occur in the opposite direction; data originating at the central computer may be sent to the user at the remote terminal through the reverse procedure.

When terminals are connected to the standard dial-up telephone network, modems with **acoustic couplers** (Figure 7–3) are used. Electronic impulses from the terminal are converted into tones that the acoustic coupler actually "speaks" into the telephone headset. These tones are then transmitted over the telephone network and are converted back to electrical impulses at the computer end. Figure 7–4 shows the transformation of signals that occurs in data transmission. Modems are normally capable of converting signals from digital to analog as well as from analog to digital forms.

Asynchronous and Synchronous Transmission

Transmission may be asynchronous or synchronous. **Asynchronous transmission** (Figure 7–5) is used with relatively slow devices such as terminals. People type so slowly that characters will tend to be transmitted one at a time, with long delays between them. Asynchronous transmission handles individual characters by enclosing their bit patterns between a **start bit** and a **stop bit** to mark the beginning and the end of each transmission. After a character is transmitted, there may be a considerable time delay before the start bit for the next character is transmitted.

Synchronous transmission (Figure 7–6) is used when high-speed transmission is required and when large groups of characters are normally ready for transmission at once. Synchronous transmission handles characters as one continuous stream of bits; there are no start bits, stop bits, or delays, so line capacity is not wasted. The hardware for synchronous transmission is more costly because it must have precisely timed clocking mechanisms to recognize where each bit and each character begin and end.

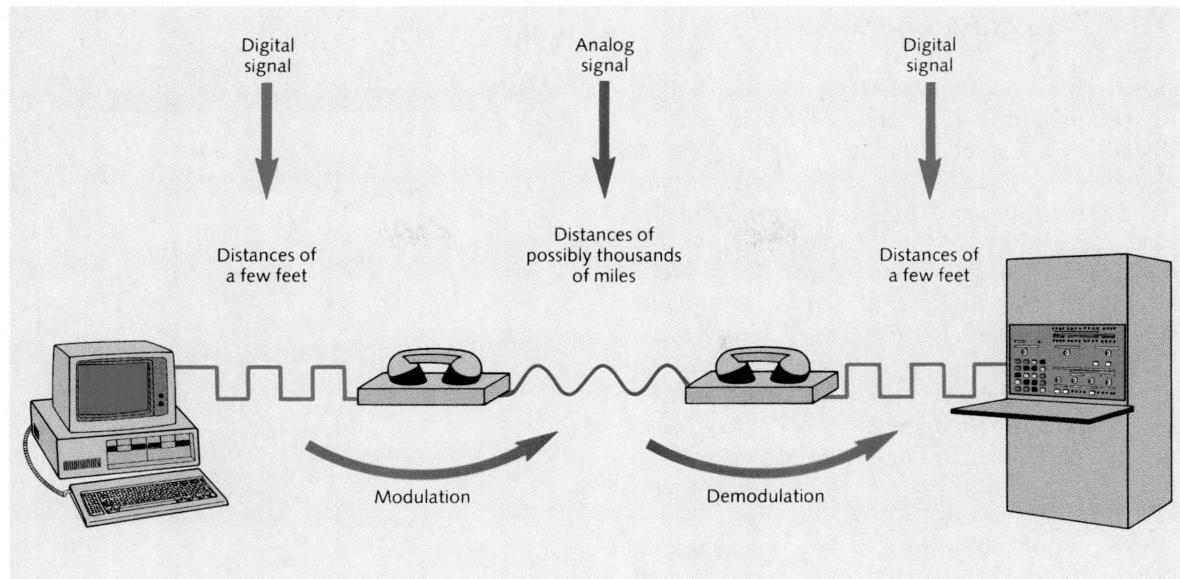

Figure 7–4 Modulation and demodulation by modems in data transmission. The "crisp" digital signals that represent bits can only be transmitted over short distances. The digital signals must first be converted to analog signals for long distance transmission.

Figure 7–5 A example of asynchronous transmission. The characters 1, 2, and 3 are transmitted one at a time. Each character is preceded by a start bit and followed by a stop bit. After a stop bit is transmitted, a considerable delay may occur before the next start bit is transmitted.

Start bit 11110001 (1) Stop bit | Delay | Start bit 11110010 (2) Stop bit | Delay | Start bit 11110011 (3) Stop bit | Delay | . . .

Time ⟶

11110001 (1) 11110010 (2) 11110011 (3) . . .

Time ⟶

Figure 7–6 An example of synchronous transmission. Here the characters 1, 2, and 3 are transmitted as a continuous group with no start bits, stop bits, or delays.

Data Transmission Codes

The two most popular character sets in use today for sending data are (as we saw in Chapter 3) EBCDIC (for Extended Binary Coded Decimal Interchange Code) and ASCII (for American Standard Code for Information Interchange). EBCDIC was developed by IBM in the mid-1960s for use in its System/360 line of computers. ASCII was developed primarily for communication of data between computer systems but is also used widely in computer systems to represent characters. Both of these character sets represent letters, digits, and special symbols by fixed-length patterns of bits. The difference in these codes necessitates that a conversion be performed for EBCDIC and ASCII devices to "talk" to each other.

It would, of course, be a lot simpler if there were only one code, so all devices would be compatible with one another. The International Standards Organization (ISO) and the American National Standards Institute (ANSI) are two groups concerned with fostering standardization in the data-processing and data communications industries.

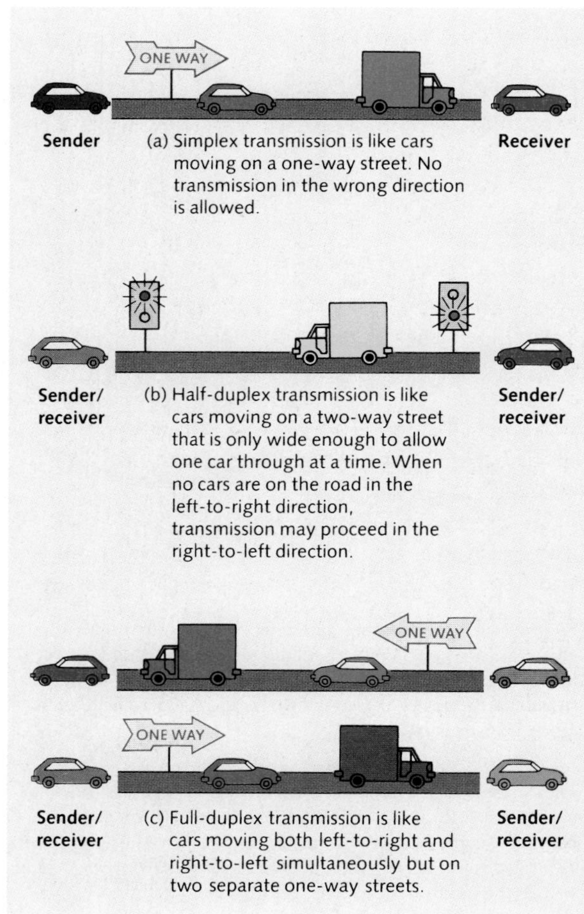

Figure 7–7 Simplex, half-duplex, and full-duplex transmission.

Simplex, Half-Duplex, and Full-Duplex Transmission

Transmission may occur through simplex, half-duplex, or full-duplex lines (Figure 7–7). With **simplex transmission**, data travels in only one direction; transmission in the opposite direction is not allowed. This form of transmission, rarely used in data communications, is common in TV and one-way radio transmissions.

Half-duplex transmission permits transmission in both directions but only in one direction at a time. It is used in **transaction-processing** systems where a user types a request to the computer (user-to-computer transmission), and the computer then processes the request and transmits a result to the user (computer-to-user transmission). Half-duplex lines are more costly than simplex lines. CB radio enthusiasts use half-duplex transmission. While one person is speaking, that person's CB radio may not receive. When the person finishes speaking (with a "10–4, good buddy"), someone else may speak and the first person's CB may now receive.

Full-duplex transmission sends data in both directions simultaneously. Normally used in higher-speed data transmission applications, full-duplex lines cost more than half-duplex lines.

Line Speed

Transmission lines may be classified according to the speed at which they carry data. This speed is often called **bandwidth. Narrowband**, or low-

speed, lines operate up to 300 bits per second (commonly written as 300 bps or 300 baud). **Voiceband**, or medium-speed, lines can handle between 300 and 9600 bps. **Broadband**, or high-speed, lines operate faster than 9600 bps.

Narrowband lines were popular in the early telegraph system, but they are being replaced by faster ones. Voiceband lines are used in the telephone network (human voice transmission requires about 2400 bps to be understandable). Broadband lines are used for rapid communications between the components of computer systems, for communications between computer systems in computer networks, and for high-speed fiber optics and microwave and satellite transmissions.

Two of the most commonly used broadband transmission rates are 19,200 bps (twice 9600) and 50K bps (50,000 bps or 50 kilobits per second). Much higher broadband transmission speeds are available. Continuing advances in communications technology point to increasing transmission speeds and decreasing costs for the next several decades.

Transmission Media

Data may be transmitted in many ways. It may be carried on a twisted-pair wire, a cable containing many twisted-pair wires, a coaxial cable, a microwave transmission, a satellite transmission, or a fiber optic glass cable.

Twisted Pairs

One of the original types of wire used in telephone communications is the **twisted-pair wire** (Figure 7–8). Each wire pair can handle one telephone conversation, or the equivalent of 2400 bps of data transmission. Twisted pairs of copper wires are still the most popular medium for local telephone and data communications. Actually, they can support various types of low-speed data terminals in the range of 300 bps to as great as 9600 bps.

Cables

As greater transmission capacities were needed, bundles of insulated twisted pairs were wrapped into a large **cable** (Figure 7–9), often several inches thick. These cables carry as many as several hundred twisted pairs. Cables carry transmissions from central telephone exchanges to local telephones.

Coaxial Cables

Coaxial cable (Figure 7–10) has a single wire with a very high capacity (that is, a large bandwidth). The conductor is wrapped in insulation, which is, in turn, covered with a wire mesh that keeps out electrical "noise" (static). The great capacity of coaxial cable allows it to carry many channels simultaneously, eliminating the need for thousands of separate wires to be strung. Cable TV companies use coaxial cable to bring many channels of subscription television programming

Figure 7–8 *Below:* A twisted pair.

Figure 7–9 *Bottom:* A cable of twisted pairs.

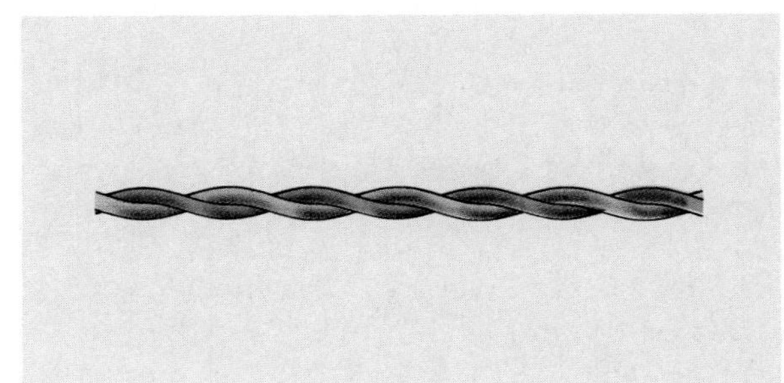

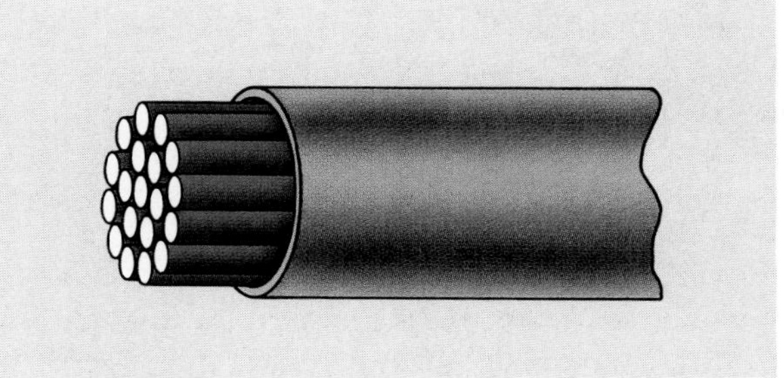

to residences. Coaxial cable is also popular in local networking, as we will see later in the chapter.

Microwave Transmission

Microwave transmission (Figure 7–11) does not use cables or wires. Rather, the signals are transmitted through the air between microwave stations. The transmission occurs in a straight line, so microwave relay towers must be within sight of one another. Normally, microwave relay stations are placed about 30 miles apart—the curvature of the earth would actually hide the signal if they were farther apart. Microwave transmissions typically have high bandwidths, so they can carry many channels of color television programming or thousands of telephone conversations.

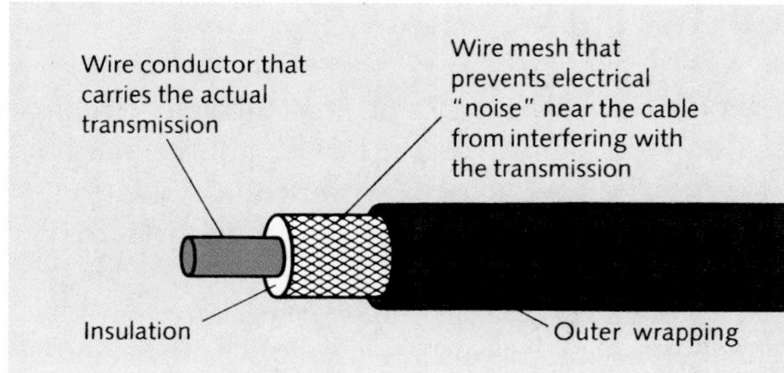

Figure 7–10 Coaxial cable.

Satellite Transmission

Satellite transmission (Figures 7–12, 7–13, 7–14, and 7–15) also uses microwaves. These are beamed at a satellite in orbit 22,300 miles above the surface of the earth. At this altitude, the satellite remains positioned at the same point above the earth at all times, even though both the earth and the satellite are moving at great speed. This is called a **geostationary orbit.** Huge microwave transmitters and receivers are aimed directly at the satellite to enable the line-of-sight transmission. Satellites make around-the-world transmission as easy as communicating with your next-door neighbor.

Figure 7–11 Micrówave transmission.

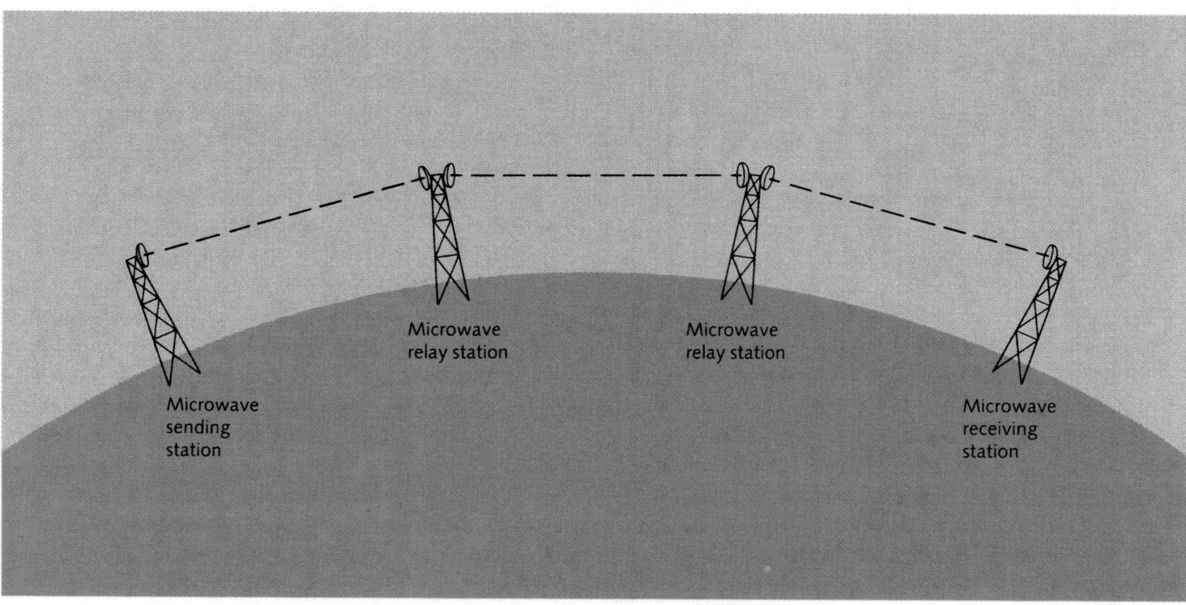

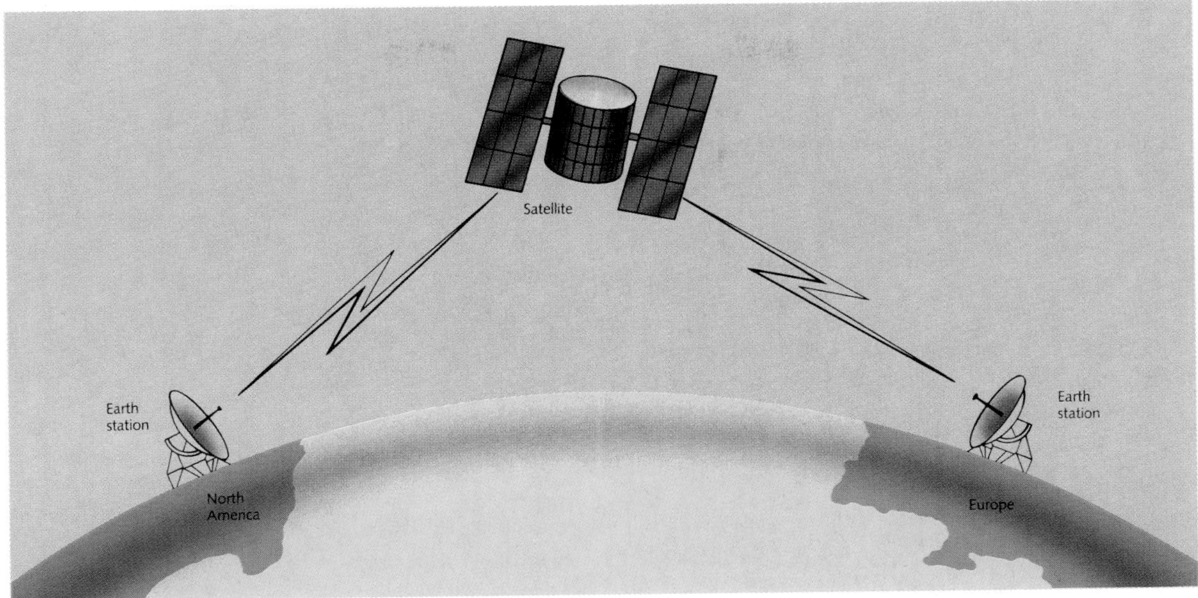

Figure 7–12 Satellite transmission.

Figure 7–13 When this communications satellite is launched into orbit, the "arms" of the satellite will spread out the reflective material, forming a huge antenna in space.

Figure 7–14 Satellite earth stations like this are now used to bring television programming to residential and office complexes. In the near future huge volumes of data will be transmitted to earth stations throughout the world. The data will be transmitted in scrambled form; subscribers will pay for the use of descramblers that will give them access to a wealth of valuable information.

Figure 7–15 This earth station operates in the superhigh frequency range. This prevents normal electronic noise in downtown city areas from interfering with the signals, so satellite signals may be received in downtown areas rather than being routed through rural stations.

Laser Talk

Theoretically, a laser beam has the capability to carry as many as 1 billion telephone conversations. If every person in America was on the phone at once, only about 100 million conversations would be in progress. A laser beam of light could potentially handle 10 times this capacity! Actual laser communications systems being developed today have much smaller capacities, but the technology for dramatic improvement is already in place.

Figure 7–16 *Below:* A colorful display of optical fibers transmitting light beams.

Figure 7–17 *Bottom:* Optical glass fibers comparable in thickness to human hairs.

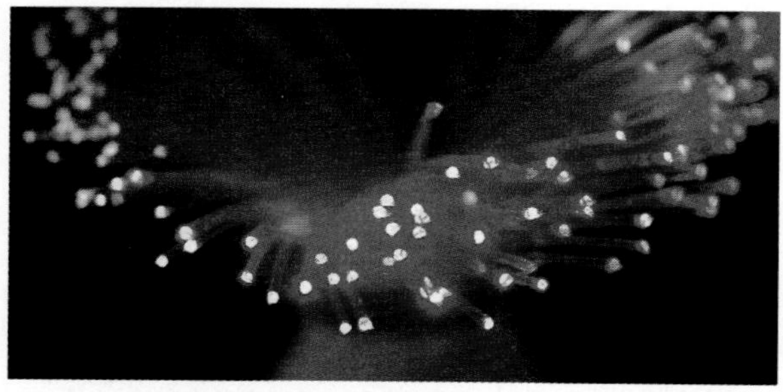

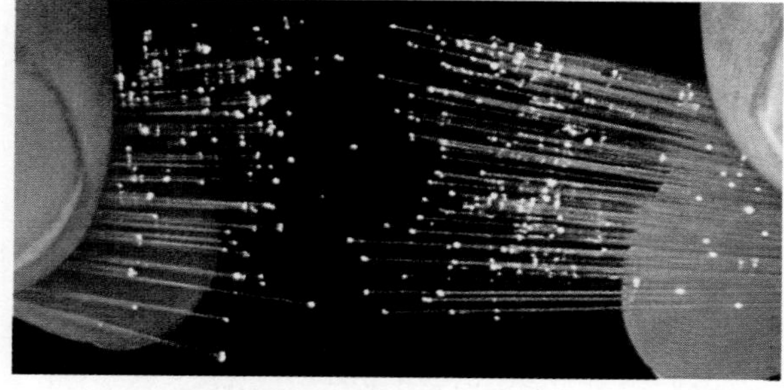

Fiber Optics

Fiber optics has established itself as the cable technology of the future. Transmission is handled by optical glass fibers, which send light rather than electricity (Figure 7–16). One of the most common light sources is lasers. Lasers produce "aligned" light beams that, when directed into the fiber, remain "on target" over great distances. The light is kept inside the fiber until it emerges at the opposite end of the cable (Figure 7–17).

Figure 7–18 shows a cross section of a fiber optic cable. The cable consists of a protective plastic **outer coating, cladding,** and a **core.** The plastic outer coating prevents the cable from being scratched or otherwise damaged. The core and the cladding both consist of strong glass materials, but each is made of a slightly different kind of glass. The effect of this is to contain light traveling in the core. The combination of the core and the cladding actually can bend a beam of light to follow the cable (Figure 7–19). This is particularly useful in applications where light needs to be brought to an inaccessible place, such as in laser surgery.

Let's refer again to Figure 7–18. A light source, often a laser, sends beams of light through the cable. Some of the beams enter at too sharp an angle and escape through the side of the cable, but most of the beams reach the light detector at the far end of the cable. Data to be sent down the

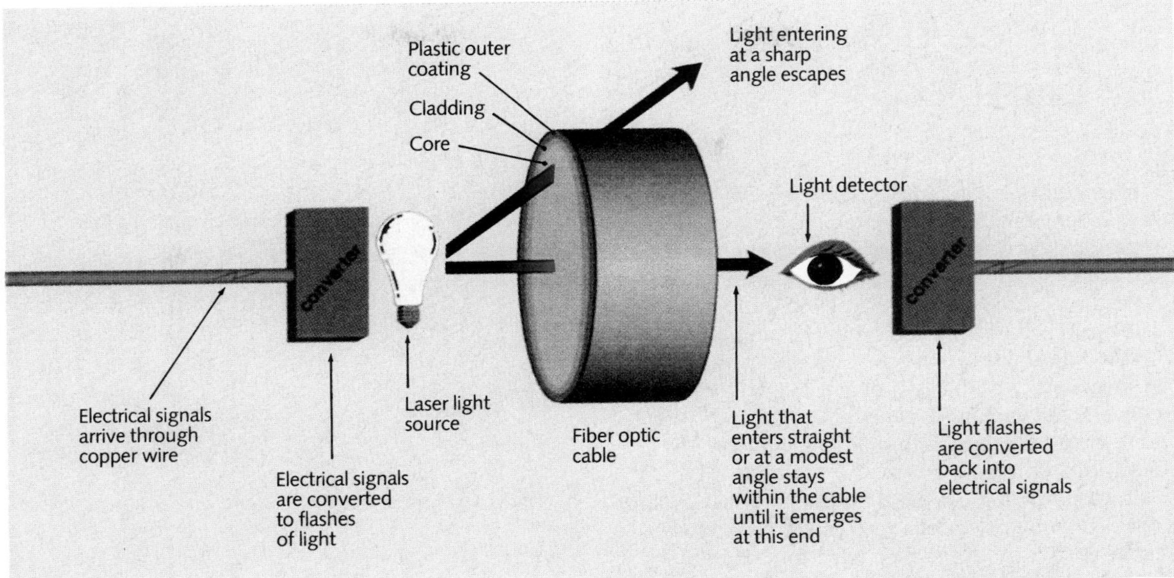

Light entering at a sharp angle escapes

Light that enters straight or at a modest angle stays within the cable until it emerges at this end

Figure 7–18 How fiber optic transmission works.

cable arrives as electrical signals. A converter accepts the electrical signals and encodes them as varying intensities of light that are then emitted by the light source. The light detector at the opposite end of the cable converts the light signals back into electrical signals that can then be sent over conventional electronic communications paths.

Fiber optic technology offers many advantages over conventional electronic communications with copper cable because of its weight, size, efficiency, immunity from electronic disturbances and physical tampering, and large capacity.

A half-inch fiber optic cable can carry 100,000 conversations, about 10 times as many as half-inch copper cable. It can be threaded through existing ductwork to increase transmission capacities.

Fiber optic cable allows the cable TV industry to offer many services to subscribers simultaneously. Speech, data, audio, and video may all be carried at one time, and many channels of each

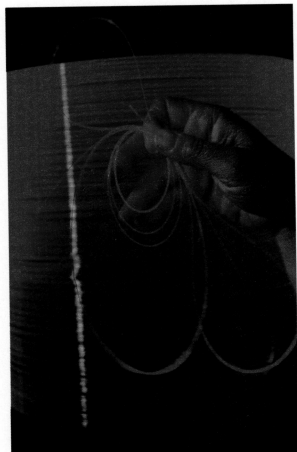

Figure 7–19 An optical fiber can actually bend a beam of light.

The Purest Glass

Alexander Graham Bell's "Photophone."

Optical transmission of data is not new. In 1880 Alexander Graham Bell invented the "Photophone" (right), a device that enables speech to be transmitted on a light beam. Sunlight is bounced off a reflector, and the beam is sharpened through a lens. The beam is then bounced off a mechanism that vibrates with the spoken voice. This causes variations in the intensity of the light beam. A detector then converts the varying signal into an electrical current to re-create the speech through a telephone receiver.

It wasn't until the 1960s that the potential of fiber optic communication as a replacement for conventional copper cable and electronic communications was demonstrated. Since then most major firms in the communications industry have committed themselves to the use of fiber optic cable for future cable installations.

To make fiber optic transmission possible, scientists needed to create a glass fiber of incredible purity and clarity, so the light would not disperse too quickly. Today's fiber optic cable glass is so pure that if the waters of the ocean were as clear, you would easily be able to see for miles underwater.

type of service can be brought into the home.

Transmissions through fiber optics are not disturbed by electrical noise generated by nearby communications lines or electrical devices. These lines are, therefore, useful in factories with large electric motors that might generate interference with conventional electronic transmissions. Because fiber optic cables do not involve the transmission of electricity, grounding to prevent electrical shocks is not necessary.

Tampering with cables made of fiber optics is nearly impossible, which makes them popular with the military, financial institutions, and other security-conscious concerns.

Fiber optics is still in its early stages of development. Advances in the field will greatly widen the scope of data communications. We will discuss anticipated developments in fiber optics under "Expectations for the Future."

Line Configuration

Point-to-Point and Multidrop Lines

Terminals and computers must be connected for data to be transmitted between them. They may be connected by either point-to-point or multidrop lines.

A terminal that is directly connected to a computer system in a data communications network with no other terminals on the line is a **point-to-point line** (Figure 7–20). The terminal transmits directly to the computer and the computer directly to the terminal, so responses are fast. Because each line is used by only one terminal, point-to-point lines are expensive.

In systems in which terminals need to communicate with a central computer for brief periods,

Figure 7–20 A point-to-point line.

it is more economical for several terminals to share a single line connected to the computer. This is called a **multidrop line** or **multipoint line** (Figure 7–21).

In a multidrop configuration only one terminal at a time can transmit data to the computer, but the computer may broadcast a message to many terminals at once. In an airline reservations system in which one computer services thousands of terminals, the terminals normally share a number of multidrop lines. Messages are transmitted to the central computer so quickly that users rarely notice any delays except during peak traffic periods.

Leased and Switched Lines

Point-to-point and multidrop lines may be either leased or switched lines (Figure 7–22). **Leased lines** are dedicated lines, that is, lines reserved for use by a particular party who is charged for the undivided attention of the line. **Switched lines** are available through the regular telephone switching system. With switched lines, each time a terminal establishes a line of communication with a computer, it may actually connect via a different set

Figure 7–21 A multidrop line shared by five terminals.

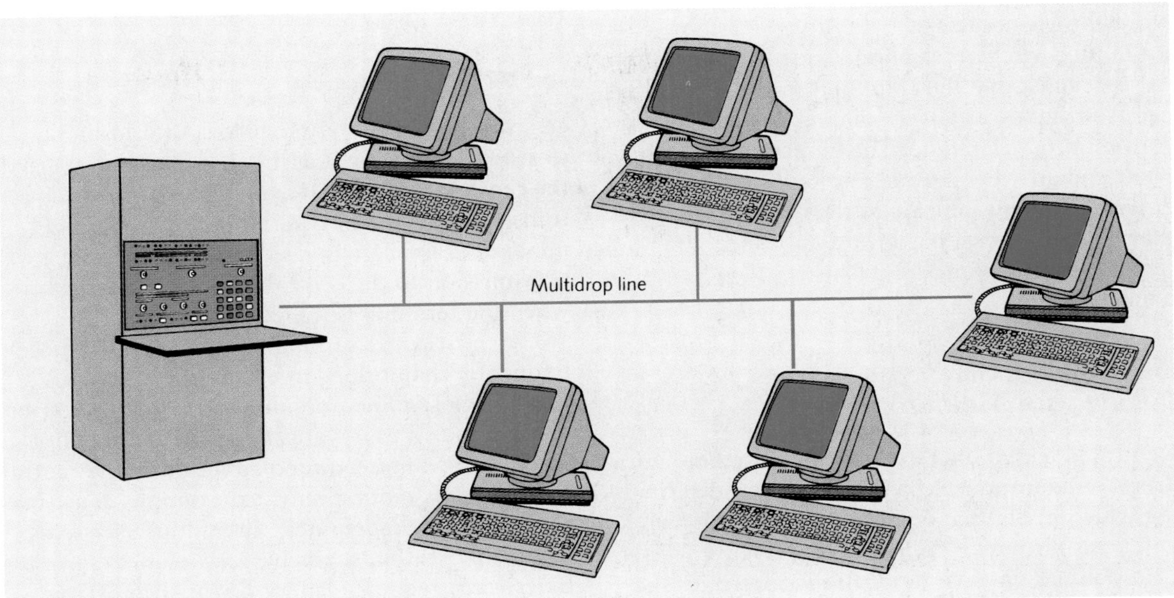

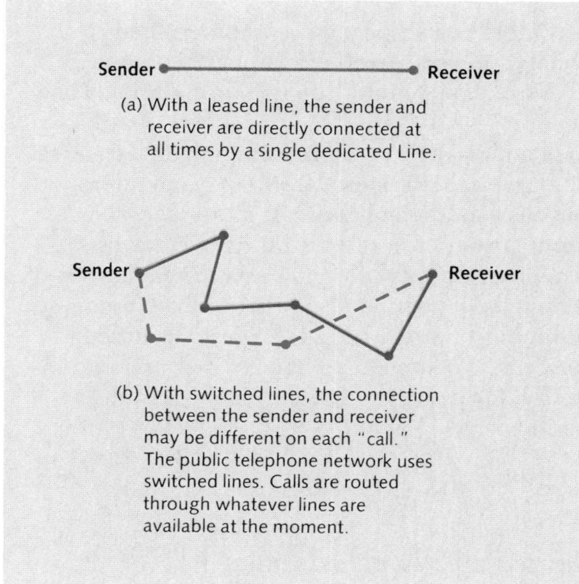

Figure 7–22 Leased and switched lines.

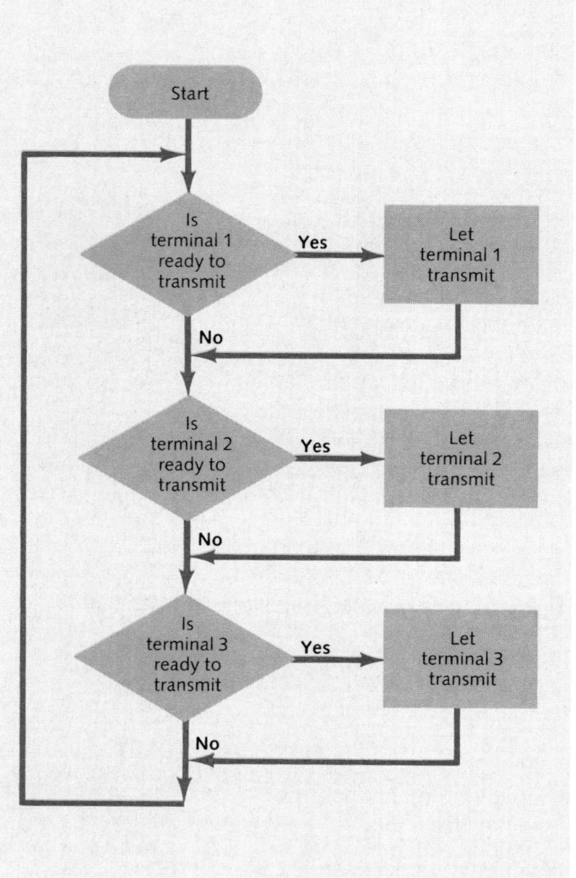

Figure 7–23 Polling.

of lines, just as happens in the public telephone network.

On leased lines the lines are always connected directly from the terminal to the computer, so communication may be initiated by typing a character at the terminal. The computer system always "listens" for these characters to be typed. No dialing is necessary.

On the switched telephone network, the terminal user must dial the computer in the same manner as if that person were dialing a friend on a conventional telephone. The modem at the computer end answers the call and sends a signal down the line to indicate to the dialing terminal that the connection has been established and transmission may proceed. This is called **handshaking**.

Polling with Multidrop Lines

Dedicated leased lines are generally used in multidrop configurations. One technique for determining which **node** (that is, terminal or computer) will transmit next is called **polling** (Figure 7–23).

In polling, the communications controller successively tests each terminal on a multidrop line to see if that terminal wishes to transmit data to the central computer. If a terminal is not ready to transmit, then the next terminal is tried. If a terminal does indicate that it wants to transmit, transmission to the central computer is initiated when the terminal is polled.

The most active terminals may be polled more frequently than others to ensure they receive good service. Sometimes, however, a polled terminal that indicates it wants to send data may not be given the uninterrupted attention of the central computer. Its request may, for example, cause it to tie up a line indefinitely. In multiuser systems where all users must receive reasonable response times, such requests cannot be satisfied. Many

systems therefore use a timer device to limit transmission time; when time runs out the line is automatically freed for use by other terminals.

Data Communications Networks

It has become common for computers to communicate with one another over data communications networks—systems with more than one computer and terminal. The Bank of Montreal, for example, operates North America's largest real-time banking computer system. The bank's computer network links 1302 branches throughout Canada by using more than 150,000 miles of telecommunications lines. A teller at any one of the 5000 branch terminals may access any customer's account information in less than three seconds. More than 3 million transactions are processed each day. This form of communication has had a tremendous impact on the sharing of programs and data across great distances or within a small area, such as one office. The most common network arrangements are star networks, bus networks, and ring networks.

Star Networks

In a **star network** (Figure 7–24), a central computer communicates with various terminals and other computers over point-to-point lines. The other computers and terminals are directly con-

Figure 7–24 A star network.

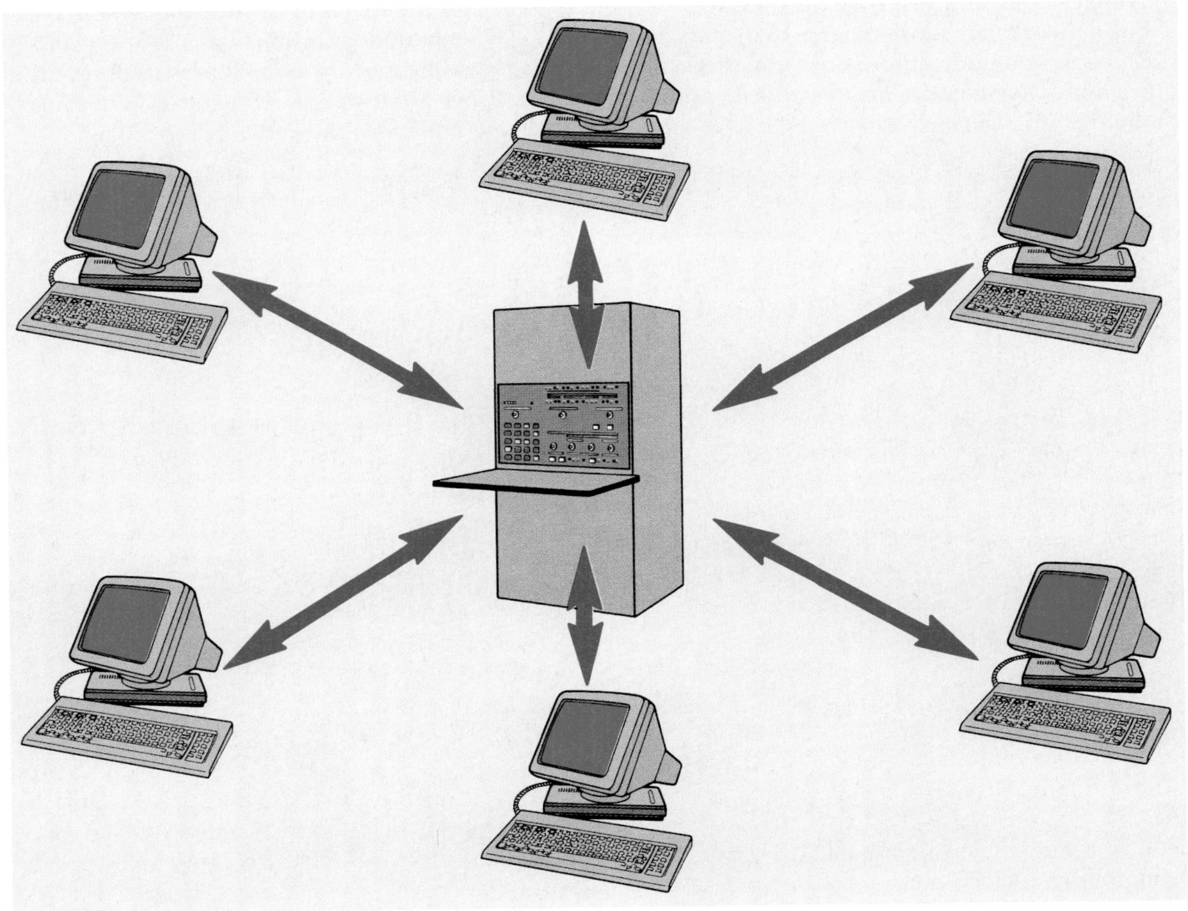

nected to the central computer but not to one another. If they wish to communicate, they must do so through the central computer system. Thus the central computer acts as a network controller. If the central computer fails, the entire network fails. Polling is commonly used to determine which node will transmit next. Star networks are used in timesharing systems with the central node being the timesharing "host" computer.

Bus Networks

A **bus network** (Figure 7–25) is essentially a single multidrop line shared by many nodes. A message to be transmitted is placed on the bus and is broadcast to all the nodes. The message contains the address of the receiving node. The receiving node pulls the message off the bus, and the other nodes simply ignore the message.

Bus networks are more reliable than stars and rings because a node failure does not affect the other nodes. New nodes may be added easily by "tapping" into the bus.

Ring Networks

Ring networks (Figure 7–26) are common network arrangements for local environments. They do not have a central computer system controlling the operation of the entire network. Instead, the various computers in the network are arranged around a ring, and each computer may communicate with any other computer in the ring. Messages from one computer to another on the ring must be **addressed**, that is, identified specifically, to the destination computer.

Token passing is commonly used to determine which node transmits next. A bit pattern called a **token** is passed from node to node. If a node that is not ready to transmit receives the token, it passes the token to the next node. If the node is ready to transmit, it removes the token, transmits the desired data to the appropriate node, and then passes the token to the next node in the ring. When a node transmits data, it also transmits the address of the node that is to receive the data. Rings are formed with point-to-point lines, so if any node fails the entire network fails.

Figure 7–25 A bus network.

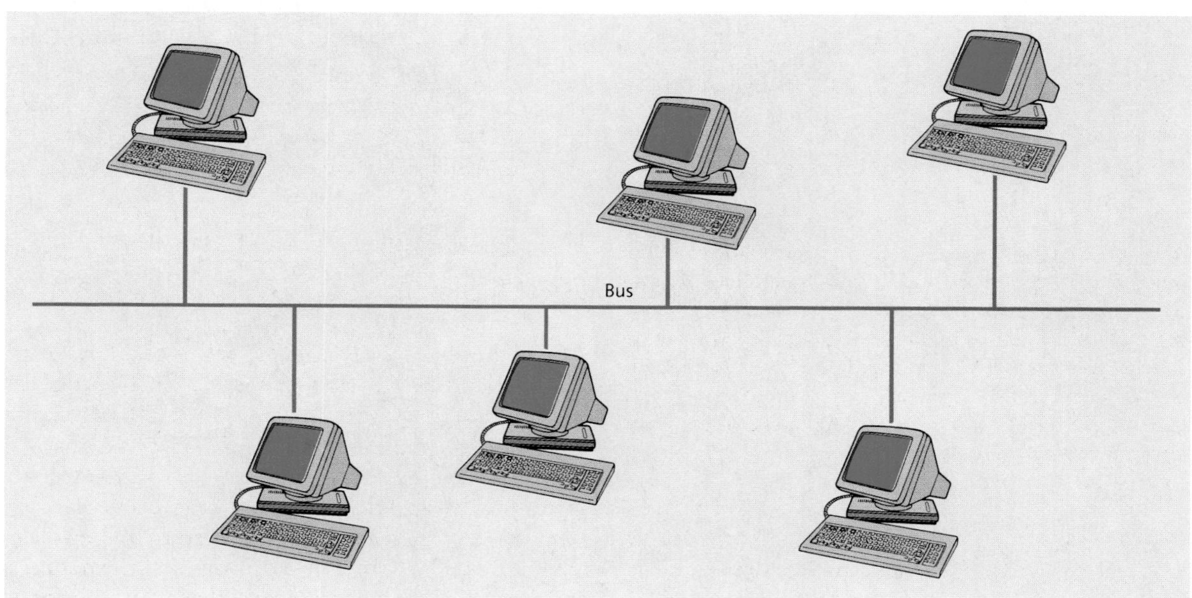

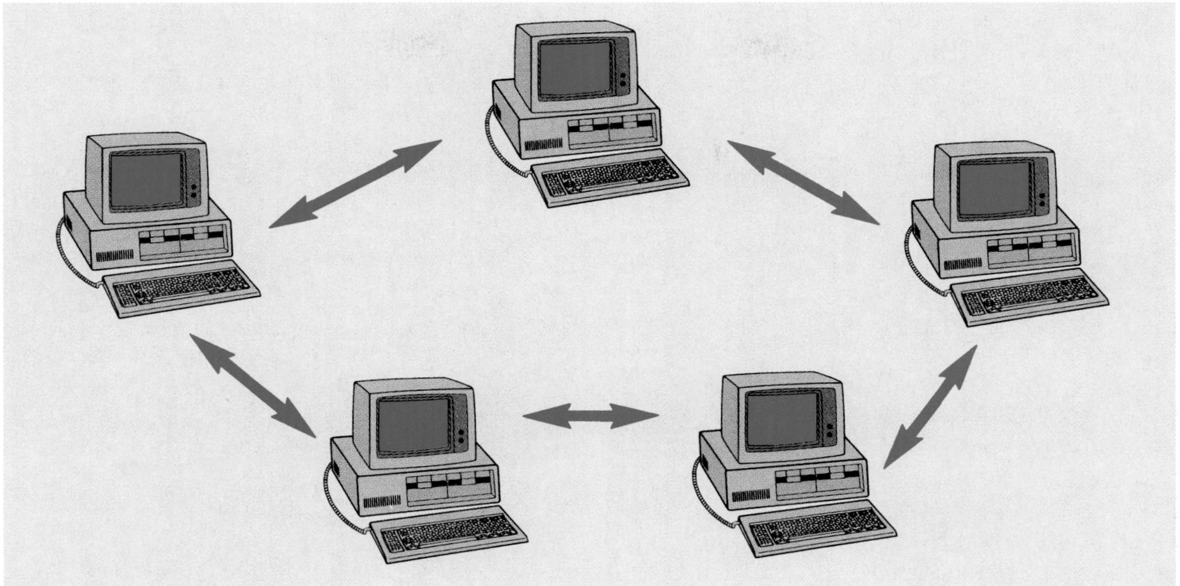

Figure 7–26 A ring network.

Local Networks

We have been discussing networks that operate across large areas, but the need to serve small locations is greater. According to Donald Massaro, former president of Xerox Office Products Division, "About 90% of all business information is distributed within a half mile." Local networks are designed to handle limited geographic areas, normally a single building or adjacent buildings. John Connell of the Office Technology Research Group sums up the case for local networking:

> The tendency in the past has been to apply technology to office work by moving the work out of the regular office and into a technology center, such as a data or word processing center. By doing this, companies inadvertently exclude nontechnical personnel from easy accessibility to technological capabilities that could enhance their productivity. With networks, the power and capabilities of all modern technologies are, quite literally, at every manager's fingertips.
>
> *Office Products News*
> September 1981

Local networks operate at greater data speeds than the telephone network. Because the local "nets" are generally company owned, they give their management greater flexibility. They are also independent of the public telephone system and its constraints.

Local networks have been developed by many major computer manufacturers. Xerox has introduced Ethernet, Wang markets Wangnet, and Exxon's Zilog offers Z-net. Nippon Electric Company of Japan has introduced its "optical highway" concept with fiber optic communications of data, voice, and video. IBM and Digital Equipment Corporation have also developed networks.

Case Study 7–1: The Ethernet Local Network

Ethernet is a local networking scheme that makes it possible to link various office machines into a single network (Figure 7–27). It uses a **coaxial copper cable** (Figures 7–28 and 7–29) to connect various pieces of information equipment. Information travels over the cable in **packets** of data (Figure 7–30) that are sent from one machine to another. Each packet contains the actual message that is being transmitted as well as infor-

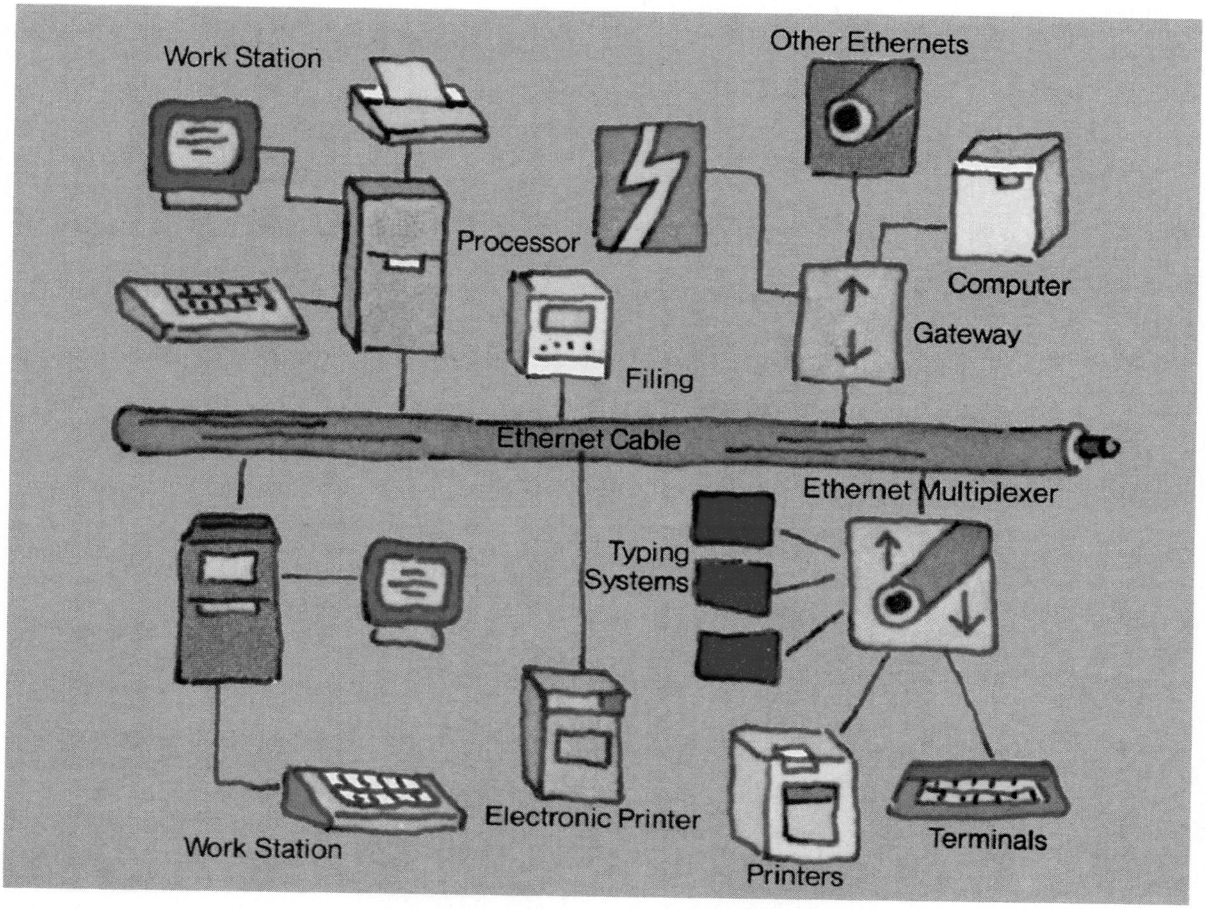

Figure 7–27 The Ethernet makes it possible to link various types of office machines in a single local network.

Figure 7–28 Ethernet coaxial cable. The single wire conductor in the cable is wrapped in various protective layers, each with its own special purpose. This cable can support data rates as high as 50 million bits per second—much faster than today's Ethernets actually operate.

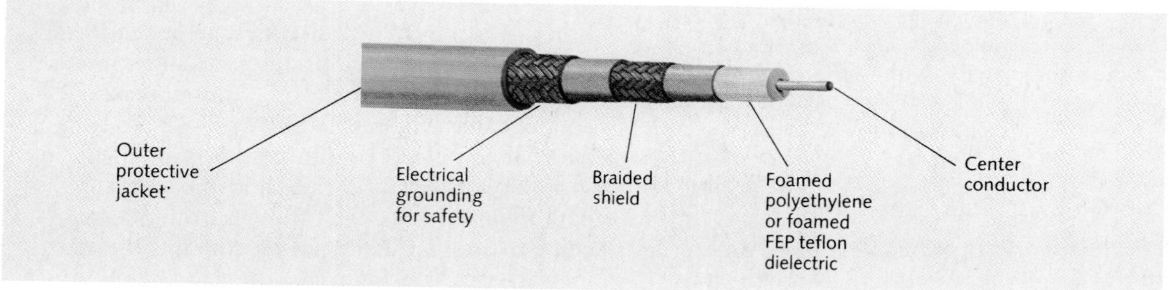

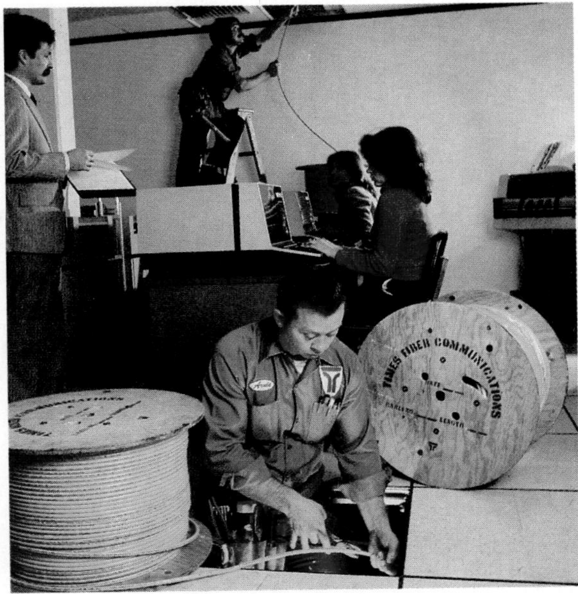

Figure 7–29 Ethernet cable may be strung in such ways as through air-conditioning ducts or under the raised flooring commonly used in computer rooms.

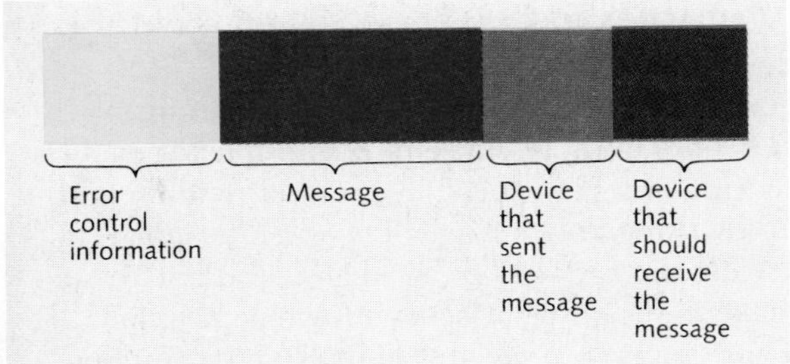

Figure 7–30 A data packet.

mation identifying the sending and receiving devices. Error control information is included to help ensure correct transmission.

Ethernet uses the **collision concept** or **contention** to decide which piece of office equipment on the network gets to communicate next. When one device is transmitting, all other devices must wait. When the current transmission stops, other devices may attempt transmission. If their transmissions collide (that is, if several devices attempt to transmit at the same time), all devices stop transmitting. Eventually, one of the devices begins transmitting again, no collision occurs, and that device is able to complete its transmission while the other devices wait. This collision concept allows Ethernet to operate without **central network control**, thus making it much easier to add new devices to the network after initial installation.

The collision approach to sharing the network may at first seem inefficient. It is, however, fast (transmitting at 10 million bits per second), reliable, and economical. The network operates so quickly and the packets are so short that each transmission lasts less than one-thousandth of a second, so the number of collisions is small. Because the control is provided by each individual device, the reliability of the network is very high. If an individual device fails, the network keeps functioning. This is called **distributed network control**.

One disadvantage of Ethernet is that it is a **baseband** rather than broadband network. A baseband network can only transmit on a single channel. Thus, Ethernet uses only a small percentage of the capacity of its coaxial cable. Broadband systems, such as Wang's Wangnet, have a much larger capacity and can transmit several channels at once. Many of the experts in the data communications industry feel that Ethernet must evolve into a broadband network before it will become widely accepted.

One objection to the Ethernet network is the coaxial cable itself. The cable is costly, and it must be routed to every device on the network. Several companies have announced **PBXs** (Private Branch Exchanges) that can handle both voice and data communications so that local networking can be implemented by use of standard telephone lines. These PBXs are often called **CBXs** (Computerized Branch Exchanges).

CBXs have their own disadvantages. CBXs use central network control, so if the CBX fails, the entire network fails. Also, interference, common on the regular telephone network, can hinder data communications. Nevertheless, CBX networks are cheaper to implement than coaxial cable networks and will appeal to organizations with limited budgets.

Multiplexors

Some devices are available that make transmission of data more efficient. A **multiplexor** enables sharing of a high-speed line, rather than tying it up by using only a single low-speed terminal. It divides the capacity of the high-speed line to make it appear to be several low-speed lines. Thus, many low-speed terminals may communicate simultaneously over a single high-speed line.

Terminals send their transmissions directly to the multiplexor instead of the central computer. The multiplexor interweaves the transmissions of the slower terminals to form a single high-speed transmission to the central computer.

When data communications became popular in the early 1960s, a typical communications system was like that in Figure 7–31. Each terminal com-

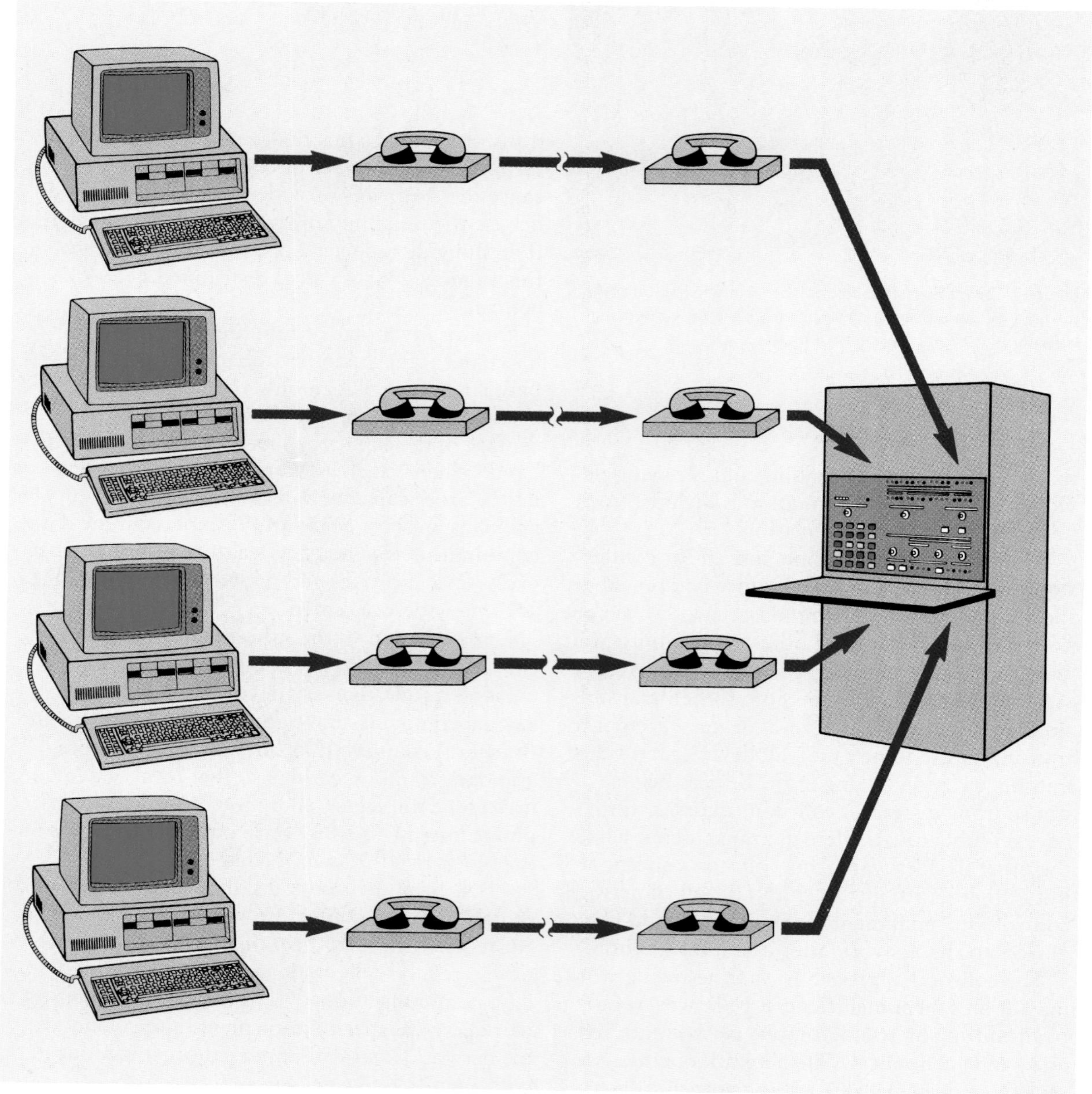

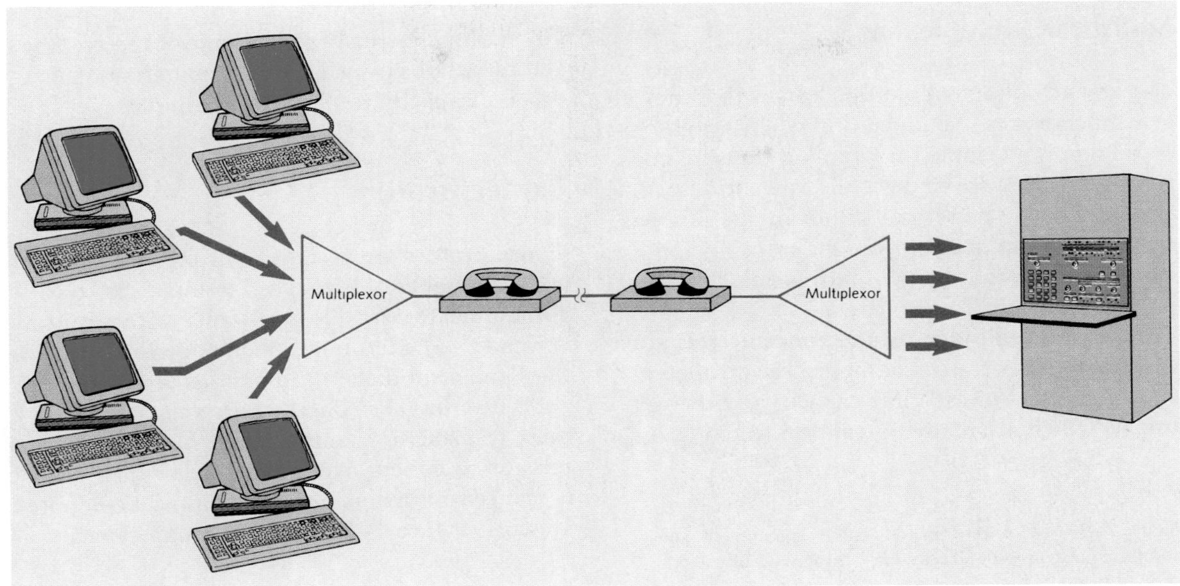

Figure 7–32 Data transmission with multiplexing.

municated with a central computer over individual telephone lines, and every line had a modem at each end. The modems were matched in speed with the terminals. As higher-speed modems became available and terminals could transmit at increased speeds over existing telephone lines, this system became less efficient. Computer systems could transmit at speeds far greater than the terminal could handle, and terminals designed to transmit at certain speeds could not be easily modified to transmit at higher speeds. Multiplexors were developed (Figure 7–32) to allow several low-speed terminals to share a single high-speed line. Multiplexors might, for example, allow four 300-bps terminals to share a single 1200-bps line.

The two approaches to multiplexing a line are **time-division multiplexing** (TDM) and **frequency-division multiplexing** (FDM). TDM dedicates the line to each terminal for brief periods of time, but it permits the line to be shared among more terminals than FDM. FDM works by assigning different frequency ranges to different terminals (radio and TV stations transmit in this manner).

Figure 7–31 *Left:* Data transmission without multiplexing.

A Popular Multiplexor

One versatile multiplexor in use today is the Bell System's Dataphone 9600, which transmits over conventional telephone lines at about the fastest rate of data communications, 9600 bps. It requires a private line with what Bell calls "high-performance data conditioning." This means that the line has to have special equipment on it besides the 9600-bps modems to make such high-speed transmission possible. The Dataphone 9600 may provide any of the following services under user control: (1) one 9600-bps channel, (2) one 7200-bps channel and one 2400-bps channel, (3) two 4800-bps channels, (4) one 4800-bps channel and two 2400-bps channels, and (5) four 2400-bps channels. Thus, the multiplexor divides one high-speed line into several lower-speed lines.

Statistical Multiplexors

The key advantage of multiplexors is that they allow much better line utilization when a high-speed line is available for handling transmissions from many low-speed devices. Conventional multiplexors have one serious disadvantage: If a particular terminal does not use the transmission capacity given to it by the multiplexor, that capacity is wasted.

Statistical multiplexors and concentrators solve this problem. A statistical multiplexor, called a **stat mux**, gives unused line capacity to other terminals which are ready to transmit. As long as any terminal is ready to transmit or receive, the stat mux skips over inactive terminals and gives the line capacity to the active terminals.

Concentrators

Concentrators are used in environments in which a large number of low-speed terminals need to communicate over a long distance with a central computer. The terminals operate on low-speed lines and send their transmissions directly to the concentrator. The concentrator then assembles these transmissions into a single high-speed transmission to be sent over a high-speed line.

Concentrators are actually complete computer systems (Figure 7–33) with fast high-capacity

Figure 7–33 A concentrator is actually a complete minicomputer system with a secondary storage (usually disk) capability.

secondary storage. When data arrives at a concentrator faster than it can be transmitted over the high-speed line, the concentrator stores the data on disk for later transmission. Unlike multiplexors, concentrators can "absorb" huge amounts of information and hold the data for long periods before transmitting it. Figure 7–34 shows how airline transportation is similar in concept to concentrator operation with data communications.

Figure 7–34 An example of a concentrator operation. An airline shuttle runs every hour from Airport A to Airport B. Customers arrive at Airport A to board the shuttle. If seats are available customers get right on the plane; otherwise the customers wait in the waiting room. During peak periods the lines in the waiting room can become very long, and customers may be delayed in reaching their destinations.

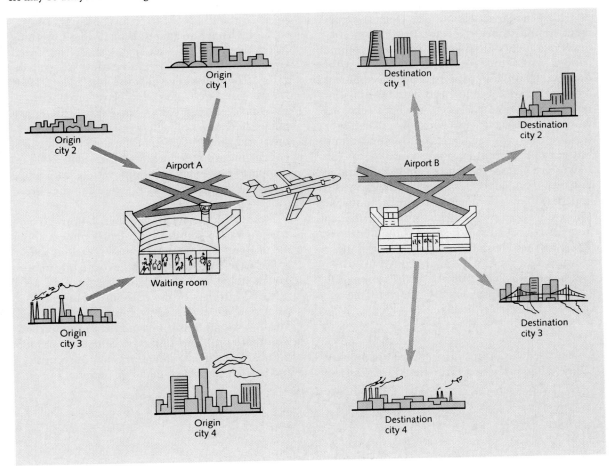

Common Carriers

Common carriers are companies authorized by the government to provide communications services to the public. Until 1968 the major telephone companies required that users of their networks install only the telephones and other equipment that they manufactured. The FCC then ruled that messages could be put through networks using devices not necessarily manufactured, installed, or controlled by the network operators. The **Carterphone decision,** as it was called, brought many more competitors into the data communications industry.

In 1971 the FCC ruled that specialized common carriers could compete with the established communications utilities for rights to offer communications services. The ultimate beneficiary has been the data communications user as competition has forced costs down.

Because of the increased competition, a number of **value-added services** are developing. For example, the communications company MCI offers Omni-Call, which automatically chooses the least costly means of making a long-distance call when a customer dials. **Teleconferencing** allows executives to hold "face-to-face" meetings with executives in other cities by using video and data communications. **Electronic mail** allows messages to be sent over computer networks instead of through the postal service.

One of the most popular value-added services is **packet switching**, which provides error correction and detection capabilities through prefixed identifiers on blocks of data. Packet switching was developed in the early 1960s in response to the U.S. government's fear of a possible nuclear attack by the Soviet Union. The Defense Department commissioned the Rand Corporation to develop a highly reliable and error-free communications system that could survive heavy wartime damage. Paul Baran proposed the development of a digital computer-controlled data transmission network that used packet switching. Packet networks like Telenet ensure virtually error-free transmission, which is particularly important to businesses that must transmit critical data.

Western Union, the nation's oldest communications company, operates a network with satellites and 10,000 miles of microwave links. It offers its Mailgram service by which customers either call in messages or submit them on computer tapes. The messages are then transmitted to U.S. post offices where they are printed, stuffed in envelopes, and delivered with the next day's mail.

Some of the improvements offered by the value-added carriers include:

1. Increased data transmission speed of a given line while providing error-free transmission
2. Ease of communication of normally incompatible devices with one another
3. Automatic conversion of data between character sets such as ASCII and EBCDIC
4. Automatic detection of the fastest (or perhaps the most economical) route for transmitting a given message

Expectations for the Future

Computers and data communications are fast-growing industries in which advancements take place constantly and greater improvements are always predicted. Most speculation now centers on developments in fiber optic and computer chip technology.

The advancements foreseen for fiber optics are expected to revolutionize cable technology. It is believed that fiber optics will enable data transmission to operate at speeds of 1 billion bps (approximately 100 million cps), a staggering speed compared to today's telephone cable transmission rates of about 2400 bps. By the mid- to late-1980s silicon chips are expected to be replaced with chips made from a compound called **gallium arsenide**. These new chips may operate at speeds a thousand times faster than those of silicon chips. For the industry as a whole, by the year 2000 computer power and communications capabilities may be a thousand times greater than they are today—for the same cost.

Along with these glowing speculations go a warning reminiscent of Lincoln's comment about the telegraph. Most data communications lines are relatively easy to tap, and private information can be stolen. It is possible for the financial activities of a business or the economy of an entire country to be disrupted by computer tampering. The data communications industry is concerned with these problems of misuse of data communications. We will examine the issues of security and privacy in greater detail in Chapter 15.

Summary

1. Data communications is the transmission of data between computer systems. The trend today is toward networks of computers that share information.
2. Recent government rulings have tended to increase competition in the data communications industry.
3. Because a computer transmits digital data and telephone lines transmit analog data, modems must be used to convert data between these different formats.
4. The data communications controller receives signals from transmission lines, converts them into computerized form, and passes them onto the central computer system, thus relieving the central computer system of these chores.
5. Simplex lines allow transmission in only one direction, half-duplex lines allow two-way transmission but in only one direction at a time, and full-duplex lines allow transmission in both directions simultaneously.
6. Leased lines are dedicated to the user who is charged for the undivided attention of the line.
7. Switched lines are available through the regular telephone switching system. Each terminal may be connected to the computer by a different set of communication lines each time the user dials the number of the computer system.
8. The most common network arrangements are star networks, bus networks, and ring networks.
9. Many low-speed terminals may communicate simultaneously over a single high-speed line by using multiplexors.
10. Time-division multiplexing dedicates a line to each terminal for brief periods of time; frequency-division multiplexing handles several transmissions over the same line simultaneously by assigning them to different frequency ranges.
11. Common carriers transmit data for the general public and are regulated by the FCC.
12. Laser-based fiber optics is the cable technology of the future. Optical glass fibers transmit light rather than electricity. The fiber optic cable has a high transmission capacity, is lightweight and immune to electrical disturbances and taps, and does not need to be grounded.
13. Local area networks are generally designed to service a limited geographical area.
14. Local networks offer high transmission capacity, management flexibility, and independence from the restrictions of public telephone systems.
15. Private branch exchanges transmit voice and data over standard telephone lines. They are often called computerized branch exchanges.

Important Terms

asynchronous transmission
bus network
CBX (Computerized Branch Exchange)
coaxial cable
collision concept
common carrier
concentrator
fiber optics
frequency-division multiplexing (FDM)
full-duplex transmission
half-duplex transmission
leased line
modem
multidrop line
multiplexor
network
packet switching
PBX (Private Branch Exchange)
point-to-point line
polling
ring network
simplex transmission
star network
stat mux
switched line
synchronous transmission
time-division multiplexing (TDM)
timesharing
token passing
twisted-pair wire

Self-Review Exercises 

Matching

Next to the term in column A, place the letter of the statement in column B that best describes it.

Column A	Column B
1. Modem	A. CB radio operates this way
2. Simplex transmission	B. Establishing connection
3. Bandwidth	C. Data travels in only one direction
4. Microwave transmission	D. Bit pattern used to see which terminal transmits next
5. Leased line	E. Requires relay towers about 30 miles apart
6. Half-duplex	F. Divides one high-speed transmission line into several low-speed lines
7. Fiber optics	G. A device that converts digital signals into analog signals
8. Multiplexor	H. Transmission capacity
9. Handshaking	I. Dedicated to one user
10. Token	J. Transmission technology of the future

Fill-in-the-Blanks

Fill in the blanks in each of the following:

1. Computers transmit ______ data while telephone lines transmit ______ data.

2. ______ transmission sends data in two directions simultaneously.

3. The three most common line speed categories are ______ , ______ , and ______ .

4. Satellites are placed in fixed orbit 22,300 miles above the earth's surface; this is called a ______ orbit.

5. Light used in fiber optic cables is generated by ______ .

6. Successively testing each terminal on a multidrop line to see which one is ready to transmit is called ______ .

7. The three most common network arrangements are ______ , ______ , and ______ .

8. Two approaches to multiplexing a line are ______ and ______ .

9. ______ uses video and data communications to hold "face-to-face" meetings.

10. Silicon chips are expected to be replaced by chips made from ______ .

Answers to Self-Review Exercises

Matching: 1 G, 2 C, 3 H, 4 E, 5 I, 6 A, 7 J, 8 F, 9 B, 10 D

Fill-in-the-Blanks:

1. digital, analog
2. Full-duplex
3. narrowband, voiceband, broadband
4. geostationary
5. lasers
6. polling
7. bus networks, ring networks, star networks
8. time-division multiplexing (TDM), frequency-division multiplexing (FDM)
9. Teleconferencing
10. gallium arsenide

Discussion Questions 

1. Compare the operation of simplex, half-duplex, and full-duplex transmission lines.

2. Discuss the differences between asynchronous and synchronous transmission. What are the advantages and disadvantages of each?

3. What are the most common network arrangements? What are the advantages and disadvantages of each?

4. What are multiplexors and concentrators used for? How do they differ?

5. How are communications satellites being used in data communications systems?

6. Briefly explain how data is transmitted over fiber optic cable.

7. Give several advantages of fiber optic transmission over transmission with copper cables.

8. What is a local network? Give some advantages of local networks over use of the public telephone system for local data transmission.

9. Briefly discuss the contention method of controlling transmissions in an Ethernet network.

10. How does a broadband network differ from a baseband network?

Projects 

1. Visit a computer store and see what types of data communications equipment are sold there. Report on your findings.

2. Some of the common carriers are listed below. Write to several of them and ask for literature on the communications services they provide. Write a report summarizing this information.

American Satellite Corporation
20301 Century Boulevard
Germantown, MD 20767

American Telephone and Telegraph Company
195 Broadway
New York, NY 10007

COMSAT
Communications Satellite Corporation
950 L'Enfant Plaza
Washington, DC 20024

General Telephone & Electronics Corporation
One Stamford Forum
Stamford, CT 06611

ITT World Communications Inc.
67 Broad Street
New York, NY 10004

MCI Communications Corporation
1150 Seventeenth Street, N.W.
Washington, DC 20036

RCA Corportaion
30 Rockefeller Plaza
New York, NY 10020

TYMNET Inc.
20665 Valley Green Drive
Cupertino, CA 95014

United Telecommunications Inc.
Box 11315
Kansas City, MO 64112

Western Union Corporation
One Lake Street
Upper Saddle River, NJ 07458

8. Structured Programming

9. Programming Languages

10. Systems Analysis and Design

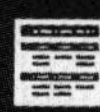

11. Database Management Systems, Management Information Systems, and Decision Support Systems

12. Operating Systems

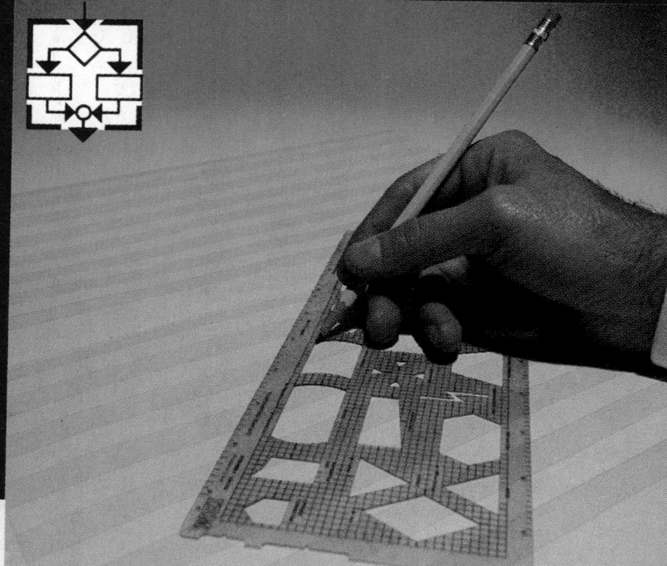

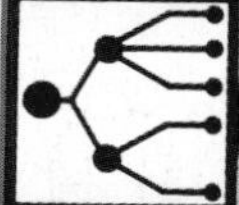

LAWS OF
PROJECT MANAGEMENT

1. No major project is ever installed on time, within budget or with the same staff that started it. Yours will not be the first.
2. Projects progress quickly until they become 90 percent complete, then they remain at 90 percent complete forever.
3. One advantage of fuzzy project objectives is that they let you avoid the embarrassment of estimating the corresponding costs.
4. When things are going well, something will go wrong.
   - When things just can't get any worse, they will.
   - When things appear to be going better, you have overlooked something.
5. If project content is allowed to change freely, the rate of change will exceed the rate of progress.
6. No system is ever completely debugged: Attempts to debug a system inevitably introduce new bugs that are even harder to find.
7. A carelessly planned project will take three times longer to complete than expected; a carefully planned project will take only twice as long.
8. Project teams detest progress reporting because it vividly manifests their lack of progress.

Part Three

Software

Without software a computer is just a marvelous device with great potential—it can't do very much. In Part Three we study software. What techniques help ensure good programs? How is pseudocode (fake code) used to develop programs (real code)? What is structured programming? Why take a structured walkthrough? How do we get bugs out of programs, and more importantly, how do we prevent them from creeping into programs in the first place?

What programming languages are used to produce software? Why has the computing profession created its own Tower of Babel? Why are most programs written in languages computers can't understand? Will there ever be an Esperanto (universal language) for programmers? When is it preferable to be "quick and dirty"? Why take a PIC? Is it difficult to write programs with a LISP? What does it mean for a language to be "very high"?

We'll show how the state-of-the-practice techniques of structured systems analysis and design are used to develop software systems. We'll discuss how to acquire software and consider the relative merits of developing versus buying software.

We'll see how database management systems, management information systems, and decision support systems help improve productivity. We'll see how VisiCalc, one of the most successful software packages of all time, helps managers plan.

We'll see how operating systems are designed to control and manage hardware and make it more "friendly" and usable to computer users.

"The computer company says call the software company. The software company says call service. Service says it's not in the contract; it's in the training manual. And nobody understands the training manual."

"We need the order-entry tracking system by the 1st. The budget consolidation in two weeks. The sales forecast next week. And the seating arrangement for my daughter's wedding by tomorrow."

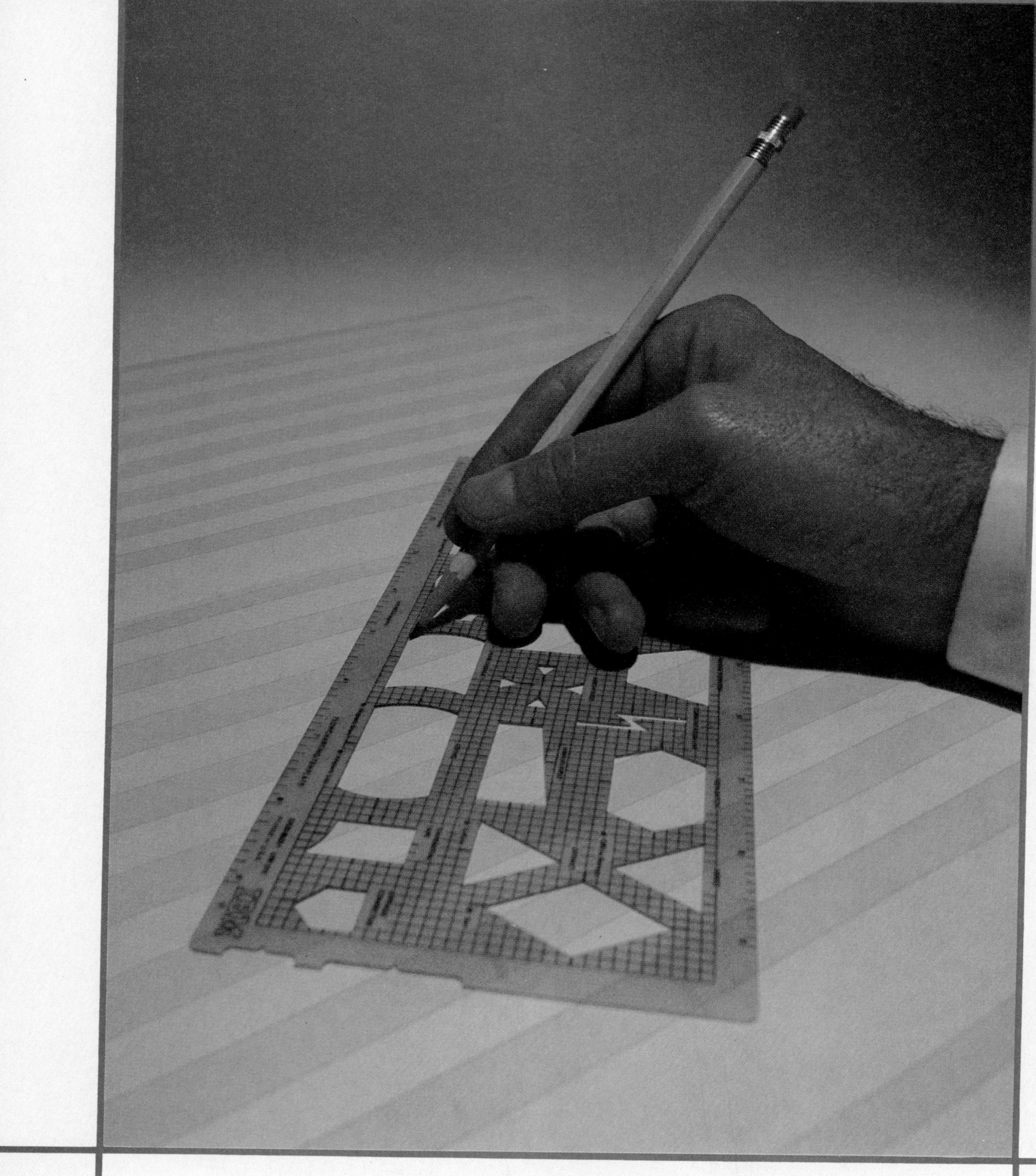

Chapter 8

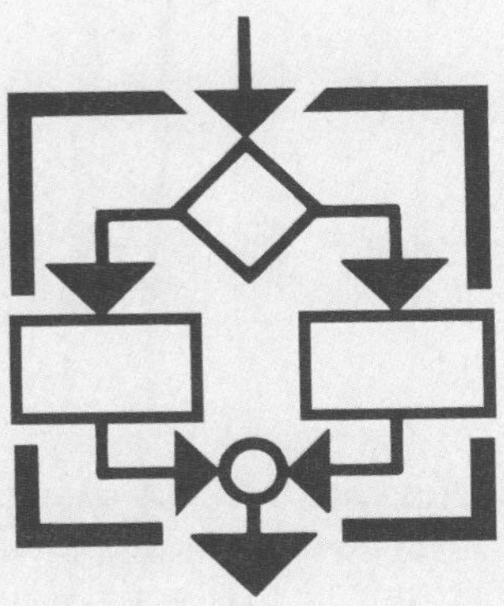

Structured Programming

After reading this chapter you will understand:

1. How computer programs are designed and what programming and design techniques help ensure good programs
2. What structured programming is and how sequence, selection, and repetition program structures are used to create structured programs
3. How flowcharting aids in program development
4. Why pseudocode has become a popular program development aid
5. How programming teams facilitate the development of large systems of programs

Left: Flowcharting helps programmers design their programs.

Outline

A debugged program is one for which you have not yet found the conditions that make it fail.
Jerry Ogdin

A computer is hardware, much as a movie projector is hardware. A computer program is software, much as a film to be shown on the movie projector is software. Films can be poorly made or they can be Academy Award winners; in this sense computer programs are similar to films.

What makes a program an Academy Award winner? In this chapter we will discuss computer programming and the practices that yield good programs. Our discussion involves the general principles of programming independent of any particular programming language. Nine case studies on important programming techniques are presented. We will look at the types of programming languages and some of the most popular ones in Chapter 9. Appendix A contains an extensive introduction to BASIC, the world's most widely used programming language. BASIC programs for each of the case studies in this chapter are presented.

What Is a Computer Program?

As we saw in Chapter 3, a computer program is a procedure followed by a computer to solve a specific problem. It is a listing of the steps, or operations, to be performed and an indication of the order, or sequence, in which those steps are to be performed to solve the problem. Correctly listing the steps and indicating the order is most important. Omitting even a single step or inserting an unnecessary one can make a program malfunction.

Computers are general-purpose instruments, just as movie projectors are. At one time a movie projector may show a space adventure film, at another time a documentary. The difference depends on which film is currently loaded. The same is true with computers. A computer may at one time perform a company's accounting tasks and at another time be used for playing games or making financial projections. Again, it depends on which program is loaded. After a given program is loaded into a computer's primary storage, the computer executes, or runs, the program. The computer performs the indicated operations correctly and in the proper sequence.

Computer programs are written in various **programming languages**. Regardless of the programming language used, a particular computer can only understand its own **machine language**. Programmers rarely write programs in machine language, however; the process is simply too tedious and susceptible to error. Thus, before most programs can be run on a computer, they must first be translated into machine language.

Programming languages have certain basic types of instructions in common. These include:

1. **Input instructions** that cause data to be read into the computer's primary storage from an input device, such as a keyboard, or from a secondary storage device, such as a disk.
2. **Output instructions** that cause data to be written from the computer's primary storage to an output device, such as a printer, or to a secondary storage device, such as a disk.
3. **Arithmetic instructions** that cause the computer to perform arithmetic operations such as addition, subtraction, multiplication, and division.
4. **Comparison instructions** that cause pairs of numbers to be compared to determine if one of the numbers is equal to, greater than, or less than the other.

 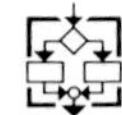

5. **Control instructions** that specify the order in which instructions are to be performed. This order often depends on the results of comparison instructions.
6. **Data movement instructions** that cause data items to be moved between locations in primary storage.
7. **Data definition instructions** that specify the data to be used by a program (for example, a count of the number of payroll checks processed, an average of a student's grades, or a report title).
8. **File and record definition instructions** that allow the programmer to specify which files of data will be processed by the program, which secondary storage devices contain these files, and what the characteristics of these files are. They also allow the programmer to specify what fields the records of each file contain (such as employee number, base salary, and number of dependents on a payroll file).

Programmers combine these instructions to produce programs that solve particular problems.

The Program Development Process

The several steps involved in writing good programs include: (1) studying the problem to be solved to determine what inputs are to be processed, what processing is to be performed, and what outputs are to be produced; (2) preparing **specifications** to describe precisely and clearly the problem to be solved; (3) developing the solution by using various design aids such as flowcharts and pseudocode to develop a solution to the problem (this is a gradual process often called **top-down stepwise refinement**); (4) writing the program by using a programming language appropriate for the type of problem (this step involves a number of clerical chores, such as typing the program into the computer and making simple edit corrections to fix misspelled items or insert omitted items); (5) testing and debugging the program (a program is tested to determine if it meets its specification; if it does not, **debugging** involves determining what is wrong and making the appropriate corrections, a process that continues until the program functions properly); (6) documenting the program (**documentation** is carried on throughout all phases of program development, but once a program is put into regular use—when it becomes a **production program**—it is important to have complete and accurate documentation. This helps other people understand the program and facilitates program modification).

The Program Design Phase

The phrase "think before you write" is especially important in programming. A carefully designed program is understandable, easy to manage and modify, and relatively free of bugs. Programs should be designed for efficiency, correctness, reliability, robustness, and maintainability.

They should be efficient; that is, they should execute quickly with minimal use of relatively expensive resources such as primary storage. They should be correct, in that they meet their specifications. Programs should be reliable in that they continue to operate under unforeseen circumstances. They should be robust in that they operate properly under a wide range of legitimate inputs, and they should be easy to modify.

Flowcharting

One of the most popular means for designing programs is through **flowcharting**. Symbols of various shapes are connected by **flowlines** ending in arrows to show the order of operations. The shapes of the symbols indicate the nature of the operations to be performed, and the flowlines designate the order in which the operations should be performed. Figure 8–1 shows some of the more frequently used flowcharting symbols; these are all that most people need to produce useful flowcharts (Figure 8–2). Figure 8–3 shows a plastic **flowcharting template** containing many more useful symbols. These symbols have been standardized for the industry by the American National Standards Institute (ANSI).

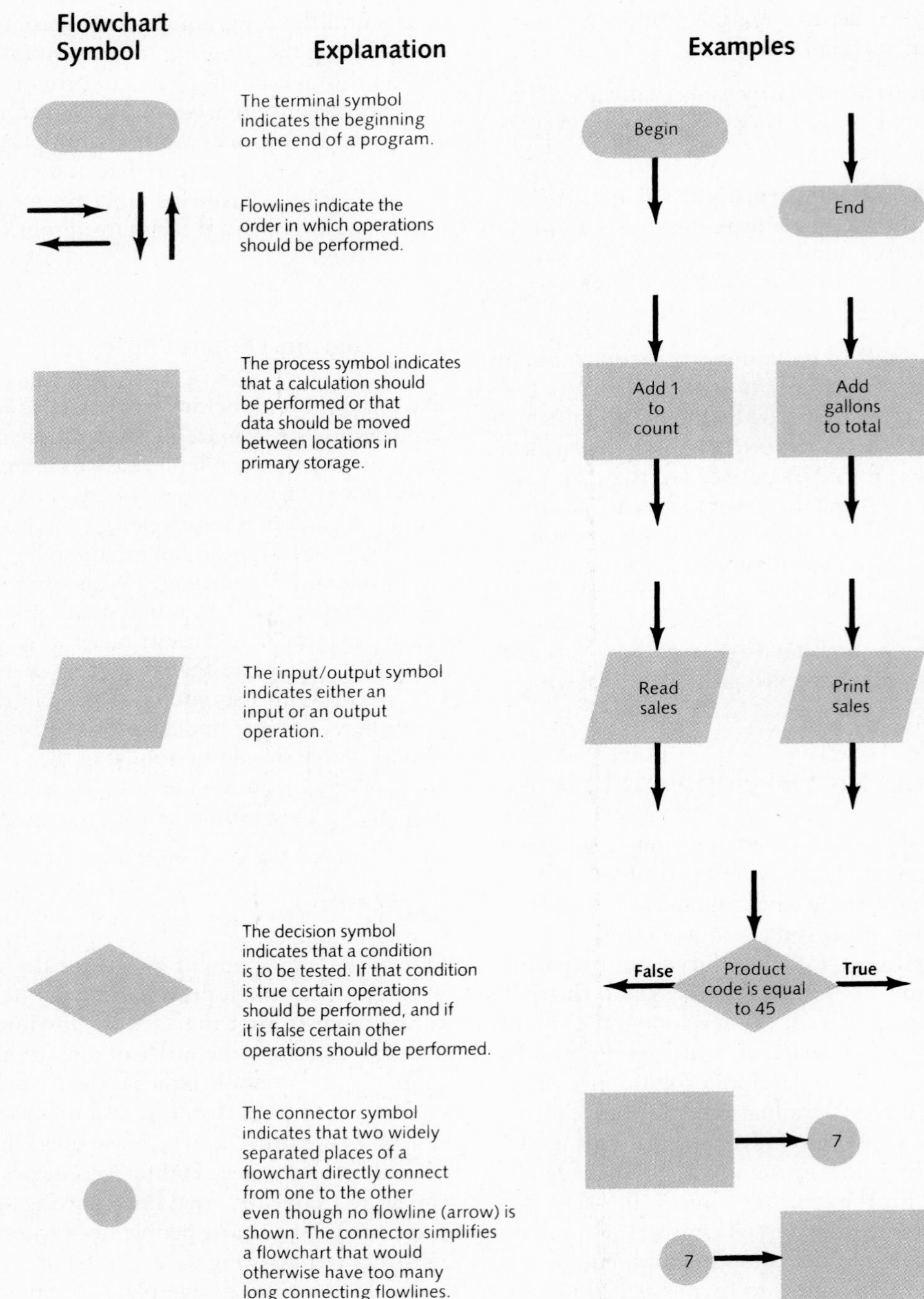
Flowchart Symbol
Explanation
Examples
The terminal symbol indicates the beginning or the end of a program.
Begin
End
Flowlines indicate the order in which operations should be performed.
The process symbol indicates that a calculation should be performed or that data should be moved between locations in primary storage.
Add 1 to count
Add gallons to total
The input/output symbol indicates either an input or an output operation.
Read sales
Print sales
The decision symbol indicates that a condition is to be tested. If that condition is true certain operations should be performed, and if it is false certain other operations should be performed.
False
Product code is equal to 45
True
The connector symbol indicates that two widely separated places of a flowchart directly connect from one to the other even though no flowline (arrow) is shown. The connector simplifies a flowchart that would otherwise have too many long connecting flowlines.
7
7

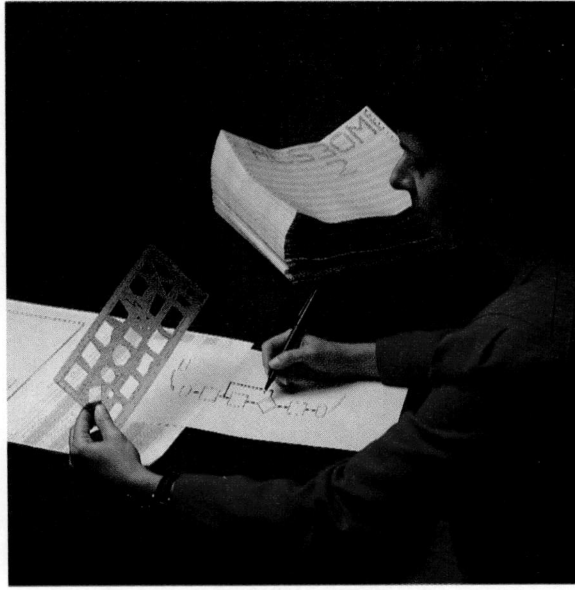

Figure 8–2 Programmers use a plastic flowcharting template to trace the shapes of the various symbols.

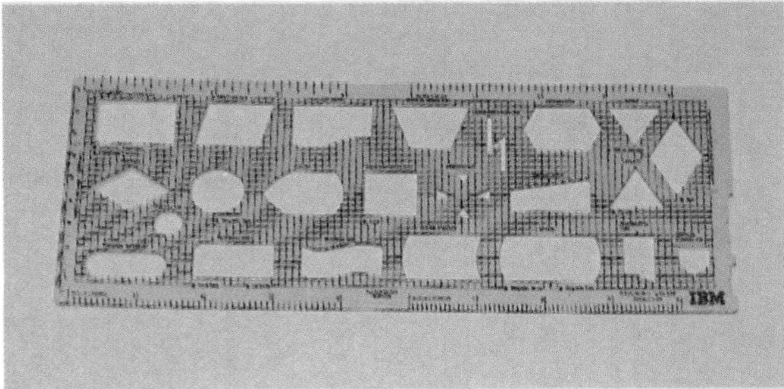

Figure 8–3 A flowcharting template.

The greatest benefit of flowcharting is that it graphically illustrates the decision-making operations in programs. The diamond-shaped decision symbol has two arrows leaving it, one to be followed when the condition in the diamond is false and the other to be followed when the condition is true. A **condition** is simply a comparison statement such as "count is greater than 10" or "inventory is less than reorder point." Figure 8–4 lists the comparison operations that may be used to write conditions in most programming languages.

Figure 8–1 *Left:* The most commonly used flowcharting symbols.

Flowcharting also has its problems. For example, flowcharts are time-consuming to draw, must often be completely redrawn when program changes are made, may not precisely represent the program, and may be out of date. Also, different programmers attempting to solve the same problem may produce dramatically different flowcharts.

Testing and Debugging

In computerese a **bug** is an error. Debugging simply means removing the errors from a program, but the process of debugging a program may not be simple at all.

Bugs may appear in a program before, during, or after the program is executed. Bugs that appear before execution are normally **syntax errors.** The syntax of a programming language is the set of rules that governs the writing of valid statements in that language. A syntax error occurs when a programmer writes an invalid statement. Simply misspelling a word of the language will cause a syntax error.

Run-time errors, or **execution errors**, occur while a program is executing. These can occur because of invalid or insufficient data read at execution time. Invalid data might, for example, cause a program to attempt to divide by zero, an operation that is forbidden on most computer systems. When a program requests data and none is available, possibly because the user failed to provide it, an insufficient-data error occurs.

Figure 8–4 The comparison operators. Note that three of the operators require two keystrokes each.

Comparison Operator	Meaning
=	"is equal to"
<>	"is not equal to"
>	"is greater than"
<	"is less than"
>=	"is greater than or equal to"
<=	"is less than or equal to"

Logic errors can be the most difficult errors to find because they do not always cause a program to terminate. Instead, the program runs to completion, and a sharp-eyed user may spot an error in the output reports. Worse yet, the error could go undetected. An example of a logic error is a mailing list program that prints addresses without zip codes. Such an error can be very costly to a mail-order company that has printed, sealed, and stamped a million catalogs! Another logic error is the failure of a payroll program to pay an employee time-and-a-half for overtime. Organizations designate certain people as **output controllers** to help spot these problems as early as possible.

The best way to locate bugs is to execute a program with a series of carefully designed test cases. We'll discuss testing and test case design in Chapter 10, "Structured Systems Analysis and Design; Systems Acquisition."

Ideally, programs should be made bug-free not by extensive testing and debugging but by writing the program correctly in the first place. The remainder of this chapter presents many of the techniques of structured programming that help to achieve this goal.

Structured Programming

During the 1960s one horror story after another emerged about major programming efforts taking much longer than anticipated, producing systems that were unreliable, and costing millions of dollars more than were budgeted. It became clear that programming would have to evolve from an art into a disciplined science if this situation were to improve.

Perhaps the real breakthrough came in 1966 when the mathematicians Bohm and Jacopini proved that the most complex program logic could be expressed by the use of three **control structures** (Figure 8–5): sequence, selection, and repetition.

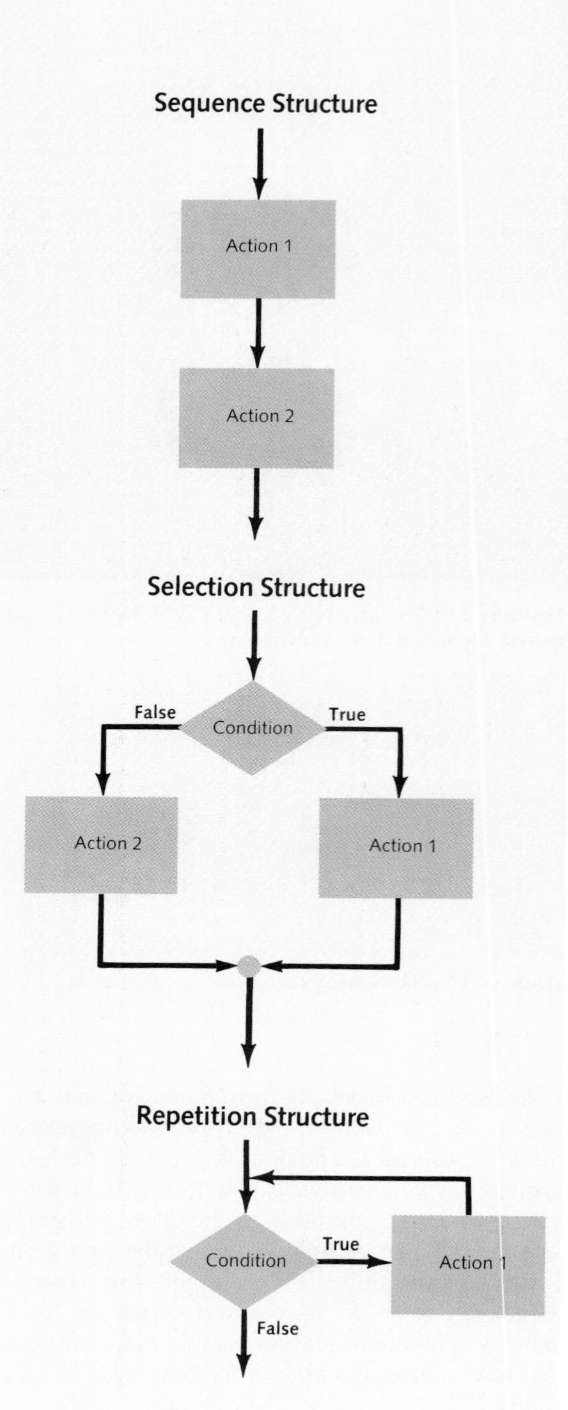

Figure 8–5 *Right:* The basic control structures.

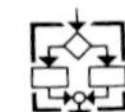

The **sequence structure** indicates that one operation is to be performed immediately after another, that is, in sequence. The **selection structure** designates that the operations to be performed in the future depend on whether a certain condition (such as "marital status is equal to single") is true or false. This structure indicates which actions are to be taken in each case. The **repetition structure** indicates that certain operations are to be repeated while some condition remains true (such as "more employee paychecks must be printed").

Programmers use these three simple structures as building blocks to construct neat, understandable programs—certainly a first step toward bringing discipline to programming. The proper use of these and of some closely related control structures is the key to the programming methodology called **structured programming**.

An important feature of these structures is that they each have only one entry point and one exit point, thus the term **single-entry, single-exit structures**. This helps make programs easier to read.

Before this structured approach was developed, programs were so individualized that one programmer might have had difficulty understanding another's programs. When a programmer left a project, that person's programs were sometimes scrapped and rewritten from scratch—a serious waste of resources. Documentation during the coding process helps to prevent this kind of waste.

Pseudocode

Flowcharting has been the primary program design aid for many years. Another technique, called **pseudocode**, is rapidly increasing in popularity. Also known as **structured English**, pseudocode allows a programmer to use English-like sentences to write an explanation of what a program is supposed to do. The programmer uses certain keywords in much the same manner as if writing in a structured programming language.

When a correction is made to a flowchart, the entire flowchart often must be redrawn. With pseudocode, however, the text can be maintained quite easily by a computerized text-editing program. Figures 8–6, 8–7, and 8–8 show pseudocode segments that correspond to each of the basic control structures. Systems that can automatically produce a neatly drawn structured flowchart from pseudocode have been developed.

Figure 8–6 An example of the sequence structure.

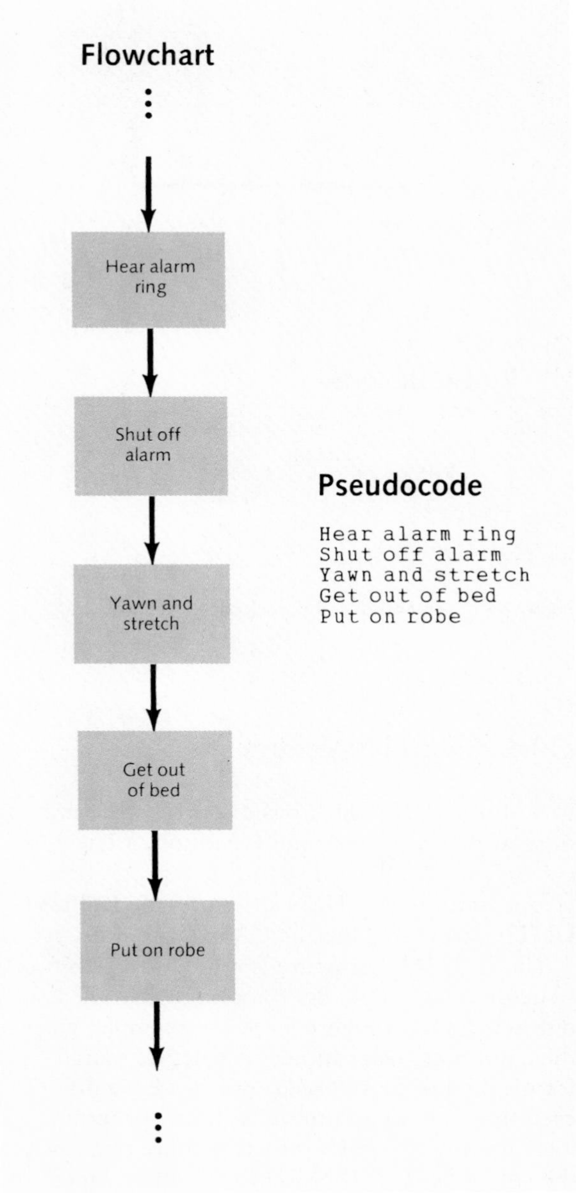

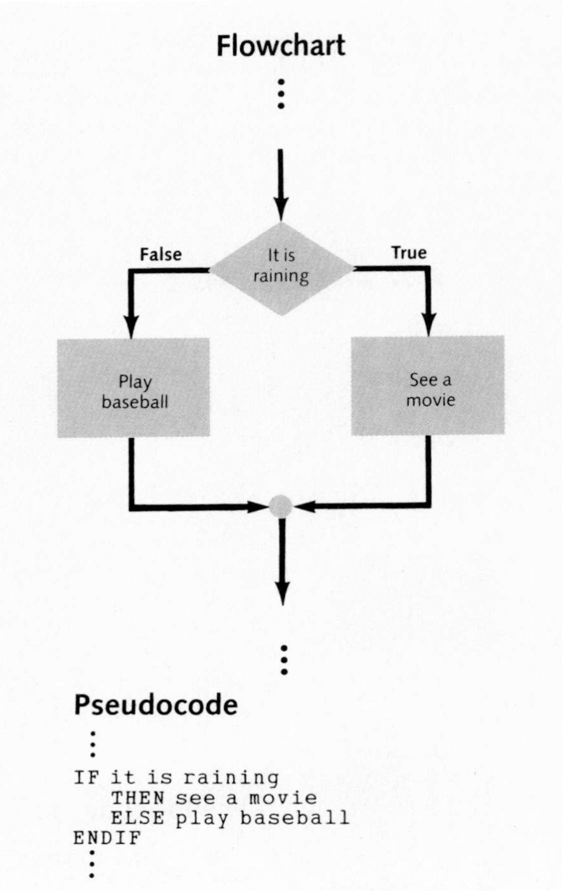

Figure 8–7 An example of the selection structure.

Flowchart

More subjects to do

True

Complete next subject's homework

False

Pseudocode

```
⋮
WHILE more subjects to do
   DO complete next subject's homework
ENDWHILE
⋮
```

Figure 8–8 An example of the repetition structure. This structure is often called the WHILE-DO, because WHILE the condition remains true the program will repeatedly DO a certain action.

Other Control Structures

In addition to the three basic control structures of sequence, selection, and repetition, a few others are commonly used to facilitate program development: the **IF-THEN structure**, the **REPEAT-UNTIL structure**, and the **CASE structure**.

The IF-THEN structure is a modified selection structure that simply does nothing when the condition is false. In Figure 8–9, for example, when the condition "it is raining" is true, we search frantically for an umbrella; otherwise we don't even think about an umbrella. Many programmers use the IF-THEN structure more often than the complete IF-THEN-ELSE structure, which might say, "IF it is raining THEN look for an umbrella, ELSE look for sunglasses."

The REPEAT-UNTIL structure (Figure 8–10) is a variation of the WHILE-DO structure of Figure 8–8 in which the test to determine if looping should continue is made after, rather than before, the action is performed. The REPEAT-UNTIL is useful when it is known in advance that the action will be performed at least once. The WHILE-DO should be used when the action may not have to be performed at all.

The CASE structure (Figure 8–11) is useful in selection situations in which the program must

 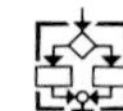

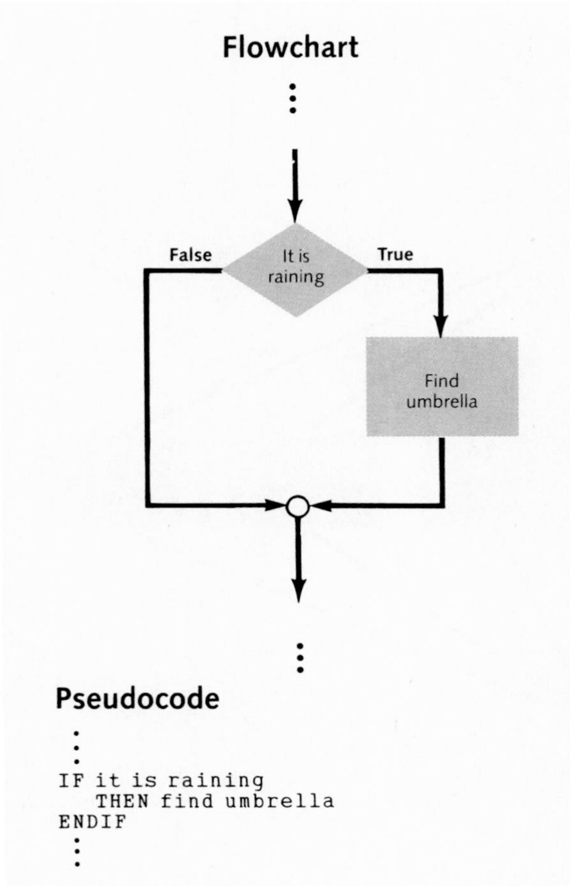
Flowchart
False
It is raining
True
Find umbrella
Pseudocode
IF it is raining
THEN find umbrella
ENDIF

Figure 8–9 An example of the IF-THEN structure.

Flowchart

Complete next subject's homework

No more subjects to do

False

True

Pseudocode

```
:
REPEAT complete next subject's homework
UNTIL no more subjects to do
:
```

Figure 8–10 Repetition with the REPEAT-UNTIL structure.

choose from more than two alternatives. For example, a program that keeps count of how many people fall into the various categories of marital status would need five separate alternative actions to account for people who are single, married, separated, divorced, or widowed. Some versions of the CASE structure, such as that shown in Figure 8–11, provide an ELSE alternative to handle errors.

GOTO Elimination

Built into each of the control structures is the use of the **transfer of control**, that is, the ability of a program to resume execution at some point in the program, possibly other than at the next instruction. In the sequence structure, control automatically transfers to the next instruction. In the selection structure, control transfers to one of two different areas in the program, depending on whether the condition being evaluated is true or false. In the repetition structure, control is transferred to the statements being repeated or to the next instruction in the program, also depending on whether the condition being evaluated is true or false.

Before these structures became widely used, programmers tended to make excessive use of the **GOTO statement** provided in most programming languages. GOTO simply causes a transfer of con-

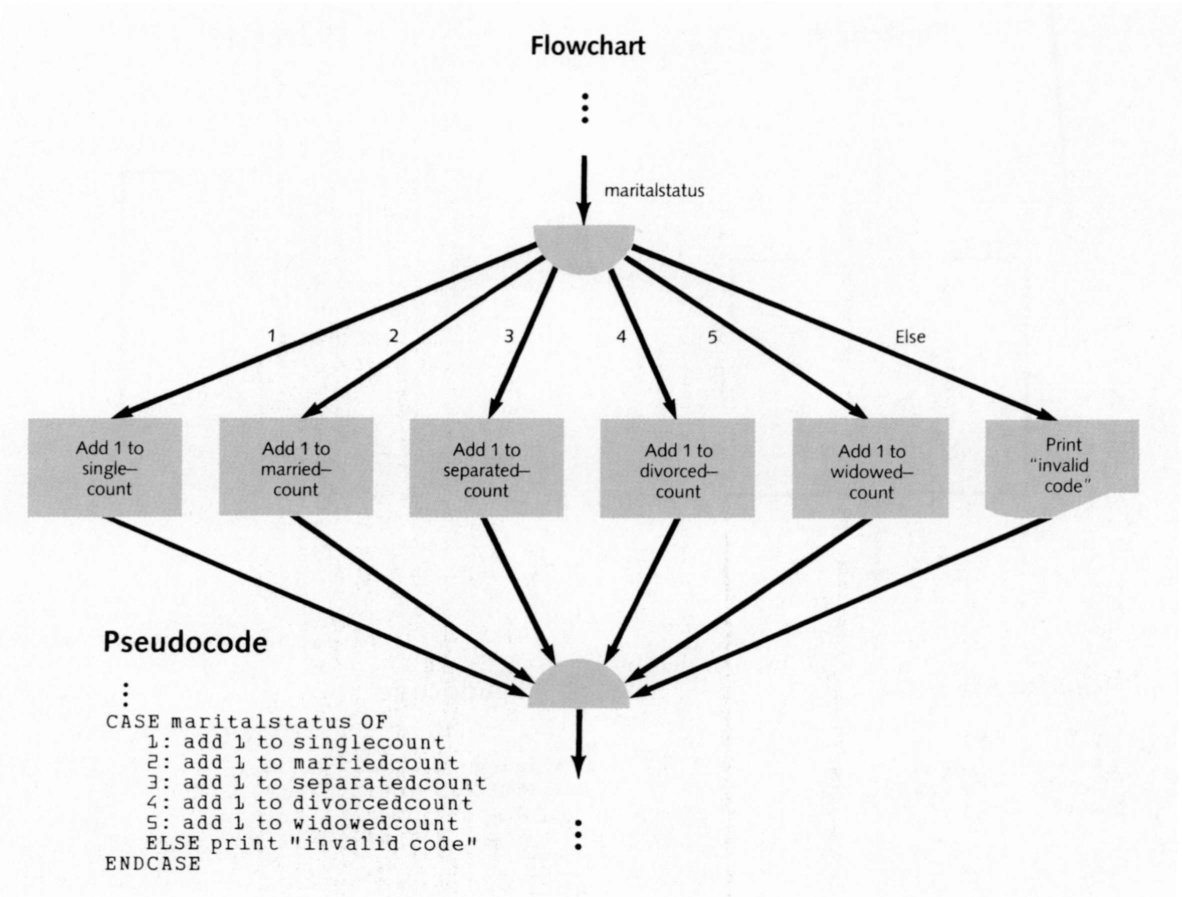

Figure 8–11 Selection with the CASE control structure.

trol to a designated place in the program. Using the GOTO indiscriminately results in programs with a rat's nest appearance, with flowcharts that contain arrows pointing in all directions. Such programs can be difficult to understand and especially difficult to debug.

Soon after publication of Bohm and Jacopini's conclusion about control structures, Edsger Dijkstra sent a letter to the *Communications of the ACM*, one of the leading professional journals in the computer field, in 1968. His letter, captioned "Go To Statements Considered Harmful," argued that the use of GOTO statements should be severely reduced, or even completely eliminated. Dijkstra suggested that this would prevent the production of "spaghetti code," in which the program flowchart is so complex and has so many crossing lines that it looks like a bowl of spaghetti. Programmers started taking this advice seriously, and significant improvements in programmer productivity and system reliability were reported on many large projects undertaken in the early 1970s. Many people equate "GOTO-less programming" with structured programming, but in some special cases even well-structured programs should use the GOTO.

In Chapter 10 we will discuss the techniques of structured systems analysis and structured systems design used in the development of large software systems.

 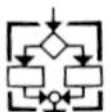

Ode to the Indomitable GOTO

I think that I shall never see
A program from all GOTO's free;
One that after such ablution
Is freed of every convolution
Whose nested modules at a look
Read exactly like a book.
A program saved from coder's guile
Replete with simples like DO-WHILE,
Of purest code whose modules tout
A single IN, a single OUT,
Exempt from all the sins of Sodom
And structured carefully from top-to-bottom.
Where dwells so potent a software genie
Worthy of Boehm and Jacopini?
Programs are made by fools like me—
Not even God is GOTO-free.*

—William J. Wilson

* In his first recorded GOTO in *Genesis* 11:7 he said, "Go to, let us go down, and there confound their language that they may not understand one another's speech."

Programming Psychology

For decades programming was viewed as an individual activity. With the frequency of large multiple-programmer projects in the late 1960s and early 1970s the goal was simply to produce a program that would work properly when plugged into the rest of the system.

Gerald Weinberg analyzed this attitude in his 1971 publication *The Psychology of Computer Programming* (New York: Van Nostrand Reinhold). He said that programmers tended to view their programs as extensions of themselves; they didn't want other people to examine their programs, were averse to criticism, and were reluctant to divulge their methods to other programmers. Weinberg proposed the notion of **egoless programming**, which he felt would foster a beneficial, cooperative spirit that would make programming a more open activity. Egoless programming encourages all members of a project to share their techniques and to review one another's work. Under egoless programming, project standards are more rigidly adhered to than under individual programming, and many obvious errors are removed much sooner and at much lower cost.

Structured Walkthroughs

Weinberg's concept of egoless programming led to the use of the **structured walkthrough**, a peer group review of an individual's work. The members of the programmer's working group (and often some outsiders) check for accuracy, adherence to standards, use of proper coding techniques, and the like. The review is intended to be constructive, but a programmer whose work is found inferior may suffer considerable embarrassment. The person being reviewed and the group as a whole will benefit, because errors may be corrected sooner and because better techniques will be learned in time for improvements to be made.

People tend to make a greater effort to produce better programs and adhere to standards if they know that their work will be carefully examined. Structured walkthroughs are not used universally, but they are becoming increasingly popular, especially in large organizations.

The Chief Programmer Team

The team concept of programming has many advantages but suffers from one key disadvantage: The designs that emerge from a team can lack **conceptual integrity**, or unity of design—that is, the system just doesn't seem to hang together. In the **chief programmer team** concept, as discussed by Baker and Mills[1] in 1973, the chief leads the team, and all the other team members function in support of the chief. The chief is responsible for the design decisions that shape the system, as well

1 Mills, H. D., and Baker, F. T., "Chief Programmer Teams," *Datamation*, Vol. 19, No. 12, December 1973, pp. 58–61.

as for coding, testing, debugging, and documenting the system. The team members support these functions under the strict supervision of the chief.

Fred Brooks, in his thoroughly entertaining work, *The Mythical Man Month* (Addison-Wesley, 1975), likens the chief programmer team to a surgical team in which the surgeon is supported by many specialists. The team members are (Figure 8–12):

The **chief programmer**, who does it all from problem definition to programming, testing, debugging, and even documentation. In every sense, the chief must be a "super programmer," most likely with 10 or more years' experience in computing, plus considerable expertise in the area of the application being designed.

The **copilot**, who serves as the alter ego of the chief. The copilot is less experienced than the chief but is able to take over in the chief's absence.

The **administrator**, a skilled person designated to handle administrative matters that the chief can't attend to because of limited time.

The **editor**, who frees the chief from much of the tedium of the clerical work, proofreading, and edit corrections associated with producing the documentation. The chief writes or dictates the generalized versions of the documentation.

Two **secretaries**, one to serve the administrator and the other to serve the editor.

The **program clerk**, who handles all inputs, outputs, program files, backup files, and the like.

The **toolsmith**, who constructs the special programs that support the chief's efforts. The toolsmith builds programs, called **utilities** or **software tools**, that make the chief's job easier.

The **tester**, who prepares test cases and appropriate test data to ensure that the programs written by the chief run properly.

The **language lawyer**, an expert in the structured programming language being used in the project.

The chief programmer team concept has grown in popularity since the early 1970s. The most serious problem with the concept is that chief programmers are hard to find: They must be both superior computing professionals and first-rate administrators. Copilots may be thought of as chief programmers in training; other team members may also eventually make it to the top.

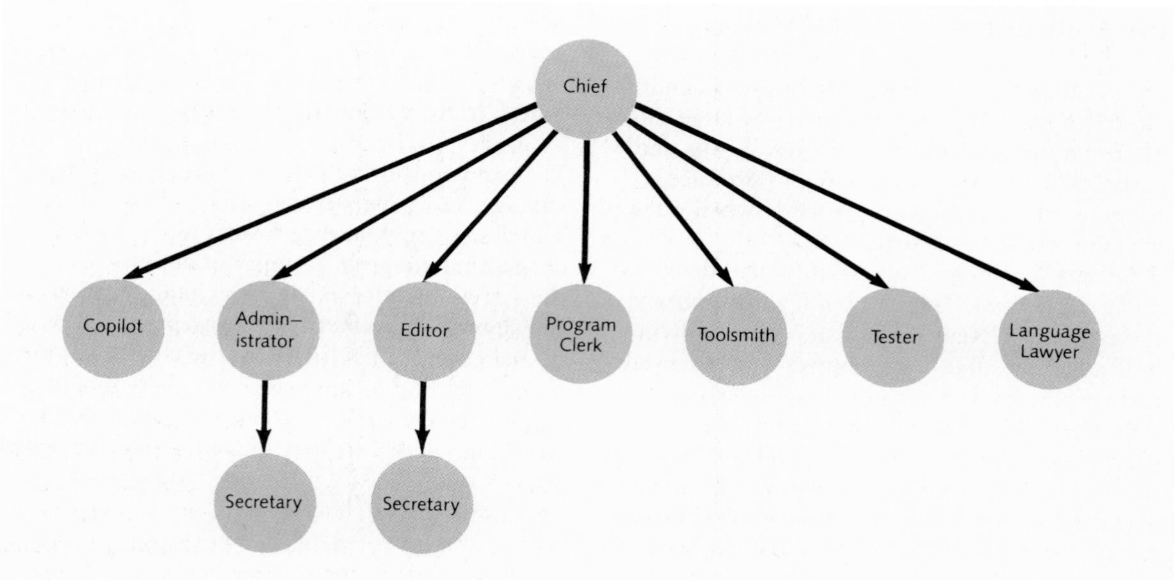

Figure 8–12 Chief programmer team structure.

 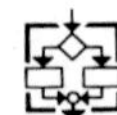

By nightfall, your entire program will be a total disaster.

Case Studies in Structured Program Development

In this section we present nine case studies designed to show the use of program structures, flowcharting, and pseudocode in structured program development. The case studies emphasize the **IPO method** (for input-processing-output), in which sample input data is shown, a structured flowchart and the corresponding structured pseudocode are presented to show what processing is to be performed, and the outputs that would be produced from the processing of the sample inputs are given. Each case study contains a narrative discussion as well as some brief exercises to try after reading the case study. These case studies serve as an important introduction to Appendix A on BASIC programming. In the appendix, we present the BASIC programs that correspond to each of the structured flowcharts and pseudocode examples in the case studies.

We show only finished flowcharts and pseudocode. Chapter 10 explains the gradual process of top-down stepwise refinement used to develop structured programs and systems of programs.

Case Study 8–1: Simple Decision Making

Problem Statement:

Develop a program that inputs two numbers and outputs the larger number followed by the message "is larger." Assume both numbers are different.

Discussion:

The solution is shown in Figure 1. The input/output symbol is used to indicate that two numbers are to be read. The variable names *A* and *B* are used; the first number is read into variable *A*, and the second number is read into *B*. By using variables in this manner, the program will work for any pair of numbers that is supplied.

A selection structure is used to determine which number is larger and to print the result. The decision symbol in this structure contains the condition "*A* is greater than *B*." This condition can be true if *A* is indeed greater than *B*, or it can be false. If the condition is true, the right flowline is followed to the symbol that prints the value of *A* followed by the message "is larger." If the condition is false, the left flowline is followed to the symbol that prints the value of *B* followed by the message "is larger." Whichever path is taken within the decision structure, the flowlines converge to a common point from which a single flowline directs the program to the end symbol.

We have used certain conventions in the pseudocode that will be used throughout the case studies. The name of the program is followed by a colon (:). BEGIN and END are used as "bookends" for the entire pseudocode procedure. The BEGIN and END are indented three spaces from the program name. The body of the program is then indented three more spaces from the BEGIN and END. Certain keywords in each of the structures are capitalized, in this example IF, THEN, ELSE, and ENDIF. Note that within the IF-THEN-ELSE structure, the THEN and ELSE portions are indented three spaces from the IF. The ENDIF is aligned directly below the IF. Even though pseudocode is informal, observing a reasonable set of

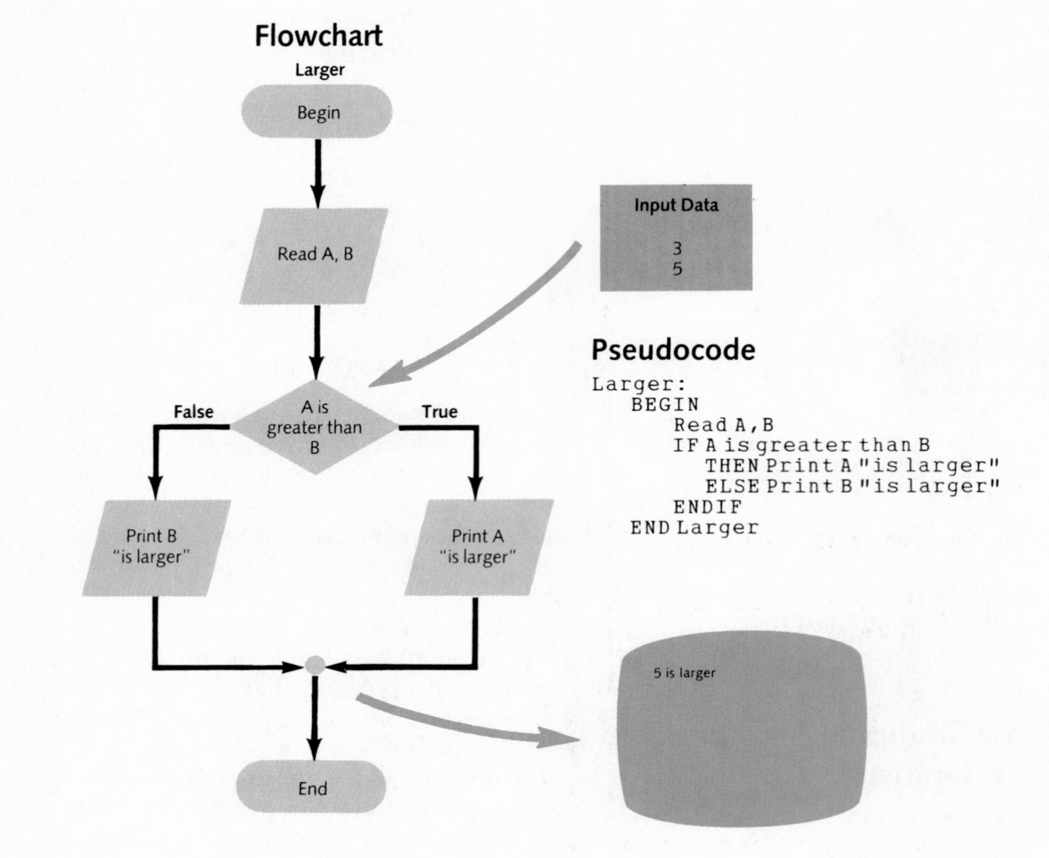

Figure 1 An example of the selection structure: finding the larger of two numbers.

conventions helps make the pseudocode more readable and useful, especially when it is being used on a project in which several programmers may read one another's pseudocode programs.

Exercises:

1. For the input data shown, which path is followed within the selection structure—the "true" part or the "false" part?
2. If the input data were 16 and 14, what output would be produced? Which path would be followed?

Case Study 8–2: Complex Decision Making

Problem Statement:

Develop a program that inputs three numbers and outputs the largest of the numbers followed by the message "is the largest." Assume that all three numbers are different.

Discussion:

The solution is shown in Figure 2. In the first case study we had to compare only two numbers, so just one decision operation was necessary. With three numbers, the decision process becomes more complicated because three comparisons must be made (we'll use a simpler technique than

 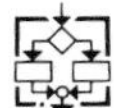

Flowchart

Largest

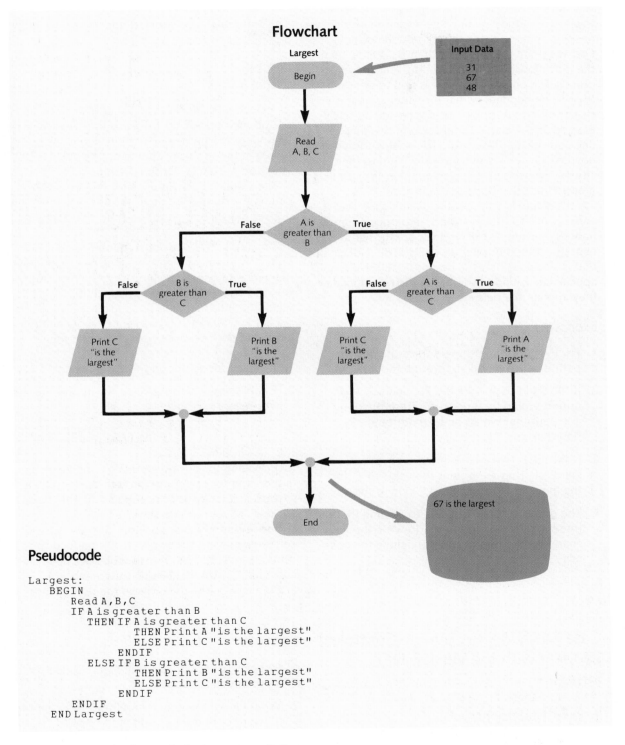

Input Data
31
67
48

Begin

Read
A, B, C

False
A is greater than B
True

False
B is greater than C
True

False
A is greater than C
True

Print C "is the largest"

Print B "is the largest"

Print C "is the largest"

Print A "is the largest"

End

67 is the largest

Pseudocode

```
Largest:
   BEGIN
      Read A,B,C
      IF A is greater than B
        THEN IF A is greater than C
              THEN Print A "is the largest"
              ELSE Print C "is the largest"
            ENDIF
        ELSE IF B is greater than C
              THEN Print B "is the largest"
              ELSE Print C "is the largest"
            ENDIF
      ENDIF
   END Largest
```

Figure 2 An example of a nested selection structure: finding the largest of three numbers.

this in Case Study 8–6). Let's trace one of the decision-making paths through the flowchart. First we test if "*A* is greater than *B*." If it is, then the right flowline is followed. This leads to another selection structure that is said to be nested (that is, embedded) within the outer selection structure. This is simply called a nested IF-THEN-ELSE structure and is common in more complex decision-making situations. The **nested structure** now tests if "*A* is greater than *C*." If it is, then clearly *A* must be the largest number because it is greater than *B* and greater than *C*.

Let's carefully consider the pseudocode that corresponds to this flowchart. In particular, note how the nested IF-THEN-ELSEs are further indented within the outer IF-THEN-ELSE. Notice that in the flowchart the nested IF-THEN-ELSEs appear side by side, whereas in the pseudocode they appear one below the other.

Exercises:

1. For the input data shown, trace the precise path that will be taken through the flowchart.
2. If the input data were 82, 76, and 55, what output would be produced? Trace the precise path that would be taken through the flowchart.
3. Notice that two of the flowchart symbols are identical: They both print the value of *C* and the message "is the largest." Why is this so?
4. The problem statement said to assume that the three numbers are different. Rewrite the flowchart and the pseudocode to handle the possibility of a tie.

Case Study 8–3: Counter-Controlled Looping with the WHILE-DO Structure

Problem Statement:

Develop a program that prints the numbers from 1 to 10. Use a single print statement that prints a single number at a time. Use the WHILE-DO repetition structure.

Discussion:

The solution is shown in Figure 3. The restriction on the print statement forces us to repeat the execution of the print statement 10 times. As required in the problem statement, the WHILE-DO structure is used to control the repetition.

The variable *count* is used for two purposes. It counts the number of times through the loop, and it gives the successive values from 1 to 10 to be printed.

Obviously, we may use a counter to control a loop only when we know in advance exactly how many repetitions of the loop are required. Later in the case studies we'll see how to control loops when this information is not available.

Four key ingredients appear in every counting loop, and each of these is shown in the figure:

1. Defining a counter (in this case, "count")
2. Establishing a starting value for the counter (in this case, 1)
3. Establishing and testing for a terminating value for the counter (in this case, 10)
4. Providing for the adjustment of the value of the counter each time through the loop by a certain increment or decrement (in this case, 1)

Notice that the DO portion of the WHILE-DO contains several statements. This is perfectly acceptable in all the control structures we have discussed in this chapter. These statements are aligned one below the other in the pseudocode.

Exercises:

1. Notice that the flowchart in Figure 3 does not input any data. Why?
2. What would this program print if "Set count to 1" were changed to "Set count to 5"?
3. What would this flowchart print if "Add 1 to count" were changed to "Add 2 to count"?

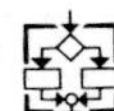

Flowchart

Countingloop 1

Begin

Set count to 1

Count is less than or equal to 10

True

Print count

Add 1 to count

False

End

1
2
3
4
5
6
7
8
9
10

Pseudocode

```
Countingloop1:
    BEGIN
        Set count to 1
        WHILE count is less than or equal to 10
            DO Print count
               Add 1 to count
        ENDWHILE
    END Countingloop1
```

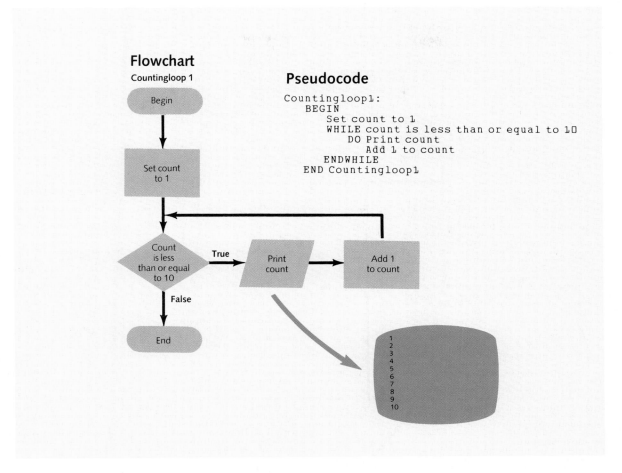

Figure 3 An example of a counter-controlled loop using the WHILE-DO structure.

4. Suppose you wanted the flowchart to print all the whole numbers from 1 to 1 million. What would you change?

Case Study 8–4: Counter-Controlled Looping with the REPEAT-UNTIL Structure

Problem Statement:

Modify the program developed in Case Study 8–3 to control the looping with a REPEAT-UNTIL structure instead of the WHILE-DO structure.

Discussion:

The solution is shown in Figure 4. Here, too, notice that the body of the REPEAT-UNTIL contains several statements. Again, this is perfectly acceptable with all the control structures we have discussed.

The WHILE-DO structure first tests to see if looping should continue, and if it should the body of the loop is executed. The REPEAT-UNTIL structure performs the body of the loop first and then makes the test. The WHILE-DO continues looping as long as the test condition remains true. The REPEAT-UNTIL, on the other hand, continues looping as long as the condition remains false. Thus, the condition we use in the REPEAT-UNTIL decision symbol is the opposite of the condition we used in the WHILE-DO decision symbol.

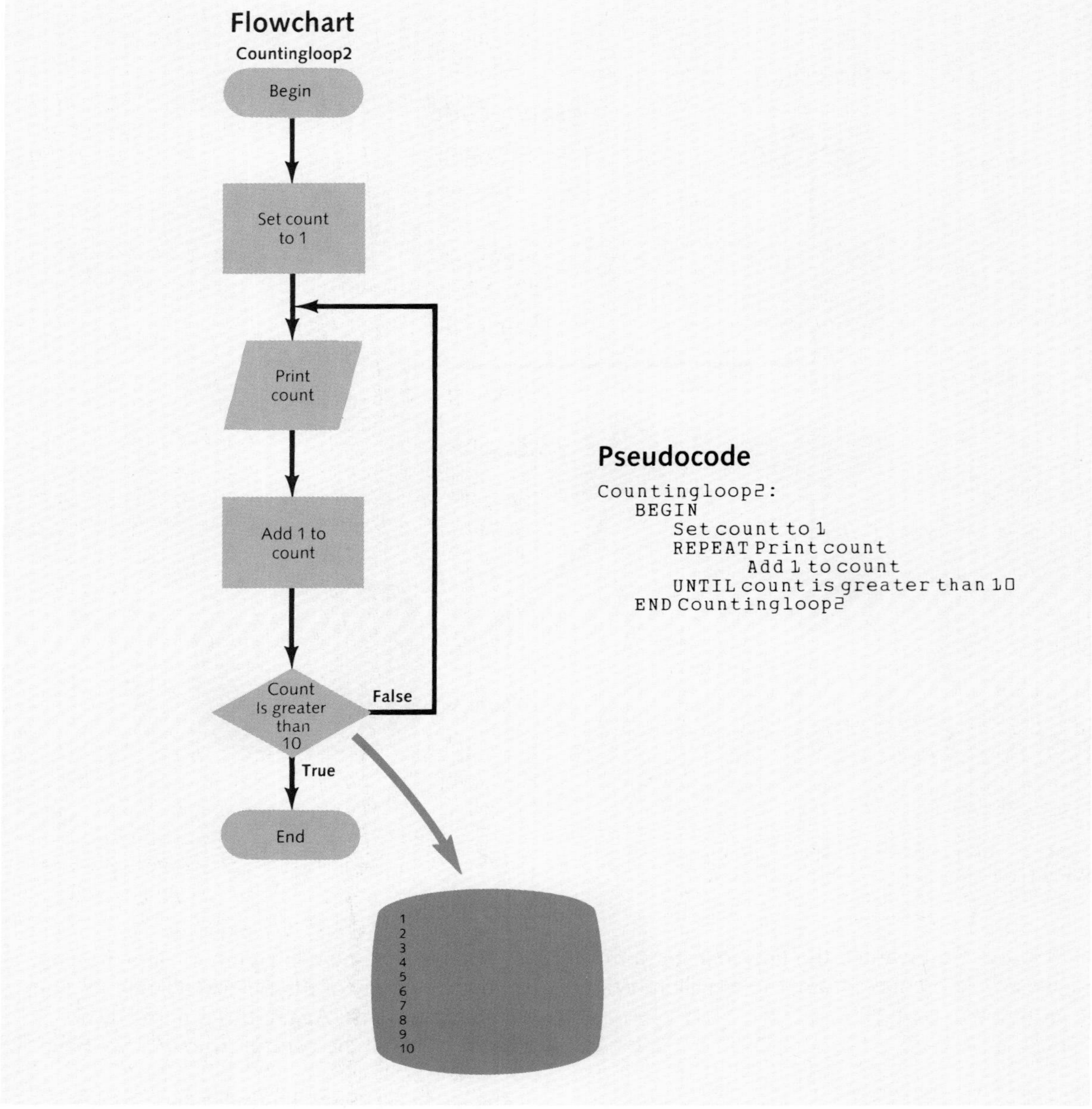
Flowchart
Countingloop2
Begin
Set count to 1
Print count
Add 1 to count
Count Is greater than 10
False
True
End
1
2
3
4
5
6
7
8
9
10
Pseudocode
Countingloop2:
BEGIN
Set count to 1
REPEAT Print count
Add 1 to count
UNTIL count is greater than 10
END Countingloop2

Figure 4 An example of a counter-controlled loop using the REPEAT-UNTIL structure.

Exercises:

1. Which method of implementing a counter-controlled loop do you prefer, the WHILE-DO or the REPEAT-UNTIL? Why?
2. Modify the flowchart and the pseudocode so that instead of printing the numbers from 1 to 10 with an increment of 1, they will print the numbers from 20 to 2 with a decrement of 2.

 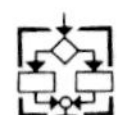

Case Study 8–5: Counting, Totaling, and Averaging with a Sentinel-Controlled Loop

Problem Statement:

Develop a program that reads a series of numeric grades for a student and produces that student's grade point average. The number of grades is not known in advance. The program should determine that it has finished reading grades when it encounters the **sentinel value** (that is, the special marker) −1. Use the WHILE-DO structure to control repetition.

Discussion:

The solution is shown in Figure 5. Because the WHILE-DO loop must begin with a test, the loop must be preceded by a symbol that reads the first number. The WHILE-DO decision will process this number only if it is not the sentinel −1. In the example shown, the program will loop five times to process the student's grades. At the end of the fifth pass through the loop, the sentinel will be read and the program will go on to print the total and the average of the student's grades.

Notice that the DO-part of the WHILE-DO ends with a second read statement. This obtains the next number in preparation for the return to the WHILE-DO decision.

Each time we pass through the loop, we add 1 to the count to keep track of how many grades have been processed, and the current grade is added to a total of all the grades. This total will be divided by the count to produce the average.

Exercises:

1. Notice the use of the value −1 for the sentinel indicating "end of data." Would 1.0 have been an acceptable sentinel for this problem? Why? State a rule for determining an appropriate sentinel for a given set of data.
2. How many times is the condition "number not equal to −1" tested in this program for the given input data?
3. Why couldn't we remove the "Read number" symbol from inside the loop and redirect the flowline entering it to the top flowline entering the "Read number" symbol before the loop? Wouldn't this be more efficient in the sense that duplicate symbols would be eliminated?

Case Study 8–6: Finding the Largest of a Series of Numbers with a Sentinel-Controlled Loop

Problem Statement:

Develop a program that reads a series of two or more numbers representing the weights of several football players trying out for a team. The coach needs one more player and wants to choose the heaviest candidate. Your program should determine and print the weight of the heaviest candidate followed by the message "is the largest." Assume no two candidates weigh the same.

Discussion:

If we attempt to use the technique of Case Study 8–2, we will wind up with a hopelessly complex flowchart. In fact, because we don't know the number of players, we aren't even able to write the flowchart unless we "overprovide" decision symbols to handle the largest possible number of players. We need a better technique. The solution is shown in Figure 6.

The first value is read directly into the variable *largest*. This certainly makes good sense. After reading only one value it is clearly the "largest so far." Each of the remaining values is read, one at a time, into the variable *number*. After a value is read into number, number is compared to largest. If it is larger, then we have found a new largest value, so we move number to largest. If, on the other hand, number is not larger than largest, we simply ignore this number and go on to read the next one. This is the familiar IF-THEN structure that does nothing if the condition is false.

Note again the use of the "Read number" input symbols both before the loop and as the last symbol inside the loop.

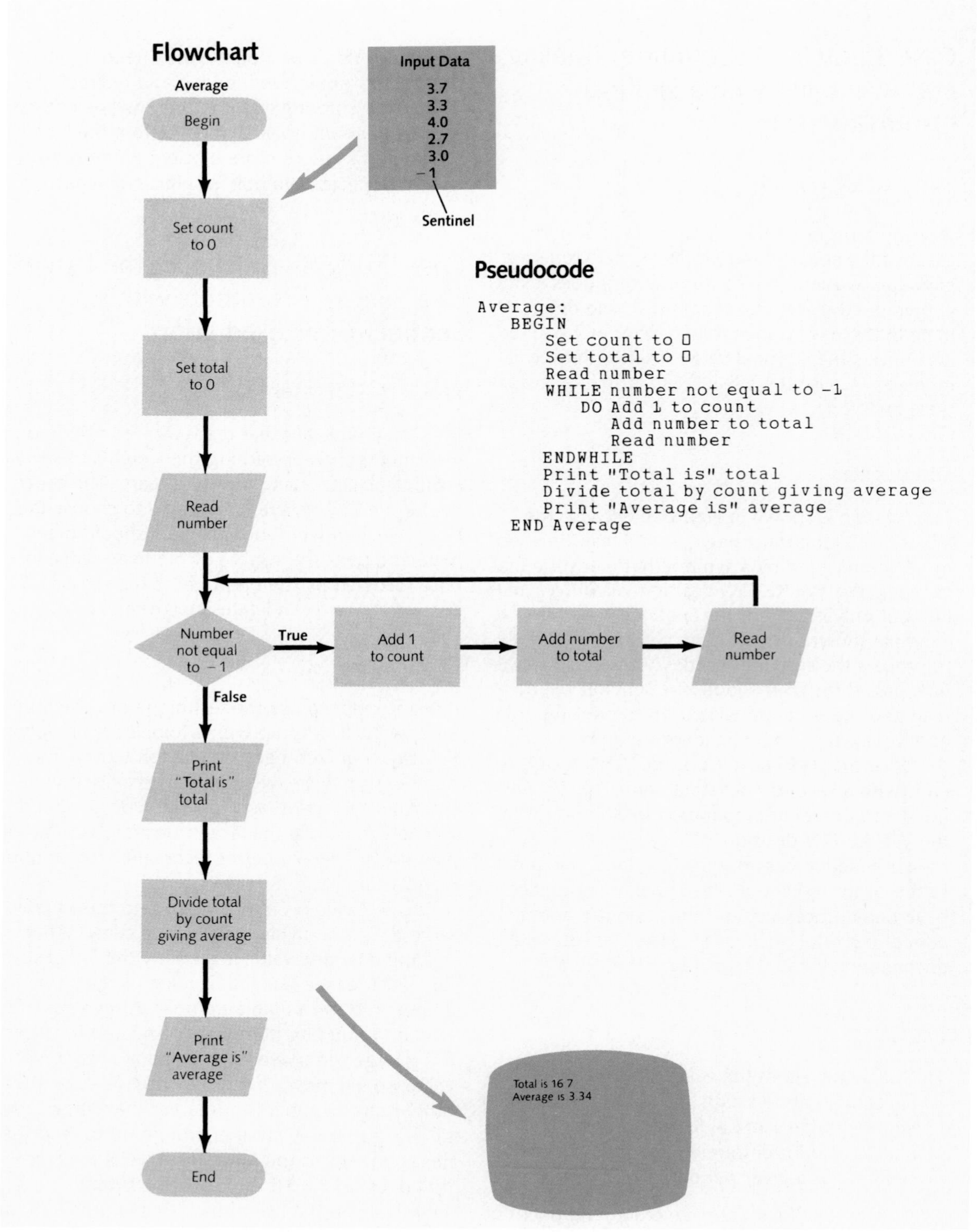

Flowchart

Average

Begin

Set count to 0

Set total to 0

Read number

Number not equal to −1

True

Add 1 to count

Add number to total

Read number

False

Print "Total is" total

Divide total by count giving average

Print "Average is" average

End

Input Data

3.7
3.3
4.0
2.7
3.0
−1

Sentinel

Pseudocode

```
Average:
   BEGIN
      Set count to 0
      Set total to 0
      Read number
      WHILE number not equal to -1
          DO Add 1 to count
             Add number to total
             Read number
      ENDWHILE
      Print "Total is" total
      Divide total by count giving average
      Print "Average is" average
   END Average
```

Total is 16.7
Average is 3.34

Figure 5 An example of a sentinel-controlled loop using the WHILE-DO structure: finding the total and average of a series of numbers.

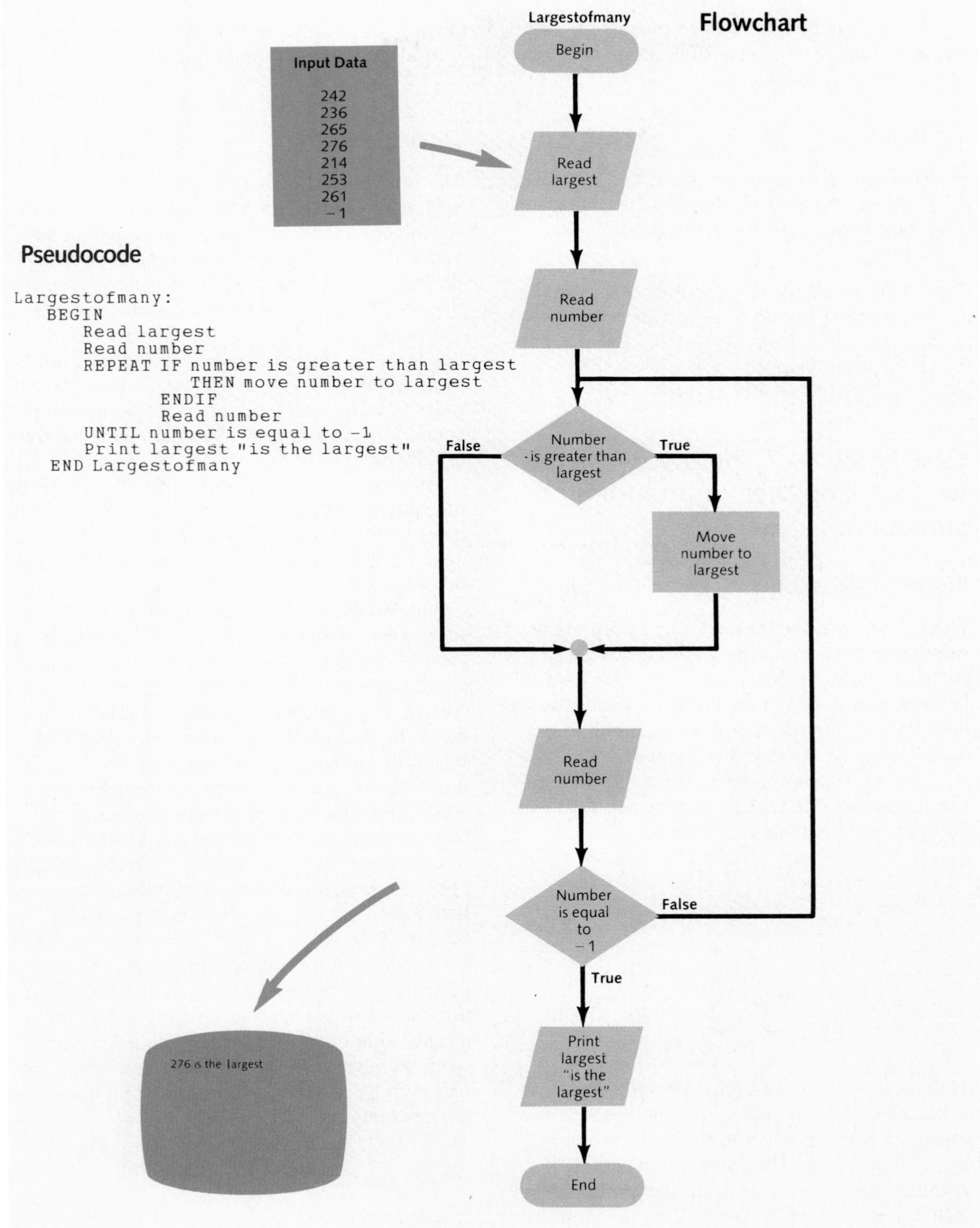


```
Largestofmany:
   BEGIN
      Read largest
      Read number
      REPEAT IF number is greater than largest
                THEN move number to largest
             ENDIF
             Read number
      UNTIL number is equal to -1
      Print largest "is the largest"
   END Largestofmany
```

Figure 6 An example of a sentinel-controlled loop using the REPEAT-UNTIL structure: finding the largest of two or more numbers.

After all numbers have been processed, the value remaining in largest is printed followed by the message "is the largest."

Exercises:

1. How would this program have to be modified to handle 1000 input values rather than simply 7 as shown in the example? Explain your answer.
2. Modify the flowchart and the corresponding pseudocode so that they find and print the two largest values. *Hint*: Use an additional variable called secondlargest.

Case Study 8–7: Piecework Payroll for One Employee: Introducing Subroutines

Problem Statement:

To provide incentive for their employees, many companies base employee wages on so-called piecework rates by which employees are paid a fixed amount for each item they produce. The pay rates vary according to the time required to produce each item. An item that requires more time is paid at an appropriately higher piecework rate. The piecework rate table shown below is used in this and the remaining case studies.

Item Code	Piecework Rate
13	.85
18	1.05
21	.55
42	.80
57	.60
64	.45

As you can see, six different types of items are produced by this company. An employee can earn anywhere from 45 cents to $1.05 for producing one of these items. The company maintains counts of the quantity of each item produced by each employee each week. Assume the input data is in the form shown in Figure 7; the information on only one employee is to be processed. The output should be in the form shown in the figure.

Discussion:

The solution is shown in Figure 7. We use a sentinel-controlled loop because the number of records for each employee is not known in advance. The sentinel 999 in the employee field indicates "end of data." We have placed zeros in the item and quantity fields for employee 999.

The program begins by printing the report headings. In the actual program written in a real programming language, the precise contents of these heading lines would have to be spelled out column by column so the program would know exactly what to print.

There are two heading lines. The first prints the report title "PIECEWORK PAYROLL REPORT," the date, and the page number. The second line of headings labels the columns of numbers that will be produced.

The variable *employeepay* is **initialized** (that is, set to a beginning value) to zero. The processing then proceeds one record at a time. Each record contains three fields: the employee number, the item number, and the quantity of that item produced by that employee. The WHILE-DO loop then loops as long as the employee is not the sentinel 999. For a given record, the program must search the table of item codes and piecework rates to determine the rate to pay for that item. In this flowchart we have indicated the lookup operation in a **predefined process symbol**—a rectangle with vertical bars near its left and right borders. Thus, instead of showing how the lookup is actually done, we have merely stated that it is done by a predefined process, namely, by another program segment specifically designed by this programmer or someone else to find the piecework rate that corresponds to a given item code. This is an example of a **subroutine** call. We would write something like

```
Call Lookup(item,rate)
```

in a real programming language. The computer would then automatically execute the Lookup

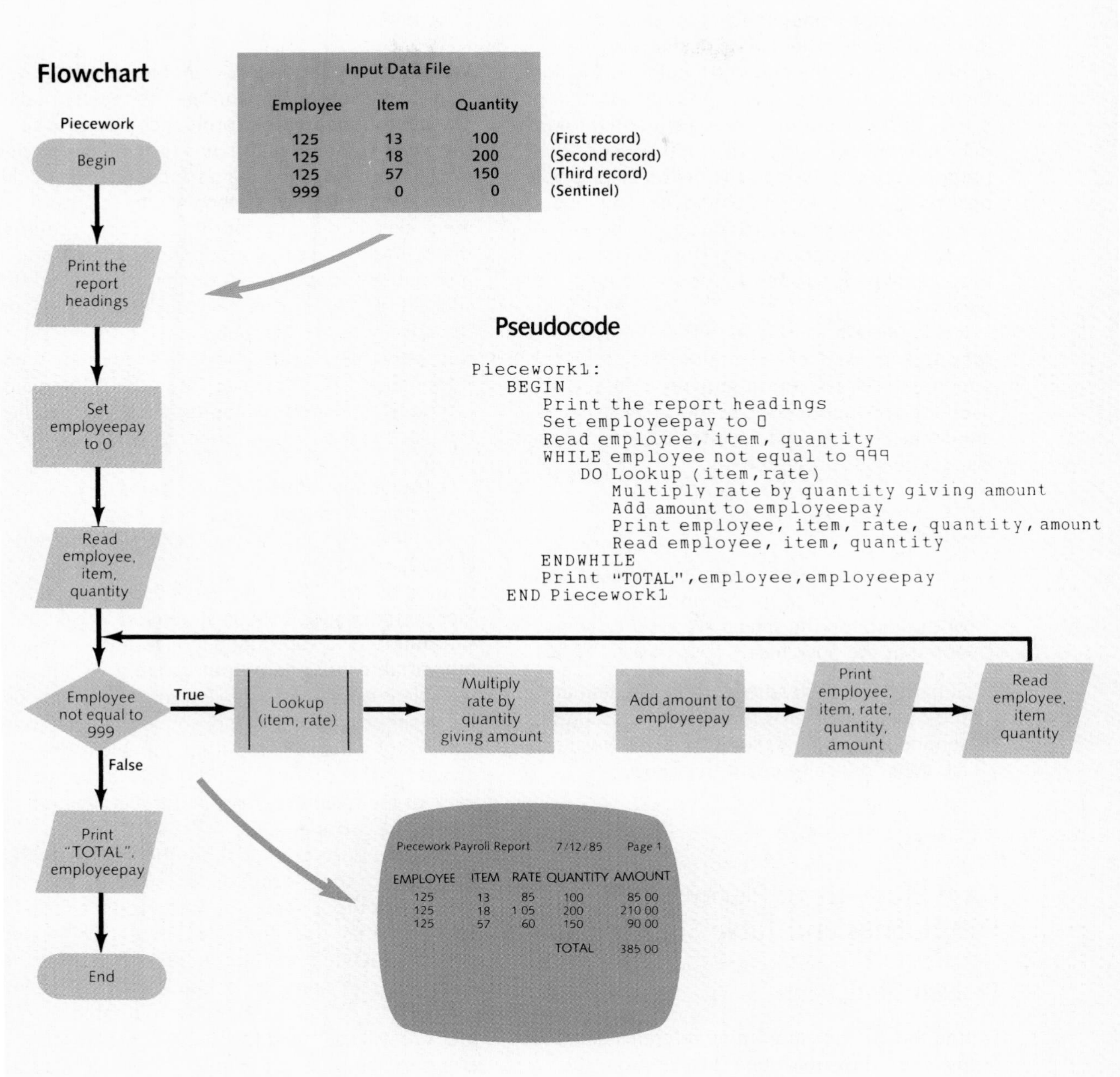
Flowchart
Input Data File
Employee Item Quantity
125 13 100 (First record)
125 18 200 (Second record)
125 57 150 (Third record)
999 0 0 (Sentinel)
Piecework
Begin
Print the report headings
Set employeepay to 0
Read employee, item, quantity
Employee not equal to 999
True
False
Lookup (item, rate)
Multiply rate by quantity giving amount
Add amount to employeepay
Print employee, item, rate, quantity, amount
Read employee, item quantity
Print "TOTAL", employeepay
End
Pseudocode
Piecework1:
BEGIN
Print the report headings
Set employeepay to 0
Read employee, item, quantity
WHILE employee not equal to 999
DO Lookup (item,rate)
Multiply rate by quantity giving amount
Add amount to employeepay
Print employee, item, rate, quantity, amount
Read employee, item, quantity
ENDWHILE
Print "TOTAL",employee,employeepay
END Piecework1
Piecework Payroll Report 7/12/85 Page 1
EMPLOYEE ITEM RATE QUANTITY AMOUNT
125 13 85 100 85 00
125 18 1 05 200 210 00
125 57 60 150 90 00
TOTAL 385 00

Figure 7 Piecework payroll for one employee.

subroutine, perform the lookup operation, and return to the first statement after the Call in the main program. Subroutines help in writing programs in a modular fashion as a collection of carefully designed program pieces called **modules**. The choice of how to modularize a program requires great care; we'll discuss this further in Chapter 10. (The Lookup subroutine is presented in the next case study.)

After Lookup finds the rate that corresponds to the item, the program multiplies this rate by the quantity produced by the employee to determine the amount of money the employee earned producing the item. Then a line of the report is printed showing the employee number, the item, the rate for the item, the quantity of the item produced, and the amount of money earned for producing items of this type during the week. The program goes on to read the next record for the next type of item for this employee. The loop continues until the sentinel value 999 is read. At this point the program prints the total earnings of this employee for all items produced during the week.

It is important to note here that the actual spacing and arrangement of information on the screen or a printed report requires a great deal of planning and careful specification. These issues are discussed further in Chapter 10 and in Appendix A on BASIC programming.

Exercises:

1. Carefully consider the output shown in Figure 7. What aspects of the columnar arrangement of this data on the screen are essentially ignored in the flowchart?
2. Suppose that instead of setting the item and the quantity to zeros for employee 999 (the sentinel), we simply didn't supply any values at all. What difficulty might this cause?

Case Study 8–8: Piecework Payroll: Subroutines and Table Searching

Problem Statement:

Design the Lookup subroutine referenced in Case Study 8–7. This subroutine is called from the main program by the statement

Call Lookup(item,rate)

The variable *item* is supplied to the subroutine. The subroutine determines the variable *rate* by searching the table for a match on the item code and then reading out the appropriate rate.

Discussion:

We're actually tackling two problems here: how to design a subroutine and how to search a table. The subroutine that performs these functions is shown in Figure 8. It contains program structures similar to those in the main program. The key difference is the **Return statement**, the last statement executed in any subroutine. Return causes the main program to continue executing at the first statement after the statement that called the subroutine. This return mechanism is handled automatically by the computer. Each time the subroutine is called (and it may be called many times from many different places throughout the main program), the computer automatically remembers the place in the main program to which it is to return.

A frequently referenced section of code is normally made into a subroutine simply to save space. It is only necessary to write the complete subroutine once. Whenever the function performed by the subroutine is needed, the programmer merely writes a single statement to call the subroutine. The subroutine in Figure 8 has one **input variable** and one **output variable.** An input variable is one that is supplied to a subroutine by the main program; in our example the item code is an input variable. An output variable is one with a value that is set by the subroutine and passed back to the main program; in our example rate is an output variable.

The pseudocode for a subroutine begins with the name of the subroutine, followed by a list of input and output variables, followed by a colon (:). Other than that, the only difference between the pseudocode for a subroutine and that for the main program is the use of the Return statement.

Now let's consider the problem of **table searching**. We will use two tables, sometimes called **arrays** in computerese (Figure 9). A table is a list of related data entries. Our first table is called tableitem; it contains the six different item codes. Notice that we have padded the table with a nonexistent entry 99, which is the sentinel value that indicates "end of table." Actually, a table is like a series of storage locations. The address of the first item is tableitem(1). The value associated with this location in the table is 13. The value of table-

Flowchart

Pseudocode

```
Lookup(item, rate):
   BEGIN
      Set index to 0
      REPEAT Add 1 to index
      UNTIL tableitem(index) equals item
      Move tablerate(index) to rate
      Return
   END Lookup
```

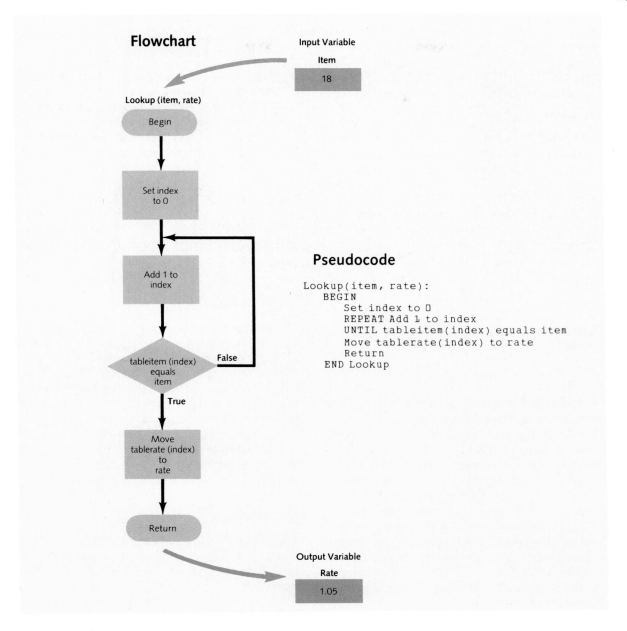

Figure 8 A lookup subroutine.

item(4) is 42. The value of tableitem(7) is 99, the sentinel value. The tablerate table contains the rates that correspond to the items in the tableitem table. The value of tablerate(3) is .55 and the value of tablerate(6) is .45.

The strategy for searching the table is to look at each entry in tableitem until we find the matching item code. Suppose the desired item is found in the fourth entry of tableitem, or tableitem(4). We then find the fourth item in the rate table and

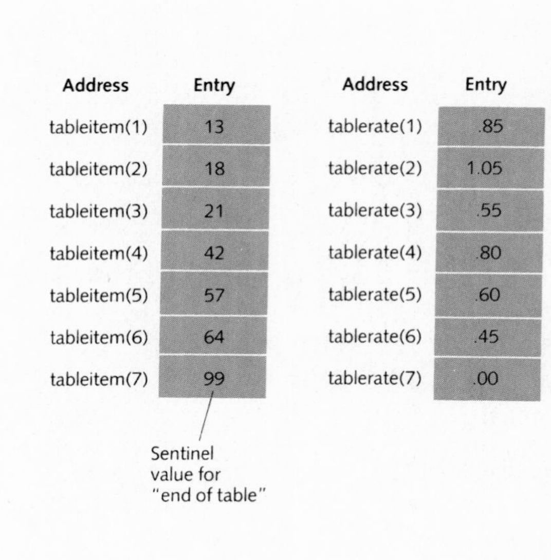

Address
Entry
Address
Entry
tableitem(1)
13
tablerate(1)
.85
tableitem(2)
18
tablerate(2)
1.05
tableitem(3)
21
tablerate(3)
.55
tableitem(4)
42
tablerate(4)
.80
tableitem(5)
57
tablerate(5)
.60
tableitem(6)
64
tablerate(6)
.45
tableitem(7)
99
tablerate(7)
.00
Sentinel
value for
"end of table"

Figure 9 The tables of piecework item codes and rates searched by the piecework payroll programs.

move this to the output variable, rate. Instead of referencing tableitem(1), tableitem(2), tableitem(3), and so on, we refer to each entry in the table by using an **index**, also called a **subscript**, which is simply the position number from the beginning of the table. If we set index to 1 and refer to tableitem(index), then we are actually referring to tableitem(1). If we add 1 to index and then refer to tableitem(index), we will actually be referring to tableitem(2). We simply keep adding 1 to index in order to search through the entire table until we find a match. Then the value of index is used to extract the appropriate rate from tablerate(index).

Exercises:

We have ignored the possibility of an incorrect item code being supplied to the subroutine.

1. What might cause an incorrect item code to be supplied to the subroutine?
2. Show how the flowchart and the corresponding pseudocode for the Lookup subroutine may be modified to detect an invalid item code and warn the main program of the error.
3. How should the main program that calls Lookup be modified
   (a) to respond to the subroutine's warning about an invalid item code?
   (b) to prevent an invalid item code from reaching the subroutine in the first place?

Case Study 8–9: Piecework Payroll for Several Employees: Control Break Processing

Problem Statement:

Modify the single-employee piecework payroll program developed in Case Studies 8–7 and 8–8 so that it handles several employees. The input data for the employees and the output report that should be produced when this input data is processed are shown in Figure 10. After the data for each employee is processed, the amount of money earned by that employee for the week should be printed. At the end of the entire report, the total amount of money earned by all employees for the week should be printed.

Discussion:

The solution is shown in Figure 10 on pages 212 and 213. Besides *employeepay*, an additional total, namely *totalpay*, is required to produce the grand total pay figure for all employees.

The program works by the technique of **control breaks**; each time it reads a new record, it checks to see if the employee number has changed. If it hasn't, we simply process the next record for this employee, calculate the amount of money earned for this item, and add this amount into both employeepay and totalpay. If indeed the employee number has changed, we have a control break, which requires special processing depending on its type. Two types of control breaks are of interest in this program. When the employee number changes from one legitimate employee number to

another, the total pay line for the previous employee must be printed, and the employeepay must be reset to zero to prepare to begin running up the total pay for the next employee. If the employee number becomes 999 (the sentinel), we must print the total pay line for the last employee and the grand total line for all employees. These operations are clearly indicated in the flowchart and the pseudocode.

The key to detecting control breaks is the use of the variable *lastemployee*. Each time we're about to read another employee record, we move employee to lastemployee and then read the new employee record. Thus, we have available both the current employee number and lastemployee. We simply compare them; if they are equal, there has not been a control break. If they are not equal, there has indeed been a control break.

Exercises:

1. Notice that after we read the first employee record, we immediately move employee to lastemployee. Why?
2. When we get an employee control break we "Set employeepay to 0." Why don't we also do this after we print the last employee pay line before printing the grand total pay line?

Summary 

1. A program is a listing of the series of steps or operations to be performed in solving a problem and the order in which those steps are to be performed.
2. Programming languages have certain types of instructions in common: input instructions, output instructions, arithmetic instructions, comparison instructions, control instructions, data movement instructions, data definition instructions, and file and record definition instructions.
3. The steps to writing a good program are studying the problem to be solved, writing a clear specification of the problem, developing the solution, writing the program, testing and debugging the program, and documenting the program.
4. Programs should be efficient, correct, reliable, robust, and maintainable.
5. In a flowchart, the shapes of the symbols indicate the nature of the operations to be performed, and the flowlines indicate the order in which the operations should be performed.
6. Bohm and Jacopini proved that the most complex program logic can be expressed in terms of the sequence, selection, and repetition control structures, and thus programs can be written without any GOTO statements.
7. Pseudocode, or structured English, allows a programmer to use English-like sentences to write an explanation of what a program is supposed to do.
8. Gerald Weinberg proposed the notion of egoless programming, by which programming becomes an open activity. All members of a project share their work, and each person's work is subject to review by the others.
9. In a structured walkthrough, a group of programmers reviews an individual's work.
10. In a chief programmer team, the chief programmer is completely responsible for the design, development, and documentation of a system of programs. The chief is supported by many specialists.

Figure 10 Control break processing: Piecework payroll for several employees.

Input Data File

Employee	Item	Quantity	
125	13	100	(First record)
125	18	200	(Second record)
125	57	150	(Etc.)
247	18	90	
247	21	195	
247	42	50	
247	64	150	
316	42	200	
316	57	250	
999	0	0	(Sentinel)

Pseudocode

```
Piecework2:
  BEGIN
      Print the report headings
      Set employeepay to 0
      Set totalpay to 0
      Read employee, item, quantity
      Move employee to lastemployee
      WHILE employee not 999
          DO IF employee not equal to lastemployee
                 THEN Print "EMPLOYEE", lastemployee, employeepay, "*"
                        Set employeepay to 0
             ENDIF
             Call Lookup(item,rate)
             Multiply rate by quantity giving amount
             Add amount to employeepay
             Add amount to totalpay
             Print employee, item, rate, quantity, amount
             Move employee to lastemployee
             Read employee, item, quantity
      ENDWHILE
      Print "EMPLOYEE", lastemployee, employeepay, "*"
      Print "GRAND TOTAL", totalpay, "**"
  END Piecework2
```

PIECEWORK PAYROLL REPORT 7/12/85 PAGE 1

EMPLOYEE	ITEM	RATE	QUANTITY	AMOUNT
125	13	.85	100	85.00
125	18	1.05	200	210.00
125	57	.60	150	90.00
			EMPLOYEE 125	385.00*
247	18	1.05	90	94.50
247	21	.55	195	107.25
247	42	.80	50	40.00
247	64	.45	150	67.50
			EMPLOYEE 247	309.25*
316	42	.80	200	160.00
316	57	.60	250	150.00
			EMPLOYEE 316	310.00*
			GRAND TOTAL	1,004.25**

Piecework 2

Flowchart

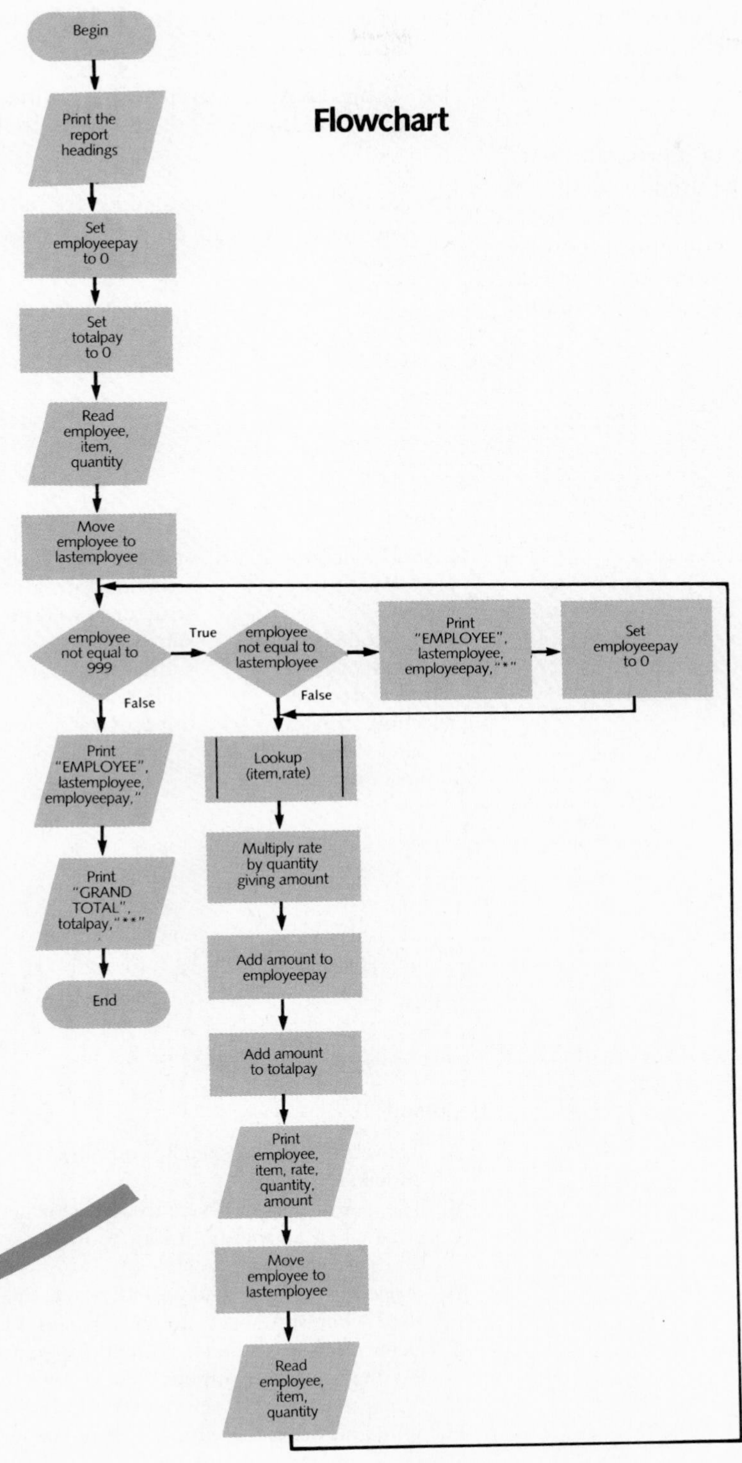

11. Counter-controlled looping is used when the precise number of repetitions is known in advance; otherwise sentinel-controlled looping is used.
12. A subroutine is a portion of a program that is written once but may be used by calling it from various locations throughout the main program. The subroutine contains a return statement that causes execution to resume at the first statement after the call in the main program.
13. The predefined process symbol is used in a flowchart to indicate a subroutine call.
14. Tables may be searched by varying an index from the lowest to the highest numbered entry in the table.
15. Control break processing is useful when various levels of totals must be shown on a report.

Important Terms 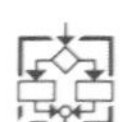

array
bug
chief programmer team
control structures
data definition instructions
data movement instructions
debugging
documentation
egoless programming
file and record definition instructions
flowcharting
GOTO statement
index
initialize
module
nested structures
predefined process symbol
pseudocode
repetition structure
return statement
selection structure
sentinel value
sequence structure
structured English
structured programming
structured walkthrough
subroutine
subscript
table searching
top-down stepwise refinement

Self-Review Exercises 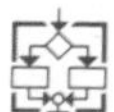

Matching

Next to the term in column A, place the letter of the statement in column B that best describes it.

Column A

1. Syntax error
2. GOTO
3. Machine language
4. Comparison instruction
5. Debugging
6. Case structure
7. Structured walkthrough
8. REPEAT-UNTIL
9. WHILE-DO
10. GOTO-less programming

Column B

A. Instructions that a specific computer can directly understand
B. The action may not have to be performed at all
C. Used when a program must choose from more than two alternatives
D. A peer group review of an individual's work
E. Used when statements are performed at least once
F. Determines if a number is equal to, greater than, or less than another number
G. A bug that appears before execution of a program
H. Sometimes equated with structured programming
I. Removing program errors
J. Transfer of control

Fill-in-the-Blanks

Fill in the blanks in each of the following:

1. A computer program is a listing of ______ to be performed in an indicated sequence.

2. The three control structures with which all programs may be constructed are ______ , ______ , and ______ .

3. A method of programming in which all members of a project share their techniques is called ______ .

4. The person in the programming team responsible for writing and proofreading the documentation is the ______ .

5. The various symbols in a flowchart are connected by arrows. These are also called ______ .

6. The ______ symbol is used to indicate a decision-making operation in a flowchart.

7. A ______ is a statement that may be either true or false.

8. Two ways of controlling a loop are counter-controlled looping and ______ looping.

9. ______ instructions specify the order in which instructions are to be performed.

10. The ______ structure is a modified selection structure that simply does nothing when the condition is false.

Answers to Self-Review Exercises

Matching: 1 G, 2 J, 3 A, 4 F, 5 I, 6 C, 7 D, 8 E, 9 B, 10 H

Fill-in-the-Blanks:

1. steps or operations
2. sequence, selection, repetition
3. egoless programming
4. editor
5. flowlines
6. diamond-shaped
7. condition
8. sentinel-controlled
9. Control
10. IF-THEN

Discussion Questions 

1. What types of instructions are found in programming languages?

2. What are the steps involved in writing a good program?

3. List the characteristics that good programs should have.

4. What are the three major control structures and their functions? What other control structures are often used?

5. Why is pseudocode popular?

6. What is a transfer of control?

7. What is meant by "spaghetti code"?

8. Explain the functions performed by each member of a chief programmer team.

9. Compare and contrast counter-controlled looping with sentinel-controlled looping.

10. What is a control break? Describe how control break processing might be used in a program that summarizes sales for an international firm by city, by state or province, by country, and worldwide.

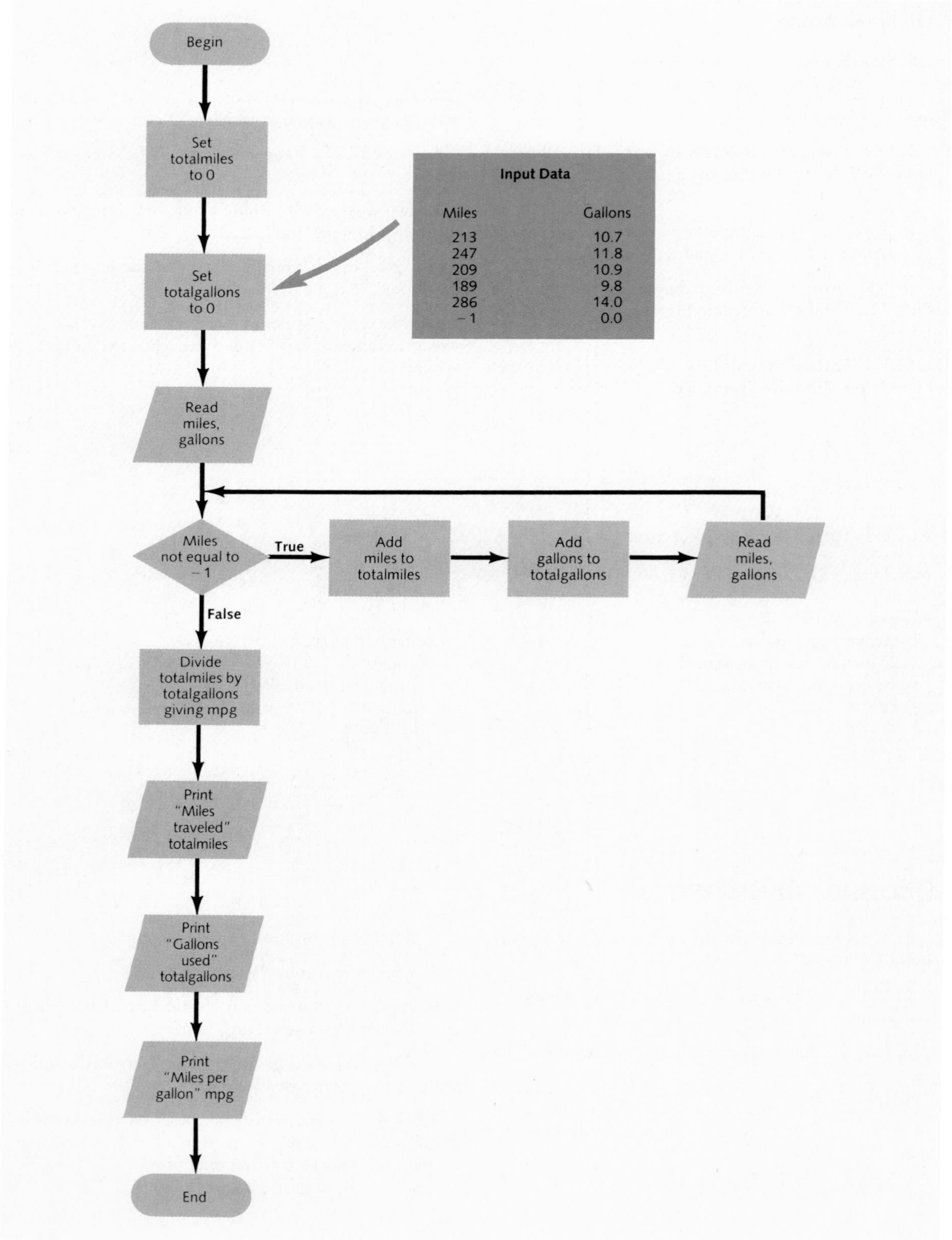

Begin

Set totalmiles to 0

Set totalgallons to 0

Read miles, gallons

Miles not equal to −1

True

Add miles to totalmiles

Add gallons to totalgallons

Read miles, gallons

False

Divide totalmiles by totalgallons giving mpg

Print "Miles traveled" totalmiles

Print "Gallons used" totalgallons

Print "Miles per gallon" mpg

End

Input Data

Miles	Gallons
213	10.7
247	11.8
209	10.9
189	9.8
286	14.0
−1	0.0

 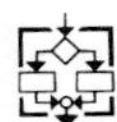

Projects

1. Mr. Smith drove 1144 miles on a business trip. He filled his tank with gas before the trip began. During the trip, he stopped for gas five times. Each time he filled his tank he recorded the miles driven since the last fillup and the gallons used. Develop a program that will read this information and will determine and print the total miles traveled, the total gallons used, and the average miles-per-gallon for the entire trip. Figure 8–13 contains the input data and the flowchart for this program. You are to write the pseudocode that corresponds to this flowchart, and then show the precise outputs that will be produced when the given input data is processed.

2. A company has asked you to write a program that will update one of its customer's balances. Your program should begin by reading the customer's name, account number, and balance at the beginning of last month. Your program should then read a series of records for this customer. Each record contains a code and an amount. If the code is 1, the amount represents a payment received from this customer last month, so your program should subtract the amount from the balance. If the code is 2, the amount represents a purchase made by this customer last month, so your program should add the amount to the balance. If the code is 3, all records for this customer have been processed, so your program should print the customer's name and final balance. Figure 8–14 contains the input data and the pseudocode for this program. You are to write the flowchart that corresponds to this pseudocode, and then show the precise outputs that will be produced when the given input data is processed.

Input Data

Name	Account	Balance
Mrs. H. Jones	237453	215.95

Code	Amount
2	23.95
2	116.49
1	100.00
2	19.95
3	0.0

```
Balanceforward:
  BEGIN
     Read name, accountnumber, balance
     Read code, amount
     WHILE code not equal to 3
        DO IF code is equal to 1
              THEN subtract amount from balance
              ELSE IF code is equal to 2
                      THEN add amount to balance
                   ENDIF
           ENDIF
           Read code, amount
     ENDWHILE
     Print "New balance for" name "is" balance
  END Balanceforward
```

Figure 8–13 *Left:* Input data and flowchart for Project 1.

Figure 8–14 *Right:* Input data and pseudocode for Project 2.

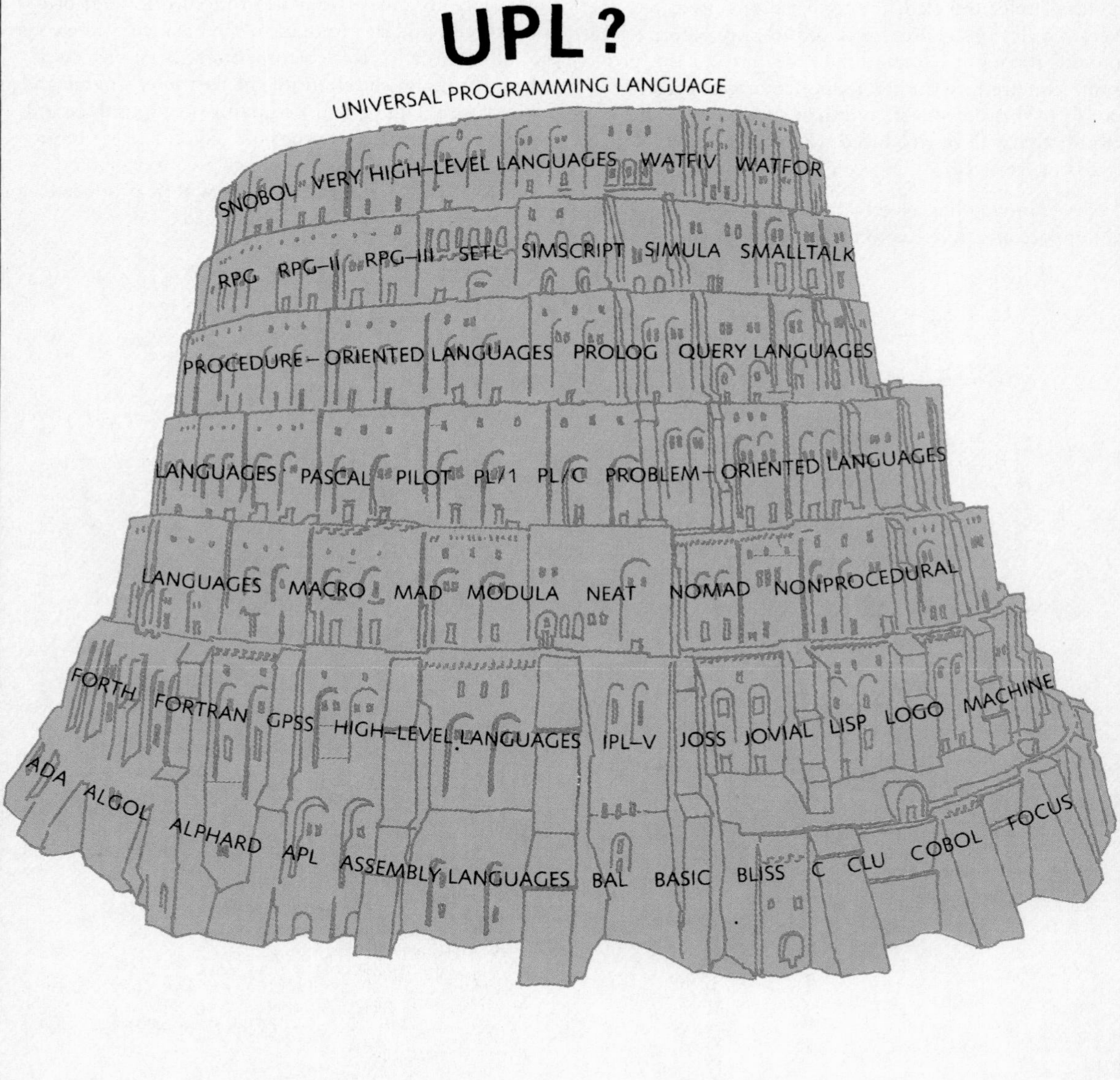

UPL?

UNIVERSAL PROGRAMMING LANGUAGE

SNOBOL VERY HIGH-LEVEL LANGUAGES WATFIV WATFOR

RPG RPG-II RPG-III SETL SIMSCRIPT SIMULA SMALLTALK

PROCEDURE-ORIENTED LANGUAGES PROLOG QUERY LANGUAGES

LANGUAGES PASCAL PILOT PL/1 PL/C PROBLEM-ORIENTED LANGUAGES

LANGUAGES MACRO MAD MODULA NEAT NOMAD NONPROCEDURAL

FORTH FORTRAN GPSS HIGH-LEVEL LANGUAGES IPL-V JOSS JOVIAL LISP LOGO MACHINE

ADA ALGOL ALPHARD APL ASSEMBLY LANGUAGES BAL BASIC BLISS C CLU COBOL FOCUS

Chapter 9

Programming Languages

After reading this chapter you will understand:

1. The differences among machine, assembly, and high-level programming languages
2. The operation of program translators such as assemblers, compilers, and interpreters
3. The advantages and disadvantages of procedure-oriented languages and problem-oriented languages and of different types of compilers
4. The more important features of some popular languages including BASIC, FORTRAN, COBOL, PL/1, RPG, APL, Pascal, C, Ada, Forth, LISP, and LOGO
5. What is meant by query languages and program generators

Left: With the hundreds of programming languages that have been developed, many people believe that the computing profession has created its own Tower of Babel.

Outline

High thoughts must have high language.
Aristophanes

We have been discussing the instructions computers are given in order to calculate, create, produce, and serve us in numerous ways. For instructions to work effectively, they must be given in specialized ways using programming languages.

Hundreds of programming languages have been developed for writing computer programs. In this chapter we consider the evolution of computer programming languages, the features of some of the most widely used languages, and several important trends that are dramatically changing the way computers are programmed.

Programming Languages

Machine Language

Each computer can directly understand only one language—its own **machine language**. With machine language a programmer can instruct a computer to perform its most fundamental operations.

Machine languages consist of strings of numbers ultimately reduced to 1's and 0's. The computer responds to these numbers by performing different operations. For example, the number +20 may instruct one particular computer to add two numbers; the number +21 on the same system might indicate that subtraction is to be performed. Machine languages are so closely related to the structure of a particular computer that they are said to be **machine dependent**. Programs written in machine language are not portable, that is, they may not be run on other computers with different machine languages.

Machine language programs are easy for computers to understand, but, for people, machine language programming is tedious work susceptible to error. The following machine language instructions of one particular computer system indicate that two numbers are to be added and the result saved for future use:

+10 00 97	Get the number stored in location 97 and load it into the accumulator register.
+20 00 96	Add the number stored in location 96 to the number in the accumulator leaving the sum in the accumulator.
+11 00 98	Store the result of these calculations in primary storage location 98.

Computers that can be programmed in machine language generally have a row of switches that can be set manually. The programmer sets a switch one way to represent a "1" and the opposite way to represent a "0." One group of switches is set to the address of the storage location; another group is set to the machine language instruction or data item that is to be placed in that location. The programmer then presses an "ENTER" key; the machine reads the contents of the switches into the appropriate locations in primary storage. When the entire program has been entered, the programmer presses a "RUN" key to execute the program.

As computing increased in popularity, it became clear that a more convenient method for programming computers was needed. One better method, called **assembly language programming,** evolved in an interesting way.

Telling a computer what to do

Imagine trying to instruct a visitor from another planet on how to boil an egg. To begin, a common language has to be learned. But even after that is accomplished, the visitor has to be given explicit, step-by-step directions, since he does not know an egg from an orange. For example: 1. Walk to the cupboard. 2. Open the doors. 3. Take out the big pot. 4. Go to the sink. 5. Turn on the cold water tap. 6. Fill the pot half-full of water. And so on. If he misses just one of the dozens of steps, the visitor will be confused and unable to complete his task.

That scenario is not unlike what a programmer goes through in writing the software, a set of instructions to perform a job on a computer. Writing a computer program is a most rigorous and exacting job that requires the utmost attention to detail. Even a misplaced comma can cause the computer to forget what it is doing and begin turning out garbage.

With the most basic computer languages—such as Assembler—programmers have to write one line of instruction, or computer code, for each tiny chore that the computer is to execute. The so-called higher-level languages such as FORTRAN and COBOL incorporate instruction subsets in the language so that one line of code can contain about six instructions. Even easier to write—because the language itself is more complex—are the software programs in the new query languages that understand English-like commands. Unlike COBOL or FORTRAN, however, which can be used to program the computer to do a wide variety of functions, query languages will instruct the computer only in how to file or retrieve information.

Shown below are portions of three programs—one in Assembler, one in COBOL, and one in a query language. Each is designed to generate the same report showing the account balances for a list of customers. But to do the job, the Assembler program takes more than 3,000 lines. The COBOL program runs more than 600 lines. But the one sentence in query language is all that is needed.

Assembler

```
215   LA   R2,@IDTWO(,R9)
216   LA   R1,@PTENDL+@PTNEXT(,R1)
217   B    PTM1
```

COBOL

```
330820   IF PRIORBAL    NOT NUMERIC MOVE 'Y' TO YES-NON MOVE
330822   'PRIORBAL    'TO MVLAB PERFORM NONNUM-1 THRU NONNUM-1-EX
330824   MOVE ZEROES TO PRIORBAL.
```

Query language

```
I WANT A REPORT FOR BUSINESS TYPE 17 IN ORDER BY BRANCH, SHOWING
ACCOUNT NUMBER, NAME, AND BOTH CURRENT AND PRIOR BALANCES.
```

Data: Cullinane Corp., BW

Assembly Language

Today programmers rarely write programs in machine language. Instead, they use the clearer **assembly languages** or **high-level languages**. These languages are partly responsible for the current widespread use of computers.

Programmers, burdened by machine language programming, began using English-like abbreviations for the various machine language instructions. Called **mnemonics** (memory aids), these abbreviations related to the action to be taken and made more sense to the programmer. For example, instead of writing "+20" to represent addition, a programmer might write the mnemonic "ADD"; "SUB" might be used for subtraction, "DIV" for division, and the like. Even the storage locations were given names. If location 92 contained a total, it might be referred to as "TOTAL" or "SUM" instead of 92. The resulting programs were much easier to understand and modify. For example, in a payroll program that subtracts total deductions from gross pay to calculate net pay, the following assembly language instructions might appear:

```
LOAD   GROSSPAY
SUB    DEDUCTS
STORE  NETPAY
```

Unfortunately, computers could not understand these programs, so the mnemonics still had to be translated into machine language for processing. An aristocracy arose in the programming profession. The "upper class" consisted of programmers who wrote programs using the English-like mnemonics. The "commoners," called **assemblers,** then took these programs and manually translated them into machine language, a rather mechanical job. In the 1950s, programmers realized that this translation could be performed more quickly and accurately by computers than by people, and so the first assembler program, or **translator program,** was written (Figure 9–1). The program of instructions written in assembly language is known as the **source program**; an assembler program translates it into a machine language program, called an **object program.**

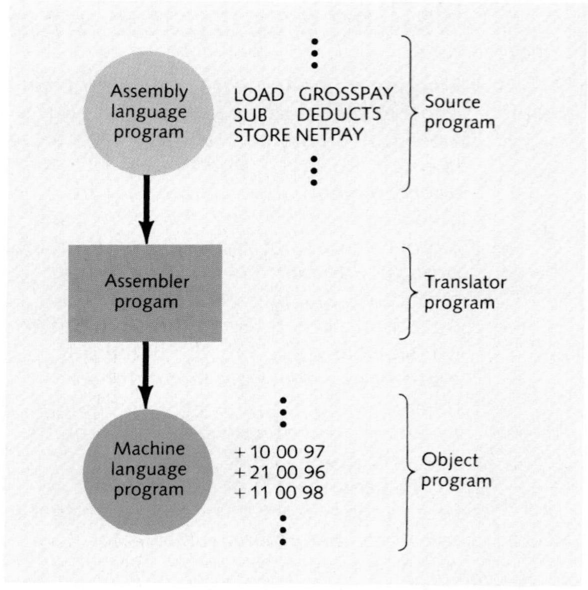

Figure 9–1 An assembler program translates an assembly language program (the source program) into a machine language program (the object program).

Figure 9–2 A sampling of assembly language mnemonics used with certain IBM mainframe computers. The complete instruction set offers about 200 mnemonic codes. The operation codes are shown in the hexadecimal (base 16) number system.

Assembly Language Mnemonic	Machine Language Operation Code	Function Performed
A	5A	ADD
C	59	COMPARE
CVB	4F	CONVERT TO BINARY
CVD	4E	CONVERT TO DECIMAL
D	5D	DIVIDE
ED	DE	EDIT
L	58	LOAD
MVC	D2	MOVE CHARACTERS
M	5C	MULTIPLY
ST	50	STORE
S	5B	SUBTRACT
SVC	0A	SUPERVISOR CALL
TR	DC	TRANSLATE
ZAP	F8	ZERO AND ADD

Programs could be written faster with assembly language than with machine language, although they still had to be translated into machine language before they could be executed (see Figure 9–2). The work involved in translation was more than justified by the resulting increased programming speed and fewer errors.

Assembly language programs are also machine dependent and not portable. Programmers must write large numbers of instructions to accomplish even simple chores, and the programs still appear to be in computerese (Figure 9–3).

Perhaps the major use of assembly languages today is in the writing of operating systems—the programs that control the hardware and make it more accessible to computer users (see Chapter 12).

Macro Instructions

The next step in the evolutionary process was the introduction of **macro instructions.** A macro instruction is one instruction that is translated into several machine language instructions. With a

Figure 9–3 This assembly language program constructs all the points of a circle. It is written in the assembly language of one of the most popular 8-bit microprocessors, the Z80. Assembly language programs can be difficult for anyone but their original authors to understand.

```
       LD  (YVAL),A
       LD  (XVAL),A
BEGN   LD  A,(SHIFT)
       LD  B,A
       LD  DE,(YVAL+1)
       LD  A,(YVAL)
       LD  C,A
       RL  D
       JP  C,DYNEG
       RR  D
YEPSP  SRL  D
       RR  E
       RR  C
       DJNZ  YEPSP
       LD  A,(XVAL)
       ADD  A,C
       LD  (XVAL),A
       LD  A,(XVAL+1)
       ADC  A,E
       LD  (XVAL+1),A
       LD  A,(XVAL+2)
       ADC  A,D
       LD  (XVAL+2), A
       JP  YBGN
DYNEG  RR  D
       LD  A,D
       XOR  255
       LD  D,A
       LD  A,E
       XOR  255
       LD  E,A
       LD  A,C
       XOR  255
       INC  A
       LD  C,A
YEPSM  SRL  D
       RR  E
       RR  C
       DJNZ  YEPSM
       LD  A,(XVAL)
       SUB  C
       LD  (XVAL),A
       LD  A,(XVAL+1)
       SBC  A,E
       LD  (XVAL+1),A
       LD  A,(XVAL+2)
       SBC  A,D
       LD  (XVAL+2),A
YBGN   LD  A,(SHIFT)
       LD  B,A
       LD  DE,(XVAL+1)
       LD  A,(XVAL)
       LD  C,A
       RL  D
       JP  C,DXNEG
       RR  D
XEPSP  SRL  D
       RR  E
       RR  C
       DJNZ  XEPSP
       LD  A,(YVAL)
       SUB  C
       LD  (YVAL),A
       LD  A,(YVAL+1)
       SBC  A,E
       LD  (YVAL+1),A
       LD  A,(YVAL+2)
       SBC  A,D
       LD  (YVAL+2),A
       JP  YEND
DXNEG  RR  D
       LD  A,D
       XOR  255
       LD  D,A
       LD  A,E
       XOR  255
       LD  E,A
       LD  A,C
       XOR  255
       INC  A
       LD  C,A
XEPSM  SRL  D
       RR  E
       RR  C
       DJNZ  XEPSM
       LD  A,(YVAL)
       ADD  A,C
       LD  (YVAL),A
       LD  A,(YVAL+1)
       ADC  A,E
       LD  (YVAL+1),A
       LD  A,(YVAL+2)
       ADC  A,D
       LD  (YVAL+2),A
```

single macro instruction, the programmer can specify an action that would ordinarily require several assembly language instructions. For example, the simple macro SUM A,B,C might be used to add A to B and store the results in C.

Whenever the assembler program encounters a macro instruction, it first performs a **macro expansion.** It produces a series of assembly language instructions to perform the function of the macro. For example, SUM A,B,C might be expanded to

```
LOAD  A
ADD   B
STORE C
```

and the assembler would then translate these instructions into machine language.

High-Level Languages

Assembly language programming with macro instructions represented a big leap forward, allowing programs to be written faster and with fewer bugs than before. These programs were easier to understand and modify, but they still consisted mostly of individual assembly language instructions and had the appearance of computerese.

This led to the development of high-level languages in which programmers code programs that look almost like everyday English and use familiar mathematical notations. The assembly language instructions in the previous example can be written in high-level language as a single statement:

```
COMPUTE NETPAY =
                GROSSPAY - DEDUCTIONS.
```

Compared to machine and assembly languages, high-level languages are easier to learn and use. High-level language programs can be produced more quickly, are easier to debug, and are easier to maintain. This makes them popular with both beginning programmers and with experienced users who want to get their programs written and debugged as quickly as possible.

High-level language programs must also be translated to machine language before they can be executed. The translator programs that do this are called **compilers** (Figure 9–4). Compilers for

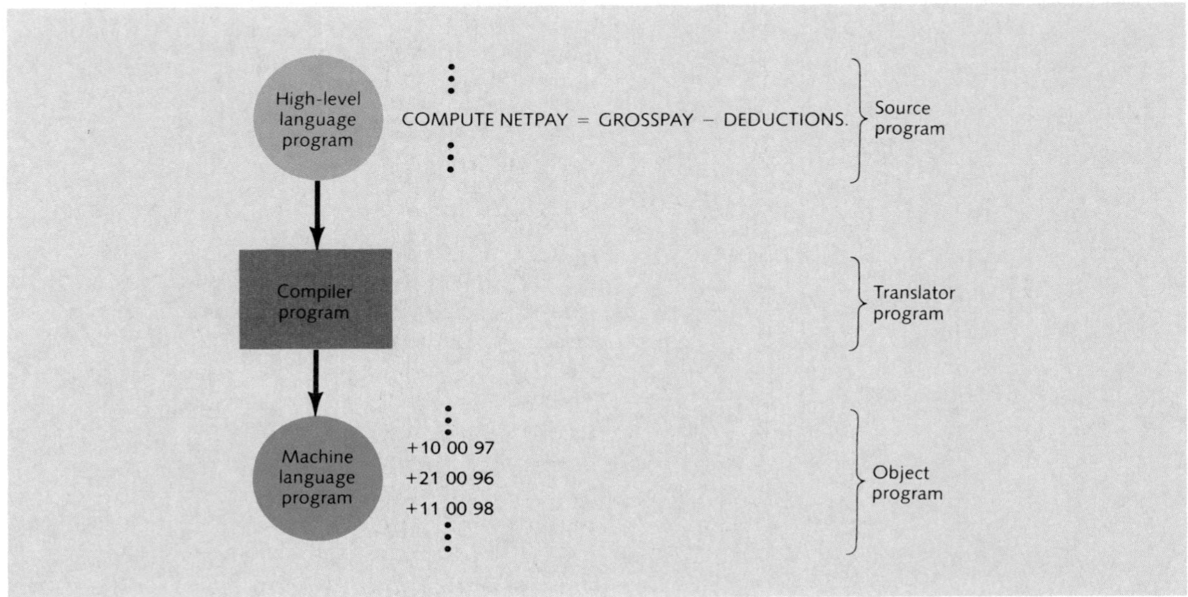

Figure 9–4 A compiler is a translator program that converts a high-level language source program into a machine language object program.

a particular high-level language can be produced for various computers with different machine languages. This makes high-level language programs portable (Figure 9–5).

An alternative to a compiler is an **interpreter**, a translator program that actually runs a source program directly. An interpreter does not produce a machine language object program. Thus, every time a given statement is executed, the interpreter has to determine exactly what that statement means. This task is very much like compiling, but it is performed only for those statements that are actually executed on a given run of the program.

Interpreters are especially useful in program development. Each time a new bug is found, the programmer can correct it, try the program again, and almost immediately expose the next bug. There are no long delays for recompiling programs.

Once a program is functioning properly, it may be best to compile it into machine language and save the machine language version for future use. When that program is executed, the machine language version will run much faster than the interpreted program. As faster processors become more economical, interpreters will become more widely used.

Figure 9–5 Compilers make high-level language programs transportable between different computers.

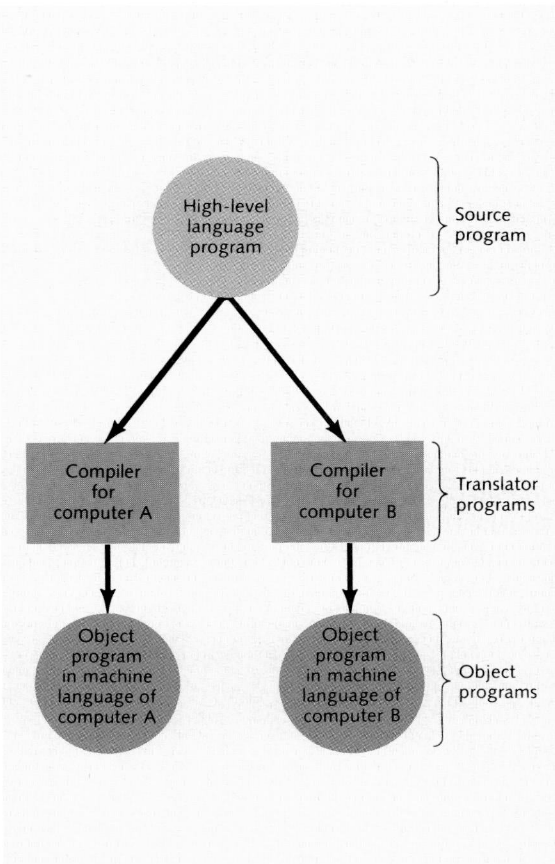

Procedure-Oriented and Problem-Oriented Languages

High-level languages may be categorized as either procedure oriented or problem oriented. **Procedure-oriented languages** are general purpose—they may be used to solve many different types of problems. Most of the popular programming languages are procedure oriented. **Problem-oriented languages** are designed to solve specific types of problems. They allow programmers to solve problems with fewer statements than are needed for procedure-oriented languages, but their use is limited to the particular problem areas for which they were designed. RPG, one of the many high-level languages we will consider later in this chapter, is a problem-oriented language designed to simplify the task of producing business reports.

"Quick-and-Dirty" Compilers and Optimizing Compilers

When programs are being developed they generally run for only a short while before a bug appears. In such **program development environments**, programmers are more concerned with debugging programs than with having them run efficiently. While a program is being debugged, **"quick-and-dirty" compilers** are used. These translate programs very quickly, but the machine language programs produced do not run as fast as possible and may use more primary storage than they really need.

Once a program has been debugged, it is then put into **production**—it is run regularly to accomplish useful work, such as preparing a company's weekly payroll. In **production environments**, programs must run efficiently—if a large weekly production job can be made to run in 3 hours instead of 10, the savings will be enormous. Efficient operation of production programs can save resources and can help an installation avoid adding unnecessary hardware. In production environments, **optimizing compilers** are used. These may take considerably more time to translate programs, but the resulting machine language programs run faster and occupy less primary storage.

"Basic, my dear Watson, Basic!"

A Survey of High-Level Languages

The next several sections present a survey of some of the more important high-level languages. Appendix A of the text contains a minicourse on BASIC programming. For each of the high-level languages discussed in this chapter, an attempt is made to give the flavor of the language, and the types of applications for which the language is useful are listed.

BASIC

BASIC (for Beginner's All-purpose Symbolic Instruction Code) was developed in the early 1960s at Dartmouth College by John Kemeny and Thomas Kurtz. It was designed to be simple to learn and easy to use, especially for novice programmers. Originally developed for interactive use on timesharing computers, BASIC is now available on virtually all personal computers and has become the most widely used programming language in the world. Both compiled BASICs and interpretive BASICs are available. Most of the other popular computer languages only have compiled versions; these other languages were simply not designed to be interpreted efficiently.

A sample BASIC program is shown in Figure 9–6. The program consists of a series of numbered statements. Statements are ordinarily processed in increasing statement number order, but this sequence can be modified by certain BASIC

Figure 9–6 A sample BASIC program that obtains two numbers typed in by a user and determines if the numbers are identical.

```
10 REM  ARE TWO NUMBERS THE SAME?
20 PRINT "PLEASE TYPE IN FIRST NUMBER"
30 INPUT F
40 PRINT "PLEASE TYPE IN SECOND NUMBER"
50 INPUT S
60 IF F = S GOTO 90
70 PRINT "THE NUMBERS ARE DIFFERENT"
80 GOTO 100
90 PRINT "THE NUMBERS ARE THE SAME"
100 END
```

instructions. The language contains simple English words and abbreviations such as REM (for REMark), PRINT, INPUT, IF, GOTO, and END. This contributes to BASIC's user-friendliness. BASIC is ideal for writing small programs and systems of programs quickly. For the design of large systems or complex mathematical programs, other programming languages are often selected.

To make a correction to a BASIC program, the programmer merely retypes the line of the program containing the error. Most other programming languages require the programmer to make changes by using separate editing programs. In BASIC the editing capability is built right into the language.

BASIC is not a structured language in terms of its syntax, although some extended versions of the language do offer control structures and enable programmers to minimize the use of GOTO statements. It suffers from a lack of standardization; many customized versions are in use. These "dialects" have wide followings, and it is unlikely that a single standard version of the language will emerge soon.

FORTRAN

FORTRAN (for FORmula TRANslator), the first widely used high-level language and the oldest such language still in use, was developed by IBM during the mid-1950s (Figure 9–7). It is oriented to performing complex mathematical computations. FORTRAN did become widely used by businesses for data-processing applications, but only because a better language for that purpose was not yet available.

One key to FORTRAN's success is the availability of libraries of mathematical routines—collections of programs that user programs may call on to perform frequently used mathematical computations.

IBM made FORTRAN freely available to anyone who wanted to use it. Soon most major computer vendors offered their own versions of the language. In the early 1960s a group of computer companies and users met to try to standardize FORTRAN. The standard was published in 1966 by a government agency that eventually became the **American National Standards Institute** (ANSI). FORTRAN was the first programming language to undergo such standardization. Its popularity persists and it continues to evolve into a more structured language.

COBOL

COBOL (for **C**ommon **B**usiness **O**riented **L**anguage) was developed for business data-processing applications that must efficiently handle large volumes of data and edit it for neat presentation.

COBOL was developed by CODASYL (the Conference on Data Systems Languages) in 1959. Participants included people from government, industry, and many universities, including Grace M. Hopper, a pioneer in high-level language programs and a moving force in the development of COBOL (Figure 9–8). The language has evolved through many versions and has been standardized through the efforts of ANSI.

COBOL programs use English words (Figure 9–9), contain paragraphs and sentences, punctuate sentences with commas, and end sentences with periods. This "grammar" makes COBOL more user-friendly than FORTRAN, at least to business programmers, but many people complain that COBOL programs are too wordy.

"AM I FAMILIAR WITH FORTRAN? I MAY BE—WHAT'S HIS FIRST NAME?"

```
C
C  THIS PROGRAM READS THREE VALUES WHICH ARE
C  PROPOSED TO BE THE SIDES OF A TRIANGLE.
C  THE PROGRAM CALLS A SUBROUTINE THAT
C  DETERMINES WHETHER OR NOT THE THREE SIDES
C  DO INDEED FORM A TRIANGLE AND IF THEY
C  DO, THE SUBROUTINE CALCULATES THE AREA OF
C  THE TRIANGLE.
      PROGRAM FIG117
      INTEGER FLAG
10    READ(5,25,END=50)SIDE1,SIDE2,SIDE3
25    FORMAT(3F5.0)
      CALL SUB1(SIDE1,SIDE2,SIDE3,AREA,FLAG)
C
C  FLAG IS CHECKED WHICH INDICATES WHETHER
C  THE GIVEN SIDES DID OR NOT FORM A TRIANGLE
C
      IF(FLAG .EQ. 2)THEN
         WRITE(10,35)SIDE1,SIDE2,SIDE3,AREA
35       FORMAT(5X,3(F7.2,3X),'AREA FOR THIS TRIANGLE IS',
     1   3X,F8.2)
                    ELSE
         WRITE(10,45)SIDE1,SIDE2,SIDE3
45       FORMAT(5X,3(F7.2,3X),'THESE THREE SIDES DO NOT',
     1   'FORM A TRIANGLE')
      ENDIF
      GO TO 10
50    STOP
      END
C
C  THIS IS THE SUBROUTINE THAT DETERMINES WHETHER OR NOT
C  GIVEN THREE SIDES DO INDEED FORM A TRIANGLE
C
      SUBROUTINE SUB1(A,B,C,TA,K)
      TA=0.0
      K=2
C
C  IS SIDE ONE GREATER THAN THE SUM OF SIDE TWO AND THREE?
C
      IF(A .GE. B+C)THEN
         K=1
                    ELSE
C
C  IS SIDE TWO GREATER THAN THE SUM OF SIDE ONE AND THREE?
C
          IF(B .GE. A+C)THEN
             K=1
                       ELSE
C
C  IS SIDE THREE GREATER THAN THE SUM OF SIDE ONE AND TWO?
C
              IF(C .GE. A+B)THEN
                 K=1
                            ELSE
                 S=.5*(A+B+C)
                 TA=SQRT(S*(S-A)*(S-B)*(S-C))
              ENDIF
          ENDIF
      ENDIF
      RETURN
      END
```

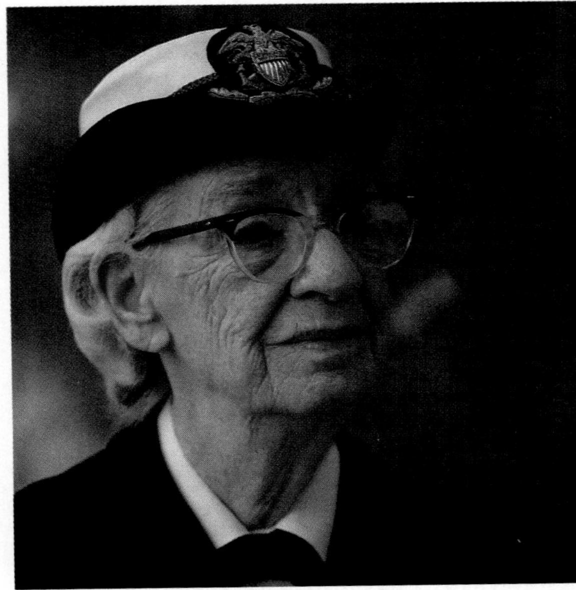

Figure 9–7 *Left:* A sample FORTRAN program. (Reprinted with permission of Macmillan Publishing Company from *FORTRAN 77, A Top-Down Approach* by Nonna Kliss Lehmkuhl. Copyright 1983 by Macmillan Publishing Company.)

Figure 9–8 *Above:* Captain Grace Murray Hopper, U.S. Navy, pioneered the design and implementation of the COBOL language.

Figure 9–9 *Below:* Some commonly used COBOL verbs.

Every COBOL program is broken up into four major divisions (Figure 9–10). The **Identification Division** includes the author's name, the date the program was compiled, the name of the installation where the program was developed, and other identifying information. The **Environment Division** defines, in the **Configuration Section**, the computer on which the program is to run and specifies in the **Input-Output Section**, the files to be processed and the auxiliary storage devices that contain those files. The **Data Division** specifies the format of each of the data items to be used by the program. This division's **File Section** shows how data is organized in the records for each file, and its **Working-Storage Section** defines the variables and constants used in the program. The **Procedure Division** specifies the actual calculations to be performed.

COBOL tends to be **self-documenting**, requiring fewer additional comments and remarks than assembly language programs. Long variable names like YEAR-TO-DATE-EARNINGS and EMPLOYEE-STREET-ADDRESS, for example, help make COBOL programs more understandable. The structure imposed by divisions, sections within divisions, and paragraphs within sections helps the reader of a COBOL program locate items quickly.

Cobol Verb	Typical Usage	Cobol Verb	Typical Usage
ACCEPT	Read information from user's terminal into primary storage.	MERGE	Combine two sorted files to form a single file.
ADD	Add two numbers.	MOVE	Move data between primary storage locations.
CALL	Call upon another program to perform a job.	MULTIPLY	Multiply two numbers.
CLOSE	Close a file after processing is complete.	OPEN	Make a file available for processing.
COMPUTE	Perform a calculation. Ex: COMPUTE X = A + B − C.	PERFORM	Repeat a group of statements.
DISPLAY	Write information from primary storage to the user's terminal.	READ	Read a record from a file into primary storage.
DIVIDE	Divide two numbers.	SEARCH	Locate an item of information in a table.
GO TO	Instead of executing the next statement, jump to another point in the program.	SORT	Sort the records of a file into some specified order.
IF	Make a decision and based upon the result of the decision, choose between alternative courses of action.	STOP	Terminate execution of a program.
		SUBTRACT	Subtract two numbers.
		WRITE	Write a record from primary storage to a file.

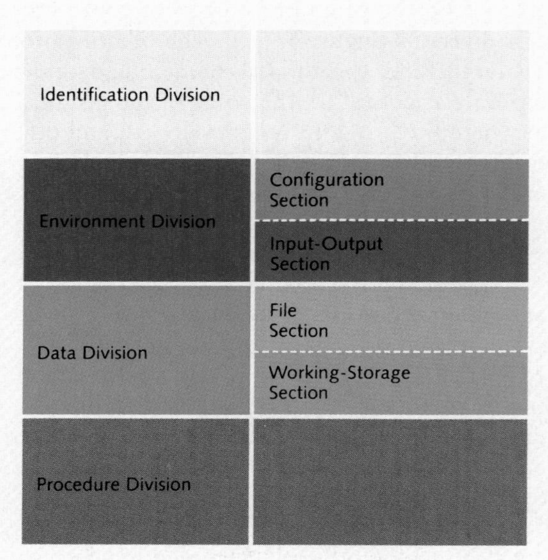

Figure 9–10 The four divisions of a COBOL program and some of the important sections within those divisions.

One interesting feature of COBOL is its ability to specify the structure of data in increasing levels of detail. This is called **hierarchical data structuring** (Figure 9–11). In this figure, PIC X(10) means that the FIRST name has a PICture of 10 characters. PIC is used to specify the form and style of data items in COBOL. Just as "X" means "any character," a PIC of "9" means "any digit." For example, a seven-digit telephone number might be given a picture clause of PIC 9(7).

COBOL is a large language designed to exercise the substantial data processing capabilities of large computers. It has not been widely adopted for personal computers, possibly because it is too large to be learned easily by the typical personal computer user and because COBOL compilers require much more primary storage than is generally available on personal computers. But as primary storage sizes continue to increase, COBOL is being "discovered" by a growing number of small businesses. A sample COBOL program is shown in Figure 9–12. The output produced by this program is shown in Figure 9–13.

PL/1

In the early 1960s most high-level language programmers used either FORTRAN or COBOL, depending on whether their applications were oriented more to mathematics or to data processing. In 1964, when IBM announced its System/360 series of computers, it also announced the development of a new programming language—**PL/1** (for Programming Language 1). PL/1 is a structured language that contains the better features of both FORTRAN and COBOL. Business programmers can include more mathematical calculations when needed, and scientific programmers can easily provide for the manipulation of massive amounts of data.

PL/1, although widely used, did not displace FORTRAN and COBOL from their premier positions. PL/1 is a huge language attempting to be all things to all people. As such, it requires a substantial amount of effort to learn. Some people believe it is simply too powerful and gives programmers too many options. Like FORTRAN, PL/1 has a large library of mathematical routines. It has been used mostly on large IBM computers, although some "subset" languages (languages that offer only a small portion of PL/1's features) have become popular on microcomputers.

Figure 9–11 An example of hierarchical data structuring in COBOL. NAME may be viewed as a single 26-character field, or it may be viewed as three subfields—a 10-character FIRST name, a 1-character MIDDLE-INITIAL, and a 15-character LAST name.

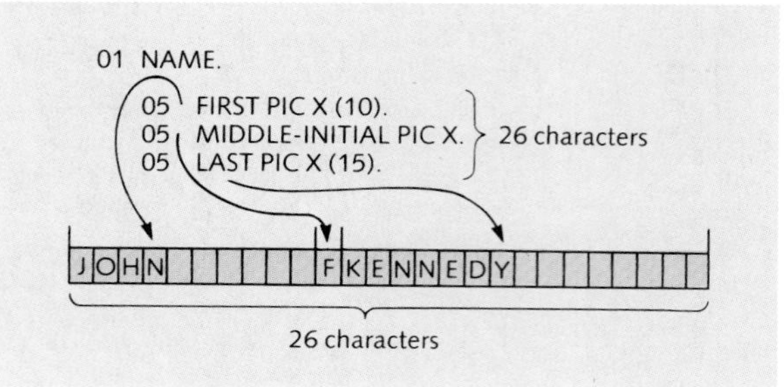

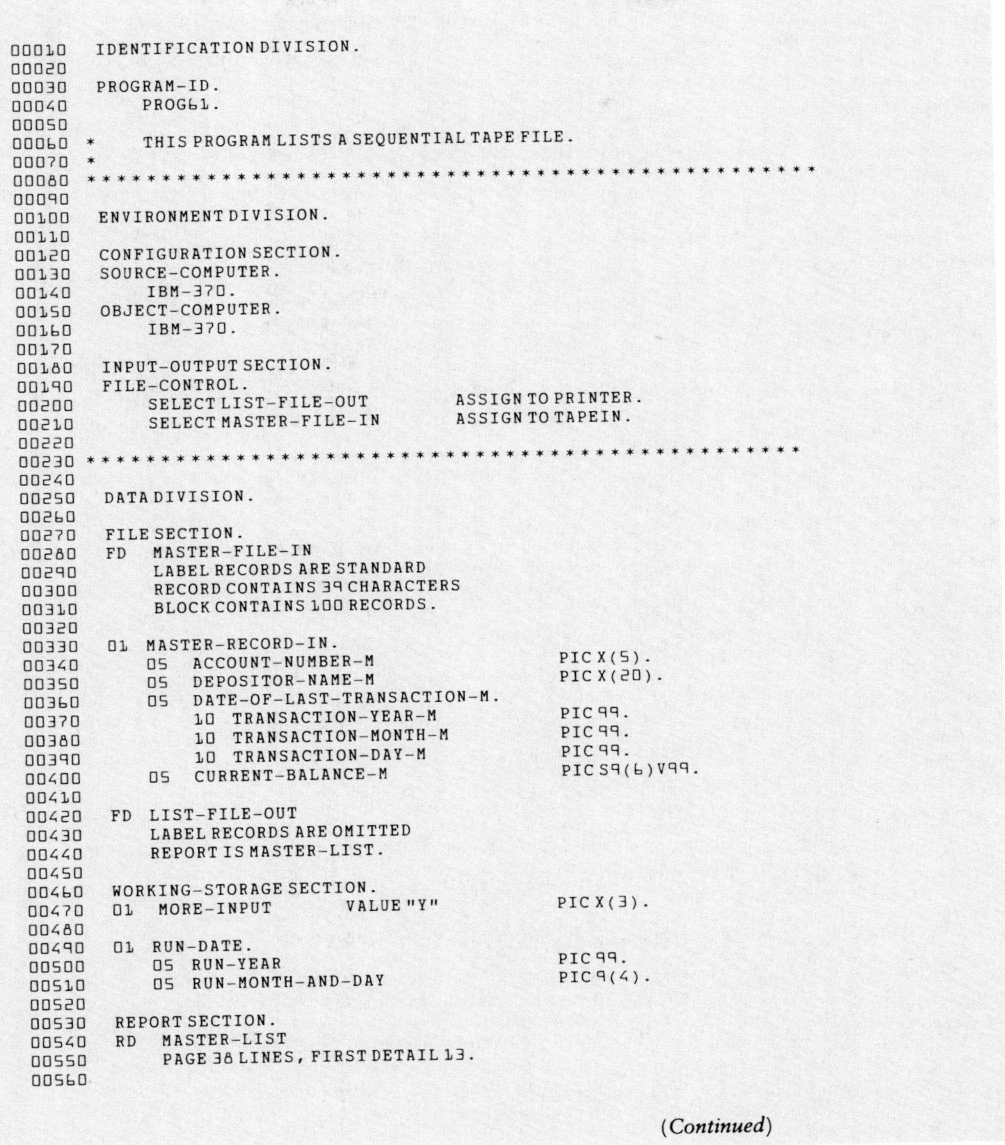

```
IDENTIFICATION DIVISION.
PROGRAM-ID.
    PROG61.
*   THIS PROGRAM LISTS A SEQUENTIAL TAPE FILE.
*
*******************************************************
ENVIRONMENT DIVISION.
CONFIGURATION SECTION.
SOURCE-COMPUTER.
    IBM-370.
OBJECT-COMPUTER.
    IBM-370.
INPUT-OUTPUT SECTION.
FILE-CONTROL.
    SELECT LIST-FILE-OUT         ASSIGN TO PRINTER.
    SELECT MASTER-FILE-IN        ASSIGN TO TAPEIN.
*******************************************************
DATA DIVISION.
FILE SECTION.
FD  MASTER-FILE-IN
    LABEL RECORDS ARE STANDARD
    RECORD CONTAINS 39 CHARACTERS
    BLOCK CONTAINS 100 RECORDS.
01  MASTER-RECORD-IN.
    05  ACCOUNT-NUMBER-M                         PIC X(5).
    05  DEPOSITOR-NAME-M                         PIC X(20).
    05  DATE-OF-LAST-TRANSACTION-M.
        10  TRANSACTION-YEAR-M                   PIC 99.
        10  TRANSACTION-MONTH-M                  PIC 99.
        10  TRANSACTION-DAY-M                    PIC 99.
    05  CURRENT-BALANCE-M                        PIC S9(6)V99.
FD  LIST-FILE-OUT
    LABEL RECORDS ARE OMITTED
    REPORT IS MASTER-LIST.
WORKING-STORAGE SECTION.
01  MORE-INPUT          VALUE "Y"                PIC X(3).
01  RUN-DATE.
    05  RUN-YEAR                                 PIC 99.
    05  RUN-MONTH-AND-DAY                        PIC 9(4).
REPORT SECTION.
RD  MASTER-LIST
    PAGE 38 LINES, FIRST DETAIL 13.
```

(*Continued*)

Figure 9–12 This sample COBOL program reads records from a file on magnetic tape and produces the printed report shown in Figure 9–13. (From Gary S. Popkin, *Advanced Structured COBOL*, Boston: Kent Publishing Company, 1983. pp. 230–232. Copyright 1983 by Wadsworth, Inc. Reprinted by permission of Kent Publishing, a division of Wadsworth, Inc.)

```
 01  TYPE PAGE HEADING.
     05  LINE 5.
           10 COLUMN 41  VALUE     "SAVINGS ACCOUNT MASTER"
                                                        PIC X(22).
     05  LINE 6.
          10  COLUMN 29  VALUE     "DATE"               PIC X(4).
          10  COLUMN 34  SOURCE    RUN-MONTH-AND-DAY    PIC Z9/99/.
          10  COLUMN 40  SOURCE    RUN-YEAR             PIC 99.
          10  COLUMN 63  VALUE     "PAGE"               PIC X(4).
          10  COLUMN 68  SOURCE    PAGE-COUNTER         PIC Z9.
     05  LINE 9
              COLUMN 47  VALUE     "DATE OF LAST"       PIC X(12).
     05  LINE 10.
          10  COLUMN 21  VALUE     "ACCOUNT"            PIC X(7).
          10  COLUMN 34  VALUE     "CURRENT"            PIC X(7).
          10  COLUMN 47  VALUE     "TRANSACTION"        PIC X(11).
          10  COLUMN 62  VALUE     "DEPOSITOR NAME"     PIC X(14).
     05  LINE 11.
          10  COLUMN 21  VALUE     "NUMBER"             PIC X(6).
          10  COLUMN 34  VALUE     "BALANCE"            PIC X(7).
          10  COLUMN 48  VALUE     "YR  MO  DA"         PIC X(10).
 01  DETAIL-LINE
     TYPE DETAIL
     LINE PLUS 1.
     05  COLUMN 22  SOURCE ACCOUNT-NUMBER-M       PIC X(5).
     05  COLUMN 31  SOURCE CURRENT-BALANCE-M      PIC Z,ZZZ,ZZZ.99-.
     05  COLUMN 48  SOURCE TRANSACTION-YEAR-M     PIC 99.
     05  COLUMN 52  SOURCE TRANSACTION-MONTH-M    PIC 99.
     05  COLUMN 56  SOURCE TRANSACTION-DAY-M      PIC 99.
     05  COLUMN 62  SOURCE DEPOSITOR-NAME-M       PIC X(20).
 01  NO-INPUT-DATA
     TYPE DETAIL
     LINE PLUS 1.
     05  COLUMN 22  VALUE "NO INPUT DATA"         PIC X(13).
************************************************
 PROCEDURE DIVISION.
 CONTROL-PARAGRAPH.
     PERFORM INITIALIZATION.
     PERFORM MAIN-PROCESS UNTIL MORE-INPUT = "N".
     PERFORM TERMINATION.
     STOP RUN.
 INITIALIZATION.
     OPEN INPUT MASTER-FILE-IN,
          OUTPUT LIST-FILE-OUT.
     ACCEPT RUN-DATE FROM DATE.
     INITIATE MASTER-LIST.
     READ MASTER-FILE-IN
         AT END
             MOVE "N" TO MORE-INPUT.
     IF MORE-INPUT = "N"
         GENERATE NO-INPUT-DATA.
 TERMINATION.
     TERMINATE MASTER-LIST.
     CLOSE MASTER-FILE-IN,
           LIST-FILE-OUT.
 MAIN-PROCESS.
     GENERATE DETAIL-LINE.
     READ MASTER-FILE-IN
         AT END
             MOVE "N" TO MORE-INPUT.
```

Figure 9–12 (*continued*)

SAVINGS ACCOUNT MASTER

DATE 5/04/82 PAGE 1

ACCOUNT NUMBER	CURRENT BALANCE	DATE OF LAST TRANSACTION YR	MO	DA	DEPOSITOR NAME
00014	990.00-	82	05	03	ROBERT DAVIS M.D.
00021	252.50	82	05	03	LORICE MONTI
00028	5,654.36	82	05	03	MICHAEL SMITH
00032	25.00	82	04	30	JOSEPH CAMILLO
00035	150.00	82	04	30	JOHN J. LEHMAN
00049	150.00	82	04	30	JAY GREENE
00056	1.00	82	04	30	EVELYN SLATER
00070	500.00	82	04	30	PATRICK J. LEE
00077	160.37	82	05	03	LESLIE MINSKY
00084	5,074.29	82	05	03	JOHN & SALLY DUPRINO
00091	2,300.00	82	05	03	JOE'S DELI
00098	500.00	82	05	03	GEORGE & ANN CULHANE
00105	50.00	82	04	30	ONE DAY CLEANERS
00112	250.00	82	04	30	ROSEMARY LANE
00126	1,100.00	82	05	03	JAMES BUDD
00133	3,563.00	82	05	03	PAUL LERNER, D.D.S.
00140	25.75	82	05	03	BETH DENNY
00161	1,280.84	82	05	03	ROBERT RYAN
00175	202.02	82	05	03	MARY KEATING
00189	35.00	82	04	30	J. & L. CAIN
00196	150.00	82	04	30	IMPERIAL FLORIST
00203	5.00	82	04	30	JOYCE MITCHELL
00210	1,000.00	82	05	03	JERRY PARKS
00217	50.00	82	04	30	CARL CALDERON
00224	175.50	82	04	30	JOHN WILLIAMS
00231	555.00	82	04	30	BILL WILLIAMS

SAVINGS ACCOUNT MASTER

DATE 5/04/82 PAGE 2

ACCOUNT NUMBER	CURRENT BALANCE	DATE OF LAST TRANSACTION YR	MO	DA	DEPOSITOR NAME
00238	10.00	82	04	30	KEVIN PARKER
00245	35.00	82	04	30	FRANK CAPUTO
00252	15.00	82	04	30	GENE GALLI
00266	99.57	82	04	30	MARTIN LANG
00273	2,000.00	82	05	03	VITO CACACI
00280	2,337.00	82	05	03	COMMUNITY DRUGS
00287	15.00	82	04	30	SOLOMON CHAPELS
00294	1,500.00	82	04	30	JOHN BURKE
00308	2,050.00	82	05	03	JOE GARCIA
00315	250.00	82	04	30	GRACE MICELI
00329	10.00	82	04	30	GUY VOLPONE
00343	1,000.00	82	04	30	JOE & MARY SESSA
00350	2,500.00	82	04	30	ROGER SHAW
00357	10.00	82	05	03	ROBIN RATANSKI
00364	1,500.00	82	05	03	JOSE TORRES
00371	300.00	82	05	03	ALISE MARKOVITZ
00392	75.00	82	05	03	INEZ WASHINGTON
00398	10.00	82	05	03	JUAN ALVAREZ
00413	100.00	82	05	03	BILL HAYES
00420	1,500.00	82	05	03	JOHN RICE

Figure 9–13 The report produced by the COBOL program of Figure 9–12. (From Gary S. Popkin, *Advanced Structured COBOL*, Boston: Kent Publishing Company, 1983. pp. 230–232. Copyright 1983 by Wadsworth, Inc. Reprinted by permission of Kent Publishing, a division of Wadsworth, Inc.)

RPG

RPG (for Report Program Generator) is a problem-oriented language developed by IBM in the 1960s. In most programming languages, the programmer writes statements that tell the computer **how** to solve a problem. In RPG, the programmer fills in **specifications** forms (Figure 9–14) that tell the computer **what** is to be done. The RPG translator then writes the program to accomplish the desired task. Thus, RPG is actually a **program generator** rather than a simple compiler that converts programs from high-level language to machine language.

This concept was well ahead of its time. Today, with the wide use of personal computers and the possibility that almost everyone will soon be using a computer, it is more important than ever to make computers user-friendly. Many people believe that the best way to accomplish this is to allow people to tell the computer what they want and then let the computer automatically generate working programs to accomplish the desired tasks.

Most business data-processing programs produce printed reports. These reports have certain common features such as report titles, page numbers, page headings, page footings, formatting of numbers into neat columns, column totals, row totals, page totals, and report totals. Programmers found that there was so much similarity among their various report programs that they repeated a great deal of the code each time they wrote a new report program. RPG was developed to make it easier to produce report-writing pro-

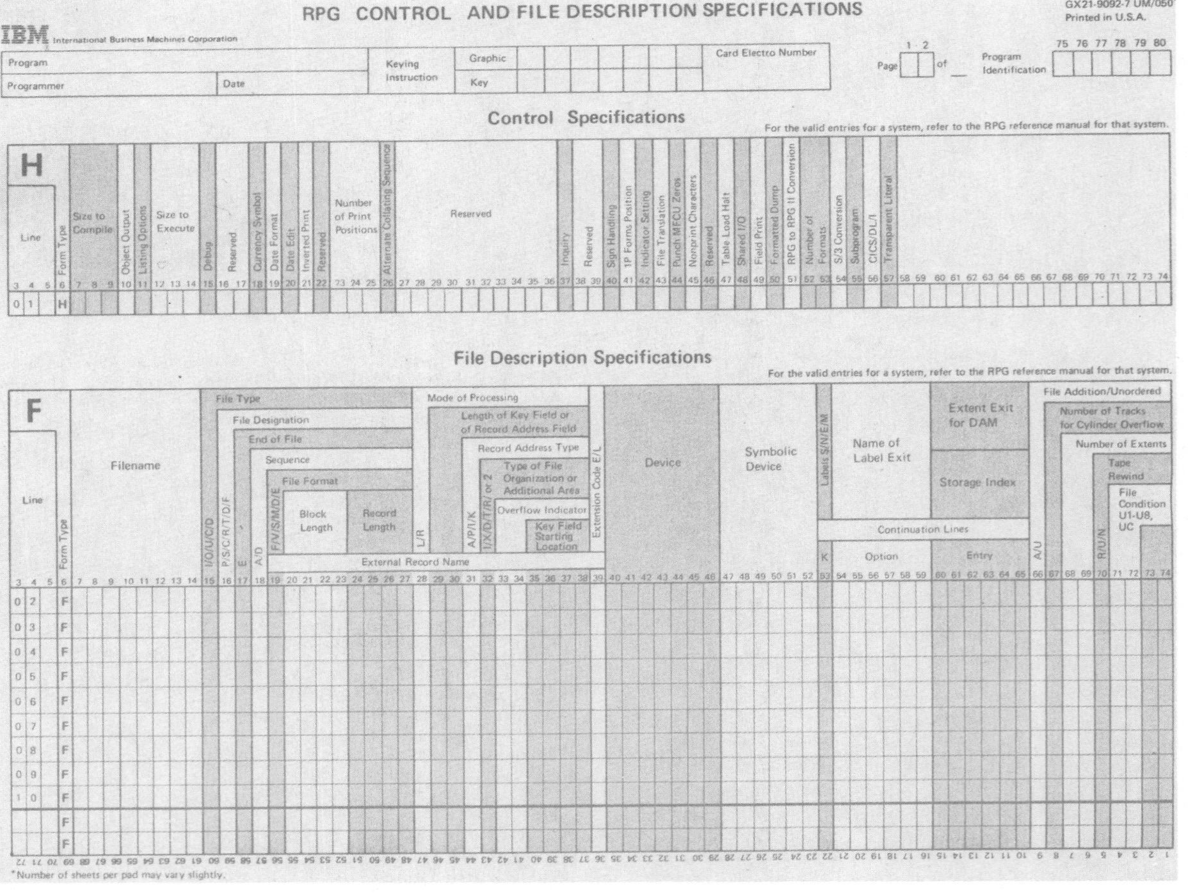

RPG CONTROL AND FILE DESCRIPTION SPECIFICATIONS

IBM International Business Machines Corporation

GX21-9092-7 UM/050
Printed in U.S.A.

Program | Programmer | Date | Keying Instruction | Graphic | Key | Card Electro Number | Page of | Program Identification

Control Specifications

For the valid entries for a system, refer to the RPG reference manual for that system.

H — Line; Form Type; Size to Compile; Object Output; Listing Options; Size to Execute; Debug; Reserved; Currency Symbol; Date Format; Date Edit; Inverted Print; Reserved; Number of Print Positions; Alternate Collating Sequence; Reserved; Inquiry; Reserved; Sign Handling; 1P Forms Position; Indicator Setting; File Translation; Punch MFCU Zeros; Nonprint Characters; Reserved; Table Load Halt; Shared I/O; Field Print; Formatted Dump; RPG to RPG II Conversion; Number of Formats; S/3 Conversion; Subprogram; CICS/DL/I; Transparent Literal

0 1 H

File Description Specifications

For the valid entries for a system, refer to the RPG reference manual for that system.

F — Line; Form Type; Filename; I/O/U/C/D; File Type; P/S/C/R/T/D/F; File Designation; E; End of File; A/D; Sequence; F/V/S/M/D/E; File Format; Block Length; Record Length; L/R; Mode of Processing; Length of Key Field or of Record Address Field; A/P/I/K; Record Address Type; I/X/D/T/R/ or 2; Type of File Organization or Additional Area; Overflow Indicator; Key Field Starting Location; Extension Code E/L; External Record Name; Device; Symbolic Device; Labels S/N/E/M; Name of Label Exit; K; Continuation Lines; Option; Entry; Extent Exit for DAM; Storage Index; A/U; File Addition/Unordered; Number of Tracks for Cylinder Overflow; Number of Extents; Tape Rewind; File Condition U1-U8, UC; R/U/N

0 2 F
0 3 F
0 4 F
0 5 F
0 6 F
0 7 F
0 8 F
0 9 F
1 0 F
F
F

*Number of sheets per pad may vary slightly.

Figure 9–14 One of the several types of specifications forms used by the RPG programmer.

Courtesy International Business Machines Corporation

grams by handling a good part of the programming automatically. The programmer specifies what features each report is to have, what the inputs look like, what types of calculations are to be performed, and so on. The RPG translator then generates a program that meets these specifications.

In 1970 IBM provided RPG II for use with its System/3 computers. In 1979 IBM introduced RPG III for use with its System/38 computers. RPG III provides the capabilities for users to manipulate information stored in a database (see Chapter 11).

APL

APL (A Programming Language) was developed by Kenn Iverson at IBM in the late 1960s. It is a highly mathematical language requiring the use of many special symbols strange to the average computer user. It is a particularly powerful language for those who can understand it. APL can create and manipulate grids of data quite easily, so it is useful for complex routing problems such as those encountered in the airline and trucking industries.

APL has a character set different from that of ASCII (see Chapter 3, "The Processor"), so it requires a special keyboard (Figure 9–15); this has hindered its use. The language allows programmers to write very brief programs to accomplish complex tasks, but these programs can be hard for others to understand.

Figure 9–15 Some APL keyboards have the special mathematical symbols on the sides of the keys.

Pascal

The language that is currently enjoying the most explosive growth is **Pascal** (Figures 9–16 and 9–17), developed by Nicklaus Wirth in 1971 and named after the seventeenth-century mathematician and philosopher Blaise Pascal. Pascal is a structured language with powerful features for defining and manipulating complex data structures. It is a descendant of **ALGOL**, a high-level language originally developed and used in Europe in the early 1960s.

Pascal is a relatively concise language that encourages programmers to produce neatly structured and correct programs. It is a general-purpose, procedure-oriented language. Programmers can define their own data types such as

```
DAYOFWEEK = (MON, TUE, WED, THU, FRI,
             SAT, SUN)
```

or

```
PRIMARYCOLORS = (RED, BLUE, YELLOW)
```

Most Pascal compilers do not generate machine language instructions. Rather, they produce instructions in an "intermediate language" called **p-Code**, which is executed interpretively. This makes Pascal more transportable than other languages; only a new p-Code interpreter need be written for the new machine.

One particularly popular version of the language is the UCSD p-System developed at the University of California at San Diego. It is actually a complete programming environment including its own operating system (see Chapter 12), editors, file handlers, assembler, compiler, and debugger. UCSD Pascal is widely used on personal computers.

Pascal is becoming extremely popular among experienced microcomputer users, but it is not yet challenging BASIC's dominance of the personal computing marketplace. As originally defined, Pascal is weak in many areas important in data processing, including input/output, string processing, and editing. The real surge of interest in Pascal has come from the universities. Pascal has proven to be the best available language for expressing algorithms, particularly those that manipulate data structured in a complex fashion.

C

The **C** programming language was developed at Bell Laboratories and used to code the UNIX operating system (see Chapter 12). C is a structured language resembling Pascal. C programs consist of functions, some created by the programmer and others selected from a large library of standard functions that are part of the language. C is interesting because it has aspects of both assembly and high-level languages. This makes it useful for writing operating systems as well as user applications programs. The use of C is increasing very rapidly, particularly among UNIX users.

Ada

It may seem as though there are already too many programming languages. Nevertheless, the U.S. Defense Department in the mid-1970s sponsored and coordinated the development of yet another language, **Ada**, named after Augusta Ada Byron, Countess of Lovelace, whom many consider the world's first computer programmer. Using suggestions from industry, government, the military, and universities, the Defense Department chose Pascal as a base from which to begin; Pascal's influence is apparent throughout the final version of Ada.

Ada allows a programmer to specify that many tasks (activities) are to be performed simultaneously. Called **multitasking** (see Chapter 12), this capability is particularly useful in military command and control systems.

The first Ada compilers went into use in 1984. It remains to be seen if Ada will indeed meet its goals of improving programmer productivity, reducing software development costs, and improving the reliability and maintainability of large software systems.

Forth

Forth was developed by Charles More at the Kitt Peak Observatory in Arizona. It is not a particularly user-friendly language and is not appropriate for novices.

```
yp:=-radius;
xp:=0;
xold:=round(xp)+xcen;
yold:=round(yp)+ycen;
epsilon:=1/shiftit;
npoint:=npoint DIV 2;
FOR linenum:=1 TO npoint DO
BEGIN
  xp:=xp+epsilon*yp;
  yp:=yp-epsilon*xp;
  x2:=round(xp)+xcen;
  y2:=round(yp)+ycen;
  IF (y2<>yold) THEN
    patternline(x2,y2,2*round(abs(xp)));
  xold:=x2;
  yold:=y2;
END;
```

Figure 9–16 This segment of a Pascal program accomplishes the same task as the assembly language program shown in Figure 9–4.

In a sense, each Forth programmer creates a unique language. The programmer defines functions in terms of already defined functions, building up an ever-richer set of capabilities. Forth automatically saves these functions; each time the programmer uses Forth, all previously defined functions become available.

Forth is available for many personal computers, but it is well behind BASIC and Pascal in user acceptance.

LISP

LISP (for LISt Processor) was developed by John McCarthy at the Massachusetts Institute of Technology in Cambridge in 1960. It is probably the most unconventional of all the languages considered in this chapter. LISP programs are saturated with parentheses, giving them a very strange appearance (Figure 9–19).

LISP was one of the first **symbol manipulation languages**. Instead of "crunching" numbers, LISP manipulates lists of symbols. It can perform such

```
program checkorder (input, output);
{read three characters and report whether they are in
 alphabetical order. loop until reading '***'    }

var
    c1, c2, c3 :char;
    working    :boolean;

function inorder (x:char; y:char; z:char)  boolean,

{the function inorder returns true if and only if
 x < = y < = z    }

begin
    if x < = y then
        inorder : = y < = z
    else
        inorder : = false
end; {inorder}

{the main program starts here}

begin
    working : = true;
    while working do
    begin
        readln(c1, c2, c3);
        write(c1, c2, c3);
        if (c1 = '*') and (c2 = '*') and (c3 = '*') then
            working : = false
        else
            if inorder (c1, c2, c3) then
                writeln ('are in order')
            else
                if inorder (c3, c2, c1) then
                    writeln ('are in reverse order')
                else
                    writeln ('are not in order')
    end {while loop}
end. {program checkorder}
```

Figure 9–17 Blank lines and indentation are used in this complete Pascal program to emphasize program structure. (From *An Introduction to Programming and Problem Solving with Pascal*, second edition, by G. Michael Schneider, Steven W. Weingart, and David M. Perlman. Copyright 1978, 1982. Reprinted by permission of John Wiley & Sons, Inc.)

Figure 9–18 This Ada procedure prints the dollar value of a number of coins consisting of pennies, nickels, dimes, quarters, halves, and dollars.

```
PROCEDURE count your money IS
    USE simple io;
    count, money, cents, dollars: INTEGER;
    values: CONSTANT ARRAY (1..6) OF INTEGER : =
            (1, 5, 10, 25, 50, 100);
  BEGIN
    money: = 0;
    FORiIN 1...6 LOOP
      GET(count);
      money:=money+values (i) * count;
    END LOOP;
    IF money = 0 THEN
      PUT("You are broke.");
    ELSE
      dollars : = money / 100;
      cents := money MOD 100;
      PUT("dollars:"); PUT (dollars);
      PUT ("cents:"); PUT (cents);
    END IF;
END count your money;
```

operations as forming a list from individual elements, combining two lists, splitting a list into separate lists, and determining if an item is contained in a list.

LISP was one of the first languages used for text processing, and it's easy to see why. A word is actually a list of characters. A sentence is a list of words. A paragraph is a list of sentences. A section of a chapter may also be viewed as a list—its first element is a section heading, and the remaining elements are paragraphs. A chapter may then be viewed as a "list of section lists," and so on.

This capability of building increasingly complex structures has made LISP the preferred language in the field of artificial intelligence. More will be said about LISP in Chapter 16.

Figure 9–19 LISP programs are composed of functions. The function LENGTH shown here calculates the length of a list. If the list is empty (NULL X) then the length is zero. If the list is not empty, then the length is one plus the length of the list remaining after the first element is "chopped off" (CDR X). Thus, in LISP the LENGTH function is defined in terms of itself—this is called recursion.

```
==>.pp(length)
    (LENGTH
         (LAMBDA (X)
              (COND
                   ((NULL X)
                        0)
                   (T (PLUS
                        1
                        (LENGTH (CDR X)))))))
    NIL
==>.(length(quote(a b c d e f g)))
    7
```

Query Languages

Query languages allow computer users to request information from computers by typing simple English sentences. In a business application for example, the user may type:

PRINT A REPORT LISTING THE TOTAL SALES FOR JANUARY IN OUR 10 LARGEST STORES.

Query languages have a bright future. Many people believe that they are one of the keys to making computers more user-friendly. Query languages will be discussed further in Chapter 11.

A Universal Programming Language

Should a **universal programming language** (UPL) be developed? Should all future programs be required to be written in it? This idea has generated considerable interest, but no such language has ever been developed. Its advantages are obvious: All programs would be portable, fewer translators would have to be written, more effort could go into developing an excellent UPL translator, and people would only have to learn one language.

But there are also disadvantages. From a practical standpoint, a huge amount of working software in use would have to be replaced. A universal language would have to be very large because it would need to contain all the features of existing languages. It would be constantly changing, because as new ideas emerge the language would have to be adjusted. Its size would make it more difficult to learn than other languages, and its compilers would demand large primary storages and very fast processors. It is unlikely, therefore, that a UPL will ever be developed.

Software Packages

People who want to listen to rock and roll usually buy hit records instead of writing and recording their own music. Similarly, computer users often purchase software packages from software vendors instead of developing their own software. Many "hit floppies" are offered.

By purchasing software packages, users can obtain needed capabilities immediately and at less cost. Most likely the packages will be superior to the software the users could have developed themselves. More purchased software than custom-developed software is already used on personal computers and small business computers. This use of purchased software is certain to increase in the foreseeable future.

Trends

Many trends are taking shape in the field of programming languages. **Very-high-level languages** (VHLLs) will enable programmers to write programs with fewer statements. **High-level language machines** will run high-level language programs directly without the need for compiling. **Concurrent programming languages** will allow programmers to specify that many tasks are to be performed simultaneously.

Future computers may understand free-form English sentences (natural language) well enough to enable them to be programmed in English. But English is an ambiguous language, so the computer may have to ask questions to resolve any uncertainties. Computers equipped with speech recognizers may be programmed by spoken commands. Languages will be developed that are even easier than BASIC to learn and use. More powerful problem-oriented languages will appear that greatly facilitate writing programs for solving very specific types of problems.

"Well, it's not cobol and pretty sure it's not fortran and..." ©Creative Computing

The computer user population will shift from experienced computer professionals to the general public. People will program computers early in their education. An increasing portion of all programs will be produced by program generators rather than by programmers. The flow of excellent software packages will increase and software prices will continue to decline. As more users plug in to worldwide data communications networks, they will have access to ever-growing software libraries. Users will be able to search these libraries by computer to locate and use programs of almost any type. Software libraries will also contain program pieces or modules that programmers may use as building blocks to construct programs.

A Brief Introduction to LOGO

LOGO is a unique programming language often associated with the use of computers by children. In fact, it is a powerful language that experienced programmers can use to create certain types of programs much faster than is possible with other popular high-level languages.

LOGO was developed over the last two decades by researchers in industry and at MIT, most notably Seymour Papert. As head of MIT's LOGO effort, Papert drew on his experience in the fields of computing, artificial intelligence, and psychology to create a programming language that could facilitate the educational process.

LOGO contains particularly powerful graphics capabilities. It uses **turtle graphics**, in which a pen is attached to a mechanical device (the turtle) that makes marks on a sheet of paper according to user commands. On personal computer versions of LOGO, the turtle is a dot that moves around the screen leaving a trace of its path. The following boxed piece briefly introduces the operation of turtle graphics in LOGO.

Building Turtle Designs with Procedures

The most common introductory Logo activity is creating designs with the turtle. At first this is done simply by typing a sequence of commands. To draw a square you could type these commands:

FORWARD 50
RIGHT 90
FORWARD 50
RIGHT 90
FORWARD 50
RIGHT 90
FORWARD 50
RIGHT 90

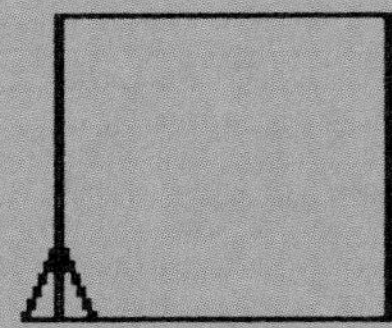

You can achieve the same result using the Logo command REPEAT, which needs two *inputs*: a number telling how many times to repeat something and a list of instructions to be repeated. Lists in Logo are always set off with square brackets.

REPEAT 4 [FORWARD 50 RIGHT 90]

The power of programming in Logo comes when you teach the computer a new command, or more properly, procedure. For example, to teach the computer to draw a square, you define a new procedure called SQUARE. (The actual name is entirely arbitrary — you could call it BOX, R2D2, HENRY, or MOMMA if you like. The only name you cannot use is one that already identifies a built-in Logo command.)

TO SQUARE
REPEAT 4 [FORWARD 50 RIGHT 90]
END

SQUARE is now a word in the computer's vocabulary. You can use it to teach the computer other words. FLOWER, for example, uses SQUARE as a subprocedure.

TO FLOWER
REPEAT 12 [SQUARE RIGHT 30]
END

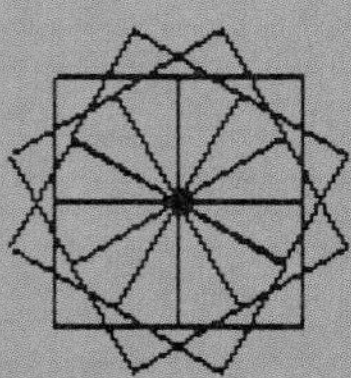

SQUARE could also be combined with other shapes to make a truck, a house, or other designs based on squares.

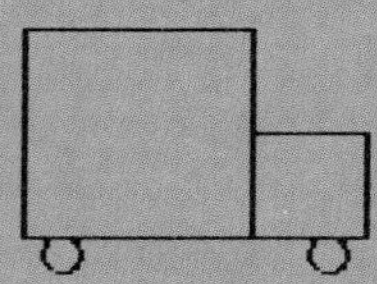

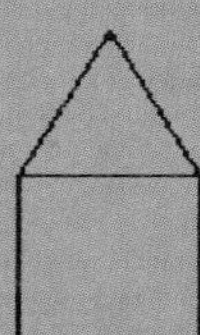

At this point you might be wondering whether you have to teach the computer a brand-new command every time you want it to draw a square of a different size. Actually all

Summary 

1. Each computer can only understand programs written in its own machine language.
2. Machine languages are machine dependent because they are so closely related to the structure of a particular machine.
3. Most programs today are written in assembly languages or high-level languages.
4. Assembler programs translate assembly language programs into machine language programs.
5. Assembly language programs can be written faster, have fewer bugs, and are easier to understand and modify than machine language programs.
6. Macro instructions are single statements that an assembler expands into several assembly language statements.
7. High-level languages use English phrases and common mathematical notations. They can convey in one statement what may take many statements in machine and assembly languages.
8. High-level languages are easier to learn than assembly languages.
9. High-level languages are categorized as either procedure oriented or problem oriented.
10. In program development environments, "quick-and-dirty" compilers are used. These translate programs quickly, although the resulting machine language programs may not run as efficiently as possible.

you have to do is modify the square procedure so that it can accept an input just as the Logo commands FORWARD, RIGHT, and REPEAT do. Modify the procedure as follows:

```
TO SQUARE :SIZE
REPEAT 4 [FORWARD :SIZE RIGHT 90]
END
```

SIZE is called a *variable*, and :SIZE tells the computer to use the current *value* of the variable named SIZE. If you designate :SIZE as 20, the computer draws a square with sides 20 turtle steps long. If :SIZE is 50, the square will be the same as our original fixed square, and so on. To specify a value for the variable SIZE, you type the command with an input number, as in SQUARE 20.

Suppose you wanted to make a set of nested squares as shown below. Simply type a series of SQUARE commands with different inputs.

```
TO GROWSQUARES
SQUARE 20
SQUARE 40
SQUARE 60
SQUARE 80
SQUARE 100
END
```

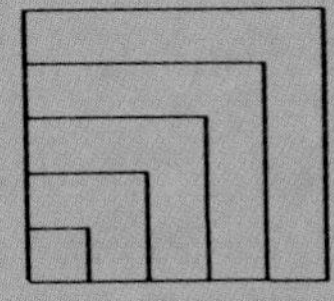

Logo does offer a simpler way to write procedures like GROWSQUARES; it's known as *recursion* — a process in which a procedure calls another version of itself. To establish this recursive process, GROWSQUARES needs an input that changes every time it calls another GROWSQUARES.

```
TO GROWSQUARES :SIZE
IF :SIZE > 100 STOP
SQUARE :SIZE
GROWSQUARES :SIZE + 20
END
```

When you give the command GROWSQUARES 20, GROWSQUARES checks to see if its input is larger than 100. If not, it goes on to the next step and calls on SQUARE, giving it an input of 20. Then it calls *another* GROWSQUARES but gives this one an input of 40 (:SIZE + 20). This new GROWSQUARES calls a SQUARE procedure with an input of 40 and then calls a new GROWSQUARES with an input of 60, and so on. Finally one GROWSQUARES procedure receives an input of 120 and the whole process stops.

A Sampler of Turtle Drawings

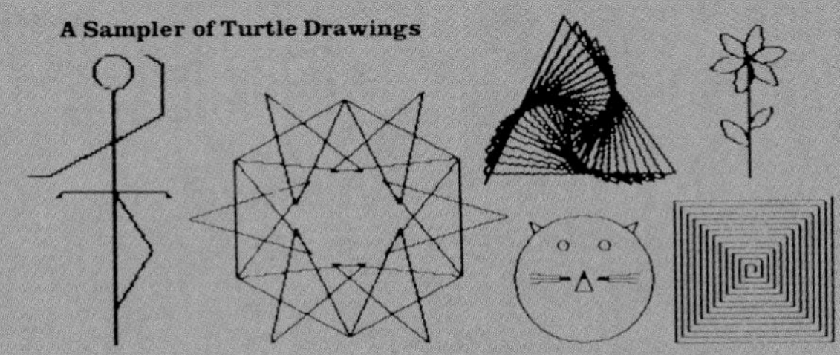

This text and the accompanying drawings are reprinted with the permission of the author, Daniel H. Watt, from the article, "Logo: What Makes It Exciting?" which appeared in *Popular Computing* Magazine, August 1983. The illustrations themselves were taken from the book *Learning With Logo* by Daniel H. Watt (Byte Books/McGraw-Hill, 1983) and are reprinted with the permission of the publisher.

11. In production environments, optimizing compilers are used. They take more time to translate programs, but the machine language programs they produce run faster and use less main storage.
12. Some of the more popular high-level languages are BASIC, FORTRAN, COBOL, PL/1, RPG, APL, Pascal, C, Ada, Forth, LISP, and LOGO.
13. Query languages allow users to request information from computer systems by writing simple English sentences.
14. A universal programming language would make all programs portable and allow programmers to communicate programs in a common language. Such a language is unlikely to emerge because it would have to be very large, would require substantial computer resources, and would always be changing.
15. Some important trends are the development of very-high-level languages, high-level language machines, and concurrent programming languages. More programs will be produced by program generators, an increasing portion of software used will be purchased rather than home grown, and data communications networks will give programmers access to huge libraries of existing software and program building blocks.

Important Terms 

Ada
ALGOL
American National Standards Institute (ANSI)
APL
assembler
assembly language
BASIC
C
COBOL
compiler
Forth
FORTRAN
hierarchical data structuring
high-level language
interpreter
LISP
LOGO
machine dependent
macro instruction
optimizing compiler
Pascal
PL/1
problem-oriented language
procedure-oriented language
production environment
program development environment
"quick-and-dirty" compiler
RPG
translator program
universal programming language

Self-Review Exercises 

Matching

Next to the term in column A, place the letter of the statement in column B that best describes it.

Column A

1. Mnemonic
2. COBOL
3. Query language
4. LOGO
5. Compiler
6. RPG
7. Macro
8. Optimizing compiler
9. Ada
10. Pascal

Column B

A. One instruction that is translated into several machine instructions
B. Useful in military command and control applications
C. Technique to aid memory
D. Uses turtle graphics
E. Handles complex data structures
F. Translator program
G. Used in business data-processing applications
H. Allows users to request information
I. Program generator
J. Used in production environments to produce fast-running machine language programs

Fill-in-the-Blanks

Fill in the blanks in each of the following:

1. Each computer can directly understand only its own ______ .

2. A translator program that actually runs a source program directly is called an ______ .

3. High-level languages may be categorized as either ______ oriented or ______ oriented.

4. ______ compilers translate programs quickly, but the machine language programs they produce do not run fast and may use more primary storage than they need.

5. The four major divisions of a COBOL program are ______ , ______ , ______ , and ______ .

6. ______ is a structured language that contains the better features of FORTRAN and COBOL.

7. ______ is a somewhat mathematical language that requires a special keyboard.

8. ______ allows many tasks to be performed simultaneously.

9. Machine languages are said to be ______ because they are so closely related to the structure of the computer.

10. ______ languages use everyday English and mathematical notations.

Answers to Self-Review Exercises

Matching: 1 C, 2 G, 3 H, 4 D, 5 F, 6 I, 7 A, 8 J, 9 B, 10 E

Fill-in-the-Blanks:

1. machine language
2. interpreter
3. procedure, problem
4. "Quick-and-dirty"
5. identification, environment, data, procedure
6. PL/1
7. APL
8. Multitasking
9. machine dependent
10. High-level

Discussion Questions

1. Distinguish between machine, assembly, and high-level programming languages.

2. Explain the differences between compilers and interpreters.

3. What are the four divisions of every COBOL program? Briefly describe the purposes of each.

4. List some of the common features found in business data processing reports.

5. Discuss some of the features of Pascal that have contributed to its popularity.

6. Why was Ada developed?

7. Why is LISP particularly well-suited for text-editing applications?

8. Describe how you would determine the most appropriate programming language for a particular application.

9. List several important trends in programming languages.

10. Briefly describe the operation of turtle graphics in LOGO.

Projects

1. Write to the following companies for information about the program generators they offer. Write a report comparing and contrasting the features of these program generators.

Generator	Company
dBASE II	Ashton-Tate Company Los Angeles, CA
FORMULA	Dynamic Microprocessor Associates or Lifeboat Associates New York, NY
Personal Pearl	Relational Systems, Inc. Salem, OR
Programmer's Apprentice	Lifeboat Associates New York, NY
The Last One	D.J. "AI" Systems, Ltd. Los Angeles, CA
The Programmer	Advanced Operating Systems Inc. Michigan City, IN

(Source: Jon Levine, "Programming Made Easy," *Venture*, September 1982, p. 20)

2. Visit a computer store and ask to see a demonstration of a program generator. Try using it yourself. Write a report describing its capabilities and ease of use.

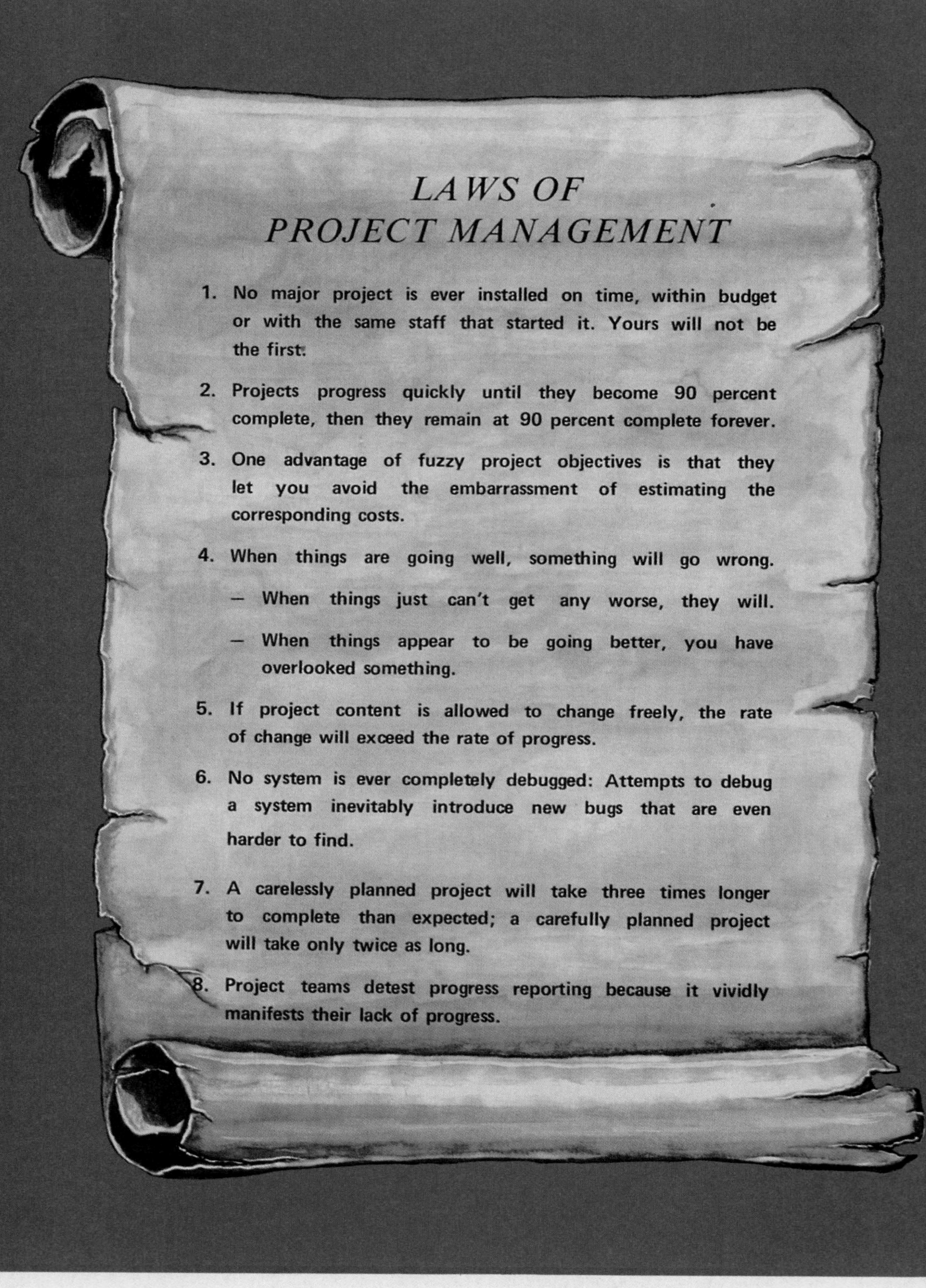
LAWS OF
PROJECT MANAGEMENT
1. No major project is ever installed on time, within budget or with the same staff that started it. Yours will not be the first.
2. Projects progress quickly until they become 90 percent complete, then they remain at 90 percent complete forever.
3. One advantage of fuzzy project objectives is that they let you avoid the embarrassment of estimating the corresponding costs.
4. When things are going well, something will go wrong.
— When things just can't get any worse, they will.
— When things appear to be going better, you have overlooked something.
5. If project content is allowed to change freely, the rate of change will exceed the rate of progress.
6. No system is ever completely debugged: Attempts to debug a system inevitably introduce new bugs that are even harder to find.
7. A carelessly planned project will take three times longer to complete than expected; a carefully planned project will take only twice as long.
8. Project teams detest progress reporting because it vividly manifests their lack of progress.

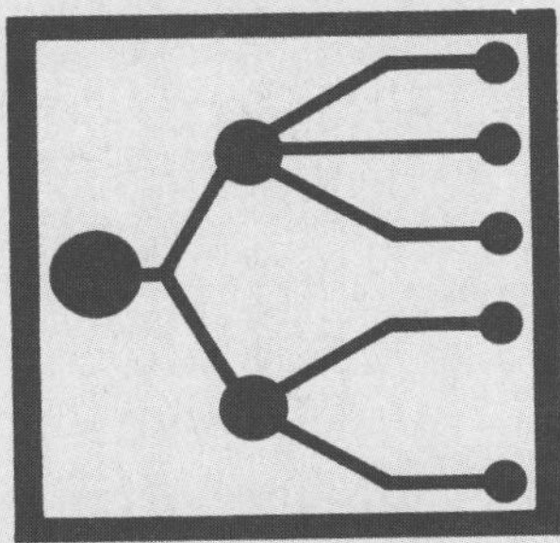

Structured Systems Analysis and Design; Systems Acquisition

After reading this chapter you will understand:

1. What a system is
2. What the systems life cycle is and what its key stages are
3. What is meant by structured systems analysis
4. What a feasibility study is
5. How to evaluate a system

Left: These "Laws of Project Management" are meant to be humorous. All too often, however, they are also true.

Outline

Nothing endures but change.

Heraclitus

The more things change, the more they remain the same.

Alphonse Karr

The Random House Dictionary of the English Language defines a system as "an assemblage or combination of things or parts forming a complex or unitary whole." An automobile is a system by this definition, as is a person, a baseball team, a computer, and even a single computer program. Some of the most common business systems and their functions are listed in Figure 10–1; case studies on these systems are presented in Chapter 11.

A computer-based system is one with "things or parts" that consist primarily of hardware and software that work together to perform some common goal. In the previous chapters we have focused on individual aspects of these systems. In Chapters 10, 11, and 12, we take the **systems view**, seeing how these components may be combined to form systems.

In this chapter, we discuss the systems development process in detail. Developing new systems is a costly and time-consuming process. The benefits gained from a successful system can be great; the problems caused by an unsuccessful one can be devastating. For those individuals and organizations that do not wish to develop their own systems, we discuss several popular means for acquiring systems from various types of systems suppliers.

At the end of the chapter we present a detailed case study in the state-of-the-art techniques of structured systems analysis and design. These are the latest methodologies that have evolved as part of the "structured revolution" that began with structured programming in the late 1960s. After studying the case of the FutureCar Company, the reader will be up-to-the-minute in the field of structured systems development.

Figure 10–1 The most common business systems.

System	Main Purpose
Payroll	Pay employees.
Accounts Payable	Pay other companies for goods and services they supply.
Invoicing	Bill customers for goods and services they purchase.
Accounts Receivable	Keep track of money owed by customers and send regular statements requesting payment for outstanding amounts.
Order Entry	Accept customer orders for goods and services and see that these orders are fulfilled.
Sales Analysis	Monitor the sales of goods and services.
Inventory Control	Keep track of all items in warehouses and on the shelves. When quantities get low, reorder.
General Ledger	Keep track of financial transactions so that the profitability of the business can be determined. Prepare income statements (showing profit or loss), and balance sheets (showing assets and liabilities).

Why Develop or Modify Systems?

Businesses develop new systems or modify existing ones for various reasons. They may do so to improve profits, provide better customer service, take advantage of improved technologies, comply with new or revised laws and regulations, adjust to changes in suppliers' procedures or customer requirements, satisfy the terms of new labor contracts, provide for the handling of new product lines, facilitate growth, or handle the extension of their operations into international markets.

Some changes are made to polish the system itself. These modifications help to improve system security, speed information processing, increase storage capacity, facilitate operating procedures, accommodate new hardware devices, add new capabilities such as data communications, improve reliability, and make information more accessible.

Whenever an existing system is modified or a new system is added, it is essential to consider how these changes may affect other systems in the organization. An organization's set of systems is sometimes called its **management information system** (MIS). Management information systems are discussed in Chapter 11.

The Systems Life Cycle

As new systems are developed or existing ones are changed, they evolve through a series of phases called the **systems life cycle** (Figure 10–2). In the following sections, we discuss what happens in each of these phases, what types of people are involved, and the techniques they use to perform their functions.

The Requirements Definition Phase

When it becomes apparent that a new system is needed or that changes must be made to an existing system, the users who will be affected begin by listing and justifying their new needs in the **requirements definition phase**. This list, called the **requirements document**, provides management and the systems staff with information indicating what is needed, when it is needed, and why it is needed. The requirements document, often produced by users who know little about computers, is normally written from a nontechnical viewpoint.

Commitments to change a system or develop a new one are not to be taken lightly. They can be costly, they can demand significant human resources, and, if not handled properly, they may upset the organization's operations. A major commitment to a new system could affect the company for years to come, having an impact on departments that are not directly affected as well as on clients and suppliers. Therefore, the users must make a convincing case in the requirements document. Management may reject the requirements document, or it may give the go-ahead for further investigation.

Figure 10–2 The systems life cycle.

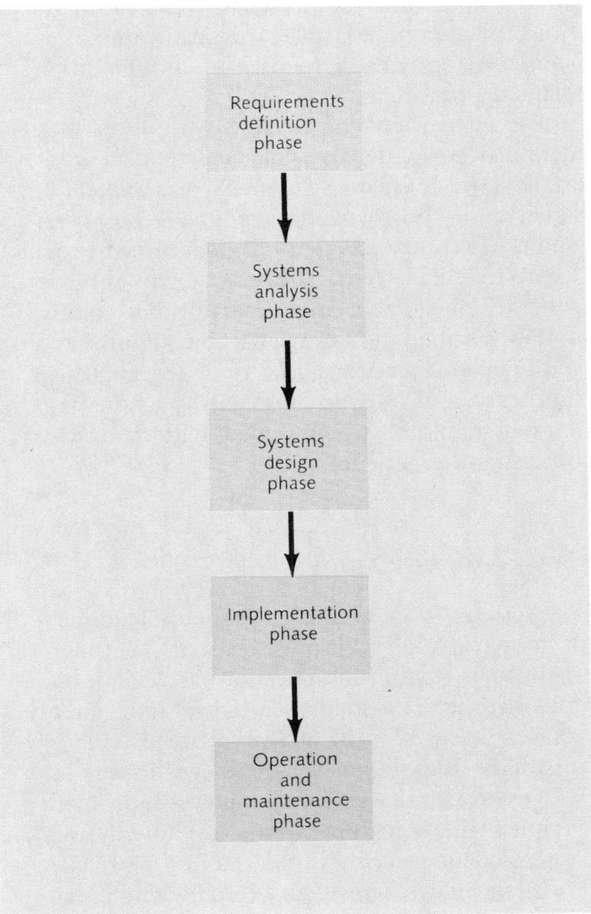

The Systems Analysis Phase

If management finds that the requirements document has merit, the users' needs are translated by **systems analysts** into a more precise document, called the **specification**. The specification restates the needs in terms that are meaningful to systems people, and it describes the type of system that the analyst feels would be appropriate to satisfy those needs. It is detailed enough so that people called **systems designers** may use it as a basis for actually designing the system.

In this **systems analysis phase**, systems analysts act as intermediaries between users, management, and systems designers, helping each of these groups to understand the needs and problems of the others. The requirements document may state that "we need to get the monthly statements out three days sooner to improve our cash flow." The analyst may translate this into a series of suggestions for obtaining faster hardware, improving software, reorganizing personnel, and modifying manual procedures.

The systems analyst consults with users, the data processing department, management, customers, the company's suppliers, government agencies, hardware vendors, software suppliers, and other companies that have developed systems to meet similar needs. The analyst should be personable, an effective communicator, both orally and in writing, and knowledgeable about the business, its operations, government regulations, hardware, and software. Obviously, a systems analyst should be highly skilled, with many years of business experience.

The Feasibility Study

The systems users may say, "It should be done" or, more forcefully, "It must be done," but the analyst has to ask such questions as "Can it be done within a reasonable amount of time and at acceptable costs?" The analyst proceeds with a **feasibility study** to answer these questions.

In the feasibility study, the analyst thoroughly examines the users' operations and how these relate to, or **interface** with, the rest of the organization. The analyst considers alternative potential solutions to the users' problems. Written questionnaires are used to gather needed information. Personal interviews are conducted; these can be particularly revealing, especially if the interviewer's style encourages the subject to speak frankly. Interviews can be time-consuming, however, so only key people should be interviewed.

The analyst determines what inputs are currently being gathered, how they are processed, and what outputs are being produced. How might each of these change in the new system? What problems are being experienced? What benefits would the new system provide? What problems might develop?

The analyst can often see many additional benefits of a new system, which the users have ignored. The analyst's interpretation may, then, strengthen the user's case that a new system is needed. Next, the analyst must evaluate the available alternatives for meeting the users' needs and narrow the choices to a few effective approaches.

The specification produced by the analyst should be brief. It should state the current problems, indicate the alternative solutions and their anticipated costs and benefits, and propose an implementation schedule. It should give a concise summary of the data gathered in the feasibility study and include names, addresses, and phone numbers of key people consulted in the study whom users and management may also want to contact.

The level of detail that should be used in the specification depends a great deal on the relationship between the systems analysts and the systems designers. If they work together regularly and understand one another, the specification will tend to be less detailed, especially if this project is similar to others they have handled. If they haven't worked together regularly, or if this project is different from previous ones, then the specification should be much more detailed.

In some cases, the analyst will specify mainframe hardware, peripherals, input formats, report and screen layouts, report frequency, placement of terminals throughout the organization, and the like. In other cases, the designer assumes these responsibilities. Often the analyst specifies these items informally and lets the designer handle the details. The interface between

 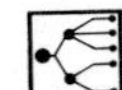

systems analysis and systems design is not crisply defined and often varies among organizations.

The analyst should discuss the specification with the users and management to make sure that they understand it, that it accurately states the users' needs, and that it addresses management's concerns.

Data Collection

Collecting input data is one of the most costly, time-consuming, and error-prone operations in computer-based systems. Careful thought must go into the specification and implementation of data collection mechanisms.

Often a company that has computerized some of its operations will discover that it is already collecting and computerizing most, and possibly all, of the data it needs to feed a new system. This could greatly reduce the implementation and operation costs of a new system. Thus, it is critical for the analyst to determine if the needed data is already being collected, even if by a different part of the organization.

Involving the Users

As a system evolves, it is handled by people who are increasingly distant from the user. These people may lose sight of the users' needs and problems. Although the goals of the systems development people may be met in that a working system is delivered on schedule and within budget, the users may say, "Sorry, it's very nice but it's not what we need." The best way to keep this from happening is for the systems analysts to involve the users throughout the systems development effort, rather than merely to consult with them during the systems analysis phase.

The Systems Design Phase

The specification that emerges from the systems analysis phase describes *what* the desired system is to do. In the **systems design phase**, the **systems designers** decide *how* to do it. In the next several sections, we consider some of the tools and methods used by systems designers to produce well-designed systems.

Systems Flowcharts

The concept of a **systems flowchart** is similar to a structured program flowchart, which was discussed in Chapter 8. A systems flowchart indicates how information flows between the various components of a system. Systems flowcharts use a much larger variety of symbol shapes to show the nature of the processing operations to be performed. Figure 10–3 shows the systems flowcharting symbols that are commonly used. We will use systems flowcharting in Chapter 11 in the case studies on the major business systems.

Top-Down Stepwise Refinement

Structured design begins with the **top-down stepwise refinement process**, in which the design is developed gradually through a series of increasingly detailed refinements. The highest level, simply called the **top**, represents a functional statement of the problem. The next lower level is obtained by breaking the single top **module** into separate modules for its separate functions (that is, the first refinement). As this process continues, each level represents a more detailed refinement. The process terminates when each module needs no further refinement—when it is clear that each module is sufficiently detailed to be programmed easily in the chosen programming language. Pseudocode, as we discussed in Chapter 8, is then used by the designers to "frame out" each module for the programmers.

The stepwise refinement process yields a **hierarchical module structure**, as shown in Figure 10–4. This is the kind of structure that is used in large corporations, where one boss has several employees, but each employee has only one boss. Such a structure has clear lines of authority. Similarly, in a hierarchical module structure, each module performs its function only when called on by the module immediately above it in the hierarchy; each module may only call on modules that are directly below it. In the case study at the end of this chapter, we will see how the hierarchical module structure emerges quite naturally.

Input/output function in card medium (all varieties):
PUNCHED CARD
★ Card Deck
A collection of punched cards.
★ Card File
A collection of related punched-card records.
Other specific media:
DOCUMENT
★ Magnetic Tape
TRANSMITTAL TAPE
Proof or adding machine tape, or other batch-control information.
PUNCHED TAPE
ONLINE STORAGE
Input/output using any kind of online storage—magnetic tape, drum, disk.
An operation using a key-driven device—such as punching verifying, typing.
KEYING
Other specific media for input/output functions:
★ Magnetic Disk
★ Core
★ Magnetic Drum
MERGE
Combine two or more sets of items into one set.
Removal of one or more specific sets of items from a set.
EXTRACT
★ Collate
Merging with extracting; forming two or more sets of items from two or more other sets.
★ Sort
Arranging a set of items into sequence.
★ Offline Storage
Storing offline, regardless of recorded medium.
DISPLAY
Information display by online indicators, video devices, console printers, plotters, etc.
Information input by online keyboards, switch settings, pushbuttons.
MANUAL INPUT
MANUAL OPERATION
Any offline process (at "human speed") without mechanical aid.
Offline performance on equipment not under direct control of central processing unit.
AUXILIARY OPERATION
COMMUNICATION LINK: Function of transmitting information by a telecommunication link. (Vertical, horizontal, or diagonal, arrowheads for clarity; bidirectional flow shown by two opposing arrowheads.)

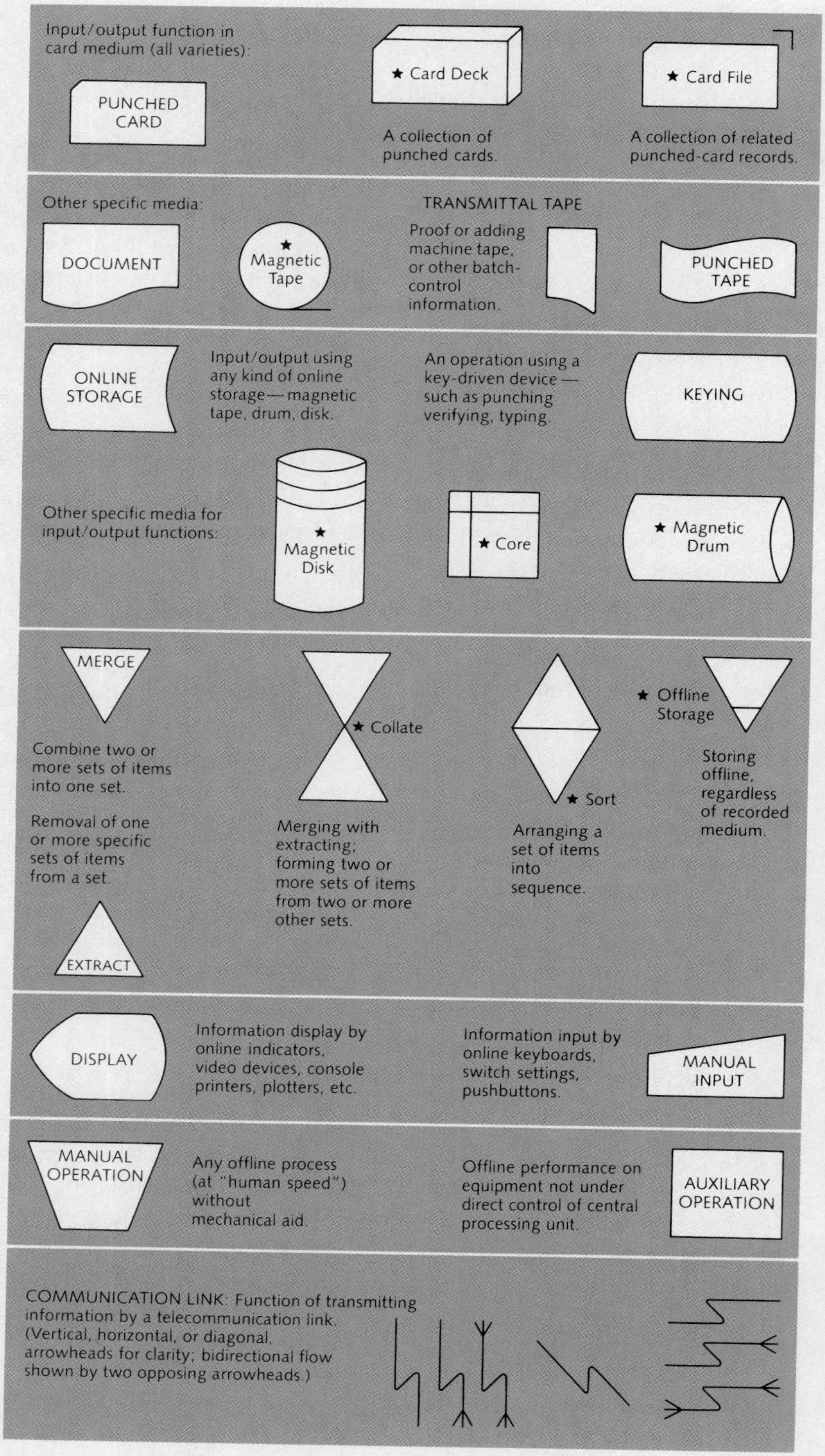

Courtesy of International Business Machines Corporation

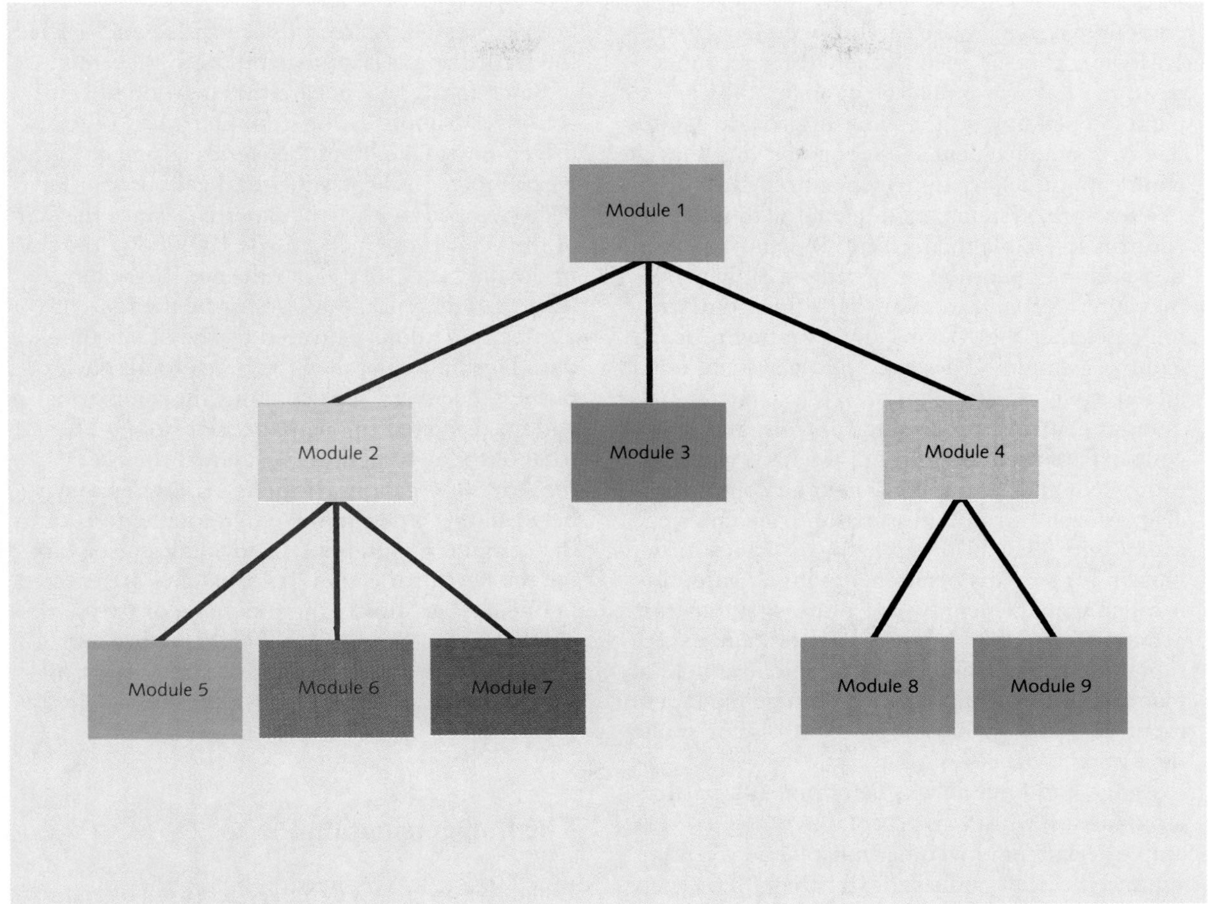

Figure 10–3 *Left:* Some commonly used systems flowcharting symbols. Symbols marked by a star (*) are drawn by adding to or combining shapes provided by cutoffs in the flowcharting template. Symbols marked "IBM" indicate IBM usage beyond the ANSI standard.

Figure 10–4 *Above:* A hierarchical module structure typical of that which emerges from the top-down, stepwise refinement process.

Cost/Benefit Analysis

Businesses operate with limited budgets for developing and modifying systems. Systems analysts and designers must choose between alternative systems and designs by considering their costs and what benefits the organization may expect. This evaluation process is called **cost/benefit analysis.**

The costs of hardware, software, people, and supplies can usually be estimated with reasonable precision. Benefits such as "50 percent faster processing" can often be translated directly into dollars. Benefits such as "making information more accessible" or "making the system more user-friendly" are more difficult to measure.

Controls

The proper functioning of an organization depends on the careful design of its computer-based systems. A bank could not operate properly if its computer systems were carelessly designed—deposits might be applied to the wrong accounts, customer balances might be in error, and companies depending on the bank to provide day-to-day cash management services might find that the bank cannot deliver funds when needed.

Therefore, systems are designed with many **controls** to enable them to check their own operation and the operation of systems with which they interface, and to allow personnel to determine whether the systems are operating properly. Controls should be designed into a system, not added as an afterthought.

Input controls, **processing controls**, and **output controls** are used to ensure that data is entered, processed, and output correctly and completely. They prevent invalid information from entering the system. They also highlight suspicious information for systems personnel to investigate; this is called **management by exception**. Routine transactions are handled by the computer, and exceptional items are examined by people. In the remainder of this section, we'll examine the types of input, processing, and output controls commonly used in data-processing systems.

Range and limit checks determine if a particular value lies within an acceptable range. For example, a date in November must be between the 1st and the 30th; values greater than 30 or less than 1 are unacceptable.

Reasonableness checks are used to determine if certain values are suspicious. A payroll system computing an hourly employee's gross pay may input a figure of 102 hours worked in one week. It is certainly possible for an employee to work that many hours, but it is highly unlikely; the payroll system should insist on confirmation from the payroll manager before this employee's paycheck is issued.

Validity checks determine if the input is in the proper format. A numeric field, for example, should not contain a question mark. A year-of-birth field should certainly not contain the word *tree*.

Record counts are used to ensure that files are complete. The record count is stored with the file and also recorded externally. Each time the file is processed, the computer recounts the records to be sure the file is intact and that all records have been processed. As records are added and deleted, the record count is adjusted to keep it current.

Batch totals help ensure that a group of transactions is complete. For example, a fuel oil truck driver may make 40 oil deliveries in one day. The truck's meter indicates the total gallons that have been pumped by the truck, perhaps since the start of the year. If the meter reads 100,000 at the start of the day, and 108,000 at the end of the day, then the difference, 8000, must be the total number of gallons delivered by the driver that day. This figure is called the batch total. Each of the 40 delivery slips contains the number of gallons delivered to one particular home. The total of these 40 figures must equal the batch total of 8000 gallons. If there is a discrepancy between the slips and the batch total entered into the computer, an **input control clerk** must examine the batch for errors. If 15 batches are entered in one day, it is likely that only one or two of the batches will be in error. Thus, the input control clerk will only have to examine about 40 or 80 slips out of a total of perhaps 600 slips.

The Implementation Phase

When the proposed design is accepted by management, it is turned over to the **implementation team**. They acquire the needed hardware, program the system, test it to uncover any bugs, correct the bugs, and retest the system until they can demonstrate that it is functioning properly. This is called the **implementation phase**. At this point the system that has been under development enters **production**—it runs on a regular schedule to perform the functions originally requested in the user requirements document.

Even the most detailed designs should still leave the implementers some flexibility in deciding how to build the system. But certainly there should not be so much flexibility that a colossal mismatch with the intent of the design could result. This is aptly indicated by the following anecdote:

> Two construction engineers were studying a set of blueprints for building a tunnel and were trying to de-

cide how to get the tunnel started. The first suggested that the crew begin at one end of the mountain and dig straight through to the other end. The second engineer disagreed, saying that the best way to dig the tunnel is to have two crews working; one crew starts at one end of the mountain, the other crew starts at the other end, and both crews dig toward the center of the mountain until they meet.

The first engineer couldn't help wondering, "But what happens if the crews don't meet in the center of the mountain?" "That's even better," replied the second engineer, after careful deliberation. "We'll get two tunnels!"

Hardware Acquisition

Hardware may be acquired from many sources, including manufacturers, retailers (such as computer stores), previous owners, or dealers of used computers. The three popular ways of acquiring hardware are **purchasing**, **leasing**, and **renting**. Financing computer equipment is a complex task that can have many consequences for a business. Management should consult with an accountant, a tax attorney, or both, before committing itself to any financing arrangements.

One disadvantage of purchasing is that when the organization wants to upgrade to better equipment, it may be difficult to dispose of the original equipment in the used computer marketplace. Instead of purchasing hardware, many companies lease it. Inflation encourages leasing because the fixed payments are made with ever-cheaper dollars. A company may feel that newer and better equipment will become available, so at the end of a lease, it need not renew.

As a rule, if the computer will not be kept for a long period, such as five or more years, it is better to lease than to buy. But the pace of change is so rapid today that systems are often replaced much faster than this. Because obsolescence is such a serious concern, some leases allow the lessee to upgrade equipment during the term of the lease. Some leases contain a clause that allows the lessee to cancel the lease upon payment of a penalty.

Many leases contain purchase options. The longer the machine has been leased when the decision is made to purchase it, the lower the purchase price. Because some organizations tend to resist change, leased equipment is often retained longer than anticipated even though it may be obsolete. For this reason, these organizations would be better off buying the equipment they are leasing rather than continuing with their leasing agreement.

Obtaining used computers can be an attractive option for many companies. Used machines can be purchased or leased for less than new machines, and they may provide the same performance and service.

When equipment is rented, the costs can be relatively high, but the risks are lower. Rental agreements are usually for a relatively short term (such as a year or two) and may contain early termination penalty clauses. The customer pays a fixed monthly fee and builds up no ownership credits.

Modules, Coupling, and Cohesion

Most of today's systems are built as groups of interacting program pieces called modules. A large system works best using the famous "divide and conquer" strategy, in which it is broken into manageable pieces. The more detail in a design, the easier it is for the programmers to translate the design into working programs. Deciding how to partition a system into modules is a difficult process that can greatly affect the ease or difficulty with which the system can be programmed, tested, debugged, and modified.

Two measures of how well a system has been modularized are **coupling** and **cohesion**. Coupling should be minimized—modules should be as independent of one another as possible. Cohesion should be maximized—functions placed within a single module should be as closely related to one another as possible.

If modules are closely coupled (an undesirable aspect of design), unanticipated **side effects**, which can be devastating, often result. The troubles frequently occur in debugging; each time one bug is fixed new ones appear. This can make it virtually impossible to debug a large system.

Training the Personnel

People have to learn how to operate the system, use its information, and keep its information current. Thus, user training is an important part of the systems implementation process.

The users can't simply be handed a pile of manuals and told to go read them. Training can be a slow and costly process, but its rewards are valuable; the users will accept and benefit by the system more readily if they understand it.

When minor changes are made to a system, it is usually sufficient to send a short memo describing the changes to the people affected by them. When major changes are made, it may be appropriate to hold training seminars. Many companies provide regular training to keep their employees aware of new developments. Such training pays off handsomely when the systems affected by these developments are actually changed.

"Here's the latest in computer technology. The only drawback is this operating manual."

Documentation

Documentation provides the "user's view" of the system. A user who tries to operate a computer without an instruction manual will most likely not be able to get the machine to do much. So documentation is especially critical. When a new system is under development, its documentation describes the state of the system at any moment—what portions exist, what portions have yet to be developed, what the known problems are, and the like.

Many people view producing documentation as a tedious chore and don't bother to document their programs, or they do a poor job. If they leave the company and someone else has to handle their poorly documented work, their programs may be too unclear to follow and have to be scrapped. Larger companies often employ documentation specialists to ensure that systems are properly documented. Too much documentation can be just as bad as too little. People who can't get the information they need quickly and easily will become discouraged.

User documentation tells how to use the system. **Operations documentation** tells the computer operators how to set up and run the programs. **Systems documentation** describes how the system is actually implemented; it is important for locating and correcting problems and for modifying the system.

Most organizations have documentation standards that describe the form and style of acceptable documentation. Unfortunately, these standards may vary considerably among organizations and even among departments and divisions within an organization.

Testing and Debugging

Testing is the process of demonstrating that the system operates according to its specification. **Test cases** are developed by a **test team**, people other than those who write the software. The test team considers the specification and designs a series of test cases to check out the system. In some large systems there are so many possibilities that the test team must select only a reasonable set of test cases without attempting to be complete.

The goal of testing is to demonstrate that the system functions properly. Tests often expose bugs in a system. Locating and removing these bugs is a task that can require a great deal of skill and patience.

Removing a bug does not guarantee that a system will pass a particular test case; instead, another bug that was hidden by the first one may appear. When the system can survive a brutal attack by the test team without any bugs surfacing, it is considered ready for installation at the user's site. Even the most thoroughly tested and debugged systems may still contain bugs, some of which may not surface until years after the system is installed (these are called "lurking bugs").

In **unit testing**, each module is tested by itself to see if it runs properly before an attempt is made to incorporate that module into the system. In **integration testing**, a module is incorporated into the current working version of the system to see if it indeed functions properly. Integration testing often exposes **interfacing problems**, flaws in the manner in which modules communicate with one another.

Systems contracts generally provide for a period of **acceptance testing**, during which users test the system in a production environment to determine if it does indeed fulfill their requirements.

The Operation Phase

After a system is implemented and accepted by the user group, it goes into operation, or production. Most systems are large and complex enough that it is impossible to anticipate every eventuality when the system is still "on paper." So the **operation phase** requires the careful attention of users, management, and the systems staff.

Converting to a New System

Changing from the old system to the new one is called **conversion**. In a **parallel conversion**, both the old and new systems are run together for some period of time. This allows the organization to function smoothly while any remaining bugs and operational problems are eliminated from the new system. Parallel conversion is a conservative approach—if the new system has problems, the old one can still handle the organization's needs. But parallel conversions are costly because they require people and resources to run two systems.

The opposite extreme is the **crash conversion**, in which the business simply stops using the old system the moment the new one is installed. Of course, if the new system has serious problems, a crash conversion can be devastating. If the new system is reliable, this method results in a fast and economical conversion. Few organizations use this approach with major systems; they simply can't risk having their operations disrupted.

A wiser approach is the **phased conversion**, in which the new system is phased in a portion at a time. This gradual process costs less and requires fewer people than the parallel conversion. Employees have time to familiarize themselves with each portion of the system.

In a **pilot conversion**, only a small portion of the business is converted over to the new system at once. For example, a company with 10 branch offices may initially convert only one of the branches. This is called a **pilot project**. Any bugs remaining in the system affect just that one branch. Pilot projects are usually conducted only with the best managed and most cooperative branches. Once the pilot project is running smoothly, the remainder of the organization may quickly convert to the new system.

Evaluation: The Systems Performance Audit

A prominent systems consultant was called in to examine a large company's computer-based systems. Management felt that these systems could be greatly improved, but they weren't sure how. The consultant observed that the system was producing weekly reports of every conceivable description for user groups throughout the company. He wanted to determine which of these reports were really needed. Without telling anyone, he simply took all the reports coming from the computer, locked them in a closet, and waited. When any user group called the data-processing department asking where certain reports were, the consultant had those reports delivered immediately. After a month, the consultant made a list of the reports still in the closet. He recommended to management that those reports be eliminated, and he enclosed a rather large bill for his services. Management happily paid the bill.

After a system is installed and running, **systems performance audits** are performed regularly to evaluate the system and determine if it is operating properly. Most systems require some fine tuning to get them functioning smoothly. No matter how carefully a system was designed and implemented, problems normally arise when it is actually put into production. The users may have omitted certain cases in the requirements. The system may be awkward to use. It may not respond quickly enough to user requests, or it may have substantial excess capacity, which can be sold to help cover costs. Changes may have occurred in the business since the requirements document was written, or government regulations may have changed. The business may have grown, requiring some additional reports and no longer requiring others. The systems performance audit often finds a need for futher modifications, and thus the requirements process may begin anew.

A performance audit may reveal that bottlenecks are causing the system to function inefficiently. **Bottlenecks** are hardware, software, or people who cannot handle the volume of work directed their way. Locating and removing bottlenecks require considerable systems expertise. Often, removing one bottleneck may not immediately improve performance, because this one could have been hiding others.

Maintenance

Systems need to keep in tune with ever-changing government regulations and organizational needs. Once a system is in operation, regular maintenance is performed; bugs are corrected as they appear, and new features are added as needed.

Some organizations set up a group of users, systems people, and managers, called a **change control board,** to consider all proposed changes and determine which ones should actually be implemented. Many organizations allocate as much as 50 to 70 percent of their software budgets to maintaining existing systems.

Computer Auditing

To verify that a system is functioning properly and fraud is not occurring, and to help locate problems when they do occur, systems are designed to include **audit trails.** An audit trail allows a person (or another system, for that matter) to trace outputs back through the system to the inputs that caused them. Any modifications to inputs must be **logged** (recorded for later reference) and **secured** so that the logged entries can't be modified or deleted to aid in the detection of potential frauds.

Because computers process huge volumes of data at great speeds, it is impractical for an auditor to reconstruct even a few seconds' worth of computer processing. For this reason, computers are often used to audit other computers.

There are two common approaches to auditing computer systems. **Auditing through the computer** means that the **computer auditor,** or an **audit program,** traces outputs back to inputs by examining the detailed processing of data inside the computer system. This requires a highly skilled auditor who is thoroughly familiar with the internal operation of the computer and the applications software system being audited. Such people are rare.

Auditing around the computer means that the auditor traces only the processing that occurs outside the computer. The auditor relies heavily on the computer system and its software being properly designed and controlled. Auditing through the computer is essential to detecting and blocking today's sophisticated computer criminals, as we will see in Chapter 15.

Service

Computers are complex devices that can and do break down. When they do, it is essential to get them up and running as quickly as possible. Service can be performed as it is required, or regular preventive maintenance can be performed to help reduce the risk of breakdown. Before it acquires hardware, the business should check with other clients of that vendor to see if they are satisfied with the vendor's service. Service is also available from independent companies that may offer it more economically and even more reliably than the computer vendors. Service is normally included with rented equipment; it must be purchased separately for leased or purchased equipment.

One problem to beware of is the finger-pointing that can occur when a company configures a system with equipment from several vendors. What does the company do when the system malfunctions? Suppose the company calls vendor A and the problem is with vendor B's equipment; vendor A may charge for a nuisance call.

Vendors now build their machines with **self-checking hardware and software** that automatically diagnoses most problems and, in some cases, even repairs them. This helps reduce service calls. When a service call is needed, the repair can usually be performed quickly.

Many service companies can perform **remote diagnostics** that check the status of a computer over the telephone. Diagnostic programs can be transferred (or "downloaded") from the service company's computer to the client's computer. Those programs are then run to determine the problem.

Prices for service generally vary according to the response time guaranteed in the service contract. **Immediate-response service** is very expensive, **four-hour-response service** is moderately priced, and **next-day service** is relatively economical.

Systems Acquisition

Not every organization has the resources, the experience, or the desire to develop its own systems. The next several sections present some popular means for acquiring systems instead of developing them. The vast majority of businesses today will use one or more of these techniques as they computerize their operations, or as they improve existing computing systems.

Software Packages

In the past, most of a company's software systems were "home-grown"—programs were written by company employees or hired consultants. Over the years, this practice has lost favor because of increasing labor costs. An important development in recent years has been the increase in the number of excellent **software packages** on the market. A software package is a program or system produced by an individual or company for sale to other individuals or companies. A huge assortment of high-quality and reasonably priced packaged software is now available from thousands of software vendors. It has been estimated that home-grown software can cost 10 to 100 times as much as a purchased package, so time spent shopping around can be worthwhile. By 1990 as much as 80 percent of new software produced and installed may be in the form of widely marketed software packages.

Using software packages has many advantages, especially for a company that may not have the expertise or resources to develop the software itself. The price is known in advance and can be budgeted. Packages are more likely than most home-grown software to be bug-free. The software can be used immediately, and vendors supply documentation and training. A disadvantage is that it may be difficult to get the vendor to make changes to accommodate the client's unique needs.

Some software vendors supply the source programs for their packages. This makes it possible for clients to do their own tailoring. But many vendors refuse to supply source programs, which makes it more difficult for competitors to produce a similar product.

Before buying a package, it is wise to see it in operation. Some vendors allow a trial period, after which the software may be returned without charge if it doesn't meet the client's needs. Some vendors offer **software service contracts**, whereby they agree to provide regular program updating.

Service Bureaus

Service bureaus are companies that develop a centralized installation with hardware, software, and databases, and make these available to users for a fee. Batch-processing service bureaus use pickup and delivery vehicles to obtain input data from the clients and to deliver finished reports, or they may have remote job entry capabilities. Time-sharing service bureaus install terminals on the client's premises.

Service bureaus enable users to obtain computing capabilities without the hassles of hardware and software acquisition. Users gain access to substantial computer resources, specialized equipment, and specialized software that they might not otherwise be able to afford.

Service bureaus provide a convenient way for first-time users to gain the benefits of computing quickly and economically. The clients pay only for services actually used. As they increase their usage, however, their monthly bills often grow to the point that they are better off acquiring their own computing capabilities. A company with its own computers may use a service bureau to handle its excess processing during peak periods.

Often service bureaus develop considerable expertise in specialized areas. Clients will purchase these services to take advantage of capabilities that they could not develop themselves.

Turnkey Systems

A **turnkey system** is a complete computing system including hardware, software, documentation, and even training programs supplied by a single vendor. The user installation runs the system with its own people.

Turnkey systems are attractive to novices who lack the expertise to develop their own systems. If the system malfunctions, the turnkey supplier is responsible and will handle the problem—there's no finger-pointing. Costs are known in advance, so budgeting is easier. In fact, many turnkey suppliers have financing arrangements worked out with banks, which can save the user a considerable amount of effort. A turnkey system can be used immediately after it arrives. There is no long period of debugging as there is with a home-grown system. The user can see the system working properly before buying, can ask other users if they're happy with the system, and can examine the documentation and training materials.

The gambles associated with developing a home-grown system are eliminated. How much will it cost? Will it be ready on schedule? Will it work properly? The company doesn't even have to have a development group. Even if it does, the group may be committed to other projects. A real advantage to turnkey systems is that the vendors continually improve their systems to make them more marketable products.

But there are disadvantages. As happens with service bureaus, a company acquiring a turnkey system must give up some degree of control over its business. If the turnkey supplier is not cooperative, it may be difficult to have the system modified. Even if the supplier will make changes, they may be costly and they may not be made according to the user's time schedule.

The software could have bugs. The hardware may be serviced by a third party that may not perform well. The turnkey supplier could go out of business. The user may have to bend its procedures to fit the system rather than the other way around. A company may have to modify certain business practices upon which it has built its reputation.

But turnkey suppliers are producing an increasing portion of business systems. They are particularly effective with the major business systems such as accounts receivable, accounts payable, and inventory control.

Facilities Management

A **facilities management** company is hired by a client to do it all—to create and run the client company's entire data-processing operation. The facilities manager acquires the hardware, acquires and develops the software, and even staffs the client's data-processing operation with all necessary personnel including systems analysts, systems designers, programmers, and operators. The facilities manager *is* the client's data-processing department.

The advantages are known costs and the use of the services and expertise of firms that really understand data processing. The main disadvantage is that the company is relinquishing control—the information lifeline of the business is being entrusted to outsiders. The company becomes dependent on the facilities manager. What happens at contract renewal time? The company doesn't know how to run its own data-processing operation, and the facilities manager may ask for substantial fee increases.

Facilities management is attractive to companies that need to have their operations cleaned up. At the end of the contract period, some companies will assume control of their now smoothly functioning data-processing operations.

Consultants

Consultants are experienced people from outside the organization who are hired to assist with various phases of the systems development and acquisition processes. They provide expertise and advice, but the client company still makes its own decisions.

Case Study: Structured Systems Analysis and Design

In this section, we consider how the **structured systems analysis** and **structured systems design** methodologies may be used in the development of a simple business system. Our approach is greatly simplified. Any real systems development effort would involve much more detail than we provide. A series of exercises immediately follows the case study.

Requirements

The FutureCar Rental Company has called in a consultant to aid with the systems analysis and design of a state-of-the-art car reservation system for the company. FutureCar has only one location at which it rents two types of cars, limousines and subcompacts. It has 5 limousines and 20 subcompacts. All rentals are for one day only. Cars must be returned by midnight on the day they are rented.

The company requires a system that operates as follows: A customer with a personal computer will dial FutureCar's toll-free number and connect with the FutureCar computer. The customer will then carry on an interactive dialogue to reserve a limousine or a subcompact car for a given date. During this dialogue, the customer's request will be checked for validity. The computer will not accept a request that is incorrectly typed—it will ask the user to reenter the request. The customer's credit will be checked, and if the credit is acceptable and the requested car is available, the system will make the desired reservation.

FutureCar requires payment by check when the car is returned. It maintains a history on each customer, indicating whether the customer has ever bounced a check. At the time of the reservation, the FutureCar computer is to dial a computerized credit bureau. The customer's driver's license number is to be transmitted to the credit bureau. The credit bureau computer will then search and retrieve the credit history of the customer and transmit a credit rating.

Systems Analysis

The analyst observes that a single personal computer with communications capability should be sufficient to handle the reservations workload for this relatively small company. The computer will keep track of all customers who have previously rented from FutureCar and will record any bounced checks. The analyst investigates the local credit bureaus and discovers that many of them have been computerized for years. The analyst chooses one particular credit bureau that operates as follows. FutureCar's computer will dial their number automatically and pass to their computer the customer's driver's license number. The credit bureau's computer will check that person's credit and then pass to FutureCar's computer a credit rating from 1 to 5, with 5 being the best credit and 1 being the worst. FutureCar's computer will then decide if this customer should be allowed to reserve a car.

Determining if a car is available for the customer is straightfoward. The computer will store for each of the next 365 days two counts, one for limousines reserved and one for subcompacts reserved. If a customer wants a limousine on a certain date, the computer will check that the limousine's reserved count is fewer than 5 for that date. If it is 5, then the computer will inform the customer that a limousine is not available on that date, will apologize, and will ask if the customer would like to try to make a different reservation. If the count is fewer than 5, the computer will add one to it and confirm the reservation with the customer. A similar procedure is followed for the customer who wants to rent one of FutureCar's 20 subcompacts.

All of this will be completely computerized. In fact, there will be no reservations clerk. The FutureCar computer accepts calls from the customer's computer directly, so FutureCar personnel are free to handle other chores while the computer routinely handles the reservations.

The Data Flow Diagram:

The analyst's job in structured systems analysis is to produce the **structured systems specification**, a clear and precise description of what the proposed system is supposed to do. The first portion of this specification is the **data flow diagram**, a graphical model of how data will flow through the FutureCar system. The analyst uses only the four types of symbols identified and explained in Figure 1, and draws the data flow diagram shown in Figure 2. Let us consider this diagram in detail.

The customer dials FutureCar's toll-free number, connects with its computer, and makes a Reservation-request. Because the customer is external to the system, a circle is used to indicate that the customer is a **source**. The computer receives the Reservation-request, which is indicated as a **data flow** in the diagram. A data flow may be either an individual piece of data or a bundle of data. Reservation-request is a bundle that must contain the following information:

Reservation-request
  License-number
  Date-of-rental
  Car-type

The indentation used here indicates that a Reservation-request consists of the three listed fields. Notice that for now we're not concerned with the exact form in which this data is to be typed; that's something for the systems designer to specify. The meaning of these three fields is clear to both the analyst and the users.

The system begins by checking the customer's credit. It uses two sources of information. The first is the credit bureau's credit rating of this customer, again a number from 1 to 5, with 5 the best and 1 the worst. It also checks the Customer-information data store to see if this customer's previous checks have been good. Based on these facts, the system decides whether the customer's credit is acceptable. If the customer's credit is not

Figure 1 The symbols commonly used in data flow diagrams.

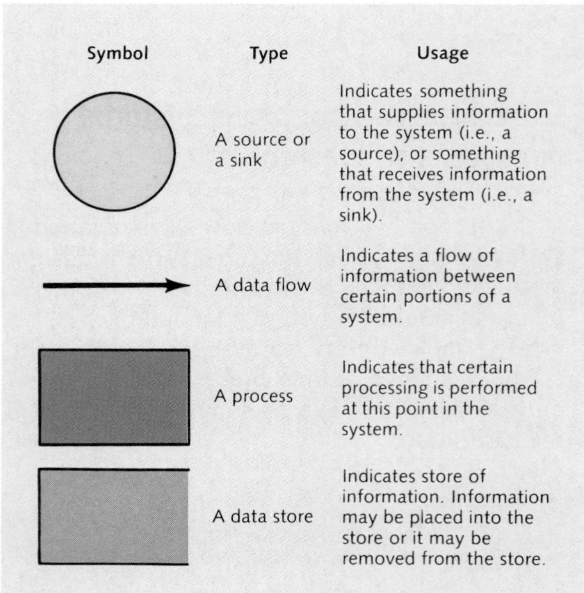

Symbol
Type
Usage
A source or a sink
Indicates something that supplies information to the system (i.e., a source), or something that receives information from the system (i.e., a sink).
A data flow
Indicates a flow of information between certain portions of a system.
A process
Indicates that certain processing is performed at this point in the system.
A data store
Indicates store of information. Information may be placed into the store or it may be removed from the store.

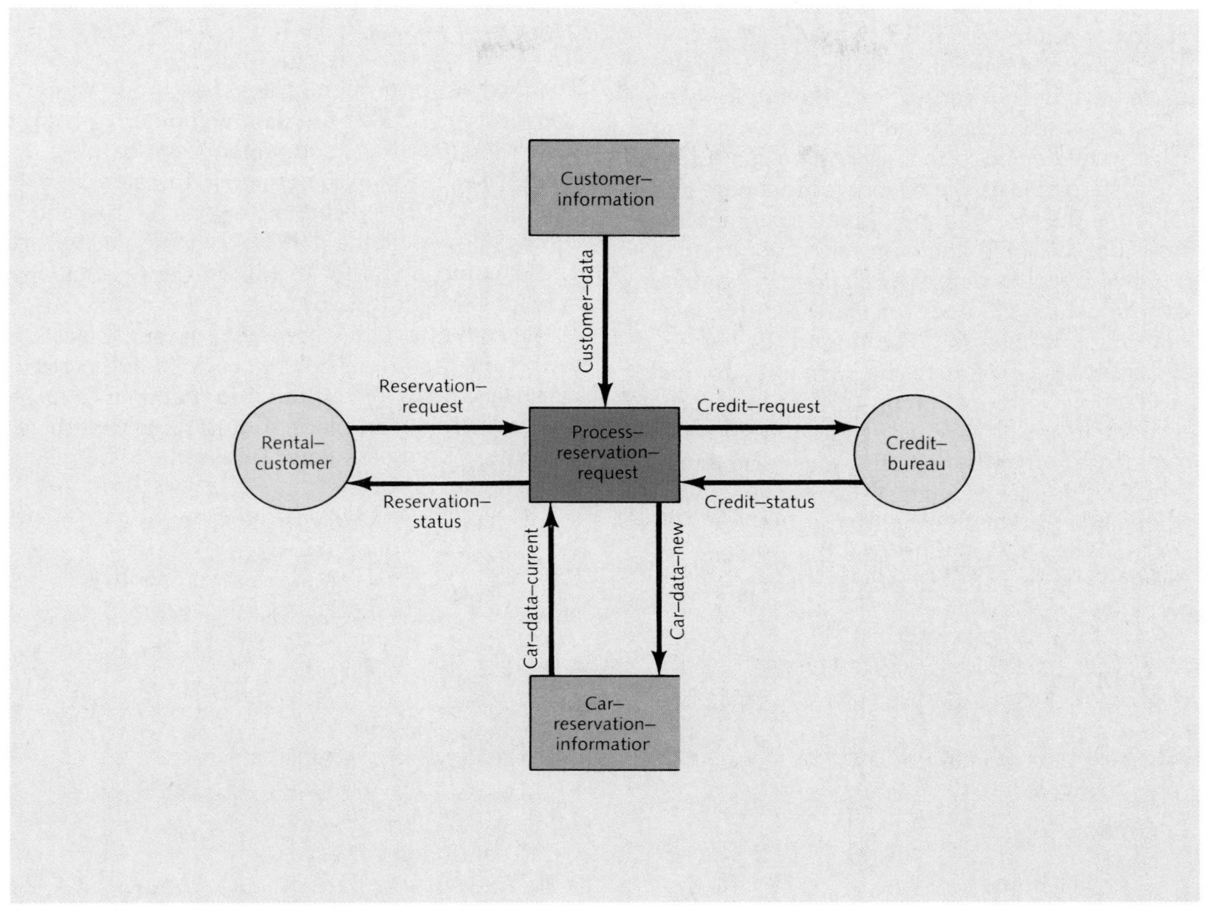

Figure 2 Data flow diagram for FutureCar reservations system.

acceptable, then the system so informs the customer and apologizes for not being able to do business with the customer. Notice that the Credit-bureau is drawn as a circle in the data flow diagram. It is both a sink and a source because it receives information from and provides information to the FutureCar system.

If the customer's credit is acceptable, the system will then check if the desired type of car is available on the specified date. It needs to examine information about all future rentals; this is kept in the Car-reservation-information data store. Again, in the analysis phase we are not concerned with the format of the information in the data store, we merely must determine what information needs to be maintained there. Obviously, this data store must contain a table of information such as the following:

Date	*Limousines Reserved*	*Subcompacts Reserved*
January 1	4	18
January 2	5	17
January 3	3	20
⋮	⋮	⋮

Note that in this example, all 5 limousines have already been reserved for January 2, so that if a customer request arrives for a limousine on this date it must be denied. Similarly, all 20 subcompacts have been reserved for Janunary 3, so a request for a subcompact on this date would also have to be denied. If the reservation can be made, the system adjusts the counts for that date and confirms the reservation with the customer. If a car is not available, the customer is so informed.

Obviously, this data flow diagram is greatly oversimplified and does not show the total picture. For example, some portion of the FutureCar system will have to keep the payment information in Customer-information up-to-date to reflect any recent bad checks. We will ignore this for now as we focus on the reservations aspect of the system. This, in fact, is what systems analysts would normally do as they flesh out a system. Of course, the analyst will have to resolve this problem before the systems analysis phase is complete.

The Data Dictionary:

The next major portion of the structured system specification is called the **data dictionary**, a complete listing of all the components and data elements of the system as defined in the data flow diagram. The data dictionary shows the detailed composition of all the data flows and data stores. The data dictionary for the FutureCar reservations system is shown in Figure 3.

Notice that a data store must contain at least the information that is to be provided in the outward data flows. And if this information is to be in the store in the first place, it must be placed there by some inward data flow. This seems to be the

Figure 3 Data dictionary for FutureCar reservations system.

Sources:

Credit-bureau
Rental-customer

Sinks:

Credit-bureau
Rental-customer

Processes:

Process-reservation-request

Data stores:

Car-reservation-information
  Car-date (For all dates, one year in advance)
  Car-limousine-count (Limousines reserved for this date)
  Car-subcompact-count (Subcompacts reserved for this date)
Customer-information (For all customers)
  Customer-license-number
  Customer-previous-checks ("Good" or "Bad")

Data flows:

Car-data-current
  Car-data-current-date
  Car-data-current-limousine-count
  Car-data-current-subcompact-count
Car-data-new
  Car-data-new-date
  Car-data-new-limousine-count
  Car-data-new-subcompact-count
Credit-request
  Credit-request-license-number
Credit-status
  Credit-status-license-number
  Credit-status-rating (From 1 to 5)
Customer-data
  Customer-data-license-number
  Customer-data-previous-checks ("Good" or "Bad")
Reservation-request
  Reservation-request-license-number
  Reservation-request-date
  Reservation-request-type ("Limousine" or "Subcompact")
Reservation-status
  Reservation-status-license-number
  Reservation-status-action ("Confirmed" or "Car not available" or "Credit not acceptable" or "Invalid request")

case with the Car-reservation-information data store. The data flows and the data store itself are composed of a date, a count of limousines rented, and a count of subcompacts rented.

But notice that the Customer-information data store has no inward data flow. Clearly this can't be. What it means is simply that the reservations system is tapping a data store that is replenished by some other subsystem of the FutureCar system. The analyst must carefully specify all such interfaces with other subsystems.

The Process Explosion:

The data flow diagram of Figure 2 shows only a single process, namely, Process-reservation-request. This is the "top" in the top-down stepwise refinement process. The analyst refines this by **exploding** the process to show more of its internal structure, that is, its subprocesses, internal data flows, and internal data stores, if any. This explosion is shown within the dotted line in Figure 4.

We have exploded Process-reservation-request into four subprocesses. The explosion is not done arbitrarily. Rather, we have tried to isolate separate functions into each subprocess. Notice that the original data flow diagram greatly influences how these subprocesses are chosen. In fact, each of the subprocesses appears to be localized to a single source, sink, or data store. Only the Check-credit process deals with more than one of these directly, but this is because its decision making is indeed influenced by both the credit bureau and the accumulated customer information.

Specifying the Operation of Processes:

The next step in preparing the structured system specification is to specify the internal operation (sometimes called the "logic") of each process. In some cases a simple English narrative will suffice—of course, we prefer structured English in the form of pseudocode (as we studied in Chapter 8).

When modules contain complex decision making, the analyst may prefer to use either **decision trees** or **decision tables** to show the logic more graphically. Let's specify the detailed logic of the Check-credit subprocess using all three alternatives (including pseudocode) so that the reader may consider the relative advantages and disadvantages of each.

It is not the analyst's job to set policy for FutureCar, so the analyst discusses credit policies with management. Management explains that the credit requirements must be much more stringent for customers wishing to rent expensive limousines. As long as the customer has never bounced a check with FutureCar, and if the credit bureau gives that customer a solid rating, then the customer's credit is acceptable for renting a limousine. If the customer has indeed bounced a check, then under no circumstances should the customer be allowed to rent a limousine.

Management is less concerned about credit with customers who rent economical subcompacts. If the customer hasn't bounced a check and the credit rating is "medium" or better, then the credit is acceptable. Even if the customer has bounced a check with FutureCar in the past, management is willing to allow the customer to rent a subcompact if the credit bureau provides a strong credit rating.

The analyst and management agree that the credit bureau's credit ratings shall be interpreted by the FutureCar system as follows:

4 or 5	"strong" or "solid" credit
3	"medium" credit
1 or 2	"poor" credit

A Decision Tree:

Based on these discussions, the analyst prepares the decision tree shown in Figure 5 to explain the FutureCar credit-checking policy. The tree is interpreted by beginning at the left and following the **branches** that apply to the particular customer. Let's walk one path of the tree for a customer who wants to rent a limousine, has never bounced a check, and has a credit rating of 3. At the first **decision point**, we follow the upward branch for "Limousine." At the next decision point we again choose the upward path for "Good past checks." But at the last decision point we choose the lower branch because the customer's credit rating is only 3. This leads us to a **leaf** indicating that this customer's credit is not acceptable for renting a limousine.

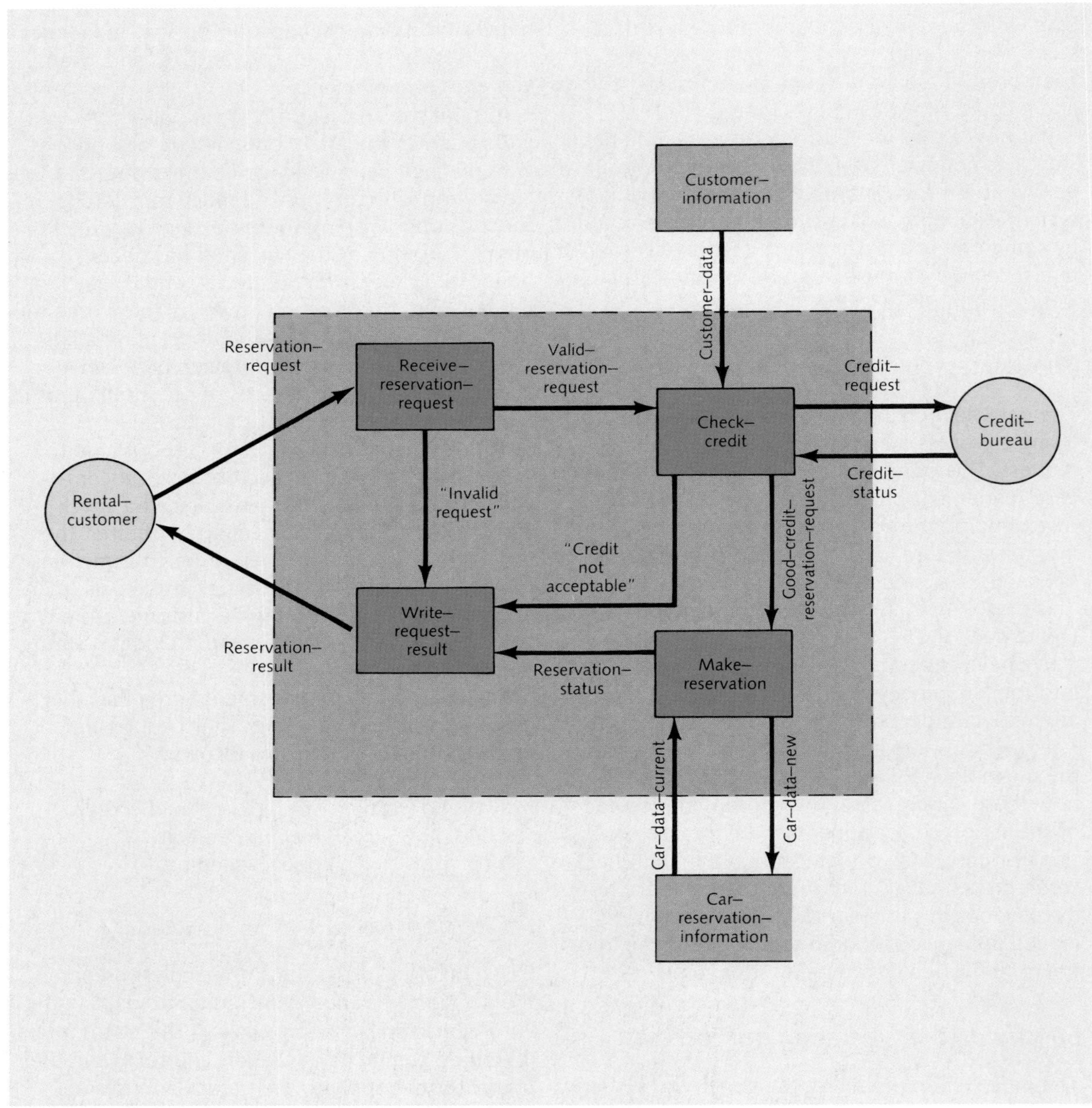

Figure 4 Exploding Process-reservation-request of Figure 2 yields this more detailed data flow diagram for the FutureCar reservations system.

A Decision Table:

Now let's consider how the Check-credit process could be described with the decision table shown in Figure 6. The upper left portion of the decision table lists the various **conditions** to be considered in determining if the customer's credit is acceptable. Condition1 is true if the customer wants a limousine and false otherwise. Condition2 is true if the customer has never bounced a check with FutureCar and false otherwise. Condition3 and Condition4 provide the other tests we need to de-

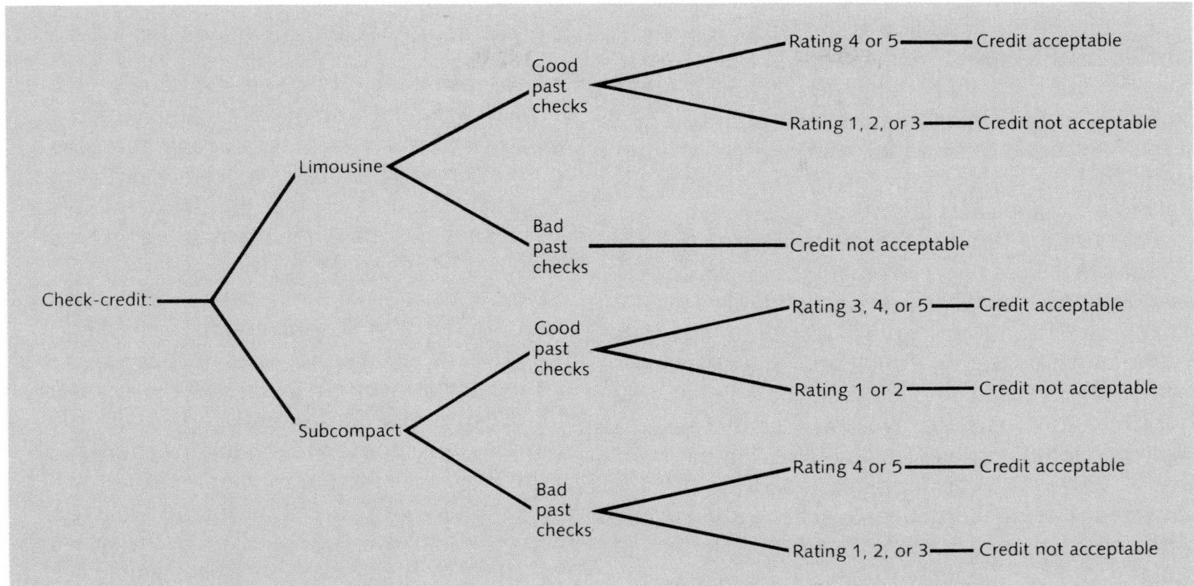

Check–credit	Rule 1	Rule 2	Rule 3	Rule 4	Rule 5	Rule 6	Rule 7
Condition 1: Limousine?	Yes	Yes	Yes	No	No	No	No
Condition 2: Good past checks?	Yes	Yes	No	Yes	Yes	No	No
Condition 3: Credit rating greater than 3?	Yes	No	—	—	—	Yes	No
Condition 4: Credit rating greater than 2?	—	—	—	Yes	No	—	—
Action 1: Credit is acceptable	X	—	—	X	—	X	—
Action 2: Credit is not acceptable	—	X	X	—	X	—	X

Figure 5 *Top:* A decision tree for the Check-credit module of the FutureCar reservations system.

Figure 6 *Above:* A decision table for the Check-credit module of the FutureCar reservations system.

termine if the credit rating is acceptable.

At the bottom left, we list the **actions** that are to be taken. There are only two. Action1 rates the customer's credit as acceptable; Action2 rates the credit as not acceptable.

The right half of the decision table is divided into a series of vertical columns called **rules**. The top portion of each rule contains the **condition entries**; these are simply "Yes" and "No" entries indicating which conditions apply to this rule.

"Yes" means the condition at the left of this row should be true for this rule to apply, "No" means this condition should be false, and "-" means this condition should be ignored. The bottom half of each rule contains the **action entries**. An "X" indicates that the action at the left of this row is to be taken; a "-" indicates it is not to be taken.

Let's use the decision table to determine the credit worthiness of a customer who wants to rent a subcompact, has previously bounced a check with FutureCar, and has a credit rating of 4.

We begin by testing Condition1. Since the customer wants a subcompact, the condition entry for Condition1 must be "No." We see that Rule4, Rule5, Rule6, and Rule7 all have "No" in this entry. Now we consider Condition2. Because the customer has indeed bounced a check, the condition entry for Condition2 must also be "No." Of Rules 4, 5, 6, and 7, only Rule6 and Rule7 have the proper entry. In both of these rules only Condition3 has yet to be tested; the dashed entries for Condition4 indicate that Condition4 is not applicable to either of these rules. Well, the customer's credit rating is 4, so the condition entry for Condition3 must be "Yes." This is true only for Rule6 and, therefore, Rule6 is the rule that applies in this case. To determine what action to take, we simply look at the action entries at the bottom of Rule6. The "X" for Action1 indicates that this customer's credit is to be considered acceptable for renting a subcompact.

Pseudocode:

In Figure 7 we show a pseudocode program for the Check-credit subprocess. The reader should read this pseudocode carefully to confirm that it functions identically to both the decision tree and the decision table we have presented.

Beginning the Structured Design:

The structured design process is concerned with translating the logical model of what the system does (as presented in the structured system specification) into a physical model that describes how the system is to be built and how it is to operate. We'll only introduce structured design briefly here and leave a complete presentation to more advanced texts.

Hierarchical Module Structure:

The designer's job is to create a module structure that will make the system easy to implement. We want a structure that is easy to code, test, and debug. We are particularly concerned with choosing a structure that will facilitate future modifications. Experience has shown that a hierarchical module structure meets all these criteria nicely.

We can usually determine an appropriate structure from the data flow diagrams, particularly those that show how processes may be exploded into their subprocesses. Observing the explosion of Process-reservation-request into its subprocesses, we choose the module structure of Figure 8. Here Process-reservation-request is the "boss module"; the other four modules are "worker modules." The real work of the system is performed by the workers; the boss simply acts in a management capacity calling on each worker module as needed.

Programming such a structure is handled by the use of a **procedure call/return mechanism** (this is essentially the subroutine mechanism we discussed in Chapter 8). Each module is implemented as an independent procedure, as shown in Figure 9. The boss is a relatively sparse "shell" that calls the worker modules in appropriate sequence. Boss modules may call the worker modules sequentially, or they may contain decision structures that call the modules selectively or repeatedly. The modules are implemented as called procedures that return to their caller upon completion of their tasks.

Stubs and Drivers:

Testing and debugging modules organized in such a hierarchical structure can begin early in the implementation effort. The system is implemented top-down; first the boss is programmed and then the workers are programmed. Once the boss is implemented, it can be tested by writing *stubs* for each of the worker modules. A stub is a "hollow" module that merely returns a preprogrammed result when called.

As a simple example of a stub, suppose that we want to test the boss, and the Make-reservations module has not as yet been written. We simply produce a short stub that does nothing more than

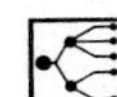

```
Check-credit:
    BEGIN
        IF customer wants limousine
            THEN
                IF customer's past checks have been good
                    THEN
                        IF customer's credit rating is greater than 3
                            THEN "Credit acceptable"
                            ELSE "Credit not acceptable"
                        ENDIF
                    ELSE "Credit not acceptable"
                ENDIF
            ELSE (customer wants subcompact)
                IF customer's past checks have been good
                    THEN
                        IF customer's credit rating is greater than 2
                            THEN "Credit acceptable"
                            ELSE "Credit not acceptable"
                        ENDIF
                    ELSE (customer's past checks have been bad)
                        IF customer's credit rating is greater than 3
                            THEN "Credit acceptable"
                            ELSE "Credit not acceptable"
                        ENDIF
                ENDIF
        ENDIF
    END Check-credit
```

Figure 7 *Above:* Pseudocode for the Check-credit module of the FutureCar reservations system.

Figure 8 *Below:* Hierarchical module structure for the FutureCar reservations system.

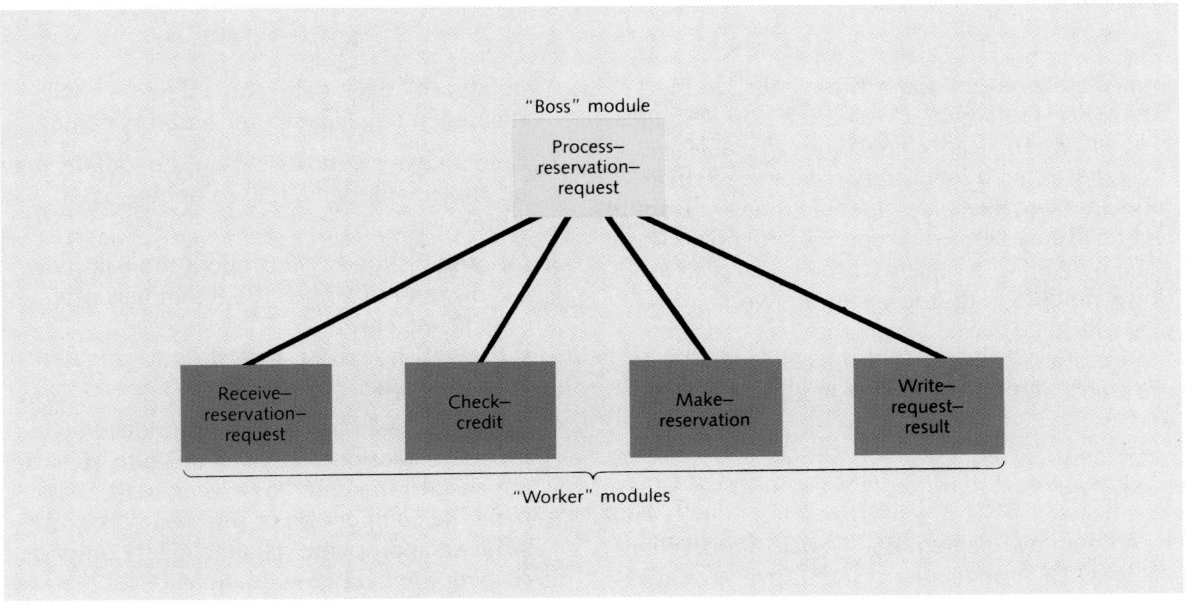

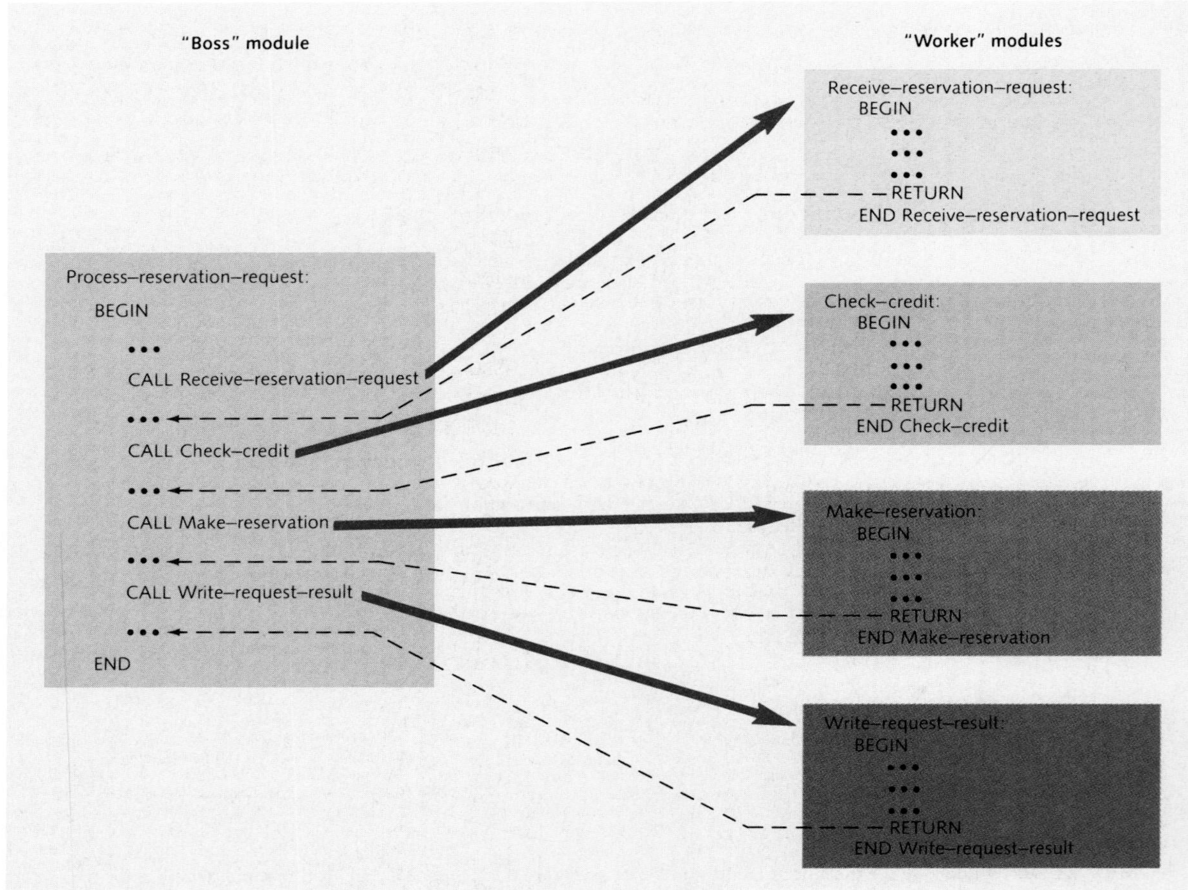

Figure 9 Procedure structure for the FutureCar reservations system.

immediately return "Car not available" to the boss. This would help us test if the boss responds properly when a car is indeed not available.

Suppose that a few but not all of the worker modules have been implemented, and we want to test how they perform in specific situations. This is done by writing a version of the boss called a **driver module** that simply calls the worker modules with the specific information needed for these test cases. Thus, to test a boss module we use stubs, and to test worker modules we use drivers.

Exercises:

1. A data flow diagram is a "logical" rather than "physical" model of a system. Give several examples of how a data store might be implemented in a real computer-based system.
2. Give several examples of how a data flow may be implemented in a real computer-based system.
3. (a) What is the key fact about the data flow diagram of Figure 10–8 that tells us it is incomplete?
   (b) What should the analyst do to complete the diagram?
4. What new data flows were introduced by the process explosion that yielded Figure 10–10?
5. For each of the data flows listed in (4), determine the composition of the data flow and write an appropriate data dictionary entry describing the data flow.

 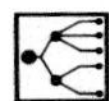

6. Redraw the decision tree of Figure 10–11 to ignore the customer's history of good or bad checks with FutureCar. A limousine should be rented to anyone with a credit rating of 4 or 5, and a subcompact should be rented to anyone with a credit rating of 3, 4, or 5.
7. Redraw the decision table of Figure 6 to reflect the new credit policy stated in exercise (6).
8. Rewrite the pseudocode program of Figure 10–13 to reflect the new credit policy stated in exercise (6).
9. Answer each of the following questions about the decision table of Figure 6.
   (a) Which conditions are tested in Rule5?
   (b) Which action is performed in more rules?
   (c) Which rule results in the customer's credit being considered acceptable if the customer wants to rent a limousine?
   (d) Which rules result in the customer's credit being considered unacceptable even if the customer has never bounced a check with FutureCar?
   (e) Which rule completely ignores the customer's credit rating? Why?
   (f) Which rule applies to the customer with a very poor credit rating who has bounced a check with FutureCar and who wants to rent a limousine? Will this customer be allowed to reserve the limousine?
   (g) Assuming that the credit policy of this decision table is rigidly enforced, how is it possible for a customer to bounce checks with FutureCar repeatedly and yet still be able to rent a car? Which rule applies?
   (h) How should FutureCar's credit policy be changed to avoid the problem exposed in (g)?

Summary

1. A computer-based system is a collection of hardware and software components that work together to reach a common goal.
2. The systems life cycle consists of the requirements definition, systems analysis, systems design, implementation, and operation phases.
3. The requirements document is a description of new capabilities needed by a user group. It is generally written by computer users from a nontechnical and applications viewpoint.
4. Systems designers specify how the system is to be built to meet its specification, a clearly stated description of what the system is supposed to do.
5. A management information system is an organization's set of systems.
6. Systems analysts and systems designers perform cost/benefit analysis to help choose between alternative systems and designs on the basis of their anticipated costs and benefits.
7. The implementation team acquires hardware and software; programs, tests, and debugs the system; and trains the users.
8. Most systems are built as program modules that interact with one another. This makes it easier to program, debug, and modify the system. Coupling between modules should be minimized; cohesion within modules should be maximized.
9. Home-grown software is developed by a company for its own use. Software packages are programs developed by one company or person and sold to others.
10. User documentation describes how to use the system. Operations documentation describes how the operators are to run the system. Systems documentation describes how the system is actually implemented; it helps programmers locate and correct problems and modify the system.
11. Testing demonstrates that the features tested operate according to the system specification. It is impractical to test a large system exhaustively.
12. Conversion is the process of switching from an old system to a new system. Companies may use parallel, crash, phased, or pilot conversions.

13. Systems performance audits help determine if the new system is operating properly. In acceptance testing, users test the new system in a production environment to determine if it fulfills their requirements.

14. Maintenance involves fixing bugs and adding new features as needed.

15. Input, processing, and output controls help ensure that systems are operating properly.

Important Terms 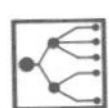

acceptance testing
auditing around the computer
auditing through the computer
cohesion
conversion
coupling
data dictionary
data flow diagram
decision table
decision tree
facilities management
feasibility study
implementation phase
module
operation phase
requirements definition phase
requirements document
service bureau
software package
specification
structured systems analysis
structured systems design
structured systems specification
systems analysis phase
systems design phase
systems life cycle
systems performance audit
testing
top-down stepwise refinement
turnkey system

Self-Review Exercises 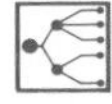

Matching

Next to the term in column A, place the letter of the statement in column B that best describes it.

Column A	Column B
1. Management by exception	A. Generates increasingly detailed designs
2. Reasonableness checks	B. Ensures that a file is complete
3. Management information system (MIS)	C. Determine if input is in the proper format
4. Module	D. Performed by users
5. Stepwise refinement process	E. Determine if values are suspicious
6. Acceptance testing	F. Determines if a system operates according to its specification
7. Validity checks	G. Acquires the needed hardware
8. Record count	H. A program piece
9. Testing	I. Information highlighted for investigation
10. Implementation team	J. An organization's set of systems

Fill-in-the-Blanks

Fill in the blanks in each of the following:

1. When new systems are developed or existing ones are changed, they go through a series of phases called the ______ .

2. The document written by computer users that informs management of what new systems they need or what changes to existing systems are necessary is called the ______ .

3. A ______ determines if proposed changes are justified.

4. In a ______ module structure, each module performs its functions only when called on by the module immediately above it.

5. A ______ helps ensure that a group of transactions is complete.

6. The three popular ways of acquiring hardware are ______ , ______ , and ______ .

7. The two measures of how well a system has been modularized are ______ and ______ .

8. When both the new system and the old system are run together for a period of time we have what is called a ______ conversion.

9. When a business uses only its new system as soon as it is installed a ______ conversion takes place.

10. ______ allow outputs to be traced back through the system to the inputs that caused them.

Answers to Self-Review Exercises

Matching: 1 I, 2 E, 3 J, 4 H, 5 A, 6 D, 7 C, 8 B, 9 F, 10 G

Fill-in-the-Blanks:
1. systems life cycle
2. requirements document
3. feasibility study
4. hierarchical
5. batch total
6. purchasing, leasing, renting
7. coupling, cohesion
8. parallel
9. crash
10. Audit trails

Discussion Questions

1. What functions are performed in each of the phases of the systems life cycle?

2. What is a requirements document? What is a specification? How do they differ?

3. What is home-grown software? Why might you choose packaged software over home-grown software? When might home-grown software be better?

4. Briefly describe the purposes of user documentation, operations documentation, and system documentation.

5. What is a conversion? List the various types of conversions and briefly explain how each is handled.

6. What kinds of problems might be discovered in a systems performance audit?

7. Briefly explain the various types of systems controls.

8. Discuss the differences between auditing through the computer and auditing around the computer.

9. Compare and contrast the following popular means of acquiring systems: software packages, service bureaus, turnkey systems, and facilities management.

10. How are stubs and drivers used in testing and debugging modules arranged in a hierarchical structure?

Projects

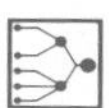

1. The computer services industry is represented by a professional group called ADAPSO (for the Association of Data Processing Service Organizations. Write for information to: Director of Public Communications, ADAPSO, 1300 North 17th Street, Arlington, VA 22209.

2. Use the techniques developed in the FutureCar case study to design a system for a business with which you are familiar.

3. List five businesses run by your relatives, friends, and neighbors. Briefly describe each. Which of the systems acquisition techniques discussed is appropriate for each? Justify your answers.

"We need the order-entry tracking system by the 1st. The budget consolidation in two weeks. The sales forecast next week. And the seating arrangement for my daughter's wedding by tomorrow."

Chapter 11

Database Management Systems, Management Information Systems, Decision Support Systems

After reading this chapter you will understand:

1. What database management systems (DBMS) are
2. The hierarchical, network, and relational database organizations
3. What management information systems (MIS) are
4. What decision support systems (DSS) are
5. Case studies on relational DBMS, MIS, and what-if planning with a typical DSS

Outline

As the electronics revolution takes hold and offices and factories become computerized, data can flow directly from shop floor to executive suite, making many middle managers redundant. Those who survive will have far different jobs to do; those who don't will be hard put to maintain their middle-class existence.

"A New Era for Management"
Business Week

"We've got information coming out of our ears. What we need is a way to make sense out of it!"

A frustrated manager

"My job has changed drastically. The computerized system has eliminated 95% of my emergencies—I know what we need and when. Now I spend my time planning, not reacting."

James H. Collins of Litton Industries, Inc.

In this chapter we consider computer applications systems, particularly those used in businesses. We discuss several major types of applications systems including **database management systems** (DBMS), **management information systems** (MIS), and **decision support systems** (DSS). Each of these plays an important part in managing the huge amounts of information that businesses must process quickly and accurately. We present many case studies and point out important trends that are shaping the applications systems of the future.

Data as a Business Resource

A business's data is one of its most precious resources. It is important to keep that data current and in a form that is easy to update, access, and associate with related data items.

We have previously considered the data hierarchy in which data is arranged into increasingly complex structures including bits, bytes, fields, records, files, and databases. A **database** is ordinarily a large collection of data. Some businesses view the collection of all their operating information as a single database, while others have separate databases devoted to different types of information. The latter view is more common.

Most businesses store data in separate files on various types of secondary storage devices. Different files are used for different purposes, and large companies might have hundreds of files. Typically, these include employee files, customer files, accounts payable files, accounts receivable files, inventory files, and so on. Manufacturing companies might have files containing information about work in progress, shipping, receiving, material requirements, production capacity, and the like.

The process of keeping files correct, complete, and up-to-date is called **file maintenance**. With many separate files, maintenance can be costly.

The same data often appears in more than one file. This repetition is called **redundancy**. Redundancy can be useful as a security measure; if certain data is lost, it can be reconstructed from the extra copies. But redundancy is costly, because the same information must be maintained in many separate areas. Unfortunately, redundancy makes it possible for the same information to exist in different versions in one system. This could result in programs using out-of-date information.

Database Management Systems

A **database** is a collection of related data items. It is generally stored on secondary storage devices that allow rapid direct access to individual data items. Redundancy is minimized; where possible, only a single copy of a data item exists. The database may be used by many different applications systems at once, eliminating the need for separate systems to maintain the data for each application. When a user program inquires if a particular item is in the database, a database management system (DBMS) does the actual searching. The user does not need to be familiar with the format in which the data is stored or the actual physical location of the data.

The DBMS creates the database, keeps it up-to-date, and provides ready access to authorized users. Database management systems also provide extensive security measures to prevent unauthorized access. They make it convenient for expressing relationships between related data items and facilitate the design of user applications systems. They provide backup and recovery capabilities to prevent against loss or destruction of vital information. They ensure **database integrity**, that is, what is supposed to be in the database is there, and what is not supposed to be there isn't.

A person called the **database administrator** determines who may access the database, modify it, add new relationships, and the like. This is a very important responsibility. The database administrator exerts great control over a business's information lifeline.

The real question in database management systems is how to organize information to provide rapid answers to the kinds of questions users are likely to ask. The same data organized differently can yield dramatically different access speeds.

Three common ways are used to structure a database to indicate the relationships among the data items; these are the hierarchical database, the network database, and the relational database.

Hierarchical Database

In a **hierarchical database**, data records are arranged in a strict parent/child (or boss/employee) relationship, as we studied in Chapter 10. Each parent record may have many children, but each child record has exactly one parent. Figure 11–1 shows a simple hierarchical database, indicating the relationship between a customer and the orders it has placed with a company. Customer A has three orders outstanding, namely Order 1, Order 2, and Order 3. The box labeled Customer A is actually a record containing several fields of information about Customer A, such as its name, account number, address, city, state, and zip code. Similarly, each of the order boxes is actually a

Figure 11–1 A hierarchical database.

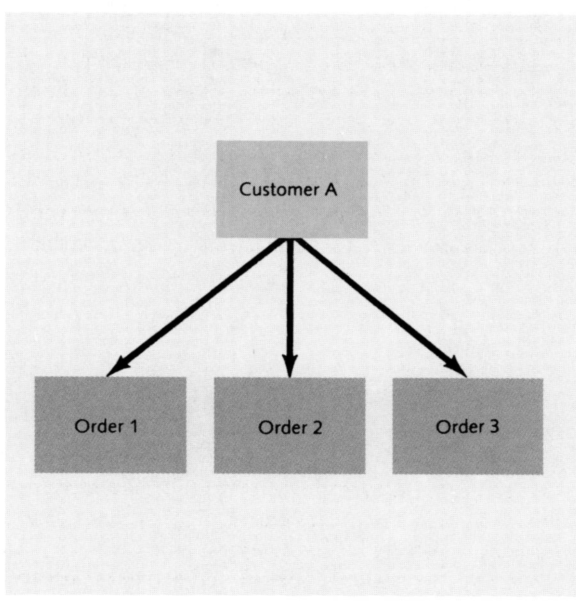

record containing detailed information about the order, such as order number, date, and parts and quantities ordered. The simple example shows a single level of hierarchy, but most hierarchical databases have many levels. Figure 11–2 shows a similar customer and orders database with each of the parts in an order listed below that order in the hierarchy.

Searching a hierarchical database is rapid and convenient as long as it is searched from the top down. The problem with the hierarchical organization occurs when the user wants to search the database in a different manner. Suppose, for example, that a user wants a rapid answer to the question: "What quantity of part 317 do we need to meet all outstanding orders?" Such a search would begin at the top of the hierarchy in Figure 11–2, walk down each branch to the order record, and then search every part record for a match on 317. The entire database would have to be searched to answer the user's inquiry. This could be quite time-consuming.

One solution to this problem would be to produce a second database in which part number is at the top of the hierarchy. Then we could search for part 317 and below it find a list of all orders and quantities ordered for that part number. Unfortunately, producing multiple databases greatly increases the amount of storage needed. What we really need is a way to organize the database so

Figure 11–2 A hierarchical database with multiple levels of hierarchy.

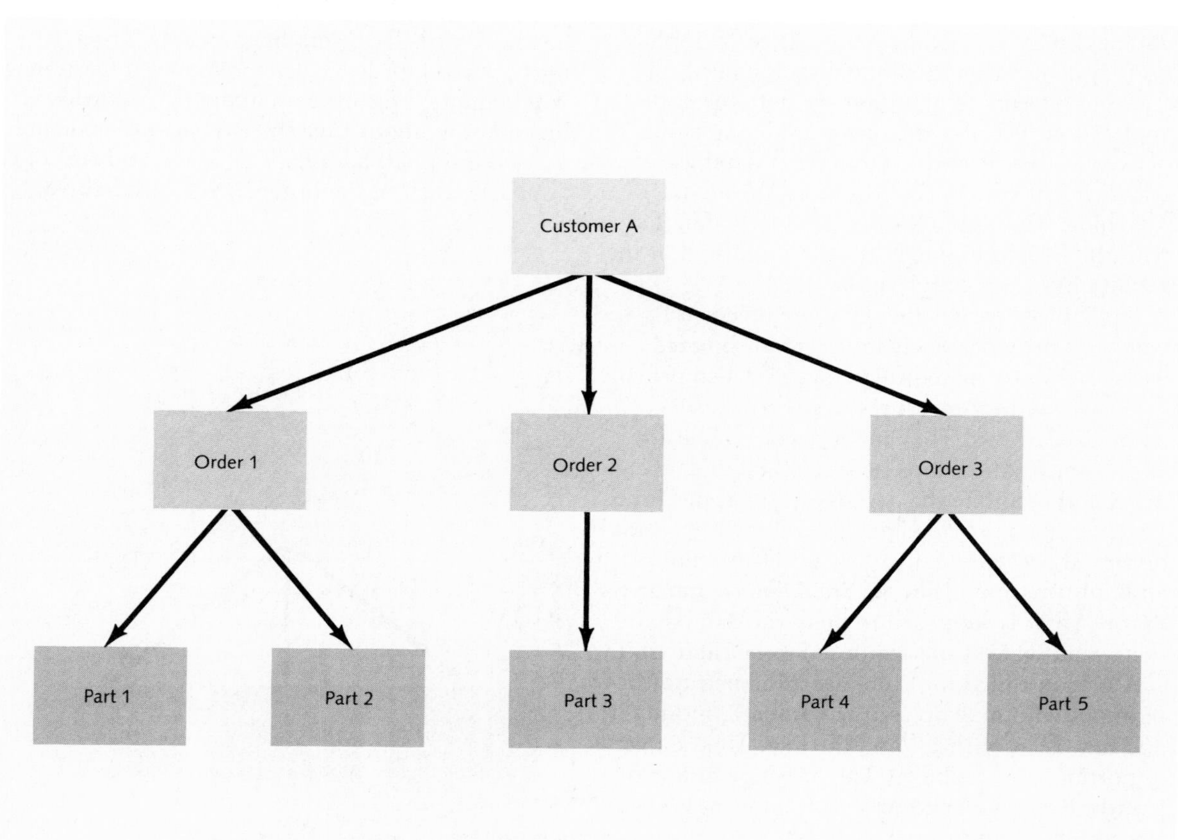

that **multiple views** of a single copy of the data can be made available simultaneously to answer many different types of queries.

Network Database

The **network database** is a more general structure that can answer a wide variety of questions without having to provide duplicate data or to reorganize the database. Figure 11–3 shows a network database that relates suppliers and the parts they supply. Notice that in this example the arrows point in both directions, so we can either start the search at a particular supplier to find out what parts it supplies, or start at a particular part and find out what suppliers supply that part. Thus, this database offers two views; general network structures can offer many more views. Not all the arrows in every network database point in both directions.

The primary disadvantage of the network database structure is complexity. Maintaining many views involves careful manipulation of **pointers** (special data items inside the computer that correspond to the arrows in the diagram) stored in the database. The interconnections can become very complicated, modifying the database can be tricky, and searching it can require highly detailed programs.

Figure 11–3 A network database.

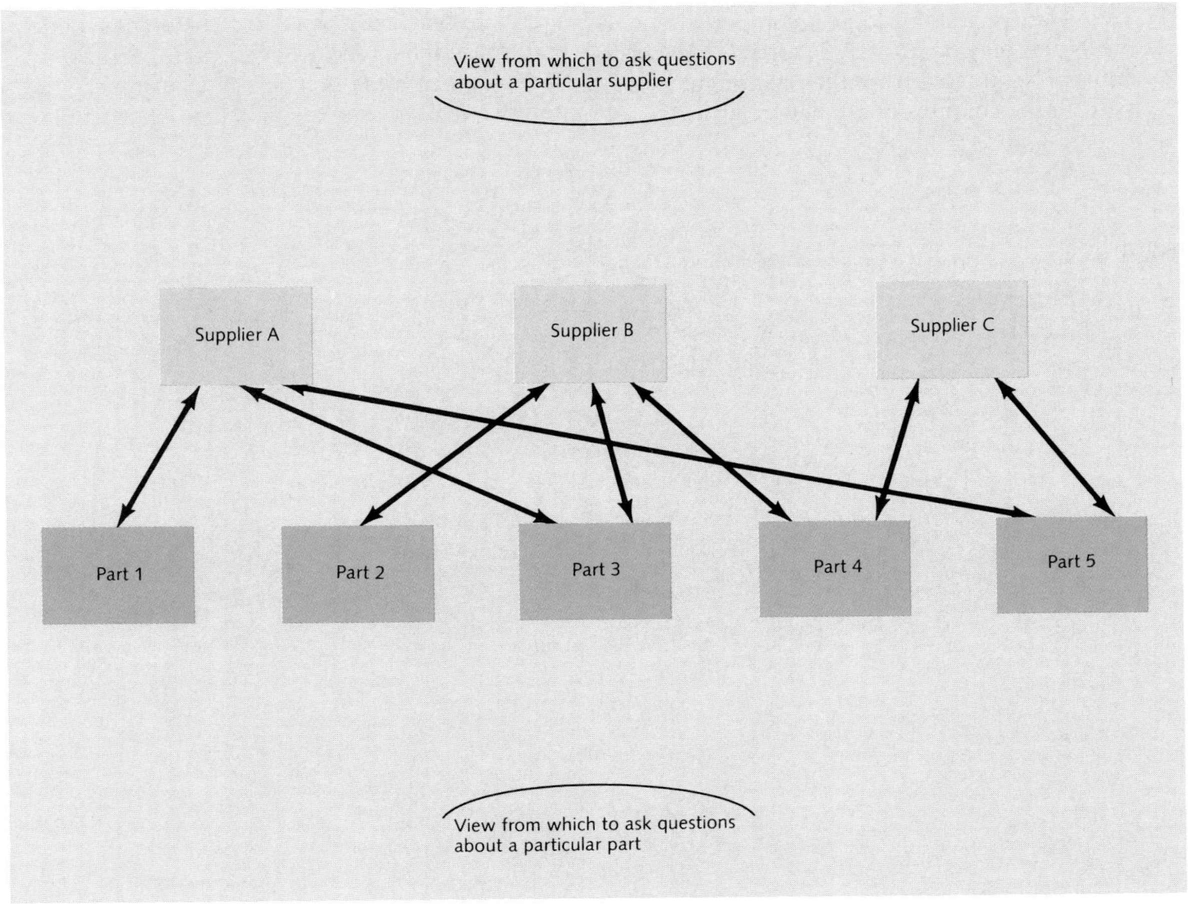

Relational Database

In the early 1970s the **relational database** approach was developed to provide a much more user-friendly organization. Instead of using complex structures of pointers, the relational database stores information simply as tables called **relations**, as shown in Figure 11–4. These tables are sometimes called **flat files** because the rows of the table really are very much the same as the records of a file.

Each row in a relation is called a record or a **tuple**. Each column corresponds to a particular field within the record (fields are also called **domains**). A relational database consists of one or more relations. A relational DBMS performs three primary operations on relations to form new relations:

1. Two relations may be **joined** (combined).
2. A relation may be **projected** (some of the columns are extracted from the relation and used to form the columns of the new relation).
3. Records may be **selected** according to various user-specified criteria.

One disadvantage of the relational database organization is that computers are not yet designed to manipulate relations efficiently. Researchers in the area of database machines are developing new approaches to designing hardware and software that should solve this problem.

Case Study 11–1: A Simple Relational DBMS

The FutureStore Company uses a relational DBMS to manage its information about customers, outstanding orders, and parts stocked at its warehouses. Periodically, it prints invoices and mails them to its customers. Figure 11–4 indicates facts about FutureStore's customers. Six facts are shown for each customer: the customer's name, account number, address, city, state, and zip code. One of these domains, the customer number, is used as a key field (see Chapter 6).

Figure 11–4 A relation that contains customer information.

Customers

Name	Customer number	Address	City	State	Zip
⋮	⋮	⋮	⋮	⋮	⋮
Jackson, A.	413251	15 Green Street	White Cliffs	Georgia	14716
James, B.	414624	191 Blue Lane	Orangetown	Wyoming	02932
Jones, C.	415917	4 Purple Drive	Blackburg	Montana	07623
⋮	⋮	⋮	⋮	⋮	⋮

The relation of Figure 1 contains information about outstanding orders. The key field of this relation is order number. Each record contains six fields. Notice that the orders relation also contains the customer number field. The relational DBMS uses the customer number to associate information in the orders relation with information in the customers relation.

The relation of Figure 2 contains information about all parts stocked in the company's inventory. The key field is part number, and each record contains five fields. Notice that the part number is also contained in the orders relation. The relational DBMS uses the part number to associate information about parts with the parts listed in an order.

Suppose the billing department receives confirmation from the shipping department that all outstanding orders numbered 250 to 300 have been fulfilled, and that the bills for these orders should be prepared and mailed. The select operation is used to extract the records for orders 250 to 300 from the orders relation to form a new relation (it might be called "Fulfilled-orders," for example). This relation is joined with the customers relation to get the name and address information that must be printed on the bills. The resulting relation is joined with the parts relation to get the parts descriptions and selling prices. Because the bills will contain neither the quantity on hand nor the cost of each part, the parts relation can first be projected to remove these fields. The result of the select, project, and join operations is a new relation containing all the information needed to print bills for orders 250 to 300. The name of this relation is then passed to the billing system, which then formats and prints the bills.

It is important to note that each of these relations may be used by many different systems at FutureStore. The orders relation, for example, is also used for sales analysis, for calculating sales commissions, and for forecasting manufacturing and purchasing needs. The parts relation is used for inventory control and for preparing "price books" for the salespeople. The customers relation is used for preparing monthly statements and analyzing sales in various ways, such as by customer and by territory.

Figure 1 A relation that contains order information.

Orders

Order number	Date	Sales-person	Customer number	Part number	Quantity
⋮	⋮	⋮	⋮	⋮	⋮
273	3/15/85	117	415917	3742	12
274	3/15/85	291	413251	7413	5
275	3/16/85	214	415917	3974	100
⋮	⋮	⋮	⋮	⋮	⋮

Figure 2 A relation that contains part information.

Parts

Part number	Description	Quantity on hand	Cost	Selling price
⋮	⋮	⋮	⋮	⋮
3742	Widget	400	21.00	35.00
3819	Gadget	200	17.50	28.75
3974	Thingy	0	2.50	3.95
⋮	⋮	⋮	⋮	⋮

Data Dictionary

Before database systems were in use, programs had to contain detailed descriptions of all the data they processed. If the size or structure of the data was altered, all the programs that referenced that data had to be modified. With database systems, the detailed descriptions of all the data items are kept in a centralized **data dictionary**. For each data item, the dictionary contains the name, type, size, and other useful information about the data item. It's much easier to write and debug programs in a DBMS environment because the programmer is freed from having to specify the physical details of the data. On large projects where many programs share common data items, the data dictionary helps ensure standardization.

Data Independence

In database systems, each program works with its own view or views of the database. If new fields are added to a database record, the DBMS preserves the existing views so that existing programs don't have to be changed. For example, Figure 11–5(a) shows a database record and the views that program A and program B have. In

Figure 11–5 With data independence, the views of existing programs remain unchanged as (a) new fields are added to the database record, and (b) new program views are defined.

DATA BASE RECORD

CUSTOMER NUMBER	NAME	STREET	CITY	STATE	ZIP CODE	INDUSTRY TYPE	SALES TERRITORY

PROGRAM A

INDUSTRY TYPE	ZIP CODE	NAME

PROGRAM B

ZIP CODE	NAME	STREET	CITY	STATE

(a)

EXPANDED DATA BASE RECORD

CUSTOMER NUMBER	NAME	STREET	CITY	STATE	ZIP CODE	INDUSTRY TYPE	SALES TERRITORY	CREDIT LIMIT	OUTSTANDING BALANCE

PROGRAM C

NAME	STREET	CITY	ZIP CODE	CREDIT LIMIT	OUTSTANDING BALANCE

(b)

Figure 11–5(b), two fields have been added to the database record—a credit limit field and an outstanding balance field. This doesn't affect programs A and B at all. With the new fields, a new view can be defined for program C. The ability to modify the structure of the database without affecting existing programs that reference the database is called **data independence**.

Management Information Systems

The key function of a manager is making decisions. These decisions are based on the information available to the manager at the time. Ideally, this information should be accurate, complete, and up-to-the-minute. The better the information, the better the decisions will be. Once a business's day-to-day transaction processing is under control, information can be extracted from the flow of computerized data to help managers in their **planning, organizing, directing,** and **controlling** functions; this is the thrust of management information systems (MIS).

One of the earliest buzzwords in the field of computerized business systems was **electronic data processing** (EDP). The primary goal of EDP systems is to reduce clerical costs by computerizing the flow of day-to-day business transaction data. EDP was the state of the practice throughout the 1950s and early 1960s. Each department tended to have its own set of computerized systems that functioned independently of the other departments' systems. A tremendous amount of effort was duplicated.

Management thought of tying these separate systems together to form a company-wide management information system. The MIS would provide management with total computerized control of the business. It was a grand plan, but the technology of the 1960s was not yet right. Business data at that time was maintained primarily as sequential files on tape. Large files comprised many reels of tape; finding a particular piece of information could take minutes or even hours. Another problem was that data communications at that time was much slower and more expensive than it is today, so it was not feasible to create corporate-wide networks for geographically dispersed companies.

The real breakthroughs came in the 1970s as

"These are the figures of the last 3 months."

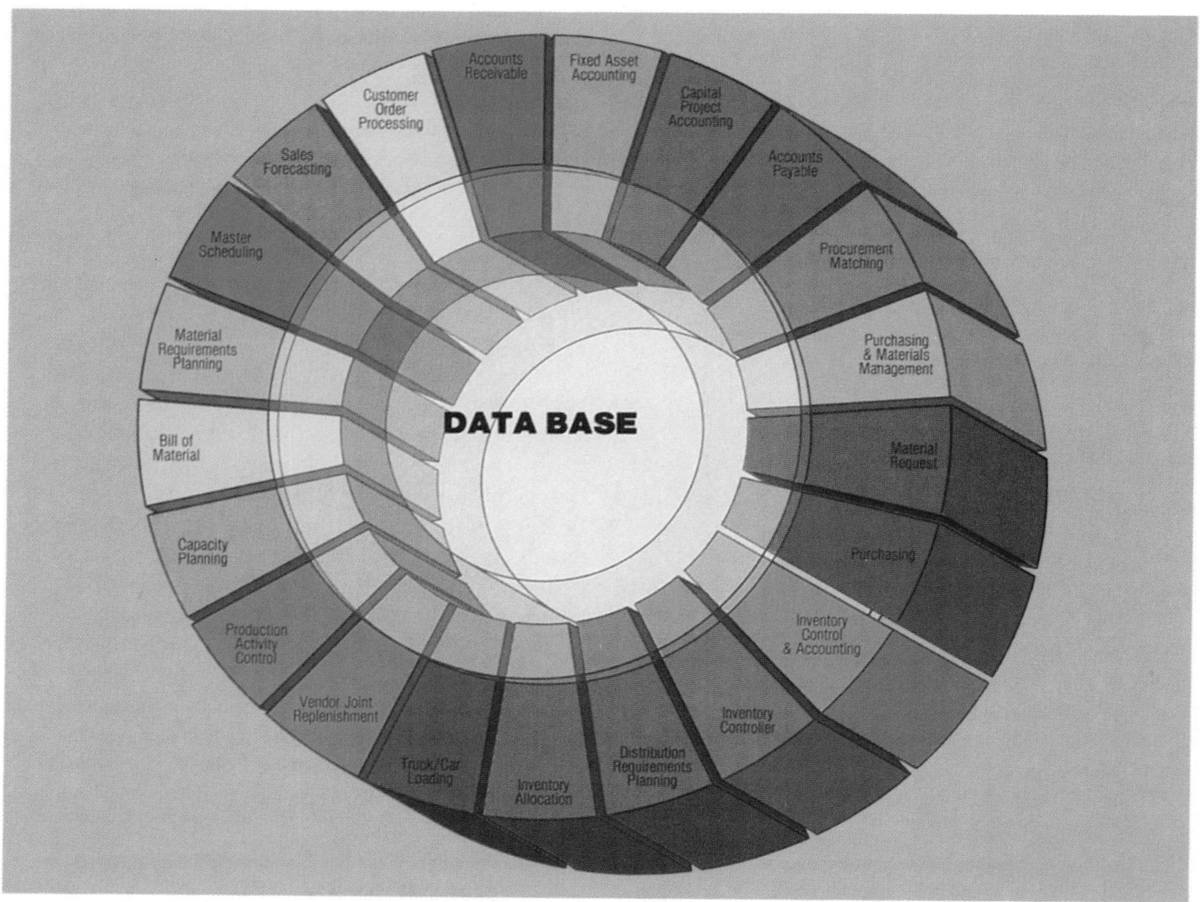

Figure 11–6 Today's view of an MIS is a set of related applications systems that share a company-wide database.

disk storage costs declined dramatically, database systems gained acceptance, and data communications capabilities improved. It is now perfectly reasonable for a company to maintain the vast majority of its current information on disk. Effective MIS systems have indeed become a reality in the 1980s (see Figures 11–6 and 11–7).

The number of managers is small compared to the number of operations people who handle the day-to-day transactions. Managers simply don't have the time to look at the huge volume of raw data. As we move up the **management hierarchy** (Figure 11–8), the data provided to each level of management must be less detailed and more summarized. Lower-level managers tend to be involved with the day-to-day transactions of the business. Medium-level managers tend to deal with short-term, **tactical planning.** Upper-level managers tend to deal with long-term, **strategic planning.** Each level of management must also receive information indicating how well all lower levels are performing.

Cullinet Application Matrix

Business Requirement

Module	Manufacturing	Finance/ Accounting	Customer Service	Human Resources	Purchasing	Cost Analysis	Production Control	Material Control	Distribution
Inventory	X		X		X	X	X	X	X
Material Requirements Planning	X							X	X
Purchase Control	X				X			X	X
Cost Control	X					X			
Bill of Material	X						X	X	
Order Entry	X		X					X	X
Master Production Schedule	X						X	X	X
Shop Floor Control	X					X	X	X	
Accounts Payable		X			X				
Accounts Receivable		X	X						
Fixed Assets		X							
General Ledger		X	X	X	X	X			
Customer Information Service			X						
Billing			X						
Payroll				X					
Personnel				X					
Pensions				X					
Part List and Catalog			X		X				X

Figure 11–7 *Above:* This applications matrix lists several of the more common computer systems in the left-hand column and several of the major areas of a typical company's operations across the top. An *X* indicates that a particular computer system is important to a particular operations area.

Figure 11–8 *Below:* The management information systems pyramid shows how an MIS supports managers at various levels.

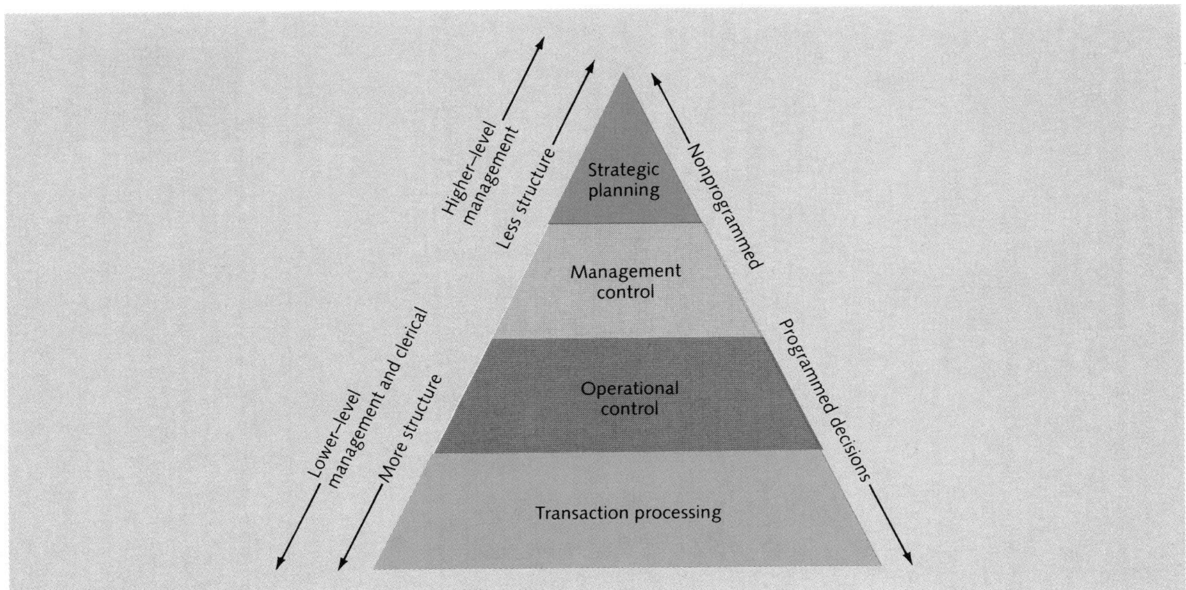

Case Study 11–2: An MIS for FutureStore

The FutureStore Company manufactures various products that it sells through independent retail stores. It has nine warehouses in major cities throughout the United States, and one factory where all its products are made. It operates a corporate-wide data communications network with a central computing facility at its corporate headquarters. All its applications systems share a centralized integrated relational database.

FutureStore is typical of many manufacturing companies (Figure 1). It receives orders, keeps a certain amount of each item available in inventory, manufactures products to meet existing orders and future needs, bills its customers, makes repeated requests for payment on overdue accounts (this is called dunning), pays its employees, pays its suppliers, pays taxes to the government, and maintains detailed financial records on all of its business activities.

In the next several sections, we discuss FutureStore's operations in detail. In particular, we will consider nine of the key computer systems that constitute a major portion of FutureStore's management information system. As we examine the company's systems, however, we shall use illustrations from many commercially available systems. All the systems we discuss involve people, hardware, and software. When we refer to accounts payable, for example, we generally mean the people, hardware, and software that cooperate to perform FutureStore's accounts payable functions.

Order Entry System

The FutureStore **order entry system** accepts customer orders for merchandise and puts in motion the mechanisms to ensure that the orders are fulfilled. The customer or a sales representative calls in an order, and an operator enters the order on a display terminal (Figure 2) Order entry checks with inventory control to see if the items are in stock. It then checks with credit and collection to

Figure 1 The flow of information and products in a typical manufacturing company.

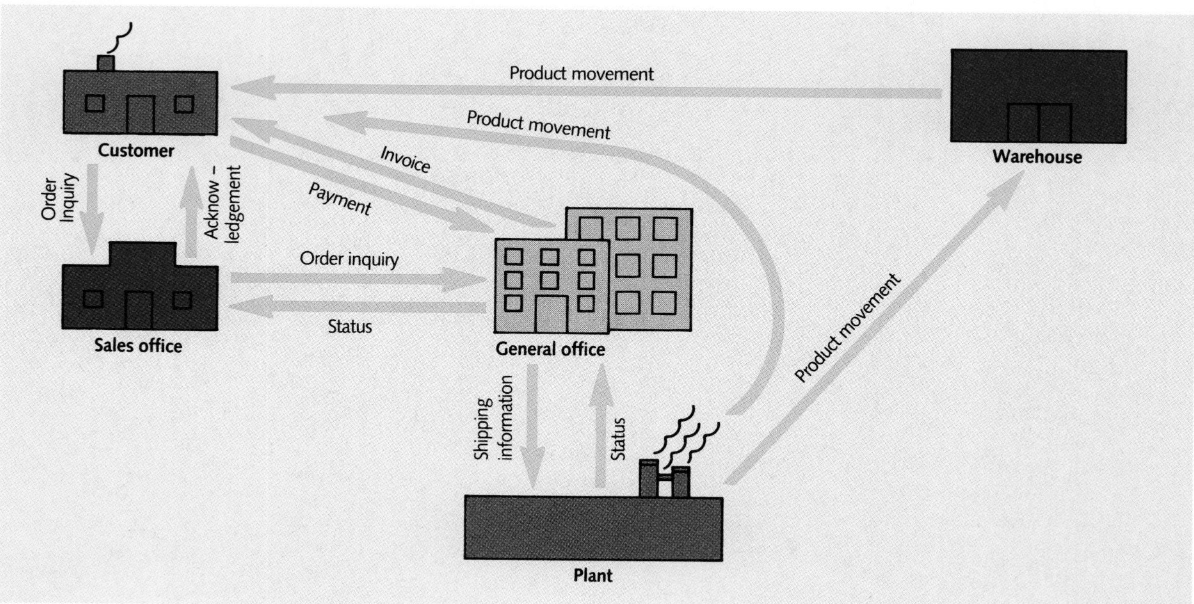

confirm that the customer's credit is acceptable, and it instructs warehousing to ship the goods. Warehousing confirms the shipment, and order entry passes the order to billing, which prints and mails a customer invoice. Billing passes the invoice information to accounts receivable, which monitors the invoice until it is paid. Order entry passes information to sales analysis so that sales statistics may be maintained and sales commissions calculated.

Order entry keeps track of the status of every order so that customer inquiries can be answered. It monitors the responses to advertising campaigns and can calculate the gross profit per invoice from pricing information maintained by inventory. Order entry interfaces with warehousing to determine which warehouse to ship from (Figures 3 and 4) and what form of transportation to use to ensure on-time delivery at reasonable cost.

FutureStore's order entry system prepares and mails a printed order acknowledgment confirming that the order has been accepted and is "in progress." If needed items are not in stock, order entry checks with manufacturing to ensure that they will be produced in time to meet the customer's needs. Order entry handles standing orders, such as to deliver a certain amount of a product to a customer on the same day each week. It can change or cancel orders that are in progress.

Inventory Control System

FutureStore must keep a certain amount of each product on hand to satisfy production needs and customer requests—this is its **inventory**. Inventory costs money, so one goal of the **inventory control system** is to minimize the amount of inventory. But a larger inventory means less chance of running out of a needed item. Such "stock-outs" result in lost sales and, if needed parts are not available to manufacturing, could actually force FutureStore's factory to shut down. Either situation could result in lost customers.

An inventory relation is maintained in FutureStore's DBMS with one record per item carried by

Figure 2 A data entry screen for use with an order entry system.

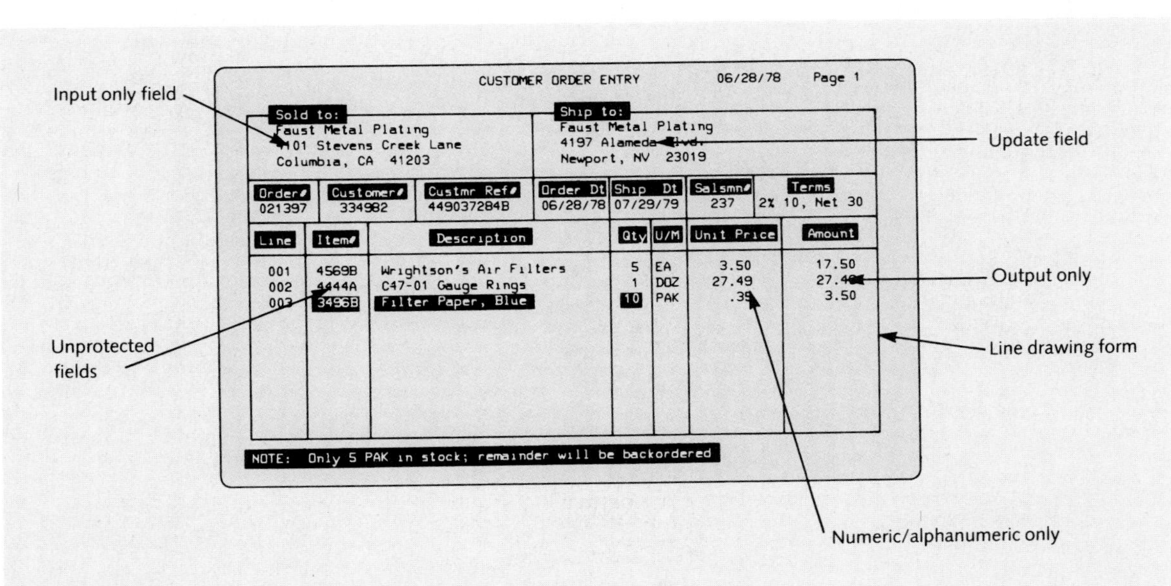

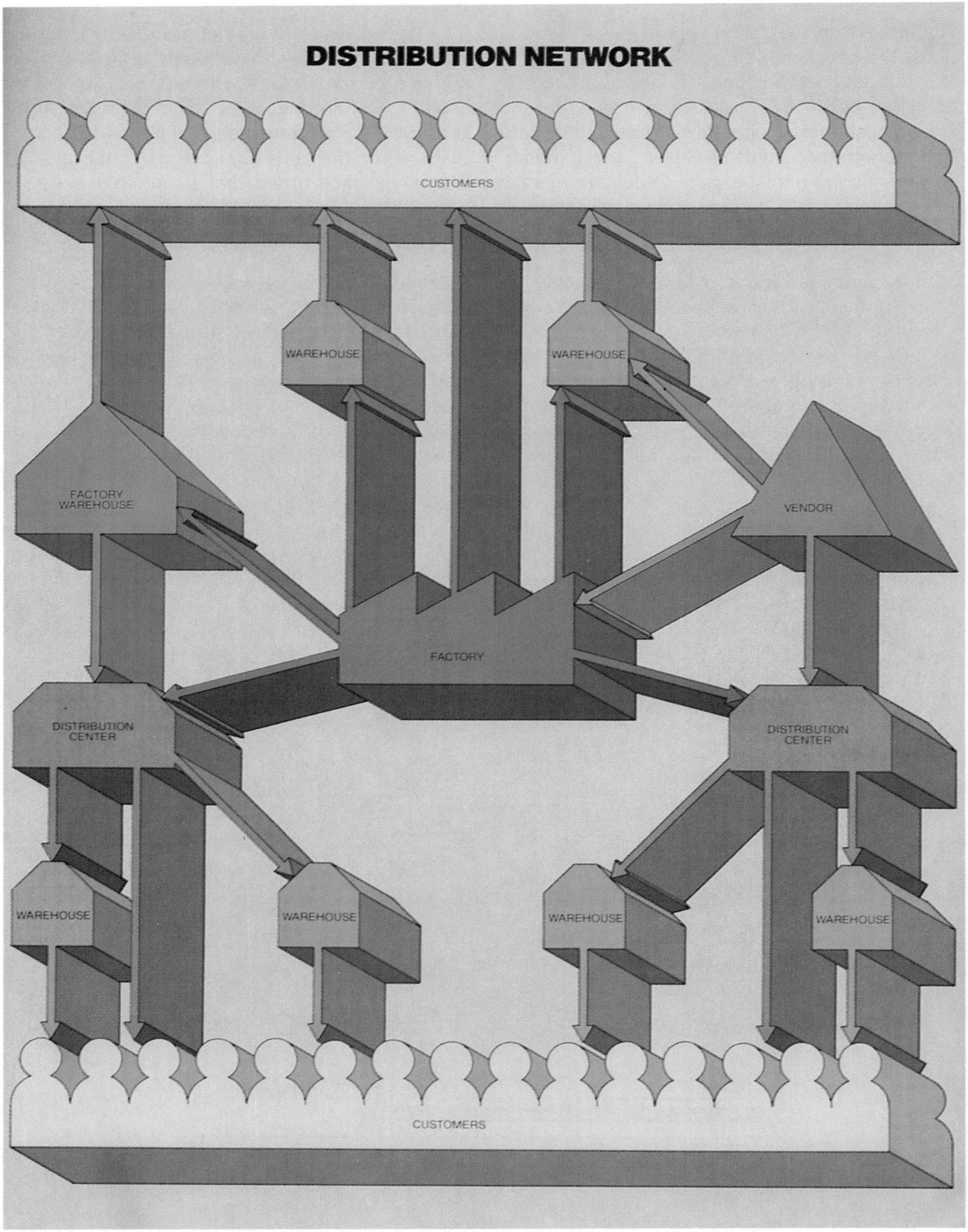

DISTRIBUTION NETWORK

CUSTOMERS
WAREHOUSE
WAREHOUSE
FACTORY WAREHOUSE
VENDOR
FACTORY
DISTRIBUTION CENTER
DISTRIBUTION CENTER
WAREHOUSE
WAREHOUSE
WAREHOUSE
WAREHOUSE
CUSTOMERS

the company. Each record (tuple) has various fields (domains) including

ITEMCODE

ITEMDESCRIPTION

QUANTITYONHAND

REORDERPOINT

REORDERQUANTITY

SUPPLIERCODE

ITEMCOST

As new shipments arrive or as customer returns come in, QUANTITYONHAND is increased. As goods are sold, QUANTITYONHAND is decreased (Figure 5). Whenever QUANTITYONHAND slips below REORDERPOINT, the computer indicates that "REORDERQUANTITY of ITEMCODE must be ordered from SUPPLIERCODE." The computer prints the **purchase order** itself, but all purchase orders require a supervisor's signature before they are mailed.

Management can determine fast-moving items and can stock up on them. Slow-moving items are

Figure 4 The warehouses are on-line to the company-wide database. Warehouse personnel can check the status of any item.

Figure 3 *Left:* The distribution network in a typical distribution system.

Figure 5 An inventory control system's display of the status of one type of part: 1110 are on hand, 500 have been allocated, 610 are available, and year-to-date 5210 parts have been issued from inventory and 5500 parts have been added to the inventory.

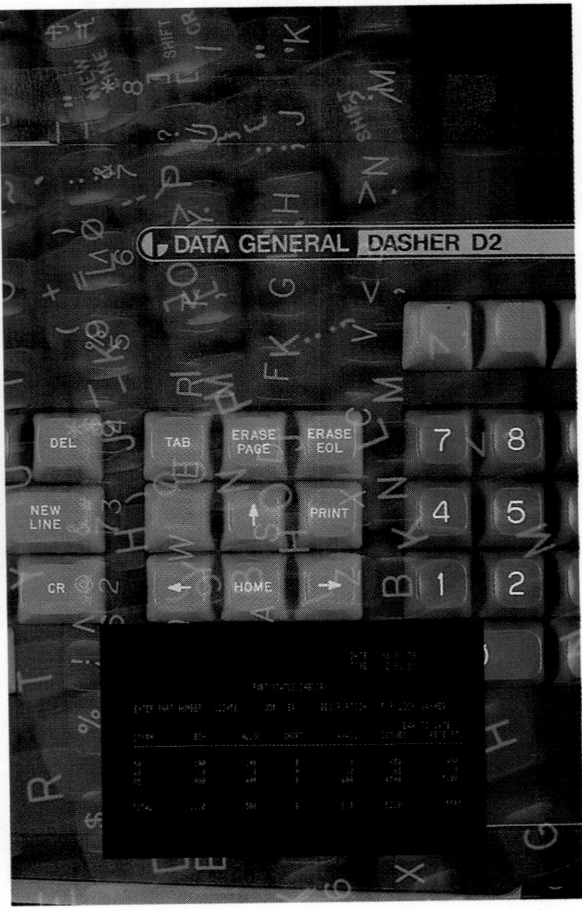

expensive to carry, and they may become obsolete while sitting in a warehouse.

The forecasting features of inventory control calculate the rate of decrease of inventory and estimate when QUANTITYONHAND will fall below REORDERPOINT for each item. This enables FutureStore management to determine when orders will have to be placed, and when FutureStore will need the cash to pay its suppliers for the ordered items.

Management can quickly determine the most important items in the **distribution-by-value report**. This report lists every item in the inventory, the quantity sold for the period (such as a month, a quarter, or a year), and the dollar volume for each item. The report is sorted in decreasing order by dollar volume. The items that generate the most business appear at the top. The report generally reveals that some small portion of the items account for the vast majority of the company's sales. Management sometimes decides to discontinue items listed at the bottom of the report.

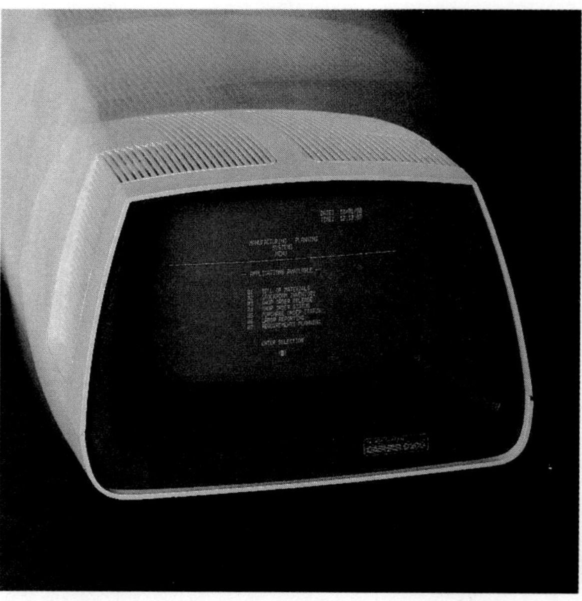

Figure 6 A user-friendly menu display for a manufacturing planning system.

Manufacturing Resources Planning System

FutureStore uses a **manufacturing resources planning system** (MRP) to help with the complex planning, resource allocation, and progress reporting functions associated with manufacturing its products (Figure 6). The manufacturing capacity of its factory depends, of course, on the capabilities of its equipment and personnel. MRP interfaces with order entry to determine what products need to be produced and when. It interfaces with inventory control to determine if the component raw materials are available, and with purchasing to ensure that needed materials will be in stock when the products are to be manufactured.

One of the key subsystems is called the **bill of materials**. For each item to be produced, the bill of materials for that item contains a complete listing of all the components that go into manufacturing that item (Figure 7). These components are made up of subcomponents, and so on right down to the smallest bolt or screw. Thus, the parts may be viewed in a hierarchical top-down arrangement very much like that used in structured systems analysis and design, as discussed in Chapter 10.

Figure 7 This display lists all of the component parts of a cathode ray tube as described in the bill of materials.

All these factors go into determining a tentative production schedule, which, in turn, dictates **material requirements** (what parts will be needed and when) and **capacity requirements** (what production capabilities will be needed and when). There is rarely a precise match between requirements and available capabilities, so these differences must be resolved to develop a viable production schedule. This may mean asking suppliers to alter scheduled delivery dates of certain components, asking customers to take delivery of ordered items at different times, or hiring or laying off production workers.

MRP interfaces with sales to obtain forecasts of needs and with order entry to ensure that desired shipping dates can be met. Customers frequently change or cancel orders, often at the last minute; MRP must respond quickly to avoid producing unwanted items.

Billing System

When the products are shipped to the customer, **billing** generates an invoice (Figure 8) listing the products shipped, the quantities and pricing for each item, and the total bill. FutureStore uses discount terms of "2% 10 days, net 30 days," indicating that the customer may deduct 2 percent of the bill amount as a discount for prompt payment (within 10 days), or that the full amount is due within 30 days. The invoice is mailed to the customer, and the information is passed to accounts receivable, which then monitors the invoice until it is paid.

Some of the complexities in billing are special pricing and discounting arrangements, calculation of sales taxes that vary by state, and assignment of freight charges. Also, bills are often mailed to a different address than the one to which the goods are sent.

Figure 8 An invoice used in an invoicing system to bill the customer for goods and services rendered.

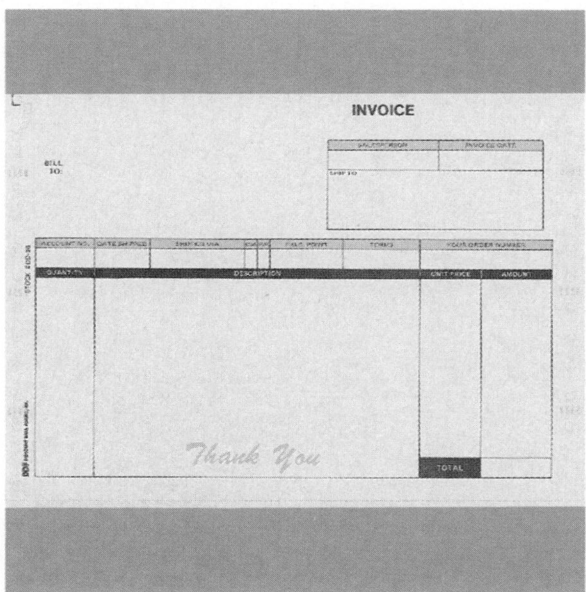

INVOICE

BILL TO:

SALESPERSON | INVOICE DATE

SHIP TO

ACCOUNT NO. | DATE SHIPPED | SHIPPED VIA | F.O.B. POINT | TERMS | YOUR ORDER NUMBER

QUANTITY | DESCRIPTION | UNIT PRICE | AMOUNT

Thank You

TOTAL

Accounts Receivable System

The financial health of FutureStore depends very much on how quickly its customers pay their bills. The more money owed by the customers, the more FutureStore must borrow to meet its financial commitments. When interest rates are high, borrowing costs could prevent the company from remaining competitive and could conceivably put it out of business. The **accounts receivable system** handles most collections routinely. It highlights the "poor payers" so that credit and collection can focus its activities on these customers.

The two major types of accounts receivable systems are **balance forward** and **open item**. In an open item system, incoming cash is applied either to a specific invoice or to the oldest invoice. In a balance forward system, cash is applied to the outstanding balance; each month a statement is issued showing the starting balance, purchases, payments, and the new ending balance. FutureStore uses a balance forward system.

Besides sending monthly statements, accounts receivable sends past due notices (Figure 9) to customers who are behind in their payments. Accounts receivable posts all payments and charges to the proper accounts. It calculates discounts that customers have earned because of on-time payments or volume purchases. It monitors each customer's payment patterns. Its forecasting features can often predict within a day or two when a customer's payment will arrive, helping management anticipate the company's cash needs.

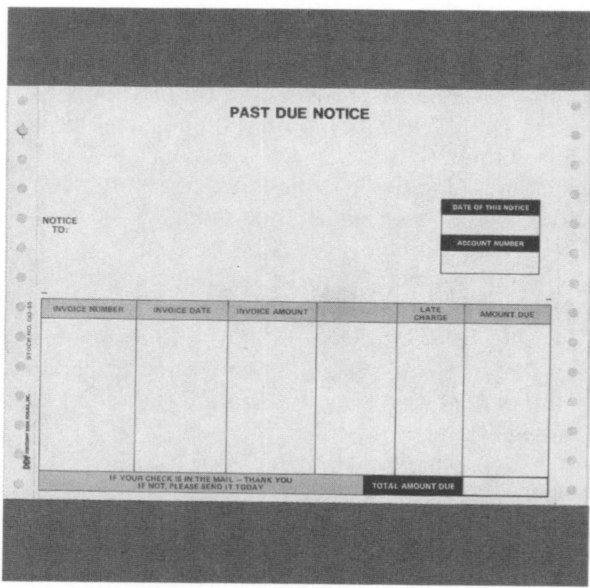
PAST DUE NOTICE

NOTICE TO:

DATE OF THIS NOTICE

ACCOUNT NUMBER

INVOICE NUMBER	INVOICE DATE	INVOICE AMOUNT		LATE CHARGE	AMOUNT DUE

IF YOUR CHECK IS IN THE MAIL – THANK YOU
IF NOT, PLEASE SEND IT TODAY

TOTAL AMOUNT DUE

Figure 9 A past due notice used in an accounts receivable system to remind customers that their balances are now overdue.

The key report is the **aged trial balance** (ATB) that shows the status of each customer, including outstanding balance, current payments, and current purchases (Figure 10). The ATB shows how much of the balance for each customer is less than one month old, how much is one to two months old, and so on. Ideally, a business wants all its receivables to be current. Normally, however, some portion is old, and the ATB shows how much of it is how old.

Accounts receivable summarizes all transactions by types. Sales are summarized by product. Discounts are summarized so that management may determine if FutureStore's discount policy needs revision. Cash receipts information and sales information are supplied to the general ledger system. Finance charges are calculated on overdue amounts.

Inevitably, some portion of the charges and payments cannot be processed immediately. For example, a customer may send in a check without also enclosing the return portion of the statement containing the customer's account number. These transactions appear on **suspense listings**; the transactions are "suspended" until they can be resolved manually.

Figure 10 A portion of an aged trial balance report.

FUTURESTORE CORP.

AGED TRIAL BALANCE

DATE: JUNE 1, 1985

CUSTOMER NUMBER	CUSTOMER NAME	TELEPHONE NUMBER	LST PYMT MO DA YR	OUTSTANDING BALANCE	CURRENT AMOUNT	OVER 30 DAYS	OVER 60 DAYS	OVER 90 DAYS
105378	AAA AUTO SUPPLY	203-123-4567	05 27 85	4,214.63	4,214.63			
114917	ACE CAR PARTS	916-123-4567	05 08 85	100.00		100.00		
119385	ARROW TRANSMISSION	402-123-4567	05 03 85	15,962.21	6,726.00	4,412.95	3,915.49	908.77
127614	BARNES MUFFLER SHOP	717-123-4567	03 18 85	763.98				763.98

Credit and Collection System

Every transaction requires a routine credit check to determine if the customer's credit purchase should be allowed. The **credit and collection system** maintains in-house records on all customers. It also uses credit information supplied by outside credit bureaus and facilitates the collection of money from overdue accounts.

Credit and collection in any organization is a delicate function. It must help collect overdue money without offending customers. Also, collection procedures must comply with very strict legislation.

Credit and collection decides which of the overdue accounts should be worked manually and tracks the status of each account throughout the collection process (Figure 11). It maintains a historical record of all previous collection attempts, keeping track of when the customer was contacted, promises to pay, refusals to pay, "disconnected phone," "no answer," "message left," when the account was turned over to a collection agency, and other useful information (Figure 12).

Credit and collection maintains performance statistics on all accounts to help determine which ones are likely to be collectible and which are not. It keeps track of disputed amounts in which the account has become overdue because the customer has claimed poor service, inferior product, or simply a billing error. It tracks progress on resolving these amounts with the customer.

FutureStore uses various "computer-originated-mail" services in which a computerized letter is transmitted electronically to a post office near the customer, where it is printed and delivered in a specially marked envelope to get the customer's attention.

Credit and collection interfaces with accounts receivable to keep informed of all payments that have arrived so that it can promptly cease collection activity on an account that has paid its bill.

Payroll System

The **payroll system** is one of the first areas companies computerize. Today thousands of companies have not yet computerized their business

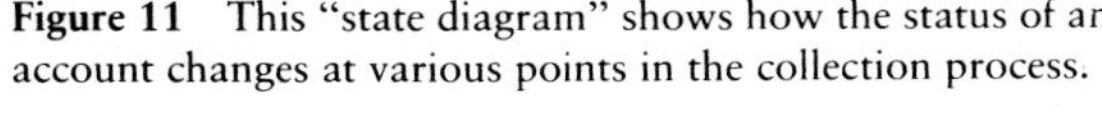

Figure 11 This "state diagram" shows how the status of an account changes at various points in the collection process.

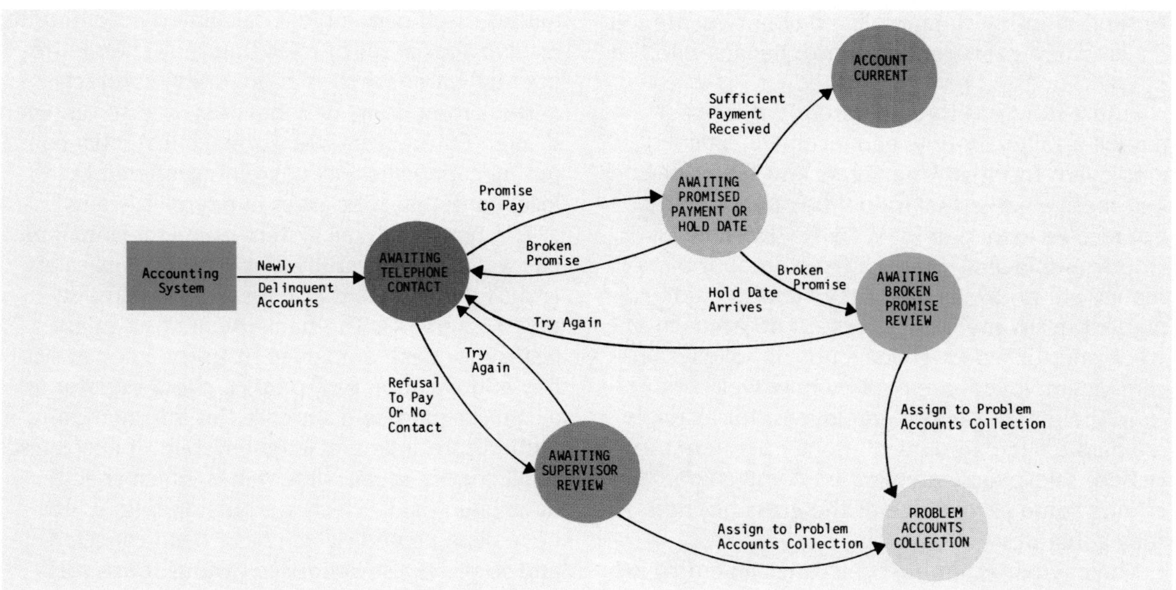

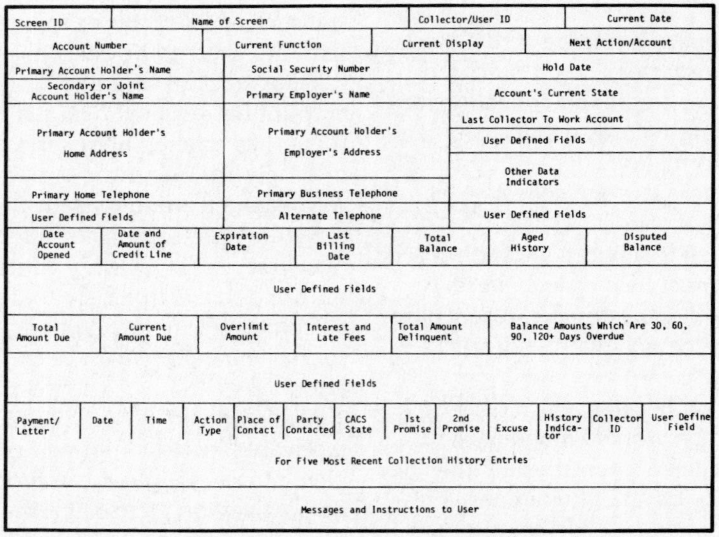

Screen ID | Name of Screen | Collector/User ID | Current Date
Account Number | Current Function | Current Display | Next Action/Account
Primary Account Holder's Name | Social Security Number | Hold Date
Secondary or Joint Account Holder's Name | Primary Employer's Name | Account's Current State
Primary Account Holder's Home Address | Primary Account Holder's Employer's Address | Last Collector To Work Account | User Defined Fields | Other Data Indicators
Primary Home Telephone | Primary Business Telephone
User Defined Fields | Alternate Telephone | User Defined Fields
Date Account Opened | Date and Amount of Credit Line | Expiration Date | Last Billing Date | Total Balance | Aged History | Disputed Balance
User Defined Fields
Total Amount Due | Current Amount Due | Overlimit Amount | Interest and Late Fees | Total Amount Delinquent | Balance Amounts Which Are 30, 60, 90, 120+ Days Overdue
User Defined Fields
Payment/Letter | Date | Time | Action Type | Place of Contact | Party Contacted | CACS State | 1st Promise | 2nd Promise | Excuse | History Indicator | Collector ID | User Define Field
For Five Most Recent Collection History Entries
Messages and Instructions to User

Figure 12 Display of customer information in a credit and collection system.

operations, but have been using an outside service bureau or bank to prepare their paychecks by computer for many years.

Paychecks must be prepared on a regular schedule, be delivered to employees on time, and be correct. It's one thing for accounts receivable to send monthly statements a day or two late, but it's an entirely different matter to be late with the payroll.

FutureStore has three different types of payroll—salary, hourly, and incentive. Salaried employees (normally managers and senior personnel) receive a fixed salary per pay period and do not receive extra pay for working overtime. Hourly employees receive a fixed amount of money per hour worked. They are also paid higher rates for work in excess of 40 hours in a week and for working weekends or holidays. Incentive employees are paid by how well they perform their jobs. Factory employees, for example, are paid a fixed amount of money per item processed; salespeople are paid on commission, receiving some percentage of the gross business they generate.

The payroll system first calculates an employee's gross pay. It then calculates all the deductions that must be withheld, such as federal taxes, state taxes, social security taxes, union dues, health insurance premiums, pension plan contributions, savings bond purchases, credit union deposits, charitable contributions, and life insurance premiums. Each deduction is calculated according to its own special set of rules that may change frequently with new legislation, union contracts, raises, promotions, new benefits, and so on. Even though FutureStore has its own substantial computing capabilities, its payroll is prepared by a local bank that specializes in payroll systems.

The bank's payroll system prints the actual paychecks, as well as stubs that list the gross salary and all deductions that have been taken (Figures 13 and 14). The bank maintains a salary history for each employee. It keeps track of sick pay and vacation pay, prints a **check register** of all checks paid, and supplies this information to FutureStore's general ledger system. It keeps track of all checks issued, determines which checks have been paid, which are outstanding, which have been voided, which have been canceled, and so on. It also produces various forms and

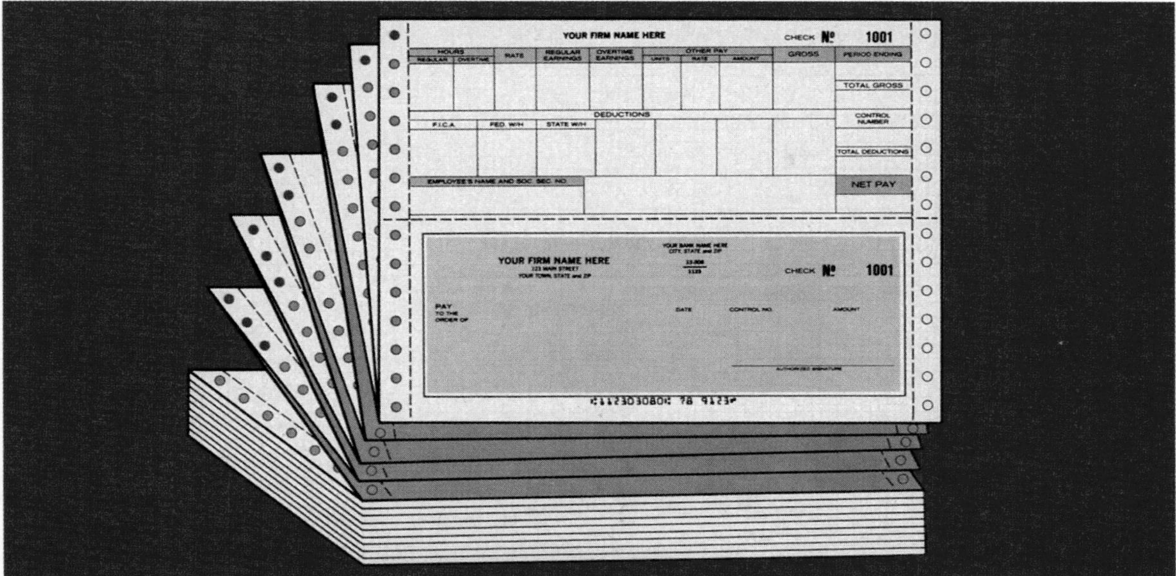

Figure 13 These paychecks and stubs are designed on continuous forms for use in computerized payroll systems.

Figure 14 Manufacturers of preprinted continuous forms used in various types of computer systems provide "print grids" such as this to aid programmers in placing the right information at the correct location on the page.

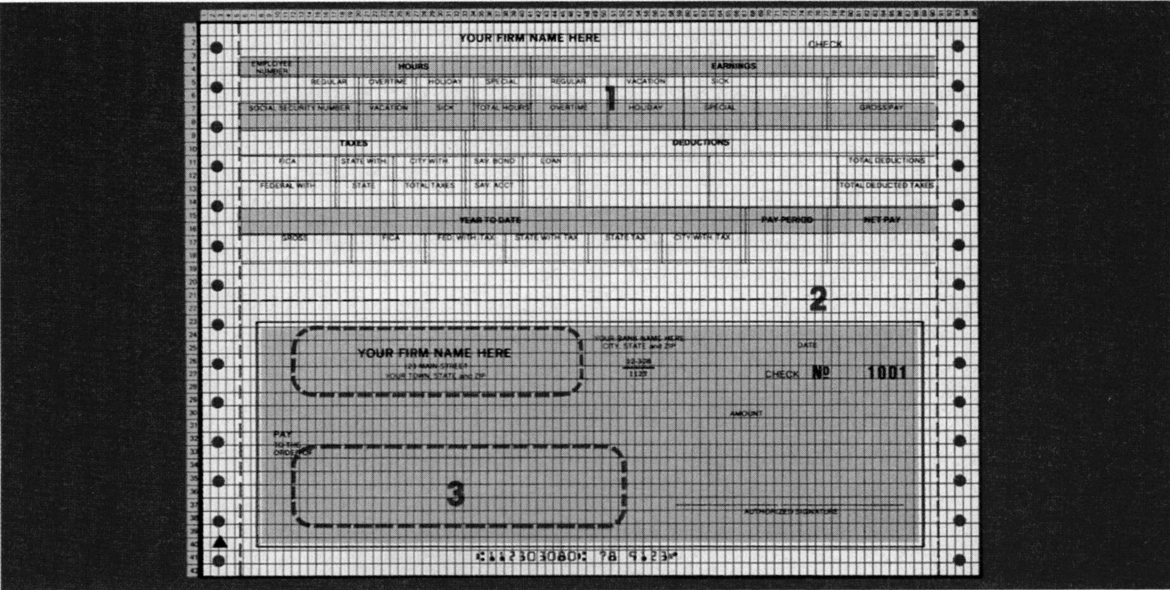

reports periodically to meet various legislated requirements.

Instead of receiving printed paychecks, many of FutureStore's employees take advantage of **direct deposit**; their net pay is deposited electronically by computer directly to their own bank accounts (see Chapter 15). This reduces paperwork and makes the funds available to the employees immediately.

Accounts Payable System

FutureStore's **accounts payable system** pays its suppliers on time to maintain good business relationships and takes advantage of discounts offered by suppliers for prompt payment. It monitors expenses by category and by supplier. Accounts payable pays bills as closely as possible to their due dates in order to conserve cash, and it avoids duplicate payments. It automatically handles such repetitive payments as rents and leases. It plans bank borrowings and reduces them by carefully controlling when payments are made. It keeps track of discounts that have been taken, discounts that are available to be taken, and discounts that have been lost because payment was not made on time.

As bills arrive, operators enter the information into the accounts payable system. Each bill must be approved for payment before the system actually issues the check. Accounts payable can "hold" checks—sometimes the company may be waiting for a supplier to fulfill some commitment before the company will pay. All payment information is passed to the general ledger system.

The **cash requirements report** shows how much money is needed, usually week by week, to handle forthcoming payments. The **check register** is a complete list of all checks that have been issued. The **vendor master report** is a complete list of FutureStore's suppliers, their addresses, their payment terms, and the like. Checks are printed with a stub that shows which vendor invoices are being paid.

General Ledger System

The **general ledger system** keeps track of FutureStore's financial records and produces reports summarizing the financial health of the company. The **chart of accounts** is a listing of all the categories to which general ledger applies charges and payments.

The two most important reports produced by general ledger are the **balance sheet** and the **profit and loss statement**, also called the **income statement** (Figure 15). The income statement summarizes by category all the income and expenses the business had for the reporting period. The difference between income and expenses is FutureStore's profit or loss. The balance sheet summarizes **assets** (what the business owns) and **liabilities** (what the business owes). The difference between these figures is FutureStore's **net worth**.

The income statement and the balance sheet are usually certified by an outside auditing firm as having been prepared "in accordance with generally accepted accounting principles." Upon completing an audit, the auditor will generally give an **unqualified opinion** if the financial statements are in good order, a **qualified opinion** if certain areas are weak, and an **adverse opinion** if the financial statements as a whole are not acceptable.

General ledger also produces the **sales journal** and the **cash receipts journal**, listing and summarizing all FutureStore's financial transactions (Figure 16). The general ledger statement summarizes how the transactions have been applied to each of the accounts in the chart of accounts.

Decision Support Systems

Decision support systems (DSS) are interactive computer systems that support management decision-making activities. They are designed to be used primarily by executives who need not have

Figure 15 *Right, top:* Samples of the two key reports produced by a general ledger accounting system—the balance sheet and the profit and loss statement.

Figure 16 *Right, bottom:* A system structure chart for a portion of a general ledger accounting system. This chart shows inputs, files, and outputs for the processing of cash receipts (CR) and sales journal (SJ) information.

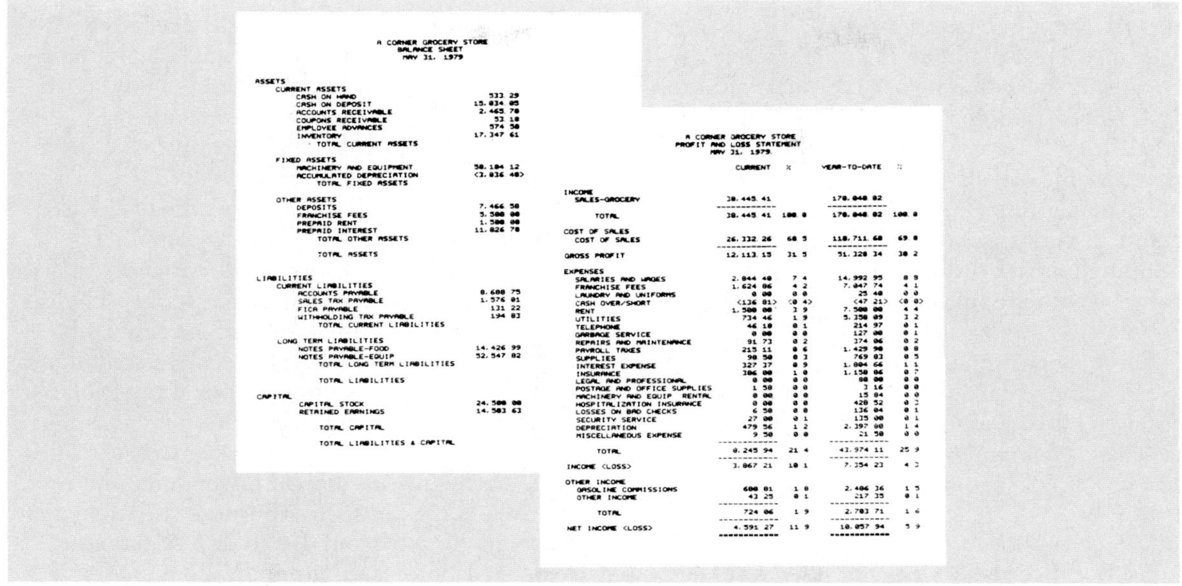

A CORNER GROCERY STORE
BALANCE SHEET
MAY 31, 1979

ASSETS	
CURRENT ASSETS	
CASH ON HAND	533.29
CASH ON DEPOSIT	15,034.05
ACCOUNTS RECEIVABLE	2,465.70
COUPONS RECEIVABLE	53.10
EMPLOYEE ADVANCES	574.50
INVENTORY	17,347.61
TOTAL CURRENT ASSETS	
FIXED ASSETS	
MACHINERY AND EQUIPMENT	50,104.12
ACCUMULATED DEPRECIATION	<3,036.40>
TOTAL FIXED ASSETS	
OTHER ASSETS	
DEPOSITS	7,466.50
FRANCHISE FEES	5,500.00
PREPAID RENT	1,500.00
PREPAID INTEREST	11,026.70
TOTAL OTHER ASSETS	
TOTAL ASSETS	
LIABILITIES	
CURRENT LIABILITIES	
ACCOUNTS PAYABLE	8,608.75
SALES TAX PAYABLE	1,576.01
FICA PAYABLE	131.22
WITHHOLDING TAX PAYABLE	194.83
TOTAL CURRENT LIABILITIES	
LONG TERM LIABILITIES	
NOTES PAYABLE-FOOD	14,426.99
NOTES PAYABLE-EQUIP	52,547.02
TOTAL LONG TERM LIABILITIES	
TOTAL LIABILITIES	
CAPITAL	
CAPITAL STOCK	24,500.00
RETAINED EARNINGS	14,503.63
TOTAL CAPITAL	
TOTAL LIABILITIES & CAPITAL	

A CORNER GROCERY STORE
PROFIT AND LOSS STATEMENT
MAY 31, 1979

	CURRENT	%	YEAR-TO-DATE	%
INCOME				
SALES-GROCERY	38,445.41		170,040.02	
TOTAL	38,445.41	100.0	170,040.02	100.0
COST OF SALES				
COST OF SALES	26,332.26	68.5	118,711.68	69.8
GROSS PROFIT	12,113.15	31.5	51,328.34	30.2
EXPENSES				
SALARIES AND WAGES	2,844.40	7.4	14,992.95	8.9
FRANCHISE FEES	1,624.86	4.2	7,047.74	4.1
LAUNDRY AND UNIFORMS	0.00	0.0	25.40	0.0
CASH OVER/SHORT	<136.81>	<0.4>	<47.21>	<0.0>
RENT	1,500.00	3.9	7,500.00	4.4
UTILITIES	734.46	1.9	5,358.09	3.2
TELEPHONE	46.10	0.1	214.97	0.1
GARBAGE SERVICE	0.00	0.0	127.00	0.1
REPAIRS AND MAINTENANCE	91.73	0.2	374.06	0.2
PAYROLL TAXES	215.11	0.6	1,429.90	0.8
SUPPLIES	98.50	0.3	769.83	0.5
INTEREST EXPENSE	327.37	0.9	1,804.66	1.1
INSURANCE	386.00	1.0	1,158.86	0.7
LEGAL AND PROFESSIONAL	0.00	0.0	80.00	0.0
POSTAGE AND OFFICE SUPPLIES	1.58	0.0	3.16	0.0
MACHINERY AND EQUIP RENTAL	0.00	0.0	15.84	0.0
HOSPITALIZATION INSURANCE	0.00	0.0	420.52	0.3
LOSSES ON BAD CHECKS	6.50	0.0	136.04	0.1
SECURITY SERVICE	27.00	0.1	135.00	0.1
DEPRECIATION	479.56	1.2	2,397.80	1.4
MISCELLANEOUS EXPENSE	9.50	0.0	21.50	0.0
TOTAL	8,245.94	21.4	43,974.11	25.9
INCOME <LOSS>	3,867.21	10.1	7,354.23	4.3
OTHER INCOME				
GASOLINE COMMISSIONS	680.81	1.8	2,486.36	1.5
OTHER INCOME	43.25	0.1	217.35	0.1
TOTAL	724.06	1.9	2,703.71	1.6
NET INCOME <LOSS>	4,591.27	11.9	10,057.94	5.9

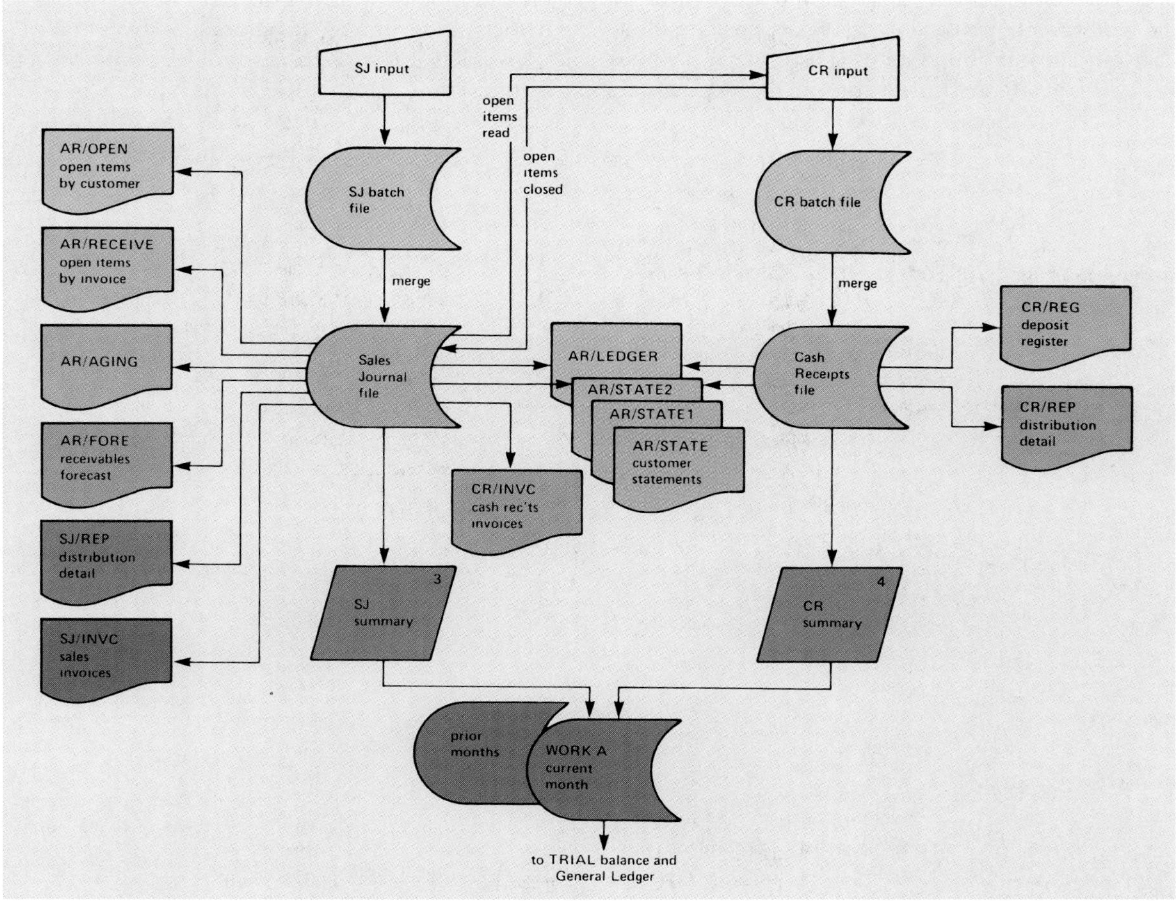

SJ input
CR input
open items read
open items closed
AR/OPEN open items by customer
AR/RECEIVE open items by invoice
AR/AGING
AR/FORE receivables forecast
SJ/REP distribution detail
SJ/INVC sales invoices
SJ batch file
CR batch file
merge
merge
Sales Journal file
AR/LEDGER
AR/STATE2
AR/STATE1
AR/STATE customer statements
Cash Receipts file
CR/REG deposit register
CR/REP distribution detail
CR/INVC cash rec'ts invoices
3
SJ summary
4
CR summary
prior months
WORK A current month
to TRIAL balance and General Ledger

extensive computer backgrounds. The users engage in **what-if planning** in an interactive dialogue with the computer. A typical application in sales forecasting, for example, would have the user asking "*What* would be the increase in sales *if* we double our advertising budget?" DSS allows the manager to try many alternatives on paper before committing company resources. DSS has been used most productively in financial planning, but other applications are becoming popular.

The strong emphasis being placed on computer use in management schools and training programs is making managers keenly aware of the benefits of computer-supported decision making. The use of DSS should become widespread in the 1980s.

DSS can assist an executive in making decisions, but it certainly does not fully automate the decision-making process. We can look forward to the widespread use of what may come to be called **decision automation systems** (DAS) in the 1990s. We will investigate this notion further in Chapter 16, where we discuss artificial intelligence.

Some DSS systems provide the executive with access to the company's integrated database, as well as access to external databases maintained by various information services companies.

Decision support systems must provide user-friendly interfaces that make it easy for executives to access computer systems. English-based dialogues are clearly superior to computerese (Figure 11–9). The ultimate user-friendly interface has yet to be developed, but spoken English is probably the optimal form of executive-to-computer and computer-to-executive communications. Touch-sensitive screens are also popular.

Unlike management information systems that produce standard reports on a regular schedule, DSS is generally used in **ad hoc inquiry and reporting**, that is, in special purpose situations that may vary greatly from day to day. A manager who needs information rapidly simply doesn't have the time to wait for the data-processing department to write new programs. So DSS makes it convenient for managers to make a wide variety of requests for information on the spot. These include both what-if requests and straightforward information retrieval requests (Figure 11–10).

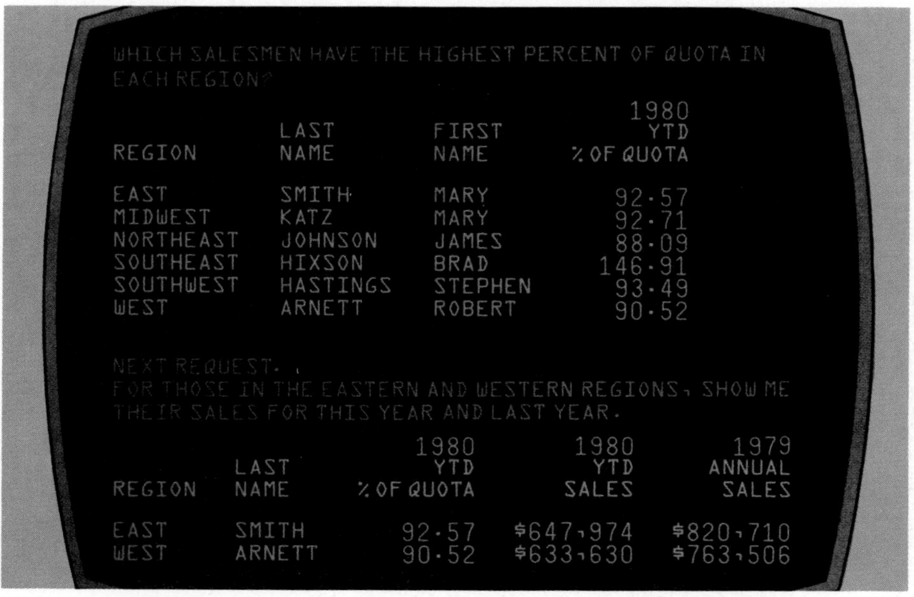

Figure 11–9 Simple English query languages like the one used in this example are essential to the acceptance of DSS by executives.

1. Using a brief question-and-answer dialogue, the computer "prompts" you with the instructions you need to specify the parameters of the report.

2. If you don't know your options, you type the word "HELP," and the computer will list them for you.

3. When you're ready, you push a button. The computer then automatically creates its own program that accesses the files, assembles all the information required, and prints the desired report.

Once the report has been generated, the specifications can be automatically retained by the computer, so if you ever require the report again, you simply request it by name. The Qantel Report Generator. One more element in a spectrum of software that gives you total control.

ENTER A NAME FOR THIS REPORT
COST DEVIATION
ENTER THE NAME OF THE FILE TO BE REPORTED ON
YOUR FILES ARE:
CUSTOMER
VENDOR
SALESMAN
STATISTICS
INVENTORY
SHIP TO
INVENTORY
LIST, IN ORDER OF IMPORTANCE, THE INFORMATION ELEMENTS WHICH WILL CONTROL THE ORDER OF INFORMATION REPORTED

1

LIST, IN ORDER OF IMPORTANCE, THE INFORMATION ELEMENTS WHICH WILL CONTROL THE ORDER OF INFORMATION REPORTED
HELP
INFORMATION ELEMENTS IN THE INVENTORY FILE ARE:
INVENTORY NUMBER
ITEM DESCRIPTION
STOCK TYPE
STOCKING UNITS
VENDOR
FIRST COST
COST DIFFERENCE
QUANTITY ON ORDER
QUANTITY ON HAND

2

3

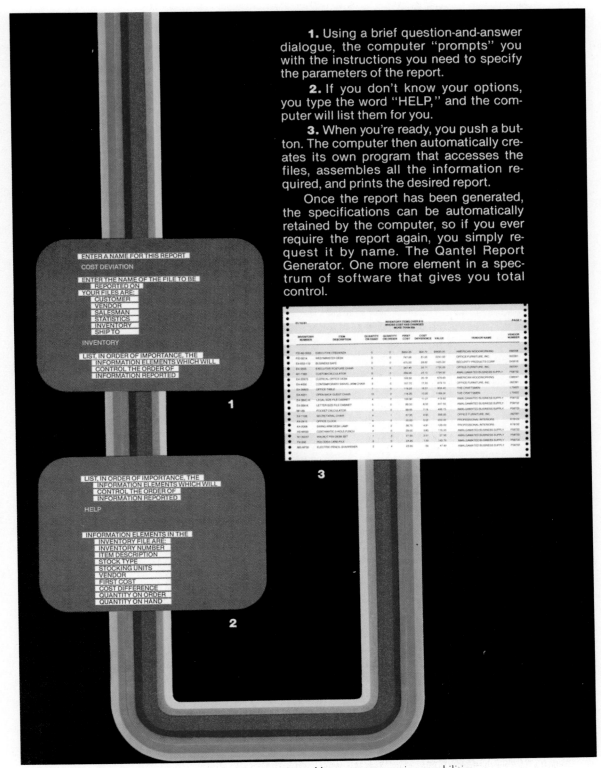

Figure 11–10 Decision support systems provide convenient ad hoc report generation capabilities.

HOW VISICALC WORKS

By Stewart Alsop II

Here's an example of how VisiCalc, the best-selling financial-analysis program, works when you sit down to use it on a personal business computer. The example, a kid's roadside cookie stand, is terrifically simplified so we can fit the explanation on one page. But VisiCalc is capable of more complex analyses. At the Boston office of Laventhol & Horwath, an accounting firm, I saw accountants create five-year income and cash-flow statements for a proposed 300-room hotel: The statements were based on 43 revenue and cost assumptions. I also saw them working up 10-year projections for tourism revenues for Grand Cayman island, that were based on hundreds of assumptions.

Anyway, we've got this 14-year-old kid who wants to make some spending money selling chocolate chip cookies to homebound commuters on a four-lane road near his house. In the Printout # 1 (below), you can see that he's gotten traffic forecasts from his town's engineering department and cost estimates from his mother, who's his exclusive distributor. He's decided that he will get an increasing percentage of cars to stop despite the uneven traffic count, and that he will have a constant average sale to each car of six cookies. He's put a price of 15¢ on each cookie and has decided that he will need his younger brother to help 12½ hours a week for $1.25 an hour.

In Printout #2 (below), you can see the profit and loss forecast the kid constructed based on his assumptions. (It took him about two hours to create the whole format.) Each position on the P&L uses a formula based on the assumptions in order to come up with the figure. For instance, the formula for NET SALES under WEEK 1 is (# CARS multiplied by STOP %) multiplied by (AV. SALE multiplied by UNIT SALE) multiplied by HRS/WEEK. To enter that formula, the kid typed (B5*B6)*(B7*B9)* B10 [R] into the computer. The letter-and-number combination identifies the position of each assumption; the asterisk signifies the multiply function; the parentheses group the functions; and hitting the return key tells the machine to calculate the formula.

As you can see, in order to use VisiCalc, you have to learn which keys stand for different functions or commands. The program, for example, is able to "replicate" the formula we just detailed into the next three columns. In order to start the replicating process, you

PRINTOUT #1

KID'S COOKIE BUSINESS ASSUMPTIONS

	WEEK 1	WEEK 2	WEEK 3	WEEK 4
# CARS/HR	825	900	875	750
STOP %	.025	.03	.0325	.04
AV. SALE	6	6	6	6
#/BATCH	36	36	36	36
UNIT $ALE	.15	.15	.15	.15
HRS/WEEK	12.5	12.5	12.5	12.5
LABOR/HR	1.25	1.25	1.25	1.25
BATCH COSTS:				
PKG CHIPS	2.16	2.16	2.16	2.16
BUTTER	0.85	0.85	0.85	0.85
EGGS	0.16	0.16	0.16	0.16
BROWN BAG	.12	.12	.12	.12
OTHER	1.23	1.23	1.23	1.23
TOTAL	4.52	4.52	4.52	4.52

PRINTOUT #2

KID'S COOKIE BUSINESS P&L PROJECTION

	WEEK 1	WEEK 2	WEEK 3	WEEK 4
NET SALES	232.03	303.75	319.92	337.50
CHIPS	92.81	121.50	127.97	135.00
BUTTER	36.31	47.53	50.06	52.81
EGGS	6.95	9.09	9.58	10.10
PACKAGE	5.16	6.75	7.11	7.50
OTHER	52.85	69.19	72.87	76.88
MFG COSTS	194.08	254.06	267.59	282.29
G. PROFIT	37.96	49.69	52.33	55.21
OVERHEAD	15.63	15.63	15.63	15.63
N. PROFIT	22.33	34.06	36.71	39.58

VisiCalc

The availability of economical personal computers has made it possible for many more executives to take advantage of DSS. **VisiCalc**, one of the most successful personal computer software packages of all time, is an excellent example of a "what-if" DSS system (see the box "How VisiCalc Works"). VisiCalc is often called an **electronic worksheet**, as we will see.

Modeling

DSS systems provide modeling capabilities that enable executives to project the effects of their decisions. Lower-level executives may need to determine the sales for each of the last several weeks; this is a simple information retrieval problem that can be solved by making a standard query to a database system. Upper-level execu-

have to know that the slash [/] key tells the machine that you're about to enter a command and that the R key after the slash tells the machine to start the replicate command. But it's fairly easy to remember the right keys, because it's usually the first letter of the word that identifies the command (R for replicate, for example).

Back to the kid's cookie stand. As you can see from the bottom line (labeled N. PROFIT), his forecast shows that he can make from $22.33 to $39.58 a week, depending on the traffic count and his ability to get more cars to stop. Suppose, though, that there is a major frost in the cocoa-producing regions of South America, and the price of chocolate chips goes through the roof in WEEK 3. The kid enters 2.73 (up from 2.16) for BATCH COSTS: PKG CHIPS in WEEK 3 and 4, and discovers that his bottom line goes to hell (to $2.94 and $3.96, respectively) because the program automatically recalculates manufacturing costs, of which chocolate chips are a part (see Screen #1 below).

In response to this dramatic change, the kid decides not to reduce the quality of his cookies by using fewer chips. But he does think the market will bear a price increase, so he raises UNIT SALE by two cents to .17 (see Screen #2). The program recalculates his P&L, because the unit price is part of the formula for NET SALES, and the kid discovers that he can actually make more money at the higher price, as long as the market doesn't start buying fewer cookies.

I could go on and on about how the kid adjusted his forecast for such events as his younger brother striking for higher wages or a construction project near his stand cutting traffic by half. Either of these recalculations would take seconds. But the point is that, once the format for a projection is set up and the data entered, you can change your assumptions and almost instantly see what effect the changes will have on the bottom line. And you can keep changing assumptions until you're satisfied that you understand which ones are truly critical to your operation.

What becomes clear from using VisiCalc is that the assumptions you thought were important, such as price of materials cost, aren't really crucial, and that the variables you thought were minor, such as overhead as a percent of gross profit, are absolutely critical. To get that kind of sophisticated understanding about your company's financial picture can be worth a lot of money.

Stewart Alsop is executive editor of INC.

SCREEN #1

D15 (V) 2.73 C! 14

	A	C	D	E
10	UNIT $ALE	.15	.15	.15
11	HRS/WEEK	12.5	12.5	12.5
12	LABOR/HR	1.25	1.25	1.25
13				
14	BATCH COS			
15	PKG CHIPS	2.16	2.73	2.73
33	BUTTER	47.53	50.06	52.81
34	EGGS	9.09	9.58	10.10
35	PACKAGE	6.75	7.11	7.50
36	OTHER	69.19	72.87	76.88
38	MFG COSTS	254.06	301.36	317.92
41	G. PROFIT	49.69	18.56	19.58
42	OVERHEAD	15.63	15.63	15.63
45	N. PROFIT	34.06	2.94	3.96

SCREEN #2

D10 (V) .17 C! 14

	A	C	D	E
10	UNIT $ALE	.15	.17	.17
11	HRS/WEEK	12.5	12.5	12.5
12	LABOR/HR	1.25	1.25	1.25
13				
14	BATCH COS			
15	PKG CHIPS	2.16	2.73	2.73
33	BUTTER	47.53	50.06	52.81
34	EGGS	9.09	9.58	10.10
35	PACKAGE	6.75	7.11	7.50
36	OTHER	69.19	72.87	76.88
38	MFG COSTS	254.06	301.36	317.92
41	G. PROFIT	49.69	61.22	64.58
42	OVERHEAD	15.63	15.63	15.63
45	N. PROFIT	34.06	45.59	48.96

tives, however, need to answer much harder questions, such as "How much business will we lose if our competitor's system is introduced next month?" A DSS can help the executive construct a **mathemetical model** to estimate what the sales would be without the competitor's product on the market, what portion of the market the competitor is likely to capture, and, therefore, what the lost sales might be. The model must be adjusted constantly to be sure that it is, in fact, an accurate representation of the business. This is called **calibration.** Case Study 11–3 illustrates how a DSS creates and manipulates a mathematical model.

Case Study 11–3: An Example of What-If Planning

Explanation (see Step 1):

Using simple English, the executive states the problem to be solved. The statement must be complete, and ambiguous statements must be avoided. When the DSS reads a problem statement, it may ask the executive to supply additional information or clarify certain points. This is not necessary here.

Explanation (see Step 2):

The DSS reads the English narrative and extracts key facts and relationships. It uses this information to develop a mathematical model consisting of a series of simple algebraic equations. The DSS prints the model for the executive to examine. The executive then types "SOLVE," indicating that the DSS should solve the model. The DSS responds with "ENTER SOLVE OPTIONS," and the executive specifies "ALL." This indicates that the values of all the variables in the model are to be shown for each of the five years. The DSS then prints the forecast for the years 1979 to 1983 showing how the company's net income should grow from $66,352 to $109,382 over the period.

The model (Step 2) contains 11 statements numbered from 10 to 20. Each of these statements was obtained by extracting information from the executive's problem statement. For example,

11 SALES = 400000, 1.12 * PREVIOUS SALES

is the mathematical model's statement corre-

"I wish to describe my projected statement of income over the next five years. I estimate sales to be $400,000 in 1979 with annual increases of 12 percent thereafter. Gross profit will be these sales less cost of goods sold, which can be considered to be 60 percent of sales. Total expenses include fixed expenses (at $25,000 in 1979, increasing with inflation at 8 percent per year) and interest paid on a long-term average debt of$80,000 at 9-1/4 percent. My tax liability is 48 percent of profit before tax. What is my net income projected to be each year?"

Step 1. Statement of the problem in everyday business language.

```
MODEL INCOME  VERSION OF  10/16/78  15:14
10 COLUMNS 1979-1983
11 SALES = 400000, 1.12 * PREVIOUS SALES
12 GROSS PROFIT = SALES - COST OF GOODS SOLD
13 COST OF GOODS SOLD = .60 * SALES
14 TOTAL EXPENSES = FIXED EXPENSES + INTEREST PAID
15 FIXED EXPENSES = 25000, 1.08 * PREVIOUS FIXED EXPENSES
16 DEBT LEVEL = 80000
17 INTEREST PAID = .0925 * DEBT LEVEL
18 TAX LIABILITY = .48 * PROFIT BEFORE TAX
19 PROFIT BEFORE TAX = GROSS PROFIT - TOTAL EXPENSES
20 NET INCOME = PROFIT BEFORE TAX - TAX LIABILITY
END OF MODEL


? SOLVE
ENTER SOLVE OPTIONS
? ALL
```

	1979	1980	1981	1982	1983
SALES	400,000	448,000	501,760	561,971	629,408
GROSS PROFIT	160,000	179,200	200,704	224,788	251,763
COST OF GOODS SOLD	240,000	268,800	301,056	337,183	377,645
TOTAL EXPENSES	32,400	34,400	36,560	38,893	41,412
FIXED EXPENSES	25,000	27,000	29,160	31,493	34,012
DEBT LEVEL	80,000	80,000	80,000	80,000	80,000
INTEREST PAID	7,400	7,400	7,400	7,400	7,400
TAX LIABILITY	61,248	69,504	78,789	89,230	100,968
PROFIT BEFORE TAX	127,600	144,800	164,144	185,896	210,351
NET INCOME	66,352	75,296	85,355	96,666	109,382

Step 2. The model.

sponding to the statement of the problem in everyday business language shown in Step 1:

> "I estimate sales to be $400,000 in 1979 with annual increases of 12 percent thereafter."

The portion of the problem statement in Figure 1:

> "Gross profit will be these sales less cost of goods sold, which can be considered to be 60 percent of sales."

translates into two statements in the model (Step 2), namely

12 GROSS PROFIT = SALES − COST OF GOODS SOLD
13 COST OF GOODS SOLD = .60 * SALES

Explanation (see Step 3):

Now the executive is prepared to ask various "what-if" questions. The executive types "WHAT IF" and the DSS responds with "ENTER STATEMENTS." In the original problem, the executive stated that the cost of goods sold was 60 percent of sales. Now the executive enters the new formula

COST OF GOODS SOLD = .70 * SALES

and then types "SOLVE" and "ALL," and the DSS solves the model once again. This time, the higher cost of the goods sold lowers the net income projections to yield $45,552 in 1979 and to grow to $76,653 in 1983.

```
? WHAT IF
WHAT IF CASE 1
ENTER STATEMENTS
? COST OF GOODS SOLD = .70 * SALES
? SOLVE
ENTER SOLVE OPTIONS
? ALL

***** WHAT IF CASE 1 *****
1 WHAT IF STATEMENTS PROCESSED
```

	1979	1980	1981	1982	1983
SALES	400,000	448,000	501,760	561,971	629,408
GROSS PROFIT	120,000	134,400	150,528	168,591	188,822
COST OF GOODS SOLD	280,000	313,600	351,232	393,380	440,585
TOTAL EXPENSES	32,400	34,400	36,560	38,893	41,412
FIXED EXPENSES	25,000	27,000	29,160	31,493	34,012
DEBT LEVEL	80,000	80,000	80,000	80,000	80,000
INTEREST PAID	7,400	7,400	7,400	7,400	7,400
TAX LIABILITY	42,048	48,000	54,705	62,255	70,757
PROFIT BEFORE TAX	87,600	100,000	113,968	129,699	147,410
NET INCOME	45,552	52,000	59,263	67,443	76,653

Step 3. Query: "What if my cost of goods sold is closer to 70 percent of sales? How does this affect my net income?"

```
? GOAL SEEKING
GOAL SEEKING CASE 1
ENTER NAME OF VARIABLE TO BE ADJUSTED TO ACHIEVE PERFORMANCE
? SALES
ENTER COMPUTATIONAL STATEMENT FOR PERFORMANCE
? NET INCOME = 70000, 1.15 * PREVIOUS NET INCOME

***** GOAL SEEKING CASE 1 *****
```

	1979	1980	1981	1982	1983
SALES	417,538	473,019	536,472	609,065	692,138

```
ENTER SOLVE OPTIONS
? ALL
```

	1979	1980	1981	1982	1983
SALES	417,538	473,019	536,472	609,065	692,138
GROSS PROFIT	167,015	189,208	214,589	243,626	276,855
COST OF GOODS SOLD	250,523	283,812	321,883	365,439	415,283
TOTAL EXPENSES	32,400	34,400	36,560	38,893	41,412
FIXED EXPENSES	25,000	27,000	29,160	31,493	34,012
DEBT LEVEL	80,000	80,000	80,000	80,000	80,000
INTEREST PAID	7,400	7,400	7,400	7,400	7,400
TAX LIABILITY	64,615	74,308	85,454	98,272	113,013
PROFIT BEFORE TAX	134,615	154,808	178,029	204,733	235,443
NET INCOME	70,000	80,500	92,575	106,461	122,430

Step 4. Query: "What level of sales do I have to generate to produce a net income of $70,000 in 1979 and increasing by 15 percent per year after that?"

Explanation (see Step 4):

Now the executive makes a different kind of inquiry. The executive types "GOAL SEEKING," indicating that a goal will be stated and that the system should perform certain manipulations to attempt to achieve that goal. The system types "ENTER NAME OF VARIABLE TO BE ADJUSTED TO ACHIEVE PERFORMANCE," and the executive responds with "SALES." This means that the system should find the level of sales that will achieve the goal about to be stated. Then the system asks "ENTER COMPUTATIONAL STATEMENT FOR PERFORMANCE." The executive types

NET INCOME = 70000, 1.15 * PREVIOUS NET INCOME

This means that the goal the executive wants to achieve is a net income of $70,000 in 1979 that increases at the rate of 15 percent per year. The DSS then prints the necessary sales levels for 1979 through 1983 to achieve the net income goals. The executive types "ALL," and the DSS once again solves the entire model for all variables. **Goal seeking** is an extremely important function of decision support systems.

"I feel kind of silly asking a computer if we should invest in more computers . . .!"

"I don't want to talk to a middleman . . . put me straight through to the computer!"

Summary

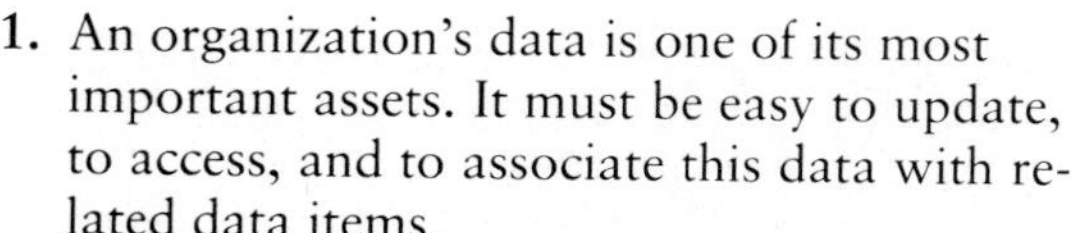

1. An organization's data is one of its most important assets. It must be easy to update, to access, and to associate this data with related data items.
2. A database is a collection of data items stored with minimal redundancy and arranged in a structure that shows how these data items are related to one another.
3. A database is stored on secondary storage devices, it can be used by many different applications at once, and applications programs are shielded from the details of exactly how data is physically stored.
4. Database management systems keep an organization's information current, readily acces-

sible to authorized users, and secure from unauthorized access.

5. A database management system creates and maintains databases, provides backup and recovery to prevent loss of vital information, and allows users to design applications systems quickly and conveniently.

6. Database integrity means that what is supposed to be in the database is, and what is not supposed to be in the database isn't.

7. In a hierarchical database, data records are arranged in a parent/child relationship. Each parent may have many children, but each child has just one parent. A disadvantage is that it is difficult to express multiple views of the data without considerable duplication.

8. Network databases are more general than hierarchical ones, and they make it easier to provide multiple views of the data. Each data record may be connected to any other. A disadvantage is that the interconnections can become complex, making it difficult to search or modify the database.

9. In a relational database, a convenient tabular representation is used. The relational organization is much more user-friendly. A disadvantage is that today's computer architectures do not manipulate relations efficiently.

10. A relational DBMS provides three fundamental operations that may be used to form new relations: the join operation combines relations, the project operation extracts only certain domains (columns) from a relation, and the select operation extracts only certain tuples (rows) from a relation.

11. Management information systems (MIS) provide managers with certain reports on a regular schedule. One key to an effective MIS is a centralized integrated database.

12. Decision support systems (DSS) are interactive computer systems that support management decision-making activities. They are used primarily by managers who need not have extensive computer backgrounds.

13. DSS is used in special (ad hoc) situations that may vary greatly from day to day.

14. A DSS works with mathematical models of a company. For the system to be useful, these models must be constantly updated to reflect changes in the business, its suppliers, its clients, government regulations, and so on.

15. Full-scale DSS systems have access to large integrated databases. They have user-friendly interfaces, ad hoc reporting capabilities, and modeling capabilities.

Important Terms

accounts payable system
accounts receivable system
ad hoc inquiry and reporting
billing system
calibration
chart of accounts
credit and collection system
database
database integrity
database management system (DBMS)
data independence
decision support system (DSS)
domain
general ledger system
goal seeking
hierarchical database
inventory control system
management information system (MIS)
manufacturing resources planning system (MRP)
mathematical model
network database
order entry system
payroll system
redundancy
relational database
strategic planning
tactical planning
tuple
VisiCalc
what-if planning

Self-Review Exercises

Matching

Next to the term in column A, place the letter of the statement in column B that best describes it.

Column A	Column B
1. Tuple	A. Report that shows the payment status of each customer
2. EDP	B. A row in a relation
3. Database administrator	C. Determines who may access the information
4. Bill of materials	D. Computerizing the flow of day-to-day business transactions
5. DSS	E. Interactive computer system that supports management decision making
6. Ad hoc	F. List of all the components that are needed to manufacture an item
7. Chart of accounts	G. A collection of related data items
8. Aged trial balance	H. Electronic worksheet
9. VisiCalc	I. Listing of general ledger categories
10. Database	J. Special purpose

Fill-in-the-Blanks

Fill in the blanks in each of the following:

1. ______ occurs when data appears in more than one file.

2. ______ means that what is supposed to be in the database is there, and what is not supposed to be there isn't.

3. Three database structures are ______ , ______ , and ______ .

4. The ability to modify the structure of a database without affecting existing programs is called ______ .

5. MIS helps managers in their ______ , ______ , ______ , and ______ functions.

6. A ______ report allows management to determine quickly what the most important inventory items are.

7. Transactions that need to be resolved manually appear on a ______ .

8. One of the first functions companies normally computerize is ______ .

9. ______ reports show how much money is needed to handle forthcoming payments.

10. The two most important reports produced by the general ledger are ______ and ______ .

Answers to Self-Review Exercises

Matching: 1 B, 2 D, 3 C, 4 F, 5 E, 6 J, 7 I, 8 A, 9 H, 10 G

Fill-in-the-Blanks:

1. Redundancy
2. Database integrity
3. hierarchical, network, relational
4. data independence
5. planning, organizing, directing, controlling
6. distribution-by-value
7. suspense listing
8. payroll
9. Cash requirements
10. balance sheet, profit and loss statement (or income statement)

Discussion Questions 

1. In what form has data traditionally been stored? How is this changing?

2. Explain what is meant by redundancy. What are its advantages and disadvantages?

3. What capabilities are provided by a database management system?

4. What are the responsibilities of the database administrator? Why is it such an important position?

5. What is the main advantage of the network database over the hierarchical database?

6. What is the primary advantage of the relational database over the hierarchical and network databases?

7. What is a management information system? Why has MIS been so much more successful in the 1980s than it was in the 1960s and 1970s?

8. List and briefly describe the major computer systems in a management information system for a manufacturing company.

9. What is DSS and how is it useful? Give examples.

10. What is ad hoc reporting? Why must a DSS have powerful ad hoc reporting capabilities?

Projects 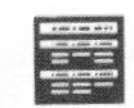

1. Prepare a research report on relational database management systems for personal computers.

2. Visit a computer store that specializes in selling personal computer systems to small businesses. Determine which MIS applications software packages are most commonly purchased by customers. Report on the capabilities of these packages.

3. Compare the features of three of the most popular electronic worksheet software packages.

"The computer company says call the software company. The software company says call service. Service says it's not in the contract; it's in the training manual. And nobody understands the training manual."

Chapter 12

Operating Systems

After reading this chapter you will understand:

1. What operating systems are, why they are needed on today's computing systems, and what their functions and capabilities are
2. The difference between systems programs and applications programs
3. What is meant by multiprocessing, multiprogramming, and multitasking systems
4. Why multiuser operating systems are so much more complex than single-user operating systems
5. The features of several of the most widely used operating systems

Outline

Machines should work. People should think.
from an IBM advertisement

As we have seen, computers require both hardware and software to accomplish their tasks. The hardware performs the basic calculations and manipulations needed to solve problems. The software instructs the hardware how to solve the problems of particular applications.

Systems programs control the operation of the computer, and **applications programs** instruct the computer how to solve specific user problems. The set of systems programs on a computer is called that computer's **operating system**. In this chapter, we discuss the types and functions of operating systems, comment on some of the more popular operating systems, and take an in-depth look at CP/M, UNIX, XENIX, and MS-DOS—some of the most popular operating systems for the 1980s.

Systems Programs

Systems programs make complex computer hardware more user-friendly. They control the hardware by performing functions that users should not have to (or are unable to) handle; they act as intermediaries between the users and the hardware.

A **systems programmer** writes and modifies the detailed systems programs. This skill requires real understanding of the internal operation of computer hardware. Computer **vendors** (companies that build computer hardware) supply general-purpose systems programs to user installations. Systems programmers at these installations then tailor the programs to the needs of the local environment.

Applications Programs

Applications programs solve a user's data processing needs. A large company might have applications programs to control its inventory, prepare its payroll, bill its customers, and the like.

Applications programmers need not know a great deal about the inner workings of a computer. Rather, they must understand the information needs of their organization and how to use a computer to meet those needs.

The various "views" of a computer system are illustrated in Figure 12–1. Systems programmers see the hardware and write programs that depend on the specifics of the hardware. Applications programmers see the operating system and the facilities it offers. The users "see" the view provided by the applications programs—this must be the "friendliest" of all the views.

Operating Systems

In the 1950s the cost of computer hardware was much greater than that of computer operators; today the opposite is true. In the late 1950s and early 1960s **operating systems** were developed. These collections of systems programs allow computer systems to handle many of the functions previously performed by computer operators. This development brought with it more efficiency because computers can handle far more details than humans and at much greater speeds.

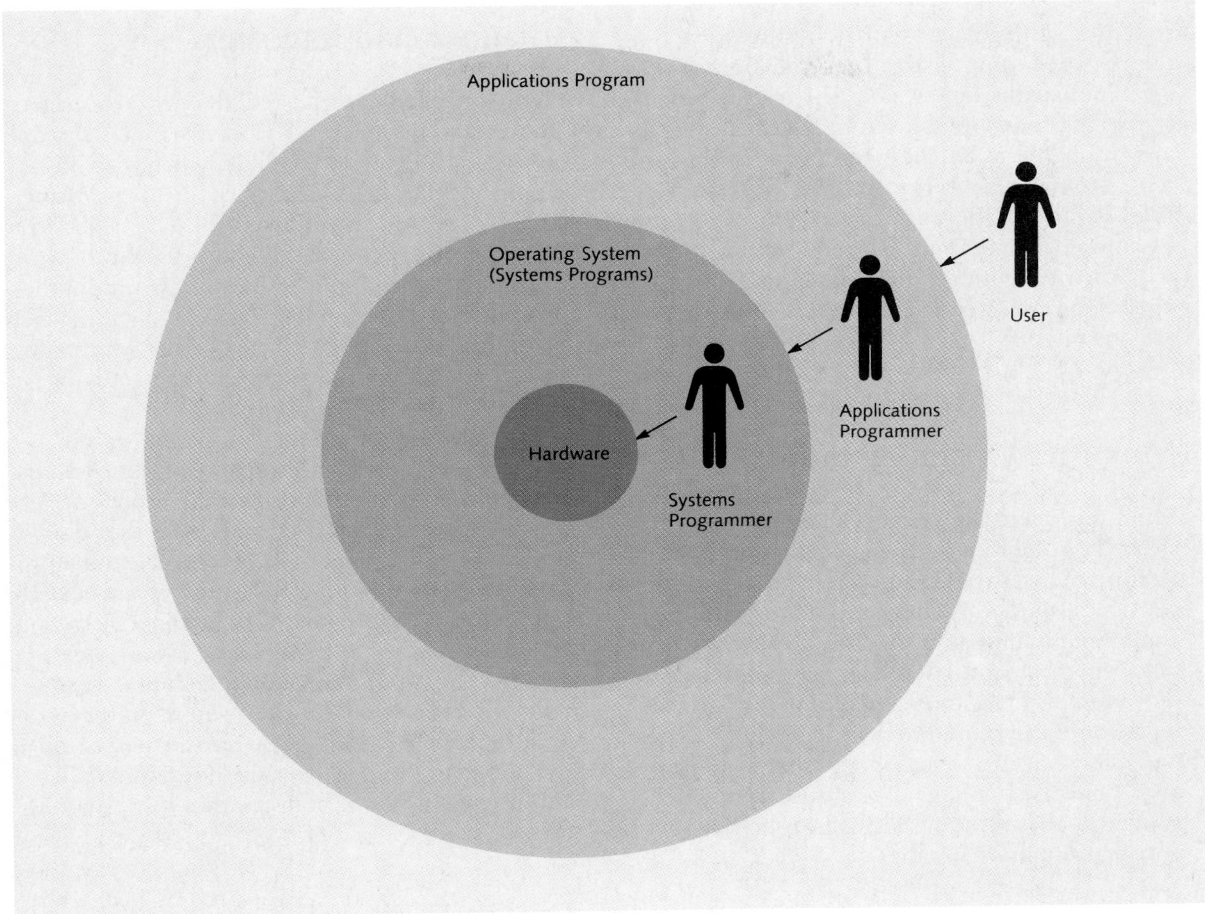

Figure 12–1 The various "views" of a computer system.

Operating Systems Functions

Operating systems are primarily **resource managers**; they manage computer hardware, programs, and data. Operating systems handle the assignment of portions of the hardware to individual users, charge those users for the resources, manage the hardware to achieve efficient operation while guaranteeing good service, and make it possible for many users to share a computer at one time without interfering with one another. They handle input and output to the various devices, manage the creation and manipulation of files, and facilitate the loading and execution of programs.

Operating systems do not perform all these functions without cost. They occupy primary storage locations, use the processor, and occupy secondary storage space on disk. The operating system's use of resources is called **overhead**. The tradeoff is simply that the benefits gained by using the operating system should far outweigh the overhead.

Batch Processing

User jobs are often classified as **batch processing, interactive**, or **real-time**. In batch processing, users submit their jobs to a central computer installation. In a single-user batch-processing system, the operating system runs one job at a time. To minimize the time wasted in "tearing down" (removing) one job and setting up the next, jobs are grouped into **batches**, and the operating system automatically performs many of the functions of job-to-job transition previously performed by computer operators. Users do not interact with their executing programs. In fact, large batch jobs are often run overnight while the users are not present.

Multiuser Operating Systems

Multiuser operating systems allow many users to share the resources of a single computer system. Sharing reduces the cost per user for accessing expensive resources. It enables users to work from a common database of information, such as in an office environment. Users may send messages to one another. If the intended receiver is not currently on the system, the message may be deposited in an "electronic mailbox," that is, a file on disk. One disadvantage of multiuser computer systems is that if the system fails, everyone's work may be brought to a halt.

Multiprogramming

Running only one job at a time can waste system resources. For example, a job that uses only a printer and a disk may leave a system's tape drives idle. Similarly, a job that does a great deal of input/output may leave the processor idle most of the time. To make better use of system resources, **multiprogramming** operating systems were developed. These allow many jobs to be run simultaneously. Of course, with only one processor, only one program may execute at a time, but the operating system switches the processor rapidly among the various jobs, creating the illusion that the jobs are indeed running at the same time. **Multitasking** is a special case of multiprogramming in which each user may have multiple activities in progress at once.

Channels and Interrupts

Hardware **channels** transfer data between primary storage and peripheral devices. Channels can operate in parallel with the CPU; when the CPU is doing calculations, channels can be transferring data. These concurrent operations are called **overlapped processing** or **parallel processing.**

To perform an input or output operation, the processor executes an instruction telling the channel to begin the operation. Instead of waiting for this lengthy operation to finish, the processor performs calculations for other users.

When the operation finally does finish, the channel generates a hardware signal called an **interrupt** to gain the attention of the processor. The processor stops what it is doing, sees that the I/O operation has finished, relays this fact to the program that requested the I/O, initiates the next I/O operation (if any) to keep that channel busy, and resumes what it was doing when it was interrupted. The processing of an interrupt is very much like what you do when you're on the phone and the doorbell rings—you ask the person on the phone to hold, answer the door, and then continue your phone conversation.

Double Buffering

Double buffering helps take advantage of overlapped processing. An area of primary storage, called a **buffer**, is set aside for communication between the processor and a channel. The CPU processes data and deposits it in the buffer. The CPU tells the channel to transmit the data from the buffer to disk. While the channel is transmitting, the CPU normally has to wait before it can put more data in the buffer. With double buffering (also known as **flip-flop buffering**), a second buffer is used (Figure 12–2). While the channel is transmitting from buffer A, the CPU can fill buffer B. When the channel finishes transmitting from A, it can immediately start transmitting from B, and the CPU can go back to filling A. This flip-flopping between the two buffers allows the CPU and the channel to operate in parallel.

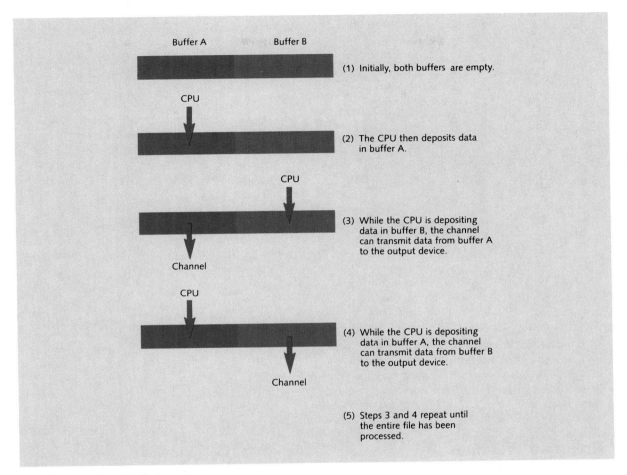

Figure 12–2 Double buffering.

Storage Protection

One difficulty with multiprogramming systems is that it is possible for the various users to interfere with one another or with the operating system. **Storage protection** mechanisms help to prevent this from occurring. One popular scheme is the use of **boundary registers.** When the operating system decides to run a particular user's program, it first loads two hardware registers with the lowest and highest main storage addresses of that user's program (Figure 12–3). If the running program then tries to refer to a storage address outside these boundaries, the hardware stops the reference before any damage can be done to another user's programs or data (this is called **error trapping**). The hardware then informs the operating system of the problem. The operating system terminates the user program and informs the user what went wrong, ideally providing enough information to help the user debug the program.

Relocatable Programs

Programs that can only run if put in certain fixed locations are called **absolute**; programs that may be placed anywhere in primary storage are said to

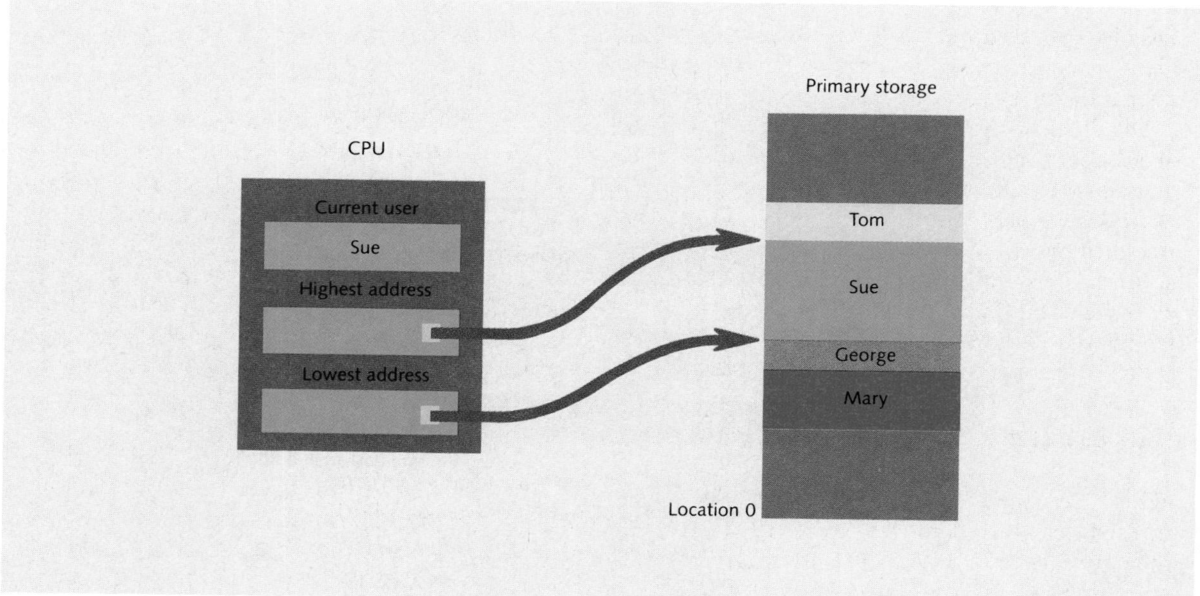

Figure 12–3 Boundary registers used for storage protection.

be **relocatable programs**. Making programs relocatable is essential in multiuser systems, because each time a program is run it may have to be placed in whatever locations are available at that time.

Reentrant Programs

Sharing may be facilitated by **reentrant programs**, that is, programs that do not modify themselves. These programs do not change while being executed, and, therefore, several users may share and execute the same copy of the program simultaneously without interfering with one another. This saves precious primary storage space.

Deadlock

One serious problem with multiuser systems is that **deadlock** (sometimes called **gridlock**) may occur. A simple example is shown in Figure 12–4. There are two users, Sam and Judy, and two resources, Disk1 and Disk2. Sam is currently using Disk1, and Judy is using Disk2. Sam needs Disk2 to proceed, but he can't have it because Judy is using it. At the same time, Judy needs

Figure 12–4 A two-user deadlock.

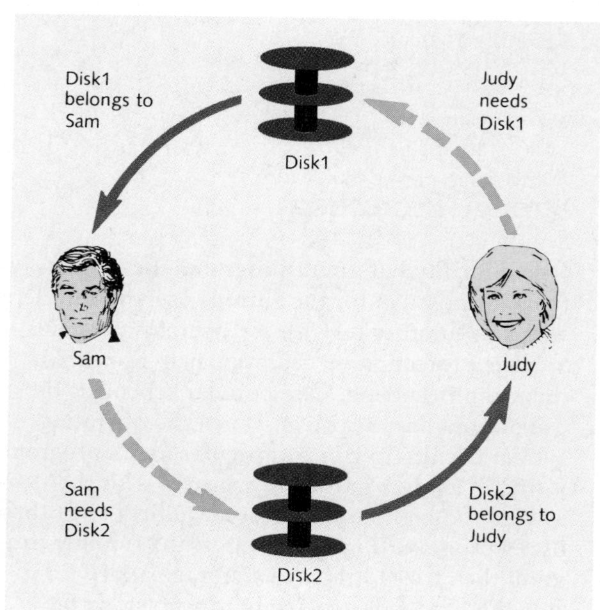

Disk1 to proceed but can't have it because Sam is using it. Neither user will release the disks, so we have a deadlock—no one can proceed.

Deadlocks of various kinds can occur in almost every operating system. Most of these can be prevented by careful design, but when deadlock does occur, normally the only way out is to terminate one or more of the deadlocked jobs to release resources. This allows other users to get the needed resources and finish, so the terminated jobs can be rerun.

Timesharing

When users interact with the computer system through terminals while their jobs are running, they are said to be **interactive users. Timesharing** operating systems multiprogram many interactive users. Timesharing systems must provide interactive users with rapid responses, otherwise the users' work would suffer. A common application on timesharing systems is **interactive program development** in which programmers type their program statements, translate and test their programs, make corrections, and continue this process until their programs execute properly.

One key to guaranteeing acceptable response times is using a hardware timer. When a user is given the processor, the timer is set to some maximum value, or **quantum**, normally a small fraction of a second. Within this quantum most user requests can be serviced. If, however, a substantial calculation that cannot be handled within that time is being performed, the quantum will expire, the timer will generate an interrupt to get the attention of the processor, and the operating system will assign the processor to the next user. This scheme of offering only brief "bursts" of time to each user is called **time slicing**. Each user receives as many time slices as are necessary to complete that user's calculations.

Real-Time Systems

Real-time systems are computer systems that respond immediately to various occurrences. They are used in industrial process control systems (such as gasoline refining), air traffic control systems, missile guidance systems, and patient monitoring systems, among others. Their most important goal is **responsiveness**. If a signal from a gasoline refinery indicates that the temperature in a mixing vat is rising too quickly, the real-time operating system must respond quickly. In a real-time air traffic control system, if a signal indicates that two planes are on a collision path, the system must respond immediately to avoid a disaster. In an implanted real-time system controlling a heart pacemaker device, rapid response to a danger signal could save a patient's life.

Scheduling

In multiuser operating systems, deciding which user gets which resources and when is called **scheduling.** The special case of scheduling the processor and assigning it to the next user is called **dispatching.** Scheduling is a complex problem and requires careful thought.

In timesharing systems, users can be dispatched in **round robin** fashion in which the jobs are viewed as arranged in a circle and the processor moves from job to job in order around the circle (Figure 12–5). Round robin is considered fair because it treats all users in the same way; it is not an effective scheme for giving priority to certain users.

A system that does enforce priorities could grant very poor service to low-priority users. The extreme case, called **indefinite postponement**, occurs when a steady stream of high-priority users

'We Call It Our "Real Time" System 'Cause Everyday We Have a "Real-Time" Getting It to Work Right.'

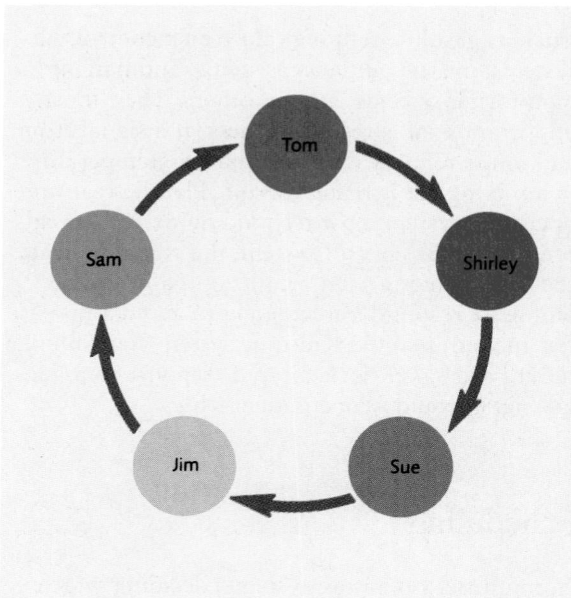

Figure 12–5 Round robin scheduling. The processor moves from job to job around the circle.

prevents low-priority users from receiving any service at all. Some systems avoid this problem by gradually increasing the priorities of low-priority users the longer they wait for service.

Print Spooling

In multiprogramming systems, several users must share the computer's input/output devices. Difficulty may occur if the system doesn't have enough printers to handle all the requests to print reports at the same time. Some of the users would then have to wait until a printer becomes available.

Print spooling allows users to run their programs even if a printer is not available. Whenever a user program tries to write to the printer, the spooling mechanism of the operating system intercepts the request and instead writes the data to disk. When the printer becomes available, the disk file may then be printed. Because disk output is so much faster than printer output, spooling makes it possible for programs that use printers (and other relatively slow devices) to run much faster.

Print spooling is even useful on single-user systems. It enables a user to run a program at the same time as a file is being printed. This is the most common form of multitasking.

Virtual Storage

The more we use computers, it seems, the more applications we would like to computerize. This trend, coupled with declining storage costs, has brought users to demand more and more storage to support their applications. But primary storage remains expensive compared to secondary storage devices like disk and tape.

In **virtual storage** systems the distinction between primary and secondary storage disappears, at least as far as the user is concerned. The operating system creates the illusion of a single massive storage that is much larger than the primary storage of the machine. In fact, it is common for a computer's virtual storage to be 100 to 1000 times larger than its primary storage. One disadvantage of virtual storage systems is that because users think storage is essentially unlimited they may tend to write programs that are longer than necessary.

Because a computer can only execute instructions and reference data that are in its primary storage, virtual storage systems must shuttle pieces of programs and data back and forth between primary and secondary storage. This shuttling can cause programs to run slowly, so operating systems attempt to minimize the number of shuttling operations.

Segmentation

The most common techniques for implementing virtual storage are segmentation and paging. In **segmentation** the program or data pieces may be of different sizes; in paging the pieces are all the same size. Segmentation allows each piece being shuttled back and forth to represent either a whole program, a whole data structure, or a whole procedure. A **segment** corresponds exactly to a meaningfully defined piece of a program. Because segments are of different sizes, as they are

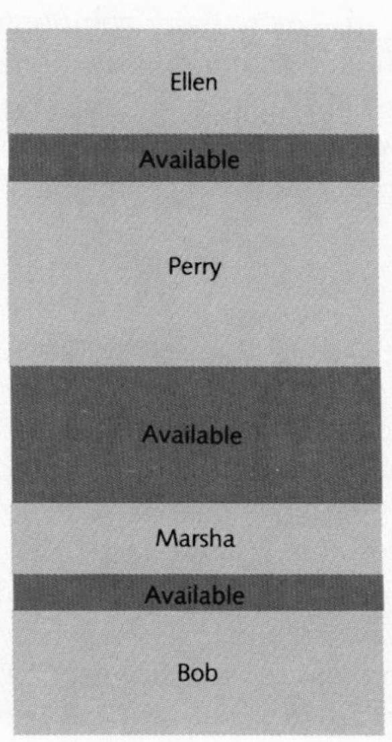
Ellen
Available
Perry
Available
Marsha
Available
Bob

Figure 12–6 Fragmentation in a segmentation system. Some of the available storage holes are too small to hold an incoming segment.

loaded and unloaded from primary storage the **storage holes** left over vary in size. Sometimes many small holes dot primary storage, and these may be so small as to be unusable. This is called **fragmentation** and is a serious problem in segmentation systems (Figure 12–6).

Reclaiming usable space is called **garbage collection**. This may be accomplished in a segmentation system by **compacting** all the occupied areas to one end of storage so that a single large usable area remains.

Paging

Paging (Figure 12–7) helps eliminate this fragmentation problem. All program and data pieces are the same size (called the **page size**). When a new page is brought into main storage, the page may be placed in the space, called a **page frame**, vacated by any previous page. Some fragmentation does occur in paging systems because the last page of a program will rarely fill a complete page frame.

Sometimes all the page frames are full, so the operating system must remove a page from primary storage to make room for an incoming page. The operating system attempts to replace pages not likely to be needed again soon.

Figure 12–7 Paging.

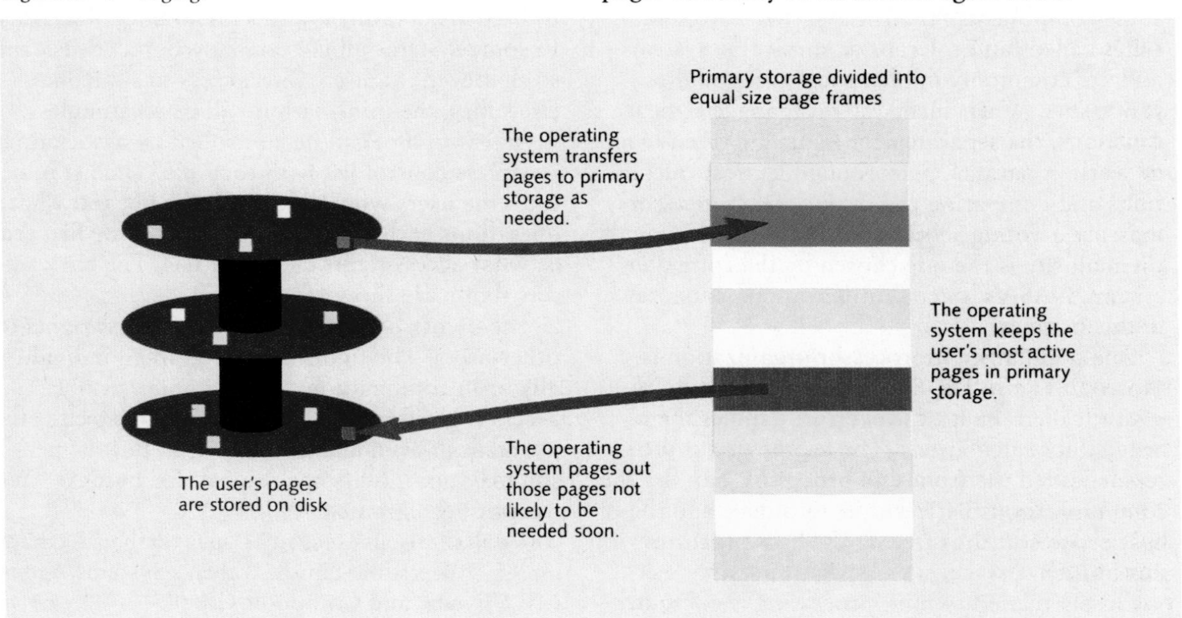
Primary storage divided into equal size page frames
The operating system transfers pages to primary storage as needed.
The operating system keeps the user's most active pages in primary storage.
The user's pages are stored on disk
The operating system pages out those pages not likely to be needed soon.

In order for a program to run efficiently in a paged system, its most active pages must be kept in primary storage. If insufficient space is available for this purpose, excessive paging activity, known as **thrashing**, occurs. Instead of doing useful work, the operating system "pages itself to death."

Some systems combine paging and segmentation. The logical program pieces and data collections correspond to segments, and each segment is divided into fixed-size pages for convenience in placing the pieces in primary storage.

Multiprocessing

Multiprocessing operating systems manage computers that have more than one processor. **Multiprocessor** computers are generally more reliable than **uniprocessor** (single processor) systems—if one of the processors fails, the others can continue operating. Multiprocessors also help improve **throughput**—the amount of work a computer can process in a given amount of time. Some multiprocessors assign a separate processor to each user; others switch the processors from user to user.

Much interest exists today in developing highly reliable systems that keep working even when some components fail. These systems are sometimes called **fault tolerant** or **survivable systems** and are commonly implemented using multiprocessors. When such systems manage critical functions, the separate processors are often made to work in parallel, performing identical calculations and comparing the results. The processors may use a **voting scheme** in which the decision of the majority is the one chosen by the computer system. NASA's space shuttle computers operate in this manner.

One popular multiprocessor organization is shown in Figure 12–8. The more powerful processor, called the **host processor**, handles the heavy duty calculations. The less powerful processor, called the **front-end processor**, handles the communications between the terminals and the host processor, thus freeing the host processor of this burden.

Closely related to multiprocessing is **computer networking** in which many computer systems are connected in a data-communications network, as we discussed in Chapter 7. A **network operating system** allows users to share the resources of many separate computer systems.

Security

With the trends toward multiuser systems and computer networking, security becomes a real concern. A common security scheme requires users to memorize secret **passwords**. The passwords are used to gain access to a multiuser system and to access files.

It is reasonable to expect a user to type a password incorrectly once or twice, but people have cracked computer systems by trying all possible passwords until the correct one is found. Therefore a wise security measure is for the operating system to monitor the number of invalid log-in attempts for the same account. If too many attempts are detected, the operating system prints a warning at the user's terminal and sends a message to the system administrator. It may even refuse to accept further communications from the terminal in order to thwart the intruder.

Encryption, the encoding of information, may be used in operating systems for additional security. In some systems all files are stored in coded form, so that even if a user gains access to someone else's files, the information will be meaningless.

Access to files can be controlled by associating an **access control list** with each file. The list indicates the users who may access the file and what operations each user may perform on the file, that is, what **access rights** each user has. The basic access rights are shown in Figure 12–9.

The owner of a file grants these access rights to other users. The rights may be granted individually or in combination. For example, "R + E" access is granted to allow someone to execute a program or even make a copy of it, but the person may not modify the original file because "W" has not been granted.

We shall discuss security issues further in Chapter 15, "Electronic Funds Transfer Systems, Security, Privacy, and Computer Crime."

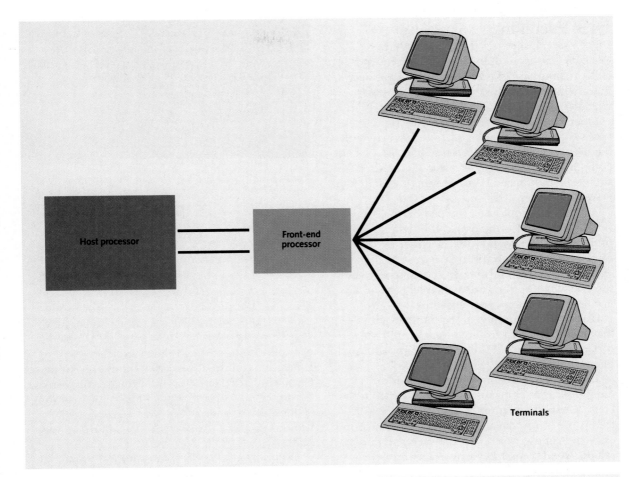

Figure 12–8 A multiprocessing system using a front-end processor to ease the burden on a host processor.

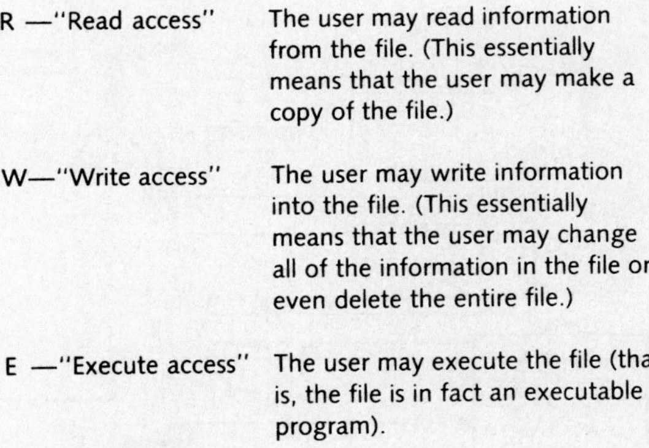

R —"Read access"	The user may read information from the file. (This essentially means that the user may make a copy of the file.)
W—"Write access"	The user may write information into the file. (This essentially means that the user may change all of the information in the file or even delete the entire file.)
E —"Execute access"	The user may execute the file (that is, the file is in fact an executable program).

Figure 12–9 The basic access rights that may be granted to users of files.

User-Friendliness

We have discussed **user-friendliness** frequently. It really means ease of use. How can operating systems help make computer systems more user-friendly?

Operating systems should provide rapid responses to user requests and communicate with the user in simple English, rather than in obscure computerese. The amount of typing required should be minimized while keeping the dialogue understandable.

A help key should be provided on the keyboard (Figure 12–10), so the user can press it at any time during a dialogue to receive assistance without having to thumb through a weighty manual.

Help menus should clearly and concisely show the user what options are available, but should not be forced upon experienced users.

Users should not have to be familiar with the messy details of controlling input/output on various kinds of devices. The operating system should handle this.

The operating system should provide error-handling capabilities to rescue the user from the consequences of certain errors. Error trapping means the hardware and operating system cooperate to "cage in" errors. If the user program attempts to do something erroneous, the error is detected, and the operating system informs the user of the problem. The operating system may suggest to the user how to correct the problem, or it may even fix the problem itself.

Figure 12–10 The help key. How the operating system responds when the help key is pressed by a user can greatly affect just how user-friendly a system is.

"This is the computer's most popular feature: whatever mistake you make, it voluntarily accepts the blame."

Positive confirmation is helpful in preventing users from accidentally committing serious errors. When the user says to erase a file, some operating systems counter with "Are you sure you really want to do this?" This at least makes the user think twice.

Utility programs are provided by the operating system to help the user accomplish certain common tasks such as renaming, copying, printing, editing, sorting, and merging files, and making backup copies of disks.

Upward mobility means that the operating system adapts easily to the growth of a computer system. This is important because as users place more and more functions on their computers, they must add primary storage, secondary storage, faster and larger disks, faster printers, and various other devices—possibly even a more powerful CPU chip.

Device independence allows users to write programs independently of considerations of how data is organized on particular devices. When the user says "read the next record from payrollfile," the user need not worry about whether that record is physically adjacent to the previous one or at the opposite extreme of the disk. The operating system handles those details.

Firmware

Most people view computer systems as consisting of hardware and software. Today's systems usually have **firmware** as well. Its very name indicates that firmware is somewhere between hardware and software in nature.

One type of firmware is called **read-only memory** or **ROM.** ROMs are hardware memory chips that have been preloaded with software. The ROM is plugged into the computer in a slot provided for this purpose. The computer reads the program in the ROM and executes it, but the computer cannot modify the program in ROM. Today, computer vendors often place major portions of operating systems in ROM chips. One benefit is security—because ROM can't be modified, the operating system can't be altered. Another benefit is that more of the conventional primary storage provided with the computer can hold user programs. These conventional memories are called **RAMs** for **random access memory.**

One popular application of ROM is to contain a special program called a **bootstrap loader.** When power is turned on or a special reset button is pressed, the computer's hardware automatically copies the bootstrap loader from ROM to RAM and begins executing it. The bootstrap loader then reads in a fresh copy of the operating system from disk and the computer begins executing the operating system. If the operating system in RAM is destroyed by a malfunctioning user program, the user must **reboot** the operating system in order to proceed.

PROMs and EPROMs are also commonly used. A **PROM** is a **programmable read-only memory.** The user programs the PROM for a particular application, but a PROM can be programmed only once. An **EPROM** (eraseable PROM) can be reprogrammed as needed. Programming PROMs and EPROMs requires special equipment.

Case Study 12–1: CP/M

CP/M (Control Program for Microcomputers) is currently one of the most widely used operating systems in the world, and is considered by many personal computer users the standard of the 8-bit microcomputer industry. A program that runs under CP/M on one computer can normally run under CP/M on any other, although in some cases minor modifications may be required. An enormous amount of software is available for CP/M. To enable their users to take advantage of this software, computer vendors make their computers **CP/M-compatible**, that is, able to run CP/M. In this case study, we discuss CP/M and its capabilities.

History of CP/M

Intel produced the first microprocessor chip in 1970. In 1973 they revealed their model 8080 microprocessor chip using 8-bit words; this was the first chip with enough power to drive a full microcomputer. The first microcomputer followed shortly—it was the MITS Altair, which sold in kit form for under $400, mostly to hobbyists.

Early microcomputers used cassette recorders for secondary storage. These devices proved to be slow and unreliable. Then Shugart Associates introduced the floppy disk, a highly reliable and relatively fast secondary storage device. The computer industry now had all the pieces it needed to build useful and economical microcomputer systems for business and personal applications.

In 1973 Gary Kildall was working as a consultant to Intel, developing a new high-level language called PL/M. He obtained a floppy disk drive and configured a microcomputer system for use in his PL/M development work. To control the micro, he wrote some software that became the root of the CP/M operating system. Kildall formed Digital Research in 1976 to develop, refine, and market CP/M.

The Console Command Processor

Figure 1 shows the major components of CP/M. The **Console Command Processor** (CCP) is the portion of CP/M that receives user requests, or **commands**, and calls upon the other components of CP/M to carry out the chores needed to service these commands. A summary of the CP/M commands is shown in Figure 2.

CCP controls the user's view of the computer

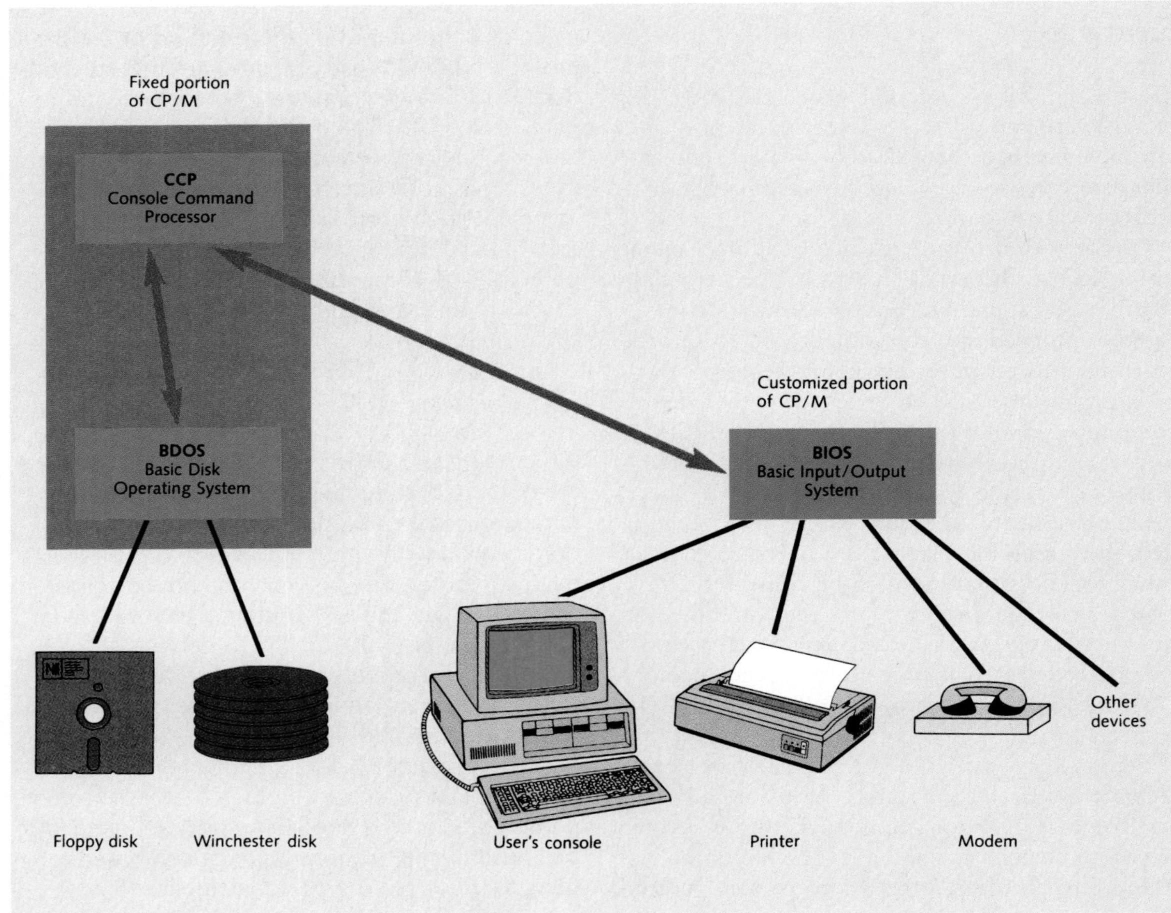

Figure 1 The major components of CP/M.

system. It carries on a dialogue with the user. The user specifies the tasks to be accomplished. CCP ensures that these tasks are performed and informs the user of errors that occur in processing.

The Basic Disk Operating System

The **Basic Disk Operating System** (BDOS) is the component of CP/M that handles all disk input/output and manipulates disk files. Disk files are normally scattered over the surfaces of disks in separate pieces called **extents**. BDOS manages these pieces so the user need not be concerned about their locations. BDOS and CCP make up the fixed part of CP/M; they are the same even in versions of CP/M implemented on different computers.

The Basic Input Output System

The **Basic Input Output System** (BIOS) is the component of CP/M that handles input/output to all devices other than disks. Some of its capabilities are reading a character from the console keyboard, writing a character to the console CRT, and writing a character to the printer. It can also check the status of any I/O device to see if the device is ready to receive or transmit a character.

ASM	translate an assembly program to machine language
DDT	help debug a program
DIR	display the names of files on a disk
DUMP	display the contents of main storage
ED	perform various editing operations on a file of text
ERA	delete (erase) a file from disk
LOAD	load a program from disk into main storage
MOVCPM	make a copy of CP/M in main storage
PIP	transfer a file between devices, for example, to make a backup copy (PIP stands for "Peripheral Interchange Processor")
REN	change the name of a file (rename)
SAVE	save the contents of main storage as a file on disk
STAT	display the status of devices and files (for example, the amount of space remaining on a disk)
SUBMIT	execute a sequence of commands from a disk file (instead of taking them from the console)
SYSGEN	prepare a new version of CP/M on a fresh disk
TYPE	display a file on the console
USER	change the user number

BIOS is the customized part of CP/M. It contains separate programs called **device drivers** to handle each type of device. Whenever a new type of device is added to a CP/M system, a device driver must be inserted into BIOS to handle it. Figure 3 shows how the various components of CP/M are arranged in primary storage.

File Extensions

All file names in CP/M have a **file extension**, a period followed by a three-letter code that helps identify the type of file. For example, the extension ".BAS" indicates a file containing a BASIC source program. Some common CP/M file extensions are summarized in Figure 4. File extensions help the user and CP/M manage files and avoid making certain types of errors.

Figure 2 *Left:* Some important CP/M commands.

Figure 3 *Below:* How primary storage is organized in a CP/M system.

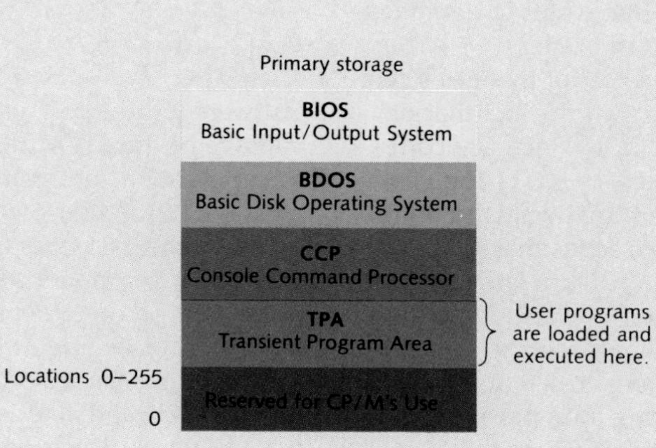

File Extension	Usage
.ASM	An Assembler source program
.BAK	The Editor's backup copy of a file
.BAS	A BASIC source program
.COB	A COBOL source program
.DAT	A data file of ASCII characters
.FOR	A FORTRAN source program
.INT	An object program from a translator
.LST	A BASIC compilation listing
.MAC	A source program for the relocatable assembler
.PRN	A compilation listing from Assembler, FORTRAN, or COBOL
.REL	A relocatable object program
.SUB	A SUBMIT command file
.$$$	A temporary ED or PIP file

Figure 4 Some common CP/M file extensions.

Logical device		Function
CON:	Logical console	Used for reading from the user's keyboard and writing to the user's CRT
LST:	Logical printer	Used for printing outputs from user programs
RDR:	Logical reader	Used for reading from a secondary storage device such as a floppy or a Winchester disk
PUN:	Logical punch	Used for writing to a secondary storage device such as a floppy or a Winchester disk

Figure 5 The four logical devices in CP/M. Applications programs "see" only these devices. CP/M automatically keeps track of which actual devices correspond to the logical devices at any moment.

Logical Devices

Applications programs written to run under CP/M see only **logical devices** (Figure 5). For example, the applications program that wants to communicate with the user does so through "CON:" the name all versions of CP/M use for the user's console. CP/M then worries about the fact that on this particular computer "CON:" actually corresponds to a printing terminal or a CRT terminal.

The applications program that wants to print lines on a hard-copy device sends these lines to "LST:" the "logical printer"; CP/M knows that on a particular system it's a daisy-wheel printer, for example. In fact, CP/M allows users to **redirect outputs**. The user who wants to see that the output is correct before printing it on paper could direct the "LST:" output to a CRT, correct any errors, and then redirect "LST:" back to a printer to print an error-free copy.

"RDR:" and "PUN:" are the logical devices that CP/M applications programs use to read and write from a secondary storage device such as a tape cassette, a floppy disk, or a Winchester disk.

System Calls

Software written to "run under CP/M" takes advantage of the CP/M capabilities. For example, the applications program that wants to write a message to the user console or receive a response typed by the user does not do so directly. Rather it executes a **system call**; it calls upon the appropriate portion of CP/M to perform the actual input/output (Figure 6). CP/M actually handles the messy details. User programs can be written more quickly and independently of the hardware details of a particular computer. Because input/output is often complex, this also means that user programs are less likely to contain errors.

System calls and logical devices simplify the

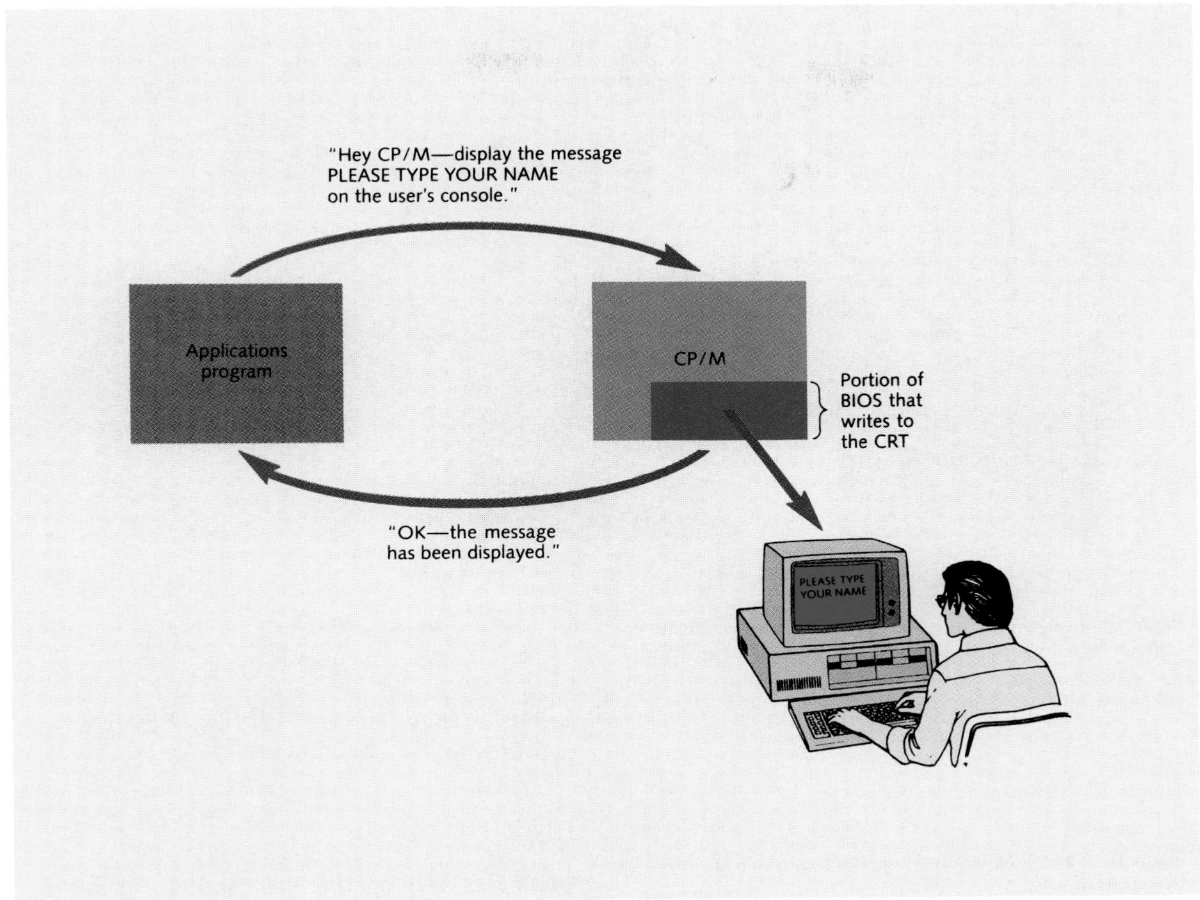

Figure 6 A system call.

task of writing applications programs to run on CP/M computers. They create an **applications programming interface**, a view of the computer that looks the same on all CP/M computers regardless of the physical differences between the machines (Figure 7). Applications software that runs on one CP/M computer can usually run on any other. This has resulted in the availability of a huge amount of applications software for CP/M systems.

One of the most important reasons users buy CP/M is to gain access to this software. Software vendors who write their packages for CP/M computers have a very large market for their products. Hardware vendors who build their machines to run CP/M can attract many more buyers. These are the benefits of any widely **standardized operating system**.

The CP/M Family of Operating Systems

The success of CP/M has led Digital Research to produce many related operating systems (Figure 8). These can all run the huge base of CP/M applications software. The systems with "-86" in their names are designed to run on 16-bit microcomputers (such as the IBM Personal Computer) based on Intel's 8086 and 8088 microprocessors.

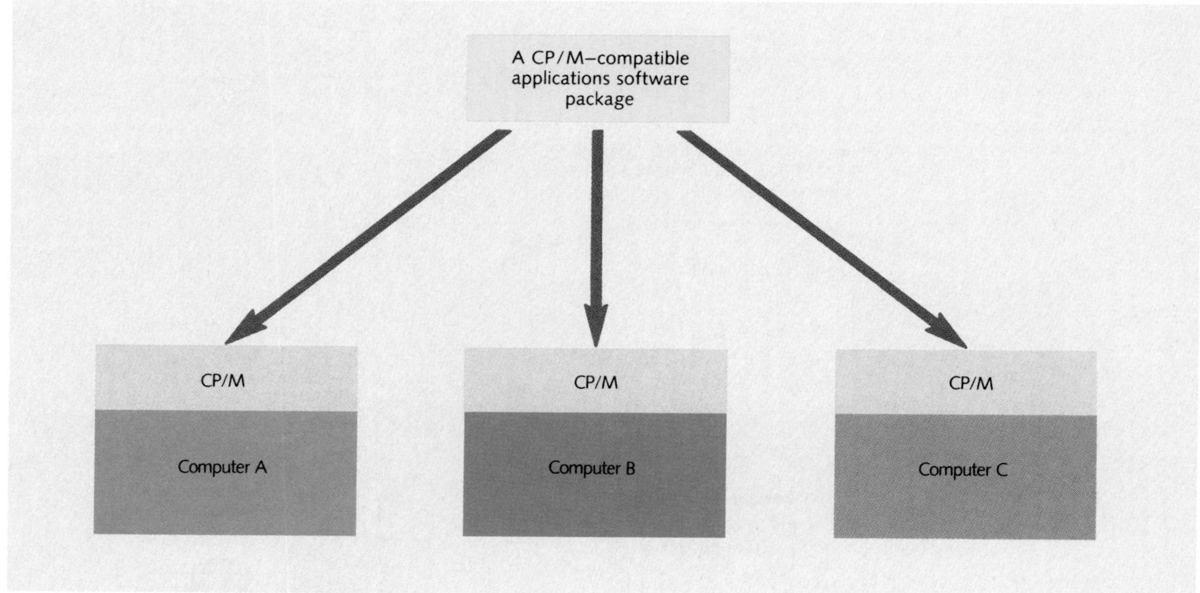

Figure 7 Even though computers A, B, and C may be quite different from one another, the views seen by the applications software package are the same, namely that of three identical CP/M machines.

Figure 8 The CP/M family of operating systems produced by Digital Research.

Single-User Operating Systems	
CP/M	For Intel 8080-based 8-bit microcomputers
CP/M Plus	A user-friendly version of CP/M for less sophisticated users
CP/M-86	CP/M upgraded to run on Intel 8086/8088-based 16-bit microcomputers
Concurrent CP/M-86	A multitasking (single-user) version of CP/M-86
Multi-User, Multitasking Operating Systems	
MP/M-II	For Intel 8080-based 8-bit microcomputers
MP/M-86	For Intel 8086-8088-based 16-bit microcomputers
Network Operating System	
CP/NET	Manages a network of CP/M and MP/M computers

Case Study 12–2: UNIX, XENIX, MS-DOS

UNIX

UNIX was developed at Bell Laboratories in the late 1960s and early 1970s. It is a multiuser, multitasking system originally used with 16-bit minicomputers, primarily PDP-11s manufactured by Digital Equipment Corporation.

UNIX supports a huge assortment of utility programs to facilitate text processing and program development. It has become popular in universities, and has been implemented on a wide range of larger computer systems.

There is great interest in UNIX today in the microcomputer marketplace. Some people believe it may soon become the industry standard microcomputer operating system. Many UNIX-like systems have become popular. Perhaps the most notable of these is the XENIX system developed by Microsoft.

Two innovative concepts in UNIX are **pipes** and **filters**. A filter is a program that reads a stream of inputs, processes them in some manner, and produces a stream of outputs. A pipe is a communi-

cation path between programs. Filters and pipes may be connected to form a **pipeline** in which inputs enter and go through a series of processing filters, and from which outputs emerge. This allows powerful programs to be composed by combining existing pieces instead of "reinventing the wheel." Many companies market filter programs for use on UNIX systems.

One of the classic examples of composing a program from pipes and filters is the development of a spelling-checker program that inputs a text file and outputs a list of misspelled words (Figure 1). The first filter inputs a file of text and outputs a stream of individual words. The second filter inputs this stream of words and outputs the same words sorted into alphabetical order. The third filter eliminates duplicate words so that only one occurrence of each word is output. The fourth filter looks up each word in a computerized dictionary and outputs only those words that don't appear in the dictionary.

UNIX has been criticized as being a "hacker's" system for computer "freaks." Some people feel it is much too difficult to learn for unsophisticated users, who form the bulk of the microcomputer marketplace.

Even though UNIX may not be a particularly user-friendly system, it excels at being a "programmer-friendly" system, which has certainly contributed to its success.

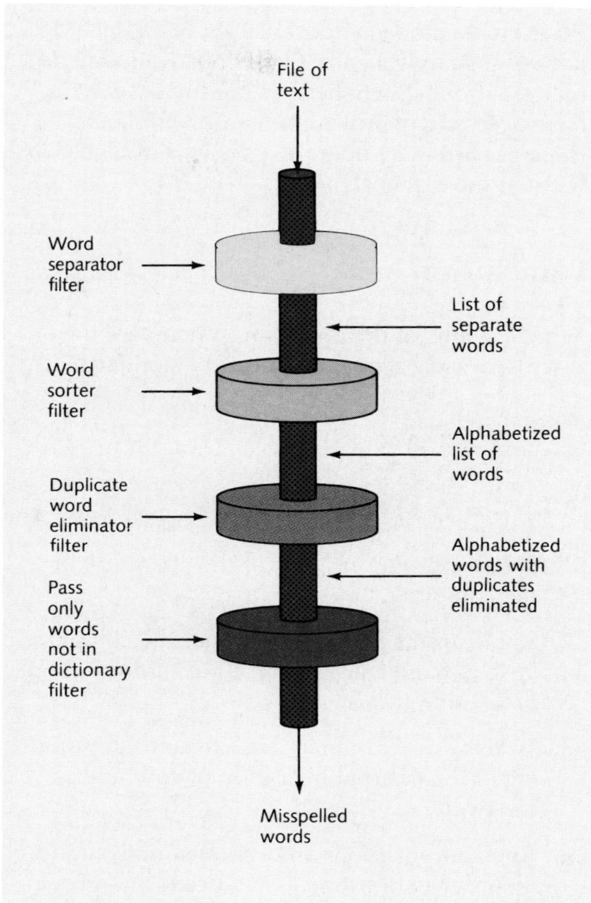

Figure 1 A UNIX pipeline that inputs a file of text and outputs only the misspelled words.

XENIX:

XENIX is a licensed version of the UNIX system designed by Microsoft especially for 16-bit microcomputers. It offers the huge UNIX library of text-editing aids and software development tools. It is a multiuser, multitasking system that contains many modifications to UNIX making it more user-friendly and more usable as a commercial product. Some people believe XENIX will eventually become the standard 16-bit microcomputer operating system.

MS-DOS

MS-DOS (Microsoft Disk Operating System) is the operating system developed by Microsoft for the IBM Personal Computer (IBM calls it PC-DOS). In its earliest versions, its capabilities were comparable to those of CP/M, but it is evolving into a much more powerful system. The latest version, for example, supports UNIX's pipes and filters. It appears that the evolution of MS-DOS will be toward Microsoft's XENIX.

MS-DOS has drawn considerable interest away from CP/M-based systems. When IBM committed to MS-DOS, many other microcomputer vendors who were considering CP/M also chose MS-DOS. But IBM simultaneously contracted with Digital Research to provide an upgraded version of CP/M, namely CP/M-86, as an optional operating system for the IBM Personal Computer. Many IBM

PC users do indeed choose CP/M-86. Which operating system will win? Quite frankly, it may not matter. The real beneficiaries are the users who have access to improved, more powerful, and more user-friendly operating systems available to them at modest cost.

Conclusion

Which, if any, of the operating systems we have discussed will become the industry standard? It appears that the field of personal computers is simply too young, too large, and changing too rapidly for any one operating system to meet the needs of all users. For the moment, personal computer users have access to several effective and modestly priced operating systems.

Summary

1. Systems programs control the operation of the computer.
2. Applications programs instruct the computer how to handle an organization's information-processing needs.
3. Systems programmers require an understanding of the internal operation of computer hardware.
4. Applications programmers must understand the information-processing needs of an organization, and how computers may be used to meet those needs.
5. Operating systems are collections of systems programs that allow computer systems to handle many functions previously performed by computer operators.
6. Operating systems are primarily resource managers. They manage hardware, programs, and data. They assign hardware to users, charge for resource usage, run many users efficiently, and guarantee good service to users.
7. Scheduling is one of the most important functions of an operating system. Priority scheduling ensures that the more important jobs are serviced first.
8. User jobs are classified as batch processing, interactive, or real-time.
9. In batch processing, users do not interact with their executing programs.
10. Multiprogramming operating systems allow many jobs to run simultaneously. Storage protection mechanisms help to prevent programs from interfering with one another. Boundary registers prevent programs from accessing a storage address outside the range indicated by the registers.
11. Timesharing operating systems multiprogram many simultaneous interactive users. They must provide rapid responses to short requests.
12. Two common techniques for implementing virtual storage are segmentation and paging. In segmentation, program pieces may be different sizes; in paging, program pieces are all the same size.
13. Multiprocessing operating systems manage computers that have several processors.
14. English dialogues, help keys, help menus, error trapping, positive confirmation, utility programs, upward mobility, and device independence all contribute to making computer systems more user-friendly.
15. Firmware is often implementated as programs stored in read-only memory (ROM) chips. Computer vendors put portions of their operating systems in ROM for security.

Important Terms

applications programs
bootstrap loader
boundary registers
buffer
channel
CP/M
deadlock
double buffering
error trapping
firmware
flip-flop buffering
fragmentation
indefinite postponement
interrupt
MS-DOS
multiprocessing
multiprogramming
multitasking
operating system
overlapped processing
paging
print spooling
real-time system
reentrant program
relocatable program
segmentation
storage protection
UNIX
virtual storage
XENIX

Self-Review Exercises 

Matching

Next to the term in column A, place the letter of the statement in column B that best describes it.

Column A	Column B
1. Channel	A. Primary goal of a real-time operating system
2. Buffer	B. Assigning the processor to the next user
3. Encryption	C. The amount of work a computer can process in a given amount of time
4. System program	D. Transfers data between primary storage and peripheral devices
5. Responsiveness	E. An area of primary storage used for communication between a processor and a channel
6. ROM	F. Memory chip that cannot be modified
7. Throughput	G. Coding of information for security
8. Dispatching	H. A multiuser, multitasking operating system
9. Device driver	I. Controls the operation of the computer
10. UNIX	J. Program that controls a computer peripheral

Fill-in-the-Blanks

Fill in the blanks in each of the following:

1. The set of systems programs on a computer is called its ______ .

2. An ______ is a signal that gains the attention of the processor.

3. Programs that can only be placed in certain fixed locations are called ______ programs.

4. Programs that do not modify themselves are called ______ programs.

5. ______ can occur when a steady stream of high-priority users prevents a low-priority user from receiving service.

6. Two techniques for implementing virtual storage are ______ and ______ .

7. A ______ operating system allows users to share the resources of many separate computer systems.

8. All file names in CP/M have ______ that consist of a period followed by a three-letter code.

9. In UNIX a ______ is a program that reads a stream of inputs, processes them, and produces a stream of outputs.

10. A ______ is a communications path between programs in UNIX.

Answers to Self-Review Exercises

Matching: 1 D, 2 E, 3 G, 4 I, 5 A, 6 F, 7 C, 8 B, 9 J, 10 H

Fill-in-the-Blanks:

1. operating system
2. interrupt
3. absolute
4. reentrant
5. Indefinite postponement
6. segmentation, paging
7. network
8. file extensions
9. filter
10. pipe

Discussion Questions

1. How do systems programs differ from applications programs?

2. What are the primary functions of operating systems?

3. Briefly define the terms multiprogramming, multiprocessing, multitasking, and multiuser.

4. What are some of the major problems that make multiuser operating systems more complex than single-user operating systems?

5. Explain print spooling and why it is important.

6. List several reasons for using virtual storage systems. What are some problems with virtual storage systems?

7. What is firmware?

8. What is a ROM? RAM? How do they differ?

9. How do PROMs and EPROMs differ?

10. Briefly discuss the functions of the three major components of CP/M.

Projects

1. Contact the following user groups for information about the wide range of software supported under each operating system:

For CP/M: CP/M User's Group
164 West 83rd Street
New York, NY 10024

For UNIX: /usr/ group
P.O. Box 8570
Stanford, CA 94305

also for UNIX: Usenix Association
Box 8
The Rockefeller University
12330 York Avenue
New York, NY 10021

For XENIX: Microsoft Corporation
XENIX Clearinghouse
10700 Northup Way
Bellevue, WA 98004

2. Two popular operating systems not discussed in this chapter are OASIS and the UCSD p-System. Write to the addresses below for information about these systems.

For OASIS: Phase One Systems Inc.
7700 Edgewater Drive
Oakland, CA 94621

For the UCSD p-System: Softech Microsystems Inc.
16885 West Bernardo Drive
San Diego, CA 92127

Part Four

Computers in Business

"Here's the story, gentlemen. Sometime last night, an eleven-year-old kid in Akron, Ohio, got into our computer and transferred all our assets to a bank in Zurich."

The vast majority of computers are used for business applications. In Part Four we consider personal computing, office automation, electronic funds transfer systems, computer security, privacy, and computer crime — all of which are essential topics in business computing.

Chapter 13 traces the history of personal computing and discusses the components, capabilities, and applications of personal computers. We present case studies on two of today's most important personal computers — IBM's PC and Apple's Macintosh. A case study on the Viewtron videotex service discusses the unique and exciting information services being made available to today's homes and businesses.

Chapter 14 examines the office automation revolution, in which networks of personal computers and automated office equipment are improving the management and flow of information. We study such innovative technologies as word processing, electronic mail, facsimile, voice mail, the electronic calendar, teleconferencing, and the electronic blackboard. The chapter features a detailed case study on word processing with Apple's extraordinarily user-friendly Macintosh personal computer.

Chapter 15 considers electronic funds transfer systems, security, privacy, and computer crime. The highlight of the chapter is a case study describing many of the most famous computer crimes that have been perpetrated by people ranging from 13-year old prep schoolers to the most sophisticated computer criminals. A summary of important electronic funds transfer and privacy legislation is included.

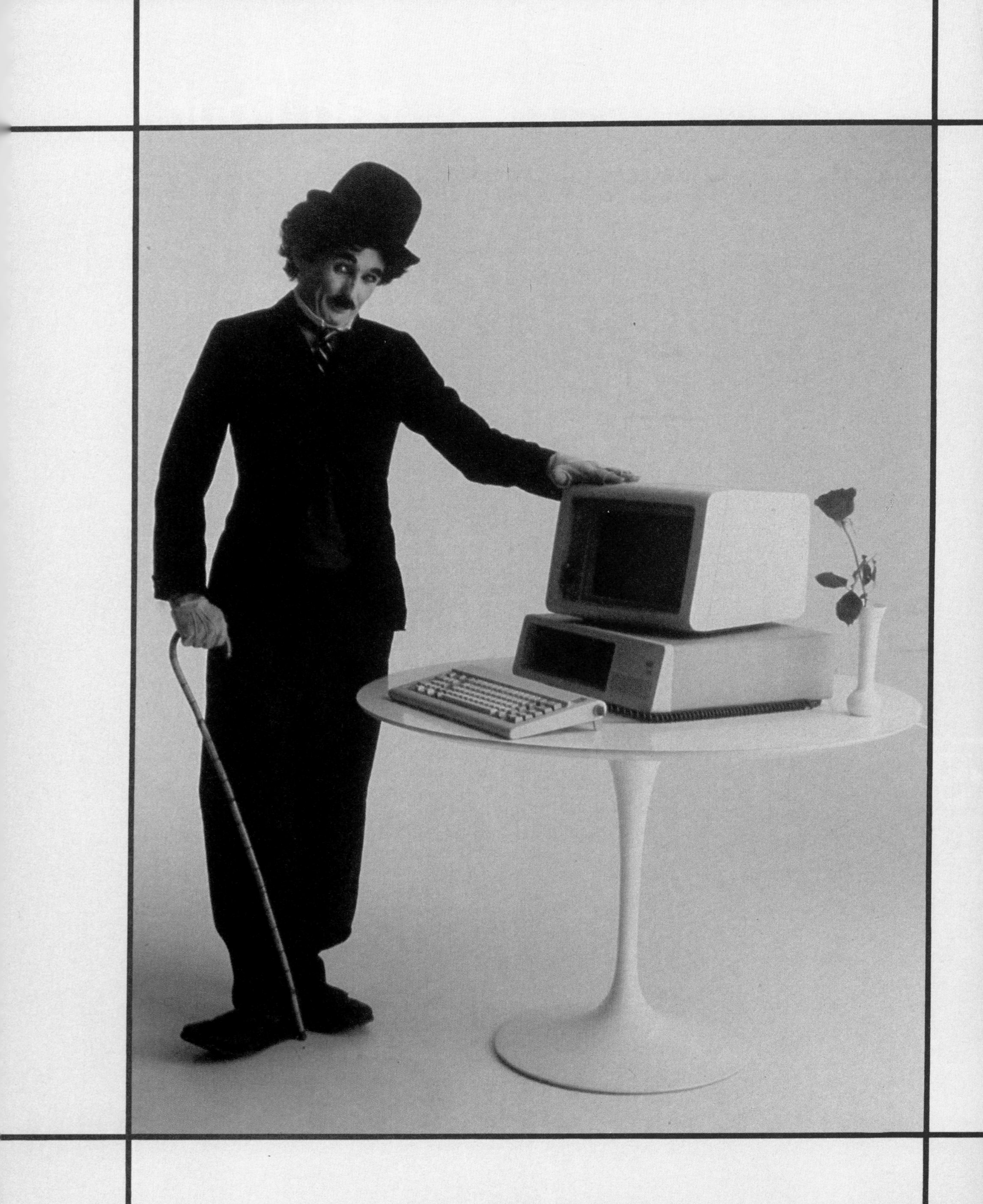

Chapter 13

Personal Computing

After reading this chapter you will understand:

1. The history of personal computing
2. The components, capabilities, and applications of personal computers
3. Case studies on the IBM Personal Computer and the Apple Macintosh
4. What teletext, viewdata/videotex, and the on-line databases are
5. A case study on the Viewtron videotex service

Left: The IBM Personal Computer (PC) was introduced in 1981, four years after companies like Apple and Radio Shack marketed the first personal computers. The outstanding features of the IBM PC, as well as a user-friendly marketing campaign featuring this delightful Charlie Chaplin character, have helped IBM become the world's leading manufacturer of personal computers.

Outline

The challenge of our industry is not only to help people learn about the computer, but to make it so easy to use that by the end of this decade it will be as common a personal tool as the bicycle.

Steve Jobs
Chairman, Apple Computer, Inc.

Don't trust any computer you can't lift.

Steve Jobs
Chairman, Apple Computer, Inc.

As recently as the late 1970s textbooks stated that people might operate and program computers if they worked for an organization large enough to afford one. Today, most people can afford to purchase their own **personal computers**. Many of these marvelous devices are far more powerful than the huge million-dollar computers of 20 years ago. Yet they are attractively and compactly packaged, and some cost about the same as a TV set.

When historians look back on the twentieth century, they may conclude that the most important development was the invention of the electronic computer. They may also conclude that the widespread use of computing made possible by inexpensive personal computers was the most important social development. Indeed, *Time* magazine reflected this sentiment in 1982 when it revised its customary practice of naming a "Person of the Year" and designated the computer its "Machine of the Year (Figure 13–1)."

What Is a Personal Computer?

A personal computer is a complete computer system that is available for the "personal" use of one or more people at work or at home. It is generally small enough to fit on a desktop and economical enough to be affordable by an individual. It should be user-friendly, so that it can be used easily by people who are not computer specialists. It should be usable directly "out of the box," reliable, and serviceable, and should have easy-to-read documentation. It should be able to run the huge variety of personal computing applications software available.

A Brief History of Personal Computing

The key development that made personal computers possible was the invention of the microprocessor at Intel Corporation in 1971. The first microprocessor chips were expensive and not very

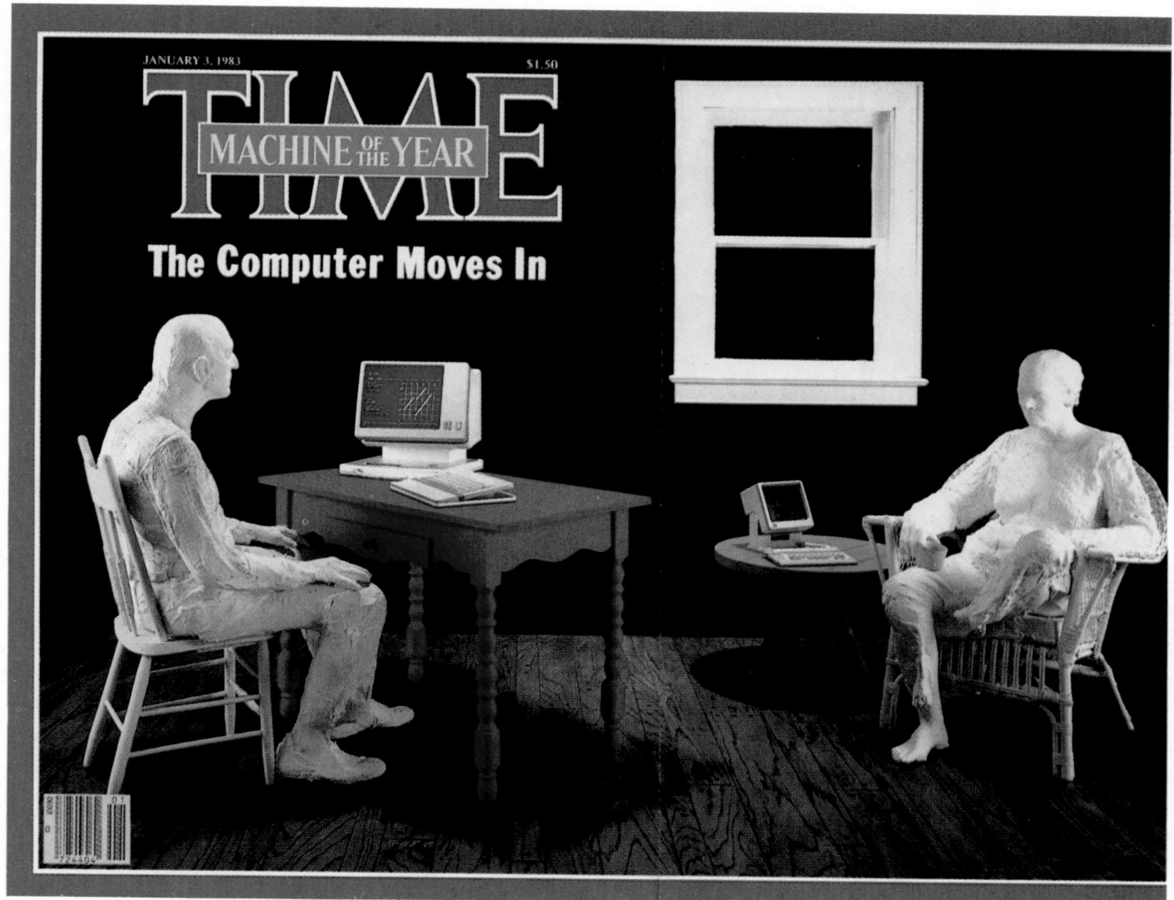

Figure 13–1 *Time* magazine's "Machine of the Year" in 1982 was the personal computer.

powerful, but the demand for them was strong. Intense competition and the economies of mass production have forced prices so low that chips as powerful as some mainframe computers of only a decade ago now sell for just a few dollars apiece.

In the early 1970s hobbyists and researchers alike began integrating these chips to form a hodgepodge of awkward devices, which they called computers. In 1975 Steve Jobs, then 19 years old and a technician at Atari, and Steve Wozniak, an electronics engineer at Hewlett-Packard, decided to build a computer in Jobs's parents' home in Palo Alto, California. They bought a microprocessor chip for $25 and went to work on a machine they later called **Apple.** Jobs and Wozniak soon demonstrated their machine to a group of hobbyists at the Home Brew Computer Club, the first computer club in the United States. They built several of their Apples for the club members, whose enthusiasm for the devices prompted Jobs and Wozniak to try to sell their machines to the public. They brought their Apple to a computer hobby shop in Palo Alto. The shopkeeper was so impressed that he ordered 50 machines. Jobs sold his Volkswagen and Wozniak pawned his calculator—Apple Computer was born with $1300 in capital. The Apple II (Figure 13–2), Apple's first widely marketed product, became the machine practically equated with the term *personal computer*. More than 100,000 Apple IIe's, an enhanced version, were sold in December 1983 alone.

Figure 13–2 The Apple II personal computer.

In 1977 Tandy Corporation marketed its first **TRS-80** personal computer through its huge network of Radio Shack retail stores (Figure 13–3). Commodore, a company with expertise in marketing electronic calculators, entered the market with its PET computer (believed to be named after the fad of the time, the Pet Rock, but later named the Personal Electronic Transactor). Atari, the world's leader in video games, also produces personal computers.

All this activity in personal computers eventually led the giants of the computer industry to enter the market in the late 1970s and early 1980s. Companies like Texas Instruments and Hewlett-Packard drew on their expertise in the field of electronic calculators; Xerox banked on its experience with business equipment.

Figure 13–3 The TRS-80 Model 1 was introduced by Radio Shack in 1977 for the then incredibly low price of $599. It had a standard 4K storage and used a cassette tape player for storing and retrieving programs and data.

But it wasn't until 1981 that IBM plunged in with its IBM Personal Computer and quickly became the world's leading manufacturer of personal computers. Apple countered with the introduction of its extremely powerful and user-friendly Lisa and Macintosh systems. Case studies on the IBM Personal Computer and the Apple Macintosh follow.

Case Study 13–1: The IBM Personal Computer

The **IBM Personal Computer** (Figure 1) was introduced in August 1981 and rapidly became the world's most popular personal computer.

The PC, as it is commonly called, features the Intel 8088 16-bit microprocessor capable of addressing more than 1 million bytes of memory and performing more than 250,000 operations per second. Even though the 8088 chip itself is smaller than a penny, the PC still requires a full-

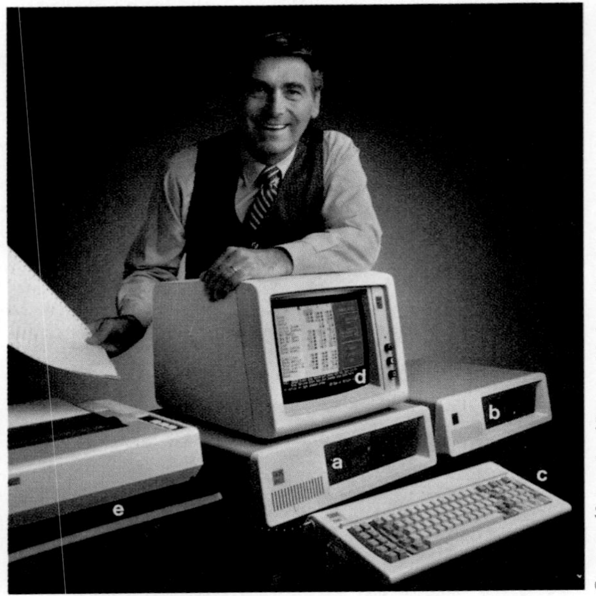

Figure 1 The key components of the IBM PC are: (a) system unit, (b) expansion unit, (c) keyboard, (d) color display, (e) printer.

Courtesy of International Business Machines Corporation

Life with a Computer

"I like BRESLIN; he's one of the family," said Carol Hawkins, looking fondly at the silent shape sitting in her husband's workroom. Breslin uttered no sound in response to the statement of affection, but, probably by coincidence, twinkled a few of the red lights mounted on "his" front panel.

Breslin is not human, nor in any way a living being: "He" exists only as a computer program. Yet, New Jerseyans Bill and Carol Hawkins and their three young daughters have accepted this abstract being as a household personality.

In a sense, this acceptance is quite reasonable considering all Breslin does for the family. The computer system and other electronic devices that manifest Breslin guard the house, remind occupants of appointments and other moments of import, provide an almost limitless amount of information and take on assorted household tasks that, at other levels of society, might be performed by a maid and butler.

Besides being eminently functional, Breslin offers the Hawkinses a charming and practical means of communication: It speaks and listens. Using a recently developed form of technology, Breslin uses the house intercom system to make his (the Hawkinses' insistence on applying a gender to the computer program is infectious) announcements and receive his instructions. . . .

Breslin runs on a regular schedule altered for weekdays, weekends and special occasions. Generally, he wakes Bill at a pre-set time by producing a series of musical tones over the intercom, then announcing the time, temperature and weather forecast (a collection of weather instruments is connected to the computer, which reads the instruments, analyzes the information and computes a forecast).

Next, Breslin turns on a radio which relays news over the intercom and activates the coffee maker in the kitchen. The computer will also announce any appointments or special reminders for the day. Various household systems—including burglar alarm, heating, outdoor lights, and air conditioning—are turned on or off automatically at dawn, as needed.

During the day, Breslin makes regular announcements over the intercom at pre-set intervals to update his weather forecast, report the current time, remind someone to do something or just speak to the family. . . .

Breslin never forgets a birthday (he plays "Happy Birthday" then offers his best wishes), says "I love you, Kristen" to the Hawkinses' 5-year-old daughter, calls the family dog by name at random intervals throughout the day and refers to Carol Hawkins as "Mom." . . .

Having a Breslin in your home can be a terrific convenience, but the question remains: Is the world ready for it? Bill Hawkins tells of the night a new babysitter was found close to hysteria after he forgot to tell her that Breslin would come on every half hour to make his announcements. She feared either the house was haunted or some burglar had a bizarre sense of humor.

On another occasion, Bill was in the backyard grilling hamburgers with the patio lights on. He told Breslin to turn on the timer. Breslin instead announced the weather. Hawkins repeated the request—Breslin set the burglar alarm, locking Hawkins out of the house. Bill ordered: "Alarm off." Breslin turned off the patio lights.

Myron Berger, "Life With a Computer," New York Daily News, *November 12, 1980. Copyright 1980 New York News Inc. Reprinted by permission.*

size system board tightly packed with components (Figure 2).

The PC hardware is modularly designed, that is, it consists of separate pieces that may be combined in various ways to tailor a system to the needs of individual users.

The main hardware units on the IBM PC are the system unit, keyboard, display, printer, and the expansion unit. The system unit contains the system board that houses the microprocessor, the user memory (random access memory, or RAM), and the permanent memory (read only memory, or ROM). The system unit also contains several expansion slots for plugging in additional hardware as the user's needs grow. It has space for one or two diskette drives, each with a capacity of 180Kb or 360Kb (Kb means kilobyte, or 1024 bytes). It also houses a power supply, connectors

Courtesy of International Business Machines Corporation

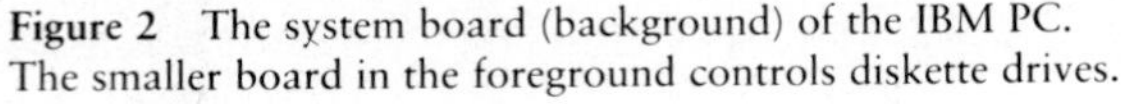

Figure 2 The system board (background) of the IBM PC. The smaller board in the foreground controls diskette drives.

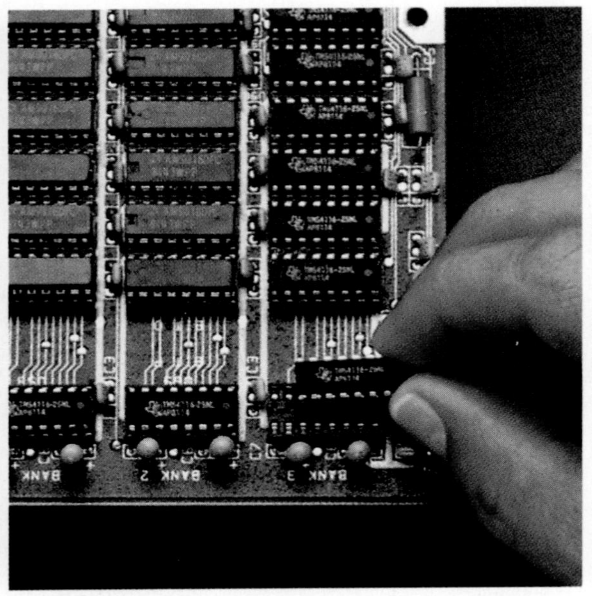

Courtesy of International Business Machines Corporation

Figure 3 The user memory of the IBM PC may be increased by simply plugging additional memory chips into the system board.

for attaching various peripheral devices, and a speaker for music and voice applications.

The expansion slots allow the user to add memory (Figure 3), diskette drives, displays, printers, communications devices, and an expansion unit. The expansion unit provides a 10Mb (Mb means megabyte) fixed disk drive, as well as several additional expansion slots.

The ROM contains a self-test program that automatically checks out key features of the PC each time it is turned on, and the version of BASIC designed to work with a cassette tape recorder. The ROM also contains the PC's basic input/output system that performs functions similar to CP/M's BIOS (see Chapter 12). User programs and portions of the operating system are executed in RAM.

The IBM PC/XT (PC "extended") model comes standard with a 10Mb fixed disk drive, 128Kb of user memory (double that of the PC), eight expansion slots, and a communications adaptor. Storing and retrieving information on the fixed disk drive is much faster than with floppy disks. Also, many applications can be kept on the fixed disk simultaneously, so that it is possible to switch quickly between applications and to integrate the outputs of separate applications. The 10Mb fixed disk drive can hold the equivalent of more than 5000 pages of double-spaced typewritten text. Both the PC and the PC/XT can handle a maximum of two 10Mb fixed disk drives, an amount of secondary storage that is more than sufficient for the vast majority of small businesses.

The PC has a detached keyboard for user convenience. The angle of the keyboard may be adjusted. The keyboard has both tactile (touch) and audio (sound) feedback; each of these features is designed for the comfort of users who enter a great deal of information at keyboards. At the right of the keyboard is a 10-key numeric pad, like that used on calculators, for rapid entry of numeric information (Figure 4). An automatic repeat feature allows the user to repeat each character many times while the key is held down. There is even a 15-character "type-ahead" buffer for fast typists; if the computer can't "digest" the characters as quickly as they are typed, it at least saves them.

Users can choose either of two kinds of displays. The IBM PC monochrome display shows crisp green characters against a dark background. It is best for users who work mostly with text,

Courtesy of International Business Machines Corporation

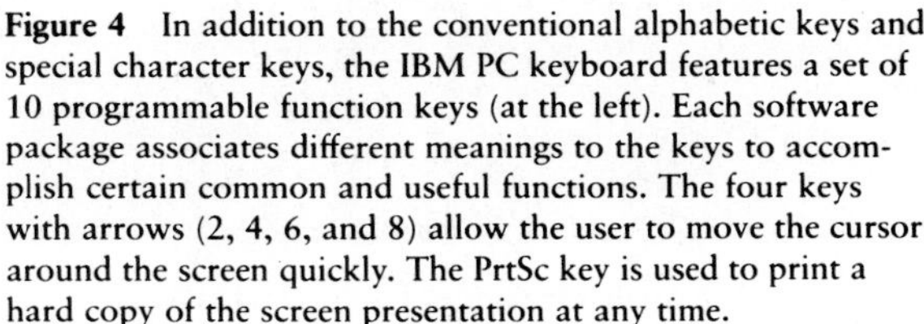
Figure 4 In addition to the conventional alphabetic keys and special character keys, the IBM PC keyboard features a set of 10 programmable function keys (at the left). Each software package associates different meanings to the keys to accomplish certain common and useful functions. The four keys with arrows (2, 4, 6, and 8) allow the user to move the cursor around the screen quickly. The PrtSc key is used to print a hard copy of the screen presentation at any time.

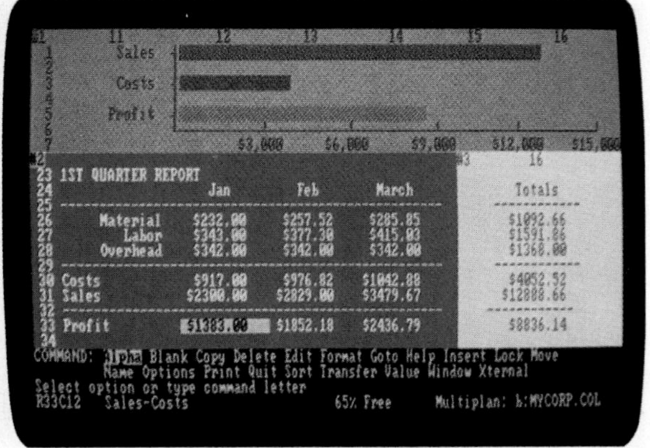

Figure 5 Many software packages (such as Microsoft's Multiplan® electronic spreadsheet shown here) take advantage of the features of the color display to create interesting presentations including text and graphics.

such as in word-processing applications. The IBM PC color display provides both text and graphics in color, but the text is not as sharp as with the monochrome display. In text mode the color display can present 25 lines of text, each containing 40 or 80 characters; the text may be displayed in any combination of 16 foreground colors against 8 background colors. The color display is popular with video game enthusiasts. Also, today's software packages take good advantage of the capabilities of color displays (Figure 5).

The BASIC language provided by IBM for use with the PC contains several commands that allow the programmer to create graphics conveniently. These include CIRCLE, PAINT, DRAW, COLOR, and LINE. The color display can mix text and graphics, control the brightness of various areas of the screen, reverse fields, underline fields, and set fields to blink on and off to draw the user's attention. The color display uses 8-by-8 dot-matrix characters; the monochrome display uses a 9-by-14 dot matrix for much sharper characters.

The IBM graphics printer prints both text and graphics. It uses **APA (all-points-addressable) graphics**—it can set any dot on the page on or off. This printer can handle 120 dots per inch horizontally and 216 dots per inch vertically. Thus it packs 26,920 (that is, 120 times 216) dots per square inch. This is sufficient resolution to draw extremely high-quality pictures. The print speed is as fast as 80 characters per second. Printing is bidirectional, that is, one line is printed left to right and the next line is printed right to left for maximum speed. The printer can print several different character sets, styles, sizes, and modes (normal, condensed, and emphasized). It can double-strike characters to make them darker, underline characters for emphasis, and print subscripts and superscripts. With all these print variations, interesting and visually pleasing reports can be prepared. A pin-feed mechanism is used to advance sprocket hole forms that may be 4 to 10 inches wide and as thick as three-part paper.

Each PC comes with two manuals: The Guide to Operations describes how to set up and operate the PC, and the BASIC manual describes the features of the BASIC programming language. Also popular are the Technical Reference manual, primarily for hardware and software designers, and the Hardware Maintenance and Service manual for persons concerned with performing preventive maintenance and repairing the PC.

Courtesy of International Business Machines Corporation

Figure 6 The IBM Personal Computer is supported by a full range of software supplied on floppy disks. Documentation is generally provided in looseleaf binders for easy updating.

Figure 1 The Apple Macintosh personal computer.

Part of the PC's appeal is the large amount of software that is available for it. Some of this software is supplied directly by IBM (Figure 6), but the vast majority of it is available through independent software suppliers.

If you are interested in the IBM PC, you may obtain more information at many local computer stores or by reading:

PC
The Independent Guide to
IBM Personal Computers
P.O. Box 2445
Boulder, CO 80322

or

PC World
The Comprehensive Guide to
IBM Personal Computers and Compatibles
Subscription Department
P.O. Box 6700
Bergenfield, NJ 07621
(800) 247-5470

Case Study 13–2: The Apple Macintosh

In January 1984 Apple introduced the **Apple Macintosh** (Figure 1), a machine it touted as "a personal computer so personable it can practically shake hands." The industry and the public reacted with rave reviews. Apple had reasserted itself as the technological leader in the personal computer field. The technological advances were in sheer computing power and in the all-important area of user-friendliness.

At the core of the Macintosh is the Motorola MC68000 32-bit microprocessor, a chip so powerful that it gives the Macintosh as much capacity as many of today's mainframe computers. The MC68000 can perform 1 to 2 million operations per second—tremendous power for a personal computer. The Macintosh takes full advantage of this power, especially in the creation and manipulation of high-resolution text and graphics.

With most personal computers, the user must

memorize a large number of commands that are then typed character by character at a keyboard. With the Macintosh, most of the dialogue with the computer occurs with the use of a **mouse** (Figure 2), one of the most user-friendly input devices. As the user moves the mouse on a flat surface, a pointer, which functions as a cursor, moves across the screen in the same manner. The user moves the mouse until the pointer is positioned next to a word or **icon** (Figure 3) that describes the operation to be performed or the application being selected. Then the user pushes the button on the mouse—this is called **clicking**—to inform the Macintosh that it should perform the indicated operation. The use of the mouse, pointing, and icon graphics was pioneered by Xerox and first offered in the Xerox Star workstations.

The Macintosh is a very intuitive machine. It tries to help the user every step of the way. One example of this occurs when the user points and clicks to select something. If it will take some time for the Macintosh to fetch the selected item from the disk, the Macintosh converts the screen pointer into a tiny watch. This action tells the user that the operation is okay, but a few moments of waiting are necessary.

The Macintosh screen layout is designed to resemble a businessperson's desktop (Figure 4). Icons are used to represent file folders, documents, applications, hardware devices, a clipboard, and even a trash can (in which you deposit items you no longer need).

The Macintosh even offers the user a series of convenient "desk accessories," including a calculator, a clock that can be set to sound an alarm, a "15-puzzle" for entertainment in lighter moments, a notepad, a scrapbook, and a control panel. The control panel (Figure 5) enables the user to set the time and date on the clock, change the background pattern on the desktop, control the sensitivity of the mouse, and so on. All of these options help make the user interface even more friendly for each user's particular needs.

As with the IBM PC, a large amount of software is available for the Macintosh, some supplied directly by Apple, but most available from independent software suppliers (Figure 6). The MacPaint software package provided by Apple turns

Figure 2 *Below:* By pressing the button on the mouse, the user tells the computer to take the action indicated by the word or icon pointed to on the screen.

Figure 3 *Bottom:* Some of the many icons provided by the Macintosh.

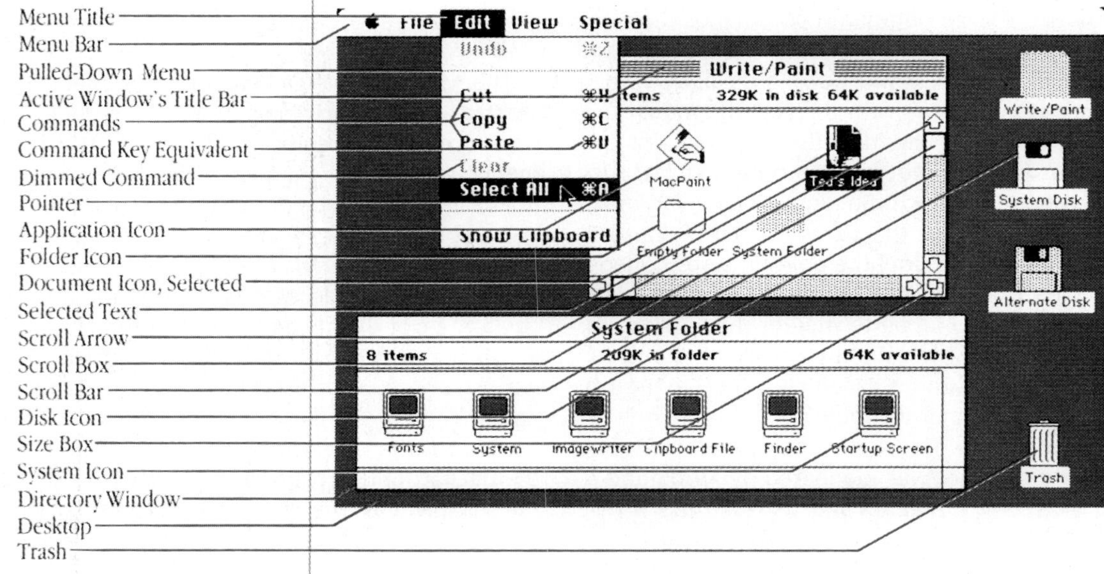

Figure 4 The Macintosh's display serves as a working desktop. It uses icons to show what the user is working on and what options are available at any time. The large boxed areas are called windows. Each application has its own window, and several windows may be on the desktop at once.

Figure 5 The Macintosh contains a control panel that lets various aspects of the user interface be adjusted to make it even more friendly for individual needs.

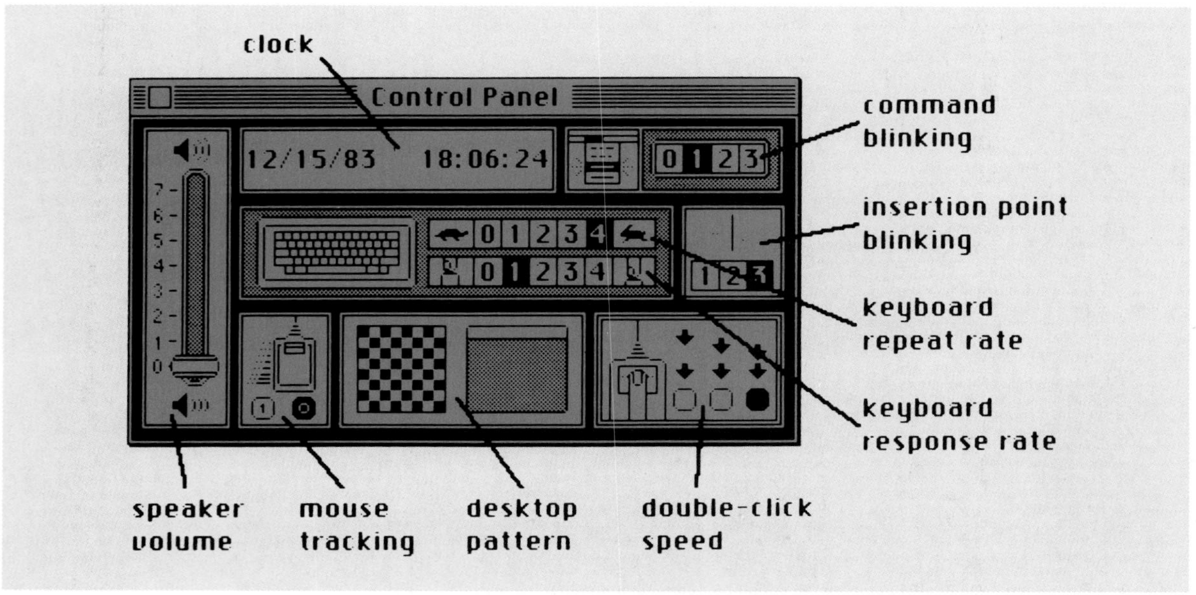

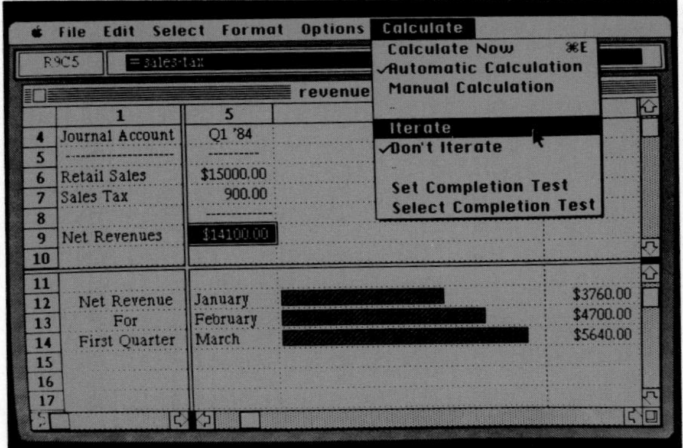

(a) Microsoft® Multiplan® Electronic Worksheet program

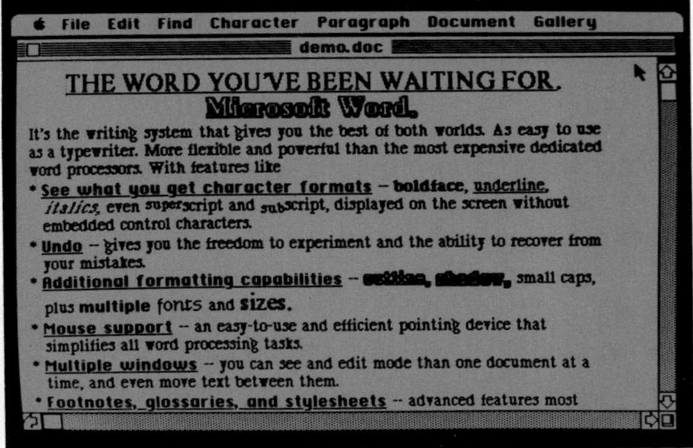

(b) Microsoft Word/Word Processing program

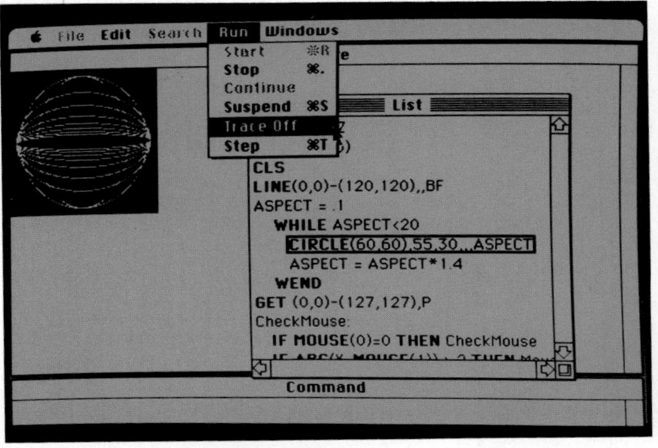

(c) Microsoft BASIC Interpreter

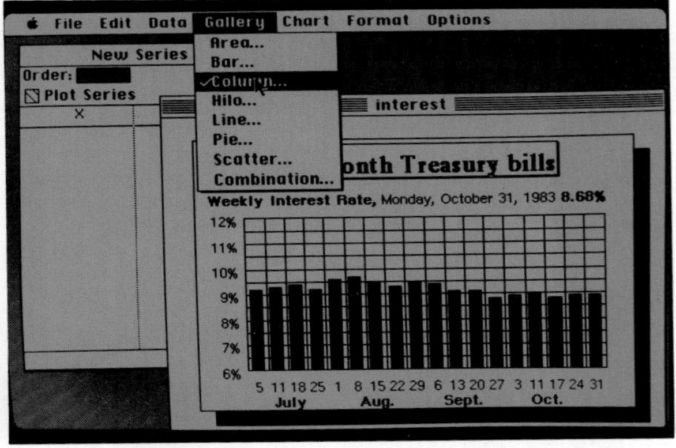

(d) Microsoft Chart/Complete Business Graphics program

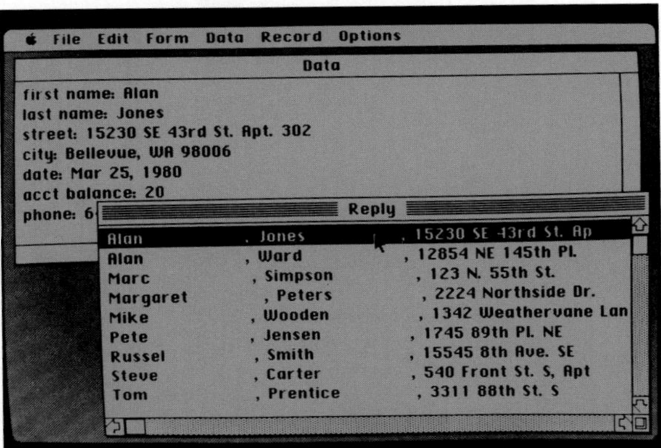

(e) Microsoft File/Data Management program

Figure 6 Several of the popular software packages available for the Macintosh from Microsoft, a leading independent software supplier. (Microsoft and Multiplan are registered trademarks of Microsoft Corporation.)

the Macintosh into an artist's sketchpad. The user moves the mouse to draw shapes, fill them with patterns, erase, crosshatch, and even spray-paint. MacWrite, also provided by Apple, is a word-processing program that uses multiple type styles, fonts, and sizes to create documents close in quality to professional typesetting.

The boxed piece on pages 346–347 shows how the mouse, icons, and the Macintosh's **pull-down menus** are used in the preparation and printing of a document with text and graphics.

The Macintosh (Figure 7) comes standard with 128Kb of RAM for user programs and 64Kb of ROM containing its operating system. The 9-inch diagonal screen has a resolution of 512 by 342 dots, or pixels. The screen is relatively small but easy on the eyes because of its crisp text and graphics and its black-on-gray colors. The complete system, including the main unit, the keyboard, and the mouse, weighs about 20 pounds, is one-third the size of an IBM PC (Figure 8), and is easily transported (Figures 9 and 10).

Instead of the popular 5¼-inch floppy disks, the Macintosh uses the newer **sturdy disks** (Figure 11). These 3½-inch disks can each hold 400Kb of data. It is believed that sturdy disks with much greater capacity will soon be available. Sturdy disk drives operate more quietly, are faster, and are more reliable than floppy disk drives.

Figure 7 The Macintosh comes in a sealed cabinet that should only be opened by authorized service representatives. For the curious, here's a peek inside so you can resist the temptation to take one apart.

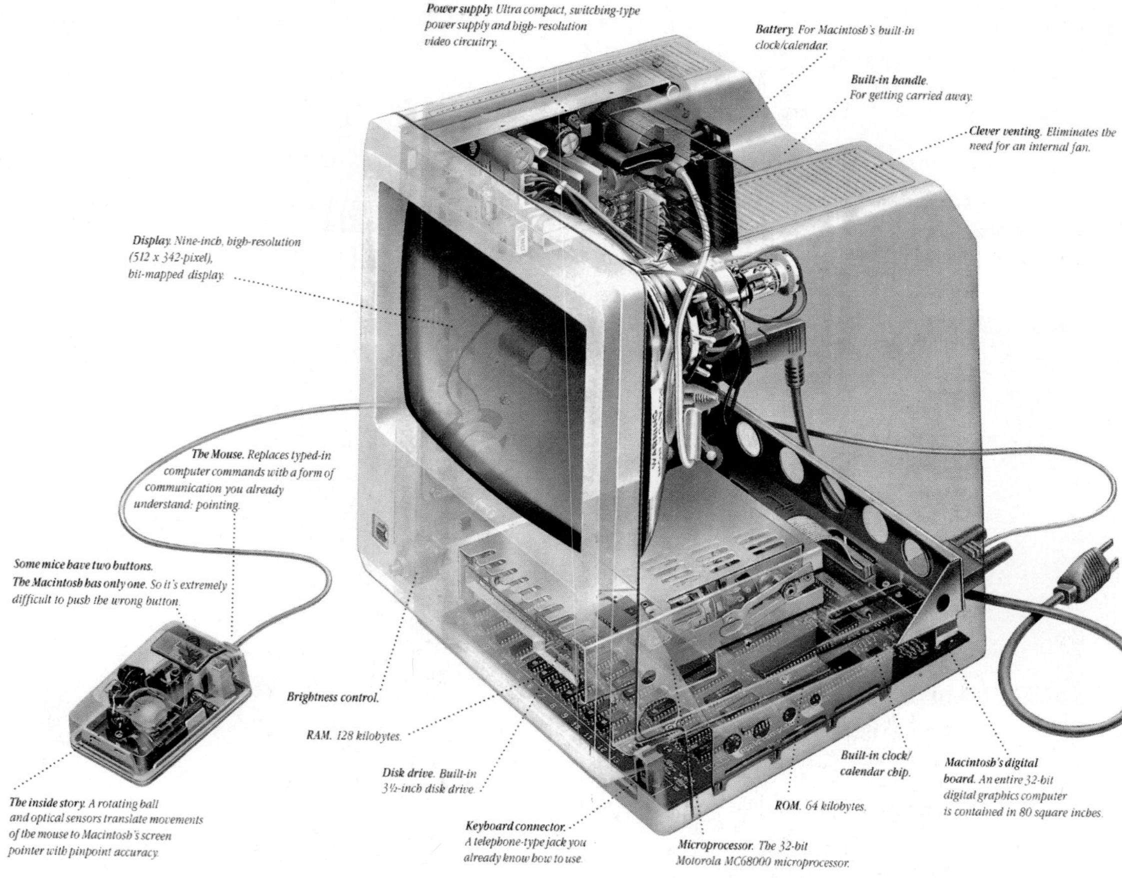

Power supply. *Ultra compact, switching-type power supply and high-resolution video circuitry.*

Battery. *For Macintosh's built-in clock/calendar.*

Built-in handle. *For getting carried away.*

Clever venting. *Eliminates the need for an internal fan.*

Display. *Nine-inch, high-resolution (512 x 342-pixel), bit-mapped display.*

The Mouse. *Replaces typed-in computer commands with a form of communication you already understand: pointing.*

Some mice have two buttons. The Macintosh has only one. *So it's extremely difficult to push the wrong button.*

Brightness control.

RAM. *128 kilobytes.*

Disk drive. *Built-in 3½-inch disk drive.*

The inside story. *A rotating ball and optical sensors translate movements of the mouse to Macintosh's screen pointer with pinpoint accuracy.*

Keyboard connector. *A telephone-type jack you already know how to use.*

Built-in clock/calendar chip.

ROM. *64 kilobytes.*

Macintosh's digital board. *An entire 32-bit digital graphics computer is contained in 80 square inches.*

Microprocessor. *The 32-bit Motorola MC68000 microprocessor.*

Figure 8 The Macintosh's designers opted to make it one of the smallest and most lightweight personal computers. Its small "footprint" means that it takes little space on a desktop.

Figure 10 Apple provides an optional security kit that you can use to make sure your highly transportable Macintosh doesn't take any unauthorized journeys.

Figure 9 Apple provides this optional padded carrying case for transporting the Macintosh.

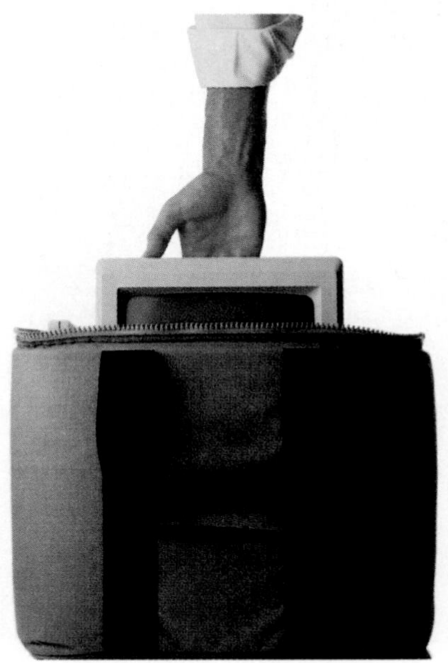

Figure 11 The new style sturdy disks are enclosed in hard plastic and can't be damaged as easily as floppy disks. The disk surface is inaccessible until the disk is inserted into the drive, so dust and other foreign matter are kept out.

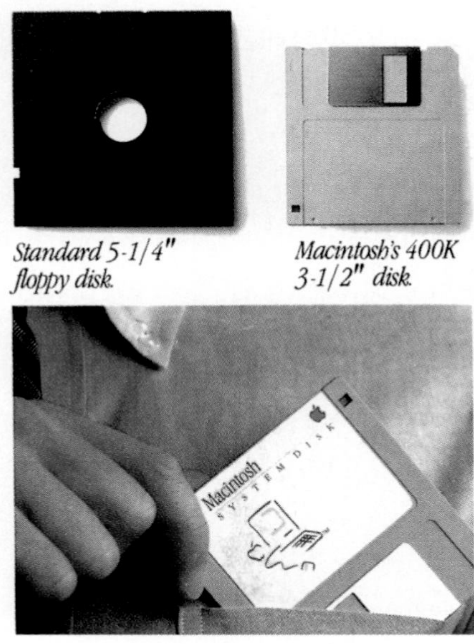

If you can point, you can use a Macintosh.

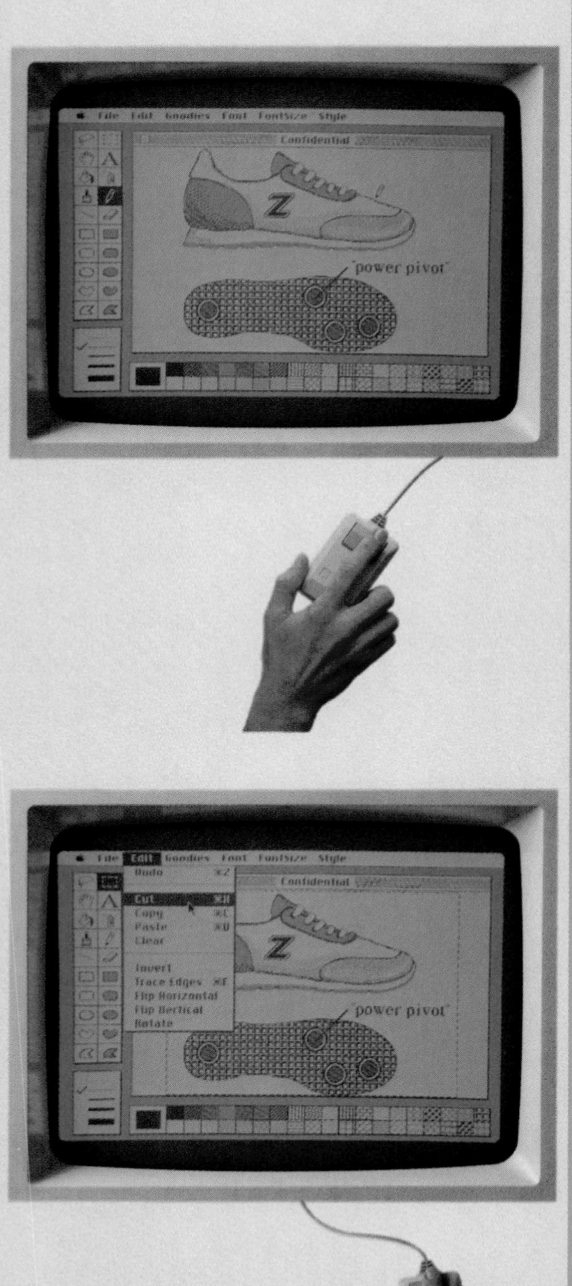

Point. Click.

To tell Macintosh what you want to do, all you have to do is point and click.

You move the pointer on the screen by moving the mouse on your desktop. When you get to the item you want to use, click once, and you've selected that item to work with.

In this case, the pointer appears as the pencil you've selected to put some finishing touches on an illustration you'd like to include in a memo.

Cut.

Once you've completed your illustration, you need to cut it out of the document you created it in, so that you can put it into the word processing program you used to write your memo.

To do this, you simply use the mouse to draw a rectangle around the illustration, which tells Macintosh what you want to cut.

Then you move the pointer to the top of the screen where it says "Edit." Hold the mouse button down and you will see a list, or "pull-down menu," of the editing commands available. Then pull the pointer down this menu and point to the command "Cut," highlighted by a black bar.

Release the mouse button and, zap, it's done.

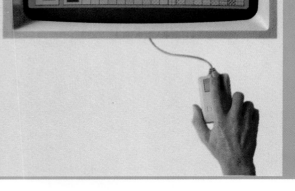

Paste.

And now, to finish your memo, bring up MacWrite,™ Macintosh's word processing program. Just pick a place for your illustration.

In the meantime, your illustration has been conveniently stored in another part of Macintosh's memory.

To paste the illustration into your memo, move the mouse pointer once again to the Edit menu at the top of the screen and hold the mouse button down.

This time, you pull the pointer down until "Paste" is highlighted. Release the mouse button and, once again, zap.

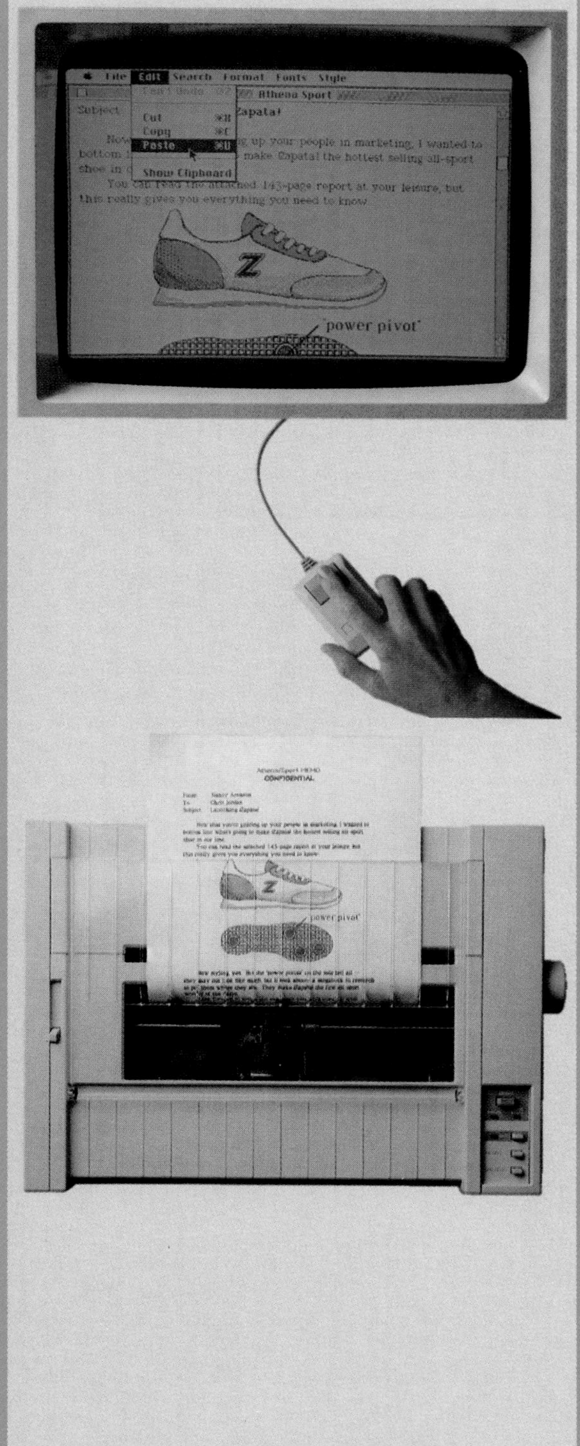

And Print.

You tell a Macintosh personal computer to print the same way you tell it to do everything else. And provided you have a printer, you'll immediately see your work in print.

All your work. Nothing but your work. Because with Macintosh's companion printer, Imagewriter, you can print out everything you can put on a Macintosh's screen.

The Macintosh has two built-in RS-232/RS-422 ports (Figure 12) that make it especially easy to connect modems, printers, and other types of peripheral devices without purchasing expensive additional hardware circuit "cards." RS-422 ports can transfer 1 million bits per second, making it easy to hook a Macintosh into a local area network. With Apple's MacTerminal software package and the Apple modem, the Macintosh can communicate over the phone with other computers at either 300 or 1200 baud.

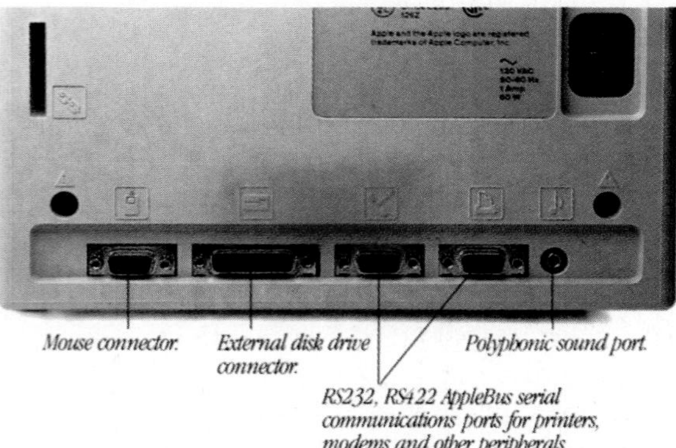

Figure 12 The Macintosh comes standard with easily accessible connectors for attaching the mouse, an external disk drive, peripheral devices, data communications equipment, and polyphonic sound generators.

The Apple Imagewriter printer used with the Macintosh actually has greater resolution than the screen. It can control 160 dots per inch horizontally and 144 vertically, whereas the screen has a resolution of 72 dots per inch both horizontally and vertically. Any image that appears on the screen can be faithfully reproduced on paper.

One of the really exciting aspects of the Macintosh is its built-in typesetting capabilities (Figure 13). It can create text in an assortment of sizes and fonts. It can then change the style of the type by setting it in regular, boldface, italic, underlined, outlined, or shadowed variations. These styles may even be combined, thus allowing the user to create boldface italic text, underlined outlined text, and so on. The ambitious user can even create customized typefaces. And as we've seen, it's easy to intermix text and graphics in the same document. The authors prepared the Instructor's Manual for this text on a Macintosh equipped with an Apple Imagewriter dot-matrix printer.

Apple provides an optional 10-key numeric pad for those users wishing to do high-speed numeric data entry (Figure 14). The Macintosh comes

Figure 13 A sampling of the type fonts, sizes, and styles that the Macintosh can create.

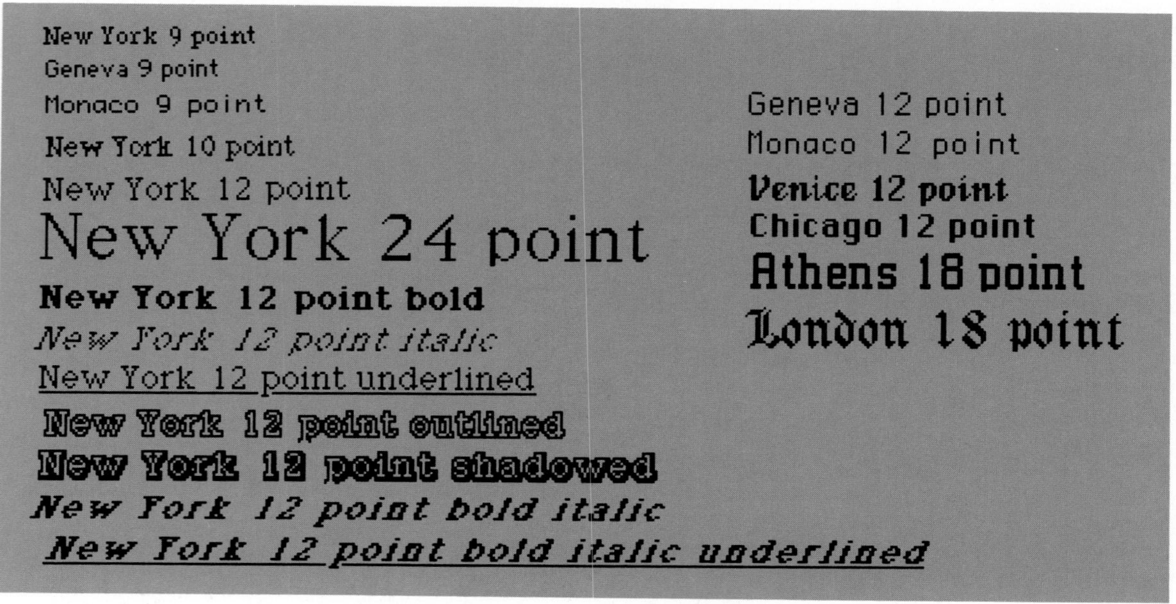

standard with a built-in sound generator that can produce four "voices" of music or even human speech (with the appropriate software, of course).

Macintoshes are produced at the rate of one every 27 seconds at a highly automated $20-million plant in Fremont, California. The assembly lines are controlled by—you guessed it—Macintoshes!

If you are interested in the Macintosh, you may obtain more information at many local computer stores or by reading:

Macworld
The Macintosh Magazine
Subscriber Services
P.O. Box 20300
Bergenfield, NJ 07621
(800) 247-5470

or by contacting Apple directly:

Apple Computer, Inc.
20525 Mariani Avenue
Cupertino, CA 95014
(800) 538-9696; in California, (800) 662-9238

Portable Computers

You might think that a personal computer should be portable—that you should be able to take it with you wherever you go. In fact, most personal computers are not portable at all. But many truly **portable computers** are available and have proven quite useful (Figures 13–4 through 13–8).

Choosing a Personal Computer

Some personal computers are sold through the mail, but most are sold at department stores and computer stores. Computer stores generally provide the best support. They sell computer books, magazines, supplies, and software packages, and they provide repair services and classes on how to use personal computers. Perhaps most importantly, experienced personnel in computer stores can answer your questions about your machine, software, or applications, and help you solve your problems.

How do you choose the computer right for

Figure 14 Apple provides an optional 10-key numeric pad for those users wishing to do high-speed numeric data entry.

Figure 13–4 The first popular transportable computers were made by Osborne Computer Corporation.

Figure 13–5 The EPSON HX-20 is a complete computer system weighing less than 4 pounds. It includes a printer, LCD screen, microcassette tape recorder/player, sound generator, and many other features. It runs for 50 hours on a rechargeable set of nickel cadmium batteries. Here the HX-20 is being used as a portable data communications terminal.

you? You should begin by writing down a complete description of your needs (see Chapter 10). Make sure that you understand exactly what you would like to accomplish by installing a computer system.

Visit friends or business associates who have already computerized similar applications and then shop around. Go to several different computer stores and discuss your needs with the salespeople. They'll recommend specific hardware and software packages, itemize supplies and service costs, and present various financing plans.

Ask for demonstrations of the hardware and software packages the salespeople recommend. Is the proposed system easy to use? Will it really save you time and money? Will you be able to get valuable information that is simply not possible to obtain in a reasonable amount of time with manual procedures?

Is the system expandable so that it can adapt to your growing needs? Is the computer store going to remain in business? How about the manufacturer of the hardware, and the software suppliers—are they stable companies?

As a rule, you should consider at least three alternatives before making a decision. And remember, if a system doesn't feel right for you, it probably isn't.

Figure 13–6 This pocket computer weighs only 22 ounces, yet packs in 16K of RAM, 34K of ROM, a full keyboard including a 10-key pad, and a thin cassette tape with a capacity of 48K bytes. Equally compact are the optional printer and RS-232 interface.

Personal Computer Data Communications

As we will see later in this chapter, there is a world of information available to people with personal computers equipped for data communications. What does a personal computer user need in order to communicate? It's actually quite simple. A modem is needed to convert the digital signals of the computer to the analog signals of the telephone system, and vice versa. In addition, your personal computer must be equipped with an **RS-232 interface**. This gives your computer the ability either to pass one character at a time to the modem for transmission or to receive one character at a time from the modem. This stream of characters must be organized in a special way that is beyond our scope here. So you'll need one more item, namely a data communications software package, which handles all the "messy" details. Information about the hardware and software for data communications may be obtained at computer stores.

Figure 13–7 A pocket computer.

Figure 13–8 The Gavilan mobile computer weighs only 9 pounds, yet offers the full power of a 16-bit computer. It has a detachable 5-pound printer, an integrated mouse, a 3-inch microfloppy disk drive, and a built-in 8-line-by-66-character LCD screen.

Applications

Personal computers may be used for an almost endless variety of applications. Today, many authors, students, and businesspeople use them as word processors. Text is typed in, and the computer stores it in its memory. Changes may then be made and a clean copy retyped at the touch of a button. If multiple copies are needed, possibly with minor changes, they can be produced much faster than typing them individually. We'll discuss **word processing** in detail in Chapter 14.

"Whither goeth literature, Emily, there also must I go."

People use database management software packages to organize household budgets (Figure 13–9), maintain their Christmas lists, store an inventory of household valuables for insurance purposes, manage organization membership rolls, and so on. A personal computer can help keep financial records and prepare reports. It can help with bill paying and energy management. It can manage mailing lists and prepare selective mailings.

Artists equip their personal computers with CRTs and plotters to draw pictures; light pens or digitizing tablets are used to record "brushstrokes." Musicians use personal computers for composing and playing music, and for printing sheet music (Figure 13–10). Music synthesizers can be controlled by personal computers.

Home computers are also used for security, energy management, income tax preparation, game playing, telecommuting (working at home via computer terminals), shopping at home, home banking, stock portfolio management, education, meal planning, and so on (Figure 13–11).

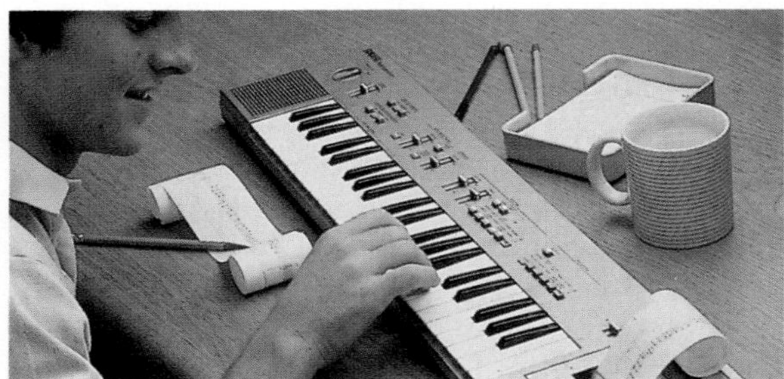

Figure 13–10 As the composer writes music, this portable electronic keyboard plays the notes through its built-in speaker, and writes out the sheet music.

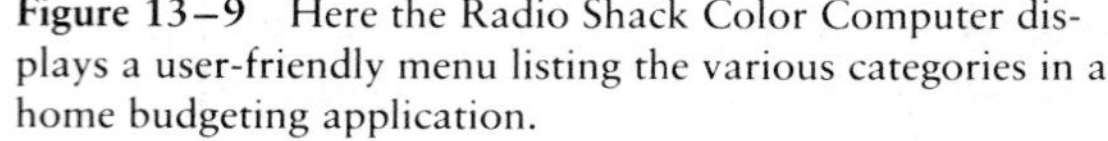

Figure 13–9 Here the Radio Shack Color Computer displays a user-friendly menu listing the various categories in a home budgeting application.

Figure 13–11 Choreographers use personal computers to design and store dance routines.

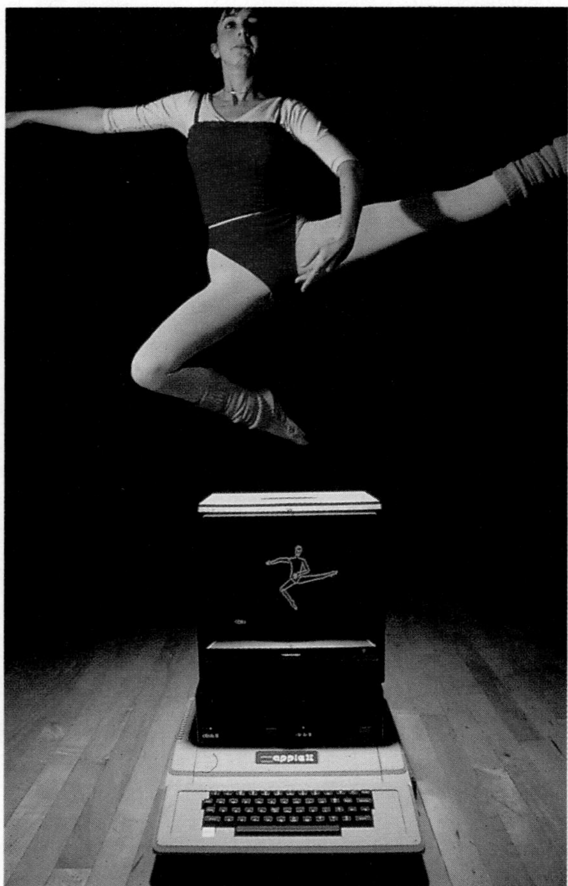

Personal Computing Software

Personal computing has completely changed the character and composition of the software industry. Today hardware vendors rarely attempt to produce their own software. Instead, software is supplied by thousands of individuals and software companies.

A great variety of software is available, but certain types of software packages are the most commonly used. These include operating systems to control the computer, word-processing packages that facilitate the creation and manipulation of text, database management packages that facilitate the storing and retrieving of user information, electronic spreadsheet packages used primarily in financial planning applications, graphics packages that enable the user to prepare charts and graphs, programming language packages that enable the user to write and debug programs, and data communications packages that enable computers to communicate with one another.

As the field of **expert systems** matures (see Chapter 16), we will be able to purchase software to provide us with expert advice on taxes, legal problems, first aid, and so on. The market for such software is huge and virtually untapped at the present time.

Education

I am anxiously awaiting the day when these kids are college freshmen, and they walk into their computer science course with ten years of programming already under their belts at age eighteen. The implications for their futures and ours staggers the imagination.

Sally Greenwood Larsen

Personal computers are great learning aids—they are fun to use, they let students learn at their own pace, they customize their presentations to the students' individual needs, and they allow education to take place at home or work, as well as in school. Computers equipped with graphics screens, speech synthesizers, and speech recognizers can create exciting visual and sound effects that hold the students' attention.

One of the early uses of computers as educational tools was the replacement of slide rules with electronic calculators (Figures 13–12 and 13–13). These devices did not meet with immediate acceptance—some teachers refused to allow students to use them, fearing the students would become lazy and not master the fundamentals. Instructors who encouraged the use of calculators often found that the students were able to accomplish a great deal more during class periods and did, in fact, learn the fundamentals. In some cases, however, students were confused by the calculators and the learning process was slowed.

The successes of electronic calculators led to an assortment of educational toys that teach math,

"THIS IS MY FATHER. HE CAN DO MATH WITHOUT A CALCULATOR."

Figure 13–12 Electronic calculators have virtually replaced slide rules.

Figure 13–13 This electronic calculator may be programmed by simply plugging in various hardware modules.

reading, and spelling at many different levels (Figure 13–14). These toys challenge children while improving their skills, and they are fun to use. Toys that teach reading and spelling have become popular, particularly those that use voice synthesizers to carry on a dialogue with the child (Texas Instruments' Speak & Spell, for example).

The marketplace for educational computing systems is very large—there are approximately 75,000 elementary schools (Figure 13–15), 30,000 secondary schools, and 3000 colleges in the United States, with a student population of

"And if you're short of time on an exam, here's a wild guess button."

Figure 13–14 (a) Speak & Read,™ (b) Speak & Spell, (c) Speak & Math, (d) The Little Professor, (e) DataMan, (f) Spelling B, (g) Math Marvel, (h) Mr. Challenger, (i) Language Tutor.

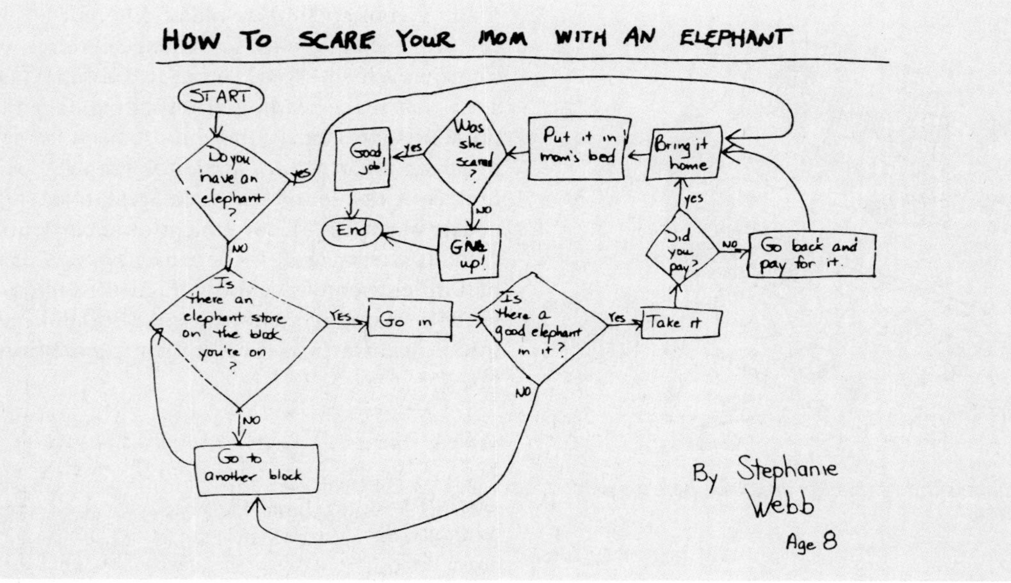

Figure 13–15 Contrary to what we might have believed only a decade ago, youngsters relate well to computers and computing concepts.

approximately 60 million. Millions of other people not in formal school programs can benefit by educational computing as well.

Computer courses have become so popular that the schools often find it difficult to get students out of the computer classrooms. Students have been known to lock themselves in closets so that they could use computers after school hours. Enrollment in computer courses offered in adult education programs has soared.

Computer camps combine computer courses with conventional camping activities. More prison inmates are enrolled in computer courses today than in the traditional favorite—lock making!

Some educators are concerned that computers may actually impede the educational process for students who do not feel comfortable working with the machines. Others are concerned with the way computer courses are displacing other valuable courses, especially in liberal arts curricula.

With **computer assisted instruction** (CAI), learning is aided by computers. Students learn at their own pace. Messages like "Press HELP if you are having a problem" encourage the student to ask for assistance. "Sorry, that is incorrect, please try again" gives the student a chance to correct mistakes.

One exciting use for computers in the class-

room is for simulation. In history classes, for example, students might use computers to reenact famous battles. In science courses, computers may be programmed to simulate space flights.

Some universities already require entering students to purchase or lease personal computers. These machines are often plugged into local personal computer networks so that students may converse with one another, share files, participate in group simulations and management games, and so on. With inexpensive floppy disks, students can have virtually unlimited storage capacity.

Personal computers are being tied to laser videodisk players (see Chapter 6) to form interactive teaching machines. A teacher's presentation is prerecorded on the videodisk. The positions of discussions, questions, and answers on the disk are prerecorded in computer storage. The computer plays a discussion from the videodisk and then asks the user a series of questions. The user's responses are checked, and the computer selects the appropriate portion of the videodisk to play next. If the user is correct, the machine offers congratulations and goes on to the next subject. If the user is incorrect, the machine explains the correct answer, plays (or replays) some material to reinforce the user's understanding, and then retests the user. Complete college degree programs may eventually be offered in this manner.

The Information Providers

The computing and communications revolutions are opening up a world of information to people with personal computers. In our personal and professional lives, we thrive on information. Acquiring it can be time-consuming and expensive; possessing it can be the root of great power. In the future, information of virtually any kind will be available instantaneously and at nominal cost. Our problem will change from obtaining useful information to sifting through mountains of it to find what we want.

Commercial enterprises called **information providers** distribute information electronically. The broad-based acceptance of cable television has proven that people are willing to pay for various kinds of entertainment and information conveniently brought to their homes and businesses via the communications media. Now companies are offering systems that flood us with a seemingly endless smorgasbord of information delights. To date, three different approaches have been used: teletext, viewdata/videotex, and on-line databases. We'll consider each of these in detail and present a case study on the Viewtron videotex service offered by Knight-Ridder Corporation.

Teletext

Teletext is a one-way transmission service. It repeatedly broadcasts a certain common base of information to its subscribers, who, through decoder boxes on their TV sets, type the numbers of the information frames they want to view. The service providing teletext receives no communication back from the subscriber.

Teletext information is transmitted in an interesting way—it is inserted in the black bands you see on your TV when the vertical hold is out of control. These bars are called the **vertical blanking intervals**, and they provide enough information-carrying capability for teletext systems to transmit a selection of about 100 pages, or frames, of text. The TV program being transmitted is unaffected. Some companies are considering transmitting teletext over full channels on cable TV systems. Perhaps 5000 to 10,000 frames could be transmitted continuously in this way, but it is generally felt that this would be too costly to be a viable commercial product.

The first widespread use of teletext was for the **closed captioning** of TV programs for deaf viewers. A small rectangle containing the text of the current dialogue is inserted in the TV picture. The adaptor for this service contains a microprocessor that extracts the information from the blanking interval and converts it to large characters on the screen.

Teletext is a relatively inexpensive system, but it does have its problems. It offers a very limited selection of information, each frame contains only a small amount of information, and there is a lengthy delay between the time a frame is selected and when it actually appears on the screen.

Viewdata/Videotex

Videotex, called **viewdata** in Europe, is a much more powerful information service than teletext. Communication is two-way, with transmissions sent over the subscriber's telephone or a two-way cable TV channel. The telephone option is currently the more popular.

Besides transmitting text, videotex uses full-color graphics, making for interesting screen presentations. The videotex provider's computer carries on a dialogue with the subscriber, who responds to questions and makes selections on a keyboard provided with the decoder box.

Only the information the user specifically requests is transmitted, and therefore the size of the database is in no way limited by the speed (bandwidth) of the communications medium, as it is with teletext. The variety of applications is enormous.

The user punches digits on a numeric keyboard (some videotex systems offer a full alphanumeric keyboard). This information is transmitted by telephone to the videotex computer, which then analyzes it and obtains the desired information from its own or a cooperating company's database. This information is then coded (so that only specially equipped decoder boxes can read it) and sent back to the user over the phone line. The user's videotex box decodes the information and displays it on a TV or personal computer screen.

Videotex graphics are generated in several different ways. With **alphamosaic graphics**, the screen is divided into 24 lines, each containing 40 blocks. A block is either a single dot-matrix character or one of a variety of small graphic shapes. Graphics produced with this technique appear boxy but may be displayed relatively fast—about 10 seconds per screen. Great Britain's pioneering Prestel videotex system uses alphamosaic graphics.

Alphageometric graphics are generated by following instructions to create certain common shapes and to locate them on the screen. The graphics are of very high quality, but it can take 30 seconds or more to generate one full screen image.

In the future, as communications capacities increase, **full definition video images** will be prepared at the videotex computer and transmitted to the user. This method will provide the highest quality graphics, but it may be decades before it is economical enough to transmit the large amounts of information required.

Videotex is intended for distribution to the general public. It uses a user-friendly, menu-driven dialogue that does not require any special technical knowledge on the user's part.

But videotex does have its problems. The costs can be substantial. The user pays for the decoder, telephone calls, and the videotex provider's fees. Some telephone companies charge considerably higher rates for data transmission than for voice transmission. The capabilities are severely limited by slow telephone transmission speeds. Home TV sets are already tied up with video game machines, personal computers, videotape and videodisk players, and of course cable TV programming and network and local television. This doesn't leave much time for using videotex. Much of what is offered for a fee on videotex can be obtained free from other sources, although perhaps not in as timely a fashion. Videotex ties up the user's telephone so that calls can't be made or received.

Case Study 13–3: Viewtron

In this case study, we investigate the Viewtron videotex service offered by Knight-Ridder Newspapers. We consider how it evolved, how to use it, and its many capabilities (Figure 1).

Figure 1 Viewtron provides its subscribers with hundreds of videotex services that use attractive color graphics. Some of Viewtron's many educational services are shown here.

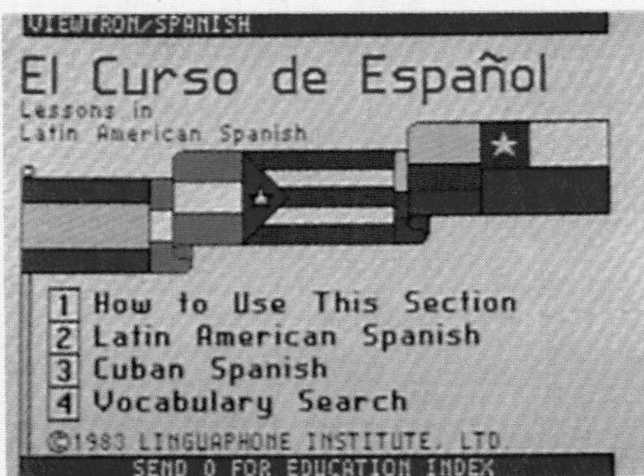

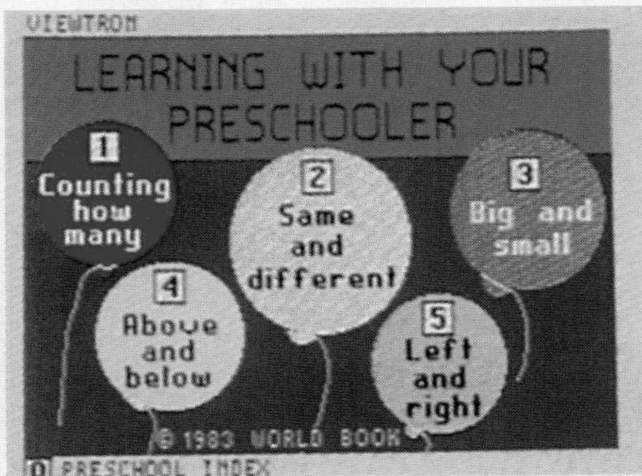

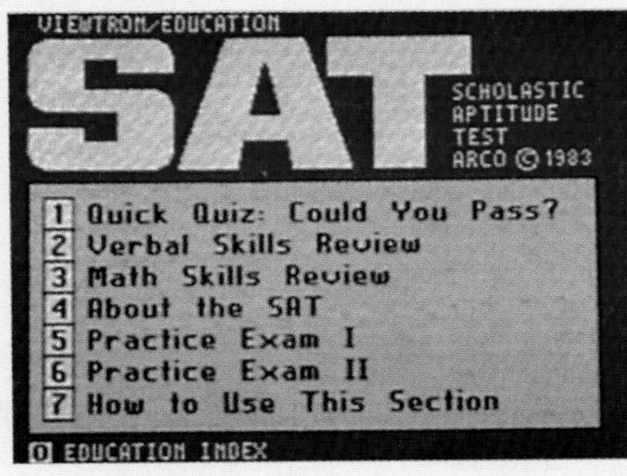

A Brief History

The first videotex service was Prestel, begun in 1979 by the British Post Office. The French followed with their Antiope service, initially intended as a means of eliminating the expenses of publishing and distributing telephone directories. The French expect to have a videotex terminal in the home of every person with a telephone by the early 1990s. The Canadian government developed the Telidon system, which has been used mostly to provide agricultural information to farmers. The **Viewtron** system developed by Knight-Ridder Newspapers was first tested in 1980–1981 with a few hundred homes in Coral Gables, Florida. In November 1983 Viewtron was offered to subscribers throughout South Florida, making it the first commercially available videotex service in the United States.

Figure 2 The Sceptre wireless remote control keypad.

How to Use Viewtron

Subscribers access Viewtron through Sceptre terminals provided by AT&T (Figure 2). The terminal has two parts: the control unit and the remote control keypad. The control unit is connected to both a TV set and a telephone jack (Figure 3). The remote control keypad is wireless and may be used from anywhere in the room (Figure 4). The keypad contains digits, letters, special symbols, and eight special function keys, F1 through F8. The Sceptre terminal is easy to connect and use (See the box on page 361, "Using Viewtron").

Figure 3 How Viewtron and Sceptre work.

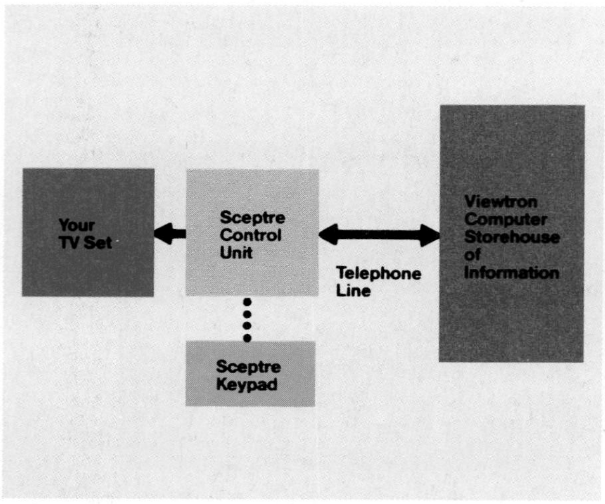

Figure 4 The wireless Sceptre may be used conveniently from anywhere in the room.

Using Viewtron

Within minutes after arriving home with the Sceptre terminal, you can have more information at your fingertips with Viewtron than you ever imagined possible.

It takes only moments to connect the Sceptre terminal to your TV set in order to begin using Viewtron. Simply,

- plug in the power cord
- connect your telephone line to the terminal
- connect your TV's antenna leads to the terminal
- connect your terminal to your TV

That's all it takes to install the Sceptre terminal.

To begin using Viewtron, turn on your TV and the terminal. Push one key and the Sceptre terminal automatically calls Viewtron.

Viewtron will ask you for your unique ID and password. (Your ID and password come in the pocket of the Viewtron handbook that is included with the terminal.) To sign-on to Viewtron, type in your ID and password and Viewtron will begin to simplify your life.

There are two ways of traveling through the world of Viewtron. First, you can start with one of 14 broad topic indexes such as news, money or education. Each topic gives you a list of sections within that topic to help lead you to the information you are interested in. Just select the number next to the section you want.

The second way of getting information on Viewtron is with keywords. Just type in a keyword such as "Weather" or "Financial News" to ask for a specific section.

Eight special keys on the Sceptre terminal give you added speed when traveling through Viewtron. Here's what the keys do:

- **More**—Takes you to the next page within a section.

- **Back**—Takes you back through the last 20 pages you looked at, one at a time.

- **Index**—Takes you to the last index page you looked at.

- **Browse**—Lets you browse within a section without returning to the index page for that section. For instance, if you are reading the first business news story on Viewtron, you can press the browse key to read the second business news story without returning to the business news index page.

- **Mark Page/Recall Page**—If you think you might want to return to a page you were looking at during the same session, simply press the mark page key. When you are ready to look at that page again, simply press recall page. You can mark up to five pages during a session.

- **Personal Magazine**—You can select up to 16 pages that you look at most often on Viewtron and place them in your personal magazine. For instance, every morning, you might want to check today's weather, headlines for news, business and sports, scores for last night's ball games, Viewtron shopping values and your biorhythm for today. Each time you press the personal magazine key on the Sceptre terminal, you'll see the next page in your personal magazine.

- **Help**—If you have a problem while traveling through Viewtron, just press the help key (or call the Viewtron Customer Service Center: it's open seven days a week from 9 a.m. to midnight.)

Viewtron service and the Sceptre terminal were designed with you in mind. You'll find the Sceptre terminal easy to install and the Viewtron service easy to use.

This boxed piece was provided by Viewdata Corporation of America, Inc.

Viewtron Services

Viewtron offers hundreds of services to its subscribers. Its advertising appeals to people who want information fast and up-to-the-minute (see the figure). The following list is only a small portion of the capabilities Viewtron provides to its subscribers 24 hours per day. Viewtron helps users to:

1. Shop at home.
2. Bank at home.
3. Get the latest sports scores.
4. Check the latest stock prices.
5. Get up-to-the-minute weather forecasts.
6. Get the latest traffic report.
7. Check real estate listings.
8. Read the latest news stories.
9. Search Grolier's on-line *Academic American Encyclopedia.*
10. Check airline fares and flight availability using the Official Airline Guide.
11. Pay bills.
12. Get consumer advice.
13. Locate and make reservations at restaurants.
14. Send electronic mail to other Viewtron subscribers.
15. Learn a foreign language or select from many other educational programs.
16. Play video games.
17. Get directions to various places.
18. Post messages on electronic bulletin boards.
19. Get the latest local, national, and international news.
20. Get calendars of events such as art shows, classes, club meetings, films, lectures, concerts, and theater presentations.
21. Receive investment advice.
22. Get product descriptions and comparisons.
23. Send a Western Union telegram.
24. Choose seats and order tickets to events.
25. Order from the J. C. Penney catalog. If the item you want is not available, the computer suggests alternatives.
26. Take advantage of eleventh hour bargains, such as deep discounts on theater tickets still unsold hours before a performance. Viewtron is a bargain hunter's paradise.
27. Place classified ads. Ads may be removed immediately after the sale to avoid needless calls.
28. Prepare for the SAT exam.
29. Solve brain-teaser puzzles.
30. Get sports score updates during a game and complete coverage within a half hour after the game is over.
31. Learn where the best fishing is.
32. Reserve a book at the library.
33. Get biographies on people listed in various Who's Who publications.
34. Keep an electronic calendar and send reminders to yourself.
35. Cast your vote in weekly polls.
36. Use your TV screen as an electronic easel.
37. Request expert advice from other Viewtron subscribers on almost any subject.
38. Browse menus and prices in local restaurants.
39. Create your own personal magazine (Figure 5).
40. Take a personality test.
41. Get first aid advice.
42. Make rental car and hotel reservations.
43. Check your biorhythms and consult your horoscope.
44. Check the latest happenings on your favorite TV programs which you may have missed.

A dozen things you'll never have to wait for again.

Service at the bank.

The clerk at the store.

Tomorrow's newspaper.

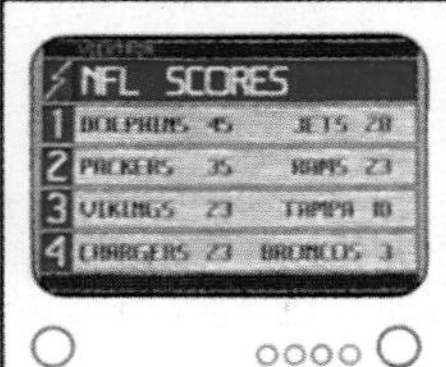

Tonight's scores.

A knowledgeable salesperson.

The market closing.

The 11 o'clock weather.

Finding a good place to eat.

Up-to-date answers.

A travel agent's attention.

The mail.

And more.

Introducing Viewtron®.

The new home information service of Knight-Ridder Newspapers.

Viewtron advertising emphasizes the service's ability to provide immediate information.

Sceptre™ is a trademark of AT&T. Viewtron® is a registered service mark applicable only to the service provided by Viewdata Corporation of America, Inc., a wholly owned subsidiary of Knight-Ridder Newspapers. This special section was adapted with permission from a special advertising section, *The Miami Herald*, November 1983. Viewtron is offered by Viewdata Corporation of America, Inc., 1111 Lincoln Road, Miami Beach, FL 33139.

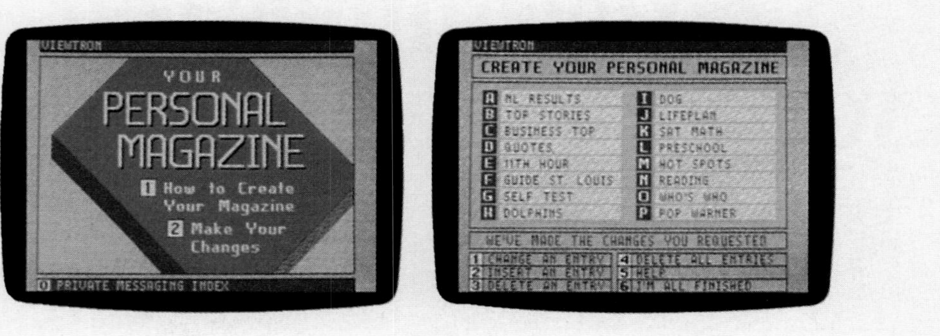

Figure 5 With Viewtron you can create your own customized personal magazine.

On-Line Databases

The third group of information providers is called the **on-line databases**. These services are offered to people with personal computers. The premier services of this category are **CompuServe, The Source**, and the **Dow Jones News/Retrieval Service**. These offer the same kinds of services that videotex provides as well as more sophisticated services appropriate for people with computer expertise. The addresses for these services are included in the Projects section at the end of the chapter.

Social Impact

How is our society changing as a result of personal computers? We now have much greater access to much more information. Many people are frustrated by this—at times there seems to be simply too much information. Some people are advocating a back to basics attitude.

The best personal computers still cost thousands of dollars, making them accessible only to wealthier people and school systems. This could widen the already wide gap that exists between the rich and the poor. Some people argue that with rapidly declining prices, this gap is actually closing quickly, and that personal computers are therefore among the most democratic of technologies.

We are able to communicate better, more often, and with more information. Ideas can be disseminated faster and to larger audiences. Information can be shared, and this sharing can be carefully controlled.

We are able to learn and to digest greater amounts of knowledge. Might we reach the point where we are learning too much? Is there some educational threshold beyond which it simply doesn't make sense to educate humans any further? Might psychological problems develop in humans who have been oversaturated with facts?

PCs enable us to **telecommute**, that is to work at home thus reducing time-consuming and costly commuting. But might this cause problems as the social interaction among people decreases?

Our privacy is threatened by having the tentacles of society's computer networks protruding into our homes, schools, and businesses. We are making information so accessible that we may never again be able to secure our cherished privacy. (Privacy issues are considered in Chapter 15.)

Our dependency on computers is increasing to the point that we simply can't live without them. A flareup on the sun or a nuclear explosion could generate electrical disturbances sufficient to cripple our lives by disrupting our abilities to calculate and communicate.

We must address many questions as the Information Revolution continues to influence the way we live and think in ever more significant ways.

Summary 

1. Today most people can afford to purchase their own personal computers.
2. The key development that made personal computers possible was the invention of the microprocessor.
3. In 1975 Steve Jobs and Steve Wozniak built their first Apple.
4. In 1977 personal computers were marketed by Radio Shack (TRS-80), Commodore (PET), and others.
5. In the late 1970s and early 1980s the giants in the computer industry entered the personal computer market. Among them were Texas Instruments, Hewlett-Packard, and Xerox. IBM entered the personal computer market in 1981 and quickly became the world's leading producer of personal computers.
6. Besides selling computer equipment, computer stores provide classes, sell computer-related books and supplies, and offer repair services.
7. The most common configuration today for a personal computer consists of a keyboard, a screen, a printer, and various kinds of disk storage.
8. Modems allow communication with other computers and computer information networks.
9. Personal computers are used in word processing, writing music, drawing pictures, keeping financial and personal records, and an almost endless variety of other applications.
10. Personal computers are useful learning aids. They are fun to use, and they allow students to work at their own pace.
11. The IBM Personal Computer, introduced in August 1981, helped IBM to establish itself quickly as the world's leading manufacturer of personal computers.
12. The Apple II, introduced in 1977, is considered the machine that spawned the personal computing industry. With the introduction of the Lisa in 1983 and the Macintosh in 1984, Apple reasserted itself as the technological leader in personal computing.
13. The Macintosh uses an extremely user-friendly interface combining high-resolution graphics, icons, and pointing with a mouse. This technology was pioneered by Xerox.
14. The information providers are companies that distribute information electronically to people with special-purpose terminals or personal computers.
15. Teletext is a one-way service that repeatedly transmits a small base of information in the black bars between TV frames. Videotex is a two-way service (for the general public) that carries on a dialogue with the user over the telephone, enabling the user to select from a vast store of information and applications. The on-line databases are similar to videotex services, except that they are specifically designed to be used by people with personal computers.

Important Terms 

alphageometric graphics
alphamosaic graphics
APA (all-points-addressable) graphics
Apple Macintosh
clicking
closed captioning
CompuServe
computer-assisted instruction (CAI)
Dow Jones News/Retrieval Service
expert systems
full definition video images
IBM Personal Computer
icon
information providers
mouse
on-line databases
personal computer
portable computer
pull-down menu
RS-232 interface
The Source
sturdy disk
telecommuting
teletext
TRS-80
vertical blanking intervals
videotex
viewdata
Viewtron
word processing

Self-Review Exercises 

Matching

Next to the term in column A, place the letter of the statement in column B that best describes it.

Column A

1. RS-422
2. APA graphics
3. Videodisk
4. Telecommuting
5. Expert system
6. Teletext
7. Viewtron
8. Simulation
9. Word processing
10. On-line database

Column B

A. The Source
B. Closed captioning
C. Author's computer application
D. First commercial videotex service in the United States
E. Computer reenacts famous battle
F. High-speed data communications interface
G. "Computerized" lawyer
H. Work-at-home
I. Used in interactive teaching machines
J. Any dot on the page can be set on or off

Fill-in-the-Blanks

Fill in the blanks in each of the following:

1. The key development that made personal computers possible was the invention of the ______ at Intel Corporation in 1971.

2. The company generally credited with inventing the personal computer is ______ .

3. The world's leading manufacturer of personal computers is ______ .

4. To enable a personal computer to communicate over the telephone, the two required pieces of hardware are a modem and an ______ .

5. Using a personal computer at home to avoid traveling to the job site is called ______ .

6. The use of computers to assist in the educational process is called ______ .

7. ______ graphics are generated by following instructions to create certain common shapes and to locate them on the screen.

8. With ______ , the information provider receives no information back from the user.

9. The input device that is essential to the Macintosh's user-friendly interface is the ______ .

10. The first videotex service was ______ , begun in 1979 by the British Post Office.

Answers to Self-Review Exercises

Matching: 1 F, 2 J, 3 I, 4 H, 5 G, 6 B, 7 D, 8 E, 9 C, 10 A

Fill-in-the-Blanks:
1. microprocessor
2. Apple
3. IBM
4. RS-232 interface
5. telecommuting
6. computer-assisted instruction (CAI)
7. Alphageometric
8. teletext
9. mouse
10. Prestel

Discussion Questions 

1. What distinguishes a personal computer from other types of computers?

2. What products and services do computer stores offer?

3. What are the parts that make up the most common configuration on today's personal computers? Explain the function of each.

4. What are some of the peripheral devices commonly used with personal computers?

5. List the most common types of software packages used with personal computers.

6. Explain how the combination of personal computers and videodisks is particularly effective in computer-assisted instruction.

7. Do you think it is wise to increase greatly the use of computers in education, or would a back to basics approach be better?

8. Compare and contrast the IBM Personal Computer and the Apple Macintosh.

9. Describe how you would choose your own personal computer.

10. Distinguish between teletext, viewdata/videotex, and on-line database services.

Projects 

1. Visit a local computer store and write a report describing the range of products it offers and the services it provides to its customers.

2. Many of the information providers listed below offer free trials of their services. Request literature from these information providers and prepare a report summarizing their capabilities:

CompuServe Incorporated
Information Service Division
An H&R Block Company
5000 Arlington Centre Boulevard
Columbus, OH 43220
(800) 848-8990; in Ohio, (614) 457-8650

The Source
Source Telecomputing Corporation
A Subsidiary of the Reader's Digest
Association, Inc.
1616 Anderson Road
McLean, VA 22102
(800) 336-3366; in Virginia, (800) 572-2070

Dow Jones News/Retrieval Service
P.O. Box 300
Princeton, NJ 08540
(800) 257-5114; in New Jersey, (609) 452-1511

3. Write to the following personal computer user groups (and others as well), and prepare a report summarizing the services and publications they offer:

The Boston Computer Society
Three Center Plaza
Boston, MA 02108
(617) 367-8080

Digital Equipment Computer Users Society
One Iron Way, MR02–1/C11
Marlboro, MA 01752

Chapter 14

Office Automation

After reading this chapter you will understand:

1. What office automation is
2. How the computing and communications technologies are being integrated with standard office equipment to create the automated office of the future
3. The operation of office automation technologies such as word processing, electronic mail, facsimile, voice mail, the electronic calendar, teleconferencing, and the electronic blackboard
4. How word processing functions with Apple's Macintosh personal computer
5. Important trends in office automation

Left: The key to automation is integration—all the computer-based devices are designed to communicate with one another.

Outline

If business implements electronic productivity tools like electronic mail today, the savings could be as much as $300 billion by 1990.

Booz, Allen, & Hamilton Inc.

And the machines will be linked to communicate with each other: the nervous system at the electronic office will carry the incessant digital chatter of zillions of bits of information racing from one smart machine to another.

Newsweek, *December 28, 1981*

Science may never come up with a better office-communications system than the coffee break.

Earl Wilson

Office automation (OA) refers to the use of the computing and communications technologies to process information in offices electronically. More than half the work force in the United States consists of white-collar workers, people whose primary task is the manipulation of information. Office automation can improve their productivity dramatically. Labor-intensive white-collar work is becoming more machine-intensive with the help of user-friendly office automation systems.

Some industry analysts project that by 1990 OA will be the largest single segment of the computer industry, so OA warrants our close attention. In this chapter we will discuss the state of the practice and future directions in OA technology. The automated office of the future in which OA is carried to its limits will be a dynamic and productive environment in which to work.

Office automation began in the mid-1960s with the introduction of **word processing** systems—computers that manipulate textual material such as words, phrases, sentences, and paragraphs. Some of today's office automation systems integrate the processing of numbers, text, graphics, voice, and video images.

Office automation is concerned with improving the productivity of managerial, professional, clerical, and administrative personnel; the interconnection of all office equipment through local and long-distance communications networks; improving the overall information flow in an organization; and the production of information that is accurate, timely, useful, and complete.

"We're moving you out of Accounts Receivable, Dickerson. The computer doesn't like you."

Goals of Office Automation Systems

Common to all OA systems are the goals of dramatically reducing the amount of paper that is produced and stored in offices, and of allowing one person's work to be handled from a single location.

Automated offices store, process, and transmit information electronically. Transmission times are reduced from the days or weeks associated with mailing paper letters and catalogs to seconds or minutes. The storage space needed for paper documents is freed for more productive use as information is stored electronically. Some people even speak of the **paperless office**, but it is unlikely that the use of paper will ever be completely eliminated.

Another fundamental principle of OA systems is that they should enable workers to transact most of their business from their own computerized **workstations** (Figure 14–1). This is a huge claim—no system yet designed makes this possible. But it is a goal that is eagerly pursued.

Courtesy of International Business Machines Corporation

Figure 14–1 One of the key marketplaces for the IBM PC has been as OA workstations in Fortune 1000 companies.

Characteristics of Offices and OA Systems

The way office work is conducted changes frequently as the requirements of a business change. New employees are hired as employees with many years of experience leave. Products and services introduced by a company may require different kinds of office support. New OA technologies may make possible dramatic improvements in office organization and work flow.

Offices are people-oriented, and office environments must make work pleasing for people. OA equipment must provide user-friendly interfaces, and offices must be comfortable places to work (Figure 14–2). Today an OA workstation may use a mouse, a touch-sensitive screen, a joystick, and even speech synthesis and recognition.

User and computer communications should be friendly. If the user makes a mistake, the computer should note the error and help the user correct it. The user should not have to plow through a thick manual for answers. OA systems should

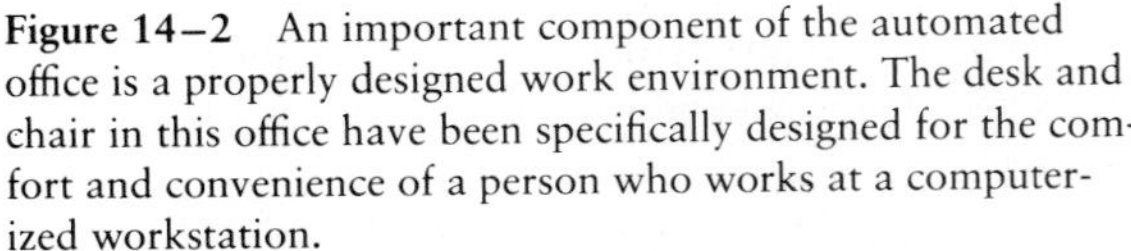

Figure 14–2 An important component of the automated office is a properly designed work environment. The desk and chair in this office have been specifically designed for the comfort and convenience of a person who works at a computerized workstation.

be easy to learn and understand; they should allow the user to choose the most comfortable information formats for input and output; several alternative forms of input and output should be available.

OA systems should be modular, that is, consisting of separate pieces of hardware and software that can be combined easily to solve the unique problems of particular offices. OA systems should be expandable so they can grow to service an organization's increased office needs.

One key to the success of OA is **integration,** that is, all the pieces of OA equipment must work together. They must be able to intercommunicate. They must, from the user's standpoint, operate in similar fashion.

Most OA stations today offer a menu approach in which the alternatives available to the user at any point are displayed on a screen. The user selects the item of interest, and the system either performs the indicated function or displays another menu that further refines the choices.

Many OA stations offer assistance through a "HELP" key on the keyboard or a word or icon (that is, symbol) on the screen. At any point, the user can press the "HELP" key, word, or symbol for assistance, and the system will respond with information to assist the user.

A more recent innovation is the **"UNDO" key** that allows a user to cancel the effects of the current activity and go back to the previous activity. The "UNDO" is the user's second-chance key. If a serious error is made, such as deleting a file accidentally, pressing "UNDO" lets the user recover from the error.

Many OA stations use **windowing** to keep track of several tasks at once. For example, while a user is editing a document, helpful information may appear in one window, indicating how to perform various types of edit functions, while in another window the user may receive electronic mail messages (Figures 14–3, 14–4, and 14–5).

Figure 14–3 Xerox Corporation pioneered the integration of the mouse, windowing, and icon graphics with the development of the Xerox Star Information System terminals shown here. The user-friendly interface they designed has become the basis for many of the OA systems currently available.

Figure 14–4 A few of the many icons used with the Xerox Star Information System.

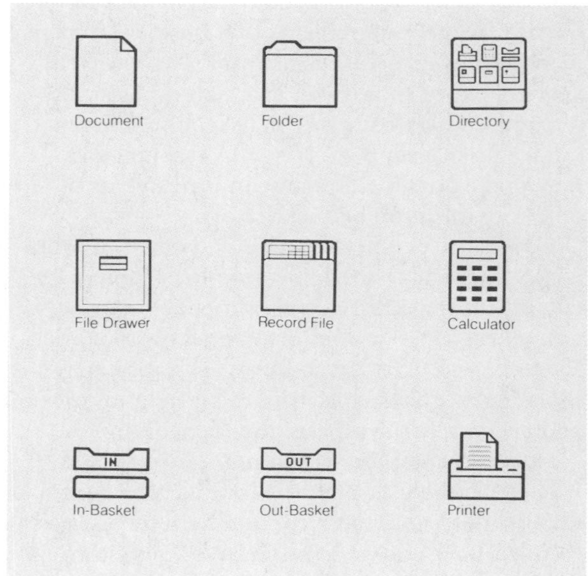

Word Processing

A **word processor** is a computer-based system that facilitates the creation, storage, editing, transmission, and display or printing of text (Fig-

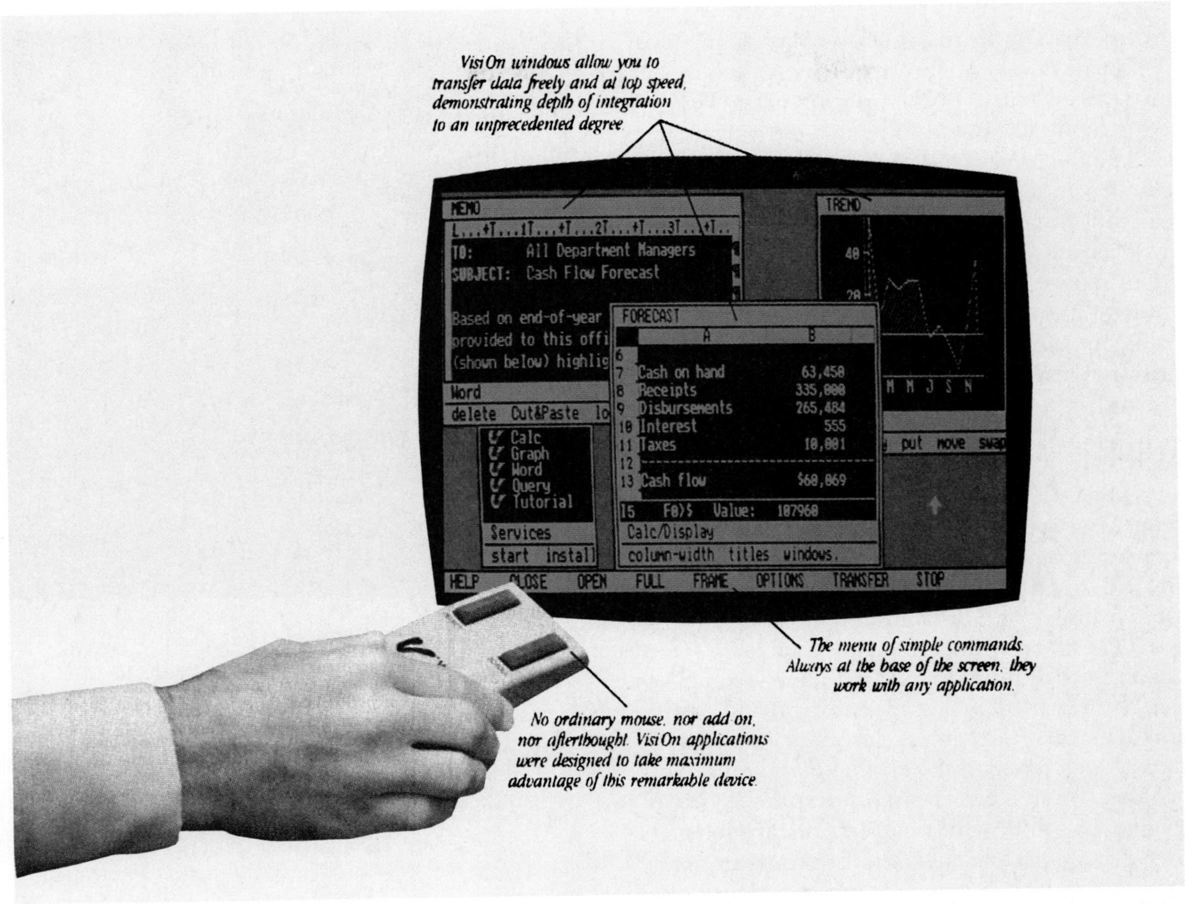

VisiOn windows allow you to transfer data freely and at top speed, demonstrating depth of integration to an unprecedented degree
MEMO
TO: All Department Managers
SUBJECT: Cash Flow Forecast
FORECAST
Cash on hand 63,458
Receipts 335,000
Disbursements 265,484
Interest 555
Taxes 10,001
Cash flow $60,869
TREND
Calc
Graph
Word
Query
Tutorial
Services
start install
Calc/Display
HELP CLOSE OPEN FULL FRAME OPTIONS TRANSFER STOP
The menu of simple commands. Always at the base of the screen, they work with any application.
No ordinary mouse, nor add on, nor afterthought. VisiOn applications were designed to take maximum advantage of this remarkable device.

Figure 14–5 The VisiOn™ system was developed by VisiCorp for use with the IBM PC/XT and other personal computers with large capacity hard disks. The system enables the user to keep track of many jobs at once, switch easily between jobs, and relate the outputs of separate jobs.

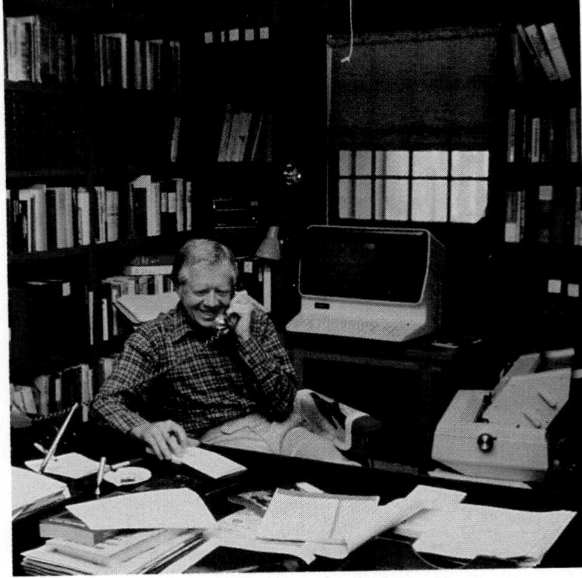

Figure 14–6 Jimmy Carter was the first president to prepare his memoirs on a word processor.

ure 14–6). The word processor may be the most significant development in writing technology since the invention of the printing press. Until you actually write with one, it is difficult to appreciate the power and convenience of word processing. Once you do, however, you may be reluctant to write any other way. Word processing is an outstanding example of technology helping to relieve people of tedious chores and to improve human productivity. The leading technology in OA is and always has been word processing. Once keystrokes are "captured" via one of many input techniques, they can be edited, stored, searched, communicated, and output in many ways.

A **stand-alone** word processor is a complete single-user system, containing a keyboard, a screen, a printer, and disk storage (Figures 14–7 and 14–8). With multiterminal systems, the separate terminals or workstations can share various system resources, thus reducing the cost per terminal. Each station in a **shared-logic system** shares the central processor, storage, and peripheral devices. If the central processor fails in a shared-logic system, the entire system fails. This problem is remedied in **shared-resource systems** (Figure 14–9) in which each workstation has its own processor, and the peripheral devices are shared. A failure in one work station does not affect the others.

The common typewriter becomes an effective input device when used with an optical character recognition (OCR) page reader. Typewritten copy may be entered directly into word processors at several hundred pages per hour. This, of course, is much faster than the data can be manually keystroked. Some of these devices make under one error per 100,000 characters—far greater accuracy than human typists. OCR page readers help free an organization's word processors so that they may be used for the text editing operations for which they were designed.

Figure 14–7 A stand-alone word processor.

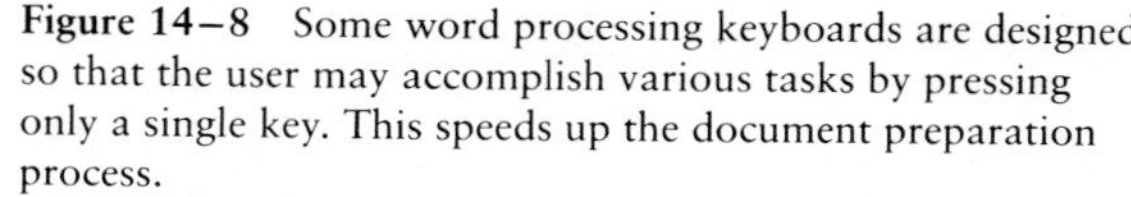

Figure 14–8 Some word processing keyboards are designed so that the user may accomplish various tasks by pressing only a single key. This speeds up the document preparation process.

Capabilities of Word Processing Systems

Let's consider some capabilities of typical word processing systems. The **word wraparound** feature may put an end to looking at the screen to

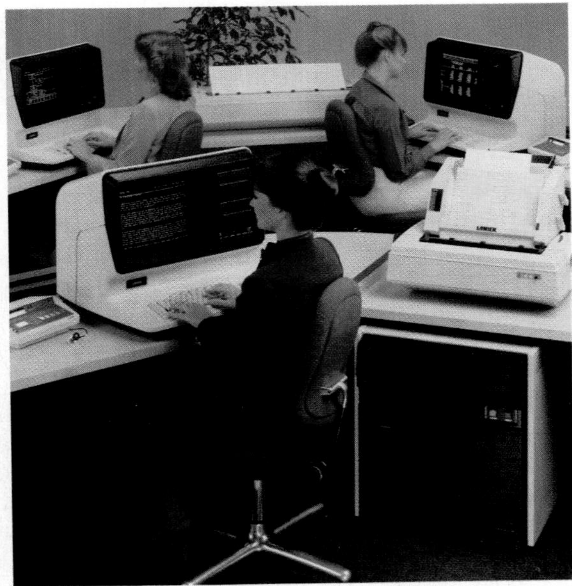

Figure 14–9 A shared-resource word processing system.

see if the end-of-line margin is near. A word typed over the margin is automatically moved down to the next line. Some systems allow **horizontal scrolling** to enable the user to create documents wider than the screen and scroll left and right to view portions of the documents. Most systems provide **vertical scrolling** to enable the user to move forward or backward in a document.

A **cut-and-paste capability** allows the user to form documents from individual pieces and to insert text and graphics at any point in a document. The term *cut and paste* refers to the conventional method of editing by cutting text from one page and pasting it on another to insert it there. The **global replace** capability allows the user to change all occurrences of a word or phrase in a document to a new word or phrase. Another feature is that words may be underlined for emphasis.

Users may specify that text is to be centered on a line—this is particularly attractive on title pages of documents. The right edge may be either jagged or right-justified. Many books are set with right-justified margins so that the text aligns at the right end of every line, just as it does at the left. But some users prefer a jagged right border (as we have used in this textbook).

Most word processors allow the user to specify **automatic page numbering** in which page numbers are automatically calculated and inserted on each page. Most allow users to insert page headings and footings, messages that appear across the top or bottom of every page.

One time-saving feature is **prestored phrases,** usually phrases and paragraphs that an organization uses frequently. Law offices, for example, often prepare wills and other legal documents by combining many prestored phrases and then keystroking only the variable information such as names, addresses, telephone numbers, dates, and any special terms and conditions. With some systems, inserting an entire prestored paragraph at a certain point in a document may be as simple as typing an abbreviation previously associated with that paragraph.

Some word processors offer a capability called **list processing** that allows the user to generate mass mailings. The user supplies the main text and a list of people to whom the text is to be mailed; the word processor then prepares individually typed letters customized to all the people on the list. For example, a college mailing several thousand acceptance letters enters the body of the letter once and supplies a file containing the names and addresses of all students being accepted. The word processor then automatically types all the acceptance letters in succession. Automatic sheet feeders can be used to feed one letterhead at a time to the typing mechanism to minimize operator intervention.

A popular feature in recent systems is the **electronic dictionary** (Figure 14–10). The word processor automatically checks each word in a document against a large number of words prestored in a computerized dictionary. Any word not in the dictionary is highlighted for the user to verify. Users may customize their electronic dictionaries to include various words that relate to their particular needs. Word processors with electronic dictionaries can perform *automatic hyphenation*—they insert hyphens at the proper points in words that are divided at the ends of lines. One problem today's systems haven't solved is words that are spelled the same but hyphenated differently depending on their meaning, such as pro-ject (verb) and proj-ect (noun).

Figure 14–10 The IBM Displaywriter has a built-in electronic dictionary that can check the spelling of about 50,000 words in English, and more than 150,000 words in five foreign languages. It verifies the spelling of words in a document against this dictionary at over 1000 words per minute.

Some word processors provide **multilingual dictionaries** to help a user convert text from one language to another. Such translation is an extremely difficult problem. It will probably be a decade or two before reasonably good interlanguage translators appear. Even then, office automation systems will do a respectable but not perfect job of translating from one language to another. Computers will always have difficulty with ambiguity and with picking up special shades of meaning that people easily convey by emphasizing words and using various facial movements as they speak.

Case Study 14–1: Word Processing with Apple's Macintosh

In this case study, a simple document will be created, edited, stored, and printed using the **MacWrite**™ word processing software package supplied by Apple for use with its Macintosh personal computer. MacWrite has many more features than can be presented in this brief introduction. As Apple continues to improve the package, features will be added that may operate differently from those described in this case study. Several independent software vendors also supply word processing packages for the Macintosh. If you have access to a Macintosh, you should perform each operation as it is discussed. Even if you don't have a Macintosh handy, a careful reading of this case study will still give you a solid understanding of word processing.

Begin by turning on the Macintosh and inserting the sturdy disk (metal end first) containing MacWrite. The menu bar and several icons appear (Figure 1). This is called the initial **desktop**.

If the write/paint icon is not blackened, move the mouse until the screen pointer is above the icon. Press the button on the mouse once and release it quickly. This is called **clicking.** Clicking **selects** the item being pointed to, in this case MacWrite/MacPaint. This causes the write/paint icon to be selected and blackened, indicating that it is now active.

Each application and each file on the Macintosh must be **opened** before it can be used. To do this, move the mouse until the pointer is above the word "File." Then **pull down** the File menu—this is done by **dragging**, that is, moving the mouse while the button is held down. Drag to the word *Open* (Figure 2) and release the mouse button. This selects the Open function.

The Macintosh now opens the write/paint window, and various icons are displayed (Figure 3). Select the MacWrite icon (that is, point to it and click), and once again pull down the File menu and select Open. At this point, the text for the new document may be entered.

MacWrite uses a blinking bar to mark the **insertion point**, that is, the place where text may be inserted (Figure 4). Now type the sentence

Using MacWrite is easy.

Notice that the blinking bar keeps moving to the right (Figure 5). Now hit the "Backspace" key once; the period disappears (Figure 6). Hit "Backspace" four more times and the word "easy" disappears. Now hold "Backspace" down; the insertion point moves left to the beginning of the line erasing the entire sentence.

The **"Return" key** may be pressed at any time to move the insertion point down to the leftmost position of the next line. Now type the following text without hitting the "Return" key:

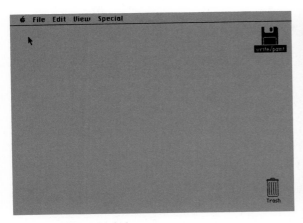

Figure 1 The initial desktop.

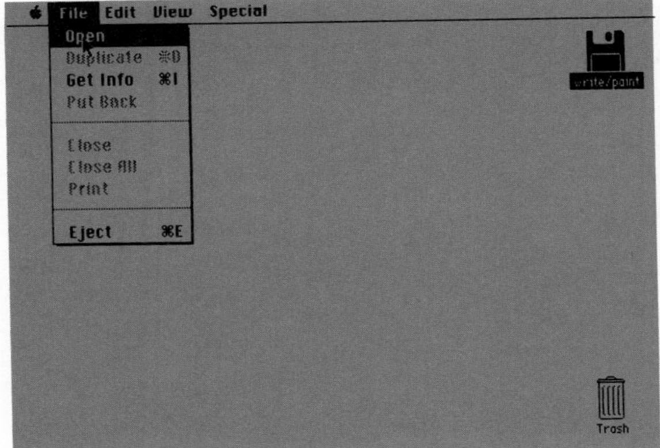

Figure 2 Pulling down the File menu and selecting the Open function.

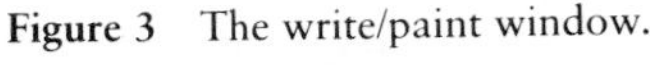

Figure 3 The write/paint window.

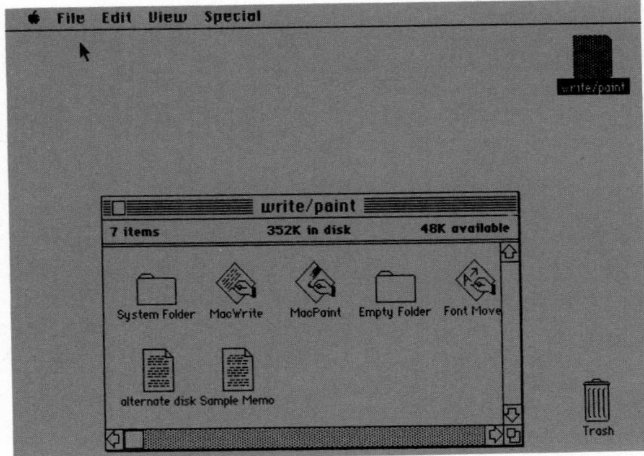

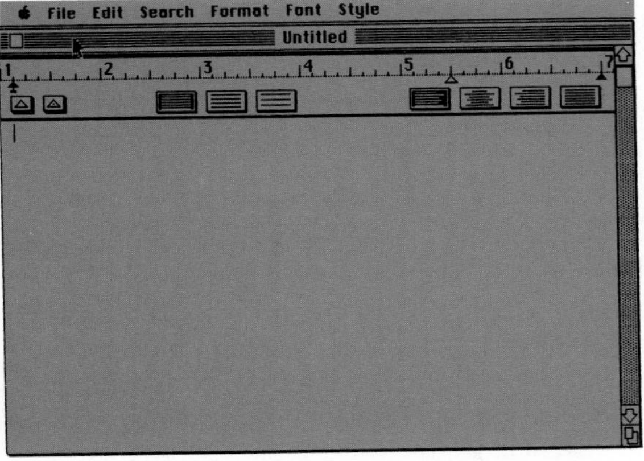

Figure 4 The insertion point (the bar at the top left of the large open rectangle) marks the place where text may be inserted.

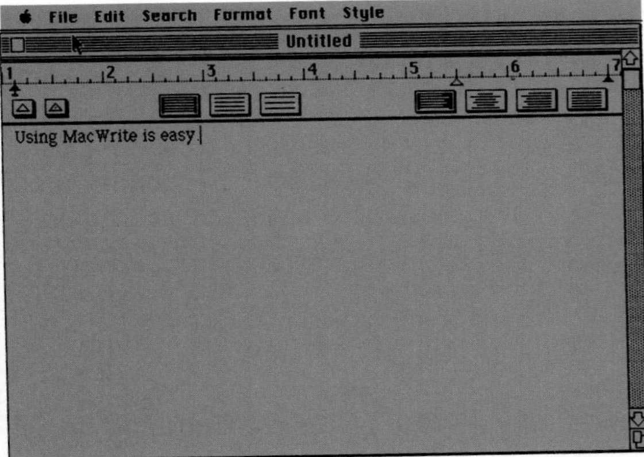

Figure 5 As text is entered, the insertion point is automatically moved.

Figure 6 Hitting the "Backspace" key once erases one character.

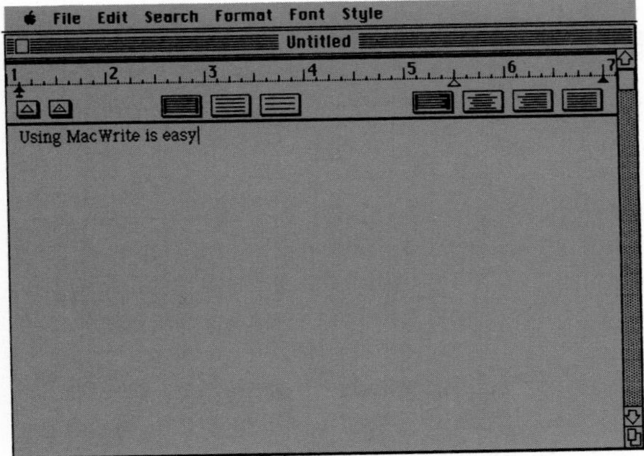

> Apple's Macintosh is an innovative personal computer that is particularly user-friendly. Its MacWrite software package uses windowing, icons, and the mouse to make word processing simple.

As you near the end of each line of the screen, do not press the "Return" key. Simply keep typing, and the Macintosh will automatically space down to the next line. If a word is typed that crosses the end of a line (Figure 7), the **word wraparound** feature will automatically move the entire word to the next line (Figure 8). Use the "Return" key only to end a paragraph or skip a line.

After you have finished typing the two sentences, move the insertion point to the beginning of the paragraph. This is done by moving the mouse so that the pointer is positioned before the word "Apple's." Notice that the pointer changes shape and becomes an **I-beam** (Figure 9); as we will see, this makes it easier to point to specific locations in the text. Then click the mouse, and the blinking bar moves to the beginning of the paragraph (Figure 10). Now type the following text:

> Office automation equipment must be easy to use.

Notice that as you type, the Macintosh moves the remainder of the paragraph to provide space for the new text (Figure 11). As you have already seen, any word that crosses the end of a line is automatically wrapped around to the next line. Now move the insertion point to the left of the word "Its" at the beginning of the third sentence (move the I-beam and click), and type the sentence

> The Macintosh was introduced in January of 1984.

Once again, the remaining text is moved automatically to make room for the text being entered (Figure 12). Now move the insertion point to the end of the paragraph and type the sentence

> This exercise shows how easy it is to use MacWrite.

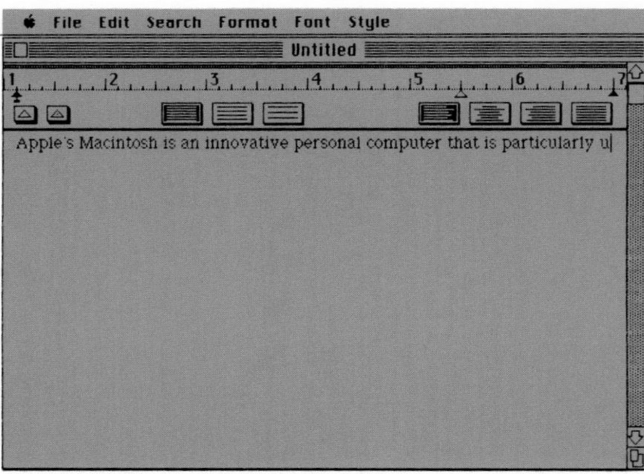

Figure 7 Typing a word that crosses the end of a line.

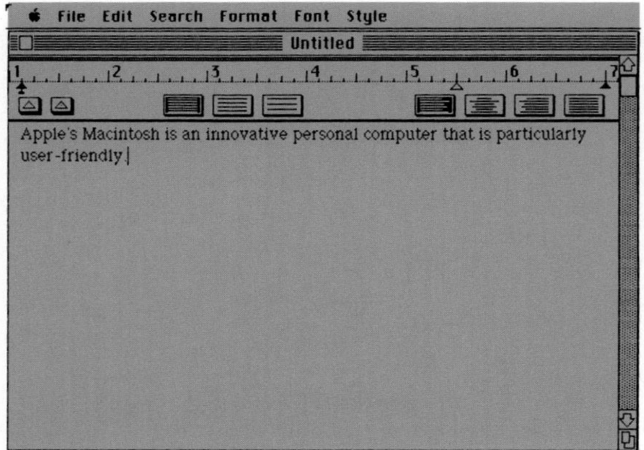

Figure 8 The word wraparound feature moves a word that crosses the end of one line down to the next line to avoid a break.

Figure 9 The pointer changes shape and becomes an I-beam.

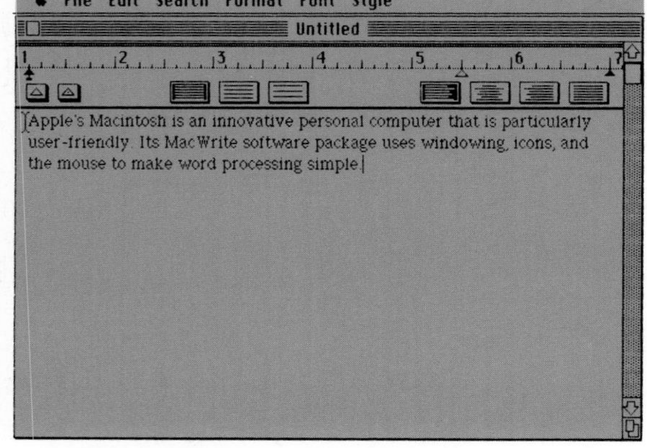

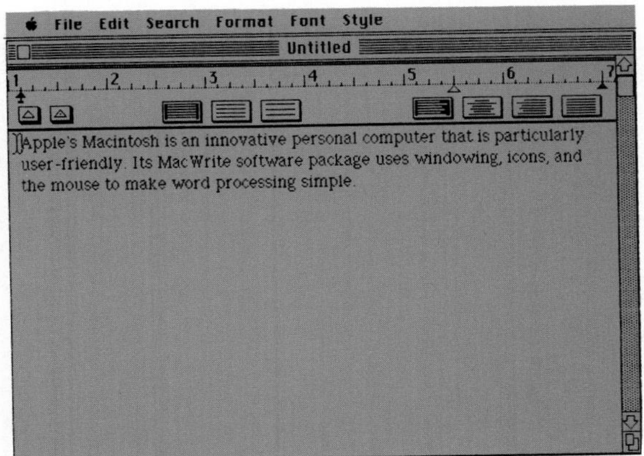

Figure 10 Clicking the mouse moves the insertion point to the location of the I-beam.

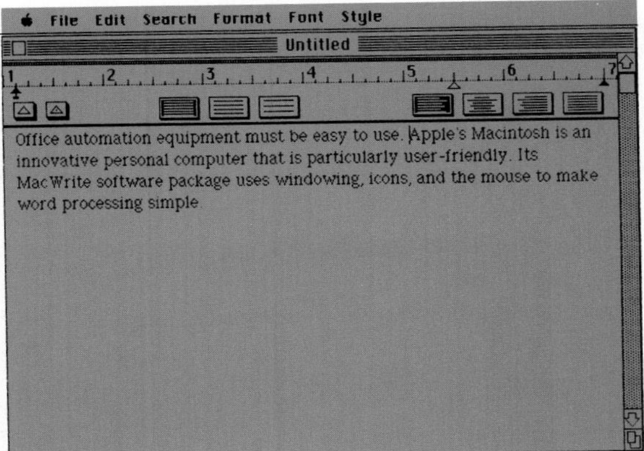

Figure 11 The Macintosh automatically moves the remainder of the paragraph to provide space for the new text.

Figure 12 Again, the Macintosh automatically moves existing text to make room for text being inserted.

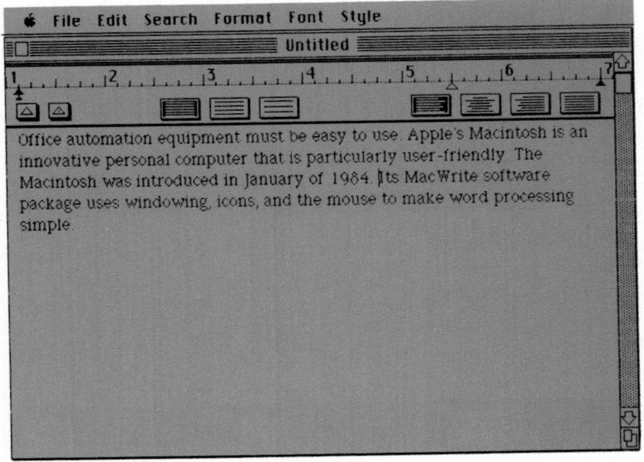

This sentence is appended to the end of the paragraph (Figure 13). Note that at any time you can undo what you have done since the last click of the mouse by selecting **Undo** from the Edit menu; the Undo itself can be undone by selecting **Redo** from the Edit menu.

Most documents, such as business letters, are generally typed single-spaced, that is, with no blank lines between text lines. But often it is desirable to insert space between lines, especially to facilitate editing. Spacing is controlled by selecting either the single-space box, the 1½-space box, or the double-space box by clicking the appropriate symbol on the **ruler** at the top of the window. Figure 14 shows the effect of selecting the 1½-space box, and Figure 15 shows the effect of selecting the double-space box. Note that the text changes almost instantaneously as these boxes are selected; this is due to the great speed of the Motorola 68000 microprocessor chip at the heart of the Macintosh.

MacWrite provides four ways to align text. Try each of these by selecting (at the right of the ruler) the left-alignment box, the center-alignment box, the right-alignment box, and then the full-justification box (Figure 16), and watch how the text changes. Notice that MacWrite does not hyphenate words when it performs full-justification, so some lines may have a considerable amount of extra space between words.

While a document is being created or edited, it can be lost if there is a power or machine failure or if the user makes a careless error. Therefore, it is wise to save the document on disk periodically. This is done by selecting **Save** from the File menu and following the instructions that appear in the Save window. (Note: At this point, save the document and name it MacWriteSample.)

After a document has been saved, the session on the Macintosh may be terminated by choosing **Quit** from the File menu. Choose **Eject** from the File menu to cause the disk to eject (pop out of the drive). To continue editing a document, reinsert the disk, select the write/paint icon, choose Open from the File menu, select the document icon for the document you wish to edit (in this case MacWriteSample), and once again choose Open from the File menu.

In the following paragraphs we explain how to

perform various editing operations. These generally require the user to select the text to be edited by dragging the pointer across it. MacWrite highlights the selected text by reversing the field, that is, displaying the text as white on black rather than black on white. The user can select anything from a single character to as much as the entire document.

The style of the selected text may be chosen from the **Style** menu (Figure 17). The Macintosh provides various text styles including Plain Text, Bold, Italic, Underline, Outline, and Shadow. These may be combined in various ways to form such interesting styles as bold italic. The size of the selected text is also chosen from the Style menu. MacWrite offers several sizes, which are measured in points, just like conventional type. These include 9-, 12-, 14-, 18-, and 24-point type. Each new MacWrite document is automatically preset to 12-Point Plain Text type.

MacWrite offers many different type fonts that may be selected from the **Font** menu (Figure 18). These include New York, Geneva, Toronto, Monaco, Chicago, Venice, London, Athens, and San Francisco. Chicago is the typeface used by the Macintosh itself in its various screen presentations. New York, a more traditional typeface, is preset in each new MacWrite document.

To continue a MacWrite session, but "wrap up" the current document, choose **Close** from the File menu. Then click the **Yes button** to save any changes.

At any time, text may be inserted at the insertion point. Blank lines may be inserted by selecting the insertion point and pressing the "Return" key an appropriate number of times.

A large block of text may be deleted by first selecting the text (Figure 19) and then choosing **Cut** from the **Edit** menu (Figure 20). The selected text disappears and the remainder of the text closes around it (Figure 21). (Note: Deletions may also be made by selecting the text and pressing the "Backspace" key once or by selecting the insertion point and pressing "Backspace" once per character to be deleted.)

To move a block of text from one point in a document to another, select the text (in this case, the first sentence) and then choose Cut from the Edit menu. The selected text is removed and

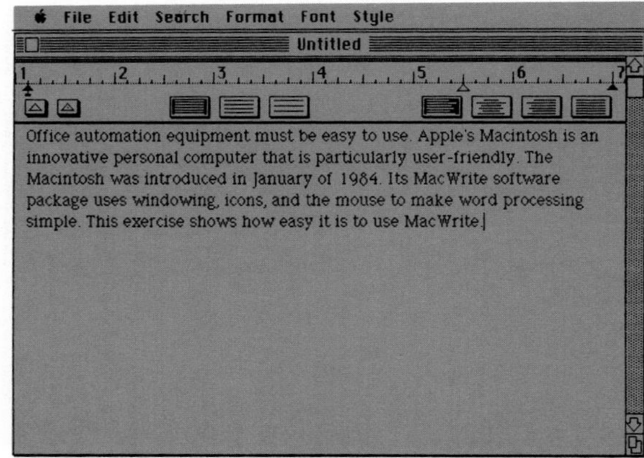

Figure 13 Appending a sentence to the end of a paragraph.

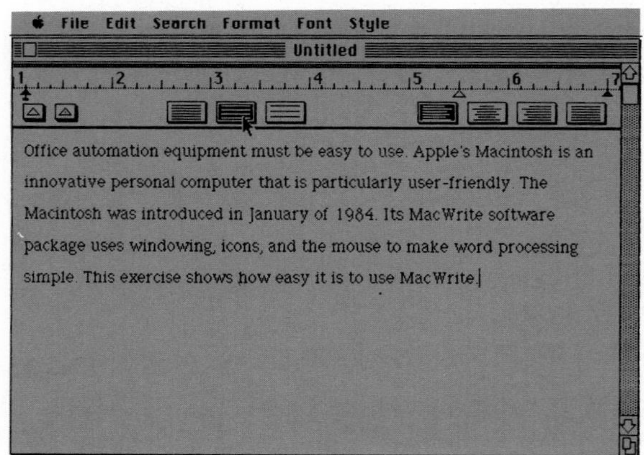

Figure 14 Selecting the 1½-space box on the ruler increases the spacing between lines of text.

Figure 15 Selecting the double-space box on the ruler inserts a full blank line between lines of text.

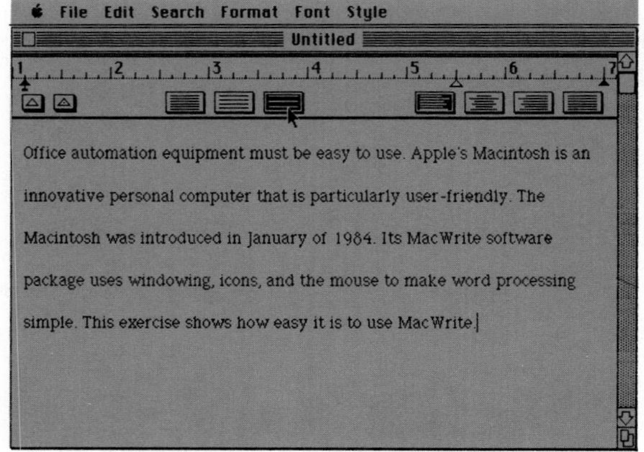

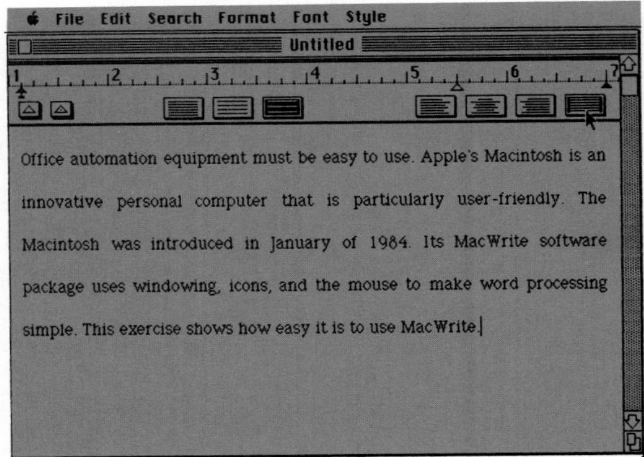

Figure 16 Selecting the full-justification box on the ruler causes the text to have even left and right margins.

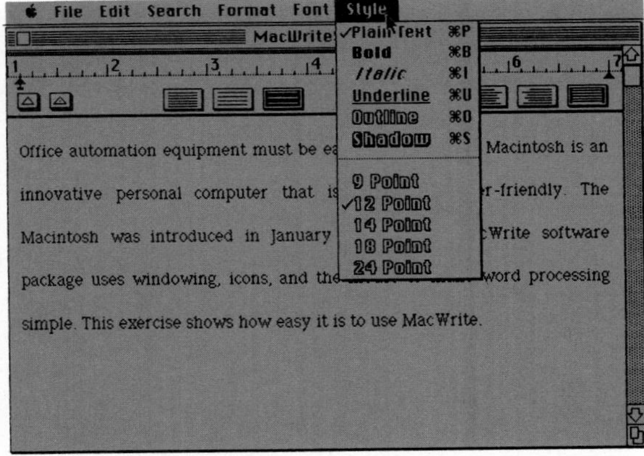

Figure 17 The style and size of type to be used on a document are selected from the Style menu.

Figure 18 The type font to be used on a document is selected from the Font menu.

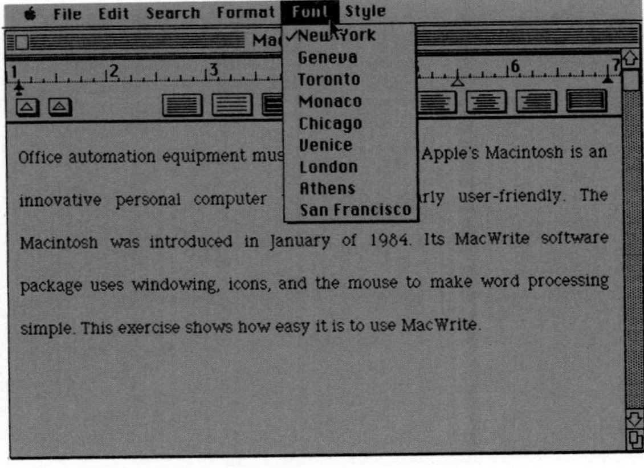

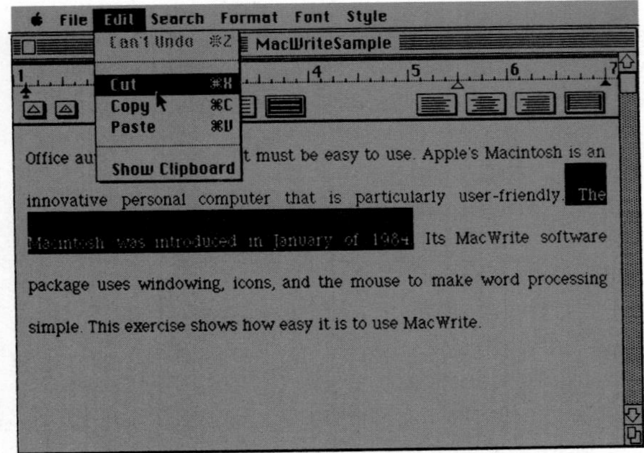

Figure 19 A block of text is selected by dragging the I-beam across it. The selected text is shown as a reversed field with light letters on dark background.

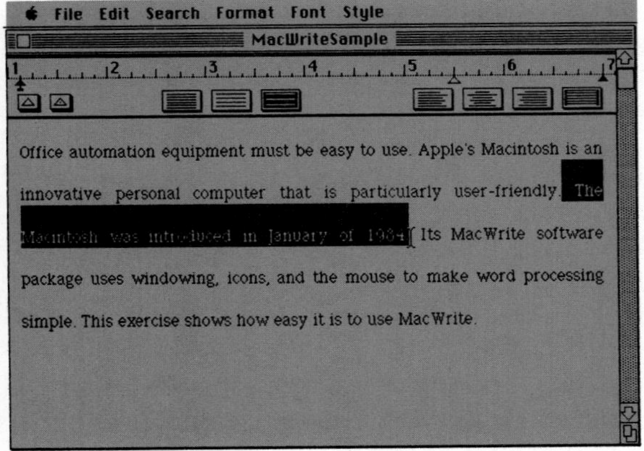

Figure 20 Choosing Cut from the Edit menu to delete selected text.

Figure 21 After choosing Cut from the Edit menu, the previously selected text disappears, and the remaining text closes around it.

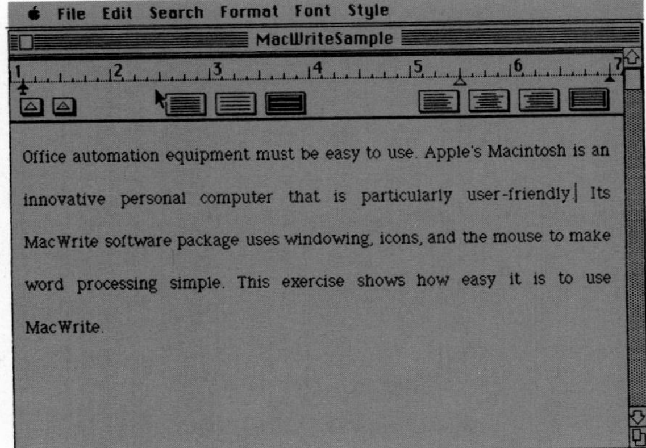

placed on the **Clipboard**, a temporary holding area. To see what is on the Clipboard at any time choose **Show Clipboard** from the Edit menu (Figure 22). Then choose **Hide Clipboard** to remove the Clipboard window from the screen. Select the point at which the text is to be inserted (in this case, at the end of the paragraph) and choose **Paste** from the Edit menu. The text from the Clipboard is moved to the insertion point (Figure 23).

To copy a block of text from one point in a document to another, select the text to be copied, choose **Copy** from the Edit menu, select the insertion point, and choose Paste from the Edit menu.

To replace a word, move the pointer to any part of the word and **double-click**, that is, press the mouse button twice quickly. Then type the replacement text. Selected text may be replaced by simply typing the new text or by pasting in the contents of the Clipboard by choosing Paste from the Edit menu.

To find text, select the insertion point where the search is to begin (in this case, the beginning of the paragraph), choose **Find** from the **Search** menu, type the characters (up to 44) to be found (in this case, "MacWrite"), and click **Find Next** (Figure 24). The Macintosh finds and selects the first occurrence of the text (Figure 25). To find subsequent occurrences of the same text, click Find Next (Figure 26). The Find window can be removed from the desktop by clicking the small square at the top left of the window, or by choosing Close from the File menu.

To find and replace text, select the insertion point where the search is to begin (in this case, the beginning of the paragraph), choose **Change** from the Search menu (Figure 27); type the characters to be replaced (in this case, "easy"); press Tab to move to the **Change To** rectangle; and type the new text (in this case, "convenient"). Click Find Next to find the first occurrence of the text. At this point there are several options (Figure 27). Click Find Next to find the next occurrence of the text; Click **Change, then Find** to change this text and find the next occurrence (this is called a **local replace**); Click **Change** to change this one occurrence of the text (this, too, is a local replace); or click **Change All** to change every occurrence of the text in the entire document (this powerful feature is called **global replace**). Clicking Change All causes a stern warning to appear because this operation is not undoable (Figure 28)—this is a fine example of how the Macintosh helps the user avoid making costly mistakes. The user responds to the warning by selecting either **Go Ahead** or **Cancel**. The Change window may be closed by choosing Close from the File menu. Now save the document with these changes by choosing **Save** from the File menu.

To print a document, choose **Print** from the File menu. A window with the various print options appears (Figure 29). **High**, **Standard**, or **Draft Quality** may be selected. The entire document may be printed by clicking **All** or a range of pages may be entered. One or more **Copies** may be

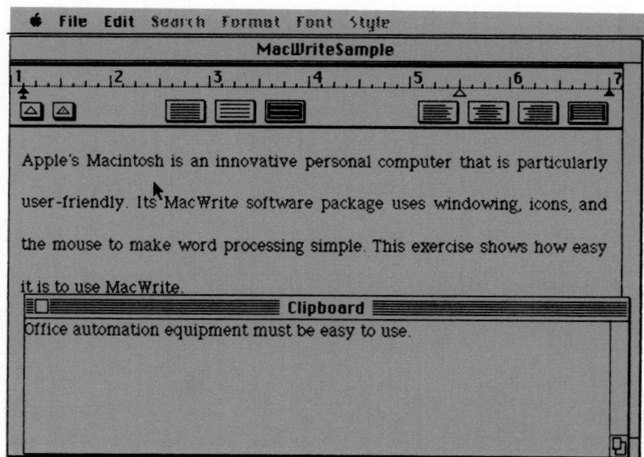

Figure 22 The contents of the Clipboard may be displayed at any time by choosing Show Clipboard from the Edit menu.

Figure 23 By choosing Paste from the Edit menu the text from the Clipboard is moved to the insertion point.

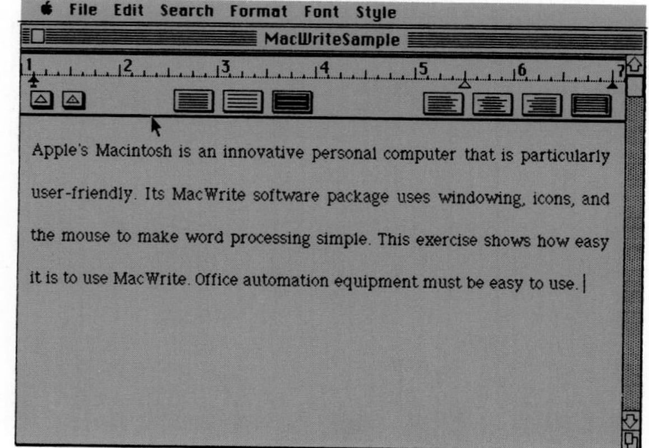

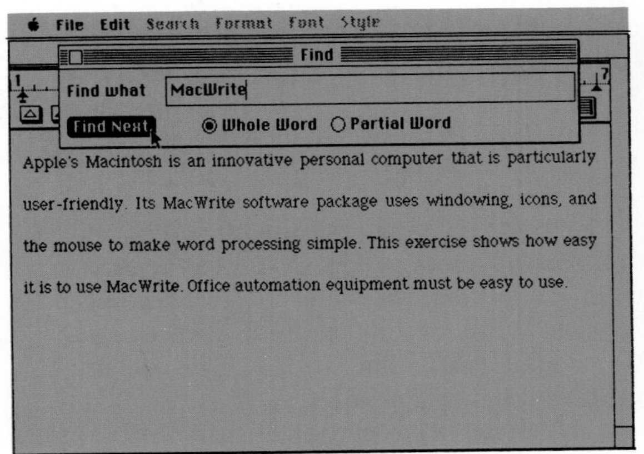

Figure 24 After typing the text to be found ("MacWrite") in the Find What box, click Find Next to find the text.

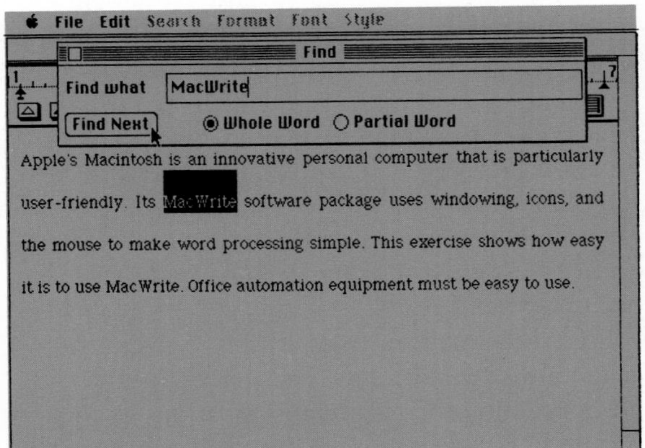

Figure 25 After Find Next is clicked, the text is found and selected.

Figure 26 After clicking Find Next again, the next occurrence of the text is found and selected.

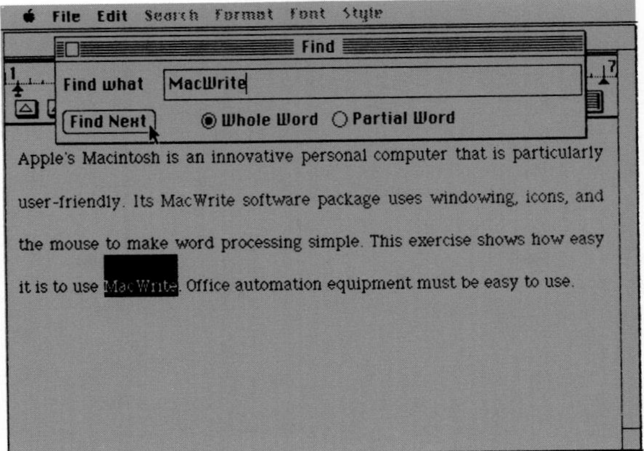

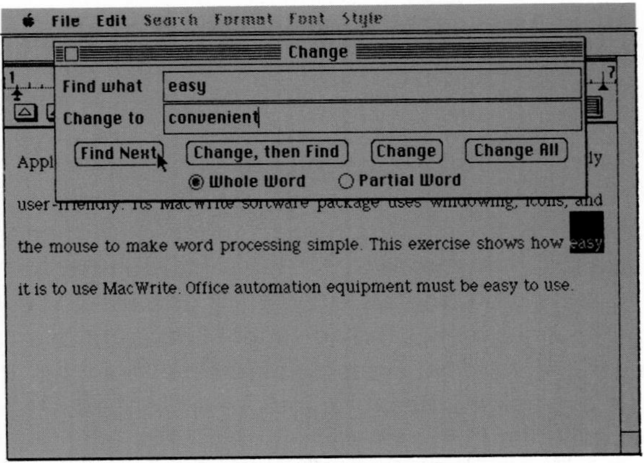

Figure 27 Choosing Change from the Search menu causes the Change window to appear.

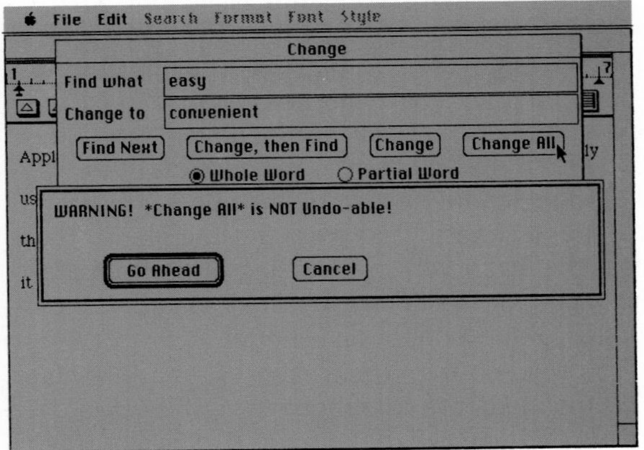

Figure 28 Clicking Change All causes a stern warning to appear because this operation is not undoable.

Figure 29 Choosing Print from the File menu causes a window with the various print options to appear.

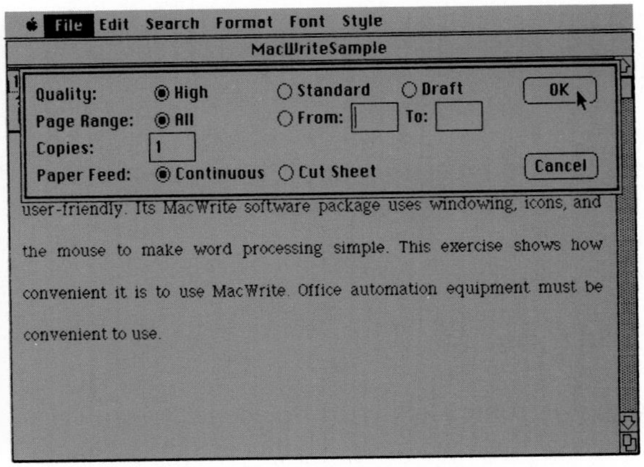

printed. And finally, the printer may use either **Continuous** form paper or **Cut Sheets**. After all of these options have been specified, the document is printed by clicking **OK**.

MacWrite displays a **scroll bar** at the right of a document window (see Figure 23). This enables the user to move a lengthy document forward or backward in the window. At the top of the scroll bar, there is a **scroll arrow** pointing upward. Clicking this once moves the document backward one line in the window. **Pressing** this arrow (pointing to it and holding down the mouse button) causes the document to scroll back continuously until the button is released. The scroll arrow at the bottom of the scroll bar is used in a similar fashion to scroll forward in the document.

MacWrite provides a feature called the **Scrapbook** in which many frequently used text selections may be stored, so that they may be used to "paste up" new MacWrite documents. To enter text into the Scrapbook, select the text, choose Copy from the Edit menu, choose **Scrapbook** from the **Apple** menu (headed by the apple-shaped icon), and choose Paste from the Edit menu. Then close the Scrapbook by choosing Close from the File menu, or by clicking the small square at the top left of the Scrapbook window.

To copy text from the Scrapbook to a MacWrite document, choose Scrapbook from the Apple menu, click the horizontal scroll arrows to display each successive text passage until the desired one is located (you may discover some interesting graphics that Apple has preloaded for your use), and then choose Copy from the Edit menu. Now activate the document window of the MacWrite document that is to receive the Scrapbook passage, select the point at which the text is to be inserted, and choose Paste from the Edit menu.

As you can see, MacWrite's use of windowing, icon graphics, pull-down menus, and mouse input makes word processing operations convenient and efficient on Apple's Macintosh personal computer.

Electronic Mail

With **electronic mail**, correspondence is sent electronically rather than by the movement of paper. The telegram was perhaps the earliest form of electronic mail. Today's electronic mail is created, edited, stored, and transmitted with computer systems. The cost of electronic mail messages has been decreasing rapidly. It may soon be more economical to send an electronic mail message than a first-class letter.

Electronic mail may be annotated with the date and time of creation. The sender can request a confirmation that the message has indeed been received. With satellite communications, electronic mail can be sent around the world as conveniently as to the next office.

Each electronic mail message is typed into the computer and then edited to correct any errors. The computer then delivers the message to the receiver's **electronic mailbox** (sometimes called an **electronic in basket**), a file on disk. A person's mailbox messages are automatically delivered when that person next uses the system.

Whenever a new correspondence arrives, the typical electronic mail system flashes a message on the user's screen. The user examines the correspondence and either answers it immediately or saves it. The receiver can make electronic notes on the message just as paper correspondence can be annotated.

Electronic mail may be sent to a select group called a **distribution list.** The sender specifies the file containing the names and locations of the people to receive the mail; the system **broadcasts**

"THE ENTIRE PACKAGE MAILING JOB IS DONE BY COMPUTER HERE—INCLUDING SEALING THE ENVELOPE"

the message to all these people. This eliminates the need to wait while a paper document is duplicated by the organization's copy center and then distributed. Some electronic mail systems feature electronic bulletin boards on which companywide messages may be posted electronically for access by any system user.

Security may be provided in several ways. Most systems require a user to supply some form of identification code and password to be able to access the mail. **Encryption** (encoding) of electronic mail messages prevents unauthorized users from reading user communications obtained by tapping a system. Only authorized system users have access to the system's **decryption** facilities for decoding encrypted messages.

Facsimile

One popular form of electronic mail is called **facsimile** transmission (Figure 14–11). Facsimile (FAX) devices are essentially long-distance copiers. A document is inserted in the sending FAX machine and optically scanned. The information is converted into electrical signals and then transmitted. At the destination, the signals are converted into their original form by another FAX machine. A hard copy duplicate of the original is provided, including text, signatures, drawings, and pictures.

Facsimile has traditionally been a relatively slow means of transmission, but high-speed communications and advances in **data compression** are pointing the way to high-speed FAX devices. One form of data compression is to avoid transmitting signals that correspond to empty areas of documents.

FAX devices with built-in microprocessors can run unattended, so correspondence can be sent overnight when phone rates are lower. FAX can be sent over high-speed computer networks much faster than over conventional telephone lines, but the costs may be greater.

Voice Mail

Voice mail is a form of electronic mail in which messages are sent as human voice rather than streams of text (Figure 14–12). Because most people prefer to talk rather than type, voice mail offers an attractive alternative to text-oriented electronic mail systems.

Figure 14–11 With this facsimile device made by Xerox Corporation, a page of information containing both text and graphics can be transmitted anywhere in the world over ordinary telephone lines in less than one minute.

Voice messages are digitized, that is, converted to 1's and 0's, and retained in computer storage for future delivery. When the called party comes in, the call is delivered as speech, exactly as the caller spoke it. Voice messages may be broadcast to many people simultaneously. The computer functions much the same as a tape recorder. It can record and play back, but it cannot understand the content of the message.

Future voice mail systems will store **voiceprints** of their users. This will enable them to verify the author of a voice message. Voiceprints are believed to be as useful as fingerprints for identifying people.

One interesting problem with voice mail systems is that electronic messages cannot relate the author's mood, and this can lead to misunderstandings. This problem may be solved by combining text and voice in electronic mail systems; important points can be made via voice and the rest conveyed as text.

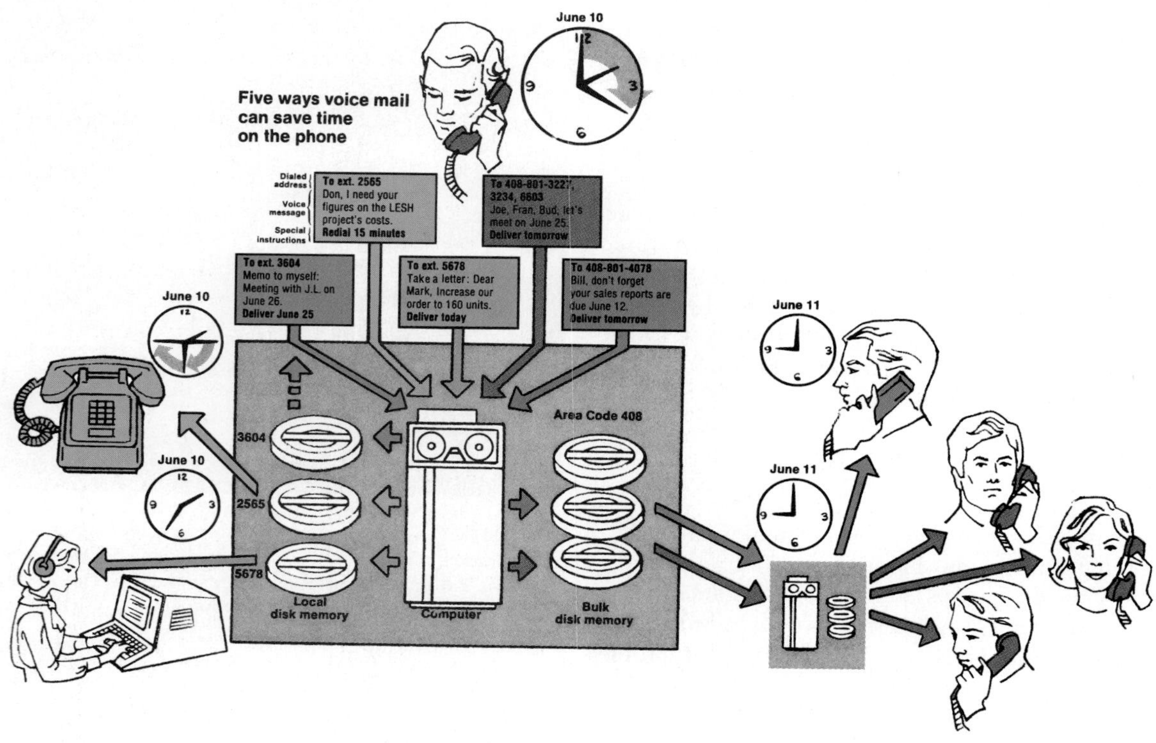

Figure 14–12 Voice mail applications.

It has been estimated that busy executives are unreachable by phone as much as two-thirds of the time, so "telephone tag," in which two people are constantly calling and returning calls but can't seem to connect, is indeed a real problem. It can be especially difficult to reach people in other countries because of time differences. Busy executives can waste considerable time on unimportant calls that they do accept. With voice mail these problems can be diminished.

Users may send voice mail **tickler messages** (reminders) to themselves. Imagine sitting at your desk. The phone rings. You pick it up and it is you calling to remind yourself to call one of your customers!

Voice mail systems may be used for dictation. An executive dictates a memo to a secretary. The secretary then plays the message back and types it. Because the dictated message is stored in a file on disk, the secretary may easily back up and replay sections as often as necessary.

Another advantage of voice mail is that the message is received exactly as it was sent, rather than as some hastily written "while you were out" slip in which the message has lost something in the translation.

A voice mail message can be edited easily if the sender wants to change it before it is transmitted. This can be a disadvantage as well because an impersonator might alter the message.

One interesting benefit of voice mail is that it can be entered during business hours but transmitted during off-hours when phone rates are considerably lower.

Eventually, computers will be able to convert the spoken word directly to stored text rather than the speech patterns used with today's voice mail systems. At that point, an executive may dictate a memo and have a computerized word processor prepare finished text. Stenographers beware!

Voice activated telephones that can respond to spoken commands are becoming popular for use with systems equipped for voice mail. They enable a person to use a telephone without having to dial numbers manually. The user may enter new names and numbers into the phone's memory by simply speaking them. Voice-activated telephones are particularly useful for handicapped or bedridden people, as well as for surgeons and others who may not be able to (or want to) interrupt their work to use the telephone.

Electronic Calendar

Each person in an automated office may maintain an **electronic calendar** containing confirmed meetings, tentative meetings, and open time slots. Someone wanting to schedule a meeting enters the desired date, time, and duration, and a list of the desired participants. An electronic scheduling system can then be used to check the personal calendars of those people to see if all are available. If they are, electronic mail messages are sent informing them of the meeting. If they are not, the system determines a more convenient time for them to get together. Scheduling systems may also be used to reserve rooms and resources such as audio-visual equipment.

Electronic calendar systems also provide convenient electronic diaries of a person's activities. Attorneys and other people who use time billing may use these systems to log the time they spend with each account. One serious concern is that these systems may violate an individual's privacy by keeping such close tabs on one's activities, especially if one person gains access to another's diary.

Teleconferencing

With the high cost of travel and with the premium being placed on the time of busy executives, business trips are often replaced by a new kind of meeting—the teleconference. **Teleconferencing** incorporates audio, video, and computer conferencing techniques (Figure 14–13).

Video teleconferencing, also called **videoconferencing**, provides much of the atmosphere of personal contact. With **continuous motion videoconferencing**, the picture is regenerated approximately 30 times per second. With **freeze-frame videoconferencing**, the conference participants

"Dial Amalgamated Industries. Ask for K. D. Campbell. Don't say who's calling, but tell him to go fly a kite. Then hang up."

Figure 14–13 A specially equipped teleconferencing room.

see what appears to be a slide show presentation with a new slide displayed every several seconds. The freeze-frame technique requires much less transmission capacity (bandwidth) and can be transmitted over conventional telephone lines, thus making it more convenient to arrange and more economical than a continuous motion videoconference.

Teleconferencing today requires expensive, specially equipped rooms. Eventually **desk-to-desk teleconferencing** may become commonplace, as AT&T and other communications companies increase transmission bandwidths and reduce costs.

Electronic Blackboard

One of the more innovative OA devices is the **electronic blackboard** (Figure 14–14). As a user writes on the blackboard with ordinary chalk, the image is digitized and transmitted by telephone to various other conference locations where it is then displayed on TV monitors. The blackboard is pressure-sensitive, so it knows where the chalk is at any time. It transmits the changing chalk positions to the receiving screens quickly enough to make it appear as if an invisible hand is writing on the displays.

OA Communications: The Computerized Branch Exchange

In Chapter 7, we presented a detailed treatment of local area networks (LANs). We compared baseband and broadband local area networks and presented a detailed case study on Ethernet, the most widely used baseband network. We talked about the trend toward broadband LANs, and explained that their wide bandwidths and multichannel capabilities will facilitate the evolution of multimedia office automation systems. In this section we will consider the evolution and capabilities of today's **computerized branch exchanges** (CBXs), devices that carry both voice and data. CBXs are sometimes referred to as private automatic branch exchanges (PABXs).

The earliest telephone systems required that each telephone in a city or large area be connected to a central telephone exchange serving that region. When the number of telephones was small, this made sense. But as organizations became more dependent on telephones, it became common to have dozens or even hundreds of phones within a company's offices in a single building. Calls from one phone to another within the organization all had to be routed through the telephone company's central exchange, possibly many miles way.

Soon companies realized that such intracompany communications could and should be controlled from within the company, thus avoiding the telephone company's charges and often busy circuits. So **private branch exchanges** (PBXs) were developed to handle these local communications.

With the advent of the microprocessor, it became possible and economical to build computerized branch exchanges (CBXs). CBXs provide many useful capabilities.

With **least cost routing**, the CBX automatically checks company tie lines, WATS lines, and other reduced rate services before finally assigning a call to the standard telephone network if all of the more economical lines are busy. With **callback queueing**, a person finding a particular line (such as a WATS line) busy is automatically called back when the line becomes available (upper-level executives may receive priority). With **call notification**, if the party being called is already talking on the phone, the CBX signals that party that someone is trying to get through. With **call forwarding**, the CBX can automatically forward

Figure 14–14 With the electronic blackboard, it is possible to transmit handwriting and hand-drawn illustrations over the telephone network for display at remote locations.

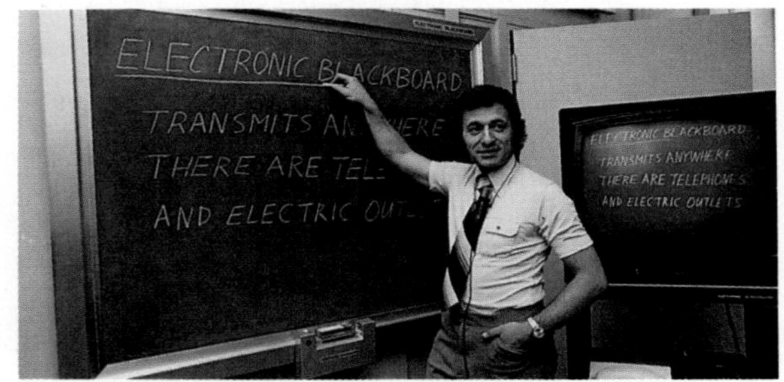

calls for someone who has moved to another number. With **station hunting**, a call to a busy extension can be automatically routed to a nearby extension. With the **conference calls** feature, calls for three or more parties can be easily arranged. With **call detail reporting**, management can keep track of all calls initiated from each extension—a feature that is helpful for billing purposes and for controlling unauthorized use of telephones. With **automatic callback**, the CBX rings a caller back when a busy party hangs up.

All these CBX features are easy to provide once computer control is built into a telephone system. But these systems are still primarily voice oriented. The newer CBXs can handle both voice and computer data.

These systems transmit information in digitized form, and so they are especially appropriate for controlling communications in the automated office. Many communications experts believe that the computerized branch exchange has a bright future in the OA marketplace. IBM has made a considerable investment in Rolm, one of the largest manufacturers of such devices.

But CBXs must evolve into far more powerful systems before they will be able to handle the bulk of OA communications. Most of today's systems operate at maximum speeds of 9600 bps, or 19,200 bps. Only a few CBXs operate at speeds as great as 1 million bps; these systems are almost indistinguishable from LANs. Today's baseband LANs operate at speeds as great as 10 million bps or more, and today's broadband LANs have yet far greater capacity spread across many channels. Besides offering only modest transmission rates, CBXs have the disadvantage of **centralized control** because of their star topology—if the CBX fails, the entire communications system fails. Most LANs, on the other hand, use **distributed control**—if one device fails, the remainder of the network continues functioning.

In the near term, companies may find it best to use both CBXs and LANs—CBXs to handle voice communications and LANs to handle higher-speed data transmission. These fundamentally different kinds of networks may be interconnected by devices called **gateways**, but the resulting hybrid networks can operate only as fast as their slowest components.

Over the longer term, economical broadband systems will become popular. These systems will provide dozens of wide bandwidth channels and permit simultaneous transmission of numbers, text, voice, graphics, and video, and, in fact, many channels of each. In the view of many industry experts, the broadband LAN will soon become the premier OA communications medium, especially for larger companies.

Computerized Typesetting

Organizations that want to prepare more professional-looking documentation may connect their word processors to computerized typesetting equipment (Figure 14–15), or they may transmit text to various typesetting companies. Typesetting is especially effective for proposals, product notices, newsletters, and certain management reports.

In the past, a major part of the high cost of typesetting was the retyping of information. But today's systems have computerized interfaces that enable them to receive computer data on floppy disks or over communications lines, thus eliminating the need to key in the data manually. One advantage of eliminating manual keying is that the data is captured exactly as it was typed; this eliminates many errors.

The typesetting process is not quite as simple as it sounds. Many special **control codes** must be incorporated into the text. These tell the typesetting machine what size, style, and font of text to use; how far to space between paragraphs; how

Figure 14–15 A computerized typesetting system.

far to indent; and the like. Some offices have skilled personnel insert these codes; others rely on the typesetting companies to perform this operation.

Computerized typesetting systems (also called **photocomposition systems**), generally operate as follows: Character images are generated on a high-resolution CRT; the CRT image is then photographed to produce the film containing the typeset material.

Archival Storage

Keeping large amounts of information on-line can be extremely costly. It is worthwhile only if that information must be readily accessible. But only a small portion of an organization's information is ever this active. Office automation systems provide **archival storage** for older and less active documents. Businesses, for example, must retain certain types of records for many years to satisfy various government requirements. Computer output microfilm (see Chapter 5) is popular for archival storage of information that will not need to be read back into a computer; computer tape is normally used for information that may eventually require further computer processing.

Obstacles to the Growth of Office Automation

Several factors tend to hold back the growth of office automation. Managers are reluctant to invest too much money in automation because it is difficult to estimate precisely what the savings will be. Managers familiar with the rapid pace of technological change in recent years may be wary of spending money for equipment that could rapidly become obsolete. Some people fear that they will lose their jobs; others fear an invasion of their turf. Managers are reluctant to do anything that might disrupt their smooth-running operations.

One of the problems facing office automation is getting executives to use the equipment. Many managers refuse to type even the shortest message (sometimes because of poor typing skills). This tends to slow information flow because messages must first be dictated or handwritten before they can be entered into the system.

Trends in Office Automation

We can expect tremendous innovation in office automation systems over the next several years. In the area of text processing, spelling checkers will go a step further than today's systems; they will suggest how to correct misspelled words,

"Hi. Me, master. You, tool."

check grammar, and in some cases even rewrite the document (see the boxed piece below).

OCR devices that scan handwritten text and convert it to computerized text will become more common. Omnifont OCR systems (see Chapter 4) will be able to read almost any type style at much higher speeds than today's relatively slow devices. Speech recognition units that can convert voice to text reliably will become extremely popular, and speech synthesis will become an essential capability in user-friendly interfaces.

"It says, 'Three percent split infinitives, 8 percent passive verbs, 16 percent compound-complex sentences, average sentence length 26 words, paperback rights $3.2 million, movie sales $8.3 million, total take $11.5 million, less 15 percent agent's fees.'"

Rewriting Lincoln's Gettysburg Address

At Bell Laboratories, language experts and computer experts cooperated in the development of the Writer's Workbench, a series of computer programs that analyze, criticize, and suggest how to improve written material. Here we show Lincoln's Gettysburg Address both before and after processing by the Writer's Workbench. Which do you prefer?

Fourscore and seven years ago our fathers brought forth on this continent, a new nation, conceived in Liberty, and dedicated to the proposition that all men are created equal.

Now we are engaged in a great civil war, testing whether that nation or any nation so conceived and so dedicated can long endure. We are met on a great battlefield of that war. We have come to dedicate a portion of that field, as a final resting place for those who here gave their lives that that nation might live. It is altogether fitting and proper that we should do this.

But, in a larger sense, we cannot dedicate—we cannot consecrate—we cannot hallow—this ground. The brave men, living and dead, who struggled here, have consecrated it far above our poor power to add or detract. The world will little note nor long remember what we say here, but it can never forget what they did here. It is for us, the living, rather to be dedicated here to the unfinished work which they who fought here have thus far so nobly advanced. It is rather for us to be here dedicated to the great task remaining before us—that from these honored dead we take increased devotion to that cause for which they gave the last full measure of devotion; that we here highly resolve that these dead shall not have died in vain; that this nation, under God, shall have a new birth of freedom; and that government of the people, by the people, for the people, shall not perish from the earth.

Workbench Analysis

Readability (years of education required): 10.8
Average sentence length: 26.7 words
Your average is very high. A good average would be 15 to 20 words.
Sentence types: simple, 10 percent; complex, 40 percent. Your document contains many more complex sentences than is common for this type of text. One way to improve this text would be to rephrase the most important ideas in simple sentences.
Passive verb phrases: 13 percent

Revised Version

Eighty-seven years ago, our grandfathers created a free nation here. They based it on the idea that everybody is created equal. We are now fighting a civil war to see if this or any similar nation can survive. On this battlefield we are dedicating a cemetery to those who died for their country. It is only right. But in another sense, the task is impossible, because brave men, living and dead, dedicated this place better than we can.

Hardly anyone will notice or remember what we say here, but nobody can forget what those men did. We should continue the work they began, and make sure they did not die in vain. With God's help, we will have freedom again, so that the people's government will endure.

Voice and video will be integrated with text and image-processing capabilities to create systems capable of storing, manipulating, and modifying color motion pictures with sound. Eventually, laser technology will make possible the integration of three-dimensional color motion pictures with sound. Digital photography, in which pictures of objects will be stored on magnetic media rather than on film, will experience rapid growth, and word processors will easily integrate these pictures with text. OA equipment will be able to integrate digital photographs with text and computer-generated graphics.

Highly portable computers and text processors will become more common; these let executives type or dictate while traveling, and then transmit this information over communications networks (Figure 14–16).

Figure 14–16 With this PCX™ terminal developed by Motorola, the electronic office can be carried in a pocket. The system uses two-way digital radio rather than phone lines, so it can communicate from locations in which telephones are not available.

Graphics capabilities will continue to improve. Full color books, catalogs, and newsletters will be developed on-line in offices. Color CRTs and color printers will become more popular. The ready access to information from OA stations will greatly reduce the need for hard copy reports.

Software will increasingly emphasize user interfaces that allow users to specify *what* capabilities they want, instead of having users write programs specifying *how* to implement those capabilities.

There will be much competition between the CBX-based approach and the local area networking approach to controlling OA communications. The CBX approach may become more successful because most existing buildings are already wired for the appropriate connections; local area networking normally requires that an existing building be rewired. In new buildings, local area networks may be more common.

"Miss Farber, would you please tell me what this piece of paper is doing on my desk?"

Summary 

1. Office automation is the combination of computing and communications techniques to automate information processing in offices.
2. Two important goals of office automation systems are the substantial reduction of paper usage and the ability to transact most of an individual's work from that person's own workstation.
3. One key to the success of OA is integration, that is, all the pieces of OA equipment must be able to intercommunicate and store their data in similar formats.
4. Word processors are computer-based systems that facilitate the manipulation of text. Word processing has been the leading technology in office automation systems.
5. Some popular features available on word processors are word wraparound, horizontal and vertical scrolling, cut and paste, local replace, global replace, right-justification, automatic page numbering, page headings and footings, prestored phrases, list processing, spelling checking, automatic hyphenation, and multilingual dictionaries.
6. Electronic mail systems send correspondence with both text and pictures electronically over communications networks.
7. Computers route electronic mail messages to the intended receivers. These messages are then delivered or stored in electronic mailboxes until the receiver next uses the system.
8. FAX (facsimile) machines operate essentially as long-distance copiers. They supply hard copy duplicates of original documents.
9. Encryption of electronic mail messages prevents unauthorized users from reading user communications obtained by tapping a system.
10. Voice mail digitizes human voice messages so they may be stored in and transmitted by computers. Computerized speech synthesis is used to speak the message to the intended receiver.
11. Teleconferencing reduces the need for expensive travel. Specially equipped rooms provide conference participants with video displays and communications links.
12. An electronic blackboard sends text or drawings over low capacity telephone lines and displays them.
13. Some functions available with computerized branch exchanges are least cost routing, call-back queueing, call notification, call forwarding, conference calls, and station hunting.
14. Some of the obstacles to the growth of office automation are the general reluctance of managers to adopt new technologies, fear of obsolescence, and the fact that managers are generally poor typists.
15. Some of the key trends in office automation are the development of text processors that check grammar and style and suggest how to improve writing, an increase in the use of speech recognition and synthesis, integration of voice and video with text and image processing, and the widespread use of CBXs and local area networks in controlling OA communications.

Important Terms 

archival storage
automatic callback
broadcast
callback queueing
call forwarding
call notification
computerized branch exchange (CBX)
cut and paste
electronic calendar
electronic dictionary
electronic mail
electronic mailbox
facsimile (FAX)
global replace
least cost routing
list processing
local replace
office automation (OA)
paperless office
shared-logic system
shared-resources system
stand-alone system
teleconferencing
tickler message
"UNDO" key
videoconferencing
voice mail
word processing
word wraparound
workstation

Self-Review Exercises 

Matching

Next to the term in column A, place the letter of the statement in column B that best describes it.

Column A	Column B
1. Word processing	A. Utilizes pressure-sensing
2. Teleconferencing	B. Moves word down to next line
3. Tickler message	C. Rapid entry of typewritten copy
4. CBX	D. Changes all occurrences of a phrase
5. Word wraparound	E. Long-distance copier
6. Freeze frame	F. Alternative to local area networking
7. Electronic blackboard	G. Leading technology in office automation
8. OCR page reader	H. Less bandwidth than continuous motion
9. Global replace	I. Reduces need for business travel
10. Facsimile device	J. A reminder

Fill-in-the-Blanks

Fill in the blanks in each of the following:

1. The earliest form of ______ was the telegram.

2. Unlike local area networking with its ______ control, a CBX provides ______ control.

3. The CBX feature called ______ determines the most economical path for a call.

4. An important component of a user-friendly interface is the ______ key that allows the user to unwind the effects of an operation.

5. Multimedia office automation systems integrate the processing of numbers, text, graphics, voice, and ______.

6. One key to the success of OA is ______, that is, all the pieces of OA equipment must work together.

7. A popular feature of OA stations is to split the screen into several areas called ______.

8. The ______ feature in a word processor changes only the first occurrence of a phrase.

9. The technology of ______ can reduce the problem of "telephone tag."

10. Electronic mail and voice mail systems make it easy to ______ messages, that is, to send them to many people simultaneously.

Answers to Self-Review Exercises

Matching: 1 G, 2 I, 3 J, 4 F, 5 B, 6 H, 7 A, 8 C, 9 D, 10 E

Fill-in-the-Blanks:

1. electronic mail
2. distributed, centralized
3. least cost routing
4. "UNDO"
5. video images
6. integration
7. windows
8. local replace
9. voice mail
10. broadcast

Discussion Questions 

1. What is office automation? What trends may enable office automation to become the largest segment of the computer industry by 1990?

2. List some of the features commonly used in office automation systems to make them more user-friendly.

3. What is word processing? Why is it popular in office automation systems?

4. List some capabilities of word processing systems.

5. How do you suppose current trends in computing and communications will affect the popularity of facsimile systems?

6. Explain how voice mail operates.

7. List some of the pros and cons of teleconferencing as compared to face-to-face meetings.

8. What are some of the factors holding back the growth of office automation?

9. List several of the capabilities commonly provided by CBX systems.

10. Some OA vendors have set as their goal the creation of the paperless office. Discuss the pros and cons of completely eliminating the use of paper.

Projects 

1. Write to several major computer vendors and request general information about their office automation systems. Write a report comparing these systems.

2. Request and summarize literature about the following electronic mail services

EasyLink INSTANT MAIL
c/o Western Union
P.O. Box 37472
Department 138
Omaha, NE 68137
(800) 445-4444

MCI Mail
Box 1001
1900 M Street, N.W.
Washington, DC 20036

"Here's the story, gentlemen. Sometime last night, an eleven-year-old kid in Akron, Ohio, got into our computer and transferred all our assets to a bank in Zurich."

Chapter 15

Electronic Funds Transfer Systems, Security, Privacy, and Computer Crime

After reading this chapter you will understand:

1. What electronic funds transfer (EFT) is and how it works
2. The differences between credit cards and debit cards
3. Security and privacy issues surrounding the use of computers
4. The laws and regulations governing EFT, security, and privacy
5. The various types of computer crime and how they can be prevented

Outline

The 1980's will bring a strange, increasingly cashless society that might have baffled earlier generations with its many options and its technology. But Americans who grew up with computer programming courses in school, computer terminals at work and video games at home should take on electronic banking and all its convenience with ease and confidence.

Michael D'Antonio,
Here Comes the Cashless Society

The good news: Computer security systems will be better than ever.
The bad news: Computer criminals will also be better than ever.

Donn Parker,
Computer Security Expert

It has been estimated that in the United States alone more than 40 billion checks are written annually against 100 million checking accounts in almost 15,000 banks. The age of "electronic money," which began in the 1960s, may eventually eliminate this time-honored way of paying for goods and services.

Electronic money refers to **electronic funds transfer** (EFT), the process by which money is transferred electronically by computers and data communications systems from one account to another without the use of written checks. We use plastic cards to gain access to electronic banking machines, payment systems, traveler's check dispensers, cash dispensers, and credit verification systems. Use of cash and checks has been reduced considerably. It is becoming more and more common for employers' computers to deposit salaries directly into employees' bank accounts, so workers do not have to wait for checks to clear. It is also becoming routine for bills to be paid by telephone and for **preauthorized computer-initiated payments** to cover regular installment loans.

In the late 1960s many bankers spoke of the coming of the **cashless/checkless society** in which all financial transactions would be made electronically. Today's view has been tempered somewhat—we now speak of the **less cash/less check society.** In any case, within just a few years we will be doing most of our banking electronically, so it is important to understand the evolution and operation of electronic funds transfer, a modern convenience made possible by the computer and communications technologies. The EFT computer networks are already carrying half a trillion dollars of funds transfers per day between banks.

Direct Deposit

One of the earliest forms of EFT was **direct deposit** of payroll involving a single company and a single bank. Previously, employees deposited their paychecks and then had to wait until the checks cleared—often several days—before they could use their money. With direct deposit, on payday banks can now transfer the funds by computer from an employer's account directly to an employee's account. This advance has made possible the elimination of the paper, labor, postage, and delays associated with producing and cashing paychecks. The savings to the banks are substantial, and employees appreciate the convenience of

having their money available immediately. Electronic fund transfers between banks are handled through a series of computer centers called **automated clearing houses** run by the Federal Reserve Board.

Direct deposit has been widely adopted by banks and businesses throughout the country. Its effectiveness has been critical to the evolution and acceptance of other forms of EFT.

The Social Security Administration prints about 30 million checks a month and has strongly encouraged participation in direct deposit programs. The result has been a sharp reduction in lost or stolen checks. Direct deposit is an important convenience to many elderly and disabled recipients who have difficulty getting to a bank to deposit their checks.

Figure 15–1 By using an on-line teller terminal, this bank teller can check the customer's balance instantly with the bank's central computer system.

On-Line Teller Terminals

Banks were already heavily computerized in the 1950s and 1960s, but the transactions that occurred at teller stations were not entered into the computers until after the close of the business day. Tellers used accounting machines to make entries in savings passbooks and to record on paper various other types of transactions. Today, most banks use **on-line teller terminals** (Figure 15–1) so that information can be entered directly into their computers. Data entry costs have been reduced and customer services have improved. Computers allow instant access to customer accounts. This speeds the process of verifying balances before allowing cash withdrawals or other transactions.

Figure 15–2 Computerized automated teller machines (ATMs) like this one handle routine banking transactions automatically 24 hours per day.

Automated Teller Machines

Banks used to be open to the public for only a portion of the business day. The other working hours were needed to record the transactions made that day. With the use of the now-common **automated teller machines** (ATMs), banks can offer many teller services around the clock (Figure 15–2).

An ATM is a computerized device for handling routine teller transactions automatically, without a teller. ATMs can handle deposits, withdrawals, and even installment loan payments. Today's ATMs are on-line to the bank's computers so that the funds are transferred immediately.

To operate an ATM, a client needs an identification card, a *personal identification number* (PIN) known only to the client and the bank, and an account at the bank. Insertion of the card gains access to the machine, which then asks for the PIN before proceeding. Upon correctly entering the PIN, business may be transacted in much the same manner as with a human teller. The ATM guides the client through the sequence of steps for each transaction (Figure 15–3). If a mistake is made, pressing a key notifies the computer, which begins the transaction again. ATMs have become popular because people like having ready access to their funds.

ATMs have a number of advantages:

1. ATMs can be installed in supermarkets, shopping malls, and even apartment complexes for the convenience of customers. In this way, ATMs bring banking to the customer rather than forcing the customer to come to the bank.
2. Banks can now be "open" 24 hours a day, seven days a week. (Many banks have actually cut back their office hours after installing ATMs.)
3. It is too costly for banks to keep building new branches. ATMs provide many of the benefits of new branches without most of the associated costs.
4. In the case of a robbery, bank employees are not endangered.

ATMs are not without disadvantages, however:

1. They cost tens of thousands of dollars per machine.
2. They malfunction occasionally, which can cause customer irritation.
3. Some people have been robbed at the machines after withdrawing cash. This makes customers nervous about using ATMs during off hours or at remote locations.
4. Customers need to be educated in the use of the machines. This can be costly and time-consuming for the banks (Figure 15–4).
5. Correcting an error can be difficult. For example, what happens when the customer requests a cash withdrawal and the machine confirms the transaction on paper but does not actually dispense the cash? When the customer comes rampaging into the bank, should the bank personnel believe the customer's story? Will it be a case of "It's your word against our machine's"?
6. ATMs have occasionally gone haywire and dispensed huge amounts of cash to unsuspecting customers. What if a customer keeps the money? Who is liable?
7. ATMs have become the targets of vandalism.

Figure 15–3 *Below:* This Citibank automated teller machine politely guides the customer through the steps for each banking transaction.

Figure 15–4 *Bottom:* A costumed character representing an automated teller machine tells classroom youngsters how to manage money. This public service program of the First Interstate Bancorp was the first of its kind in the nation.

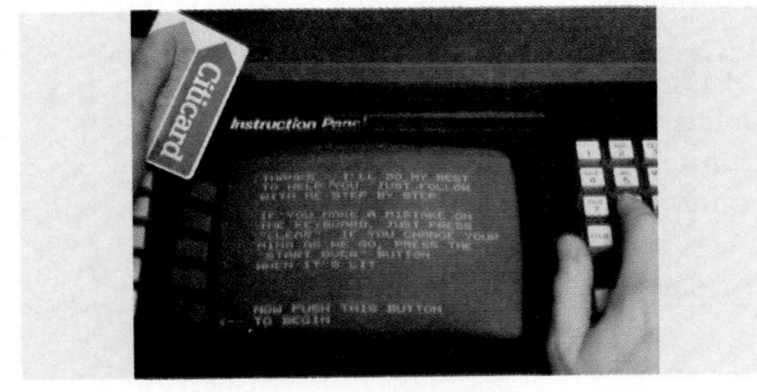

HUMAN TELLERS MAY SOON COST CUSTOMERS EXTRA.

ATMs have been well received by the general public, and their use is growing rapidly. Because ATM transactions are more economical for the banks than teller transactions, some banks have considered the possibility of charging fees for teller transactions. This has not been popular. Apparently, the public is willing to live with some problems (but not others) in exchange for the convenience the machines provide.

The success of ATMs has spurred the use of automatic machines that issue traveler's checks, dispense gasoline, prepare airline tickets, accept rental car returns, and register hotel guests. The government is even considering using automated devices to replace the use of food stamps.

Using ATMs

ATMs are easy to use. To be most effective, users should develop good record-keeping habits and beware of certain pitfalls.

1. Do not reveal your PIN to anyone.
2. Don't write your PIN on your identification card. In fact, if your bank does not assign one, choose a PIN that you will never have to write down. But do not pick something obvious like your birth date or phone number. These precautions will greatly reduce anyone's chance of gaining access to your code.
3. Insist on privacy whenever you use your card.
4. Various government rules and regulations may hold you liable for losses on your account as follows:
   (a) If you notify the bank within two business days, you may be liable for up to $50 of any losses against the account.
   (b) If you notify the bank within 60 business days, you may be liable for up to $500 against the account.
   (c) If you notify the bank after 60 business days, your liability may be unlimited.
5. Check the paper receipt dispensed by the ATM immediately to be sure all the information is correct. Save these copies for your records.
6. If you make a mistake that cannot be corrected at the machine, use the customer service phone that is normally available at the ATM. If there is no phone, report the problem to the bank as soon as possible. Do the same if you believe the machine made an error.
7. Enter each EFT transaction into your checkbook immediately so that you can maintain an accurate record of your account.
8. When your bank statement arrives, be sure to check it promptly and report any errors to the bank immediately.

Credit Authorization Terminals

When a client wants to pay for something with a personal check, how does the merchant know that the check is good? Or if a client uses a credit card, how does the merchant know if the card was stolen or revoked? **Credit authorization terminals** help merchants answer these questions.

A credit authorization terminal is normally

The United Press International carried an interesting story on February 18, 1982. A frustrated customer assaulted an automatic bank teller machine when the machine refused to give him money out of his account. The customer got angry and tossed a beer bottle at the machine's screen. The machine remained calm and took a clear picture of its assailant, allowing the police to make the positive identification needed to arrest the customer.

connected via the telephone network to a computer system that maintains current information on credit card holders and check cashers. At the time of sale, a store clerk runs the credit card through a channel on the terminal. The identification code is read automatically from the magnetic strip on the card and is transmitted to the central computer. The computer checks that the card has not been reported stolen or revoked and that the customer's credit is good. It then flashes the required approval code back to the terminal, and the sale is completed.

Use of credit authorization terminals has greatly reduced purchases made with stolen credit cards, but reporting a lost card is still the cardholder's responsibility.

The Debit Card and The Credit Card

The use of credit cards (or plastic money) has become so widespread that it is not unusual for someone to have a Mastercard, a VISA card, several gasoline company cards as well as numerous store cards.

When a client uses a credit card, that client is essentially borrowing money to pay for the item being purchased—the merchant is paid with this borrowed money, and the client repays the money to the credit card company according to certain agreed-upon terms.

With EFT usage increasing, a new kind of card has come into use, namely the **debit card**. When a client uses a debit card to buy something, the funds are transferred over the EFT networks from the client's bank account to the store's account immediately. Thus, a debit card can be used like cash to pay for items directly. No money is borrowed, and no money has to be repaid. No monthly bill is sent by the bank, but consumers do receive a statement of purchases and returns.

As debit cards become more widely used, it is possible that they may eventually eliminate the usefulness of traveler's checks. Companies like American Express are considering this carefully.

The *Guinness Book of World Records*, by Norris McWhirter, states that one person (known as "Mr. Plastic Fantastic") has the largest collection of valid credit cards—1098. He keeps them in the world's longest wallet, 250 feet long, weighing 34 pounds. Together the cards are worth more than $1,250,000 in credit.

Pay-by-Phone

Many banks offer **pay-by-phone** services for customers with touch-tone phones. The customer dials a toll-free number to connect to the bank's computers, enters the PIN, and types codes to indicate which bills should be paid. The funds may be transferred immediately to creditors' accounts, or there may be a delay period to allow enough time for an **electronic stop-payment order**.

Pay-by-phone services are growing rapidly but are limited by the telephone keyboard and the lack of a visual display. For customers with personal computers, many banks offer **bank-at-home** services that are more elaborate than pay-by-phone provides.

Home banking eliminates waiting in long lines and gives clients complete access to their up-to-the-minute financial records. One benefit of home banking is that people are able to do a better job with financial planning and home budgeting. Banks are providing many valuable services to bank-at-home customers. Those include programs for keeping tax records, preparing tax returns, and managing investments. Because of the variety of these services, some people believe that the banks may become key videotex marketers.

Point-of-Sale Terminals and Transactions

Point-of-sale (POS) terminals facilitate retail transactions in stores, supermarkets, and other places of business (Figure 15–5).

In the earliest point-of-sale applications, operators keyed in lengthy product codes, customer

charge card numbers, and other information. This was time-consuming and susceptible to error because of all the typing involved.

Today's systems use magnetic strip readers to determine customer identification numbers and, as we saw in Chapter 4, Universal Product Code scanners to read product codes off the items purchased. These systems speed the check-out process, thereby eliminating the customer irritation that made the slower POS systems unacceptable.

In early manual check-out systems, the customer watched as a clerk rapidly typed prices with one hand while reaching for items with the other—errors were common. With today's computerized check-out systems, a screen displays the name and price of each item for the customer as it is scanned by the terminal. In addition, the customer receives a detailed printout itemizing the goods purchased. Special price arrangements such as "2 for 49 cents" or "3 for $1" are handled automatically.

Some "high-tech" supermarkets already operate as follows: The customer enters the supermarket and places an EFT identification card in a terminal that displays the customer's current credit limit. Customers are, therefore, warned if their credit is bad or inadequate for the anticipated purchases, and thus they are spared the embarrassment of being denied credit at the check-out counter. The customer then shops for the desired items. At the check-out counter, the customer's EFT card is placed into the POS terminal. Each item is then automatically passed by a UPC scanner. As the items are scanned, a detailed listing is printed including the total amount of the sale. At this point, the customer enters the PIN to authorize immediate transfer of funds from the customer's bank account to the store's account. This done, the sale is completed.

Figure 15–5 This point-of-sale terminal is essentially a computer terminal sitting on top of a cash drawer. Instructions to the operator are displayed on the CRT. A built-in printer provides detailed receipts for the customer.

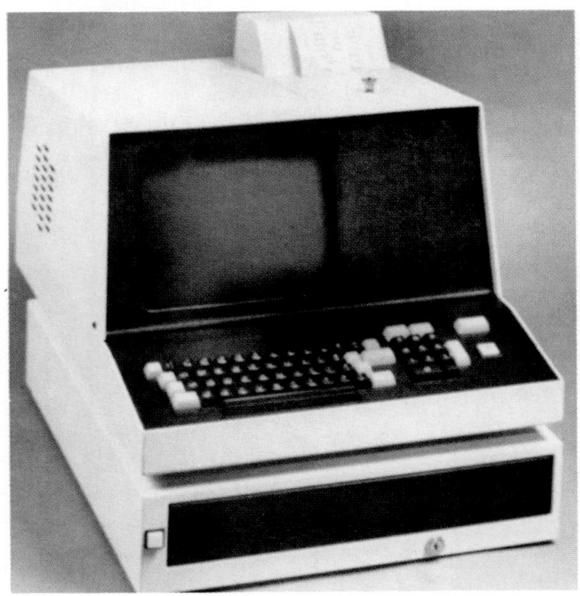

"When I was a kid, my lemonade stand didn't have a point-of-sale terminal."

Privacy and Social Issues in EFT

EFT raises a number of serious concerns about the privacy rights of individuals and about the social effects on our way of life.

Someone with access to EFT records could trace another person's spending habits and movements—surely an invasion of privacy.

Suppose merchants could get detailed credit information about individuals. It would then be possible for merchants to direct selling campaigns to wealthier people. Criminals, on the other hand, might use the information to locate people worth robbing.

How about when goods or services do not live up to expectations? Should electronic stop-payment orders be allowed to recapture electronically transferred funds? Perhaps EFT transfers should have a built-in three-day delay.

How much EFT information should the Internal Revenue Service, or any other government agency for that matter, be allowed to access? Clearly, the IRS would be delighted to have ready access to the EFT networks.

What about preauthorized computer-initiated payments such as installment loans? Suppose you agree with a bank that a car payment may be deducted electronically from your account on the same day of each month for the next 48 months. But suppose you decide to delay a given payment. How might you stop or delay a preauthorized payment?

How about credit-reporting functions? Should credit agencies be allowed to monitor the financial transactions carried by the EFT computer networks? Perhaps people should have the right to specify whether credit information about them may be given to the credit agencies.

Should government agencies be allowed to use EFT information to determine if people are complying with certain government rules? For example, some people advocate that the purchases of welfare recipients should be monitored and perhaps limited to basic necessities; others consider this an intolerable invasion of privacy.

'I Fear That If I Find the Computer Company Guilty, None of Us Will Ever Get Credit Again!'

When a court judgment is awarded, should the courts have the power to effect immediate transfer of financial settlements through the EFT computer networks, or should people and companies still have the right to decide when they will, in fact, make the payments?

Should the government or anyone else be allowed to obtain statistical information from the EFT networks—information not about individuals but rather summaries and averages? For example, it might be possible to obtain valuable information that might help control inflation or minimize the chance of a recession. One potential problem here is that people might be able to compare various summaries to infer information about individuals.

How about businesses having access to EFT information? Information about purchases could help businesses determine buying trends and help them schedule their production more efficiently. Suppose businesses are willing to pay for this information. We might actually be able to have sponsors for the EFT networks just as we have for the television networks. Should this be allowed?

With improved transportation and communications, international transactions are growing rapidly. Whose responsibility will it be to clear and guarantee international transactions, especially those involving unstable governments?

These are only a few of the many hard questions that need to be answered. Individuals, businesses, and governments must think carefully about the way they conduct their financial transactions in an increasingly EFT-based society.

EFT Legislation and Regulation

Banking is one of the most heavily regulated industries in the United States, and EFT promises to become one of banking's most heavily regulated services.

In 1974 Congress created the **National Commission on Electronic Fund Transfers** (NCEFT). This group was given the responsibility of recommending legislation that would specify how EFT

systems should be monitored and controlled. Its final report was submitted in 1977. Congress incorporated the recommendations into the **Electronic Funds Transfer Act of 1978.**

The NCEFT recommended that EFT be developed and controlled primarily by private enterprise, not the government. They encouraged the wide use of debit cards and advised that banks accept deposits at ATMs.

The NCEFT expressed concern about safeguarding consumer privacy. They advised that government use of EFT information be severely restricted and that private industry disclose customer EFT data only with the customer's consent. They recommended that consumers have the right to review their EFT records and force the prompt correction of inaccurate information.

With regard to direct deposit, the NCEFT suggested that consumers have the right to decide which bank should receive the deposits. The NCEFT also felt that the banks should have to disclose clearly all of their terms for using EFT services, send monthly statements for any month in which the customer has an EFT transaction, and dispense paper receipts at all ATMs that handle customer payments.

The NCEFT recommended that customers be fully liable for lost, stolen, or misused debit cards (but Congress disagreed and did impose limits). The NCEFT felt that the financial institution should have to prove negligence by the account holder on the security of the personal identification number (PIN).

One particularly interesting recommendation was that at the time of a sale a merchant should not be able to determine whether a customer is paying by a credit card (and thus borrowing money) or by a debit card as long as the merchant receives the proper amount. It was felt that this form of disclosure could be an invasion of the customer's privacy.

Perhaps the most significant set of rules governing EFT is **Regulation E** of the Federal Reserve Board. Reg E, as it is known, implements the provisions of the Electronic Funds Transfer Act and provides considerable protection to consumers.

The regulation requires that if banks send unsolicited debit cards to their clients or potential clients, the debit cards must first be validated before they can be used to transfer funds; this would minimize the chances of stolen cards being used, and it would give people the option of rejecting the use of the cards. If a dispute over a transaction with a customer cannot be resolved quickly, the bank must credit the customer's account with the amount in question, and the burden of proof then rests with the bank; this provision strongly favors the consumer.

The Future of EFT

EFT will soon become the dominant funds transfer technique as more financial institutions offer EFT in conveniently accessible and easy-to-use forms.

From the convenience of their own homes, some customers are already transacting business with banks throughout the country and even throughout the world. Eventually, this will become commonplace.

Strict legislation is evolving to ensure that proper security and privacy safeguards are installed. National standards are being developed for EFT equipment and for the format of EFT transactions, so that all EFT systems will operate in a similar fashion.

As the reliance on EFT increases, the size of permissible transactions will grow considerably. This demands better forms of positive identification. Computerized fingerprint recognition systems and voiceprint recognition systems are being developed that will be far more secure than the plastic card systems currently in use. Nevertheless, no system can ever be perfectly secure.

The huge bank card systems already in place, VISA and Mastercard, will expand further as they offer a full range of fund transfer capabilities, especially the wider distribution of debit cards.

Financial institutions will change drastically in response to EFT developments. Computer networks may eventually provide customers with access to the full range of banking services at all banks.

Computer Crime Techniques

As the use of computers increases, so does the potential for their misuse. In this section we consider several techniques used for committing computer crime and how some of these crimes can be prevented. Much of what is labeled computer crime can be committed without computers, but not as easily. So-called computer crimes are performed by people who use the computer as a tool; no crime has ever been performed solely by a computer.

There have been cases in which programmers who were fired by their companies planted instructions in programs that destroyed company programs and data long after they had left. This technique, called the **time bomb**, is frequently used by people who develop software to ensure that they are paid; if payment does not arrive within a reasonable period of time, the software literally destroys itself.

The **Trojan horse method** involves placing special instructions into a computer program; the instructions perform secret functions while the computer program appears to be running normally. Beware of borrowed software; as it executes, it may make copies of your programs and data for the "nice" person who lent it to you.

The **salami method** involves running a program that takes small amounts (slices) from many different accounts and places these amounts into the account of the thief. The salami method is often used in banks or other types of financial institutions where interest is earned on accounts or charged on loans. The fractions of a cent that occur when interest is calculated are placed in the account of a thief. Over a period of time, these fractions can add up to a sizable amount. The bank's books remain balanced, which makes this method difficult to detect. This type of fraud may be detected by computerized auditing programs that redo the interest calculations to check that they have been performed correctly. Periodic **software audits** in which programs are carefully examined can help determine if any programs have been modified. **Surprise audits** are essential; they help catch computer criminals off guard.

With the **super-zap method**, legitimate computer programs ordinarily used by systems programmers to override normal system controls and modify data are used for criminal purposes. Should someone obtain the use of these programs, the computer system can become vulnerable to theft or modification of any of its programs and data.

The **scavenging method** is performed in several ways. The simplest is for someone to rummage through the trash for computer printouts and documentation. The more sophisticated method involves running a memory "dump" to obtain a copy of all the programs and data in the computer; analyzing this information can give a person valuable insight into a company's operations and how to modify its computer programs.

Data diddling involves modifying a computer program so that information either entering or leaving the system can be changed. The actual processing of the information is left alone so that the computer cannot detect anything wrong.

With the **trapdoor method**, secret instructions are placed in target programs. These instructions enable the thief to bypass system safeguards whenever the thief wishes to use the programs.

Program and data theft or alteration involves the theft or modification of either programs or data for the person's own benefit. Students have changed their grades on school transcripts, employees of credit agencies have altered credit files to improve their personal credit ratings, and programmers have manipulated their company's retirement plan data files to grant themselves large pensions. Software and data audits in which programs and data files are compared to carefully secured master copies can detect this kind of crime.

Stealing computer time is one of the most common types of computer crime. Authorized users may use company computers for unauthorized purposes such as playing games, personal accounting, and doing consulting on the side. Many companies have treated this kind of activity lightly in the past, but these same companies have been getting tougher. A far more serious type of crime occurs when unauthorized users break into other companies' computer systems (usually over telephone lines) and steal computer time. No one has ever developed a completely secure computer system that can withstand any possible attack by highly skilled users.

Embezzlement involves an employee's stealing money or goods from a company. The take in computer-assisted embezzlements is often 20 times as great as in manual embezzlements.

Sabotage involves destroying computers, data, and programs by using such methods as bombing or setting fire to a computer center, turning off air conditioning or electrical systems, and even aiming high-powered microwave transmitters at a computer center to erase data from tapes, disks, and microchip storage.

Case Study 15–1: Classic Computer Crimes

In this section we discuss some of the most famous computer crimes.

Slipping in Suspicious Slips

One of our favorite computer crime stories involves a young man who opened a new checking account. The bank officer gave him the starter package containing prenumbered checks and deposit slips to use until the bank sent personalized checks.

The man noticed that the deposit slips looked just like the ones available for general use at the bank, but these slips had his account number in MICR letters across the bottom.

He went to the bank, and when no one was looking replaced a pile of the blank deposit slips with his preprinted deposit slips.

That day, dozens of unsuspecting clients unwittingly made deposits to this man's account. Shortly thereafter he withdrew a huge sum and has never been heard from since!

Here, the thief didn't actually use the computer. Rather he took advantage of the fact that the bank was heavily computerized.

How could such a crime have been prevented? Well, most people make only one deposit in any one day to their personal accounts. If the bank's computer had been programmed to check for excessive deposit activity and notify bank personnel, the dozens of deposits to this man's account would have immediately caused an investigation. As another precaution against this tactic, many banks now have tellers hand out blank deposit slips only on request.

The Prep School Gang

This case involved several students at a college prep school. The students repeatedly dialed a timesharing company's computer system trying all possible passwords until they gained entry into the system. A remarkably large percentage of today's timesharing computers have no safeguards against this simple intrusion technique.

Once on the system, the students were able to locate the passwords of the timesharing company's client accounts. Before they were done, they had examined the files of more than 20 companies and done considerable damage to several of these.

The crime was discovered when the owner of the timesharing company noticed excessive activity on the system. He notified the phone company, and they traced the calls back to the prep school. The police were notified and they informed the headmaster. It was determined that four 13-year-old boys were responsible. None of the boys was prosecuted.

This case is particularly significant because so many computers today are designed to accept telephone transmissions, and thus companies must be prepared to fend off attacks from computer criminals throughout the world. This type of crime may be thwarted in several ways. Passwords should be long enough that it would take years to try all the possibilities. Some systems allow three unsuccessful entry attempts and then hang up. Others report any excessive entry activity to system administrators who may then notify the police.

Diamonds Are a Bank's Best Friend

A computer consultant had a client company that serviced the computers at a major West Coast bank. Posing as an employee of this company, he gained access to the bank's wire transfer room, where he was able to obtain secret codes used by the bank to transfer money between banks.

Pretending to be a manager of the bank, he had several million dollars transferred to a large

East Coast bank. The transfer did not stand out because the bank handles billions of dollars in such transfers daily.

The consultant withdrew the money from the New York bank and purchased $8 million worth of diamonds. Executives at the West Coast bank did not know the bank had been robbed until the FBI told them so a week later. The consultant surrendered and returned the remaining cash and diamonds.

This story has a delightful footnote. At the time, diamond prices were rising dramatically; the bank was able to sell the diamonds for a profit of $5 million!

This crime could have been prevented with better security at the bank. Computer access codes should never be posted where they can be seen. These codes should be changed frequently so that even if they are stolen they will be of use only for a short time. Personnel entering high-security areas should be screened carefully and should have to pass several security checks.

The ATM Kidnap Caper

In this case, a person planned a kidnapping with a unique form of ransom payoff. Using false identification, the kidnapper opened an account at a large bank that had automatic teller machines located throughout a large city. After making several deposits and withdrawals at different locations, the kidnapper discovered that it took the bank about 20 minutes to update his account and determine which ATM was used.

He kidnapped the child of a prominent family and called the parents with his ransom demands. The money was to be deposited in his account at the bank. He would then withdraw it at a randomly selected ATM. When the police were notified about the demands, the detective in charge of the case figured out how the kidnapper was going to get the money. The bank quickly reprogrammed its computers so that when a withdrawal was made from the kidnapper's account, the location would be displayed immediately. Police were sent to several locations throughout the city and were able to catch the kidnapper and return the child safely.

Today, ATMs routinely take pictures of each client; this capability is especially important to the banks because legislation has placed the burden of proof in most disputes on the banks rather than the consumer.

Funding Funds with Fake Funds

A financial services company sold mutual funds to investors and used the dividends they accumulated to pay the premiums on life insurance policies for these clients. When its stock started to drop, the company needed a way to prop up its price. So the company began creating false insurance policies that they sold to reinsurers. The company guaranteed the payment of premiums on these policies, so they had to make up even more false policies to sell to other reinsurers to pay the premiums due on the first group of policies.

The fake policies were coded on the computer so that when the company was audited, these policies would not appear on any printouts; legitimate policies were coded to appear several times.

Two aspects of this case make it particularly interesting. One is that the embezzlement was perpetrated by the highest levels of management rather than by rank and file employees.

The second is that the creation and manipulation of the fake policies could have been done manually, but the computer was used as a high-tech obstacle in the path of auditors who at that time knew little about computers. Here the use of computerized auditing programs might have been able to reveal the duplicate accounts, and the crime could have been discovered sooner.

In the wake of computer crimes such as these, auditing firms have developed computer auditing techniques in which computers are used to audit other computers at electronic speeds.

The Scavenger's Delight

Each day on his way home from school a student picked various memos and computer printouts from the trash bins located behind the headquarters of a nearby telephone company. He used this information to determine how the company did its ordering and controlled its inventory. He then tapped into the company's computer and had a

regular supply of equipment sent to a number of locations where he received the goods and resold them.

His activities were exposed when one of the student's employees who had been denied a raise informed the telephone company. The student had stolen over $1 million worth of equipment in seven months. He pleaded guilty to his crime and served only 40 days in jail. After his release, he set up a business as a consultant to advise companies how to prevent computer crime.

Actually, companies can prevent this type of crime quite easily by using *paper shredders* to shred hard copy documents before disposing of them, yet few companies shred their hard copy documents today (Figure 1).

But beware: At one bank, employees accidentally shredded the day's checks and deposits. A manager promptly hired dozens of temporary workers who worked diligently to piece the documents together over a three-week period. This proves two points: (1) you had better be careful what you place in a shredder, and (2) given enough time and effort, shredded documents can be pieced back together.

Figure 1 Shredding hard copy documents.

Stealing a Stolen System

A programmer developed a series of programs for a small business. He then stole the programs, went into hiding, and demanded and received a ransom of $100,000. He was apprehended shortly afterward by a local sheriff who locked up all the tapes and programs as evidence. The owner of the business told the sheriff he had to have the tapes and programs to run his business. The sheriff refused on the grounds that they were evidence and would be needed eventually when the case came to trial. The desperate businessman then broke into the sheriff's office, stole the tapes, made copies, and returned the originals to the safe!

The Prompt Prepayment Perpetrator

A young man went into a bank and applied for an automobile loan. When the loan was approved, the bank gave the man a booklet of preprinted payment slips and told him to send in one slip with a check each month. He went home in his new car, drove it for 30 days, and then realized that it was time to make his first payment. He looked through the payment book and noticed that the slips were numbered "Payment #1," "Payment #2," and so on. He looked at the back of the book and saw that the last payment was marked "Last Payment. Thank you." So he pulled out the last slip, wrote a check for one month's payment, and sent them to the bank. A few days later he received a letter from the bank thanking him for paying off his loan so promptly! Of course, the bank immediately modified its system so this could not happen again. (This just goes to prove that computers cannot overcome programmer or management stupidity!)

The Computerized Bulletin Board Blitz

Many long-distance telephone companies require customers to enter secret access codes. Some people with automatic dialing modems set these devices to try all possible codes until they find valid ones to which phone calls may be charged. Some people then use these codes to charge calls. This is nothing short of robbery. Others have chosen instead to reveal their cleverness in a different way. They call up computerized bulletin board systems and post the access codes they have discovered. This is not a crime, but using these codes to charge calls to other people is. Some telephone companies have reported instances in which more than 1000 calls were charged to one customer's number in one day after that customer's code was discovered and placed on a computerized bulletin board system.

Long distance phone companies are considering using much longer access codes to minimize the chance of discovery. But this has met with some consumer resistance because of the longer dialing time required. What is really needed here is a stiffening of the laws and penalties for using computers to perpetrate crimes.

Computer Criminals

According to the FBI, computer criminals are generally under 30 years of age, outwardly loyal to their companies, have no previous criminal records, are intelligent, are intrigued by the challenge, fear detection worse than punishment, and do not feel anyone is being hurt by their actions.

There are normally no eyewitnesses to a computer crime, and often the thief's tracks can be completely erased. Sometimes the criminal does not want to steal anything but merely wants to disrupt a company's operations. Fearful of losing investors and business, many companies would rather suffer their losses than admit that they have been victimized by computer criminals.

The small number of cases that make it to trial often result in nominal or suspended sentences. Juries rarely view the perpetrators of computer crimes as hardened criminals. Also, laws defining computer crimes and the appropriate penalties are relatively new.

Computers and Law Enforcement

Computers are also effective in preventing crimes and in tracking down criminals. The government has more than 100 million fingerprint cards on file for citizens, military personnel, government employees, and known criminals. Matching fingerprints with those on file is a time-consuming process. Rockwell International has developed a computerized fingerprint matching system that uses optical scanning techniques and concentrates on ridge endings (Figure 15–6). The system is faster and more precise than manually scanning the card files.

Police use portable computer terminals in their patrol cars. They type in the license number of a suspicious vehicle, and the central computer system determines if the vehicle is stolen, has an excessive number of parking violations, or was used in a crime. Parking tickets and traffic citations are produced on portable dot-matrix printers in patrol cars. The information is stored in central computers to ensure that tickets are paid and that customers with excessive citations are prosecuted.

The crimes of one criminal often tend to have certain key similarities (called MOs for modus operandi or method of operation). Information

ELECTRONIC FUNDS TRANSFER FRAUD... WHAT ABOUT YOU?

Figure 15–6 The Printrak fingerprint matching system developed by Rockwell International uses optical scanning techniques to isolate splits and endings in ridge patterns. These features are then compared with those of fingerprints on file.

about past crimes is entered into computer systems accessible by terminals from around the country. When a new crime is committed, information about it is typed into the computer to determine in minutes if the MO closely matches that of any known criminal.

Many cities use computerized police dispatching systems that receive police calls, verify addresses, check for similar calls in the same area, locate the police units best able to respond, and advise on the best route to a location considering traffic, road repairs, and other factors.

Auto theft is one of the most common crimes in America, with over 1 million cars stolen per year. Several new products under development may help to reduce this problem. One microprocessor-based device prevents a car from being started until an appropriate code is keyed in by the driver. If a thief tries to enter a code, and does it incorrectly several times, a powerful alarm system goes off automatically. Other microprocessor-based security systems use speech recognition techniques to identify the driver before allowing the car to be started.

Perhaps the most important application of computers in law enforcement today is the *National Crime Information Center* (NCIC) run by the federal government. This network of computer systems handles thousands of inquiries per day on crimes, criminals, and stolen property. One of the real benefits of NCIC is that police officers are able to determine if the suspects they are dealing with are dangerous criminals.

Security

With more companies computerizing their records, and with the vast amount of information available through computer networks, securing this information has become a major problem. Companies use several forms of security to protect their computer equipment, programs, and data. There are several popular methods.

Passkeys, plastic identification cards that resemble credit cards, can be given to those employees who need access to the computers (Figure 15–7). Because passkeys can be stolen, many companies improve security by using a system that requires a person to insert a passkey and then type in a multiple-digit secret **access code** (Figure 15–8).

Fingerprints may be prestored in the computer for those employees who are given access to the computer. A computer compares the fingerprints of an employee who places his or her hand on a special pad with sets of fingerprints stored in its memory. Only when there is a match will access be allowed. A system called the **hand analyzer** identifies people by their hand geometry. **Voiceprint** identification systems match people's voices to prestored voice samples. **Signature verification** systems match signatures to prestored samples; one of these even measures the changes in pressure as people write their names.

Some hotels have installed computerized room locks. Each guest receives a thin paper card with a precise pattern of holes punched in it by a computer. When the card is inserted into a small box on the room door, an electronic motor opens the latch if the code on the card matches the one assigned to the door. When a customer checks out of the hotel or reports a missing card, a central computer automatically changes the room combination.

Figure 15–7 Using a plastic card passkey to gain entrance to a large computer center.

RICHARD TENNANT
"YOUR ACCESS CODE TOM, INPUT YOUR ACCESS CODE!!"

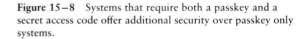

Figure 15–8 Systems that require both a passkey and a secret access code offer additional security over passkey only systems.

Disaster Recovery

Every computer system is vulnerable to fire, sabotage, floods, earthquakes, tornados, and acts of war. It is impossible to ensure that a computer will continue to operate in the wake of every conceivable disaster. Nevertheless, organizations must consider the potential disasters they face, how they should secure themselves, and how they expect to recover afterward.

One of the most effective recovery techniques is to keep backup copies of all programs and data locked in fireproof vaults, preferably at an alternate site (Figure 15–9). Many companies make arrangements with other companies that use the same type of computer equipment to make computer time available in an emergency.

One of the most common problems faced by computer centers is loss of power. A computer installation that must continue operating even during power failures may use a hardware device called an **uninterruptible power supply** (UPS).

Encryption

Because computers and data communications make data so accessible, it is easier today for important data to get into unauthorized hands. To render data useless to unauthorized users, it may be encrypted (encoded). Governments have been using **encryption** for centuries, but today even small businesses find it essential for protecting valuable information. Someone wishing to use the data would first have to decode, or decrypt it, and this requires knowledge of a secret **decryption key**.

An encrypted message is called a **cryptogram** or **ciphertext**; the unencrypted message is called **plaintext** or **cleartext**. The simplest systems use the same secret key for encrypting and decrypting messages.

Encryption is used to encode messages being transmitted over channels or lines that could be tapped. Users of timesharing systems have been reluctant to place their critical data on systems accessible by so many people; by using encryption, they need not worry (as much).

Figure 15–9 This vivid picture appeared in an advertisement for the sale of fireproof storage cabinets for computer tapes and disks. Cabinets like the one shown here keep magnetic storage media at safe temperatures even in raging fires for several hours.

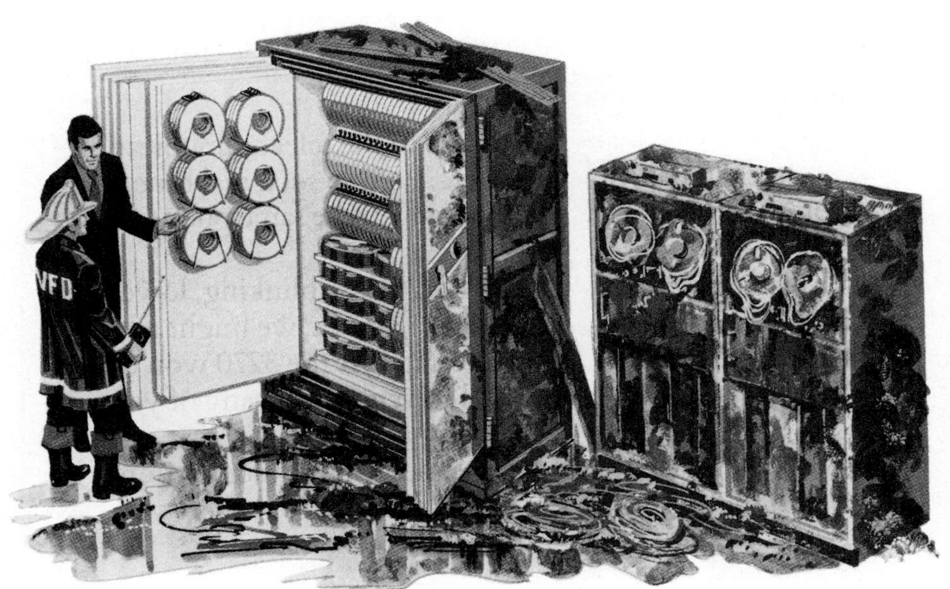

Software Protection

Because personal computers are so popular, a need has developed to protect the programs that have been designed for them. Most of these programs are now covered by copyright laws, making it a crime to make unauthorized copies.

The developers of programs used on personal computers sometimes build in **software locks** that either prevent duplication or allow a buyer to make a limited number of **backup copies**. Should copies become damaged, many software suppliers will replace them when they are returned.

Several programs currently on the market can break these software locks and allow multiple copies to be made. Such software piracy is a serious concern to the developers of the programs, because they do not receive royalties on pirated copies. No one has ever found a completely effective method of preventing software piracy. It has been estimated that for every copy of a software package that sells through proper channels, 2 to 10 illicit copies are made. Some people believe the solution will come when competitive pressures force the price of software so low that it will be more economical to buy it than copy it, but it is unlikely that this will happen soon.

Privacy

We discovered that we were collecting some information about people which didn't really relate to their jobs. And we concluded that one excellent way to protect people was to collect less information about them.

From an IBM advertisement entitled "Privacy Begins at Home"

When a person is born, attends school, makes major purchases, moves, enters a hospital, travels, earns a living, and so on, information about that person is entered into various databases (manual or computerized) maintained by public and private organizations (Figure 15–10).

What information about individuals should be recorded? Who should have access to this information? What safeguards should be taken to en-

Figure 15–10 Most people would probably be amazed to discover how much information the federal government records about them.

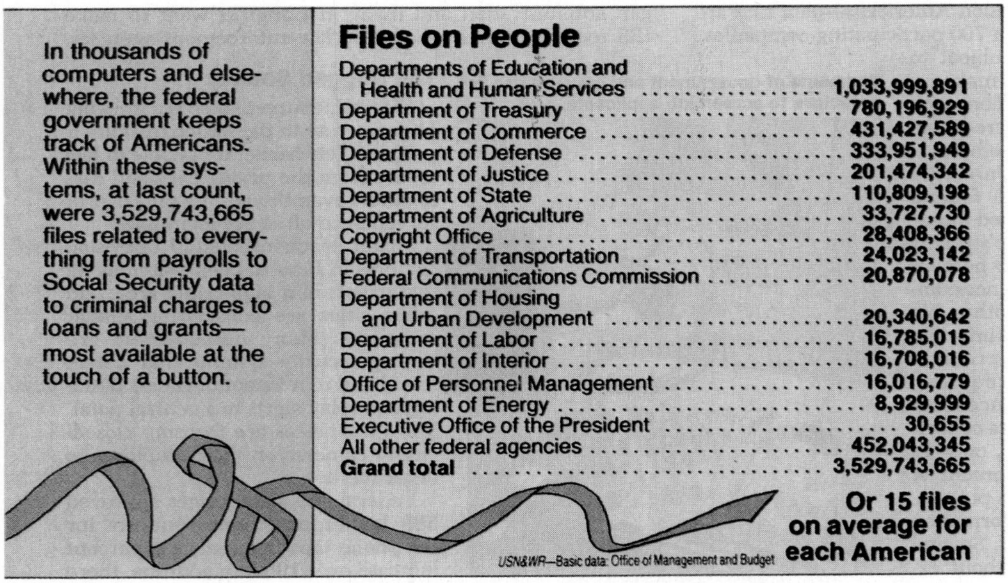

In thousands of computers and elsewhere, the federal government keeps track of Americans. Within these systems, at last count, were 3,529,743,665 files related to everything from payrolls to Social Security data to criminal charges to loans and grants—most available at the touch of a button.

Files on People

Departments of Education and Health and Human Services	1,033,999,891
Department of Treasury	780,196,929
Department of Commerce	431,427,589
Department of Defense	333,951,949
Department of Justice	201,474,342
Department of State	110,809,198
Department of Agriculture	33,727,730
Copyright Office	28,408,366
Department of Transportation	24,023,142
Federal Communications Commission	20,870,078
Department of Housing and Urban Development	20,340,642
Department of Labor	16,785,015
Department of Interior	16,708,016
Office of Personnel Management	16,016,779
Department of Energy	8,929,999
Executive Office of the President	30,655
All other federal agencies	452,043,345
Grand total	3,529,743,665

Or 15 files on average for each American

USN&WR—Basic data: Office of Management and Budget

"You never heard such a clatter as when the computer kicked out your return."

sure that the information is correct? How can we be sure that this information will not be used against us? These are just a few of the very important questions we must ask ourselves.

Some of the information kept on ordinary citizens includes religion, ethnic group, salary history, credit rating, medical history, education, debts, and previous addresses. Unauthorized access to such material could certainly threaten an individual's privacy.

Laws have been passed to ensure that only necessary information is gathered and that the information must be kept secure. The **Freedom of Information Act of 1966** gives individuals the right to know the operation and structure of federal agencies and which federal agencies keep records on them; it also allows people to access their records and make sure they are correct.

The **Fair Credit Reporting Act of 1970** was passed because of the increasing collection of credit information made possible by computers and data communications. Individuals have the right to determine what credit information is being collected about them and to force the correction of inaccurate information. Credit agencies may collect only that information which is needed to verify a person's credit, and they are obliged to protect this information from unauthorized access. When people are denied credit, this law helps them determine why.

The **Education Privacy Act of 1974** applies to schools that receive federal funds. It ensures the privacy and security of academic and behavioral records and permits access to a student's records only by that student, the student's parents, or authorized school officials.

The **Privacy Act of 1974** prevents the federal government from keeping secret files on individuals. Data may be collected by the government only for legitimate purposes. People can determine what data is being collected about them and how the government intends to use this data; they can force inaccurate data to be corrected. One of the most important provisions of this law is that federal agencies such as the FBI and the IRS cannot share the information they collect without the authorization of a federal judge.

The **Right to Financial Privacy Act of 1978** gives people the right to review the data about their personal finances that financial institutions maintain about them. Individuals may also have inaccurate financial data corrected. The law restricts access to financial records by federal agencies and generally forbids federal agencies from sharing what information they do have except for legitimate law enforcement purposes. This law is particularly significant because the Supreme Court had ruled previously that such data was the property of the financial institutions.

Various state laws give workers access to their personnel files, restrict disclosure of these files to outsiders, give citizens access to their medical records and limit disclosure of information from these records, make it illegal to intercept com-

puter communications without proper legal authorization, and so on.

Perhaps the greatest invasion of personal privacy could come as a result of the increasing use of home computers and two-way cable TV hookups. Many of these interactive systems enable users to do banking, make purchases, make travel arrangements, and participate in polls from their homes. Simple monitoring of these systems could reveal significant information about a person's finances, habits, and political beliefs.

Conclusion

Once again we face the double-edged sword of technology. The same computing and data communications techniques that can help us improve our personal lives and business enterprises can be equally effective in disrupting them and violating our privacy. A computer-literate public aware of the pros and cons of these technologies can help ensure that they are used effectively and responsibly.

Summary

1. In electronic funds transfer, money is transferred electronically by computers and data communications systems from one account to another without the use of written checks.
2. With direct deposit, employers' banks electronically deposit salaries into employees' bank accounts without checks being produced. Direct deposit was one of the earliest forms of EFT, and it has played an important part in the acceptance of other forms of EFT.
3. On-line teller terminals provide immediate access to customer records and facilitate transactions by checking rapidly that the required funds are on deposit.
4. Automated teller machines (ATMs) provide 24-hour-per-day banking at convenient locations. ATMs are expensive, break down occasionally, and sometimes make mistakes. When using ATMs, be sure to save the written receipt of each transaction, carefully choose and guard your personal identification number (PIN), and report any errors immediately.
5. Credit authorization terminals speed credit verification and reduce losses due to stolen credit cards.
6. A debit card is used to initiate immediate payment through the EFT computer networks. Because payment is instantaneous, using a debit card is like using cash. In fact, a debit card is safer than cash because it is useless without the accompanying PIN.
7. Point-of-sale terminals make it possible to enter transactions into a company's computers at the moment each transaction occurs; businesses may now have up-to-the-minute information about sales and inventories.
8. The Electronic Funds Transfer Act of 1978 is the primary legislation governing electronic funds transfers; Regulation E of the Federal Reserve Board is the key regulation implementing the provisions of the EFT Act. Regulation E provides responsible rules governing the disclosure of terms, validation of unsolicited debit cards, issuance of receipts for ATM transactions, and so on. Its provisions for resolving disputes tend to favor the consumer.
9. Most so-called computer crimes can be performed without computers; computers simply make the process easier. No crime has ever been committed solely by a computer. There are normally no eyewitnesses to a computer crime.
10. The Trojan horse method uses special instructions to perform secret functions in a computer program. The salami method uses a computer to remove small amounts (slices) from different accounts and place them in the

account of the thief. The super-zap method uses a legitimate computer program that overrides normal system controls; this program may then be used to modify programs and data freely.

11. In the scavenging method, the thief either rummages through the trash for printouts or examines a memory dump to obtain valuable information. In the data diddling method, the thief modifies a computer program that is capable of changing information before or after it is processed. The trapdoor method involves inserting special instructions into a program to enable a user to bypass system safeguards whenever the user wishes to access the system.

12. Alteration of programs and data involves the modification of programs or data for the thief's own benefit. In embezzlement, the thief uses the company's computers to steal from the company. Sabotage can involve bombs, fires, turning off air conditioning, and using microwave transmissions to destroy programs, data, and microchip storage.

13. Scanning techniques and computers are being used in fingerprint identification. Police cars are being equipped with portable computer terminals. Information about crimes and criminals is stored in databases that can be accessed by law enforcement officials worldwide.

14. Some popular security techniques are passkeys, secret codes, fingerprint identification, voiceprint identification, and hand geometry identification.

15. The Freedom of Information Act of 1966 enables people to determine which federal agencies keep records on them, and gives people access to these records to make sure they are correct. The Fair Credit Reporting Act of 1970 gives people access to their credit records and the right to force inaccurate records to be corrected. The Education Privacy Act of 1974 ensures the privacy of students' records. The Privacy Act of 1974 prevents the federal government from keeping secret files on individuals, and prevents federal agencies from sharing the information they collect unless they first obtain a judge's permission. The Right to Financial Privacy Act of 1978 restricts access to financial records by federal agencies.

Important Terms 

access code
automated clearing house
automated teller machine (ATM)
cashless/checkless society
ciphertext
credit authorization terminal
data diddling
debit card
direct deposit
Education Privacy Act of 1974
electronic funds transfer (EFT)
Electronic Funds Transfer Act of 1978
encryption/decryption
Fair Credit Reporting Act of 1970
Freedom of Information Act of 1966
National Commission on Electronic Fund Transfers (NCEFT)
personal identification number (PIN)
plaintext
point-of-sale (POS) terminal
preauthorized computer-initiated payments
Privacy Act of 1974
Regulation E
Right to Financial Privacy Act of 1978
salami method
scavenging method
super-zap method
time bomb
trapdoor method
Trojan horse method
uninterruptible power supply (UPS)

Self-Review Exercises 

Matching

Next to the term in column A, place the letter of the statement in column B that best describes it.

Column A	Column B
1. Direct deposit	A. Limits access of federal agencies to your financial data
2. On-line teller terminal	B. Legitimate computer program that overrides system controls
3. Point-of-sale terminal	C. Makes stolen data useless to unauthorized users
4. Right to Financial Privacy Act of 1978	D. Instant access to account information
5. Salami method	E. Used in computerized fingerprint recognition systems
6. PIN	F. Implements the EFT Act of 1978
7. Regulation E of the Federal Reserve Board	G. Secret access code that enables EFT transactions
8. Super-zap	H. Eliminates the need for paychecks
9. Optical scanning	I. Common computer crime involving interest calculations
10. Encryption	J. Facilitates up-to-the-minute sales and inventory information

Fill-in-the-Blanks

Fill in the blanks in each of the following:

1. Electronic funds transfers between banks are handled through a series of ______ run by the Federal Reserve Board.

2. With the use of ______, banks can offer many teller services around the clock.

3. A ______ card can be used like cash to pay for items directly.

4. Regulation E of the Federal Reserve Board implements the ______ of 1978.

5. ______ speed credit verification and have reduced losses due to stolen credit cards.

6. The ______ society would be one in which virtually all transactions are handled by EFT.

7. The ______ is a set of instructions planted in a program to destroy certain programs and data at some point in the future.

8. The ______ of 1966 gives individuals the right to know which federal agencies keep records on them.

9. A ______ is used to render hard copy documents useless to potential scavengers.

10. ______ allow people to make regular loan payments automatically.

Answers to Self-Review Exercises

Matching: 1 H, 2 D, 3 J, 4 A, 5 I, 6 G, 7 F, 8 B, 9 E, 10 C

Fill-in-the-Blanks:
1. automated clearing houses
2. automated teller machines (ATMs)
3. debit
4. Electronic Funds Transfer Act
5. Credit authorization terminals
6. cashless/checkless
7. time bomb
8. Freedom of Information Act
9. paper shredder
10. Preauthorized computer-initiated payments

Discussion Questions 

1. Give several advantages of direct deposit over using checks.

2. Discuss the advantages and disadvantages of ATMs.

3. For years, bankers have been talking about the cashless/checkless society. Give several reasons why we are more likely to have a less cash/less check society.

4. Discuss some of the more important findings of the NCEFT.

5. The NCEFT stated that merchants "should not be able to determine whether a given transaction is a debit or a credit as long as the merchant receives par value. This type of disclosure could represent an invasion of consumer privacy." Discuss the meaning of this statement. Do you agree with the NCEFT on this issue? Why?

6. Summarize the major provisions of the Federal Reserve Board's Regulation E.

7. Explain the differences between debit cards and credit cards. What are the advantages and disadvantages of each?

8. Summarize the major types of computer crime.

9. Summarize the major types of security measures that may be taken to prevent computer crime.

10. List and briefly describe the legislative acts and regulations discussed in this chapter that protect individual privacy.

Projects

1. Suppose Congress passed legislation declaring that cash would no longer be valid after a certain date and that all transactions had to be conducted through the EFT computer networks. Write an essay about the changes that would occur in our society with total EFT. Consider the following:

(a) What would it be like not having cash in your pocket?

(b) Would this total EFT concept be a convenience?

(c) Would total EFT represent an invasion of your privacy?

(d) Many cash businesses would have to change their operations dramatically. List several types of these businesses. How would their operations change?

(e) Why might the Internal Revenue Service be delighted to have total EFT?

2. Read several current magazine articles on EFT and report on recent developments.

3. Request catalogs of EFT publications from these and other sources:

Bank Administration Institute
60 Gould Center
Rolling Meadows, IL 60008

American Bankers Association
1120 Connecticut Avenue, N.W.
Washington, DC 20036

Summarize their contents.

4. One definite trend is for banks to share their ATMs. Eventually it may become possible for any bank customer to use any ATM of any bank in the world. Discuss the advantages and disadvantages of such a development to both the banks and their customers.

5. If a national encryption code is developed and used to code all data stored in computers throughout the United States, government agencies as well as industry could gain access to important and secret information.

(a) Should the government develop its own codes?

(b) Should different codes be used for each agency? Why?

(c) Why should private industry be encouraged to develop its own codes?

(d) Should the banking industry have different codes for EFT transactions? Give some suggestions and your reasons.

6. Comment on the following scenario:

Your doctor has placed you on a restricted diet. You feel like cheating a bit. You go into a restaurant and order a dish you are not supposed to have. The waiter takes your order, but returns a few moments later and informs you that the restaurant cannot serve you the dish because the restaurant's computer checked with a public medical database and discovered your dietary restrictions.

7. In the text we stated that "no crime has ever been performed solely by a computer." Discuss this point. Explain why it is true today. In other chapters we have referred to the fields of artificial intelligence and robotics. In the next chapter we discuss these in depth. As you read the next chapter, consider the possibility that "artificial criminal intelligence" could develop as a consequence of current research efforts. You may then wish to adjust your discussion for this project.

8. Write to: American Civil Liberties Union
132 West 43rd Street
New York, NY 10036

Request literature on computers and the invasion of privacy. Report on this subject.

 16. Robotics and Artificial Intelligence

 17. Computers and Medicine

 18. Computers and the Handicapped

 19. Computers and Transportation

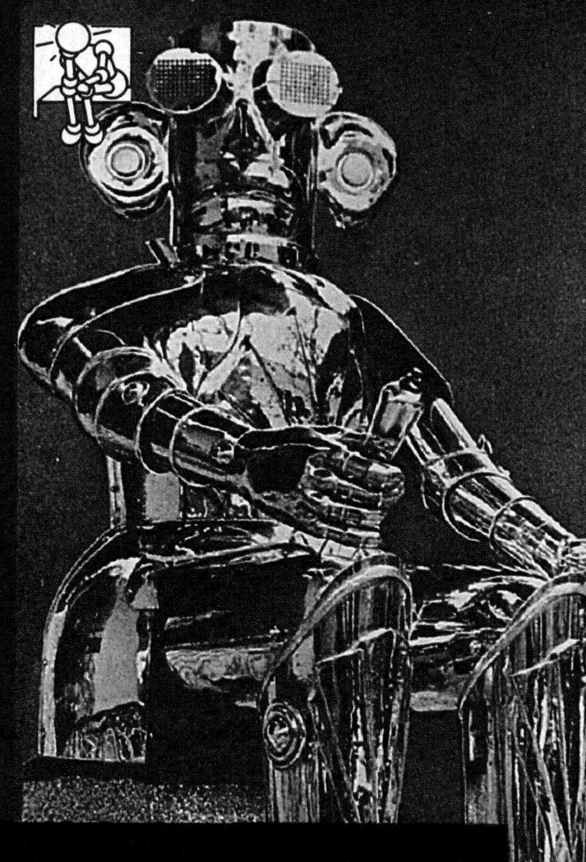

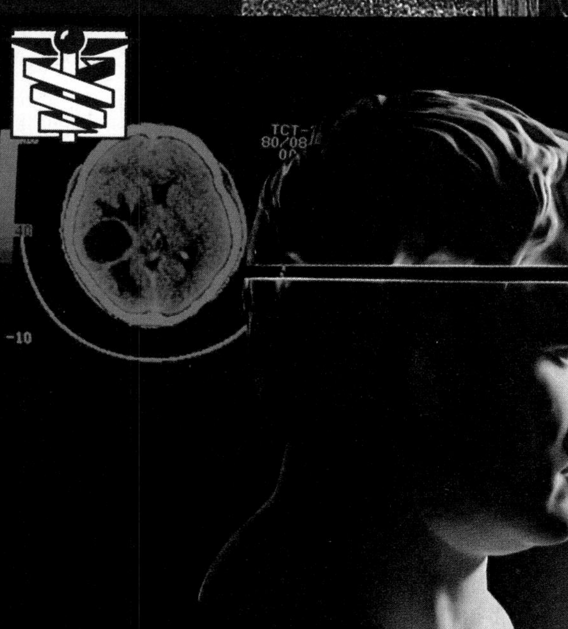

Part Five

Computers in Society

The applications of computers are limited only by the reach of human imagination. How will computers change our lives? Will the quality of life improve?

In Chapter 16 we'll consider whether computers can think and reason intelligently. Will they ever surpass our human abilities? Will powerful intelligent robots take over our jobs and perform our labors for us? Are robots better than people in certain ways? Will we always be able to "pull the plug"?

In Chapter 17 we'll see how computers are revolutionizing the field of medicine. We'll discuss how the CAT scan makes it possible for doctors to see inside the human body without the need for diagnostic surgery, and we'll look at how microprocessors are being used in the development of artificial organs.

In Chapter 18, one of the most important chapters in the book, we'll see how computers are helping handicapped people overcome their handicaps to live more normal lives and gain useful employment. We'll consider why microprocessors may hold the key to restoring sight to the blind, hearing to the deaf, and mobility to the paralyzed.

In Chapter 19 we'll look at how computers are playing critical roles in evolving transportation systems. We'll see how they help reduce energy consumption and pollution, help vehicles navigate safely through congested travel lanes, and train the drivers, pilots, captains, and engineers of today's sophisticated transportation systems.

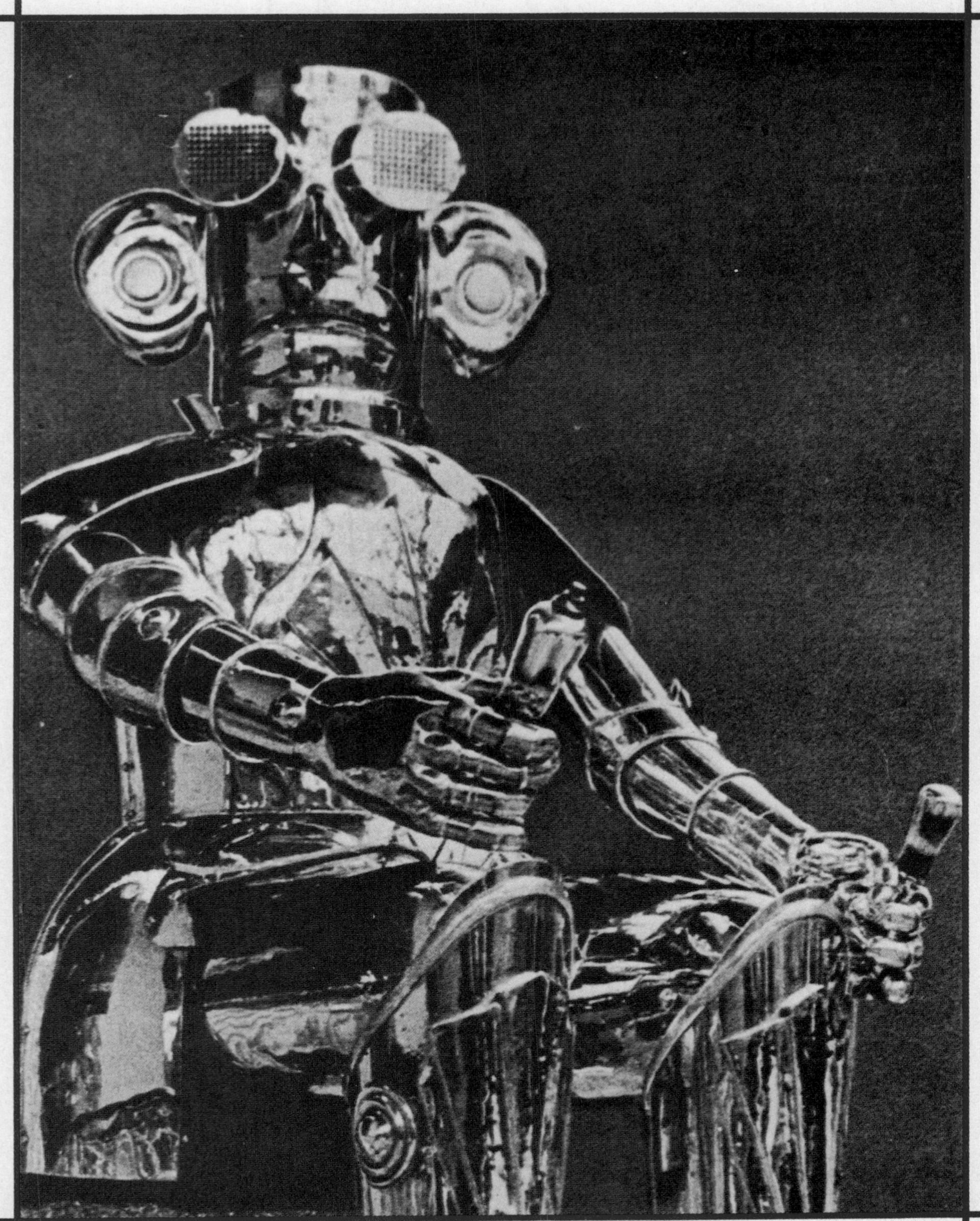

Chapter 16

Robotics and Artificial Intelligence

After reading this chapter you will understand:

1. What robotics and artificial intelligence are
2. How robots are being used today and what jobs they will be doing in the future
3. How organized labor is dealing with robotics
4. What natural language processing and expert systems are
5. Many of the controversial social and philosophical issues raised by robotics and artificial intelligence

Left: The "Roboter" shown at the London Radio Exhibition in 1932 typifies the common conception of a robot.

Outline

DOMIN. Robots are not people. Mechanically they are more perfect than we are; they have an enormously developed intelligence, but they have no soul.
HELENA. How do you know they have no soul?
DOMIN. Have you ever seen what a Robot looks like inside?

Karel Capek,
Rossum's Universal Robots, 1923

I can't give you brains, but
I can give you a diploma.
(The Wizard of Oz to the Scarecrow)

Lyman Frank Baum
The Wizard of Oz

If intelligent machines make us really uncomfortable, we can always pull the plug.

Hans Berliner

Artificial intelligence is the study of making machines that exhibit intelligent behavior. This is generally considered to be the most controversial field in computer science. There are philosophical, theological, psychological, and sociological overtones to the creation of "smart" machines. No one really understands what intelligence is in the first place, so how can we ever say that we have built an intelligent machine? If we do build these machines, could we (should we) make them exhibit emotions? If they are put to a task, could we (should we) program them to feel upset if they do not succeed? Could we (should we) program them to feel fear and defend themselves in the face of danger? If we build intelligent machines, could we (should we) always keep the ability to "pull the plug" if they get out of control? There are many hard questions like these that must be dealt with soon, because we may well be on the brink of creating truly intelligent machines.

Robotics

A **robot** is:

"a machine that resembles a man and does routine tasks on command as though it were alive."

(*The Random House Dictionary of the English Language*, Unabridged)

"a reprogrammable multifunctional manipulator designed to move material, parts, tools or specialized devices through variable programmed motions for the performance of a variety of tasks."

(Robot Institute of America)

Most of today's robots are not the familiar steel people from science fiction, movies, and television (Figures 16–1 and 16–2). Instead, they are relatively dumb machines that often consist of nothing more than a single metal arm connected to a box of controls, and are used for industrial

purposes (Figure 16–3). They generally cannot see, hear, feel, or walk, but robots with these capabilities have been developed.

Many of these **industrial robots** are controlled by small computers, but they need not be—they could easily be built with simple electrical and mechanical parts. However, computers are certainly critical to the operation of the more advanced robots now being developed. The highly intelligent robots likely to appear in the 1990s will owe their existence to computer technology.

Inflation has pushed labor costs so high that industrial robots can now perform many tasks at a fraction of the cost of human labor. But there are other motivations for developing robots. Our de-

Figure 16–2 NBC's 25th-century lovers Twiki and Tina from the series *Buck Rogers*.

Figure 16–1 Star Wars good guy Artoo-Detoo.

Figure 16–3 A high-speed, computer-controlled industrial robot.

sires to explore deep space or miles below the ocean surface are hindered by human limitations—robots can easily survive in these and other hazardous environments (Figures 16–4 and 16–5). They can be designed to walk through fire, handle radioactive materials (Figure 16–6), repel bullets, and chase and apprehend criminals. They can also be immune to poisonous fumes. It is believed that the military is interested in developing robot soldiers.

The Mechanical Human

The most common conception of a robot is that of a mechanical human being (Figure 16–7) that walks, talks, and understands verbal commands; the robot has great strength and can walk through walls leaving a dusty pile of rubble behind; it is not invulnerable—it can be destroyed by bombs, rayguns, or more powerful robots.

People have always been fascinated by **anthropomorphic robots**, that is, robots that have the form and attributes of humans. Since the 1950s, Disney's "Imagineers" have constructed electromechanical people and animals that they call **audio-animatrons** to entertain their millions of visitors. Vacationers visiting the Hall of Presidents at Disneyland in California or at Walt Disney World in Florida are often brought to tears by an Abraham Lincoln audio-animatron describing the early history of America.

Figure 16–4 This robot made by Bell Laboratories is used to repair phone cable along the ocean bottom.

Figure 16–5 *Below:* The surface of Mars as seen from the camera eye of the Viking 2 lander. The picture, enhanced by computer processing, shows the lander's robot arm that was used to sample the Martian soil. The robot arm fed the samples into a complete laboratory in the lander which then analyzed the chemical composition of the soil.

Figure 16–6 *Bottom:* This robot vehicle in West Germany handles deadly nuclear contaminants.

Today, anthropomorphic robots like Harvey (Figure 16–8) at the University of Miami School of Medicine help educate medical students. Harvey is a teaching tool with plastic skin and realistic looking veins and arteries. Under computer control, he can breathe and simulate many common cardiac disorders. Harvey can have a simulated heart attack on command—and with various levels of severity. Robots like Harvey are making it possible for medical students to experience treating many more health problems than they would normally see during their education.

Figure 16–7 *Below:* Elektro and his faithful robot hound, Sparko, were exhibited at the 1939 New York World's Fair.

Figure 16–8 *Bottom:* Harvey is a robot in use at the University of Miami School of Medicine in Miami, Florida. He is a teaching tool with plastic skin and realistic veins and arteries. He simulates breathing and can demonstrate many common heart disorders.

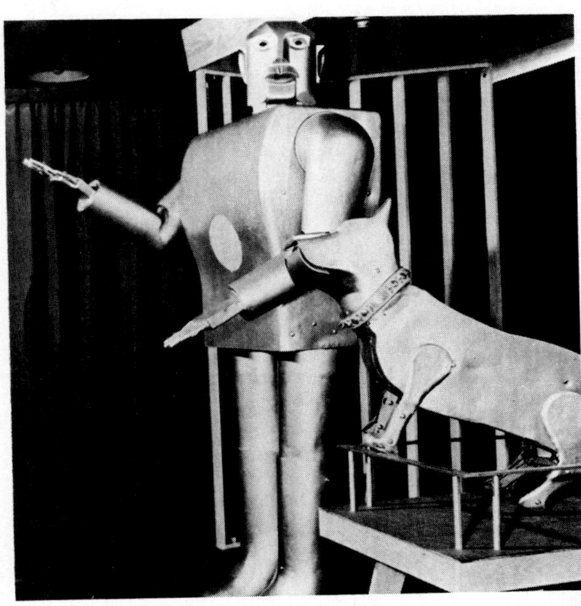

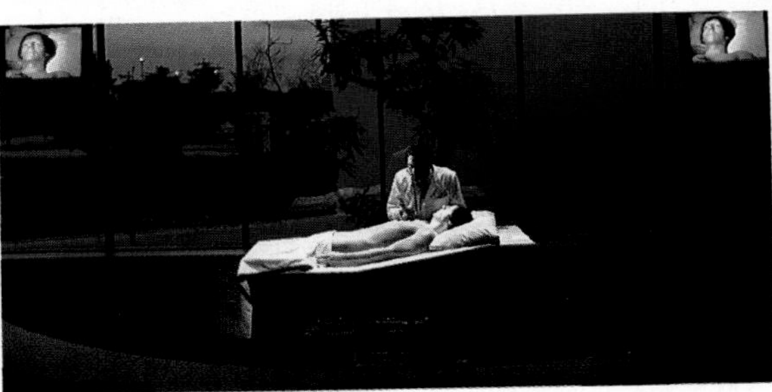

A Brief History of Robotics

The word robot comes from the Czech noun "robota" meaning "forced labor." It was coined by the Czech playwright Karel Capek in his 1920s play *R.U.R. (Rossum's Universal Robots)* about humanoid machines that ultimately destroy humanity.

The Atomic Energy Commission used robotlike devices in 1959 in high risk radiation areas. The first production line robot was built by Unimation and installed at General Motors in 1961. Joseph Engelberger, who served as president of Unimation, is generally recognized as the father of industrial robotics. The relative costs of robots and labor in the 1960s and early 1970s was not favorable to the machines; Unimation did not become profitable until the mid-1970s.

The first generation robots in wide use today are little more than dumb mechanical manipulators (Figure 16–9). Second generation robots, now starting to appear in industry, often have elementary vision and touch capabilities. Many are equipped with arms, hands, and optic sensors

Figure 16–9 This robotic superworker is used by Storage Technology Peripherals Corporation to load disk platters onto spindles.

Figure 16–10 This robot is equipped with arms, hands, and optic sensors. It is used in the precision assembly, adjustment, and inspection of small electronic devices.

Asimov's Laws of Robotics

The term **robotics** was coined by Dr. Isaac Asimov, one of the world's foremost science fiction writers. Asimov, considered the father of fictional robotics, stated three laws robots must obey in his book *I, Robot* (1950).

1. A robot may not injure a human being, or, through inaction, allow a human being to come to harm.
2. A robot must obey the orders given to it by human beings except where such orders would conflict with the First Law.
3. A robot must protect its own existence as long as such protection does not conflict with the First or Second Law.

Handbook of Robotics, 58th edition, 2058 A.D.

These laws are widely quoted and may someday form the basis of a more detailed body of laws governing the existence of robots.

for use in the precision assembly, adjustment, and inspection of small electronic devices (Figure 16–10). Third generation robots, expected to appear in the late 1980s, will have highly developed sensory capabilities and limited intelligence. Highly intelligent fourth generation robots will probably not appear until the late 1990s. When they do, society will be in for monumental changes.

Productivity Concerns

Industrial productivity in the United States increased slowly in the 1960s and 1970s and actually decreased in the early 1980s. The prospects are for only modest productivity gains in the next several years.

Contrary to this trend, Japanese productivity has been increasing dramatically in recent years. Certainly a portion of these gains is due to the fact that Japan is by far the largest user of industrial automation and robots in the world.

The poor performance of American industry in the early 1980s has brought the productivity issue to the forefront. It is clear that the United States must dramatically improve productivity if it intends to stay competitive in world markets.

When goods are manufactured in repetitive assembly line fashion, technological improvements can often result in productivity improvements. But the vast majority of goods made in America are not mass produced—they are, instead, assembled in small batches as sizes and styles change. The automation techniques of the last several decades were useful for mass production environments, but they are not applicable to small batch environments. What is needed is more adaptable automation, sometimes called **flexible automation**. Industrial robots offer this adaptability.

Industrial Robots: "Steel Collar" Workers

Industrial robots are the mechanical arms used in industry for jobs such as welding, spray painting, lifting, tending hot ovens, and manipulating nuclear fuel rods. Industrial robotics is an infant industry in the United States, but it is growing at a

staggering pace. The forecast is for the $100 million industry of 1980 to grow to a $2 billion industry by 1990, and to a $40 billion industry by the year 2000.

In 1984 the typical automobile assembly worker earned a substantial hourly wage, worked one shift per day, and, with consideration of breaks, sick days, and vacations, was productive about six hours per day. Industrial robots available today cost a few dollars per hour to run, work around the clock, and are productive almost all the time. Their main drawback, however, is their high initial cost, usually tens of thousands of dollars per robot. During the remainder of this decade, it is expected that wages will rise considerably, while robots will become more economical as they are mass produced. Most large assembly plants will be using robots extensively by 1990 (Figure 16–11).

General Motors had 500 robots in 1982 and may have more than 10,000 robots by 1990. General Electric is considering replacing half its assembly workers with robots eventually. By the year 2000, most automobile assembly work in the United States may be performed by automated machines. It is interesting to note that Communist countries are generally a decade or more behind the West and Japan in their use of robots.

How Robots Work

Most robots in use today are one-armed industrial robots used to perform various tasks on highly automated assembly lines. Figure 16–12 shows a typical industrial robot and the movements it can perform. Attachments such as paint sprayers, welding guns, riveters, claws, and scoops are connected to the end of the arm. The robot is programmed to move the arm to a certain location and then to activate the attachment.

Pick-and-place robots are relatively simple and dumb devices that merely pick up objects from one place and put them in another. They repeatedly perform only one task sequence on command.

The power of today's robots is only partly due to hardware; complex software generally guides the robot through its intricate actions. Programming a robot is not an easy task—it has been likened to trying to write down how to tie a shoe (you might try this as an interesting exercise). For this reason, robot manufacturers have developed a number of interesting schemes to help make the programming process easier.

With **programmable robots** a person leads the robot's arm manually through the series of movements and tasks it is to perform. The robot is designed to remember these movements and faithfully repeat the sequence upon command.

Figure 16–11 *Below:* Automobile assembly lines using robot welders. These machines work 10 times faster than humans, and they produce much higher quality work; in particular, the machines are more consistent than humans.

Figure 16–12 *Bottom:* An industrial robot. The arrows indicate the directions in which the robot may move.

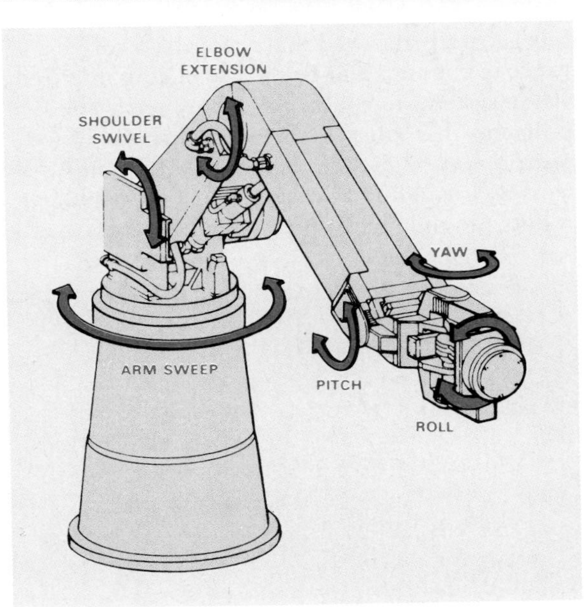

Reprogramming these robots is a tedious manual process.

Computerized robots are software programmable. Their task sequences are prepared and saved on a computer system. The instructions are transmitted electronically from the computer to the robot. They can be reprogrammed in an instant simply by transmitting new instructions.

Sensory robots have one or more artificial senses. These robots are generally computerized robots with limited vision or touch capabilities. Robots with a sense of hearing have been put to work evaluating musical instruments. Robots with senses of taste and smell are at work in wineries and breweries.

Once robot touch and vision capabilities are sufficiently developed, **assembly robots** will be put to work on assembly lines. They will have to be able to reach into a bin containing many different loose parts positioned at different angles, pick out the part they need, and attach it properly to the item being assembled. This problem is so difficult that it has been given its own name, the **bin picking problem**, and robot developers are aggressively attempting to solve it.

Robot Vision

It is generally believed that the next major advance in robotics will be the use of computerized vision systems to enable robots to "see." The problems that must be solved are incredibly complex; it may be decades before robot vision systems will rival human vision. Most of today's robots can only pick up an object that is properly positioned—an object not in exactly the right place might be crushed by a robot's arm. Today's blind welding robots expect an object to be positioned precisely; if the object is not there when the robot is ready to weld, the robot will perform its welding sequence anyway. With vision, robots will be able to determine if objects to be processed are in the proper position.

Robot vision systems currently under development convert signals from a TV camera into tens of thousands of dots of varying intensities. Computer programs analyze the dots and attempt to draw conclusions about what is being seen (Figure 16–13).

A robot vision system at the National Bureau of Standards (Figure 16–14) is able to locate and lift an egg without breaking it. If the robot is not quite in the right position, it moves to another location, takes another look at the egg, and tries again.

The pictures actually seen by robots normally contain only the most significant features of the objects being observed (Figure 16–15). This is done to reduce the amount of information the computer has to process so that the computer can decide what the object is in a reasonable amount of time.

Some basic vision systems are already at work in industry, especially as parts inspectors on assembly lines (Figure 16–16). But these systems have only the most primitive vision capabilities. They can recognize only a small number of parts and are easily confused by overlapping parts, similar parts, and shadows.

Researchers are currently developing computer programs capable of recognizing various kinds of objects and identifying the separate parts in a scene consisting of many objects. One problem they face is that vision requires so much computer power that it may take many minutes to see an object. With the more powerful computer systems currently being developed, it will eventually become possible for vision systems to see at the rapid speeds required on automated assembly lines.

Future computer systems are expected to be so powerful that robot vision should eventually surpass human vision in precision, speed, clarity, and detail. Robots will be built that can see micro-

Rampant Robots

Robots do fail occasionally. A component burned out in a robot at a major university causing the machine to hit itself so hard that it chopped off its own arm! At another university, a ping pong playing robot is reputed to have gone wild, smashed the game table, and chased its opponent around the room. Perhaps robots are poor sports!

Figure 16–13 To the human eye, a tank looks like the picture in Frame 1. But to a computer, the picture is simply a large array of numbers stored in its memory. It has to process that data to "recognize" the tank. In Frame 2, it analyzes light intensities of the picture. In Frame 3, it manipulates its stored data to identify edges of the tank. And in Frame 4, it has eliminated background and now has abstract edges and shapes from which it can proceed to recognize the tank.

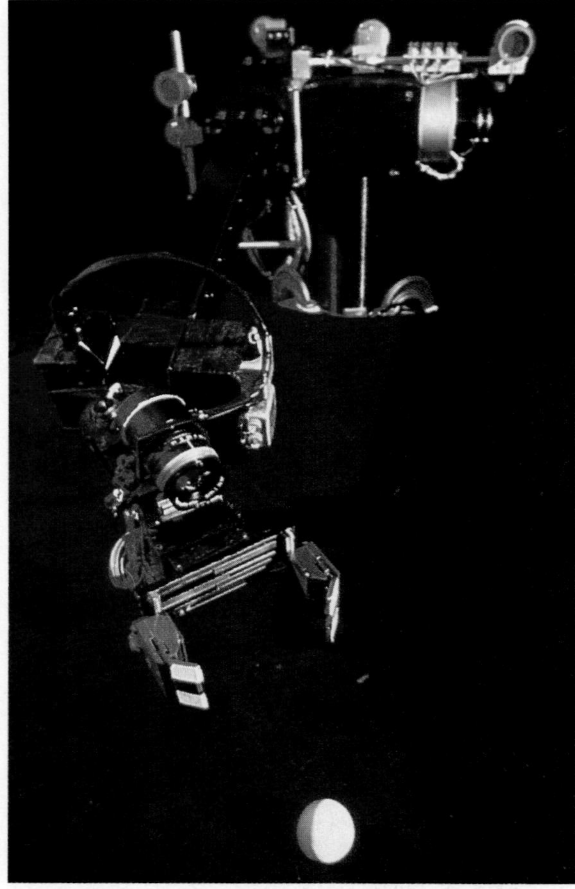

Figure 16–14 This robot arm uses a television camera "eye" and a sense of touch to pick up an egg without breaking it.

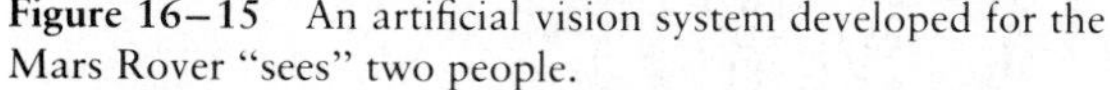

Figure 16–15 An artificial vision system developed for the Mars Rover "sees" two people.

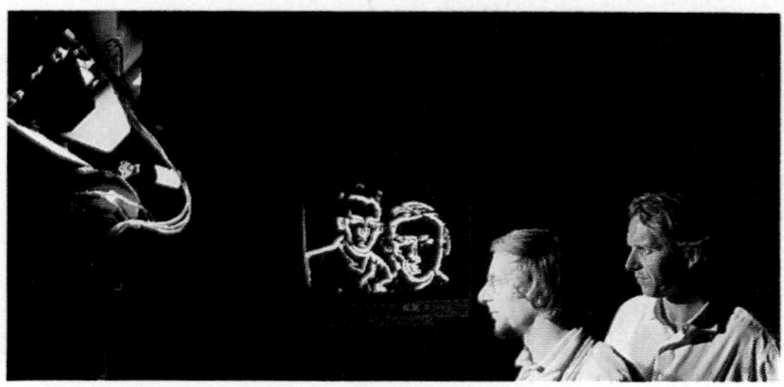

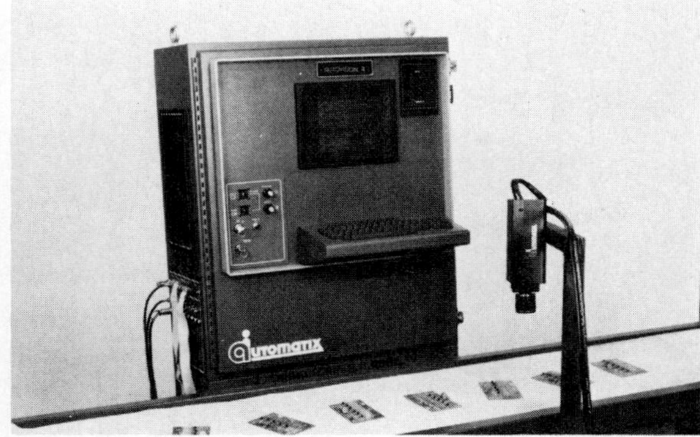

Figure 16–16 This visual inspection system can reject parts due to defects or missing components.

scopic parts, shadings, and color variations not perceivable by humans; some will be sensitive to infrared light so that they will be able to see in the dark.

An Artificial Sense of Touch

Today's industrial robots use crude gripper mechanisms to lift objects. These mechanisms operate either without a sense of touch, or with a primitive one that determines how much pressure the gripper exerts on an object.

Researchers are developing grippers that closely resemble the human hand and mimic its motions (Figure 16–17). Perhaps one useful test of such a robot hand would be to attach it to a robot programmed to play concert piano pieces! Another interesting experiment would be to build a robot sculptor that could use a vision system in conjunction with robot hands to make clay sculptures of objects it sees. A robot arm and hand with a built-in sense of touch has been developed that can grip and toss a baseball (Figure 16–18). Perhaps robot baseball players will help bring down high ticket prices!

Researchers at the Massachusetts Institute of Technology have constructed a robotic skin from thin sheets of rubber lined with a net of fine wires. The sheets are piled in several layers and wrapped around a robot's fingers and hand.

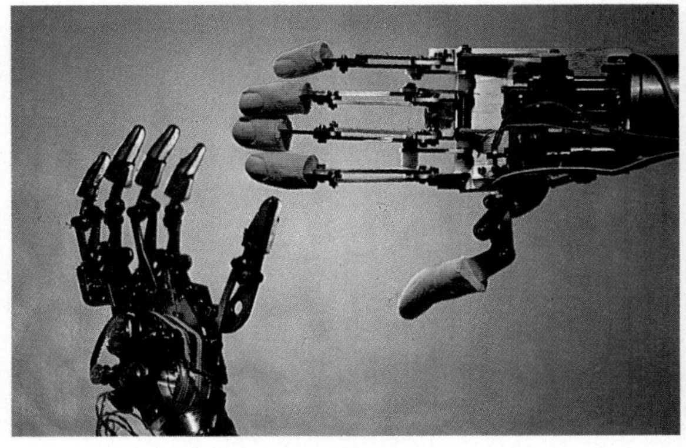

Figure 16–17 A robot's hand developed at Waseda University in Tokyo.

Figure 16–18 This robot hand, developed at the University of Tokyo, has sensors built into the fingers to provide the robot with an artificial sense of touch.

When the robot touches an object, the sheets come into contact causing different amounts of current to flow in the wires depending upon how much pressure is sensed. This robotic skin is connected to a computer system that analyzes the electric signals. The system can actually construct, from the touch signals alone, a video image of the object being touched.

Robot toys for children have been popular for decades, but these have been mostly "dumb" devices. New generation robot toys will carry on intelligent conversations with children and will have vision capabilities. Toy manufacturers in the United States are reputed to be spending more money developing robot toys than NASA spends developing space exploration robots.

Household Robots

Robots will eventually become economical enough to have around the house. Chores like cleaning, painting, and mowing the lawn may be routinely performed by household robots. Home security will improve greatly—what burglar would enter a home and confront a growling 300-pound guard robot!

Actually, a typical home is a far more complex place for a robot than an assembly line. The furniture is always being rearranged. The kids' toys are everywhere. The lighting varies day and night. Strange new voices and faces appear with visiting guests or with the arrival of a new baby. Even the most dedicated household robot might put your artificial fruit in the refrigerator, vacuum your jewelry, toss a salad in your favorite hat, mow your high pile carpeting, water your artificial plants, hang wallpaper over a fine painting, or attempt to resuscitate your child's dolls.

Organized Labor and Robotics

Unions generally have not been as violently opposed to robots as might be expected. There are several reasons for this:

1. The robotics industry in the United States is growing quickly, but it is still quite small. The time has not yet come when large numbers of blue-collar workers should feel threatened by robots. (But that time is rapidly approaching.)
2. So far, robots have generally been given jobs that are monotonous, hazardous, or dirty. (This, too, will change as more powerful robots begin to replace assembly workers, and eventually even white-collar workers.)
3. Companies have generally avoided firing workers whose jobs were eliminated by robots. Instead, they have relied on retirement and other factors to reduce the number of workers.

4. Unions know that American industry has been losing its competitive edge in world markets; and that this poses a much greater threat to blue-collar workers than robots do.
5. The number of people choosing to enter the manufacturing trades is declining rapidly each year. This has relieved some of the pressures against automation, while actually spurring interest in it as a means of filling the developing labor gap.
6. As the robotics industry grows, many new jobs are being created in the design, construction, programming, sales, and repair of robots.
7. An interesting irony is that among industrialized nations, the countries with the greatest numbers of robots have some of the lowest unemployment rates. (Why do you suppose this is so?)

A major issue of concern to the unions is job security for current workers. The unions recognize that industry must change, but they want this to be a gradual and responsible process in which the needs of current workers are not ignored.

Many workers have their suspicions. They hear that robots will be used only in boring and hazardous jobs. Of course a very large number of humans are employed in such jobs today. What is going to happen to them?

"Here, we've introduced robotics."

Social Issues

We cannot ignore the fact that robots can already perform many tasks better than humans can. They work faster, more economically, more accurately, in hostile environments, 24 hours per day, with no complaints, no vacations, no lunch breaks, and no time off for "personal reasons."

The smug human says "Ah, but they're just machines, they can't think or reason." That person may be in for a surprise. Robots may eventually be able to reason intelligently, and do so perhaps millions of times faster than humans!

Eventually, the ego of the human race may be shattered by the intelligence displayed by robots fresh off the assembly line. Instead of saying "ga ga," these robots may be able to carry on Ph.D.-level discussions in physics, economics, or any of hundreds of other fields. They may be built in hours instead of developing over a 9-month pregnancy. They may emerge from the robot factory as fully developed "adults" instead of having to "grow up" for 15 or 20 years while requiring the attention of adult "parents."

We currently view the robots we are creating as nothing more than mechanical slaves that will

Clapp's Laws of Robotics

Neale Clapp, a social scientist and industrial relations consultant, has suggested the following guidelines for smoothing labor-management relations when installing robots:

1. Organizations may not install robots to the economic, social or physical detriment of workers or management.
2. Organizations may not install robots through devious or "closed" strategies that reflect distrust for the work force, for surely they will fulfill their own prophecy.
3. Organizations may only install robots on those tasks which, while currently performed by humans, are tasks where the human is like a robot, not the robot like a human.

Quoted in *Creative Computing*, August 1980

Silent Sam

"Silent Sam," a product of Queens Devices, Inc. of Long Island City, N.Y., is an automated safety robot flagperson. He is used in hazardous areas to warn motorists to slow down and drive carefully. He works 24 hours per day in any weather. Union resistance to this kind of automation has been minimal; each year many human flagpersons are killed or injured by passing vehicles.

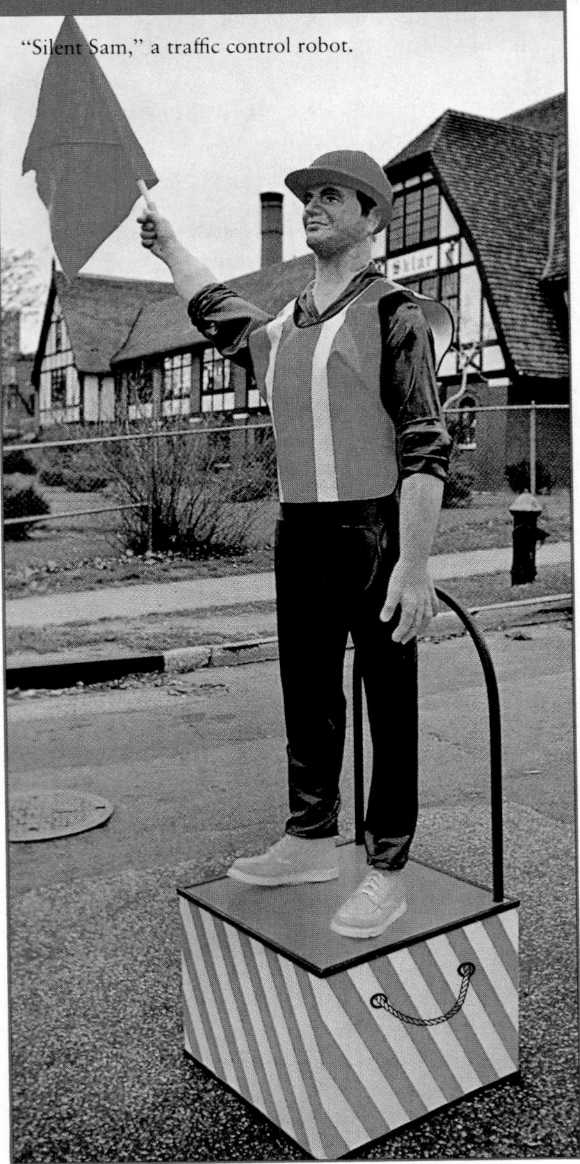

"Silent Sam," a traffic control robot.

free us from dirty jobs and boring, arduous labor. But as we make robots more intelligent, we must be careful to ensure that Asimov's Laws of Robotics be followed. If not, we may face the danger that the robots may rebel against us. A robot rebellion has been a favorite theme in science fiction. Technology is reaching the point that the fears of such a revolt may have a basis in reality.

Elimination of the Work Ethic

We are told that working makes us valued members of society, and, in fact, a partial measure of that value is the income we earn. The expectation of a young person today is to become gainfully employed, work a regular work week consisting of five eight-hour days, and have weekends and occasional vacation time and sick days off. In exchange for time spent working, this young person expects to make a living and provide for retirement at about age 65.

In contrast, our great grandparents, many of whom worked 14 hours per day, every day, might have considered these expectations absurd or even sinful. We can hear them saying "What will they do with all their free time—wander around and get into trouble?" Well, let's see how you react to this: Your great grandchildren may not have to work at all!

What Will People Do?

It is reasonable to predict the eventual decline of the work ethic. Our robots may build products better than we ever could. We may have an abundance of high-quality inexpensive goods to enjoy. Material wealth may become commonplace.

When robots can do our work better than we can, what will we do? Build more robots? Supervise factories run by robots? Surely we can envision the time when the world will have enough robots. We can also envision the time when new robots will be completely designed and constructed by other robots. In fact, the Japanese already have robot factories run by robots. In one such enterprise, there are more humans serving as tour guides than there are humans assisting with the operation of the factory.

Isaac Asimov feels that humans will redirect their energies:

"Robots will leave to human beings the tasks that are intrinsically human, such as sports, entertainment, and scientific research."

Quoted in *Time*, December 8, 1980

Joseph Engelberger has some interesting suggestions:

"You can keep the same level of material wealth but work only 20 hours a week. Leisure is, after all, another form of wealth. Or you can keep people working 40 hours a week, and produce great material wealth for everybody. Or you can use the extra productivity to clean the air and water. Quality of life may be what you want."

Quoted in *NEXT*, May/June 1980

Who Will Control the Wealth?

The wealth the robots generate may eventually be sufficient to fulfill our basic needs. But who, if anyone, will see to it that people receive this wealth? How will the wealth be distributed—to whom, and in exchange for what, if anything? One can't help but think that we may be heading toward the most massive welfare state of all time.

But welfare, until now, has involved the redistribution of relatively scarce resources. Goods and material wealth may become so abundant that distribution of wealth may involve merely seeing that people get what they need. We won't be allocating scarce resources—we may simply be ensuring that abundant resources do reach the people.

Should the government nationalize all robots and forbid private ownership? If it does, then it will certainly have the responsibility of deciding where these robots work, and on what projects. It must also then assume responsibility for distributing the wealth produced by the robots. To most Americans, this would be unacceptable. We want a government that serves our needs, not one that controls our lives.

It seems as though the best approach for now is to let the free market and free society forces operate as they may. If robots are good investments, then people will invest in them. If unions feel threatened by robots, then they will negotiate with industry through the collective bargaining process to limit their use. If robots destroy property or injure workers, then they will be liabilities to their owners who may be sued by the injured parties. If people feel that the robots are getting out of control, then they will initiate efforts to control them. If the government needs to change to respond to the needs of a heavily roboticized society, then it will change, because the people, looking out for their own best interests, will demand the changes.

"Sometimes I ask myself, 'Where will it ever end?' "

Philosophical Issues

As computer technology advances, we will eventually be able to build extraordinarily intelligent robots. They may have all the senses that humans possess plus many others. They will have great strength, a huge memory capacity, and may reason millions of times faster than humans. Some will be able to fly and others will swim to depths of thousands of feet. Perhaps most frightening of all, they may be able to reproduce themselves quickly with future members of the species designed to be better than current members—something humans cannot do (but may eventually be able to do with progress in genetic engineering).

Should we build these creatures? It is unlikely that humans will be deterred by the potential

"Arthur, there's a thing at the door says it's escaped from M.I.T. and can we please plug it in for the night."

Drawing by Chas. Addams; ©1971 The New Yorker Magazine, Inc.

dangers. We could legislate that all robots be built to obey Asimov's Laws, but such legislation would be difficult to enforce. The people who worked on the Manhattan Project developing the atom bomb in the early 1940s knew that they were creating weapons that might ultimately destroy humans—but that did not temper their zeal. Genetic engineers know that they may accidentally create disfigured mutations that might destroy the human race, yet they work at a more feverish pace each day.

We envision that it will eventually become necessary for humans to design laws to control the robots they create. The robots (many more decades hence) may feel the need to design laws to control humans!

As robots become highly intelligent and independent, should they be subject to the laws of human society, or should they have their own laws? Should these laws be imposed by humans or by robots themselves? Should a human sit as judge in a robot court or should there be robot judges? Could humans ever accept the ruling of robot judges in human cases?

Should we install robots as teachers in our children's classrooms? Could we trust these robots not to program our children with ideas contrary to human beliefs?

Would you "go under the knife" of a robot surgeon? Would you allow robot police to carry weapons and patrol our streets? Would you allow robot soldiers to control the weapons of destruction that humans have created and fight our wars? Should humans allow robots to create their own weapons of destruction?

Questions like these need to be deliberated carefully, and soon. Factories around the world are churning out robots at an ever-increasing pace. Universities are receiving substantial funds for research and development of intelligent robots. But, unfortunately, few people are actively investigating the implications of this work.

MIT's Marvin Minsky, one of the founding fathers of the field of artificial intelligence, says

> "Some will see extremely intelligent machines as a threat to our survival, others as a natural stage to our development."
>
> *U.S. News & World Report*, Nov. 2, 1981

Genetic engineers are now tinkering with DNA, the building block of life. The link between genetic engineering and computers is becoming increasingly clear. Some scientists believe that we may eventually be able to build living creatures to our own specifications. Minsky observes

> "Does it really matter if our descendants are made of flesh or of silicone or even of something completely different? Perhaps we should only care that they propagate our deepest wishes and aspirations."
>
> *U.S. News & World Report*, Nov. 2, 1981

We have the option today to bring all this to a halt. We can immediately destroy all these fearsome mechanical creatures. But they will probably be built sooner or later. Humans may eventually have to deal with a race of machines stronger and perhaps more intelligent than they are—a race that they seem destined to create.

"If it's human to err, what do computers do?"

The Turing Test of Intelligence

Alan Turing, a British mathematician, proposed the following test to determine if a machine could exhibit intelligent behavior. A person is situated in one room, and a machine in another. Another person, the interrogator, does not know which room the other person is in or where the machine is. The interrogator asks questions that are directed at the occupant of one of the rooms. The questions are given to an intermediary, and the responses from the occupants are passed to the interrogator through the intermediary. After asking as many questions as desired, the interrogator must attempt to determine which room contains the machine and which room contains the person. If the interrogator cannot distinguish between the person and the machine, then the machine is said to have passed the Turing test and thus exhibited intelligent behavior.

The **Turing Test** is elegant because of its simplicity and reasonableness. It has stood the test of time and is today considered the standard test of machine intelligence.

Expert Systems

A major area of research within the field of artificial intelligence is the development of **expert systems**. These are computer systems that can provide intelligent answers to questions in specialized areas of expertise and can do this as effectively as human experts in the area. One expert system might provide tax advice; another might suggest first aid in emergencies; yet another may counsel a high school student on how to apply to college and which colleges are most appropriate for the student's level of accomplishment. Expert medical diagnostic systems have been built (see Chapter 17) and expert prospecting systems have located hundreds of millions of dollars of mineral deposits.

There are many motivations for developing expert systems. They reduce dependence on human experts who may change their jobs. They "immortalize" expertise that is lost when a human expert dies. An expert system may be duplicated easily and put to use in many places simultaneously. Expert systems can work tirelessly around the clock, and they can exercise infinite patience while processing massive amounts of information at computer speeds.

Another motivation for developing expert systems is that the world's knowledge is doubling every few years. It is becoming ever more difficult for a human to master a significant portion of this knowledge. Expert systems, however, can easily retain ever larger amounts of knowledge.

It has been suggested that teachers and other professionals might eventually be replaced by expert systems. Imagine having a robot judge, for example. After both sides of your case have been presented, the judge makes a decision. To some people this is inconceivable. But aren't the vast majority of cases, especially civil cases, very similar and don't they have relatively straightforward verdicts? More likely, expert systems would be used to assist human judges who would then decide the cases, but only after the expert system had "heard the testimony" and made its recommendations.

A college professor we know often asks his classes to consider the following situation. If you cut your finger and ask an expert system what to do, what if the expert system tells you to amputate your finger? Almost invariably the students respond "Don't be ridiculous, I'd never blindly obey a machine's commands!" Our instructor friend then asks, "Well, what if you are driving around one morning at 3 A.M. and you reach an intersection where the light is red. Suppose there

are no cars in sight. Would you stop?" A very large part of the class inevitably responds, "Yes." Our instructor asks, "Why?" The class responds, "Because the law says that if the light is red we must stop." Our instructor responds "So, in fact, you are obeying a machine because our society tells you to obey a machine." Now the class perks up and listens more intently. Our instructor then asks "What if it became law that you must obey an expert system policeperson, or judge, or teacher, or boss? Would you?" At this point, a heated debate usually follows.

"It gives the answer as 12,621,859,007. But, it says it's just a hunch."

Expert System Components

An expert system generally consists of several key components. The **knowledge base** contains the factual knowledge and the rules of thumb of the given area of interest, sometimes called the **domain** of interest. The **inference engine** is a set of programs that reasons from the information contained in the knowledge base. The **natural language processor** is a set of programs that enables the user and computer to carry on a user-friendly dialogue. The **workspace** is a large area of memory in which the user's problem statement is placed, and which the computer uses as a scratchpad while solving the problem.

Expert systems with only the above major components could certainly produce answers. But users almost always want to know why and how expert systems reach their conclusions. So expert systems generally contain one additional component, an **explanation system**, that details for the user precisely how each conclusion is reached. In most envisioned applications, the expert system acts only as a consultant—not as a final authority. Actions are taken by humans after studying the problems themselves, developing their own analyses, as well as considering the recommendations made by expert systems. Therefore, effective explanation systems are essential if the advice of expert systems is to be seriously considered.

One bottleneck in the development of expert systems is in obtaining the information for the knowledge base. This is a complicated and tedious process in which a **knowledge engineer** painstakingly interviews a human expert called a **domain expert**. It is hoped that computer science schools will be producing increasing numbers of qualified knowledge engineers.

Natural Language Processing

Natural language processing is concerned with the problems of developing machines that understand natural languages such as English, French, German, and Spanish. The central problem in the field is called **natural language translation** where a machine is put to work translating text from one natural language to another, such as English to French, German to Russian, and so on. Researchers envision the day when machines will be able to translate from any one language to any other; this could eventually eliminate the language barriers that hinder international communications.

Will computers ever perform natural language translation perfectly? In fact, computers should eventually do about as well, or even a little better than humans do, but **ambiguity** (uncertainty of meaning) will always prevent perfect translation.

What is ambiguity? Consider, for example, a business enterprise known as "The Red Brick Factory." What product does it manufacture? Some people respond that it makes red bricks. But, in fact, it is possible that it is a red building that is a brick factory in which case we cannot say anything about the color of the bricks it manufactures! It could also be a factory built of red bricks in which case we cannot say anything about what it manufactures!

What problems does ambiguity cause? We simply cannot tell what an ambiguous sentence really means, so we may misinterpret it. Consider, for example, what happened when computers were used (legend has it) to translate the biblical phrase

"... the spirit indeed is willing, but the flesh is weak."
Matthew 26:40–41

from English to Russian and back again. The result was

"... the wine is agreeable, but the meat has spoiled."

Surely, something was "lost in the translation!"

Natural language processing is essential to the development of user-friendly interfaces. When coupled with successful speech synthesis and recognition mechanisms, it will enable humans to converse with their machines. When this finally happens people will warm up to and accept machines more readily. Somehow a device with a voice takes on a personality of its own. How does one design a personality for a computer voice? There may soon be angry computer voices, cheerful ones, or even "poker player" voices that show absolutely no emotion whatsoever.

One exciting application of natural language processing will be the development of systems that can read magazines and extract and summarize useful information for busy executives. Lawyers look forward to being able to ask subtle questions about legal issues and then have computer systems read through the legal literature to search for precedents. Intelligent books have been envisioned; these would carry on discussions with their readers about the meaning of stories and why characters behaved the way they did.

Heuristics

A **heuristic** is a rule of good judgment or a rule of thumb based on experience or intuition that human experts may use to attempt to solve a hard problem, usually one for which there is no known solution procedure. Heuristics rarely guarantee success; rather they increase the likelihood of success. For example, in the game of chess, experts often play strategies that help them gain control of the center board; they know from past experience that this is good to do, but they are in no way assured that control of the center board will lead to a win. This is the flavor of a heuristic. One test of the reasonableness of a heuristic is whether or not human experts agree it has merit; another is whether it does, in fact, yield successes when tried. Another popular chess heuristic (that is applicable to many other games as well) is to make the move that gives your opponent the smallest number of return moves to choose from; this is called the "fewest-replies" heuristic.

With computer systems, we choose heuristics that we can program. These are often rules that enable the computer to attach a "point value" to

Eliza and the Turing Test

Perhaps the most famous natural language-based system was the Eliza program developed in the early 1960s at MIT by Joseph Weizenbaum. Eliza played the part of a psychiatrist; the user played the part of a patient. Eliza really could not understand the sentences typed by the person. It merely looked for certain keywords and made its responses accordingly. If the user typed something Eliza could not understand, Eliza would respond with a canned question just to keep the dialogue moving.

Eliza became a phenomenon of its time. People enjoyed their conversations with the program. Psychiatrists indicated that Eliza-like programs might eventually perform psychiatric services for humans. This enraged Weizenbaum; he could not tolerate the notion that humans should even entertain the thought of using machines in this capacity. His concerns are expressed in his thought-provoking book *Computer Power and Human Reason*, W. H. Freeman and Company, San Francisco, 1976.

Another research group developed a program that simulated a psychopath. One day, these people called the MIT computer and let their psychopath program converse with Eliza. Many people who have seen the dialogue insist that it could have been two people talking, and that, therefore, these programs have passed the Turing Test.

©INFOSYSTEMS

"That's carrying automation a little too far!"

A Chess Machine That Couldn't Lose

Several chess playing computer games have been developed that use robot arms to move the machine's pieces. The designers of one of these games once challenged a chess master to a match. They bet him that the machine's special programming prevented it from losing. Certain he could beat any machine he accepted the bet. As the game progressed the master clearly outplayed the machine. But just as he was about to make the winning move, the robot arm knocked all the pieces off the board! The chess master lost the bet, but with a smile.

each of the possible alternatives. The computer then makes its decision by choosing the alternative with the highest point value. Heuristics that are poorly chosen may cause a computer to play a game poorly. Heuristics that may be appropriate for choosing opening moves in a game may, for example, not be appropriate for the "end game."

Knowledge engineers try to determine the heuristics of an area of expertise when they interview domain experts. These are then inserted into an expert system's knowledge base.

The Game of Chess

Chess is one of the most complex games devised by humans. The number of possible games is so large that playing a perfect game of chess is well beyond the range of any human, or of any imaginable computer system for that matter.

Artificial intelligence researchers have always viewed as a worthwhile goal the creation of a chess playing computer that could beat the world's best human player. A $100,000 prize has been offered for this accomplishment. Initially, it was thought unlikely that the prize would have to be paid before the turn of the century. But researchers have made so much progress in recent years that the payoff may come before 1990!

But suppose a machine is created that plays chess better than any human. Is that machine necessarily intelligent? No one can say for sure. What can be said is that such a machine would be solving a problem that humans have always associated with intelligent behavior. Until we understand what intelligence really is, the best we can say is that our machines are exhibiting what appears to be intelligent behavior. Actually, it does not matter whether or not we label such machine behavior as intelligent. The fact is that if we can build machines that do so well at chess, then we can probably build machines that can make complex business decisions, or diagnose illnesses reliably, or show creativity in designing buildings or painting pictures or writing poetry. The most interesting question, then, becomes how will the widespread use of such machines affect our lives?

Lisp: The Programming Language of Artificial Intelligence

The Lisp programming language (see Chapter 9) was developed in the late 1950s at MIT, but it is only now receiving widespread attention. Most conventional programming languages like COBOL, Fortran, Pascal, and BASIC are designed to manipulate numbers. Lisp, on the other hand, was designed to manipulate lists of symbols, and it is particularly adept at processing words and phrases.

Lisp makes it easy to relate items to one another. Each symbol stored in the computer's memory in a Lisp environment is also stored with directions on where to find related symbols in other parts of the computer's memory. So Lisp is ideal for storing the kinds of **knowledge structures** like the **if-then rules** used in many expert systems.

For example, a knowledge base may contain rules like: If it is dark and cloudy, then it is likely to rain; if it is raining, then a person could get wet; if clothes get wet, then they could be ruined; if a person doesn't want to get wet from rain, then that person should use an umbrella.

From rules like these, an expert system might conclude that if it is dark and cloudy, and if you do not want to risk ruining your clothes, then you should carry an umbrella.

Lisp programs are themselves lists of symbols, so they may be processed by other Lisp programs. In fact, a Lisp program may even process itself! This intriguing capability facilitates the writing of programs that learn; based upon a program's success rate with certain game playing strategies, that program might modify itself to play future games differently.

Lisp runs best on very powerful computers with very large memories. Special-purpose computers have been developed that run Lisp programs efficiently, but these **Lisp machines** are still relatively expensive; increasing demand coupled with mass production should make it possible to produce inexpensive Lisp machines within the next several years. Many people believe that when this occurs Lisp will become very widely used, and artificial intelligence will experience a great surge in interest.

Serial Versus Parallel Computers

Most computer systems today employ a single CPU, or processor, to execute instructions, so these systems can "concentrate" effectively on only one task at a time. But what about situations in which many tasks must be managed at once, in particular where the computer is used to model the human brain?

It is known that electrical signals travel through our nerves at only a few hundred miles per hour—a snail's pace compared to the speed of electricity through a wire. So how is it that the human brain can simultaneously control our sight, smell, touch, taste, hearing, muscular system, nervous system, and various organs. The answer is believed to be that the brain consists of many billions of processors that function in parallel. Some of these processors handle hearing, others handle sight, and yet others control the slightest motions of the smallest muscles. Thus, today's **serial processors**, that is, processors that process one task at a time, are simply not effective at performing human tasks such as seeing, hearing, and even thinking.

Researchers are currently developing highly parallel computers, that is, computers with many processors that function simultaneously. Computers with a few such processors are called **multiprocessors. Massive parallelism** refers to computers with hundreds, thousands, or even more processors; so many processors, in fact, that a different processor may be set to work on each separate activity that may be accomplished in parallel. Such computers may eventually enable us to simulate the functions of the human brain effectively. But that time is at least decades away.

Current technology allows circuit designers to place hundreds of thousands of components on a single chip. It may well be necessary to place hundreds of millions of components on a chip before a computer can be built in a small enough space for us to give robots human-sized brains that rival our own. Researchers appear confident that such an accomplishment will be within reach in the next century.

Summary 

1. Most of today's robots are dumb machines. They often consist of nothing more than a metal arm connected to a box of controls.
2. Computers are critical to the operation of the more powerful robots now being developed. Industrial robots perform many tasks more economically than humans can. Robots are particularly useful in hazardous environments.
3. The term robot comes from the Czech noun "robota" meaning "forced labor." Dr. Isaac Asimov, the father of fictional robotics, coined the term "robotics" and wrote the widely quoted Laws of Robotics.
4. The first production line robot was built by Unimation and installed by General Motors in 1961. Joseph Engelberger, who served as president of Unimation, is generally recognized as the father of industrial robotics.
5. First generation robots are dumb mechanical manipulators. Second generation robots are more powerful and often have elementary vision and touch capabilities. Third generation robots now being developed will have highly developed sensory capabilities and limited intelligence. Highly intelligent fourth generation robots will probably not appear until the 1990s.
6. Pick-and-place robots lift objects from one place and move them to another. Programmable robots are programmed by having a human lead the robot's arm through its task sequence. Computerized robots are programmed electronically by having a computer transmit instructions to the robot. Sensory robots are computerized robots with one or more artificial senses, usually sight or touch. Assembly robots are computerized robots with sensors specifically designed to perform assembly jobs such as fetching parts from bins.
7. Robot vision systems use a TV camera attached to a computer system that analyzes the data from the camera to determine what is being seen. Future computer systems are expected to be so powerful that robot vision may surpass human vision. Grippers for robots have been constructed that resemble the human hand. At MIT a robotic skin has been constructed from thin sheets of rubber lined with fine wires and connected to a computer system.
8. Labor unions have adopted a wait-and-see policy toward robotics, but this is likely to change as increasingly intelligent robots replace assembly workers.
9. Artificial intelligence is the study of making machines exhibit intelligent behavior. The Turing Test of artificial intelligence considers a machine to be intelligent if its responses to an interrogator's questions are indistinguishable from a human's responses.
10. An expert system is a computer system that can provide intelligent answers to questions in specialized areas of expertise about as well as, or even better than, a human expert in that area can.
11. The key components of an expert system are the knowledge base that contains knowledge obtained from a human expert, the inference engine that enables the expert system to draw conclusions, the natural language processor

that allows the expert system to carry on user-friendly dialogues with human users, a workspace for holding the problem definition, and an explanation system that explains to human users how and why the expert system reaches its conclusions.

12. The field of natural language processing is concerned with developing computer systems that understand natural languages such as English, French, German, and the like. Ambiguity is one of the key problems in this area.

13. A heuristic is a rule of good judgment or a rule of thumb based on experience or intuition that human experts may use to attempt to solve a hard problem, usually one for which there is no known solution procedure.

14. Lisp is the favored programming language in the field of artificial intelligence because of its symbol manipulation capabilities. Economical Lisp machines to appear in the near future should cause a surge of activity in artificial intelligence.

15. One development that may increase the pace of activity in artificial intelligence will be the development of economical computers that exhibit massive parallelism.

Important Terms

ambiguity
anthropomorphic robot
artificial intelligence (AI)
Asimov's Laws of Robotics
assembly robot
audio-animatron
bin picking problem
Clapp's Laws of Robotics
computerized robot
domain expert
expert system
explanation system
flexible automation
heuristic
if-then rules
industrial robot
inference engine
knowledge base
knowledge engineer
knowledge structures
Lisp machine
natural language processing
pick-and-place robot
programmable robot
robot
robotics
sensory robot
steel collar worker
Turing Test
Unimation

Self-Review Exercises

Matching

Next to the term in column A, place the letter of the statement from column B that is most closely associated with it.

Column A

1. Joseph Engelberger
2. Programmable robot
3. Karel Capek
4. Alan Turing
5. Neale Clapp
6. Isaac Asimov
7. Natural language translation
8. Marvin Minsky
9. Fourth generation robots
10. Computerized robot

Column B

A. A founding father of the field of artificial intelligence
B. Father of fictional robotics
C. Can be reprogrammed electronically
D. The first highly intelligent robots
E. Ambiguity prevents this from being 100 percent effective
F. His laws are meant to serve as guidelines for smoothing labor-management relations when installing robots
G. Father of industrial robotics
H. Reprogrammed by leading its arm through the new task
I. Wrote *R.U.R.* and coined the term "robot"
J. Developed a test for machine intelligence

Fill-in-the-Blanks

Fill in the blanks in each of the following:

1. The country that is the largest user of industrial automation and robots in the world is ______.

2. ______ robots resemble humans.

3. ______ robots are the simplest kind of robots; they are essentially mechanical transfer devices.

4. More adaptable automation called ______ automation is appropriate for small batch environments.

5. One type of knowledge structure used in expert systems is a set of ______ rules.

6. ______ are computer systems that can provide intelligent answers to questions in specialized areas of expertise.

7. A rule of good judgment or a rule of thumb based on experience or intuition is called a ______.

8. ______ is the preferred programming language in the field of artificial intelligence.

9. ______ refers to a computer with so many processors that different processors would be available to work simultaneously on all separate activities that may be accomplished in parallel.

10. The expert system component that reasons from the facts contained in the knowledge base in order to generate conclusions is called the ______.

Answers to Self-Review Exercises

Matching: 1 G, 2 H, 3 I, 4 J, 5 F, 6 B, 7 E, 8 A, 9 D, 10 C

Fill-in-the-Blanks:
1. Japan
2. Anthropomorphic
3. Pick-and-place
4. flexible
5. if-then
6. Expert systems
7. heuristic
8. Lisp
9. Massive parallelism
10. inference engine

Discussion Questions

1. Discuss Asimov's Laws of Robotics. Suggest some other laws of robotics.

2. Give several reasons why robots are likely to explore deep space before humans do.

3. Programming a robot has been likened to trying to write down how to tie a shoelace. Do this and comment on any difficulties you experience.

4. List and discuss briefly each of the types of industrial robots.

5. List several reasons why unions haven't been as violently opposed to robots as might be expected.

6. Comment on Clapp's Laws of Robotics. Are they realistic?

7. What is an expert system? List and briefly describe each of the major components of a typical expert system.

8. What is natural language processing? Why is there so much interest in this field? What would be the ultimate development in this field?

9. List several factors that have held back the use of Lisp. What developments are likely to foster the widespread use of Lisp?

10. What is massive parallelism? Why is it important to the future of artificial intelligence?

Projects 

1. The following companies are vendors of industrial robots. Write to several of them requesting their literature. Visit some of them if possible. Report on the types, costs, capabilities, and applications of industrial robots.

Advanced Robotics Corp.
Newark Ohio Industrial Park, Bldg. 8
Hebron, OH 43025

American Robot Corp.
P.O. Box 10767
Winston-Salem, NC 27108

ASEA Inc.
4 New King St.
White Plains, NY 10604

Automatix Inc.
217 Middlesex Turnpike
Burlington, MA 01803

Cincinnati Milacron
4701 Marburg Ave.
Cincinnati, OH 45209

Cybotech
P.O. Box 88514
Indianapolis, IN 46208

Devilbiss-Trallfa
300 Phillips Ave., P.O. Box 913
Toledo, OH 43692

International Robomation/Intelligence
2281 Las Palmas Drive
Carlsbad, CA 92008

Planet Corp. Robot Division
27888 Orchard Lake Rd.
Farmington Hills, MI 48018

Robot Systems Inc.
50 Technology Parkway
Technology Park Atlanta
Norcross, GA 30092

Seiko Instruments
2990 W. Lomita Blvd.
Torrance, CA 90505

Unimation Inc.
12 Shelter Rock Lane
Danbury, CT 06810

United States Robots Inc.
1000 Conshohocken Rd.
Conshohocken, PA 19428

2. Assume that intelligent robots that move about freely among humans will be common in the 21st century. Write an essay describing what you think the world will be like then.

3. Write an essay describing the benefits and dangers to society if intelligent superhuman robots are developed.

4. Contact the national offices of several large labor unions and request any literature they may offer on automation and robotics. Report on the issues discussed in this literature.

5. Visit a university or a company doing research in robotics. Report on your findings.

6. Write an essay on household robots. Describe several functions that household robots might usefully perform.

7. Suppose robots will make it possible for people not to have to work for a living in the future. Write an essay describing what society might be like. Do you think this would lead to a welfare state?

8. Play a game such as chess, checkers, or backgammon with a computer. Write a report comparing your experience with that of playing against human opponents.

9. Write an essay in which you argue both for and against the development of robot soldiers to replace all human soldiers and thus eliminate the draft.

10. Write an essay examining the issues of using robots in sports. Should robots and humans play on the same sports teams? Would sports fans enjoy watching robot athletes? Design a set of rules for holding a world championship heavyweight robot boxing match—this would make a marvelous TV special!

11. Suppose you hear a knock at the door, and you look through the peephole to see a robot standing there. Would you open your door to a strange robot? Suppose it is a door-to-door vacuum cleaner salesrobot and you happen to need a new vacuum cleaner. Would

you let the salesrobot in to give you a demonstration? Explain your answers. Compare your attitudes toward salespeople with your attitudes toward salesrobots.

12. Write an essay examining the pros and cons of using intelligent robot teachers in our classrooms.

Chapter 17

Computers and Medicine

After reading this chapter you will understand:

1. How computer technology is being used in the medical field to improve health care
2. How computer-based scanning devices work and how they are used to diagnose various illnesses
3. How computers are used in matching donors and recipients for organ transplants
4. How database management systems are used to maintain extensive medical libraries and detect drug conflicts
5. Some of the controversies raised by using computers in the medical field

Left: This strange illustration shows the effect obtained by a CAT scan, one of the miracles of modern medicine made possible by computer technology. The device compiles pictures of "slices" of the human body without any surgery. (The operation of the CAT scan is explained in the text.)

Outline

"I'd like to call in a colleague to recommend a diagnosis," he tells the patient. The consultant he has in mind has decades of medical experience, an infallible memory for past cases and an encyclopedic knowledge of symptoms and diseases. The consultant, whose only shortcoming is a rather cold bedside manner, is a computer.

Richard Stengel
Calling "Dr. SUMEX"

Says Myers, "CADUCEUS is about on a par with a good human internist." In fact, he says, it has passed the certifying examination of the American Board of Internal Medicine, the test that is used to assess the credentials of internal medicine specialists in the United States.

Kevin McKean
DISCOVER

The low cost and small size of microprocessors has made it possible to build **intelligent control** into medical diagnostic, monitoring, and control equipment at a nominal expense. The enhanced capabilities of today's medical equipment are dramatically changing the practice of medicine and improving the outlook for the patient.

The American Medical Association, recognizing the importance of computers, publishes a journal called *Computers in Medicine* and has created a number of groups to foster development of computers for medical applications. Many of the professional societies in the computer field have created special interest groups to increase communication between individuals and organizations interested in medical computing.

With computerized diagnostic tools, the vast majority of exploratory surgery may be eliminated. In fact, surgery is often performed today on suspicion of an ailment rather than because of positive confirmation.

'Our Computer's on the Blink, but I'll Take a Shot in the Dark — It Could Be Gall Stones.'

'There's No Easy Way to Tell You This, Mr. Brown, But Our Diagnostic Computer Says You're Dead.'

Computer Doctors

The patient, a 67-year-old man, was anemic and feverish. His liver was enlarged, and his legs were swollen with fluid and peppered with blue and purple splotches. After many tests, doctors at Pittsburgh's Presbyterian-University Hospital were still not sure what was wrong. They had narrowed their choice to cancer of the bone marrow, an infection in the heart, or amyloidosis, a buildup of abnormal protein in the body's organs.

The physicians ordered biopsies of the liver and of the bone marrow. They also consulted CADUCEUS, a medical computer system capable of diagnosing 500 diseases. Even before the biopsies were analyzed, CADUCEUS made the correct diagnosis: amyloidosis.

Named after the emblem of the medical profession, CADUCEUS was conceived a decade ago by Jack Myers, a white-haired, cigar-smoking internist, and Harry Pople, a computer expert at the University of Pittsburgh. Using a computer at Stanford University Medical Center, CADUCEUS identifies the relationship between a patient's problems and the diseases that may be causing them. It does this with two scales ranging from zero, indicating a weak connection, to five, a very strong connection. The first scale, based on Myers's clinical experience, assesses the likelihood that a patient's complaint is caused by a given disease. The second, based on medical literature and interviews with experts, assesses how likely it is for a patient with a specific disease to have a particular complaint. For example, when CADUCEUS is told that a patient has an abdominal mass on the lower right side, it provides a list of 18 diseases that might cause such a lump. The disease with the highest numbers, and thus the most likely cause, turns out to be cancer of the right colon. Its numerical rating, 2-3, signifies that a significant minority of patients with such a mass have cancer of the right colon and that about half of all patients with colon cancer on the right side have such a mass.

Patients, though, sometimes have many complaints, not just one or two. So after a doctor tells CADUCEUS all the problems he has found—as well as those he has looked for but not found—the computer finds all the diseases evoked by each complaint. CADUCEUS then culls this list until it determines the diseases that have the strongest connection to them. If CADUCEUS has not received enough information to reach a diagnosis, it will ask for more—and in a startingly blunt fashion. Sometimes it will demand additional test results, and sometimes it will curtly interview the physician, insisting on only yes or no responses. These questions can suggest a new approach and possibly eliminate unnecessary and costly tests. "In many difficult cases, the doctor orders everything and sees how it sorts out," says Randolph A. Miller, who assists Myers with the project. "CADUCEUS allows a more directed work-up so that the patient needn't see everyone and his brother."

In spite of CADUCEUS' rudeness, the relationship between doctor and computer has so far worked well. Myers has demonstrated in trial runs that CADUCEUS can take different cases from the wards of Presbyterian-University Hospital and, more often than not, find the correct diagnosis. This spring formal field trials of about 10 cases a day will begin. If successful, they are expected to be repeated at half a dozen other hospitals. Myers hopes doctors across the country will be using CADUCEUS within a decade.

As promising as CADUCEUS seems, it still has not mastered some of the finer points of medical thinking. For one thing it cannot handle subtle reasoning about time, and, to a doctor, the order in which things happen can be very important. A patient with severe abdominal pain, for example, is more likely to have appendicitis if the pain was not preceded by a fever. The computer also gets mixed up when a patient has several unrelated ailments.

CADUCEUS will soon be endowed with a second-generation program that, Myers hopes, will solve some of these bugs. Still, he has no fear that CADUCEUS will someday make internists like him obsolete. "Patients can't be objective," he says. "If a patient sat down and put in things, the patient would get back a garbled analysis." Nor has Myers or anyone else taught a computer to smile, hold a patient's hand, or, for that matter, make house calls.

Gerald Lanson, *SCIENCE 81/Cross Currents,* March 1981, pp. 89 and 92. Reprinted by permission of *SCIENCE 84* Magazine, copyright the American Association for the Advancement of Science.

Computer-Based Scanning Systems

Some of the more dramatic applications of computers in medicine have come from various types of **computer-based scanning systems.** These systems use techniques such as x-rays, gamma rays (see the box on page 453), and **ultrasound** (Figures 17–1 and 17–2) to obtain thousands of separate pieces of data about a person's internal organs. Computers then reassemble this data into still or moving pictures. The various scanning techniques are **noninvasive diagnostic techniques,** which means they do not use surgery in order to obtain a precise picture of the inside of the human body. In the next several sections we discuss some of the popular computer-assisted scanning techniques.

Figure 17-1 An ultrasound scanner.

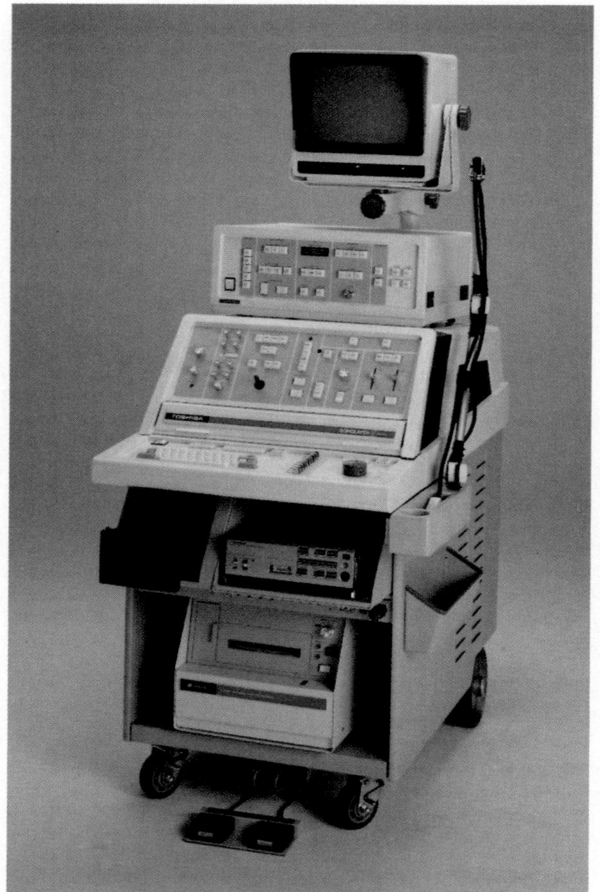

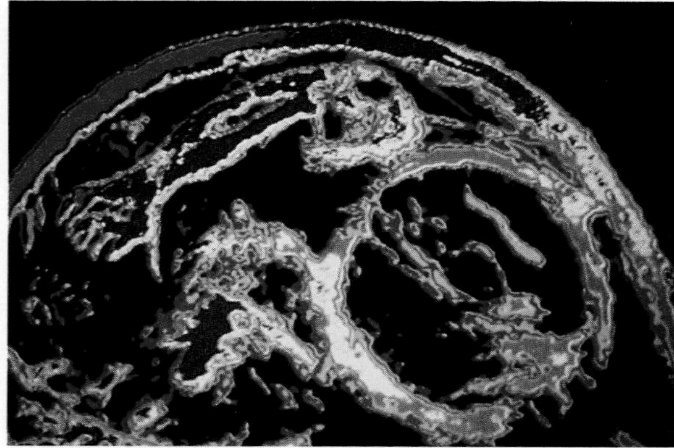

Figure 17-2 An ultrasound picture of a fetus in the womb. The head is at the right and one arm is clearly visible across the top.

The CAT Scan

The most significant application of computers in modern medicine is probably the **CAT scan.** This device combines x-ray equipment and computer technology to produce detailed pictures of "slices" of the human body.

The CAT scan was pioneered by Godfrey Hounsfield of EMI Ltd. in Great Britain and independently by Allan Cormack, a Tufts University physicist. They shared the 1979 Nobel Prize for medicine or physiology for their contributions. The first EMI system, designed for brain scanning, was delivered to the Mayo Clinic in 1973. Since that time, several thousand systems have been installed throughout the world; about half are in use in the United States. With a price tag in the range of half a million dollars or more, the CAT scan is one of the most expensive medical devices in use today.

The CAT scan (for computer-assisted tomography or computer-axial tomography) uses the principles of **tomography** that have been well-known for half a century, but it took computer technology to make them practical. Tomography means "the description of slices," an accurate explanation of what the CAT scan provides.

A patient is injected with a radioactive fluid and lies on a couch that passes slowly through the scanning unit. The machine shoots x-rays through the patient's body. These x-rays strike detectors and produce signals that are then transmitted to a computer. The computer processes

Elscint's Newest Marvel

Elscint has developed the Apex 115 gamma camera, a $130,000 machine to help doctors make difficult diagnoses. It is the first to combine the camera and a powerful specialized computer into a single apparatus, thus yielding especially sharp and detailed TV-like pictures. Radiation from a patient's body is transformed into electrical signals; these are fed through tubes and computers to give a moving image of an internal organ. How it works: ❶ A radioactive isotope in a chemical solution with an affinity for a specific organ or malignancy is injected into the patient's bloodstream. ❷ The area under examination (in this case the heart) emits gamma rays. ❸ The collimator, a sieve-like filter, focuses the rays. ❹ A thin crystal of sodium iodide, bombarded by 700,000 gamma rays per second, changes them into photons, or flashes of light. ❺ Light guides convey the photons to photocathode tubes, which measure the photons and convert their energy into electrical impulses. ❻ Circuitry translates these impulses into binary code that computers can use. ❼ A moving image of the heart is created by computer, with a total delay of only 30 seconds. ❽ The display console exhibits the heart in operation. Different parts appear in different colors to aid diagnosis. The right screen displays measurements of the amount of blood ejected by each contraction of a ventricle, for example, and also tells what buttons to push to obtain other images, such as a close-up of part of the heart.

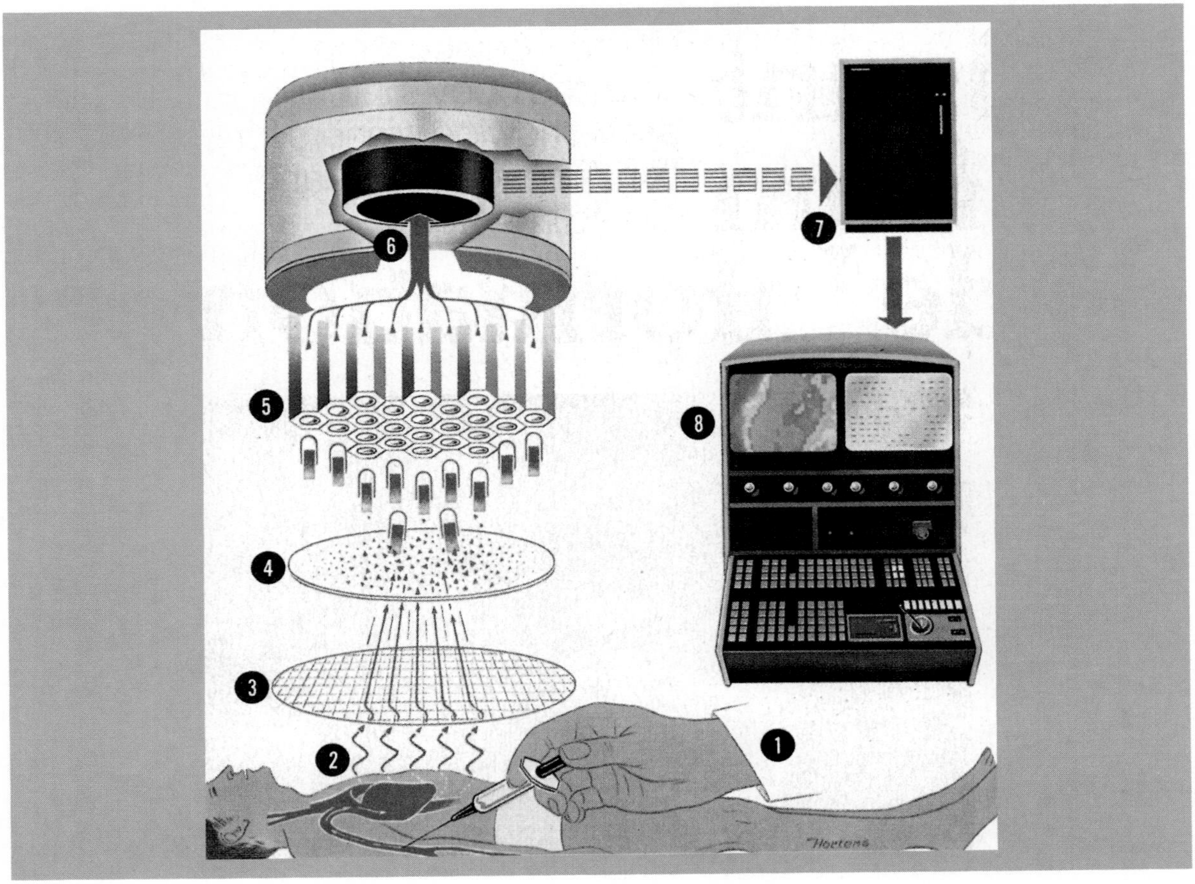

this massive amount of data into a still picture, produced on a screen and in hard copy, showing a "slice" of the person's body. The picture contains different shadings and colors for the various materials being shown such as fluids, organ tissues, and bone. CAT scan pictures rival the quality of direct photographs. Of course, such photographs of a living patient could never be taken—the patient would have to be sawed in half! The x-ray tube rotates periodically to obtain data from many different angles. The computer knows what data corresponds to which angles and through programming is able to construct on the screen an image of the slice. Each exposure, lasting less than a second, requires more than 100,000 watts of electricity!

The high cost of the CAT scan has made it the focus of much controversy. The federal government requires hospitals to file a "certificate of need" before being allowed to purchase a CAT scan. Independent businesses have been formed to share the high costs of the equipment by placing CAT scans in vans and moving them from hospital to hospital on a regular schedule. This has made it possible for smaller hospitals to use CAT scans, too. Critics point out that cheaper ways are available to diagnose many of the disorders CAT scans are used to detect. In time less expensive models should become available, enabling more people to benefit from this technology.

We can expect improvements to be made in CAT scans so that models will be developed that use far less radiation than the current ones. Eventually CAT scans will actually be able to produce motion pictures. The more versatile scanners of the future may completely eliminate invasive diagnostic techniques.

CAT scans are also being designed to assist industry. For example, electrical workers use CAT scans mounted on the arm of a crane to find faults in light poles. Scientists at General Electric are using CAT scanning to study how coal burns at various temperatures. Their hope is to use this information to develop more efficient coal furnaces.

The PET Scan

Researchers are experimenting with a new technique called the **PET scan** (positron emission tomography) that can map brain activity (Figure 17–3). The PET scan monitors glucose (sugar)

Figure 17-3 A woman being prepared for a PET scan.

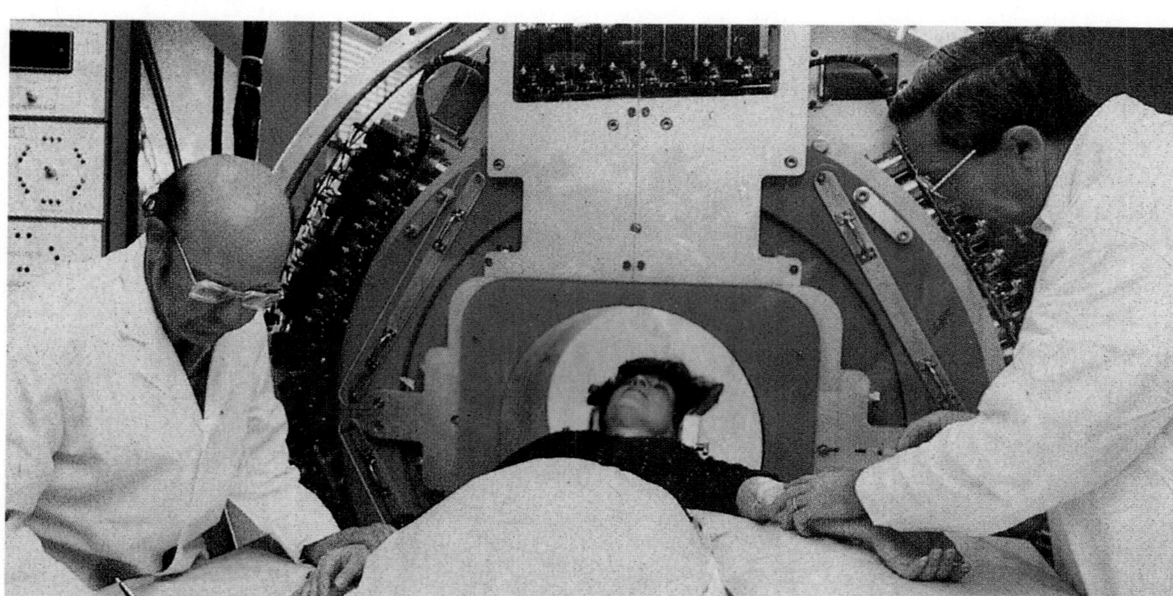

Bernard Gotfryd — Newsweek

activity to determine areas of abnormal metabolism (the rate of "body function"). It can determine if a patient is manic-depressive (one who suffers from alternating extremes of excitement and depression) or schizophrenic (one who exhibits withdrawn behavior or delusions and suffers intellectual and emotional deterioration).

The patient receives an injection containing a glucose-related compound and radioactive fluorine. As the radioactive chemical is absorbed by the brain cells, a complex interaction causes radiation to be emitted. Information about this radiation is processed by a computer, which then generates a color picture on a screen. The different shades of color in the picture indicate the levels of glucose metabolism in various areas of the patient's brain. These shadings and colorings can reveal the presence of serious mental disorders (Figure 17–4).

The PET scan may also be useful in the treatment of epilepsy, a disorder of the nervous system usually characterized by seizures followed by a loss of consciousness. The scan can locate the portions of the brain involved in epileptic seizures and can direct surgeons to destroy those cells.

Many heart patients have to suffer through a painful and dangerous diagnostic procedure in which a catheter (thin flexible tube) is inserted into a blood vessel and pushed directly into the chambers of the heart. The PET scan can monitor blood flow without catheterization and can help diagnosticians see inside tiny capillaries (the minute blood vessels between the ends of the arteries and beginning of the veins) inaccessible to catheters.

Another form of computerized scanning being used to diagnose heart and blood vessel problems is called **angiography**. It uses x-rays to locate internal bleeding, heart disease, and obstruction of blood vessels by tumors. A dramatic angiograph picture is shown in Figure 17–5.

Figure 17-4 Normal, manic-depressive, and schizophrenic brain scans.

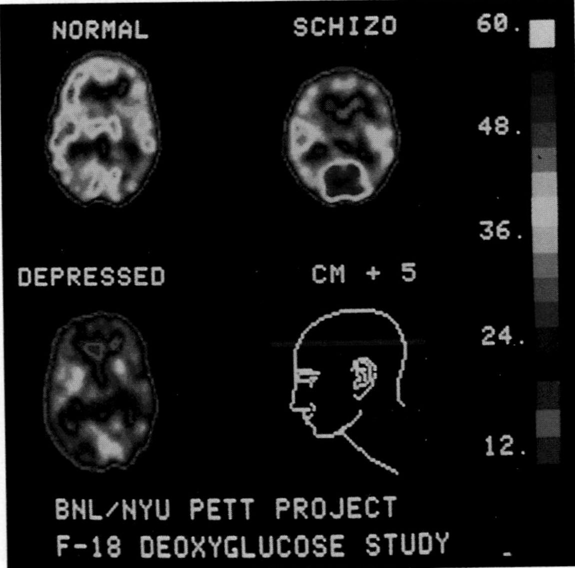

Figure 17-5 A view inside the body provided by angiography.

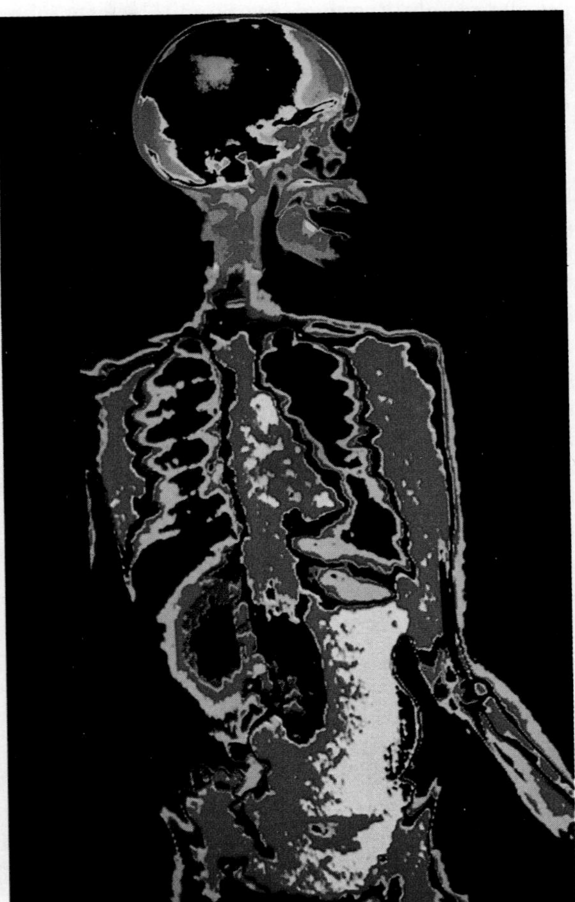

Dynamic Spatial Reconstructor

The state of the art in computerized x-ray scanning technology is a device constructed by Raytheon for the Mayo Clinic. Called the **Dynamic Spatial Reconstructor** (DSR), this 25-foot x-ray machine weighing 17 tons provides three-dimensional motion pictures of organs. These images may be rotated or sliced to allow physicians to probe into places ordinarily hidden in conventional x-rays. Computer processing can even look through the muscle tissue of an organ to show only the blood vessels on the display screen.

Heart Research

The human heart is about the size of a clenched fist and weighs less than one pound. It beats more than 100,000 times each day and services about 60,000 miles of blood vessels. Microcomputers are now being integrated into **implantable devices** (Figure 17–6), such as **pacemakers**, to provide precise control of heart functions. The battery-powered devices previously used are being replaced with mechanisms powered by body heat, so regularly scheduled surgery to replace batteries is no longer needed. This is important because heart patients always suffer a great risk when undergoing surgery. Approximately 500,000 Americans have pacemakers in their chests. According to Abigail Trafford (*U.S. News & World Report*, March 15, 1982, p. 57), "No longer a simple, cumbersome device, today's computerized pacemakers are designed to monitor and correct many types of abnormal rhythms." She quotes Dr. Donald C. Harrison, president of cardiology at Stanford University School of Medicine, in Stanford, California, as saying, "It's like putting a computer in your chest."

Heart monitoring devices are being developed that allow physicians to obtain readings from inside the body without surgery; the external monitors receive signals broadcast from transmitters that have been surgically implanted.

Researchers are building **externally programmable control devices** that perform many more functions than the common pacemaker and can

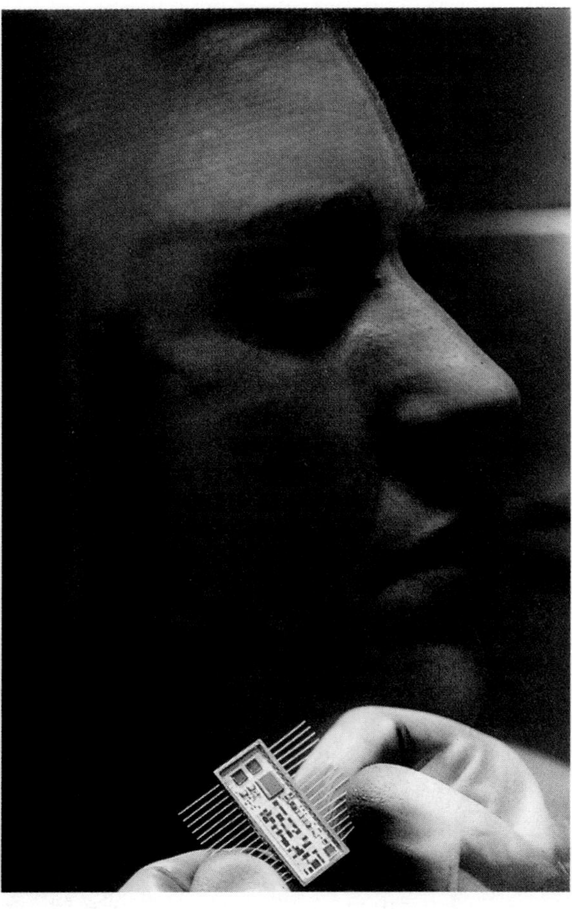

Figure 17-6 Microcircuits like this are key components of implantable medical devices such as pacemakers and drug delivery systems.

be altered to react to changes in the patient's heart activity. These devices can be reprogrammed from outside the patient without the need for surgery. When changes in the patient's heart function occur, doctors can send electronic signals to the implanted microprocessor to modify its program.

A patient with an implanted monitoring device would no longer need to travel to a heart specialist's office for examination. Instead, the patient could dial a special phone number, place a modified telephone receiver near the appropriate portion of the chest, and transmit current information directly from within the chest to a diagnostic computer system. If the computer detects any irregularities, it can warn the patient to see a

Device Pinpoints Location of Heart Victims

Two years ago, when a friend suffered a fatal heart attack on a lonely country road, Reginald M. Spencer, president of American Computer Information Systems, Inc., decided to find a way to help future victims. The result is Heart Alert, an electronic beeper device weighing six ounces that can be attached to a belt or pocket. When heart patients feel an impending attack, they press a button which sends out a radio signal to a receiving station. By using computer technology, the victim's location is accurately pinpointed and the nearest fire department's rescue squad is quickly dispatched.

Venture, August 1982, p. 8

doctor immediately and can notify the doctor of the patient's problem. For less serious problems the computer can transmit signals back over the phone to the implanted control device to alter its functions.

Electrocardiograms (or EKGs as they are commonly called) are graphical records of a patient's heart activity. Ordinarily, taking an EKG requires a time-consuming office visit during which sensors from an electrocardiograph machine are taped to the patient. It is now possible for patients to use portable devices to take their own EKGs and then transmit the signals over the telephone to a central office where these signals are examined by computer. If an abnormality appears in the EKG, the computer notifies the patient and the doctor. This technique makes it possible for many heart patients to have more frequent EKGs and thus for problems to be detected sooner.

Cancer

You may one day be able to walk into your local medical center, stand in an odd-looking chamber as a technician twists dials for a few minutes, and walk out with the reassuring knowledge that there is no cancer anywhere in your body.

Raymond Damadian

Cancer is one of the most dreaded, mysterious, and widespread diseases known to our society. Actually, cancer is a series of related diseases in which certain cells begin to grow wildly out of control. Cancer research is heavily funded by the federal government and private benefactors, but its cure remains elusive. Progress has been made, however, in reducing the suffering, extending the lifespan, and even curing the disease in many patients. Computers are expected to play an important part in finding a cure.

Radiation has long been useful in killing tumors and in controlling cancers, but radiation is dangerous and is itself capable of causing cancer in the treated patients. The precise control of **irradiation devices** in cancer therapy (Figure 17–7) is often performed by computers.

The reporting of cancer cases is an important part of cancer research. Using statistical analysis techniques, researchers are able to draw conclusions about the incidence of cancer in people of different races, geographic locations, occupations, and the like. They are able to determine if certain diets or medications affect cancer rates. All of these analyses are greatly facilitated by high-speed computer processing of the data.

Many researchers believe that the cure for cancer will come only when the structure and operation of human cells are better understood. In

"Computer No. 9 just discovered a cure for which there is no known disease!"

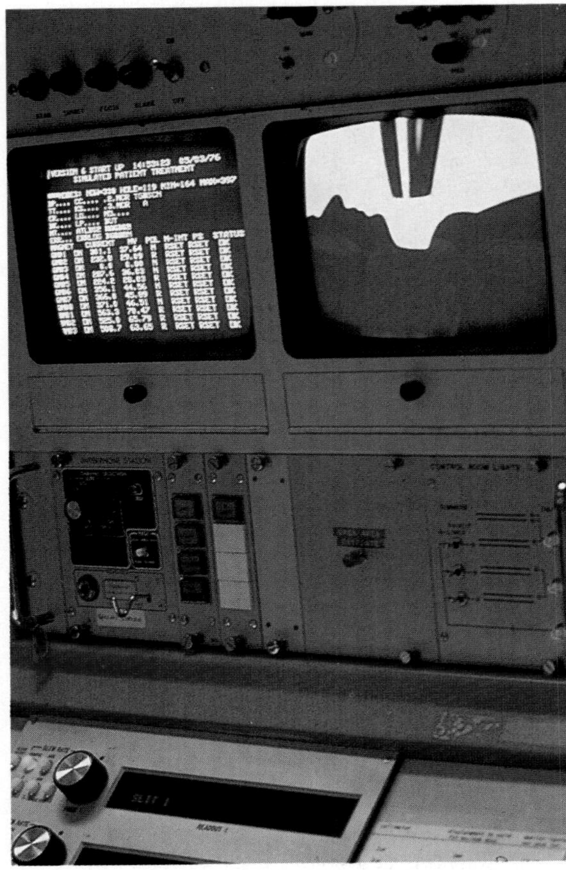

Figure 17-7 Computer-controlled irradiation of a cancer patient.

recent years the field of **genetic engineering** has been developing rapidly. Scientists in the field are concerned with the structure of DNA, said to be the building block of life. Computers with high-resolution graphics screens and plotting equipment draw DNA molecules and allow researchers to rotate the pictures to examine them from different angles. The equipment helps give the researchers information about DNA that would otherwise be impossible to obtain. The marriage of computers and genetic engineering is being used in attempts to generate interferon, a chemical present in the human body in small quantities that is believed to be a possible cure for cancer and for a large number of diseases caused by viruses.

Organ Matching

Organ transplants have become everyday occurrences within the last decade. Thousands of organ transplants are performed in the United States each year, and this number is increasing rapidly. People with a life expectancy of months, weeks, or even days have received organ transplants and have lived relatively normal lives for many years. Computers facilitate organ transplants particularly in **organ matching.**

Organ matching involves locating organs with the proper tissue types, from people with appropriate blood types and other characteristics, for transplanting to people with similar (and often identical) characteristics. It also involves locating people who can successfully receive available organs. Without a careful match, the odds are overwhelming that a transplanted organ will be rejected. The time element is often critical. Once an organ is removed from a donor it must be transplanted within hours (or perhaps a day or two at most).

Organizations such as the South-Eastern Organ Procurement Foundation (SEOPF) in Richmond, Virginia, maintain computerized databases of registered organ recipient candidates. When organs become available, usually because of the death of the donor, doctors transmit the appropriate information to the organ matching organization, where a computerized search locates any matches in minutes. Once a match is made, the recipient is located, brought to a nearby hospital that does transplants, and prepared for the surgery. The organ is rushed to the hospital, and if all goes well, the organ is often transplanted and functioning in the recipient within hours of the donor's death.

With today's high-speed transportation and highly sophisticated communications networks, computers are matching organ donors and recipients throughout the world.

Anesthesiology

Why do patients need monitoring under anesthesia? Think of an anesthetic as a reversible poison, because that is exactly what it is. Curare and eserine, both used

in medicine, are a South American arrow poison and an African "trial by ordeal" drug, respectively. "Trial by ordeal" means that if you did not die after taking the drug, you were obviously innocent of the crime of which you were accused.

Inhalation anesthetic drugs such as halothane and enflurane are fluorocarbons that melt plastic and are excellent dry cleaning fluids, as well as potent anesthetics. Despite this, used carefully in the correct dosage, they are very safe, but the patient needs to be monitored closely.

Phil Wilkinson

The dangers of improper monitoring and possible overdoses of anesthetics are great. The anesthetist needs to respond quickly and accurately to rapid changes in a patient's vital signs (such as heart rate and breathing) during complex and sometimes dangerous surgery. The patient's response to the anesthetic itself needs to be monitored carefully; some patients have violent reactions to improper doses of certain anesthetics.

The anesthetist uses readings from electronic equipment to determine how the patient is doing, but the anesthetist can only respond at human speed and can only monitor and control a relatively small number of items effectively. A computer-based system can monitor many more items, detect much finer changes in the patient's vital signs, and respond to multiple situations faster than the anesthetist.

One of the primary research goals in **computer-assisted anesthesiology** is to reduce the amount of anesthetics that need to be administered to make a patient unconscious and immobile. This should result in fewer complications due to anesthetics.

Surgery

The skilled hands of surgeons are already being assisted by the precision of computers. In delicate eye surgery, for example, **computer-controlled lasers** have been used to kill tumors and to fuse detached retinas. Computers can be used to control cutting and sewing in areas thousands of times smaller than a surgeon's hands could safely reach.

The process of opening up a patient in surgery carries great risk. Computers can be used to control tiny probes inserted through the skin and directed to the area requiring surgery. Miniature optical devices allow the surgeon to see the surgical area from the tip of the probe. Low dosage computer-controlled x-ray devices can monitor the surgery from outside the patient, permitting, for example, surgery to be done to correct birth defects on a fetus.

Intensive Care

The **intensive care unit** (ICU) in any hospital is probably the most carefully staffed and well-equipped area outside of the operating room itself. Patients in intensive care need to be monitored constantly. They are often unconscious or incapable of communication. The slightest changes in vital signs may require immediate attention. Many hospitals place a highly skilled nurse with each patient, but monitoring a patient for 24 hours a day is expensive.

Computerized patient monitoring is being used successfully for patients in intensive care. The computers are programmed to monitor many vital signs simultaneously. They control intravenous feeding and drug flow, make fine adjustments to electronic devices connected to the patient, and display variations in the patients' conditions that require the attention of skilled nurses and doctors.

Computers in intensive care can be connected to a central hospital computer system that constantly knows the nurses' and doctors' locations. If a patient requires the attention of a particular specialist not currently at the ICU, that nurse or doctor can be located immediately.

Obtaining Medical Histories

Obtaining **medical histories** of patients is a time-consuming operation that can easily be handled by a computer system. Today, many hospitals, small clinics, and even individual doctor's offices use computer systems for this purpose.

The patient sits at a display terminal and receives instructions on how to respond to the machine's questions. The patient is instructed to notify the attendant after completing the computer's questions or if any difficulties should arise.

The computer is programmed to ask a long series of routine questions. Based on the patient's responses, the computer may vary its dialogue and ask other related questions. While the history is being taken, the computer records the information so that reports may be produced after the session is over. Results from these systems have been interesting. Patients generally accept the systems quite readily, and many report that the systems are helpful and even pleasant to use. Staffs have been able to reduce the amount of time spent taking histories. Most computers provide neatly printed reports or screen presentations of the histories.

One fascinating phenomenon has been that patients seem more willing to "discuss" certain personal problems with a computer than with a nurse or doctor! Even though the patient knows this information may eventually be seen by a person, the patient tends to be more frank with the computer.

The time spent taking these histories can be precious, especially in emergency situations. A number of different **smart cards** have been developed that an individual may carry in a wallet or purse. Each card contains a complete medical history in a tiny yet high capacity computer memory which is updated by a computer device every time the person receives medical attention. The card can be crucial in a medical emergency because it reveals important information about allergies, drug restrictions, or other medical problems.

Drug Conflict Warnings

The range of prescription medications available today is enormous. Doctors and pharmacists are concerned about possible interactions between the various medications taken by a patient. Some common foods or alcoholic beverages should not be taken with certain medications. The problem is made worse by the fact that one patient may see many doctors and fill prescriptions at different pharmacies.

Computers are being used to catalogue facts about known drug interactions and to provide pharmacists and doctors with **drug conflict warnings**. When conflicting medications are prescribed, the computer can often suggest an alternative drug or combination of drugs that could be used in treating the patient.

One concern about these systems is that they may violate a person's privacy, so many doctors and pharmacists require special consent forms to be filled out before they will enter a client's information into a computer system.

Searching Medical Libraries

It is impossible for a doctor to perform professional duties and keep completely current with the medical literature. Vast amounts of medical information are being kept in **computerized medical libraries** to help medical professionals locate information quickly.

New articles and reports of important developments are regularly entered into computerized databases. A person requesting information from a database may list a series of keywords or some other identifying information, such as author, subject, title, institution, or the like. The computer then searches the database to obtain any and all articles that contain these facts. Communications networks enable medical professionals to obtain important information from computerized databases throughout the world.

Artificial Organs and Body Parts

Many researchers feel that microprocessor-controlled **artificial organs**, such as hearts, lungs, kidneys, and livers, may soon be in wide use. An artificial pancreas that will automatically secrete insulin into the bloodstream of a diabetic is expected to become available. Artificial eyes and ears are being developed.

One intriguing possibility is that software could be developed to customize artificial organs to the needs of the individual. Surgeons performing transplants today rely on a close match of tissue types, blood types, and other characteristics, but most of the time a matching organ is simply not available. In the future, organs may be built with precisely the right characteristics needed by the patient.

Summary 

1. The low cost of microprocessors has made it possible to build intelligent control into medical diagnostic, monitoring, and control equipment.
2. The 1979 Nobel Prize for medicine or physiology was shared by Godfrey Hounsfield and Allan Cormack for their independent efforts in developing the CAT scan.
3. The CAT (computer-assisted tomography) scan produces pictures of "slices" of the body.
4. The PET (positron emission tomography) scan maps brain activity and can help determine if a patient is manic-depressive or schizophrenic.
5. The Dynamic Spatial Reconstructor (DSR) developed by Raytheon for the Mayo Clinic can take three-dimensional motion pictures of organs.
6. Microcomputers are being integrated into implantable devices, such as pacemakers, to provide much more precise control.
7. Organ monitoring devices are being developed that give doctors readouts from inside the body without the need for surgery.
8. Computer-controlled irradiation devices are used in cancer therapy.
9. Computers play an important part in genetic engineering.
10. Organ matching programs locate acceptable donors and donees throughout the world.
11. Computer-controlled lasers are used in eye surgery to kill tumors and fuse detached retinas.
12. Computers are particularly useful in patient monitoring and control, especially in the intensive care units in hospitals.
13. Computers are used by doctors and pharmacists to detect drug conflicts for the safety of patients who must take several different medications.
14. Databases of medical information are available on worldwide computer networks.
15. Microprocessors will play an important part in the development of artificial organs and body parts.

Important Terms 

angiography
artificial organs
CADUCEUS
CAT scan
computer-assisted anesthesiology
computer-assisted tomography (CAT)
computer-axial tomography (CAT)
computer-based scanning systems
computer-controlled lasers
computerized diagnosis
computerized medical libraries
computerized patient monitoring
drug conflict warnings
Dynamic Spatial Reconstructor (DSR)

electrocardiogram (EKG)
externally programmable control devices
genetic engineering
implantable computerized devices
intelligent control
intensive care unit (ICU)
irradiation devices
noninvasive diagnostic techniques
obtaining medical histories
organ matching
pacemaker
PET scan
positron emission tomography (PET)
smart cards
tomography
ultrasound

Self-Review Exercises 

Matching

Next to the term in column A, place the letter of the statement in column B that best describes it.

Column A

1. CAT scan
2. PET scan
3. Pacemaker
4. DSR
5. CADUCEUS
6. Tomography
7. Noninvasive procedure
8. Genetic engineering
9. Smart card
10. ICU

Column B

A. Three-dimensional moving pictures of organs
B. Computerized diagnostician
C. Diagnosis without surgery
D. May develop artificial interferon
E. Can detect schizophrenia
F. Contains a patient's medical history
G. Uses computerized patient monitoring
H. The description of slices
I. Pictures of body "slices"
J. Implantable heart controller

Fill-in-the-Blanks

Fill in the blanks in each of the following:

1. Because of the low cost and small size of microprocessors it is possible to build ______ into medical diagnostic, monitoring, and control equipment.

2. ______ is a form of computerized X-ray scanning used to diagnose heart and blood vessel problems.

3. Computer-controlled ______ are being used to kill tumors and fuse detached retinas.

4. ______ are implanted in the body, but may have their programs altered by signals received from equipment outside of the body.

5. Pharmacists and doctors use computers to detect dangerous ______ .

6. It has been observed that patients are more frank with computers than with doctors when revealing their ______ .

7. The 1979 Nobel Prize in medicine or physiology was awarded for the development of the ______ .

8. The ______ "maps" brain activity.

9. The ______ is perhaps the most powerful noninvasive diagnostic tool ever built.

10. The computer technologies of data communications and ______ are combined in the development of life-saving organ-matching systems.

Answers to Self-Review Exercises

Matching: 1 I, 2 E, 3 J, 4 A, 5 B, 6 H, 7 C, 8 D, 9 F, 10 G

Fill-in-the Blanks:
1. intelligent control
2. Angiography
3. lasers
4. Externally programmable control devices
5. drug conflicts
6. medical histories
7. CAT scan
8. PET scan
9. DSR
10. database management systems

Discussion Questions 

1. What is probably the most important application of computers to medicine in recent years?

2. What are noninvasive diagnostic techniques? Why is so much effort being devoted to developing new noninvasive diagnostic techniques?

3. How are computers being used in eye surgery?

4. Why could CAT scan pictures never be taken by a regular camera?

5. What is tomography?

6. Explain the controversy surrounding the CAT scan. Why is this controversy likely to disappear?

7. How might the PET scan be useful in the treatment of epileptics?

8. Microminiaturization has made possible the production of tiny implantable devices. Discuss several ways in which implanted microprocessors may be used in the future.

9. One way to solve the drug conflict problem would be to set up a nationwide (or even worldwide) database system accessed by all doctors and pharmacists. Any time a doctor prescribes a medication, the doctor would check the database to see what prescriptions the patient is already using—including those given by other doctors. Would you consider this an invasion of your privacy? Explain.

10. Microprocessors are making it possible to develop artificial organs and body parts. How would you feel about receiving an artificial arm? an artificial heart? an artificial brain?

Projects 

1. Contact any organ matching organizations in your area. Report on their current efforts and programs. Discuss their use of computers and communications to facilitate rapid and accurate matches. What new programs are they planning?

2. Visit a hospital that has a CAT scan. Discuss the operation of the machine with the technicians who administer patient scans. Write a brief report on the CAT scan.

3. Write to several companies in the field of biomedical engineering. Ask for literature on their computer-controlled devices. Write a report discussing recent developments in this area.

4. Read several issues of *Computers in Medicine* published by the American Medical Association. Report on some recent developments not covered in this chapter.

5. Write to:

The American Heart Association
7320 Greenville Avenue
Dallas, TX 75231

Request any literature they may have on the use of computers in heart research, particularly on artificial hearts. Report on your findings.

6. Because of the intensive research now going on, it is reasonable to believe that computers, particularly microprocessors, will greatly extend human life spans. Give several examples of how microprocessors might be used for this purpose. Discuss the social consequences of extending the human life span by an average of a year, ten years, a hundred years, or even more.

7. Visit a nearby medical school. Interview several professors, administrators, and students. Write a report on computers and the medical school curriculum.

Chapter 18

Computers and the Handicapped

After reading this chapter you will understand:

1. How some common handicaps affect people
2. How computer technology is helping the physically disabled become more self-sufficient
3. How microprocessor technology together with miniaturization techniques can create implantable devices that may enable the handicapped to regain lost movement and senses
4. How computers help improve the employability of the handicapped
5. The personal benefits that computers can bring to handicapped people

Outline

This fifty-liter rawhide bag of gas, juices, jellies, gristle and threads movably suspended on more than 200 bones, presided over by a cranium, seldom predictable and worst of all living, presents a challenge to discourage a computer into incoherence.

Biomechanician John Stapp

We have already discussed many of the positive applications of computers: how they can improve medical care, speed computing, and relieve people of many tedious tasks. Computers can also help the handicapped to improve the quality of their lives. Most of these computer applications are possible because of the relatively recent advances in microprocessor technology. Many organizations are working to improve the lives of handicapped people, and several interesting publications are devoted to work on their behalf (see "Projects" at the end of this chapter).

The computer applications that aid the handicapped, although different in many ways, are alike in their goal: All of them are designed to help people integrate more fully and independently in society despite their physical disabilities. Some of the ways computer technology is being used to improve the quality of life for the handicapped include:

1. Bringing the job site to the home instead of having the handicapped individual travel to the job. For example, a handicapped person with a computer terminal can work at home.
2. Removing some of the physical burdens faced by the handicapped. For example, a handicapped person's mobility can be greatly improved by the use of a voice-activated, computer-controlled wheelchair.
3. Helping the handicapped to make better use of their functioning senses. For example, many near-blind people are helped by computerized displays that show text in very large letters.
4. Enabling the handicapped to use their **residual capabilities** (those senses and movements that still function) to replace lost capabilities. For example, a person who can't speak can still touch words and phrases on a computerized "voice board" that then causes the words and phrases to be spoken through a speech synthesizer.
5. Making it easier for the handicapped to use computers for the very same purposes that nonhandicapped people do. Society is becoming increasingly dependent on computers. People need to use them just to keep up in this technological world.

Rehabilitation Engineering

Applying technology to improve the lives of the handicapped is called **rehabilitation engineering.** In the past, work in this area required electrical and mechanical engineering skills and was confined to expensive laboratories funded by government and industry grants. Today's microprocessors and microcomputers have made it much easier for large numbers of concerned people—not just those in engineering and the sciences—to make contributions in rehabilitation engineering. Many handicapped individuals have developed their own applications; relatives often program computers to function for the benefit of handicapped family members. It is reasonable to expect that the pace of breakthroughs in rehabilitation engineering will increase rapidly as microprocessor technology improves.

An Electronic "Human Eye"

It may be the 21st Century, but Monday morning's rush hour in the big city is as hectic as ever. Rail commuters prepare to disembark, poised to race through the underground maze of newsstands, shops, and passageways in the busy midtown subway station. Some scurry to catch connecting trains, others scout for exit signs marking the route to the surface. Moving somewhat hesitantly, yet unnoticed by the tide of humanity, is a blind man wearing glasses. He has no cane, no guide dog or escort. Instead, he is equipped with an artificial vision system designed to provide a useful level of mobility.

The system consists of a microminiature TV camera housed in a glass eye and feeding signals to a microcomputer and other very-large-scale integration components fitted inside the frame of a pair of eyeglasses. A tiny connector and cable of fine wires runs from the earpiece to a female socket connector permanently attached to the skin just above and to the rear of the ear. The socket is hidden by hair.

The connector interfaces the system with an implanted array of 512 platinum electrodes on the surface of each of two flexible Teflon wafers. Each wafer sits on one hemisphere of the occipital cortices at the lower rear of the blind man's skull.

Albert F. Shackil, Associate Editor, *IEEE Spectrum*, September 1980. Based on research headed by Dr. William H. Dobelle, Director of Artificial Organs at Columbia University.

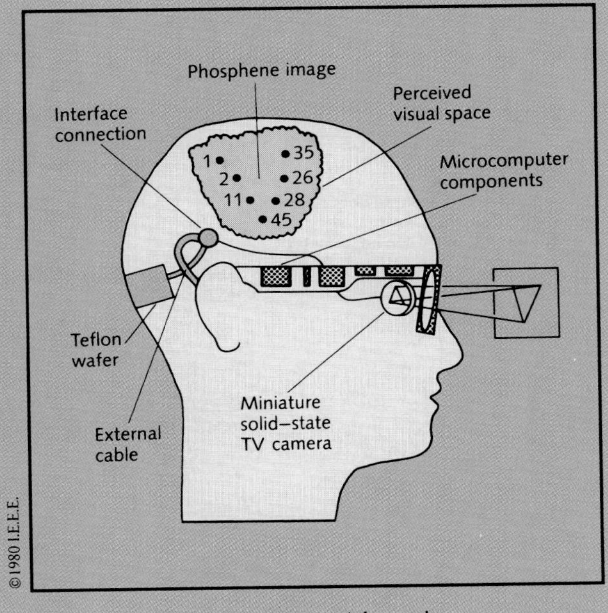

How an artificial vision system might work.

Information Amplification

Because of their disabilities, many handicapped people read or write slowly. Through **information amplification**, computers can help handicapped people work at more normal speeds. For example, a handicapped person capable of typing, but only at a slow speed, could use abbreviations that a computer program would then expand to full words and phrases. This can help the handicapped person compete effectively with non-handicapped associates not using such a program.

Computers and Blind People

Blindness, in varying degrees, affects almost 2 million Americans. Unfortunately, because of other disabilities, many blind people cannot learn the **Braille** language, a notation of raised dots embossed in paper that allows people to read by touch (Figures 18–1 and 18–2). Even if a person can read Braille, only about 3 percent of the books published in the United States are made available in that form.

Blind people are assisted by a wide range of conventional household devices using microprocessor-controlled speech synthesizers. These include talking wristwatches, bathroom scales, calculators, thermometers, and microwave ovens.

The Orator

ARTS Computer Products Inc. of Boston, Massachusetts, has developed a device called the **Orator** that allows a computer to speak its output (Fig-

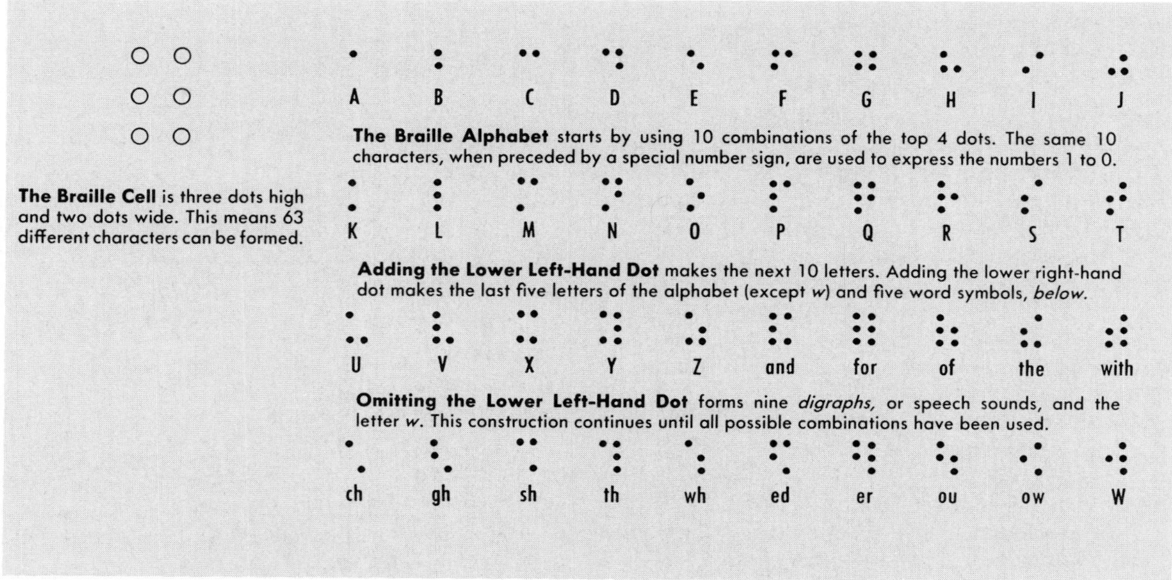

A B C D E F G H I J
The Braille Alphabet starts by using 10 combinations of the top 4 dots. The same 10 characters, when preceded by a special number sign, are used to express the numbers 1 to 0.
The Braille Cell is three dots high and two dots wide. This means 63 different characters can be formed.
K L M N O P Q R S T
Adding the Lower Left-Hand Dot makes the next 10 letters. Adding the lower right-hand dot makes the last five letters of the alphabet (except w) and five word symbols, below.
U V X Y Z and for of the with
Omitting the Lower Left-Hand Dot forms nine digraphs, or speech sounds, and the letter w. This construction continues until all possible combinations have been used.
ch gh sh th wh ed er ou ow W

Figure 18-1 The Braille alphabet.

Figure 18-2 A blind person reads Braille by touching the patterns of raised dots.

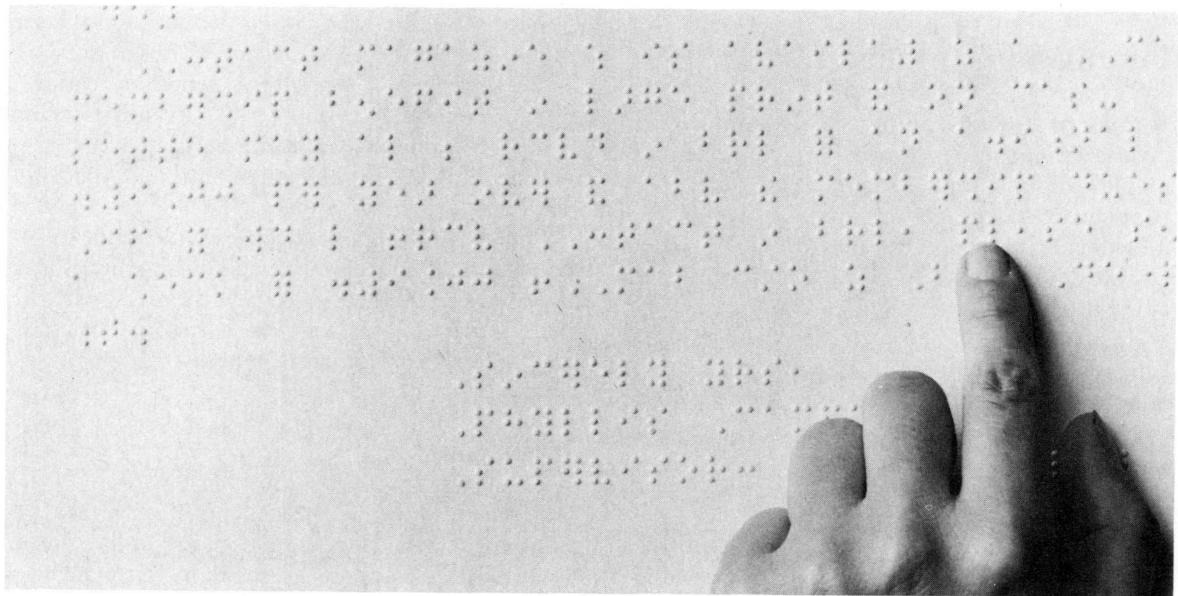

ure 18–3). The Orator uses **synthetic speech** rather than **stored speech**. In the stored speech method, human speech is recorded and stored in the computer's memory for playback. This technique allows only a limited vocabulary, although the speech quality is quite good. The synthetic speech method used by the Orator stores several hundred speech formation rules that help it analyze standard English pronunciations. As characters are scanned and recognized, they are interpreted according to these stored rules, and the appropriate sounds are mechanically produced. The greatest advantage of synthetic speech is its almost unlimited vocabulary. The quality of synthetic speech is not as good as that produced by stored speech systems, but it is improving rapidly as research in this area continues.

One problem that designers of text-to-speech translators like the Orator face is that the same thing can often be said in several ways. For example, the number 460 could be pronounced "four six zero," "four sixty," "four hundred sixty," or "four hundred and sixty." Other similar problems make the design of these devices extremely challenging.

The Orator can spell out words it doesn't understand. At times, users actually prefer the spelling mode, and they can request it. The Orator can speak words and phrases as the user types them. A poor typist can request that individual characters be called out by the machine as they are typed, which helps confirm that the correct keys are being pressed.

Figure 18-3 The Orator is an output device that allows a computer to speak its outputs.

Aids for Partially Sighted People

ARTS developed its **Large Print Video Terminal** for partially sighted people. Since many of these people eventually become totally blind, individuals with failing vision can learn to communicate with computers on a system using both the Orator and the Large Print Video Terminal. If they become totally blind, they will be better prepared for dealing with their handicap, and they can continue working effectively without a long period of readjustment.

The president of ARTS, Peter Duran, who is himself blind, says, "I hope our products will put the blind and visually impaired on an equal footing in the job market. There is no longer any reason for them to be excluded."

Microelectronics has made possible the development of portable large print devices that help partially sighted people read printed text (Figure 18–4).

Figure 18-4 As the hand-held scanner is passed over the text, greatly enlarged letters are displayed on the computerized screen. These portable devices enable partially sighted people to read conventional books and magazines without the expense of purchasing special large-type editions.

Jeff Lowenthal — Newsweek

Braille Computer Terminals

The most popular reading aid for the blind today is Braille, still in the form developed by the blind 15-year-old Frenchman Louis Braille in 1824. Computer programmers, operators, and users have been working with **Braille computer terminals** for some time (Figure 18–5). These terminals enable blind people to hold productive computer-related jobs. Inexpensive Braille printers for personal computers are quite popular.

Many users have commented favorably on the benefits of these terminals to both themselves and their businesses. Dr. John Morrison of the U.S. Department of Transportation used the Braillemboss system developed at MIT and commented:

> From a purely personal point of view, I cannot emphasize enough the almost unanticipated boost in morale the Brailler has afforded me. For the first time, I can access the computer directly and, for the first time, I can read the results of my labor. From the point of view of a productive worker, my contribution to the inhouse effort has kept pace with my colleagues, which would not have been the case had I not had the Brailler at my disposal. I consider it an indispensable instrument for my work. Should I be deprived of its use, my value to the employer would suffer commensurately.
>
> Quoted in *Computer Decisions*, October 1976
> "Braille Computer Terminals," by George F. Dalrymple, MIT

Figure 18-5 An operator who is totally blind is shown using a Braille computer terminal. The keyboard has Braille patterns on the keys; the output device is a Braille printer.

Soft copy Braille output devices have been developed. A microprocessor causes a set of metal pins to move up and down on a flat surface to form a line of Braille characters. After the person has read the material, a control key is pressed and the pins are set to the next line of output. These devices are like CRTs to sighted people.

Sonar "Sight"

Only 1 percent of the nation's blind people use guide dogs. The most popular mobility aid is currently the cane, but it has disadvantages. First, it has a very narrow range—only the person's next step; second, it is normally held low to detect ground obstacles, so it is not useful for avoiding tree branches and other obstacles above the ground.

One device provides **sonar "sight"** by using the sonar focusing element made popular in Polaroid cameras. The sound waves that bounce back are interpreted by a microprocessor that bleeps out various noises indicating the nature and distance of obstacles.

A Television Camera "Eye"

Researchers at the Smith-Kettlewell Institute of Visual Sciences in San Francisco, California, have developed an electronic device to help blind people move around more easily and safely. The aid consists of a shoulder-mounted television camera. As the person using this device walks at normal speed, a microcomputer analyzes images produced by the camera and warns of nearby objects. The computer controls a speech synthesizer that tells the user the type of obstacle, the direction in which it lies, and how close it is. The system also includes a mechanical device that taps the user on a special belt to indicate the direction and distance to the obstacle—the location of the tapping on the belt indicates the direction, and the faster the frequency of the tapping, the closer the object.

Reading by Vibrations

The **Optacon**, developed by Telesensory Systems Inc. of California, enables a blind person to "read by vibrations." The device scans letters on a page of text and converts each letter into a different vibration that the person feels by fingertip. With the Optacon, a person can read handwritten as well as printed text at about 50 words per minute, much slower than normal reading and conversation rates.

The Kurzweil Reading Machine

The Kurzweil Reading Machine has done more to liberate the blind than any invention since Louis Braille perfected raised fingertip reading in 1829.

Money magazine, October 1981

Using computer technology, Raymond Kurzweil, president of Kurzweil Computer Products Inc. of Cambridge, Massachusetts, developed an optical character recognition device that actually reads printed text to the blind. The **Kurzweil Reading Machine** (Figure 18–6) scans ordinary printed material; it recognizes individual symbols and letters, assembles them into words, and speaks the words via a **speech synthesizer**. The machine speaks at normal conversation speed (about 250 words per minute), but it appears to have a thick Swedish accent. Most users find the machine's speech quite understandable after a few hours of practice.

The machine uses the synthetic speech generation method. It stores more than 1000 English grammar rules as well as 1500 exceptions to assist in the text-to-speech translation process.

Kurzweil designed the machine for convenient use. Control buttons allow the user to make the machine pause, resume operation, repeat a single line or a single word, and skim through the text. The user may even mark several portions of the text to return to at a later time. One innovation is an operator key that, when pressed before any other key, causes the machine to speak the second key's name. This feature is particularly popular with new users. The first individual to purchase a Kurzweil machine for personal use was rock star Stevie Wonder.

Figure 18-6 The Kurzweil Reading Machine. This person is shown operating the controls of the Kurzweil machine in a public library.

Computers and Deaf People

Today, people gather information much more by hearing than by reading. Try to imagine what your information level would be without a telephone, radio or television.

Mary Robinson
Deaf Communications Institute

In the United States, more than 13 million people

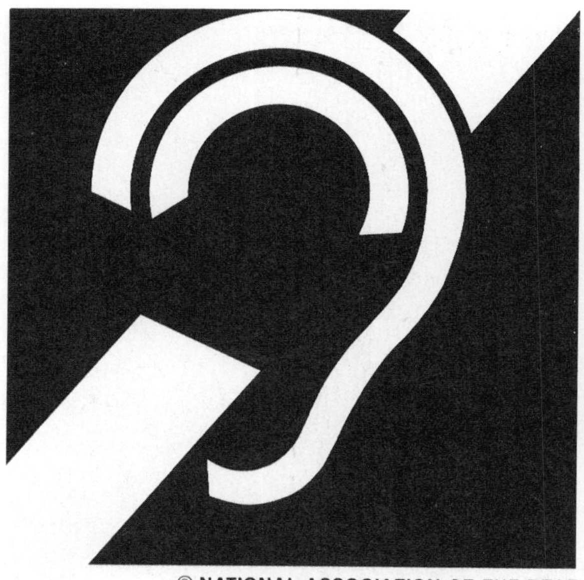

Figure 18-7 The International Symbol of Deafness is now used by the Bell System in its telephone directories. The symbol identifies telephone company numbers equipped with TDD capabilities (Telecommunications Devices for the Deaf).

Courtesy of International Business Machines Corporation

Figure 18-8 This student is using an interactive computer system to learn Ameslan, the American sign language of the deaf. The student types a word or phrase at the terminal, and the appropriate sign appears on the screen. The symbol shown here is for the word drive in Ameslan.

have significant hearing loss. Approximately 2 million of these people are totally deaf. Computers are useful in educating deaf people, helping them communicate (Figure 18-7), and improving their employment opportunities. Computers are also useful in teaching people with normal hearing how to communicate with the deaf using **Ameslan,** American sign language (Figure 18-8).

Computers can help determine the type and extent of a person's deafness. They analyze diagnostic tests and can often pinpoint the exact cause of the hearing problem. Computers are then used to design customized hearing aids; microprocessor-controlled hearing aids can emphasize certain aspects of sounds for people with special hearing difficulties.

Using microprocessor technology, SRI International has developed a hand-held printing terminal that helps hearing impaired people communicate over the telephone (Figure 18–9). Using a conventional typewriterlike keyboard, a deaf person types messages that are then sent over telephone lines to another terminal where they are printed.

Figure 18-9 A printing telephone for the deaf.

Newsweek

Deaf people may "speak" Ameslan over telephone lines using a computer-controlled device that picks up signals from reflective tape placed on gloves worn by the user. Developed by computer graphics experts, the computer encodes information about the movement of the reflective tape spots. The information—much less than is required for full video images—is then transmitted over regular telephone lines. The picture of the moving reflective spots is then reconstructed by a microprocessor on a screen at the receiving end (Figure 18–10).

Electronic Mail for the Deaf

One obvious application for electronic mail is for communications among deaf people. Using a computer terminal and a modem, both hearing and hearing impaired users may send messages over the **Deafnet** system operated by GTE Telenet. Messages may be sent 24 hours a day anywhere in the United States. If the intended receiver is not at home, the message will be stored in Telenet's central computer for delivery when the intended receiver dials in to Deafnet.

One particularly popular feature of Deafnet is its computerized electronic bulletin board system that provides much useful information for the deaf, including medical facts, want ads, show times for captioned movie and TV programs, and a schedule of various social events.

Speech Recognition Devices for the Deaf

Perhaps the ultimate breakthrough for the hearing impaired will come when **speech recognition**

Figure 18-10 Bell Labs researchers check a videotaped test of an experimental communication technique for the hearing impaired. The screen at the left shows a researcher using special gloves to "speak" in American sign language. With special lighting adjustments, only the reflective spots on the gloves appear on the screen at the right. This simplified image requires less transmission capacity than a full-screen picture and can be understood easily by sign-language users.

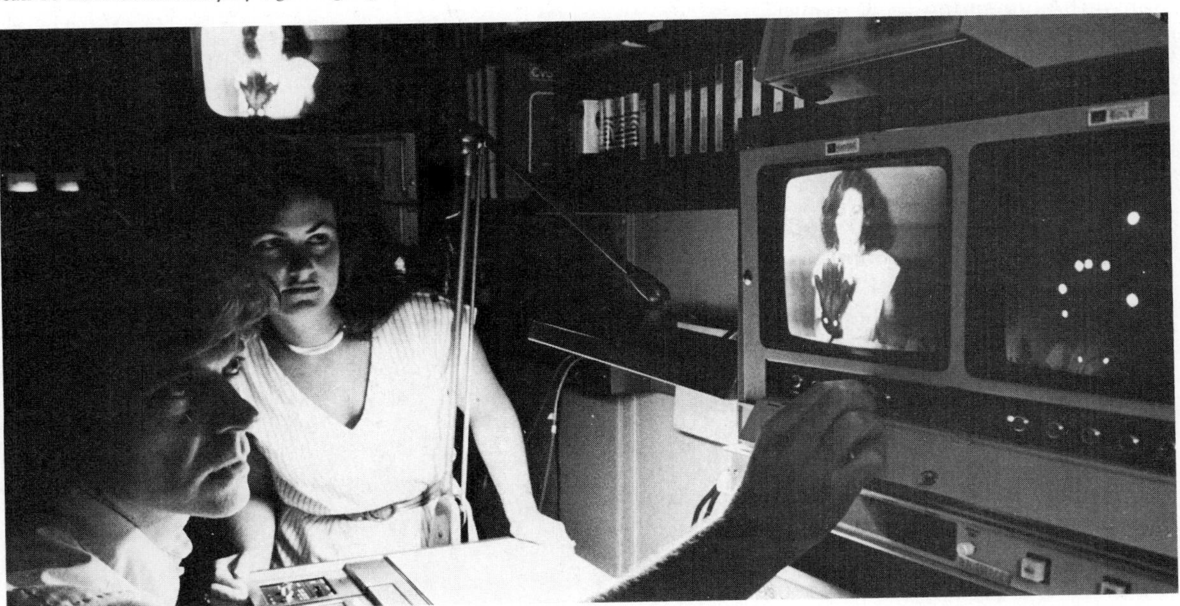

technology improves to the point that computers can easily recognize human speech. This may happen within the next decade. It will then be possible to build portable devices that recognize speech and display it as text on a small screen. A deaf person could then better enjoy a play or the pleasures of a simple conversation.

Computers and Deaf-Blind People

More than 10,000 people in the United States are both deaf and blind. Communicating is an enormous problem for them. Of their remaining senses of touch, smell, and taste, only the sense of touch is especially useful for communication.

Computerized devices that signal deaf-blind people by vibration have been built. These hand-held devices are made to vibrate at different frequencies to notify them that a phone or doorbell is ringing or that an emergency has occurred. Some of these devices key their vibrations to the Morse code.

Deaf-blind people can be provided with Braille telephone terminals. Portable Braille printers may eventually be attached to speech recognition devices so that normal speech can be converted directly to Braille and vice versa for communication with nonhandicapped people.

Computers and Nonvocal Disabled People

Many severely handicapped people cannot use a keyboard, so other communications methods are needed. At the Biomedical Engineering Center of the Tufts-New England Medical Center, a number of personal communication devices have been developed. Most of these devices allow people who can't speak to point to a letter, number, symbol, word, or phrase by using whatever muscular control they still have. The **Tufts Interactive Communicator** (Figure 18–11) helps a person form words one letter at a time. The user need merely be able to operate a switch of some kind. The letters of the alphabet are shown on a screen in order of their frequency of use in the English language (Figure 18–12) to minimize scan time. A flashing cursor first moves from row to row; the user closes the switch to indicate when to stop. Then the cursor moves column to column.

A touch-sensitive pad with common words and phrases written on an overlay sheet enables a handicapped person to form sentences by touching various words (Figure 18–13). The position of each word has been prestored in a computer. As the words are pressed, the computer converts the signals to text stored in its memory. A speech synthesizer then speaks the touched words.

For those with severe loss of muscle control, **eye-tracking devices** have been developed (Figure 18–14) that determine what the eye is looking at and thus what the disabled person wants to

Figure 18-11 With this device—developed by the Rehabilitation Engineering Center at New England Medical Center—the user merely needs to be able to operate some kind of switch. The letters of the alphabet are presented to the user; two switch closures select an individual letter. This device is based on a Radio Shack Model 100 and an Intex-talker speech synthesizer.

Figure 18-12 The letters of the alphabet arranged according to their frequency of use in the English language.

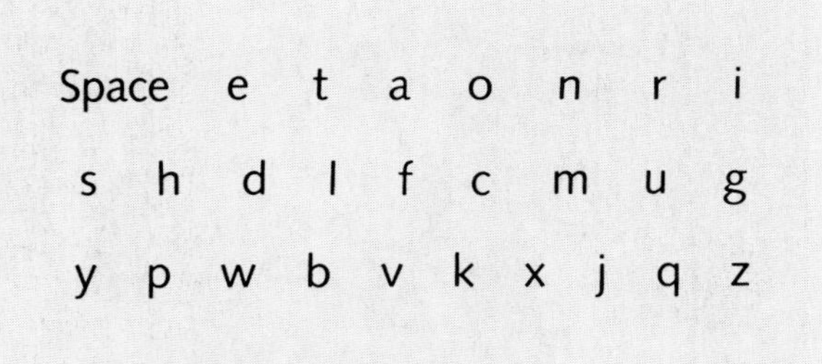

Figure 18-13 This patient at New England Medical Center communicates by pointing to words on the tablet, which is connected to an Epson HX-20 portable computer. Each word selected is then output to a speech synthesizer. The entire system is battery operated and wheelchair mounted.

say. The locations of the words or phrases are prestored in the computer; as the person stares at a particular word or phrase, the computer displays it on a screen or speaks it through a speech synthesizer.

The Abilityphone

People with such disabilities as loss of sight, loss of hearing, loss of mobility, or loss of speech can receive help in an emergency from the **Abilityphone.** The Abilityphone is a computerized telephone device made by Basic Telecommunications Corporation of Fort Collins, Colorado.

A handicapped person who needs help presses a large button marked "HELP." The device contains a speech synthesizer that calls out "help on" to confirm that it is responding to such a request. As the phone dials for help, it speaks out "I am calling for help now"; it also displays the spoken messages on a screen for the benefit of a deaf user. The user can hear the called aide's phone ringing through the Abilityphone's speakers. When the aide answers the phone, the Abilityphone speaks the message: "Emergency at (address) . . . forced entry authorized." The aide answers by pressing a beeper device. If the first

Figure 18-14 For severely disabled people with intact visual function, gaze can be utilized as a means of communication. These glasses monitor what the eye is looking at. The disabled person communicates by staring at words, phrases, or pictures on a chart. The glasses connected to a computer indicate the message the person is trying to convey.

person being called doesn't answer the call, the Abilityphone automatically dials several other prestored telephone numbers until help is reached.

The Abilityphone contains several important features. It can automatically answer incoming calls to give a handicapped person time to get to the phone. It contains an alarm clock, a calculator, an environment controller, and a calendar. It can call out reminders for a patient to take medication. It can periodically call out "Are you OK?" and if the user doesn't answer, it will dial for emergency help.

Minspeak

One of the most promising vehicles for information amplification is the **Minspeak** system under development at the Prentke Romich Company in Shreve, Ohio.

Minspeak uses a unique keyboard (Figure 18–15) with keys that contain pictures to represent concepts. The keys also contain numbers, letters, names, and words. The user presses a sequence of keys. Then the Minspeak system analyzes the concepts and the order in which they were entered. It determines that the user is trying to convey a certain idea. It then selects from among thousands of prestored sentences the one that most directly conveys the desired idea. Finally, the appropriate sentence is spoken through a speech synthesizer. Researchers have found that with a relatively small number of keys and keystrokes, a huge assortment of common thoughts, ideas, and meanings may be expressed—truly the goal of an effective information amplification system.

Computers and the Paralyzed

A quadriplegic is a person handicapped by the loss of movement in both arms and both legs. Often, quadriplegics retain the ability to make shoulder, neck, and head movements, and their remaining senses of sight, hearing, smell, and taste still function properly. Therefore, a quadriplegic's problem is usually one of mobility rather than one of communication.

This movement impairment can make an everyday task, such as eating, impossible without assistance. Figure 18–16 illustrates a system to facilitate eating. This system uses a microcomputer-controlled manipulator arm to respond to the quadriplegic's shoulder, neck, or head movements. Systems like this are becoming more economical and hold great promise for helping quadriplegics become more self-sufficient.

One device under development uses a robotic arm with a voice-recognizer. The user programs the arm by listing the chores to be done step by step. The task is then given a name (such as "feed" or "scrub") and placed into the arm's memory. The robot then performs tasks in response to the voice commands of the user.

Computer terminals that respond to the user's spoken commands may be used by nonhandicapped users as well as by paralyzed users. The computer displays a menu of options on the screen, and the user responds by calling out the number or letter of the desired option. Certain commonly used sequences of operations can be coded so that the user may cause the entire sequence of operations to occur with a single spoken command. One popular system allows a personal computer to be completely controlled by voice input.

Restoring Movement to Paralyzed Limbs

"We see the body as a mechanical system," says mechanical engineer Ali Seireg. "Therefore we should be able to describe human motion as a series of equations, feed those equations into a computer and get useful information about how humans move, and how to help them when they cannot move correctly.

Science Digest, March 1982

Computers are being used to help restore movement to paralyzed limbs. In paralysis, the problem is often that damaged nerves prevent control

Figure 18-15 *Right:* Some of the keys used with Minspeak. By striking several keys in succession, the user can convey complex thoughts and ideas that are then spoken through a speech synthesizer.

HADES 8 H HEAD

I 9 I EYE

GOD 7 E = MC² GALL-BLADDER G

JESUS 10 J JUGULAR

FRED 6 F FEET

TOM 20 T TONGUE

EVEREST 5 E EAR

29

DAN 4 D DIAPHRAGM

ANN 1 A ARM

30 O OVARY

CATHY 3 C COCCYX

50

BOB 2 B BONE

60

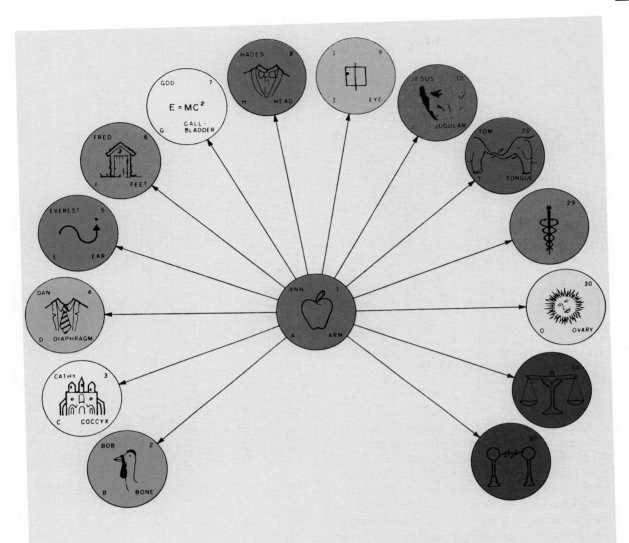

Key #	Image	Theme	Letter	Anatomy	Person
1	apple	eating or food	A	arm	Ann
2	turkey	bad or danger	B	bone	Bob
3	cathedral	wheelchair	C	coccyx	Cathy
4	tie, shirt	dressing or clothing	D	diaphragm	Dan
5	directional arrow	transport or travel	E	ear	Everest
6	privy	ablutions, bathing, or water	F	feet	Fred
7	equation	philosophy or ideas	G	gall bladder	God
8	tuxedo	formalities, departures, or greetings	H	head	Hades
9	Chinese symbol, center	personal opinions or disclosures	I	eye	I
10	Bertrand Russell	logic or modality	J	jugular	Jesus
20	elephants	tag questions	K	tongue	Tom
29	caduceus	medical	—	—	—
30	sun	positive expression or happiness	O	ovary	—
50	scales	typing mode	—	—	—
60	electric current	electricity or control	—	—	—

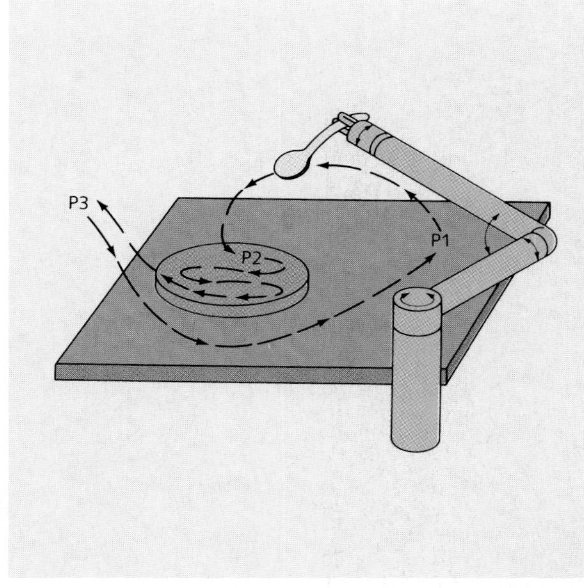

Figure 18-16 This computer-controlled manipulator arm can assist a quadriplegic in eating. The quadriplegic can start the arm in motion by using head movements. The arm is then programmed to scoop up the food and raise it to a comfortable position for eating.

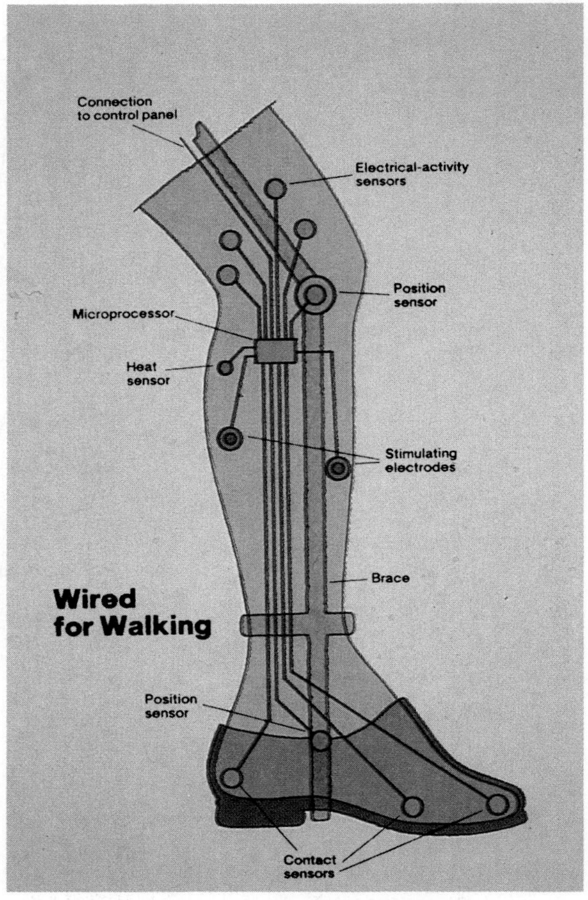

Figure 18-17 An illustration of how a leg might be wired with sensors and a microprocessor to help a paralyzed person walk. The computer would generate signals to the muscles to move—signals that would otherwise have come from healthy nerves.

signals from the brain from reaching otherwise healthy muscles. Jerrold Petrofsky, a professor at Wright State University in Dayton, Ohio, has been working on techniques for using implanted microprocessors to generate simulated brain signals. These signals are directed to the paralyzed person's muscles, which then move accordingly. The problems are enormous. A very large number of nerves and muscles must work together precisely to accomplish even the simplest movement. He is currently experimenting only on partially paralyzed patients, but it may be possible to use his techniques to restore mobility even to quadriplegics (Figures 18–17, 18–18, and 18–19).

The Handicapped at Work

Computers enable the handicapped to participate in and contribute to society, especially through productive employment (Figure 18–20). Today, many companies offer **work-at-home programs**.

Control Data Corporation, a leading manufacturer of mainframe computers, developed its HOMEWORK program in 1978. CDC trains disabled people and provides jobs for them when their training is complete. Recently, a CDC employee received a year's training in its PLATO® system for computer-assisted education. Now, with a computer terminal in her home, she has a new career tutoring students at CDC schools throughout the country. She receives and answers their problems through the PLATO system over CDC's nationwide computer network.

Computers and Special Education

Computers can play an important part in the education of physically and mentally handicapped people. Handicapped people are hindered not only by their physical disabilities, but sometimes by poor concentration and lack of motivation as well. Computers with color graphics, sound, and interaction capabilities can help hold the individual's attention.

Computers can call the student by name and customize the speed and content of their presentation to the individual's special needs. Learning is self-paced. The handicapped person need not be concerned with keeping up with the rest of the class, and the computer has infinite patience.

Computers are also fun to use and they provide immediate feedback. The student doesn't have to wait for a teacher to grade papers. Computers

Figure 18-18 *Left:* This young man, whose legs were completely paralyzed in a diving accident, is able to pedal an exercise bike because of a computer that generates the signals that move the leg muscles.

Figure 18-19 *Below:* Here a paralyzed patient is shown pedaling a wheelchair. A computer generates the signals that move the patient's legs.

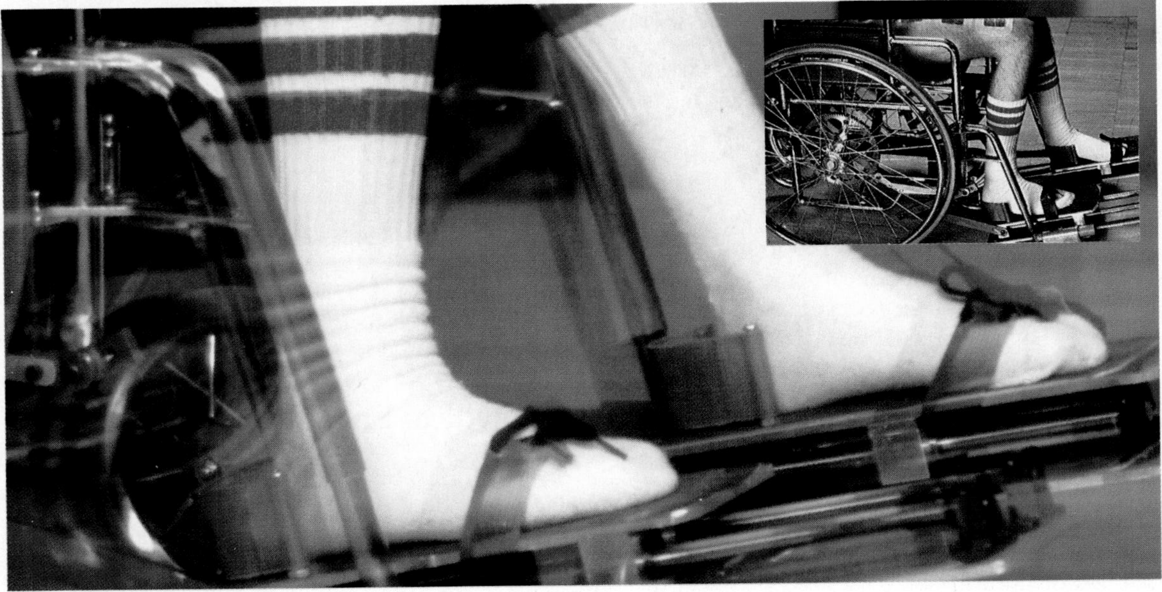

Courtesy of International Business Machines Corporation

Figure 18-20 IBM developed the Audio Typing Unit to help blind typists produce office correspondence quickly and accurately on several popular models of IBM typewriters. The voice synthesizer uses synthetic speech to guide the typist in typing as well as in reviewing each document.

Artificial Hand

Bunce Pierce's left hand hums softly as it opens. When he's nervous, the fingers move with tiny jerks and the popping, cracking sounds of frying bacon.

But when his mind wills it open, the artificial hand opens. Computerized, battery-powered, gear-driven, and life-like in appearance, the device is far removed from the metal hooks that usually replace amputated hands.

"When I tell people I have an electric hand that runs on brain waves, they just freak out," says Pierce.

"It moves because I'm telling it to with my head."

The plastic hand and forearm, covered with a flesh-colored rubber glove that simulates fingernails and veins, is probably the most realistic and advanced artificial limb that's commercially available.

It does two things: the thumb and first two fingers will spread apart and they will close up again. The other two fingers are for appearance. The wrist must be rotated manually with the other hand.

The artificial hand slips over the forearm with a specially molded plastic collar. Inside the collar an electrode picks up and amplifies minute electronic impulses that travel along nerves and produce motion. The signals go to a computer chip, which interprets them and starts the gears moving.

The three functioning fingers can exert up to 35 pounds of pressure. The device is heavy, weighing between 6 to 8 pounds, and expensive, with a cost of $5000.

Says Pierce, "I wouldn't say it's a lot better. I don't want to give the impression this is some kind of panacea. The real difference is appearance. People who pass me on the street don't know I have an artificial hand."

Condensed from "His Electric Hand Obeys Commands" by Robert Locke, AP Science Writer, *Middlesex News*, May 11, 1981. Used by permission of The Associated Press.

can produce frequent progress reports to parents, doctors, and supervising educators.

Even video games are effective rehabilitation tools. They have been used by doctors to treat stroke victims and people with cerebral palsy. They help improve hand-eye coordination, reaction time, memory, span of concentration and problem-solving skills, and they provide enjoyable recreation to handicapped individuals. Psychologists have used video games to observe how people with various types of handicaps respond to success or failure.

Biomedical Engineering

"By 1996 a marathon runner equipped with a super-efficient artificial heart might actually be disqualified because he would have an unfair advantage," says Dr. Willem J. Kolff of the University of Utah.

Newsweek, July 12, 1982

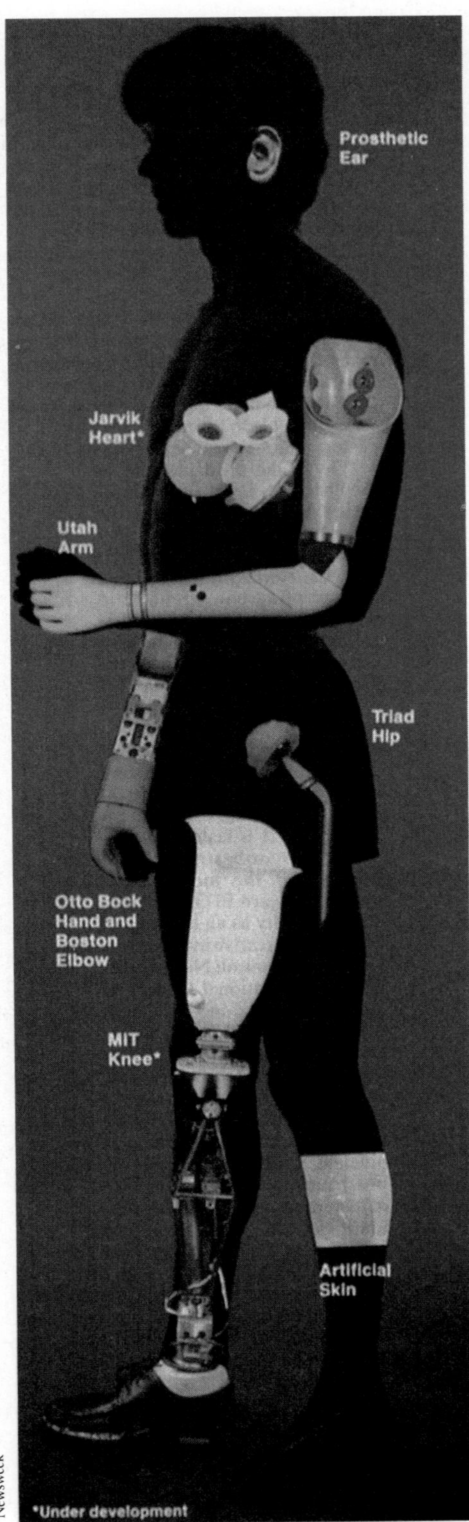

In the 1970s the lead characters of two popular TV shows, "The Six Million Dollar Man" and "The Bionic Woman," were bionic. Little did we know then that **bionic body parts** would go from fantasy to reality so quickly.

Today, the field of **biomedical engineering** is developing replacement body parts such as elbows, arms, lungs, eyes, ears, knees, hearts, and skin (Figure 18–21).

Doctors, engineers, and computer experts are working together to design these parts. Microprocessors are being built into artificial arms, legs, and hands. The microprocessors interpret electronic impulses from the brain and order the appropriate movements of the artificial limbs.

Biomedical engineers are studying every movement of the human body. These movements are entered into computers that analyze the data and help the doctors and engineers to design and construct **artificial body parts** customized to an individual's specific needs. (Figures 18–22 and 18–23.)

Microprocessors have been built into implantable insulin pumps that regulate the level of blood sugar in diabetics. Microprocessors have been used to develop an artificial ear. Sounds are converted by the microprocessor into signals that are sent to electrodes implanted in the patient, and the signals are then converted to electrical impulses that are used to stimulate the patient's auditory nerve so that the patient actually hears.

Some researchers believe that most major organs will be replaceable by artificial body parts within the next several decades.

Figure 18-21 The development of artificial body parts has received new attention with the advent of the microprocessor. The MIT Knee has a built-in microprocessor that controls the complex knee movements.

I Am Not a Robot

"He's a robot," the blond 4-year-old declared.

The rest of the preschool children in the museum looked at me as if I were an exhibit, their faces showing a combination of curiosity and fear. "The children watch a little too much televised science fiction," the teacher apologized.

I laughed and traveled on, strapped in my head-controlled electronic wheelchair. Touring the museum, I reflected on the 4-year-old's observation. It was, of course, wrong. I'm not a robot. I am a person who can't walk, talk, or use my hands, due to severe athetoid cerebral palsy. But, thanks to God, a little bit of luck, a lot of caring people, a stylus (called a headstick) attached to a headband, and computers, I'm "rehabilitated."

While I was struggling to pass my first and only programming course, Dr. Lois Schwab, head of the Independent Living Center at the University of Nebraska-Lincoln, was investigating microcomputers as rehabilitation tools. At the same time, automatic bank tellers with voice synthesizers were beginning to make their way into local banks. Recognizing the potential for "talking computers" as communication devices for people without natural vocalization, Dr. Schwab managed to convince the Rehabilitation Services Administration to allocate $250,000 for further research.

Teaming up with Mark Dahmke, a senior majoring in computer science, Dr. Schwab purchased a TRS-80 Model I and set up the machine. Mark had designed a mechanical arm for his uncle who had lost his arm in a farm accident. The young computer scientist had won a high school science-fair prize for his design but his real dream was to make a voice synthesizer. He mentioned this to Dr. Schwab. They talked. They thought of a certain person who could benefit. I was their guinea pig.

In the fall of 1978, my computer science professor told me about an exhibit featuring personal computers. He suggested I go and find out how computers could help my writing career. He sounded so enthusiastic about the "fast idiots" that I took his advice. It was at the exhibit that I met Mark.

"I'm glad we finally met," he said. "I live in the same dorm you do and I've been talking to some people at the university. We want to build a computerized voice synthesizer for you. Until now, it was too impractical. But I think we can help one another now."

I was skeptical of the idea. I was doing so badly in my computer class that I was beginning to develop a paranoia about the machines. I didn't understand programming logic or algebra and I wasn't cut out to be a computer programmer.

But the voice synthesizer had strong appeal to me. Besides solving my phone dilemma, the ability to verbalize would allow me to ask a professor a direct question instead of using an intermediary. And, more important, having a voice—even an electronic voice—would make me more acceptable to others. I felt that people assume if you don't express coherent thoughts, you don't have any.

Well, I did get a voice. It was a long, slow, arduous process of building, testing, and modifying. My voice was "up" in July 1979—ten years after Neil Armstrong took a stroll on the moon. I spent the summer putting key words and phrases into the voice's memory for later recall. Some of the selections were:

Hello, this is Bill Rush.
I need some information.
I need some Maalox.
I'm using a voice synthesizer.
What are you doing Saturday night?
Are you busy?
Can I help you?

After we programmed the voice, I spent the rest of the summer getting acquainted with it.

The voice synthesizer has been modified and altered since that summer. In 1980, Mark added a word processor; he said it would be invaluable in my writing career.

He was right. Before I had my text editor, rewriting meant retyping and when you type with your head, redoing something gets to be a pain in the neck—both literally and figuratively. But now rewriting means just that—I no longer have to worry about the mechanics; I'm free to concentrate on the message of a story.

Some people, like the child in the museum, think that because I use electronics and computers, I'm somehow sub- or superhuman. Both views are wrong. I am not R2-D2's cousin.

Computers have given me an equal footing with others. They haven't enabled me to see 60 miles away, lift 20 tons, or run 200 yards. They simply allow me to express myself to others more efficiently.

A friend from Kansas once summed up the role computers play in my life when he said, "You're using computers as tools to gain acceptance by other people."

 William L. Rush is a journalism student at the University of Nebraska. He has had cerebral palsy since birth.

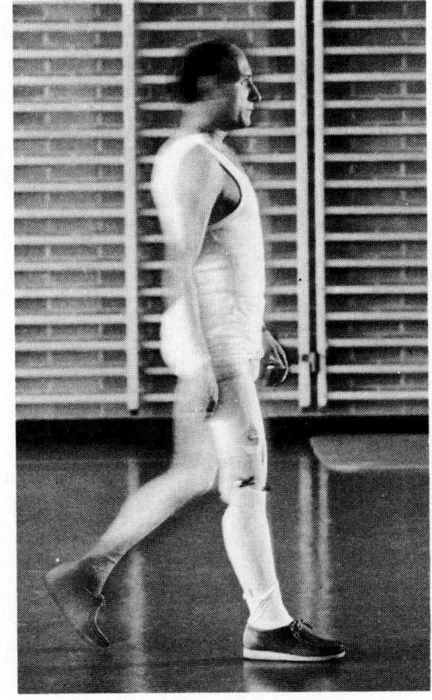

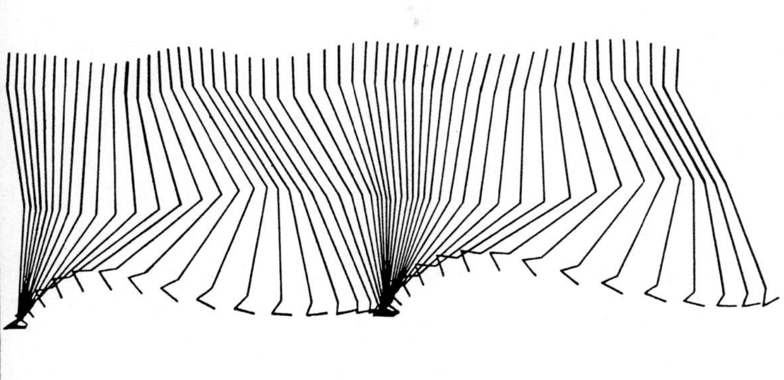

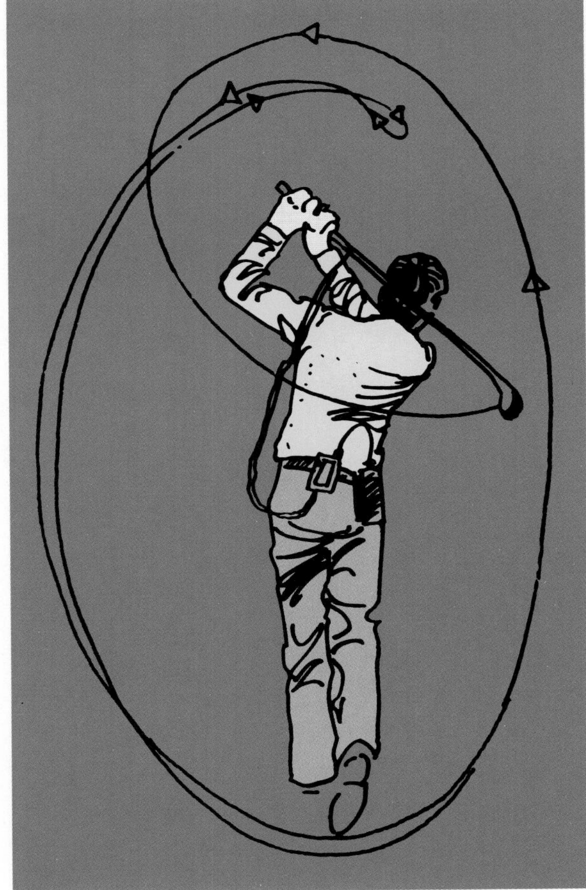

Figure 18-22 *Above:* The movements of a normal person's limbs are carefully analyzed by a high-speed camera that passes its images to a computer system. By studying these movements, designers learn important facts that help them produce artificial body limbs.

Figure 18-23 *Left:* The same motion analysis system that helps in the development of artificial limbs is used to help athletes improve their game.

Summary 

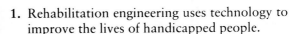

1. Rehabilitation engineering uses technology to improve the lives of handicapped people.
2. Exciting technological advances, particularly the microprocessor, hold great promise for improving the lives of handicapped people.
3. The two most popular forms of speech synthesis are stored speech, in which a vocabulary of prerecorded human speech is stored for playback, and synthetic speech, in which pronunciation rules are stored in the computer and artificial speech generators make the appropriate sounds. Stored speech generally has better quality than synthetic speech, but it is limited by a relatively small vocabulary.

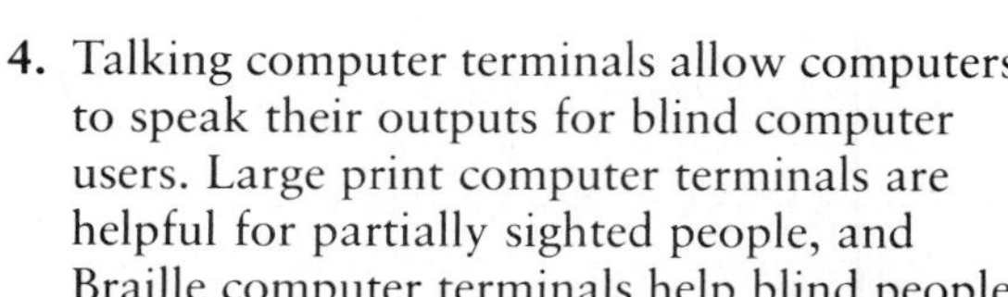

4. Talking computer terminals allow computers to speak their outputs for blind computer users. Large print computer terminals are helpful for partially sighted people, and Braille computer terminals help blind people hold computer-related jobs.
5. Sonar devices are used by blind people to detect obstacles both on and above the ground.
6. Hand-held printing terminals help the deaf communicate over the telephone.
7. Speech recognition devices that convert speech to text hold great promise for the deaf.
8. Paralyzed people are helped by devices that allow them to communicate using whatever muscular control they still have. Such devices can be hooked into speech synthesizers so that a paralyzed and nonvocal person can carry on a conversation.
9. Computerized scanning devices help nonvocal people communicate by forming words and sentences one character at a time.
10. The Abilityphone helps handicapped people obtain assistance in emergency situations. It has many features including automatic answering, automatic redialing of busy numbers, monitoring, and automatic reminders to take medication.
11. The Minspeak system uses a keyboard that contains pictures, numbers, letters, names, and words. The system analyzes the order in which entries are made and then selects and speaks an appropriate sentence from among thousands that have been prestored in its memory.
12. Microcomputer-controlled manipulator arms can help a quadriplegic eat. The quadriplegic uses remaining muscular control to direct the arm.
13. Researchers are developing a technique in which implanted microprocessors simulate brain signals to move the muscles of paralyzed people. Ultimately, it may even be possible to restore mobility to quadriplegics.
14. A device is under development that will help a blind person to move about freely. The device consists of a shoulder-mounted camera and a microprocessor that interprets the video signals. The device reports regularly on nearby obstacles.
15. The field of biomedical engineering is concerned with the design and development of replacement body parts.

Important Terms 

Abilityphone
Ameslan
artificial body parts
artificial vision
biomedical engineering
bionic body parts
Braille
Braille computer terminal
Deaf Communications Institute
Deafnet
eye-tracking
GTE Telenet
information amplification
Kurzweil Reading Machine
Large Print Video Terminal
Louis Braille
Minspeak
Optacon
Orator
residual capabilities
rehabilitation engineering
Smith-Kettlewell Institute of Visual Science
soft copy Braille output device
sonar "sight"
speech recognition
speech synthesis
stored speech
synthetic speech
Tufts Interactive Communicator
work-at-home program

Self-Review Exercises 

Matching

Next to the term in column A, place the letter of the statement in column B that best describes it.

Column A

1. Orator
2. Kurzweil Reading Machine
3. Headstick
4. Tufts Interactive Communicator
5. Abilityphone
6. Residual capabilities
7. Stored speech
8. Optacon
9. Synthetic speech
10. Ameslan

Column B

A. An answering device capable of calling for help
B. Sign language used by the deaf
C. Unlimited vocabulary
D. Stylus used to enter information into a computer
E. Speaks computer output
F. Reads books to the blind
G. Senses and movements that still function
H. Uses actual human speech
I. Scans a display consisting of letters and numbers to spell out messages
J. "Speaks" by vibrations

Fill-in-the-Blanks

Fill in the blanks in each of the following:

1. The application of technology to improve the lives of the handicapped is called ______ .

2. ______ is an electronic mail service offered to the hearing impaired.

3. The ______ system uses a keyboard consisting of pictures that represent concepts which are then analyzed, and an appropriate phrase is generated.

4. ______ is developing implantable microprocessors to simulate brain signals and restore movement to paralyzed muscles.

5. CDC developed its ______ program to provide work for disabled employees.

6. The field of ______ is developing replacement body parts.

7. To help the handicapped work at normal speeds, computers can be programmed to ______ the information being entered.

8. ______ Braille output devices use metal pins on a flat surface to form the Braille characters.

9. ______ devices can determine what a handicapped person is looking at.

10. Ultimately, the most valuable computer-related technology for the deaf will probably be ______ .

Answers to Self-Review Exercises

Matching: 1 E, 2 F, 3 D, 4 I, 5 A, 6 G, 7 H, 8 J, 9 C, 10 B

Fill-in-the-Blanks:

1. rehabilitation engineering
2. Deafnet
3. Minspeak
4. Jerrold Petrofsky
5. HOMEWORK
6. biomedical engineering
7. amplify
8. Soft copy
9. Eye-tracking
10. speech recognition

Discussion Questions 

1. What are some of the keys to improving the quality of life for handicapped people?

2. Discuss the significance of the Kurzweil Reading Machine. List some of its features and explain how they make it convenient to use.

3. What is a major problem faced by designers of text-to-speech translators? Give an example.

4. Suppose that future telephone lines will have a capacity sufficient for transmitting video as well as sound. How might this help people with various handicaps?

5. List several features of the Abilityphone. Suggest some additional features that might also be helpful.

6. Suppose intelligent robots were available. How might they be of help to handicapped people?

7. Why are work-at-home programs important for the handicapped? Why might it be better for a handicapped person to go to the job site rather than work at home?

8. Robots now being developed can feed a handicapped person. What kinds of bugs might these devices develop?

9. With artificial body parts, handicapped athletes may eventually be able to outperform normal athletes. Should people with artificial body parts be allowed to compete in the Olympics on an equal basis with normal people? (Perhaps separate record books could be kept.)

10. How do you feel about the use of artificial body parts? Is there some point at which society should draw the line?

Projects 

1. Suggest some new applications for the handicapped in any of these three areas:

(a) computer-based aids for the blind, deaf, or mentally retarded
(b) ideas for applications that help individuals with learning disabilities
(c) devices for the orthopedically handicapped.

2. The Association of Rehabilitation Programs in Data Processing (ARPDP) was formed "to better share information on adaptive devices and placing the handicapped." Write to several of the ARPDP member programs listed below requesting literature. If possible, visit one of the programs and report on its activities.

Project Director
Computer Programming for Disabled
Bureau of Rehabilitation Services
32 Winthrop Street
Augusta, ME 04330

Center for Independent Living
2020 Milvia
Room 460A
Berkeley, CA 94704

Central Ohio Rehabilitation Center
1331 Edgehill Road
Columbus, OH 43212

Crossroads Rehabilitation Center
3242 Sutherland Avenue
Indianapolis, IN 46205

Director of Handicapped Training
215 Franklin Building 16
3451 Walnut Street
Philadelphia, PA 19104

Easter Seal-Goodwill Industries
Rehabilitation Center
20 Brookside Avenue
New Haven, CT 06515

Home Industries
Goodwill Industries
2201 Glenwood Avenue, S.E.
Atlanta, GA 30316

Human Resources Center
I.U. Willetts Road
Albertson, NY 11507

Lakeshore Rehabilitation Facility
3800 Ridgeway Drive
Birmingham, AL 35209

Maryland Rehabilitation Center
2301 Argonne Drive
Baltimore, MD 21218

State Technical Institute &
Rehabilitation Center
Alber Drive
Plainwell, MI 49080

Director of Computer
Programming Training
TODCOMP
R.R. #4
Columbia, MO 65201

Woodrow Wilson Rehabilitation Center
Fishersville, VA 22939

3. Many colleges and universities offer special support services for deaf people seeking college degrees. Among them are:

Gallaudet College
Washington, DC
(a liberal arts college for the deaf with approximately 1100 students)

Rochester Institute of Technology
Rochester, NY
(a technical college with approximately 7000 students. About 10 percent of the student body is deaf and served by the National Technical Institute for the Deaf, a unit of RIT)

Obtain literature from either of these institutions or from other institutions that have educational programs and support services for the deaf. Visit one of these institutions if possible. How are computers being used? Propose other ways computers may be used to help in educating the deaf.

4. The National Association of the Deaf has developed a book entitiled *Signs for Computing Terminology*. This book contains more than 600 signs that are used for computer terms. For more information, contact:

National Association of the Deaf
814 Thayer Avenue
Silver Spring, MD 20910

5. Many handicapped people are not aware of how advances in computer technology may eventually help them. Discuss this chapter with several handicapped people and record their reactions. Ask them how they feel computers might help them. Summarize their suggestions.

6. Make a list of some handicaps not discussed in this chapter. How might computers help people who have these handicaps?

7. What computer-related services are available to handicapped people at your school or place of work?

8. Visit your local library. Does the library have any Braille publications? Is a Kurzweil Reading Machine available? If so, try using it.

9. Inquire about the status of Deafnet by contacting:

Deaf Communications Institute
Bethany Road
Framingham, MA 01701

Request and summarize literature on the latest developments in communications technology for the deaf.

10. For more information about computers and the handicapped, write to:

The Bulletin of Science and Technology for the Handicapped
American Association for the
Advancement of Science
1515 Massachusetts Avenue
Washington, DC 20005

Closing the Gap
Route 2, Box 39
Henderson, MN 56004

International Software Registry of Programs
Written or Adapted for Handicapped Individuals
Trace Research and Development Center
314 Waisman Center
University of Wisconsin
Madison, WI 53706

USA
NASA

Chapter 19

Computers and Transportation

After reading this chapter you will understand:

1. How computers are used to increase the safety and efficiency of today's cars, planes, trains, and ships
2. How computers and radar equipment work together in collision avoidance systems
3. How computerized simulators work and how they are used as training tools
4. How computers are used in traffic control
5. How computers may be used in the transportation systems of the future

Left: Between on-board and ground-based computers, the Space Shuttle is the most heavily computerized transportation system ever developed.

Outline

It may not be long before a car is equipped with an electronic voice that cries out when the driver pushes beyond the speed limit. By that time it could be too late; the computer in the policeman's car a mile down the highway will have already written out the ticket.

Natalie Angier

If computerized traffic control saves as many gallons of gasoline as the predictions indicate, then cities will have to invest in large fleets of tank trucks to haul the excess away.

John O'Connor

It is unlikely that the pioneers of computing could have imagined the many ways in which computing would touch our lives. Certainly they could not have foreseen its uses in transportation. But computers are advancing all modes of travel—automobile, airplane, train, and even shipping—by helping to speed them, make them safer, and improve their efficiency.

Computers and Automobiles

Some experts even suggest that many cars of the 1990s will be smarter than their owners.

Tappan King

The use of microprocessors is the technological breakthrough of the last twenty-five years in the automobile industry.

Robert Templin

The auto industry has gone through many changes over the years; the most dramatic of these may well be the widespread use of microprocessors. Microprocessors perform numerous functions, including helping to reduce gasoline consumption and limiting exhaust emissions. Their future applications are almost limitless (Figure 19–1).

In 1984 fully equipped U.S.-built cars used 10 to 15 chips, compared with less than one chip per car in 1978. General Motors considers microprocessors so vital to its future that it now manufactures its own chips. In fact, GM has actually become one of the world's largest computer manufacturers—just to service its own needs.

General Motors cars now come equipped with **Computer Command Control**—a system to monitor and control many engine functions (Figure 19–2). When a problem arises, the computer flashes a signal light located on the dashboard. The car can then be taken to the service department of a GM dealer, where it is plugged into a computerized readout device that tells a mechanic exactly what the problem is.

Another General Motors innovation is the microprocessor-controlled **modulated displacement system**, which was first offered in 1981 Cadillacs. Once a vehicle has accelerated to full speed, it no longer needs maximum engine power. The microprocessor detects this and automatically reduces the number of cylinders in operation from

Figure 19–1 *Right:* The driver of the 1990s will touch a touch-sensitive screen to indicate origin and destination. With the aid of satellite communications, a central traffic control computer will display the best route to take.

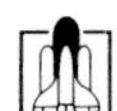

Figure 19–2 The GM Computer Command Control module slips into a carrier underneath the dashboard.

eight to six and eventually to four for easy cruising. This greatly improves fuel efficiency.

Car computers are making driving easier and more pleasurable in a variety of ways. Door keys have been replaced in some cars by a personal code that the driver punches into a computerized lock to open the door. Dashboard computers inform the driver if the oil is low, if the engine is hot, what the temperature is in the passenger compartment, and how much farther the car can go with the remaining fuel. Some car computers report distance remaining to a preset destination, estimated time of arrival, and a wide range of other facts. Microprocessors even control radios; they can seek out stations and remember a driver's favorites.

Yamaha has announced the world's first computerized motorcycle. Its monitoring system includes a microprocessor connected to sensors that report the status of brakes, battery fluid, engine oil, headlights, taillights, brakelights, and even the kickstand position. A flashing light on a small console mounted between the handlebars warns the driver if a problem arises. The driver has the option of checking all the functions by pushing a single button that causes the microprocessor to scan them in sequence. The scan also occurs automatically when the driver first starts the engine.

Cars are making increased use of computer-

"It's your computer. I'll have to call in a systems analyst."

controlled voice. Today's models generally use prerecorded voice messages to warn the driver to turn off the lights, lock the doors, take the key from the ignition, check the oil, fasten a seat belt, and so on. Future systems will use speech synthesis techniques and even speech recognition to carry on a dialogue with the driver.

Future cars will have trip guides with video displays of maps and points of interest. Collision avoidance systems will warn drivers of approaching hazards. Car computer systems will be able to communicate with central computers containing databases of information on traffic conditions, alternate routes, and where to get emergency service anywhere along the way.

In one computer system under development, a small computer in the car is linked via radio communications to a network of roadside computers that sense the traffic volume. At the start of a trip, the driver punches in a destination code. The roadside computers receive the code and relay back the best route to take to avoid construction and traffic jams. Because the roadside computers know in advance where the driver is going, they can predict potential tie-ups and avoid them. The driver is also forewarned about dangerous conditions ahead, such as snow, fog, ice, or accidents.

In Switzerland, motorists may drive under the Alps through the 10-mile St. Gotthard Tunnel with their safety ensured by a computerized control system. Computers monitor sensors placed throughout the tunnel to collect information on traffic flow, air quality, and the status of lighting and ventilation equipment. Any problems are reported immediately to engineers and emergency personnel. The tunnel has reduced considerably the time it takes to travel through the Alps, and it is a much safer trip than driving on the region's steep and icy roads.

Car Pooling

Many people turn to **car pooling** to conserve fuel and reduce commuting costs. Cities and private companies have developed computer systems that help drivers find car pool companions. Information such as starting points, destinations, passenger capacity of cars, and working schedules are just a few of the facts computers use to set up groups for car pooling. Car pooling also reduces traffic congestion, makes parking easier, and reduces pollution.

Houston offers a car pooling system free to commuters. Applications are processed on a computer that produces lists of drivers in the same areas as the applicants. The system takes car pooling one step further by offering a phone service that matches drivers and riders immediately. This feature has been particularly popular with commuters whose cars have been stolen or are being repaired.

Traffic Control

Computers are used to synchronize traffic lights in order to improve traffic flow. In New York City, thousands of intersections have been converted to computer operation, and motorists are already saving 20 million gallons of fuel per year. The Federal Highway Administration estimates that using computerized **traffic control** throughout the country would save as many as 3 billion gallons of oil per year.

Some cities considering computerizing their traffic control systems have discovered that they could share recently installed cable television lines. By tying their traffic signals and computers into the cable networks, they have reduced the

costs of their automated traffic control systems.

One devastating problem in traffic control is called **gridlock**, the situation that occurs when traffic is so congested that intersections are blocked and impassable, and all traffic comes to a dead halt. Computerized traffic control systems can quickly change traffic light patterns to unwind a gridlock. Future traffic control systems may be able to prevent a gridlock from developing in the first place.

©Creative Computing

Emergency Service

If you've ever been stranded in a car, especially if in a remote location or in bad weather, you know the importance of receiving assistance quickly. Many road service organizations use computers in their dispatching operations.

In an emergency, the driver dials a road service number. The dispatcher sitting at a CRT terminal enters information describing the problem, the car's location, the driver's name, and the telephone number where the driver can be reached. The computer automatically displays a list of garages closest to the motorist, along with their telephone numbers. The dispatcher then calls a nearby garage, confirms that it will respond, and enters this information into the computer, along with the estimated time of arrival. Motorists frequently call back before help arrives. The dispatcher can access all the information accumulated about calls to keep motorists posted about when help will arrive.

The computer system can monitor the call volume assigned to each service station; when a station becomes busy, the computer can recommend that calls be diverted to other stations.

When service has been completed, the emergency vehicle radios in the problem found, the time of completion, and whether the car was repaired or towed.

Computers also provide useful management information. They can summarize service performed by each station, spot service stations that are not responding quickly enough, and determine what geographical areas may require additional coverage.

Driving Simulators

Microprocessors have made possible the development of economical driving **simulators** that are used in driver training programs. With these simulators, a driver can experience a wider range of driving situations and conditions than is possible during the limited hours spent behind the wheel of a real car while learning to drive. The combination of simulator training and real driving makes for better prepared drivers.

Computers and Air Travel

Air Traffic Control

In the mid- to late 1980's we are planning to replace our entire existing network of air traffic control computers at a cost on the order of $1.5 billion . . . which may well be the biggest computer project ever undertaken.

S. C. Taylor

By the end of this decade collision avoidance systems will be added to air carrier cockpits already crammed with hundreds of warning devices and enough alarms, bells, chimes, clackers, gongs, buzzers, whistles, and whoopers to equip a symphonic percussion section.

Roger Rapoport

The Federal Aviation Administration (FAA) is responsible for monitoring and controlling the commercial, military, and private air traffic in American skies. Its safety record has been impressive, especially with more than 200,000 aircraft flying regularly. But the screens watched by human air traffic controllers throughout the world are becoming clogged with ever-increasing activity (Figure 19–3).

The FAA is now working with private contractors to develop the next generation of computer-based air traffic control and **collision avoidance systems**. Because of the availability of inexpensive microprocessors, it will be possible (and perhaps required) for small private planes to install the equipment.

Figure 19–3 At the regional control center in Frankfurt, Germany, air traffic controllers track flights across hundreds of square miles of busy airspace. Computerized video displays provide them with the speed, altitude, and direction of each aircraft.

Two different types of systems are being designed. The **Discrete Address Beacon System** (DABS) (Figure 19–4) will use ground-based radar and computer systems to track each aircraft individually. Every aircraft will carry a **transponder**, a device that sends a reply automatically when it receives a certain signal. When the DABS system wants the position of a given aircraft, it sends a specially coded signal unique to that plane. The transponder on the plane receives the signal and immediately transmits the plane's position. In conjunction with the DABS, the **Automatic Traffic Advisory and Resolution Service** (ATARS) computers will receive positions of the planes, monitor flight paths, detect potential collisions, and transmit collision avoidance instructions back through DABS directly to microprocessor-controlled screens on each plane.

The second system currently under development is called the **Beacon Collision Avoidance System** (BCAS). BCAS is primarily an air-based system that can operate effectively even if the ground-based systems fail. The BCAS system, installed directly in an aircraft, interrogates the transponders in any nearby planes to get their positions. If the BCAS computer determines that there is a chance of collision, it will warn the pilots and provide a new course. The Airline Pilots Association wants a collision avoidance system completely independent of ground systems and, therefore, favors the BCAS approach.

The Holding Pattern

Computers may eventually eliminate the need for planes to circle airports in **holding patterns** while waiting for landing clearance. Lockheed Corporation has developed a computerized navigation system that allows an airliner hundreds of miles away from touchdown to be placed in line to land, its time and order of arrival reserved.

The new system works with the four flight dimensions of range, course, altitude, and time. The operation starts with early communication between the pilot and the destination's air traffic controller. The system steadily computes the

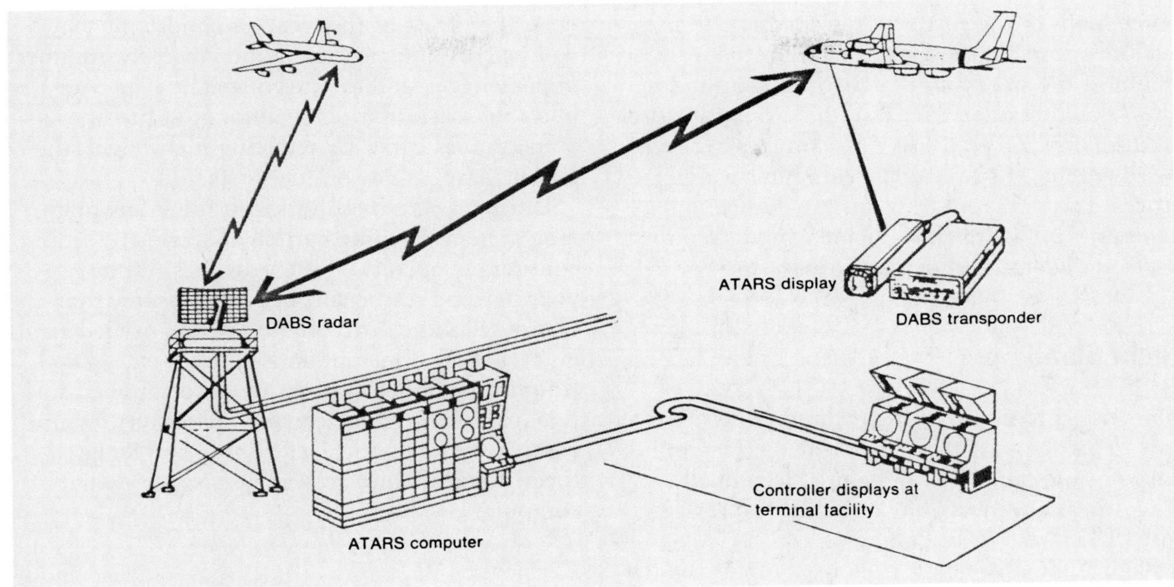

Figure 19–4 A ground-based collision avoidance system.

flight factors to control and guide the aircraft into an exact assigned spot in the landing order. No time is spent in a holding pattern, and no fuel is wasted.

The Airborne Electronic Terrain Map System

The Air Force is currently developing a new computerized system that may revolutionize navigation. Called the **Airborne Electronic Terrain Map System,** it helps a pilot fly a plane safely at night, in poor weather conditions, or over unfamiliar territory.

Detailed information about the terrain to be flown over is entered into a powerful mapping computer, creating an electronic map of the territory. In the air, a navigational computer supplies continuous readings on latitude, longitude, course, and altitude to the mapping computer. The mapping computer searches its memory for a description of the land below. Using high-speed computer graphics, the computer displays 30 pictures per second, simulating the changing scenes outside the plane (Figure 19–5). The pilot thus sees a view almost identical to what the actual view would be in clear visibility.

One possible way to accumulate detailed **elec-**

Figure 19–5 With computerized terrain maps, pilots can see the ground below even at night or in poor weather conditions.

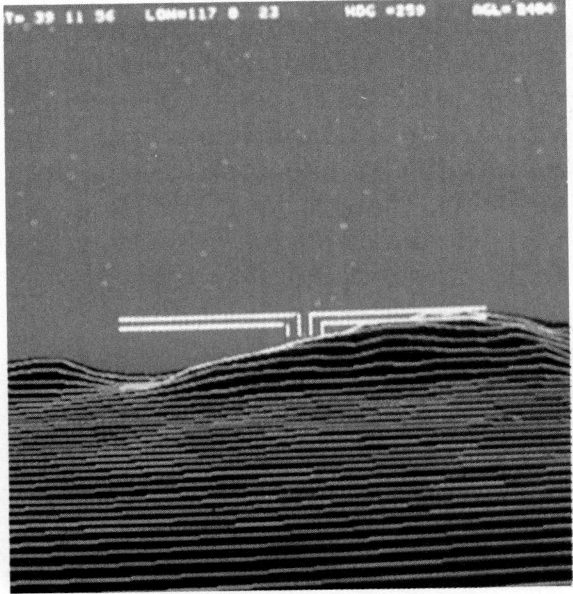

tronic maps of the entire world would be to use satellites; some of these have cameras that can see an object the size of an orange on the ground. They would regularly scan all the ground features on the earth and transmit this data to a ground-based computer system. The computer would process this data and transmit the needed maps to aircraft in flight. This scheme would keep the electronic maps current.

Flight Simulators

Pilots use computerized **flight simulators** to learn how to fly planes without ever leaving the ground. Takeoffs and landings can be practiced in all types of weather conditions, day or night (Figures 19–6 and 19–7).

Flight simulators have been used mainly by the airlines, military, and aerospace companies for larger aircraft, but they are now becoming popular even for small planes and helicopters (Figure 19–8). Helicopter pilots enter a simulator and practice the maneuvers they will have to perform during the course of a flight. Simulators also help the instructor monitor the student's performance under a wide range of challenging situations and enable pilots to practice emergency procedures (Figure 19–9).

Fuel Planning

Computers are used to determine how much fuel a plane should carry on each leg of a flight. Flight information is entered into a computer that analyzes such facts as the weather conditions that will be encountered during the flight, the number of passengers, and the cargo weight. The computer then determines the amount of fuel the plane should carry. By reducing fuel weight, the airlines save money on fuel costs.

During severe fuel shortages, these **fuel planning systems** become particularly critical to the continuous operation of the airlines. When supplies become scarce, airlines can't assume that planes will be able to obtain the fuel needed at every airport. One option is to ferry excess fuel from oversupplied stations to undersupplied stations. Planning these ferrying operations requires complex mathematical calculations to be performed quickly and accurately—exactly what computers do best.

Computerized Reservations Systems

Major airlines and travel services have been using computerized **reservations and ticketing systems** for years. At any given time the airlines know how many people are booked on a flight, how many seats are still available, where the seats are located, any special meals that were ordered, and so on. The computer records the names of children who will be traveling alone and the people who will be meeting these children at their destinations. The computer also lists people requiring special assistance, such as wheelchairs, upon arrival.

Reservations computer systems are of the type called **database/data communications (DB/DC) systems** because they maintain massive databases

Figure 19–6 Runway approach viewed from a flight simulator.

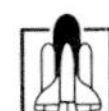

Figure 19–7 A nighttime landing as seen from the cockpit of a computerized flight simulator.

Figure 19–8 Outside view of a computerized simulator for helicopter pilot training.

Figure 19–9 Inside this computerized flight simulator, the instructor can create 200 different malfunctions. The pilot's performance is monitored on the CRT screen.

of facts about upcoming flights and because they are normally tied into computer networks.

Today, with a single call to any of several major airlines, a traveler may book a complete trip including all plane flights, rental cars, and hotel accommodations. If the airline doesn't fly to certain cities, or if a leg of the trip is completely booked, the computer will check with other airline computers and automatically confirm the flight with an airline that has space.

Microprocessors are used in **automatic ticketing machines** (Figure 19–10). Some of these devices can print tickets only for same-day flights to a limited number of cities served by that airline. Others allow customers to book multiple-flight journeys well into the future.

Figure 19–10 An air traveler purchasing a ticket at an automatic ticketing machine. She inserts a major credit card in the machine. The machine verifies the customer's credit with the credit card company and then prints the ticket and a receipt.

Computers and Trains

Canada's Intermediate Capacity Transit System

In Ontario, Canada, the Urban Transportation Development Corporation is developing a heavily computerized mass transportation system. The trains, part of the **Intermediate Capacity Transit System** (ICTS), are completely computer controlled (Figure 19–11).

ICTS trains use **linear induction motors** (LIMs). LIMs work on the familiar principle that opposite magnetic poles attract. Electric currents create magnetic fields both in a fixed rail and in plates located on the train. These currents are generated to keep accompanying magnetic fields opposite, so the train is actually pulled along the rail by magnetic attraction. Interestingly, as the train brakes, electrical energy is absorbed by the system rather than going to waste, as with conventional braking systems.

Antennas underneath each car regularly transmit the car's position and speed to cables installed along the tracks. The antennas receive instructions from a group of three computers. At least two of the three must agree on the instruction to be performed before the train will obey. This is called a **voting scheme** and is often used in situations requiring very high reliability. A pair of

Figure 19–11 These conductorless trains, part of Canada's Intermediate Capacity Transit System, are completely controlled by computers.

on-board computers drives the train; there is no conductor. Both computers must agree on what to do, otherwise an emergency braking system stops the train.

The computer systems control all movements of the train, including track switching and car coupling. They can stop the train within inches of a designated spot. The computers are so precise that separate trains may run safely very close together.

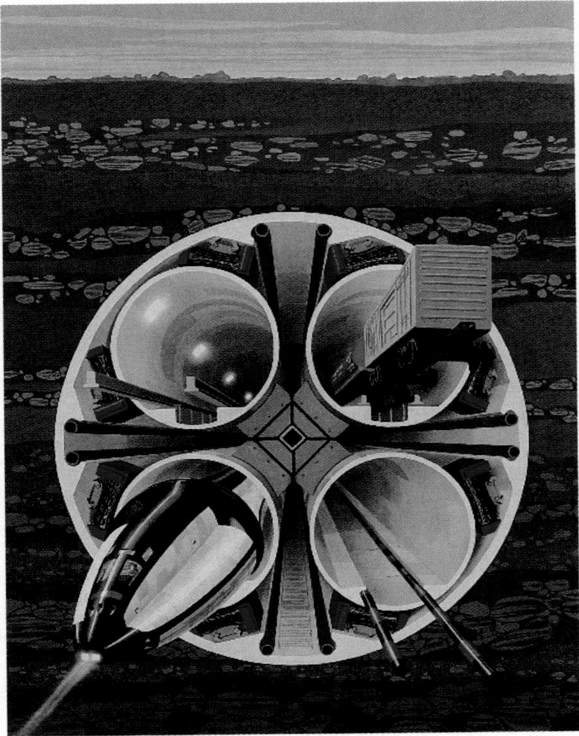

Figure 19–12 An artist's conception of the 40-foot Planetran tunnel with two Planetran tubes and two conventional rail tubes.

The Westinghouse People Mover System

Beneath the Atlanta Airport, one of the world's busiest, the completely automated **People Mover System,** built by Westinghouse, speeds 100,000 passengers per day between the main terminal and the concourses.

Electronic sensors are located throughout the microprocessor-based system. The sensors detect the position of each train and report this data back to a control room. There, larger computer systems analyze the readings to determine the speed and position of each car and make sure that the trains are operating properly and at safe distances from one another. In case of a malfunction, maintenance engineers are notified immediately. The computers tell the engineers which train is malfunctioning and provide other information to help the engineers isolate and repair the problem quickly. In case of a dangerous situation, the computers can shut down the entire system in seconds.

Magnetic Levitation Trains

The ultimate train of the future may be the *Planetran*, the brainchild of Robert Salter at the Rand Corporation. Planetran would operate via LIMs and **magnetic levitation** (called *maglev* in the industry) at speeds of 6000 miles per hour (three times faster than the Concorde SST) in huge tubes buried beneath the ground (Figure 19–12). It could travel across the United States in less than one hour!

Magnetic levitation trains actually float on air above their tracks. This is accomplished by using the simple principle of magnetism that like poles repel each other. Both the track and metal plates on the bottom of the train are given the same polarity by running electric currents through them. The train actually lifts off the track and flies through the air!

In Japan, maglev trains (Figure 19–13) are already transporting passengers comfortably at more than 300 mph. But Planetran would go about 20 times as fast, so even simple air resistance would provide intolerable drag. Therefore, the Planetran tubes would contain vacuum pumps to eliminate air friction as well.

As these trains decelerate, most of their energy would be converted back to electricity and recycled into the system. Thus, Planetran would be so efficient that it would require only a few dollars' worth of electricity to transport a passenger coast to coast!

Electronic sensors would be placed throughout

Figure 19–13 This Japanese maglev train rides on a cushion of air at 325 mph. It operates quietly and economically and is pollution-free. The conventional train in the background provides an interesting contrast.

Figure 19–14 CSX Corporation, America's largest transportation and natural resources company, operates a 27,000-mile freight distribution network. The new $71-million Queensgate railroad yard is one of the busiest interchange points in the CSX railroad system. Computers help control the processing, coupling, and routing of more than 1 million railroad cars per year.

the tubes to detect the slightest deviations in the train's speed and position. Signals would be sent to microprocessor control stations that would rapidly compute corrections and adjust the electric currents controlling the train's movement to keep it on center in the tube.

"Tracking" Railroad Cars

Computers are making conventional railroad transportation more efficient (Figure 19–14). Railroad cars are monitored by computerized **tracking systems**. Markings on the sides of the cars indicate their owners, the weight of each car both empty and full, and other identifying information. As the cars pass checkpoints, this information is entered into computers, sometimes manually and sometimes by automated scanning systems. People waiting for goods being transported can get a car's location to help determine the arrival time. The railroad companies use the information gathered from the side markings to determine how long a train can be and what type of locomotive will be necessary to pull the train. This information is updated as cars are loaded, emptied, removed from the train, or added. Computers also maintain information about the contents of each car; dangerous materials are monitored along their journey, and fresh produce cargoes are given priority so that they reach their markets quickly.

Train Simulators

Conrail has been using a train simulator since 1977. The device, called the **Train Dynamics Analyzer** (TDA), helps instruct new engineers and is useful in sharpening the train-handling skills of experienced personnel.

The simulator helps an engineer develop the feel for handling huge trains, such as the mile-long freight haulers commonly used today. Too much braking at the head of the train can cause cars at the rear to ram into the front, and too much acceleration when the brakes on the rear cars have not fully released could tear the train apart.

The simulator displays many facts for the engineer to consider, such as the length of the train, steepness of the grades, sharpness of the curves, location of heavy and empty cars, horsepower of the locomotive, and braking capacity. Engineers can push their simulated trains to the limit. They can see how the trains respond under difficult and dangerous conditions. Derailing a simulated train is a marvelous learning experience!

Computers and Ships

With fuel costs increasing and supplies becoming more uncertain, the shipping industry has renewed its interest in sailing vessels propelled by the wind. With computers controlling the sails, ships can take maximum advantage of the winds (Figures 19–15 and 19–16). The ship's computer monitors the wind direction and speed and then adjusts the sails to make the best use of this free energy. When the wind is strong, the computer slows the ship's motors to reduce fuel consumption. The computer also monitors changes in weather conditions; if a storm is approaching, the computer closes the sails to prevent them from being damaged. **Computerized sailing ships** offer

Figure 19–15 This ship is equipped with computer-controlled sails to take maximum advantage of free wind energy.

Figure 19–16 When the steel sails on the *Shinaitoku Maru* are closed, they form a wedge shape to reduce drag. When the sails are open, a microprocessor continuously analyzes wind speed and direction data and rotates the sails so they are at the best angle to the wind.

Figure 19–17 This computerized collision avoidance system, installed on the French container ship *Fort Royal*, sounds an alarm if the ship is headed on a potential collision course with another vessel.

tremendous energy savings—they may well be the ships of the future.

Computerized systems are greatly reducing the chance of ship collisions (Figure 19-17). These systems can identify targets many miles away and can differentiate between ships, debris, and land masses. Generally, the computer reports the speed and course of the approaching ship. It also estimates the closest point and time of approach and recommends an appropriate course for avoiding the collision by a safe distance. Computerized navigation systems are also popular (Figure 19-18).

Computerized simulators help train new crew members and help established crews refine their skills (Figure 19-19). Crews can practice docking in ports around the world. Today's supertankers are so huge and so loaded with complex electronic equipment that many months of intensive training on simulators are required before a person may pilot a real ship.

Figure 19–18 This shrimp fisherman uses a computerized navigational aid produced by Raytheon to help pinpoint and return to areas of productive fishing.

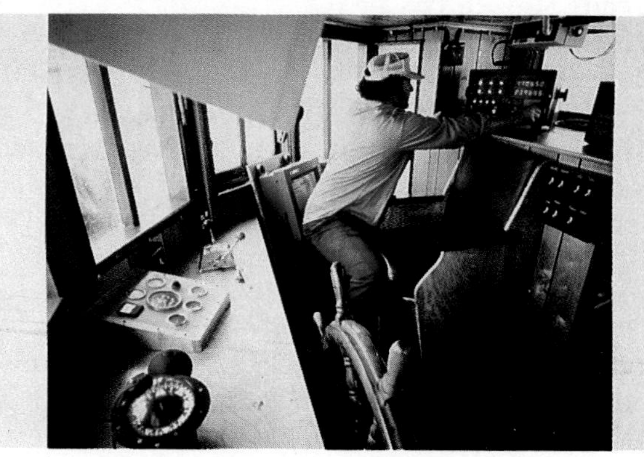

Figure 19–19 The view from the deck of this computerized ship simulator may look real, but it isn't. As the deck officers steer the ship, the simulator adjusts the pictures on the screen. These people are being trained to maneuver a bulk carrier into St. Lawrence Seaway's Iroquois Lock. The seaway handles more than 5000 ship transits per year.

Conclusion

Automobiles, airplanes, trains, and ships, which were themselves prime movers in advancing communications, are now advancing further because of the Information Revolution. Austrian Chancellor Bruno Kreisky's statement, which we quoted in Chapter 1, speaks to part of that process: "What networks of railroads, highways and canals were in another age, networks of telecommunications, information and computerization . . . are today." The chancellor might have added that these "networks of telecommunications, information and computerization" of the Information Revolution are guiding the railroads, highways, and canals ahead into another age. We look forward with great anticipation to seeing the effects of this progress.

Summary 

1. The use of microprocessors may be the most important technological breakthrough of the last 25 years in the automobile industry.
2. The Computer Command Control system developed by General Motors uses a microprocessor to monitor many critical engine functions and to report problems to the driver.
3. Collision avoidance systems warn drivers of hazards that lie ahead.
4. Computerized traffic control systems monitor sensing devices to determine traffic volumes and synchronize traffic lights to eliminate congestion.
5. The Discrete Address Beacon System (DABS) would use ground-based radar and computer systems to track aircraft individually.
6. The Beacon Collision Avoidance System (BCAS) would use computers installed on each plane. BCAS could function even if ground-based computers fail.
7. The Airborne Electronic Terrain Map System will display a computer-generated simulated view of the terrain moving beneath a plane. This would facilitate flying at night, in poor weather, or even over unfamiliar territory.
8. Computerized flight simulators help educate pilots safely while they remain on the ground. Simulators can create many malfunctions pilots would not ordinarily experience while learning to fly in a real plane.
9. Computer-based fuel planning systems help the airlines conserve fuel by indicating where each plane should fuel up, and whether fuel should be ferried from oversupplied stations to undersupplied stations.
10. At the heart of modern airline reservation systems are DB/DC (database/data communications) computer systems.
11. Canada's Intermediate Capacity Transit System (ICTS) uses computer-controlled trains powered by linear induction motors (LIMs). LIMs pull a train along a track by magnetic attraction. ICTS trains are fully automated and have no human conductors. To achieve high reliability, multiple computers perform each function and send each command. These computers must agree on the action to be performed before the train will do what it is told. This is called a voting scheme.
12. Computers in the Westinghouse People Mover System can detect malfunctions and shut down the entire system in seconds.
13. Planetran, currently in the thought stages, would propel a magnetic levitation vehicle using LIMs through a vacuum tunnel at 6000 miles per hour. Microprocessors would ensure the stability of the vehicles.

14. Because of expensive and uncertain fuel supplies, the shipping industry has renewed its interest in sailing vessels. Computers control the sails and the engines to save fuel when the winds are strong.

15. Computerized ship simulators help trainees practice docking in ports around the world.

Important Terms

Airborne Electronic Terrain Map System
automatic ticketing machine
Automatic Traffic Advisory and Resolution Service (ATARS)
Beacon Collision Avoidance System (BCAS)
car pooling
collision avoidance system
Computer Command Control
computerized sailing ships
computerized terrain map
database/data communications (DB/DC) system
Discrete Address Beacon System (DABS)
electronic map
flight simulators
fuel planning system
gridlock
holding pattern
Intermediate Capacity Transit System (ICTS)
linear induction motor (LIM)
magnetic levitation (maglev)
modulated displacement system
People Mover System
Planetran
reservations and ticketing system
simulators
Space Shuttle
tracking systems
traffic control
Train Dynamics Analyzer (TDA)
transponder
voting scheme

Self-Review Exercises

Matching

Next to the term in column A, place the letter of the statement in column B that best describes it.

Column A

1. Gridlock
2. FAA
3. Simulator
4. Planetran
5. Collision avoidance system
6. Transponder
7. DB/DC system
8. ICTS
9. Voting scheme
10. Computer Command Control

Column B

A. Automatically sends a reply when it receives a signal
B. Warns of hazards that lie ahead
C. Used in reservation systems
D. A majority of the computers must agree before an action will occur
E. Computer-controlled trains powered by LIMs
F. Monitors various engine functions
G. Controls and monitors aircraft flying over the United States
H. The blocking of intersecting streets preventing traffic from moving
I. Computerized teaching machine that gives students a feel for different types of vehicles
J. 6000 mph transportation via maglev

Fill-in-the-Blanks

Fill in the blanks in each of the following:

1. The ____ system automatically reduces the number of cylinders in operation in an automobile engine for fuel efficiency.

2. Two new air traffic collision avoidance systems now being designed are ____ and ____.

3. The Airline Pilots Association wants a collision avoidance system completely independent of ground systems and, therefore, favors the ____ approach.

4. The ____ system uses a powerful mapping computer that produces an electronic map of the territory so that pilots may see the ground even at night or in poor weather conditions.

5. ____ motors are being used to propel trains by using the principles of magnetic attraction and repulsion.

6. The ____ is a simulator used by Conrail to help train new engineers.

7. Ships are now using ____ to take advantage of free wind energy and conserve fuel.

8. The ____ is the most heavily computerized transportation system ever developed.

9. ____ vehicles work by the principle that like poles repel one another; these vehicles actually float in midair.

10. ____ systems enable the airlines to conserve fuel by indicating where each plane should fuel up, and whether fuel should be ferried from oversupplied stations to undersupplied stations.

Answers to Self-Review Exercises

Matching: 1 H, 2 G, 3 I, 4 J, 5 B, 6 A, 7 C, 8 E, 9 D, 10 F

Fill-in-the-Blanks:

1. modulated displacement
2. Discrete Address Beacon System, Beacon Collision Avoidance System
3. Beacon Collision Avoidance System
4. Airborne Electronic Terrain Map
5. Linear induction
6. Train Dynamics Analyzer (TDA)
7. computerized sails
8. space shuttle
9. Magnetic levitation (maglev)
10. Fuel planning

Discussion Questions 

1. Discuss several applications of microprocessors in today's automobiles.

2. How will microprocessors be used in the car of the future?

3. How are computers useful in ground vehicle traffic control in the cities?

4. Why does the Airline Pilots Association prefer the BCAS approach to the DABS/ATARS approach?

5. Why are computers essential in the Airborne Electronic Terrain Map System?

6. What is a DB/DC system? Why are airline reservation systems of that type?

7. What is a voting scheme? Under what circumstances are voting schemes used?

8. How would microprocessors be used in Planetran?

9. Discuss the importance of collision avoidance systems in the transportation industry, and how computers are used in such systems.

10. Discuss how simulators are used in the transportation industry. What functions do computers perform in simulators?

Projects 

1. Research the car of the future. Write to several major car manufacturers for literature on the subject. Visit an automobile show to see some displays on future cars. Write a report on what the car of the future might be like, and how computers will be essential to its operation.

2. Contact a school that uses a computerized driving simulator. If possible, use the simulator. Report on your experiences.

3. Write to several manufacturers in the transportation industry. Ask for literature on the new types of transportation systems they are developing, and how these systems will use computers. Write a report summarizing the literature you receive.

4. Contact the Federal Department of Transportation and request literature on computer applications in future transportation systems. Write a report summarizing the literature you receive.

5. Discuss how microprocessors might be used in walking, jogging, cycling, and various other forms of transportation not discussed in this chapter.

6. Visit the control tower of an airport near you. Observe the air traffic controllers and any computerized equipment they use. Report on your findings.

7. In the not too distant future, cars may be able to drive themselves. Discuss how computers might help make this possible. How would you feel as a passenger in a car driven by a computerized "chauffeur"?

Appendix A

BASIC Programming

After reading this appendix you will understand:

1. How to produce neatly structured programs in essentially unstructured BASIC
2. How to create, edit, store, retrieve, and run BASIC programs
3. How to debug BASIC programs
4. How to write the BASIC programs that solve the problems in the Case Studies of Chapter 8
5. How to use some of BASIC's more advanced features such as fancy print formatting, single-subscripted arrays, and random number generation to solve challenging problems

Outline

Module 1: Introduction to BASIC

As originally developed, BASIC was not designed to be a structured programming language, but many recent versions do provide structured programming facilities. In this appendix we use a compromise, namely, an unstructured BASIC that is written as closely as possible to the norms of a structured programming style. The BASIC we use is similar to what is called **ANSI Minimal BASIC**, a common subset of the language that is supported by the vast majority of BASICs on the market. We use only uppercase letters; some versions of BASIC allow the use of lowercase letters as well.

As you read this appendix, you should attempt to run all the programs on a computer that supports BASIC. BASIC is not as yet a standardized language, so your computer's BASIC may differ somewhat from the version shown here. Check with your instructor if you have any questions. The presentations in this appendix assume that the reader has already studied Chapter 8, "Structured Programming."

A Very Simple BASIC Program

Consider the following BASIC program:

```
100 REM    A SIMPLE BASIC PROGRAM
110 PRINT "PLEASE TYPE YOUR NAME"
120 INPUT N$
130 PRINT "HELLO "; N$
140 PRINT "PLEASE TYPE A NUMBER"
150 INPUT X
160 PRINT "PLEASE TYPE ANOTHER NUMBER"
170 INPUT Y
180 LET S = X + Y
190 PRINT "THE SUM OF THESE TWO NUMBERS IS "; S
999 END
```

This simple program carries on a **dialogue** or **conversation** with a user at a terminal. It greets the user (lines 110 through 130), requests and obtains two numbers from the user (lines 140 through 170), and then calculates and prints the sum of the two numbers (lines 180 and 190). When it is run, the program displays the following information on the screen

```
PLEASE TYPE YOUR NAME
? SUSAN
HELLO SUSAN
PLEASE TYPE A NUMBER
? 27
PLEASE TYPE ANOTHER NUMBER
? 45
THE SUM OF THESE TWO NUMBERS IS 72
```

Now let's examine the program in detail. The program contains 11 **lines** or **statements**. Each line or statement has some special meaning to the program, and each begins with a **line number** or **statement number** (the numbers 100, 110, 120, 130, 140, 150, 160, 170, 180, 190, and 999). BASIC requires only that these be positive whole numbers and in increasing order. By convention we'll start the numbers at 100, and each line number will be 10 higher than the previous one. Separating the numbers in this manner makes it easy to insert additional lines later if necessary.

After the line number in each BASIC statement is a **command**, a word that describes the action the statement is to perform. Five different commands are used in this program, namely REM, PRINT, INPUT, LET, and END; the PRINT and INPUT commands are each used in several statements. The information following the BASIC command in each statement pertains to that command.

Now let's examine each statement of the program. The statement

```
100 REM A SIMPLE BASIC PROGRAM
```

at line 100 uses the BASIC command **REM** (for "remark"). REM statements are used to insert meaningful comments at any point in a program. The words following the REM, in this case "A SIMPLE BASIC PROGRAM," provide useful information to the reader. This particular REM provides a title for the program. REM statements do not cause any action to occur; rather, they help **document** BASIC programs to make them easier to understand. A BASIC program may contain many REM statements, and these may be located throughout the program.

The statement

```
110 PRINT "PLEASE TYPE YOUR NAME"
```

is a **PRINT** statement. When the computer performs a PRINT statement, it displays the indicated information on the terminal for the user to see. In this PRINT statement, the **message** "PLEASE TYPE YOUR NAME" is displayed. A message appearing in quotes is also called a **literal** or a **string.** The user sees this message and interprets it as instructions on what to do next. The statement

```
120 INPUT N$
```

actually obtains the name from the user. When the computer performs an INPUT statement, it displays a question mark (?) on the terminal and then waits. This is called a **prompt** because it indicates to the user that a response is required. The user then types in the appropriate information (in this case, Susan types her name) and then presses the ENTER or RETURN key on the keyboard to inform the computer that the information is ready to be processed. The computer places this information ("SUSAN") into its main storage in a location that has been given the name N$ (pronounced "N-string"). Whatever name the user types will be stored in N$, and so N$ is called a **variable. Numeric variable names** in BASIC (that is, names for variables that may hold numbers such as 111 or −42.63) may be either a single letter (A, B, C, and so on) or a single letter followed by a single digit (C1, X7, P5, and so on). **String variable names** consist of a letter followed by a dollar sign (A$, B$, and so on). Some versions of BASIC allow the programmer to use much longer names; this helps make programs more understandable. Statement

```
130 PRINT "HELLO "; N$
```

greets the user. It first prints the string "HELLO " on the terminal, and then it prints the name that has been stored in N$, "SUSAN" in this case. So the message "HELLO SUSAN" appears on the terminal. Only the characters between the double quotes are printed; the double quotes themselves do not print. The **semicolon (;) separator** is used here to indicate that the two items ("HELLO " and N$) should be printed side by side. We have inserted one blank at the end of the literal "HELLO " to provide a space between "HELLO" and "SUSAN"—otherwise the two strings would run together. The **comma (,) separator** may be used to indicate that items should be printed in evenly spaced **print zones.** A print zone is normally one of five 14-character-wide printing areas per line, but the number and size of print zones may vary from one computer system to another.

Statement 140

```
140 PRINT "PLEASE TYPE A NUMBER"
```

displays the string "PLEASE TYPE A NUMBER" on the user's terminal. The next statement

```
150 INPUT X
```

actually obtains that number from the user's terminal and places it into numeric variable X (notice that there is no $ in the variable name). Statement

```
160 PRINT "PLEASE TYPE ANOTHER NUMBER"
```

displays the string "PLEASE TYPE ANOTHER NUMBER" on the terminal.

Statement

```
170 INPUT Y·
```

obtains this number from the user and places it into numeric variable Y.

At this point, the program has obtained two numbers from the user; one has been stored in X and the other in Y. Statement

```
180 LET S = X + Y
```

calculates the sum of X and Y and stores the result in numeric variable S. The **LET** statement is used to perform most calculations in BASIC. It is also called the **assignment statement**, because after the value of the expression to the right of the equal sign is calculated, this value is then assigned to the variable on the left of the equal sign. Thus the equal sign in an assignment statement really does not mean equals, but rather means "is replaced by." Statement 180 should be read "LET the value in S be replaced by the sum of X and Y." Note that only a single variable name may appear as the target location on the left of an equal sign in a LET statement. Statement

```
190 PRINT "THE SUM OF THESE TWO NUMBERS IS "; S
```

prints a literal and the result of the previous calculation. First it prints the string "THE SUM OF THESE NUMBERS IS" and then it prints the actual sum contained in numeric variable S. The semicolon separator indicates that the string and the value should be printed side by side. Statement

```
999 END
```

indicates that the end of the BASIC program has been reached. The **END** statement must be the highest numbered statement in every BASIC program. As a convention, we will use all nines in the statement number of the END statement. The reason for this will become apparent later.

Arithmetic

Most BASIC programs perform some arithmetic calculations. The following program shows how addition, subtraction, division, multiplication, and exponentiation are accomplished in BASIC.

```
100 REM   ARITHMETIC IN BASIC
110 PRINT "THE SUM OF 5 AND 2 IS "; 5 + 2
120 PRINT "THE DIFFERENCE BETWEEN 5 AND 2 IS "; 5 - 2
130 PRINT "THE QUOTIENT OF 5 DIVIDED BY 2 IS "; 5 / 2
140 PRINT "THE PRODUCT OF 5 TIMES 2 IS "; 5 * 2
150 PRINT "5 RAISED TO THE POWER 2 IS "; 5 ^ 2
999 END
```

When this program is run it prints

```
THE SUM OF 5 AND 2 IS 7
THE DIFFERENCE BETWEEN 5 AND 2 IS 3
THE QUOTIENT OF 5 DIVIDED BY 2 IS 2.5
THE PRODUCT OF 5 TIMES 2 IS 10
5 RAISED TO THE POWER 2 IS 25
```

Addition uses the plus sign (+) and subtraction uses the minus sign (−), exactly as in algebra. Division may only be performed with the slash (/). Multiplication is indicated in BASIC (and most other computer languages) by the asterisk (*), and the asterisk may not be omitted. Exponentiation is usually indicated by the caret (^), up arrow (↑), or double asterisk (**), depending on your particular computer system.

Precedence

When BASIC evaluates arithmetic expressions like 5 + 3 * 2 or 6/7 − 4 or 3 * (6 − 3) or 4 * (16 − (4 * 2)), it performs the various arithmetic operations in a very specific order. It obeys the same **rules of operator precedence** used in algebra. These are

1. Perform the operations inside parentheses first, from the innermost parentheses outward.
2. Then perform exponentiations.
3. Then perform multiplications and divisions.
4. Then perform additions and subtractions.

When there is a tie, that is, when two or more operations of the same precedence are to be performed, BASIC performs the operations left to right.

It is important for programmers to understand these rules so that they write programs that operate properly. For example, what does the statement

```
200 PRINT 5 + 3 * 2
```

print? Well, if the operations are performed left to right, we'll get 5 plus 3 is 8, and 8 times 2 is 16. But in fact the correct answer is that 11 will print because BASIC performs the multiplication before the addition. The programmer may force operations to occur in any desired order by the proper use of parentheses. Thus, the statement

```
300 PRINT (5 + 3) * 2
```

would indeed perform the addition first and print the result 16.

Program Editing

BASIC programs are typed into the computer one line at a time. While you're typing a line of your program, if you notice that you made an error, you can correct it by backspacing over it and then retyping the remainder of the line correctly. At the end of each line of typing, the ENTER key (or RETURN key on some systems) is pressed to enter the line into the computer. Once a line has been entered, it can be replaced at any time by simply retyping the complete line including the line number.

To delete a line, simply type the line number and press ENTER. To insert a line between existing lines, choose an appropriate line number and simply type the line; you can insert a line anywhere at any time in BASIC.

System Commands

BASIC provides many **system commands** that help the user perform operations such as saving, retrieving, running, and printing programs.

To list an entire program, simply type LIST; the complete program will be displayed on the screen or printed on the printer. LIST followed by a line number lists only that line. LIST 100-300 (or LIST 100,300 on some systems) lists a range of lines.

To save a program for future use, type SAVE followed by the name you have chosen for the program. The maximum size of program names varies between systems. Some systems require that you type a double quote before the program name.

A program that has been saved may be retrieved or made active again by typing LOAD followed by the program name (again the double quote may be required). At this point you may continue editing the program.

Once a program has been entered and any typing errors have been corrected, the program may be executed by typing RUN. The program will then do one of three things. It may run properly producing the desired results, it may run but not produce the desired results, or it may terminate prior to completion and print an error message.

Debugging

It is very satisfying to have a relatively large program run properly on the first try, but this rarely happens. If the program terminates with an error message, the error message will often include the line number of the statement in error and provide some hint as to what went wrong. Fix the problem and type RUN again.

On new programs, you will often get a series of error messages for **syntax errors**. These are errors in the use of BASIC itself. You may write PRENT instead of PRINT, or INPIT instead of INPUT. You may type a line number with more digits than the language allows. Syntax errors normally are easy to find and correct.

When a program runs to completion but does not produce proper results, there is a **logic error**. This type of error occurs because something is wrong with the way the program is solving the problem (that is, the algorithm is incorrect). Logic errors come in a seemingly endless variety. You can write programs for years and still discover new kinds of logic bugs.

Debugging large computer programs is more of an art than a science. But when you've got a tough bug that seems immune to your efforts to remove it, don't panic; there is no such thing as a logic bug that can't be found and removed. Be patient and follow these few simple rules:

1. Read your program listing carefully; you may have made a simple error that will become apparent immediately.
2. **Desk check** your program, that is, follow the instructions in your program manually one at a time to simulate how the computer runs your program. This is a painstaking process, but it will often lead you right to the bug. While desk checking, keep a scratch pad handy. List each variable and its current value. As you simulate each instruction, show how you think the values of affected variables are changing.
3. If after desk checking your program you still haven't found the bug, the logical next step is to see if the computer actually runs the program the way you think it does. To do this you need to "peek inside" the running program and watch its variables change values. The simplest way to do this is to insert some extra PRINT statements at key points in the program. When the program is rerun, these PRINTs may display values that disagree with what you think they should be at those points. You can then usually zero in on the bug gradually by focusing your attention in that vicinity of the program. This, too, is a painstaking process, but it works.
4. If after all this effort you still can't find the problem, ask for help. You may be too close to your own program; someone else may give it a quick glance and find the bug immediately.
5. And, finally, if all else fails don't be afraid to throw one away. Sometimes sitting down fresh and starting over can be rewarding. You will probably have learned a great deal about your program and the problem you're trying to solve. Simply rewriting the program may generate a bug-free program, or it may generate different bugs that you find more manageable.

Self-Review Exercises

Matching

Next to the term in column A, place the letter of the statement in column B that best describes it.

Column A

1. Logic error
2. PRINT
3. String
4. INPUT
5. N$
6. Semicolon separator
7. Comma separator
8. LET
9. Equal sign
10. Syntax error

Column B

A. Obtain information from user
B. Perform an assignment
C. "Is replaced by"
D. Incorrect algorithm
E. Also called a message or literal
F. Side-by-side spacing
G. Displays information
H. Print zone spacing
I. String variable name
J. Misspelled command

Fill-in-the-Blanks

Fill in the blanks in each of the following:

1. (True/False) BASIC was originally designed to be a structured programming language. ______.

2. The common subset of the BASIC language that is supported by the vast majority of BASICs on the market is called ______ BASIC.

3. (True/False) BASIC is a standardized language. ______.

4. Lines in a BASIC program are also called ______.

5. ______ statements do not cause any action to occur; rather, they help document BASIC programs to make them easier to understand.

6. The rules of ______ govern the order in which BASIC performs operations in arithmetic expressions.

7. When the computer performs an INPUT statement, it displays a ______ on the terminal and then waits.

8. Numeric variable names in BASIC may be either a single letter or ______.

9. In a LET statement, after the value of the expression to the right of the equal sign is calculated, this value is then assigned to ______.

10. Following the instructions in a program manually one at a time to simulate how the computer runs the program is called ______.

Answers to Self-Review Exercises

Matching: 1 D, 2 G, 3 E, 4 A, 5 I, 6 F, 7 H, 8 B, 9 C, 10 J

Fill-in-the-Blanks:
1. False
2. ANSI Minimal
3. False
4. statements
5. REM
6. operator precedence
7. question mark (?)
8. a single letter followed by a single digit
9. the variable on the left of the equal sign
10. desk checking

Problems

1. (a) Write a comment at statement 100 to indicate that a program performs a payroll calculation.
(b) Write a statement at line 150 that displays the string "THE WINNER IS" on the terminal.
(c) Write a statement at line 200 that obtains a weekly sales figure from a user at a terminal.
(d) Write a statement at line 230 that computes the product, P, of three values, A, B, and C.
(e) Write a statement at line 240 that displays the product calculated in (d) along with a meaningful string.
(f) Suppose the last statement before the END is at 2130. Write an appropriate END statement with the smallest possible statement number. Also, write a different END statement with a line number that follows the convention we established in this module.

2. Write a BASIC program that inputs a user's first name, and then tells that person to have a nice day.

3. Write a BASIC program that obtains five numbers from the user. The program should then print these numbers in the same order in which the user typed them. The program should then print these numbers in the reverse order (that is, the fifth, then the fourth, and so on). Use literals to label the program's outputs.

4. Write a BASIC program that inputs a person's name as three separate character strings. Input the first name first, then the middle initial, then the last name. Then print the person's full name last name first, then a comma, then a space, then the first name, then another space, and then the middle initial followed by a period.

Module 2: Structured Programming in BASIC

This module introduces the more substantial features of BASIC needed to perform decision making and looping. These features are then used to develop the selection and repetition control structures of structured programming. Finally, structured programs are developed that perform the important operations of counting, totaling, averaging, and finding the largest of a series of numbers.

Case Studies 1 through 6 of Module 2 correspond precisely to Case Studies 8-1 through 8-6 of Chapter 8. For each case study, you should (1) read the problem statement, (2) study the corresponding program flowchart and pseudocode in Chapter 8, (3) study the discussion in Chapter 8, and (4) study the BASIC program and the corresponding discussion in Module 2. For your convenience, we have repeated the flowcharts and pseudocode programs from Chapter 8 in this appendix.

Case Study 1: Simple Decision Making

Problem Statement:

Develop a program that inputs two numbers and outputs the larger number followed by the message "is larger." Assume both numbers are different.

Discussion:

Read the discussion on pages 197–198 and study the flowchart and pseudocode of Figure 1. The BASIC program and a sample execution are shown in Figure A-1.

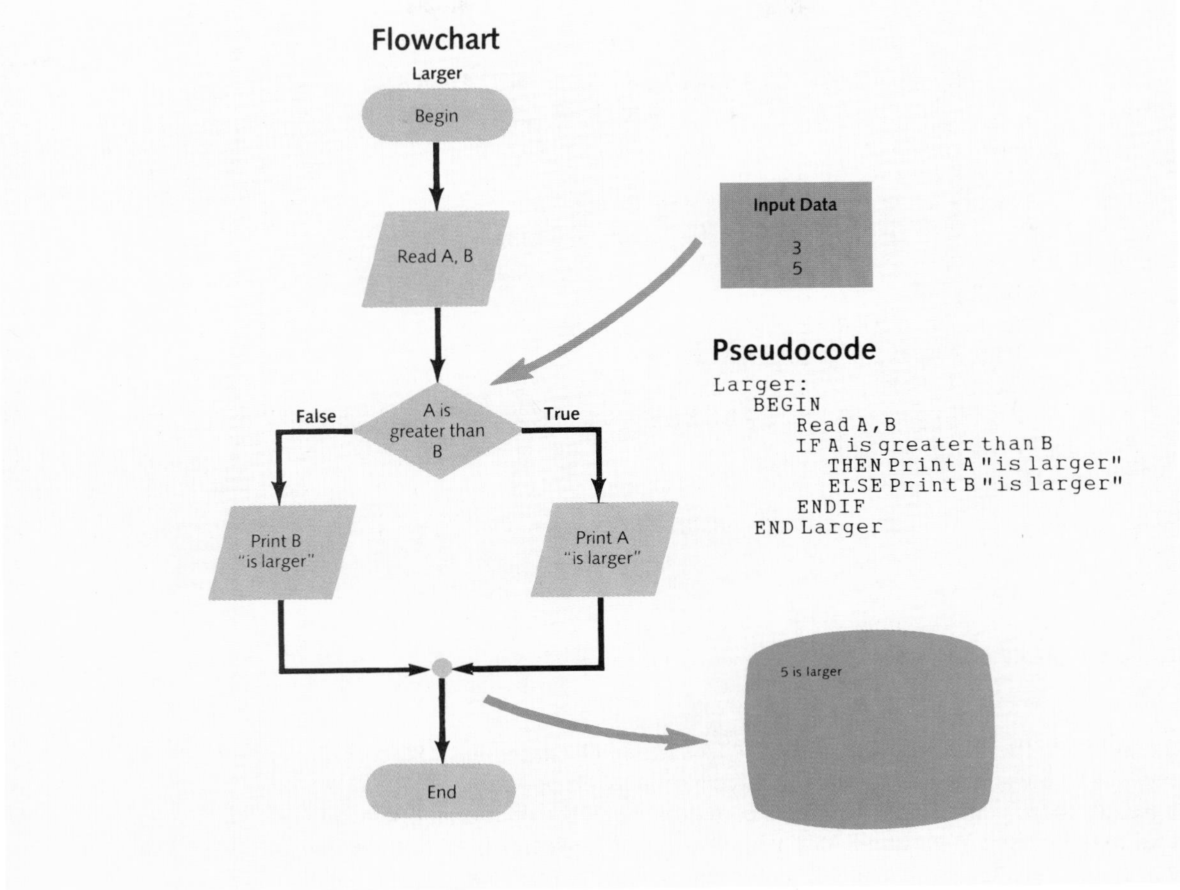

Figure 1 An example of the selection structure: finding the larger of two numbers.

We can input information with either the INPUT or the READ/DATA combination. We will use READ/DATA throughout the case studies so that the data we use may be built into our programs. As we study the program, we'll see how READ/DATA is used.

In the case studies, we introduce a number of conventions dealing with the use of remarks and indentation to make programs more readable and understandable. In Figure A-1, lines 100 through 160 are all remarks. We will use the convention that the opening remarks of every program should include the program title, the author(s), the date the program was written (or last modified), and a list of the names and purposes of the program's variables. Notice that lines 120 and 160 are used to provide vertical spacing for program readability.

The READ statement at 170 obtains two values from the DATA statement at 220. Variable A is set to 3, the first value in the DATA statement, and variable

```
LIST

100 REM   FIND THE LARGER OF TWO NUMBERS
110 REM   H + B DEITEL    JANUARY 11, 1985
120 REM
130 REM   VARIABLES:
140 REM      A: FIRST NUMBER READ
150 REM      B: SECOND NUMBER READ
160 REM
170 READ A, B
180 IF A > B THEN 210
190    PRINT B; "IS LARGER"
200    GOTO 999
210    PRINT A; "IS LARGER"
220 DATA 3,5
999 END

RUN

 5 IS LARGER
```

Figure A-1 BASIC program and sample execution for Case Study 1.

B is set to 5, the second value in the DATA statement. Statement 180 compares A to B using the relational operator (comparison operator) ">" for "greater than." (See Figure 8-4 for a complete list of the relational operators that may be used in writing BASIC programs.) If A is greater than B, then the computer transfers control to the statement whose number appears after the word THEN, namely 210. At statement 210, the value of A is printed followed by the words "IS LARGER" and the computer proceeds to line 220, skips 220 because DATA statements are ignored by running programs, and proceeds to line 999 where the program ends. If at line 180 A is not greater than B, that is, if B is greater than A (since we know from the problem statement that both numbers are different), then control passes to line 190 where the value of B is printed followed by "IS LARGER," and the computer continues at line 200 which transfers control to 999 where the program ends.

Using 999 for the END statement (or 9999, 99999, and so on in larger programs) enables us to see that program is about to end, even though control may be somewhere in the middle of the program, such as at the GOTO 999 at line 200 in this program.

Notice that lines 190, 200, and 210 each use three-space indentation. This is because these statements are all part of the IF-THEN-ELSE control structure (see Figure 1). We make careful use of indentation in our BASIC programs to emphasize our use of control structures. This greatly improves the readability of structured programs. BASIC itself ignores the indentation.

DATA statements may appear anywhere in a BASIC program, but they are most commonly grouped just before the END statement. Some programmers prefer to put the DATA statements immediately after the READ statements that reference them. There may be as many DATA statements as the user needs to list all the data. The DATA statements do not have to correspond one-for-one with the READ statements. For example, in this program it would have been perfectly acceptable for the programmer to include two DATA statements as follows:

```
220 DATA 3
230 DATA 5
```

When the user first types RUN, BASIC gathers up all the data items in order from all the DATA statements and forms a single **DATA list**. Then as the program executes, whenever a READ statement requests one or more values, these values are taken in order from the DATA list. BASIC automatically maintains a **DATA list pointer** which at all times keeps track of the next data item to be supplied to a READ statement.

Case Study 2: Complex Decision Making

Problem Statement:

Develop a program that inputs three numbers and outputs the largest followed by the message "IS THE LARGEST." Assume all three numbers are different.

Discussion:

Read the discussion on pages 198–200 and study the structured flowchart and pseudocode in Figure 2. The BASIC program and a sample execution are shown in Figure A-2.

Notice that there are three selection structures—an outer selection structure and two inner selection structures nested within this outer structure. The nesting is shown graphically in the structured flowchart. Notice that all the decision structures have a common exit point which is in fact the END statement at 999.

In the BASIC program (and the pseudocode) the nesting is made more visual by the use of indentation. We continue to use three-space indentation, that is, each new level of indentation is placed three spaces farther to the right of statements in the next higher (or outer) level. Again, BASIC ignores the indentation; it is used by the programmer to make a program more readable. If indentation is used properly, it makes the programs much clearer. If it is used poorly, it can obscure the meaning of a program, and, worse yet, BASIC is of no help in pointing out indentation problems.

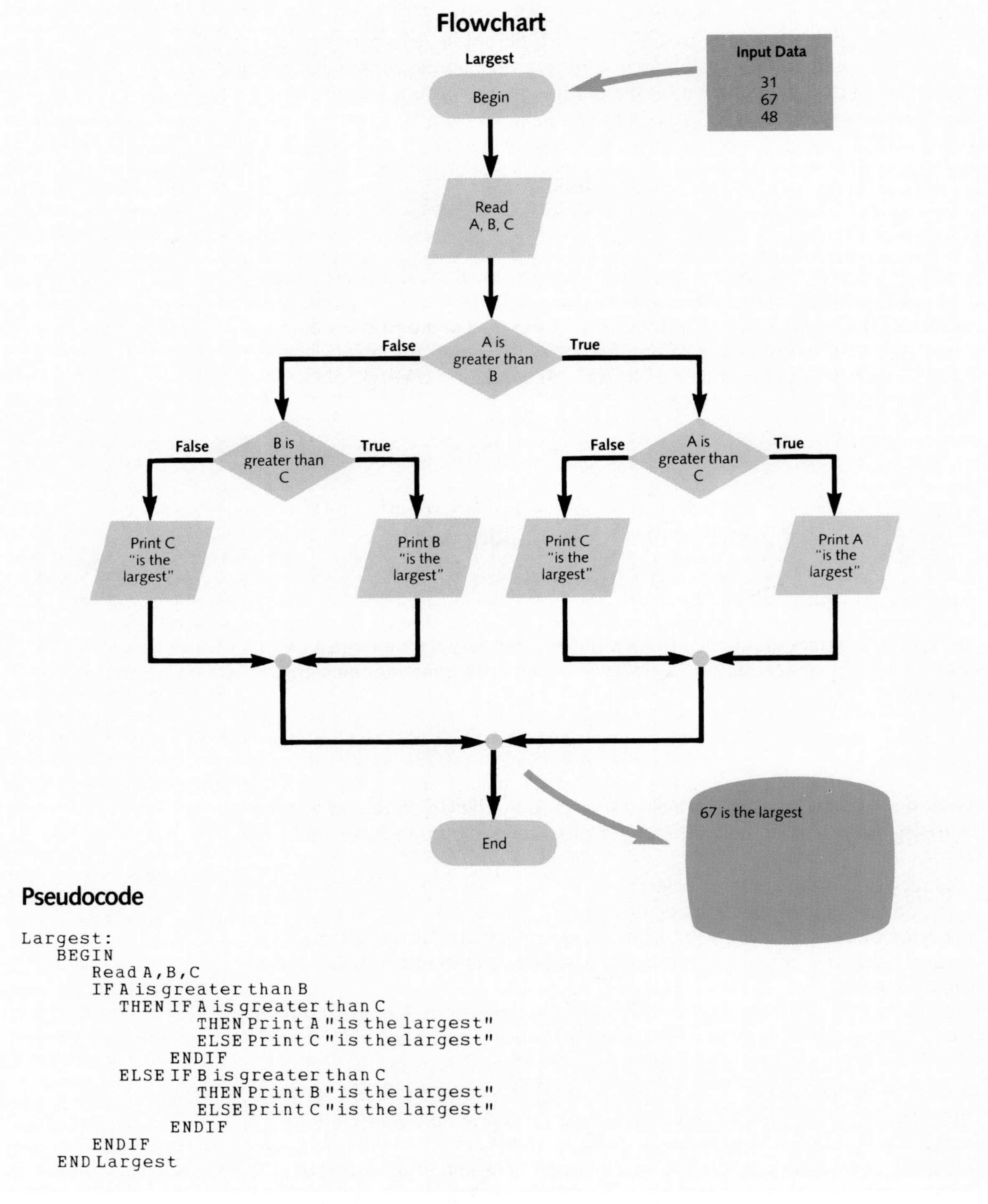

Pseudocode

```
Largest:
   BEGIN
      Read A,B,C
      IF A is greater than B
         THEN IF A is greater than C
                 THEN Print A "is the largest"
                 ELSE Print C "is the largest"
              ENDIF
         ELSE IF B is greater than C
                 THEN Print B "is the largest"
                 ELSE Print C "is the largest"
              ENDIF
      ENDIF
   END Largest
```

Figure 2 An example of a nested selection structure: finding the largest of three numbers.

```
LIST

100 REM    FIND THE LARGEST OF THREE NUMBERS
110 REM    H + B DEITEL    JANUARY 11, 1985
120 REM
130 REM    VARIABLES:
140 REM       A: FIRST NUMBER
150 REM       B: SECOND NUMBER
160 REM       C: THIRD NUMBER
170 REM
180 READ A, B, C
190 IF A > B THEN 250
200    IF B > C THEN 230
210       PRINT C; "IS THE LARGEST"
220       GOTO 999
230       PRINT B; "IS THE LARGEST"
240       GOTO 999
250    IF A > C THEN 280
260       PRINT C; "IS THE LARGEST"
270       GOTO 999
280       PRINT A; "IS THE LARGEST"
290 DATA 31,67,48
999 END

RUN

 67 IS THE LARGEST
```

Figure A-2 BASIC program and sample execution for Case Study 2.

Case Study 3: Counter-Controlled Looping with the WHILE-DO Structure

Problem Statement:

Develop a program that prints the numbers from 1 to 10. Use a single print statement that prints only one number at a time. Use the WHILE-DO repetition structure.

Discussion:

Read the discussion on page 200 and study the structured flowchart and pseudocode in Figure 3. The BASIC program and a sample execution are shown in Figure A-3.

Statement 160 sets the counter variable, C, to its initial value, and then the WHILE-DO structure beginning at line 170 tests if looping should be allowed (that is, if C is less than or equal to 10). Since C is 1 initially, the body state-

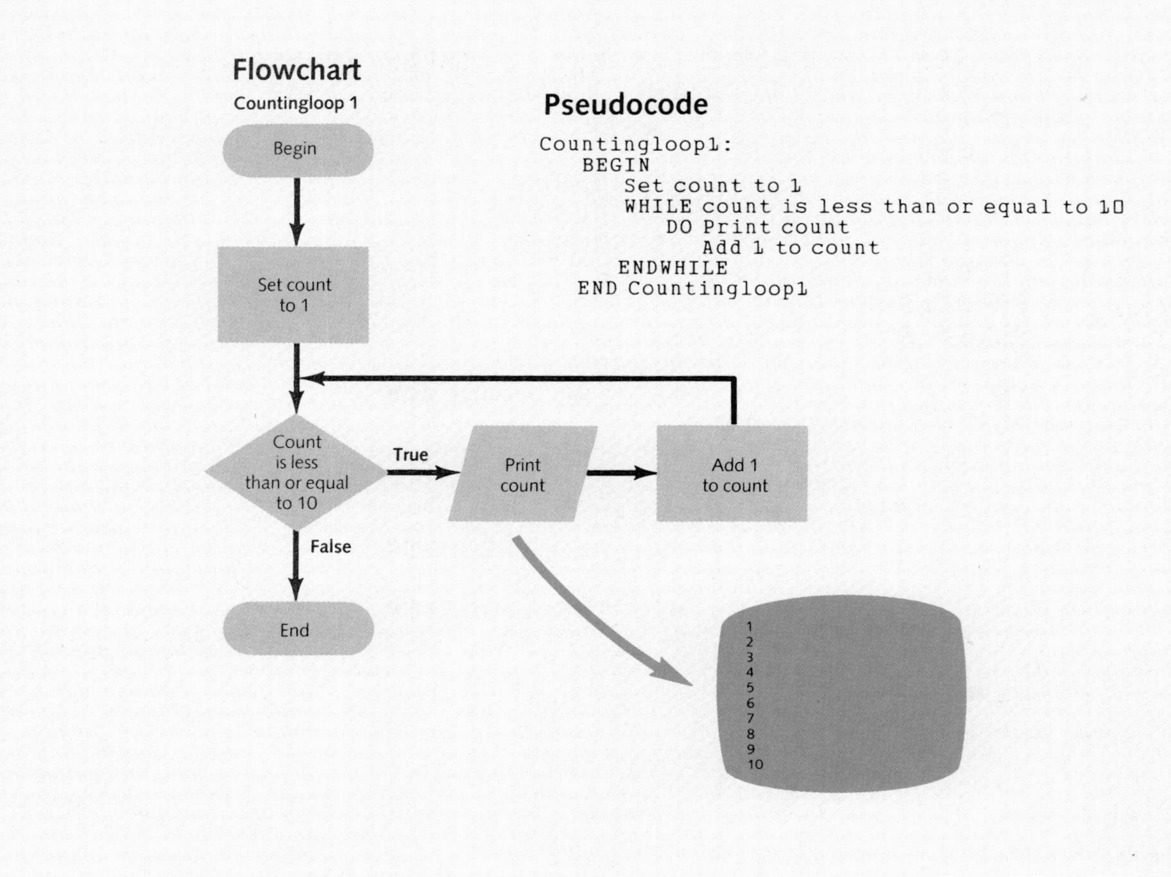

Figure 3 An example of a counter-controlled loop using the WHILE-DO structure.

ments of the loop are performed in which C is printed at line 190 and then incremented by 1 at line 200 to prepare to print the next value. The GOTO at line 210 closes the loop back to the WHILE-DO test at 170. When the WHILE-DO test eventually fails because C exceeds 10, then control passes to line 180, which causes the program to terminate looping and branch to 999, the END statement.

Notice the indentation of statements 180 through 210. These statements are all part of the WHILE-DO control structure that begins at line 170.

We have written the WHILE-DO structure using two GOTO statements. For those people who prefer to minimize the use of the GOTO, lines 170 and 180 could be replaced with

```
170 IF C > 10 THEN 999
```

```
LIST

100 REM    COUNTER-CONTROLLED LOOPING WITH THE WHILE-DO
110 REM    H + B DEITEL    JANUARY 11, 1985
120 REM
130 REM    VARIABLES:
140 REM       C: COUNTER (1 TO 10)
150 REM
160 LET C = 1
170 IF C <= 10 THEN 190
180    GOTO 999
190    PRINT C
200    LET C = C + 1
210    GOTO 170
999 END

RUN

 1
 2
 3
 4
 5
 6
 7
 8
 9
 10
```

Figure A-3 BASIC program and sample execution for Case Study 3.

which eliminates one of the GOTOs. Why do you suppose some people prefer the two-GOTO version?

Let's take a closer look at the LET statement at line 200. In algebra, a statement like

```
C = C + 1
```

makes no sense, but in BASIC the statement

```
200 LET C = C + 1
```

is perfectly reasonable. Remember that the equal sign (=) in a LET statement does not mean equals, but rather "is replaced by." So statement 200 is read, "Let the value of C be replaced by the value of C plus 1" or, quite simply, "Add 1 to C."

Case Study 4: Counter-Controlled Looping with the REPEAT-UNTIL Structure

Problem Statement:

Modify the program developed in Case Study 8-3 to control the looping with a REPEAT-UNTIL structure instead of the WHILE-DO structure.

Discussion:

Read the discussion on page 201 and study the structured flowchart and pseudocode in Figure 4. The BASIC program and a sample execution are shown in Figure A-4.

The REPEAT-UNTIL differs from the WHILE-DO in that the body of the loop is performed before the test for loop termination. Therefore, the REPEAT-UNTIL should only be used when it is known that the loop will be executed at least once. Also, the condition in the WHILE-DO is tested to determine if looping should continue, whereas the condition in the REPEAT-UNTIL is tested to determine if looping should terminate.

Initialization is performed at statement 160, the body of the REPEAT-UNTIL loop is performed at statements 170 and 180, and the termination test is made at 190. If the condition is true, control is transferred out of the loop to statement 999 and the program ends. If the condition is false, then looping continues—control passes to statement 200 which closes the loop back to statement 170 where the loop body is repeated once again.

We have indented statements 170 and 180, the body statements of the REPEAT-UNTIL control structure. Again, BASIC ignores the indentation; it is strictly to make our programs more readable.

Some people may prefer to shorten the REPEAT-UNTIL control structure by replacing lines 190 and 200 with

```
190 IF C <= 10 THEN 170
```

This has the additional advantage of eliminating a GOTO. Why do you suppose some people prefer the form with the GOTO?

The FOR-NEXT Structure: A Simple Way to Count

In Case Studies 3 and 4 we saw how the WHILE-DO and REPEAT-UNTIL structures could be used to control counting loops. Recognizing the importance of counting and its use in controlling loops, the designers of BASIC incorporated the **FOR-NEXT structure** into the original language. Its use is illustrated by the following simple program segment that also prints the numbers from 1 to 10

```
300 FOR C = 1 TO 10
310     PRINT C
320 NEXT C
```

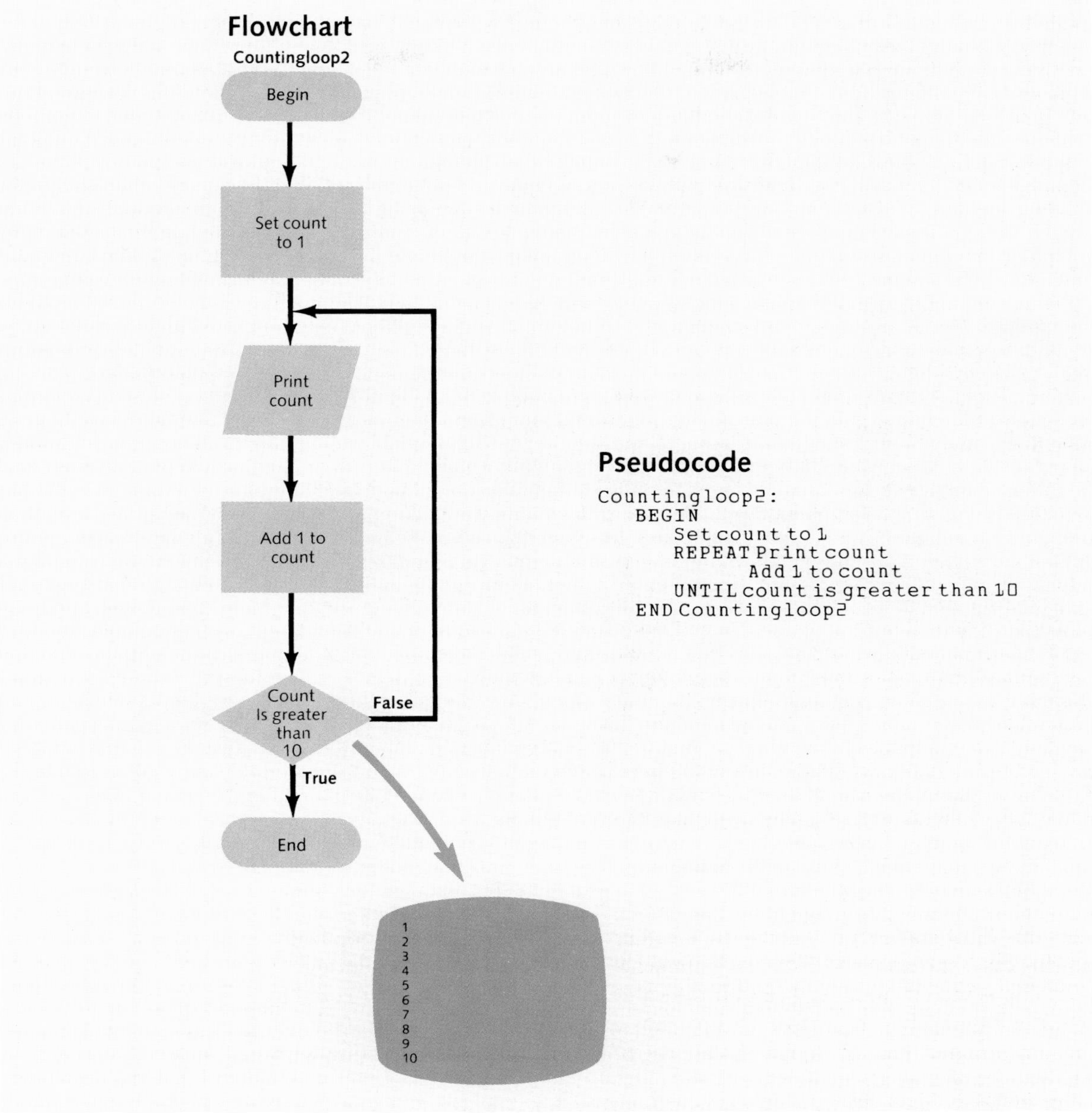
Flowchart
Countingloop2
Begin
Set count to 1
Print count
Add 1 to count
Count Is greater than 10
False
True
End
1
2
3
4
5
6
7
8
9
10
Pseudocode
Countingloop2:
BEGIN
Set count to 1
REPEAT Print count
Add 1 to count
UNTIL count is greater than 10
END Countingloop2

Figure 4 An example of a counter-controlled loop using the REPEAT-UNTIL structure.

```
LIST

100 REM   COUNTER-CONTROLLED LOOPING WITH REPEAT-UNTIL
110 REM   H + B DEITEL   JANUARY 11, 1985
120 REM
130 REM   VARIABLES:
140 REM      C: COUNTER (1 TO 10)
150 REM
160 LET C = 1
170    PRINT C
180    LET C = C + 1
190 IF C > 10 THEN 999
200 GOTO 170
999 END
```

```
RUN

 1
 2
 3
 4
 5
 6
 7
 8
 9
 10
```

Figure A-4 BASIC program and sample execution for Case Study 4.

ters this FOR statement, it sets C to 1 and proceeds to execute the loop body, in this case, statement 310. When statement 320 is executed, the counting variable is incremented by 1, and if the value of C is still less than or equal to 10, the loop body is repeated. This process continues until C does in fact become greater than 10, in which case the program continues operating with the first statement after line 320.

FOR-NEXT statements normally count by 1's, but it is possible to count by any other integer, positive or negative, as well. For example, the statement

```
400 FOR X = 4 TO 20 STEP 2
```

would vary the counter X from a starting value of 4 to a final value of 20 in steps of 2 at a time. Thus, line 400 would generate the following sequence of values for X: 4, 6, 8, 10, 12, 14, 16, 18, and 20. The statement

```
500 FOR M = 60 TO 10 STEP -5
```

would vary the counter M from a starting value of 60 to a final value of 10 in steps of −5 at a time. Thus, line 500 would generate the following sequence of values for M: 60, 55, 50, 45, 40, 35, 30, 25, 20, 15, and 10.

Obviously, when the word STEP is omitted in a FOR statement, BASIC assumes STEP 1. The reader is encouraged to use the FOR-NEXT structure to control counting loops.

Case Study 5: Counting, Totaling, and Averaging with a Sentinel-Controlled Loop

Problem Statement:

Develop a program that reads a series of numeric grades for a student and produces that student's grade point average. The number of grades is not known in advance. The program should determine that it has finished reading grades when it encounters the sentinel value −1. Use the WHILE-DO structure to control repetition.

Discussion:

Read the discussion on page 203 and study the structured flowchart and pseudocode of Figure 5. The BASIC program and a sample execution are shown in Figure A-5.

Lines 190 and 200 initialize the count, C, and the total, T, to zero. Actually, most versions of BASIC automatically initialize each numeric variable to zero each time a program is run. It is nevertheless considered good programming practice to initialize all counts and totals anyway, especially because most other languages the programmer is likely to use do not do this.

Statement 210 reads the first grade. Statement 220 begins the WHILE-DO by performing the looping test. It checks to see if the value, N, just read is not the sentinel value, −1. As long as the value read is not the sentinel value, the loop body statements (240, 250, and 260) are performed and statement 270 causes the program to return to the loop test at 220. When statement 220 finally detects the sentinel value, statement 230 is performed, causing the computer to transfer control to statement 280, the first statement after the WHILE-DO loop. Statement 280 prints the total of the grades, statement 290 calculates the grade point average, and statement 300 prints the grade point average. The program ends at 999.

Again, for those who wish to minimize the use of the GOTO, statements 220 and 230 may be replaced with

```
220 IF N = -1 THEN 280
```

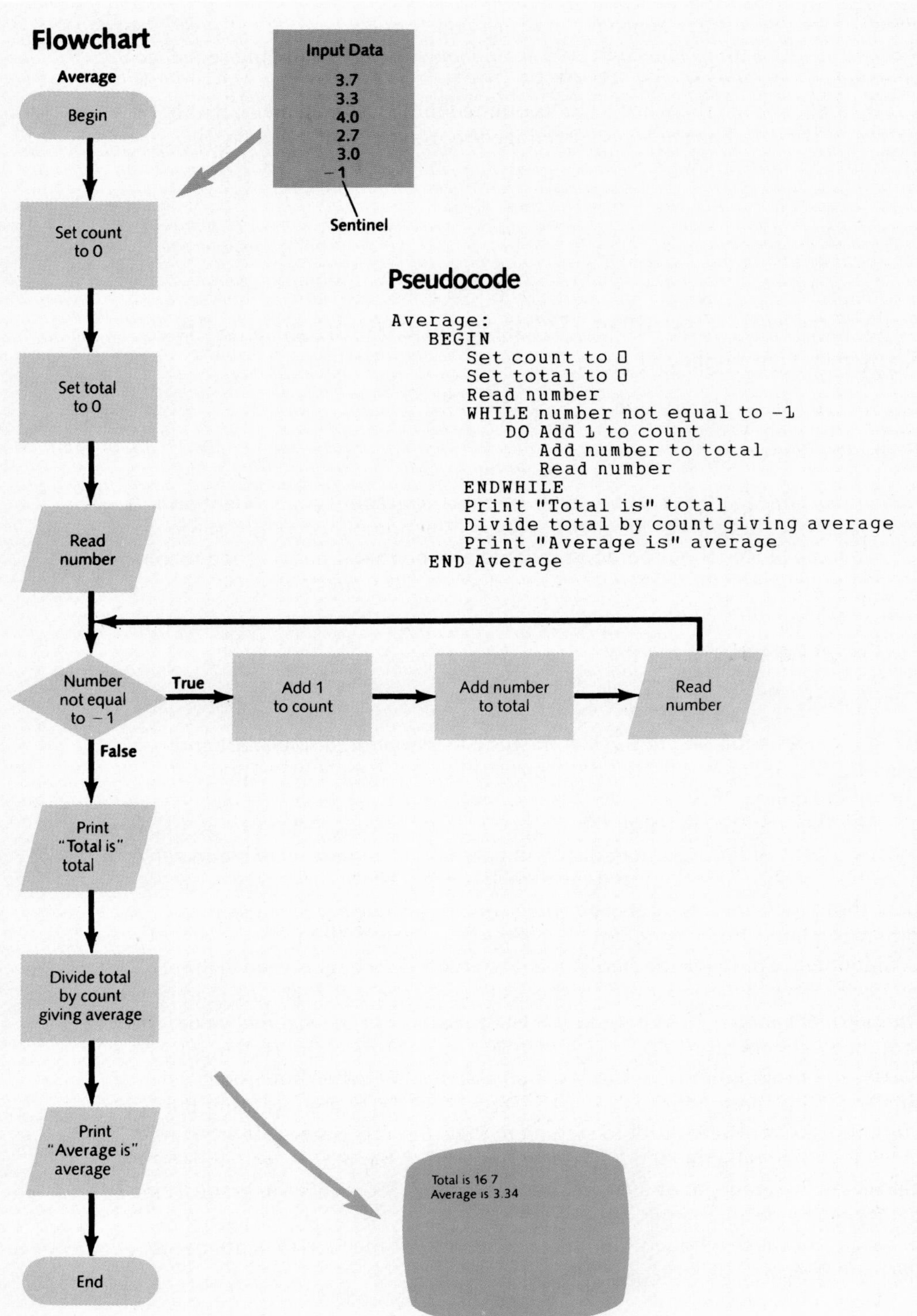

Figure 5 An example of a sentinel-controlled loop using the WHILE-DO structure: finding the total and average of a series of numbers.

```
LIST

100 REM    CALCULATE A STUDENT'S GRADE POINT AVERAGE
110 REM    H + B DEITEL    JANUARY 11, 1985
120 REM
130 REM    VARIABLES:
140 REM        C: GRADE COUNT
150 REM        T: GRADE TOTAL
160 REM        N: NEXT GRADE
170 REM        A: GRADE AVERAGE
180 REM
190 LET C = 0
200 LET T = 0
210 READ N
220 IF N <> -1 THEN 240
230     GOTO 280
240     LET C = C + 1
250     LET T = T + N
260     READ N
270     GOTO 220
280 PRINT "TOTAL IS"; T
290 LET A = T / C
300 PRINT "AVERAGE IS"; A
310 DATA 3.7,3.3,4.0,2.7,3.0,-1
999 END

RUN

TOTAL IS 16.7
AVERAGE IS 3.34
```

Figure A-5 BASIC program and sample execution for Case Study 5.

Case Study 6: Finding the Largest of a Series of Numbers with a Sentinel-Controlled Loop

Problem Statement:

Develop a program that reads a series of two or more numbers representing the weights of several football players trying out for a team. The coach needs one more player and has decided to choose the heaviest candidate. Your program should determine and print the weight of the heaviest candidate followed by the message "IS THE LARGEST." Assume no two candidates weigh the same.

Discussion:

Read the discussion on pages 203–206 and study the structured flowchart and pseudocode of Figure 6. The BASIC program and a sample execution are shown in Figure A-6.

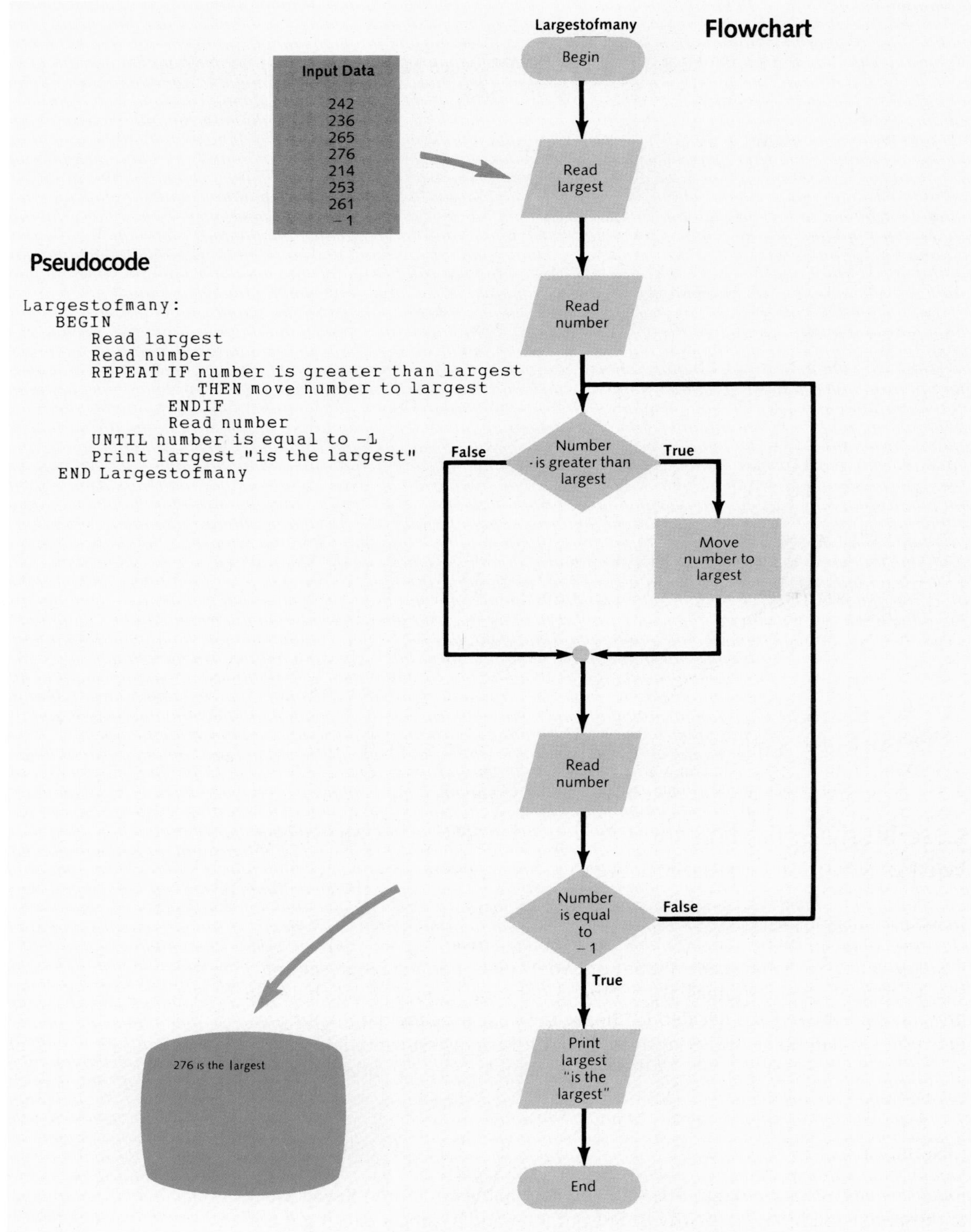


```
Largestofmany:
   BEGIN
      Read largest
      Read number
      REPEAT IF number is greater than largest
               THEN move number to largest
             ENDIF
             Read number
      UNTIL number is equal to -1
      Print largest "is the largest"
   END Largestofmany
```

Figure 6 An example of a sentinel-controlled loop using the REPEAT-UNTIL structure: finding the largest of two or more numbers.

```
LIST

100 REM    FIND THE LARGEST OF TWO OR MORE NUMBERS
100 REM    H + B DEITEL    JANUARY 11, 1985
120 REM
130 REM    VARIABLES:
140 REM       L: LARGEST NUMBER READ SO FAR
150 REM       N: CURRENT NUMBER BEING PROCESSED
160 REM
170 READ L
180 READ N
190     IF N > L THEN 210
200         GOTO 220
210         LET L = N
220     READ N
230 IF N = -1 THEN 250
240 GOTO 190
250 PRINT L; "IS THE LARGEST"
260 DATA 242,236,265,276,214,253,261,-1
999 END

RUN

 276 IS THE LARGEST
```

Figure A-6 BASIC program and sample execution for Case Study 6.

The program uses the REPEAT-UNTIL and IF-THEN control structures. The REPEAT-UNTIL (lines 190 through 240) is used to control the loop; the program reads and processes new numbers until the sentinel value −1 is read.

Inside the loop, the program uses the IF-THEN structure (lines 190 through 210) to determine if the number just read, N, is larger than the largest number read so far, L. If N is larger than L, then L is replaced by N at line 210; if N is not larger than L line 210 is skipped.

Notice the use of indentation. Lines 190 through 220 comprise the body statements of the REPEAT-UNTIL, so they are all indented. Lines 200 and 210 are indented yet one more level. This is because they comprise the body of the IF-THEN structure that is nested within the REPEAT-UNTIL.

If we are willing to reverse the conditions in the IF-THEN and the REPEAT-UNTIL structures, lines 190 through 240 can be replaced with

```
190     IF N <= L THEN 220
210         LET L = N
220     READ N
230 IF N <> -1 THEN 190
```

for a net savings of two statements both of which were GOTOs.

Self-Review Exercises 

Matching

Next to the term in column A, place the letter of the statement in column B that best describes it.

Column A

1. Nesting
2. = in LET statement
3. Condition in the WHILE-DO
4. READ/DATA
5. 240 LET A = A + 1
6. 250 LET B = B + C
7. 9999
8. INPUT
9. Relational operator
10. Sentinel value

Column B

A. Data is built into the program
B. Running a total
C. Used when number of loops not known in advance
D. <> ("is not equal to")
E. Appropriate for END statement
F. Means "is replaced by"
G. Tests if looping should continue
H. One structure is contained within another
I. Adding to a counter
J. Data is supplied by user when program runs

Fill-in-the-Blanks

Fill in the blanks in each of the following:

1. (True/False) A program with three READ statements must also have three DATA statements. ______.
2. ______ emphasizes the use of control structures, and greatly improves the readability of structured programs.
3. The REPEAT-UNTIL differs from the WHILE-DO in that with the REPEAT-UNTIL the ______ is performed before the ______.
4. Data statements are most commonly grouped just before the ______ statement.
5. Most versions of BASIC automatically initialize each numeric variable to ______ each time a program is run.
6. (True/False) With the exception of the "gathering up" of the data, DATA statements are ignored by running programs. ______
7. Using unstructured BASIC, the WHILE-DO looping structure should begin with the ______ statement.
8. The condition, A <= B is true if ______.
9. Using the conventions established in the text, what does the statement 300 GOTO 9999 probably do? ______
10. (True/False) The REPEAT-UNTIL should only be used when it is known that the loop will be repeated at least once.

Answers to Self-Review Exercises

Matching: 1 H, 2 F, 3 G, 4 A, 5 I, 6 B, 7 E, 8 J, 9 D, 10 C

Fill-in-the-Blanks:

1. False
2. Indentation
3. body of the loop, test for loop termination
4. END
5. zero
6. True
7. IF
8. the value of A is less than or equal to the value of B
9. It probably transfers control to the END statement
10. True

Problems

1. Without using looping, write a BASIC program that inputs four different numbers and determines and prints the largest number.

2. Write a BASIC program to find and print the largest of a series of numbers as well as the second largest of the series. Read each number from DATA statements

only once. Such a program might be useful in finding the two best salespersons in a company. You may assume that all the numbers are different.

3. Write a BASIC program that will calculate and print the sum of the integers from 1 to 100. Your program should not READ or INPUT any data.

4. Write a BASIC program that reads pairs of numbers from DATA statements. The first number in each pair is a 1 for "female" or a 2 for "male." The second number in each pair is the person's age. Assume that −1 is used as a sentinel. Read and process all the pairs and print a summary of the results, including separate figures for males and females indicating how many of each are seniors (65 or over), midrangers (45 to 64), and juniors (44 and under). Print the results in a neat table.

Module 3: Single-Subscripted Arrays and Subroutines

This module introduces the advanced features of the BASIC language for processing lists of information and for constructing larger programs as sets of interacting program pieces. Some of the techniques covered here are especially important to the top-down, stepwise refinement program development process. Case Studies 7, 8, and 9 of Module 3 correspond precisely to Case Studies 8-7 through 8-9 of Chapter 8. For each of these case studies, the reader should (1) read the problem statement, (2) study the corresponding program flowchart and pseudocode in Chapter 8, (3) study the discussion in Chapter 8, and (4) study the BASIC program and corresponding discussion in Module 3. Again, for the reader's convenience, we have repeated the flowcharts and pseudocode programs from Chapter 8 in this appendix.

Case Study 7: Piecework Payroll for One Employee: Introducing Subroutines

Problem Statement:

To provide incentive for their employees, many companies base employee wages on so-called piecework rates by which employees are paid a fixed amount for each item they produce. The pay rates vary according to the time required to produce each item. An item that requires more time to produce is paid at an appropriately higher piecework rate. The piecework rate table shown below is used in this and the next two case studies.

Item Code	Piecework Rate
13	.85
18	1.05
21	.55
42	.80
57	.60
64	.45

As you can see, six different types of items are produced by this company. An employee can earn anywhere from 45 cents to $1.05 for producing one of these items. The company maintains counts of the quantity of each item produced by each employee each week. Assume the input data is in the form shown in Figure 7; the information on only one employee is to be processed. The output should be in the form shown in the figure.

Discussion:

Read the discussion on pages 206–208 and study the structured flowchart and the pseudocode of Figure 7. The BASIC program is shown in Figure A-7, and a sample execution is shown in Figure A-8.

```
LIST

100 REM    PIECEWORK PAYROLL FOR ONE EMPLOYEE
110 REM    H + B DEITEL   JANUARY 11, 1985
120 REM
130 REM    VARIABLES:
140 REM       P: TOTAL PAY
150 REM       E: EMPLOYEE NUMBER
160 REM       I: ITEM NUMBER
170 REM       Q: QUANTITY PRODUCED
180 REM       R: RATE PAID FOR PRODUCING ONE PARTICULAR ITEM
190 REM       A: AMOUNT PAID (= RATE TIMES QUANTITY OF ITEM)
200 REM
210 PRINT "PIECEWORK PAYROLL REPORT", "7/12/85", "PAGE 1"
220 PRINT
230 PRINT
240 PRINT "EMPLOYEE", "ITEM", "RATE", "QUANTITY", "AMOUNT"
250 PRINT
260 LET P = 0
270 READ E, I, Q
280 IF E <> 999 THEN 300
290    GOTO 360
300    GOSUB 700
310    LET A = R * Q
320    LET P = P + A
330    PRINT E, I, R, Q, A
340    READ E, I, Q
350    GOTO 280
360 PRINT
370 PRINT ,,, "TOTAL", P
380 DATA 125,13,100
390 DATA 125,18,200
400 DATA 125,57,150
410 DATA 999,0,0
999 END
```

Figure A-7 BASIC Program for Case Study 7.

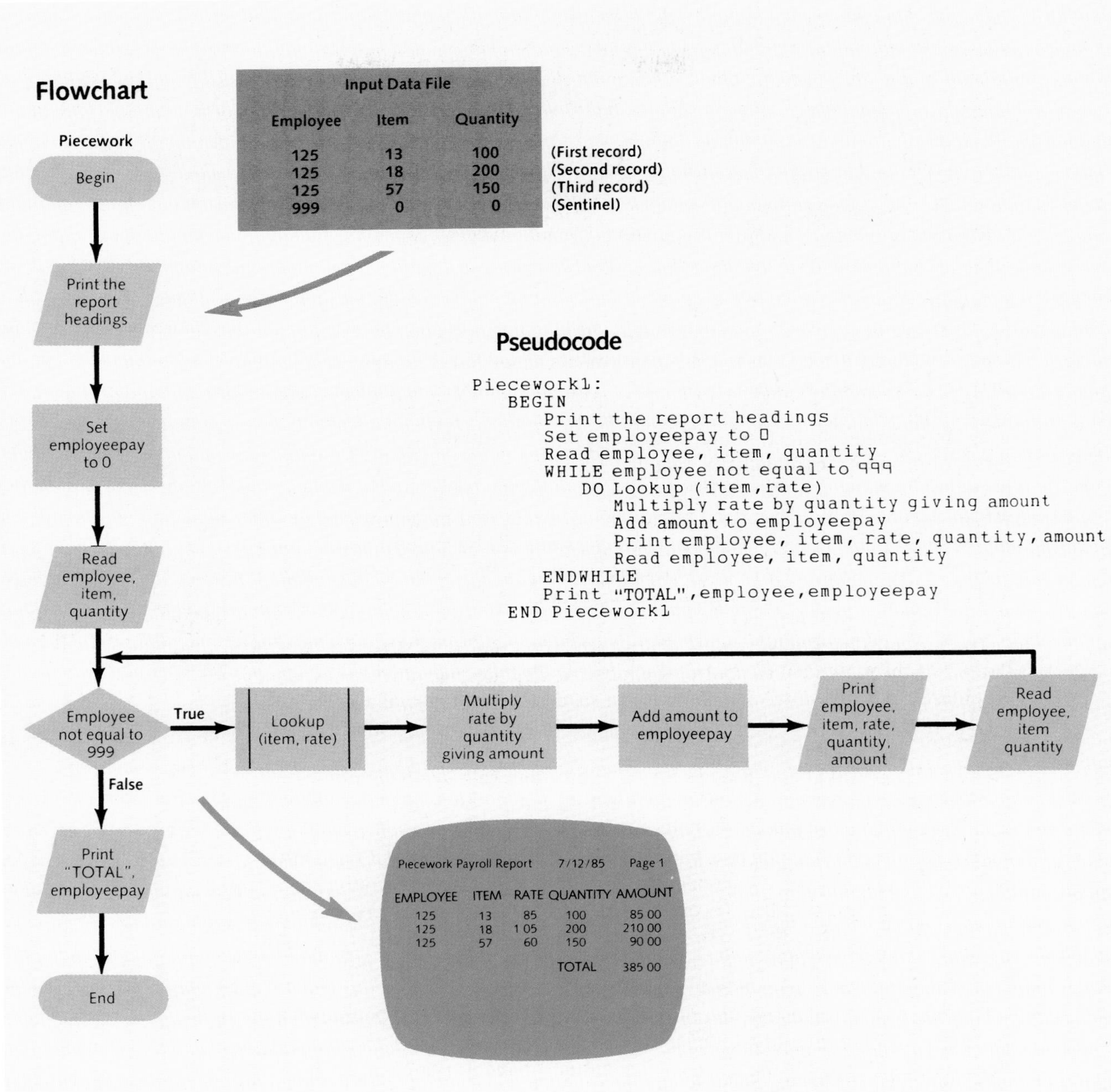

Flowchart
Input Data File
Employee Item Quantity
125 13 100 (First record)
125 18 200 (Second record)
125 57 150 (Third record)
999 0 0 (Sentinel)
Piecework
Begin
Print the report headings
Set employeepay to 0
Read employee, item, quantity
Employee not equal to 999
True
False
Lookup (item, rate)
Multiply rate by quantity giving amount
Add amount to employeepay
Print employee, item, rate, quantity, amount
Read employee, item quantity
Print "TOTAL", employeepay
End
Pseudocode
Piecework1:
BEGIN
Print the report headings
Set employeepay to 0
Read employee, item, quantity
WHILE employee not equal to 999
DO Lookup (item,rate)
Multiply rate by quantity giving amount
Add amount to employeepay
Print employee, item, rate, quantity, amount
Read employee, item, quantity
ENDWHILE
Print "TOTAL",employee,employeepay
END Piecework1
Piecework Payroll Report 7/12/85 Page 1
EMPLOYEE ITEM RATE QUANTITY AMOUNT
125 13 85 100 85 00
125 18 1 05 200 210 00
125 57 60 150 90 00
TOTAL 385 00

Figure 7 Piecework payroll for one employee.

```
PIECEWORK PAYROLL REPORT     7/12/85     PAGE 1


EMPLOYEE            ITEM          RATE          QUANTITY      AMOUNT

Undefined line number in 300
```

Figure A-8 Output produced when the program of Figure A-7 is run.

We immediately notice that the flowchart, pseudocode, and BASIC program are each considerably longer than those in the earlier case studies. But they are composed from the same kinds of elements as we have already used (with only one exception, as we will soon see). Real-world programs that perform useful functions such as calculating payrolls or monitoring air traffic can be very large indeed. In fact, many software systems in use today consist of hundreds of programs containing as many as several thousand statements each. It may take us more time to read and understand longer programs, but if they are written using the disciplined techniques of structured programming, then understanding even very large programs will normally be straightforward.

Lines 210 through 250 print the report headings. The "blank PRINTs" at lines 220, 230, and 250 each print one blank line. This is a simple technique for spacing outputs vertically.

The program uses only a single control structure, namely a WHILE-DO (lines 280 through 350) to control the loop. At 280 the program checks whether or not the employee number just read is the sentinel value 999. If it is not, then the body of the loop is performed from statement 300 through 340.

The GOSUB 700 at line 300 is a BASIC **subroutine call**. We have not included the actual subroutine statements in Figure A-7. We know from the discussion in Chapter 8 that this subroutine's job is to determine the piecework rate that corresponds to a particular item code. By writing GOSUB 700 at this point we're doing all we need to do at this early stage of writing this program to express that the piecework rate is to be determined here. We will write the subroutine in the next case study. But this should not deter us from writing and understanding the current program. This is in fact an important part of the top-down stepwise refinement methodology.

The subroutine will assign the rate to variable R. Statement 310 multiplies the rate, R, by the quantity, Q, of that particular item and places the result into an amount variable, A. Since we'll eventually have to print the person's salary for all items, statement 320 adds the amount, A, into the total pay, P.

Statement 330 then prints one line of the report containing the employee number, item code, piecework rate, quantity produced, and the amount of money the employee earned for producing items of that type. Statement 340 reads the next set of data to be processed and statement 350 closes the WHILE-DO loop returning to the loop test at line 280.

The program continues looping until it reads a set of data with employee number 999, the sentinel value. At this point, it transfers control first to statement 290 and then to statement 360 where it writes a blank line and then the totals line of the report; it prints the word TOTAL followed by this person's total pay. Notice the group of three commas in print statement 370; each of these commas causes a print zone to be skipped so that the word "TOTAL" will print in the fourth print zone and the total pay, P, will print in the fifth print zone. The program ends at line 999.

After going through all this effort to produce the program of Figure A-7, we are anxious to run the program and observe its outputs. When we do this the output of Figure A-8 is produced. Notice that only the report headings print followed by the error message "Undefined line number in 300." Checking line 300 we see that it contains the GOSUB 700 call to our rate finding subroutine which we, of course, haven't as yet written. So we're not surprised by the error.

But we are naturally curious if the rest of our program is working properly. Is there something we can do to check out most of the features of our main program even before we write the subroutine in the next case study?

The answer is that we can supply what is called a **dummy subroutine** or a **stub** (see Chapter 10). We won't actually write the subroutine in all its glory. Rather, the stub will be a means of plugging the hole in the program at 700, and doing so in a way that allows us to check out most of the rest of the program in some meaningful fashion.

Writing stubs is an important part of the program development process. It allows us to test major portions of large programs and get the bugs out much earlier. This in turn can greatly reduce program development costs since it is a proven fact that the further we are into the development process, the more it costs to remove bugs.

Actually, all the stub at 700 needs to do each time it is called is to return a reasonable rate in variable R. The program may then proceed to use this value in its calculations and run to completion. For simplicity, let's choose the first rate in our table, namely .85, the rate corresponding to item 13 which conveniently happens to be in the program's data as well.

The stub appears as lines 700 through 760 in Figure A-9. Notice that we have used dashed lines to set this stub subroutine off from the main program. The remarks clearly identify this section of the program as a stub. Statement 740 sets the rate to .85, and statement 750 returns control to the main program.

Now when we run the program it runs to completion and produces the output of Figure A-10. There are two problems with this output. First, the report differs from the desired output shown in Figure 7. This is really not a serious problem; it occurs because we are using a stub that supplies a fixed rate of .85 regardless of the item number. Remember all we're trying to accomplish at this point is to check out as many features of our main program as possible before we write the rate-finding subroutine. In this regard our stub has been quite useful since everything did in fact print in the right place and the calculations are correct considering that they are based on the fixed .85 rate.

The second problem is that the run terminated with the error message "RETURN without GOSUB in 750." What happened here is that our program ran properly, printed its final total properly at line 370, and then accidentally fell

```
LIST

100 REM    PIECEWORK PAYROLL FOR ONE EMPLOYEE
110 REM    H + B DEITEL   JANUARY 11, 1985
120 REM
130 REM    VARIABLES:
140 REM       P: TOTAL PAY
150 REM       E: EMPLOYEE NUMBER
160 REM       I: ITEM NUMBER
170 REM       Q: QUANTITY PRODUCED
180 REM       R: RATE PAID FOR PRODUCING ONE PARTICULAR ITEM
190 REM       A: AMOUNT (= RATE TIMES QUANTITY OF ITEM)
200 REM
210 PRINT "PIECEWORK PAYROLL REPORT", "7/12/85", "PAGE 1"
220 PRINT
230 PRINT
240 PRINT "EMPLOYEE", "ITEM", "RATE", "QUANTITY","AMOUNT"
250 PRINT
260 LET P = 0
270 READ E, I, Q
280 IF E <> 999 THEN 300
290    GOTO 360
300    GOSUB 700
310    LET A = R * Q
320    LET P = P + A
330    PRINT E, I, R, Q, A
340    READ E, I, Q
350    GOTO 280
360 PRINT
370 PRINT ,,, "TOTAL", P
380 DATA 125,13,100
390 DATA 125,18,200
400 DATA 125,57,150
410 DATA 999,0,0
700 REM    --------------------------------
710 REM    STUB FOR RATE FINDING SUBROUTINE
720 REM    ALWAYS RETURNS A RATE OF .85
730 REM
740 LET R = .85
750 RETURN
760 REM    ---------------------------------
999 END
```

Figure A-9 Testing with a stub subroutine.

```
PIECEWORK PAYROLL REPORT 7/12/85      PAGE 1


EMPLOYEE        ITEM          RATE          QUANTITY    AMOUNT

 125             13            .85           100         85
 125             18            .85           200         170
 125             57            .85           150         127.5

                                            TOTAL        382.5
RETURN without GOSUB in 750
```

Figure A-10 Output produced when the program of Figure A-9 is run.

into the subroutine at 700. (Remember that DATA statements and remarks are skipped by a running program.) Subroutines should only be executed by calling them via GOSUBs. This is because they always end in a RETURN to the main program to the statement after the calling GOSUB. We protect the subroutine from accidental entry by placing a GOTO statement just before it that transfers control to 999 END. This GOTO has been incorporated into the program of Figure A-11, which when executed produces the error-free output of Figure A-12.

```
LIST

100 REM    PIECEWORK PAYROLL FOR ONE EMPLOYEE
110 REM    H + B DEITEL    JANUARY 11, 1985
120 REM
130 REM    VARIABLES:
140 REM       P: TOTAL PAY
150 REM       E: EMPLOYEE NUMBER
160 REM       I: ITEM NUMBER
170 REM       Q: QUANTITY PRODUCED
180 REM       R: RATE PAID FOR PRODUCING ONE PARTICULAR ITEM
190 REM       A: AMOUNT PAID (= RATE TIMES QUANTITY OF ITEM)
200 REM
210 PRINT "PIECEWORK PAYROLL REPORT", "7/12/85", "PAGE 1"
220 PRINT
230 PRINT
240 PRINT "EMPLOYEE", "ITEM", "RATE", "QUANTITY", "AMOUNT"
250 PRINT
260 LET P = 0
270 READ E, I, Q
280 IF E <> 999 THEN 300
290    GOTO 360
300    GOSUB 700
```

(continued)

Figure A-11 Using the GOTO statement to protect a subroutine.

(*continued*)

```
310     LET A = R * Q
320     LET P = P + A
330     PRINT E, I, R, Q, A
340     READ E, I, Q
350     GOTO 280
360 PRINT
370 PRINT ,,, "TOTAL", P
380 DATA 125,13,100
390 DATA 125,18,200
400 DATA 125,57,150
410 DATA 999,0,0
420 GOTO 999
700 REM   --------------------------------
710 REM   STUB FOR RATE FINDING SUBROUTINE
720 REM   ALWAYS RETURNS A RATE OF .85
730 REM
740 LET R = .85
750 RETURN
760 REM   --------------------------------
999 END
```

Figure A-11 Using the GOTO statement to protect a subroutine.

```
PIECEWORK PAYROLL REPORT 7/12/85      PAGE 1


EMPLOYEE        ITEM          RATE          QUANTITY     AMOUNT

 125             13            .85           100          85
 125             18            .85           200          170
 125             57            .85           150          127.5

                                             TOTAL        382.5
```

Figure A-12 Output produced when the program of Figure A-11 is run.

Case Study 8: Piecework Payroll: Subroutines and Table Searching

Problem Statement:

Design the rate finding subroutine referenced in Case Study 8-7. The subroutine is called from the main (pseudocode) program by the statement

```
Call Lookup(item, rate)
```

The variable **item** is supplied to the subroutine. The subroutine determines the

variable **rate** by searching the table for a match on the item code and then reading out the appropriate rate.

Discussion:

Read the discussion on pages 208–210 and study the structured flowchart and pseudocode of Figure 8. The BASIC program complete with the rate finding subroutine appears in Figure A-13; a sample execution is shown in Figure A-14.

Flowchart

Pseudocode

```
Lookup(item, rate):
   BEGIN
      Set index to 0
      REPEAT Add 1 to index
      UNTIL tableitem(index) equals item
      Move tablerate(index) to rate
      Return
   END Lookup
```

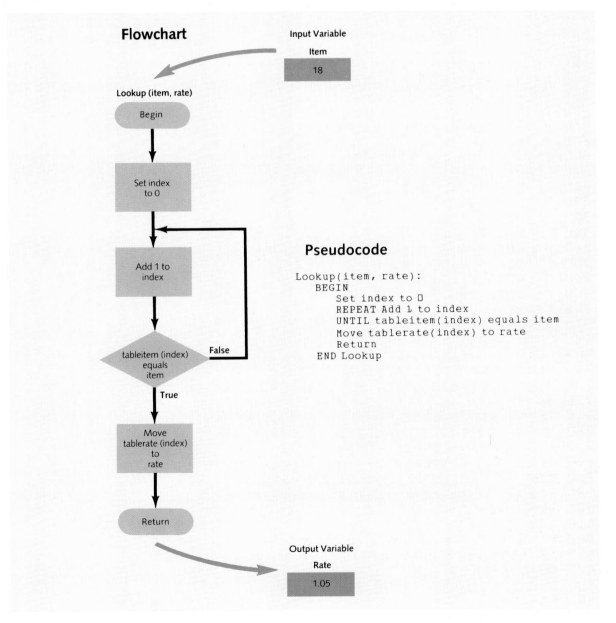

Figure 8 A lookup subroutine.

```
LIST

100 REM    PIECEWORK PAYROLL FOR ONE EMPLOYEE
110 REM    H + B DEITEL    JANUARY 11, 1985
120 REM
130 REM    VARIABLES:
140 REM       P: TOTAL PAY
150 REM       E: EMPLOYEE NUMBER
160 REM       I: ITEM NUMBER
170 REM       Q: QUANTITY PRODUCED
180 REM       R: RATE PAID FOR PRODUCING ONE PARTICULAR ITEM
190 REM       A: AMOUNT PAID (= RATE TIMES QUANTITY OF ITEM)
200 REM
205 GOSUB 2000
210 PRINT "PIECEWORK PAYROLL REPORT", "7/12/85", "PAGE 1"
220 PRINT
230 PRINT
240 PRINT "EMPLOYEE", "ITEM", "RATE", "QUANTITY","AMOUNT"
250 PRINT
260 LET P = 0
270 READ E, I, Q
280 IF E <> 999 THEN 300
290    GOTO 360
300    GOSUB 700
310    LET A = R * Q
320    LET P = P + A
330    PRINT E, I, R, Q, A
340    READ E, I, Q
350    GOTO 280
360 PRINT
370 PRINT ,,, "TOTAL", P
420 GOTO 9999
700 REM    ----------------------------------------
710 REM    RATE FINDING SUBROUTINE
720 REM    RETURNS RATE, R, CORRESPONDING TO ITEM, I
730 REM
740 REM    VARIABLES:
750 REM       I: ITEM CODE (INPUT VARIABLE)
760 REM       S: INDEX (SUBSCRIPT)
770 REM       X: TABLE OF ITEM CODES (ARRAY)
780 REM       Y: TABLE OF RATES (ARRAY)
790 REM       R: RATE (OUTPUT VARIABLE)
800 REM
810 LET S = 0
820    LET S = S + 1
830 IF X(S) = I THEN 850
840 GOTO 820
850 LET R = Y(S)
860 RETURN
870 REM    ----------------------------------------
```

(cont.)

Figure A-13 BASIC Program for Case Study 8.

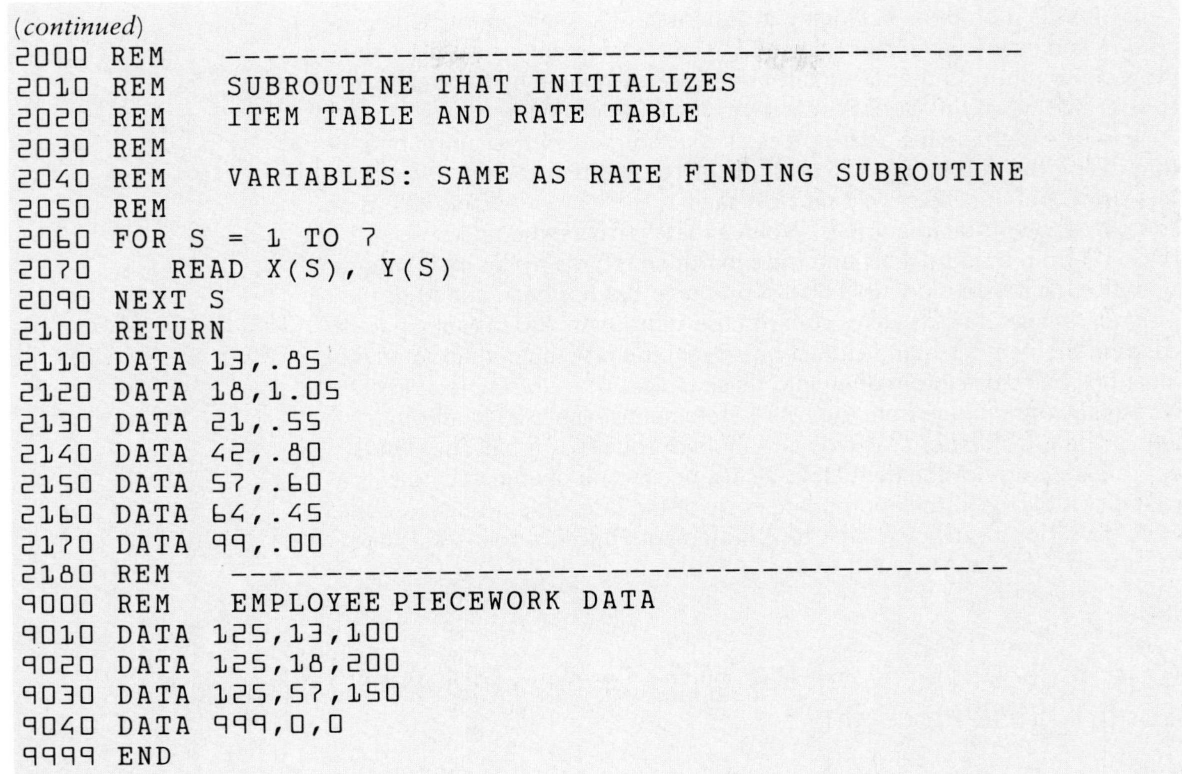

(*continued*)

```
2000 REM    ----------------------------------------------
2010 REM    SUBROUTINE THAT INITIALIZES
2020 REM    ITEM TABLE AND RATE TABLE
2030 REM
2040 REM    VARIABLES: SAME AS RATE FINDING SUBROUTINE
2050 REM
2060 FOR S = 1 TO 7
2070     READ X(S), Y(S)
2090 NEXT S
2100 RETURN
2110 DATA 13,.85
2120 DATA 18,1.05
2130 DATA 21,.55
2140 DATA 42,.80
2150 DATA 57,.60
2160 DATA 64,.45
2170 DATA 99,.00
2180 REM    ----------------------------------------------
9000 REM    EMPLOYEE PIECEWORK DATA
9010 DATA 125,13,100
9020 DATA 125,18,200
9030 DATA 125,57,150
9040 DATA 999,0,0
9999 END
```

Figure A-13 BASIC Program for Case Study 8.

```
PIECEWORK PAYROLL REPORT 7/12/85        PAGE 1


EMPLOYEE        ITEM          RATE          QUANTITY     AMOUNT

 125             13            .85           100          85
 125             18           1.05           200          210
 125             57            .6            150          90

                                             TOTAL        385
```

Figure A-14 Output produced when the program of Figure A-13 is run.

The subroutine is quite short, but it contains some powerful techniques that must be carefully understood. Statement 300 of the main program transfers control to the subroutine by using the **GOSUB**, or "GO to SUBroutine" statement in BASIC. The GOSUB performs two functions. First, it notes the statement number of the statement following the GOSUB (in this case, 310); it saves this so that the subroutine will know where to return after it completes its processing. Next the GOSUB transfers control to the statement whose number appears to the right of the word GOSUB, in this case statement 700.

The BASIC subroutine beginning at statement 700 then performs its processing and eventually it executes the RETURN statement. This causes the program to return to the statement number remembered by the program (automatically) when the GOSUB was performed, namely 310.

Now let's examine the actual processing performed by this subroutine. Before calling this subroutine, the program places the item code in variable I. The subscript S is successively set to 1, then 2, then 3. For each S, X(S) is compared to I in statement 830. When a match occurs, the rate R is set to the rate Y(S) from the rate table and the subroutine returns to the main program.

Notice that there is an additional subroutine that has been added to the program at line 2000. If we're going to use subroutine 700 to look up item codes in the item table and extract rates from the rate table, then clearly we must first place this information into these tables. The subroutine at line 2000 reads pairs of numbers from the DATA statements in lines 2110 through 2170. The first number of each pair is an item code that is placed in the appropriate entry of the item table, X. The second number in each pair is a rate that is placed in the appropriate entry of the rate table, R. Because the FOR/NEXT loop varies S from 1 to 7, statement 2070 first reads X(1) and Y(1), then X(2) and Y(2), and so on.

Case Study 9: Piecework Payroll for Several Employees: Control Break Processing

Problem Statement:

Modify the single-employee piecework payroll program developed in Case Studies 8-7 and 8-8 so that it handles several employees. The input data for the employees is arranged as in Figure 10. The output report that should be produced when this input data is processed is also shown in Figure 10. After the data for each employee is processed, the amount of money earned by that employee for the week should be printed. At the end of the entire report, the total amount of money earned by all employees for the week should be printed.

Discussion:

Read the discussion on pages 210–211 and study the structured flowchart and pseudocode of Figure 10 on pages 550–551. The BASIC program appears in Figure A-15; a sample execution is shown in Figure A-16.

Once again, although the program is large, it is understandable because of the disciplined use of structured programming techniques.

First, let's study the structured flowchart in Figure 10 and examine the use of control structures. The program contains a large WHILE-DO loop that continues processing employee information while the sentinel value has not as yet been read. Within the large loop, an IF-THEN structure tests for the control breaks. It compares the current employee number to the previous employee number; if they are different it prints the line summarizing the previous em-

```
LIST

100 REM   PIECEWORK PAYROLL FOR SEVERAL EMPLOYEES
110 REM   H + B DEITEL   JANUARY 11, 1985
120 REM
130 REM   VARIABLES:
140 REM      P: TOTAL PAY FOR ONE EMPLOYEE
145 REM      T: TOTAL PAY FOR ALL EMPLOYEES
150 REM      E: EMPLOYEE NUMBER
155 REM      L: LAST EMPLOYEE NUMBER
160 REM      I: ITEM NUMBER
170 REM      Q: QUANTITY PRODUCED
180 REM      R: RATE PAID FOR PRODUCING ONE PARTICULAR ITEM
190 REM      A: AMOUNT PAID (= RATE TIMES QUANTITY OF ITEM)
200 REM
205 GOSUB 2000
210 PRINT "PIECEWORK PAYROLL REPORT", "7/12/85", "PAGE 1"
220 PRINT
230 PRINT
240 PRINT "EMPLOYEE", "ITEM", "RATE", "QUANTITY", "AMOUNT"
250 PRINT
260 LET P = 0
270 LET T = 0
280 READ E, I, Q
290 LET L = E
300 IF E <> 999 THEN 320
310    GOTO 440
320    IF E <> L THEN 340
330       GOTO 360
340       PRINT
343       PRINT ,, "EMPLOYEE", L, P; " * "
346       PRINT
350       LET P = 0
360    GOSUB 700
370    LET A = R * Q
380    LET P = P + A
390    LET T = T + A
400    PRINT E, I, R, Q, A
410    LET L = E
420    READ E, I, Q
430    GOTO 300
440 PRINT
443 PRINT ,, "EMPLOYEE", L, P; "*"
446 PRINT
450 PRINT ,, "GRAND TOTAL",, T; "**"
460 GOTO 9999
```

(continued)

Figure A-15 BASIC Program for Case Study 9.

(continued)

```
700 REM   ------------------------------------------
710 REM   RATE FINDING SUBROUTINE
720 REM   RETURNS RATE, R, CORRESPONDING TO ITEM, I
730 REM
740 REM   VARIABLES:
750 REM      I: ITEM CODE (INPUT VARIABLE)
760 REM      S: INDEX (SUBSCRIPT)
770 REM      X: TABLE OF ITEM CODES (ARRAY)
780 REM      Y: TABLE OF RATES (ARRAY)
790 REM      R: RATE (OUTPUT VARIABLE)
800 REM
810 LET S = 0
820    LET S = S + 1
830 IF X(S) = I THEN 850
840 GOTO 820
850 LET R = Y(S)
860 RETURN
870 REM   ------------------------------------------
2000 REM   ------------------------------------------
2010 REM   SUBROUTINE THAT INITIALIZES
2020 REM   ITEM TABLE AND RATE TABLE
2030 REM
2040 REM   VARIABLES: SAME AS RATE FINDING SUBROUTINE
2050 REM
2060 FOR S = 1 TO 7
2070    READ X(S), Y(S)
2090 NEXT S
2100 RETURN
2110 DATA 13,.85
2120 DATA 18,1.05
2130 DATA 21,.55
2140 DATA 42,.80
2150 DATA 57,.60
2160 DATA 64,.45
2170 DATA 99,.00
2180 REM   ------------------------------------------
9000 REM   EMPLOYEE PIECEWORK DATA
9010 DATA 125,13,100
9020 DATA 125,18,200
9030 DATA 125,57,150
9040 DATA 247,18,90
9050 DATA 247,21,195
9060 DATA 247,42,50
9070 DATA 247,64,150
9080 DATA 316,42,200
9090 DATA 316,57,250
9100 DATA 999,0,0
9999 END
```

Figure A-15 BASIC Program for Case Study 9.

```
PIECEWORK PAYROLL REPORT 7/12/85      PAGE 1


EMPLOYEE      ITEM        RATE        QUANTITY     AMOUNT

 125           13          .85         100          85
 125           18          1.05        200          210
 125           57          .6          150          90

                          EMPLOYEE     125          385 *

 247           18          1.05        90           94.5
 247           21          .55         195          107.25
 247           42          .8          50           40
 247           64          .45         150          67.5

                          EMPLOYEE     247          309.25 *

 316           42          .8          200          160
 316           57          .6          250          150

                          EMPLOYEE     316          310 *

                          GRAND TOTAL               1004.25 **
```

Figure A-16 Output produced when the program of Figure A-15 is run.

ployee's figures, and then clears the employee pay back to zero to prepare to process the next employee.

Statements 260 and 270 initialize the totals. Statement 280 reads the first set of employee information. Statement 290 initializes the last employee number, L, to the same value as the current (first) employee number, E. It does this to prevent a fake control break on the first employee (otherwise a needless line of output would appear).

The WHILE-DO loop is from 300 through 430. It begins by testing if the sentinel value 999 has been read. If not, then the program performs the body of the WHILE-DO beginning with 320. Here the IF-THEN structure checks for the control break. If it has occurred, then line 343 prints the summary for the previous employee and line 350 reinitializes the pay to zero to prepare to process the next employee.

Whether a control break has occurred or not, the program continues at line 360 where it calls the rate-finding subroutine to determine the piecework rate, R, for the item code, I. Lines 370 and 380 calculate the amount earned, A, for this type of item and add that amount to this employee's total pay, P. Line 390 adds that amount to the total earnings, T, for all employees; T is the grand total that will be printed as part of the last line of the program's output.

Statement 400 prints the information for this employee's work on this type of item. Statement 410 sets the last employee number to that of the em-

Figure 10 Control break processing: Piecework payroll for several employees.

Input Data File

Employee	Item	Quantity	
125	13	100	(First record)
125	18	200	(Second record)
125	57	150	(Etc.)
247	18	90	
247	21	195	
247	42	50	
247	64	150	
316	42	200	
316	57	250	
999	0	0	(Sentinel)

Pseudocode

```
Piecework2:
  BEGIN
     Print the report headings
     Set employeepay to 0
     Set totalpay to 0
     Read employee, item, quantity
     Move employee to lastemployee
     WHILE employee not 999
         DO IF employee not equal to lastemployee
                THEN Print "EMPLOYEE", lastemployee, employeepay, "*"
                     Set employeepay to 0
            ENDIF
            Call Lookup(item,rate)
            Multiply rate by quantity giving amount
            Add amount to employeepay
            Add amount to totalpay
            Print employee, item, rate, quantity, amount
            Move employee to lastemployee
            Read employee, item, quantity
     ENDWHILE
     Print "EMPLOYEE", lastemployee, employeepay, "*"
     Print "GRAND TOTAL", totalpay, "**"
  END Piecework2
```

PIECEWORK PAYROLL REPORT 7/12/85 PAGE 1

EMPLOYEE	ITEM	RATE	QUANTITY	AMOUNT
125	13	.85	100	85.00
125	18	1.05	200	210.00
125	57	.60	150	90.00
			EMPLOYEE 125	385.00*
247	18	1.05	90	94.50
247	21	.55	195	107.25
247	42	.80	50	40.00
247	64	.45	150	67.50
			EMPLOYEE 247	309.25*
316	42	.80	200	160.00
316	57	.60	250	150.00
			EMPLOYEE 316	310.00*
			GRAND TOTAL	1,004.25**

Piecework 2

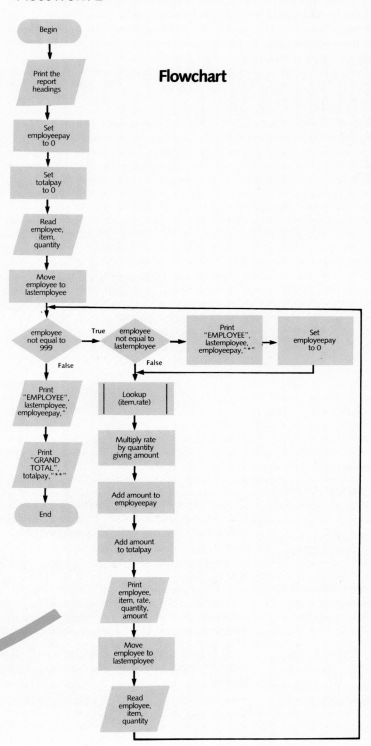

Flowchart

Begin

Print the report headings

Set employeepay to 0

Set totalpay to 0

Read employee, item, quantity

Move employee to lastemployee

employee not equal to 999

True

employee not equal to lastemployee

Print "EMPLOYEE", lastemployee, employeepay, "*"

Set employeepay to 0

False

Lookup (item,rate)

Multiply rate by quantity giving amount

Add amount to employeepay

Add amount to totalpay

Print employee, item, rate, quantity, amount

Move employee to lastemployee

Read employee, item, quantity

False

Print "EMPLOYEE", lastemployee, employeepay, "

Print "GRAND TOTAL", totalpay, "**"

End

ployee just processed; this will enable the program to compare L to the new E about to be read to test for a control break. Statement 420 reads the next set of employee information and statement 430 closes the WHILE-DO loop and returns control to the loop test at line 300.

When line 300 determines that the sentinel value has been read, control falls through to line 310 where the program transfers to its "wrapup" processing at lines 440 through 450. The last line of output for the last employee is printed at line 443, and the grand totals line containing the total of all of the employees' earnings is printed by statement 450. Statement 460 transfers control around the subroutines (the same as those in Case Study 8) directly to the END statement at 9999 where the program terminates.

Self-Review Exercises 

Matching

Next to the term in column A, place the letter of the statement in column B that best describes it.

Column A	Column B
1. 377 PRINT	A. Last statement executed in a subroutine
2. ,,	F. A BASIC subroutine call
3. REM statement	C. In a PRINT statement this skips a print zone
4. Call	D. Used to hold a table of information
5. X(3)	E. Ignored by a running program
6. 300 GOSUB 700	F. Dummy subroutine used for testing
7. RETURN	G. Might generate a needless line of output
8. Array	H. Pseudocode GOSUB
9. False control break	I. Name of an element of an array
10. Stub	J. Blank print

Fill-in-the-Blanks

Fill in the blanks in each of the following:

1. Understanding even very large programs is normally straightforward if they are written using the disciplined techniques of ______.

2. (True/False) For a program that finds the average age of a group of 10 people, 99 is an appropriate sentinel value. ______

3. When a BASIC program containing the statement 300 GOSUB 700 was run, it caused the error message "Undefined line number in 300" to appear. What was probably wrong? ______

4. The further we are into the development process, the (more/less) ______ it costs to remove bugs.

5. (True/False) When a program is run with a stub, it generally produces the same results as when it is run with the finished subroutine. ______

6. When a BASIC program that uses a subroutine was run, it produced the error message "RETURN without GOSUB in 850." What was probably wrong? ______

7. The two functions performed by the GOSUB statement are ______ and ______.

8. A ______ occurs when, after reading and processing all the records for one employee, a record is read with the next employee's number.

9. (True/False) With the top-down methodology, program testing can begin long before a program is finished.

10. One common technique for avoiding the problem in question 6 is to ______.

Answers to Self-Review Exercises

Matching: 1 J, 2 C, 3 E, 4 H, 5 I, 6 B, 7 A, 8 D, 9 G, 10 F

Fill-in-the-Blanks:

1. structured programming
2. False
3. There was no statement 700. The subroutine was missing.
4. more
5. False
6. The program accidentally executed the subroutine without calling it by using a GOSUB.
7. Save the statement number of the statement after the GOSUB so that the subroutine will know where to return to after it completes its processing, and transfer control to the statement whose number appears to the right of the word GOSUB.
8. control break
9. True
10. place a GOTO statement before the subroutine; the GOTO should transfer control around the subroutine.

Problems 

1. Write a segment of a BASIC program that will determine and print the sum and average of the 15 elements of array Q.

2. Write a segment of a BASIC program that will flip a 12-element array V, that is, V(1) and V(12) should be swapped, V(2) and V(11) should be swapped, and so on. Print the contents of the array both before and after it is flipped.

3. A class of 30 students rated their instructor on a scale from 1 to 5 with 1 meaning very poor and 5 meaning excellent. Write a BASIC program that reads the 30 responses from DATA statements and uses a 5-element array C to tally the number of responses of each type. Let C(1) count the number of 1 responses, let C(2) count the number of 2 responses, and so on. If the responses are read into variable R, then what does the following statement do?

```
400 LET C(R) = C(R) + 1
```

Implement the program without using any IF statements. After all 30 responses have been processed, print a summary of how the students voted, that is, the number of 1 votes, the number of 2 votes, and so on.

4. Read a list of 25 nonzero numbers from DATA statements. The list may contain some duplicates. Print each different number once; do not print any duplicates. **Hint**: Use a 25-element array. Initially, the array contains all zeros. Each time a number is read, search the array to see if this number has already been placed in the array. If it hasn't, then put it in the next available position in the array and print it. If the number just read has already been placed in the array, then simply ignore it.

Module 4: Advanced Topics

Modules 2 and 3 have presented BASIC programs and sample executions for all nine case studies of Chapter 8. In Module 4, we investigate four additional case studies on advanced programming topics. Case Study 10 examines fancy print formatting techniques with BASIC's PRINT USING and PRINT TAB statements. It shows how to correct the alignment problems that developed in the case studies of Module 3. Case Study 11 discusses sorting—the arranging of information into order. It explains the bubble sort which uses a single-subscripted array and nested FOR-NEXT loops. Case Study 12 investigates the use of double-subscripted arrays for manipulating tables or grids of information; again, nested FOR-NEXT loops are seen to be important. And, finally, Case Study 13 explains how to incorporate randomness or the element of chance into BASIC programs; these techniques are at the heart of problems that simulate coin tossing, dice rolling, and card dealing.

Case Study 10: Fancy Print Formatting

In Case Studies 7, 8, and 9 we discovered some weaknesses in the operation of BASIC's simple printing mechanisms. For example, a dollar amount like 362.50 prints as 362.5 without the rightmost, or **trailing zero**, and a dollar amount like 362.00 prints as 362 without a decimal point and without the two trailing zeros. Worse yet, when we print items in print zones, that is, when we use the comma print separator, we find that these dollar amounts appear left-justified at the beginning of the print zones rather than aligned vertically according to the position of the decimal point. Thus, BASIC ordinarily gives us

```
362
362.5
1367.43
```

when we may in fact prefer

```
 362.00
 362.50
1367.43
```

Many versions of BASIC provide the **PRINT USING statement** which gives the programmer the ability to control the precise formatting of printed outputs.

Problem Statement:

You have been asked to write a simple payroll calculation program for a company with five employees. For each of these people your program should read from DATA the person's employee number, hourly salary, and hours worked last week. Your program should print a neatly formatted report showing each of these facts as well as the gross pay earned by each employee for last week. The printed report must do the following:

1. Show all dollar amounts with a decimal point and two decimal digits to the right of the decimal point.

2. Align all dollar amounts in a given column according to the decimal points.

3. Compress the printouts so that the four columns of information take up much less space horizontally across the page than if they were printed in four separate print zones.

Discussion:

The program and a sample execution appear in Figure A-17. The gross pay is calculated simply as the hourly salary times the hours worked last week.

The formatting requirements are easily met with the powerful PRINT USING statement. The program is designed to produce two printed reports. Lines 190 through 230 print the report using four print zones and BASIC's elementary print formatting capabilities. Line 250 uses BASIC's **RESTORE** statement to reset the DATA list pointer back to the beginning of the DATA list so that the data may be reprocessed. Lines 260 through 320 print the report again, this time using the advanced print formatting capabilities of the PRINT USING statement. A quick glance at the second printed report in Figure A-17 shows that it indeed meets the requirements of the problem statement.

Now let's take a closer look at the PRINT USING statement in line 300. The key differences between this and the corresponding PRINT in line 220 are the word USING, a character string containing many number signs (#), spaces, and decimal points, and, finally, a semicolon separating this character string from the list of variables to be printed.

The special character string in line 300 is called a **format string**. It serves as a guide for the precise positioning and editing of the values to be printed. Notice that the format string actually consists of four separate format strings separated by blanks (Figure A-18). The PRINT USING automatically associates the first item to be printed, E, with the first format string ######, S is associated with ##.##, H is associated with ###, and S * H is associated with ####.##.

The # characters serve both as place holders and format controllers. Their spacing indicates the positions across the output line in which each of the numbers are to be placed. So the employee number will be placed in positions 2 through 7, the hourly salary in positions 11 through 15, the hours worked in 20 through 22, and the gross pay in 27 through 33.

Notice that all the employee numbers in the DATA statements are six digits long, the same length as the format string ######. In this case the format string serves only to specify that the employee number is to be placed in positions 2 through 7.

The salary will print in positions 11 through 15 under the control of format string ##.##, indicating a five-position field that will always print with a decimal point in the third position of the field and with two trailing decimal digits, even if they are zeros, in the fourth and fifth positions. The number signs to the left of the decimal point will not print leftmost zeros, also called **leading zeros**. Thus, the salary of 8.90 that prints as 8.9 in the first report will print as 8.90, with the zero printing as shown.

```
LIST

100 REM    PRINT FORMATTING WITH PRINT USING
110 REM    H + B DEITEL   JANUARY 11, 1985
120 REM
130 REM    VARIABLES:
140 REM       P: PERSON NUMBER (1 TO 5)
160 REM       E: EMPLOYEE NUMBER
170 REM       S: SALARY
175 REM       H: HOURS WORKED
180 REM
190 PRINT "EMPLOYEE", "SALARY", "HOURS", "GROSS PAY"
200 FOR P = 1 TO 5
210     READ E, S, H
220     PRINT E, S, H, S * H
230 NEXT P
240 REM    RESTORE ALLOWS THE PROGRAM TO REPROCESS THE DATA
250 RESTORE
255 PRINT
260 PRINT "EMPLOYEE  SALARY  HOURS  GROSS PAY"
280 FOR P = 1 TO 5
290     READ E, S, H
300 PRINT USING " ######   ##.##    ###     ####.##"; E, S, H, S * H
320 NEXT P
330 DATA 345679,8.90,38
340 DATA 457868,9.00,40
350 DATA 555763,7.95,37
360 DATA 675431,5.00,15
370 DATA 778693,32.50,39.5
999 END
```

```
RUN

EMPLOYEE        SALARY          HOURS           GROSS PAY
 345679          8.9             38              338.2
 457868          9               40              360
 555763          7.95            37              294.15
 675431          5               15              75
 778693          32.5            39.5            1283.75

EMPLOYEE  SALARY  HOURS  GROSS PAY
 345679    8.90     38     338.20
 457868    9.00     40     360.00
 555763    7.95     37     294.15
 675431    5.00     15      75.00
 778693   32.50     40    1283.75
```

Figure A-17 A program that demonstrates some of the capabilities of the PRINT USING statement.

```
     E             S             H            S * H
  345679         8.90           38           338.2
  ######        ##.##          ###          ####.##
  345679         8.90           38           338.20
```

Figure A-18 How a format string controls positioning and formatting.

The hours worked figures in the DATA statement are for the most part two-digit numbers. Notice that the format string ### really provides for integers as large as three digits. In this case, BASIC will print the numbers in the rightmost two positions, namely 21 and 22, and will print a blank in position 20 (instead of a zero). We have intentionally included an hours worked figure of 39.5 for the last employee to illustrate a potential problem with the PRINT USING statement. The format ### calls for the printing of three-digit integers. But 39.5 has a fractional part (.5). Examining the printed report shows that when the PRINT USING tries to print 39.5 using format ### it rounds off the number to 40. And of course 40 times 32.50 is not 12.8375! So even though the PRINT USING is very powerful, it can also be very dangerous. The point here is that the programmer must carefully consider the range and formats of available inputs in any program. If the programmer really wants to allow fractional numbers in the hours worked figures, a better format than ### might be ###.# or perhaps ###.##.

The gross pay is printed in positions 27 through 33 under the control of format string ####.##. The decimal point will print in position 31, two decimal digits, including trailing zeros will print in positions 32 and 33, and four decimal digits will print in positions 27 through 30, but with leading blanks instead of leading zeros. In data processing terminology, replacing leading zeros with blanks is called **zero suppression**.

One additional fancy printing capability of BASIC is the **PRINT TAB** that is used to position to any printing position. The statement

```
600 PRINT TAB(35); "*"
```

would print an asterisk in print position 35. The statement

```
700 PRINT TAB(15); "X"; TAB(30); "Y"
```

would print an "X" in position 15 and a "Y" in position 30. One caution here is that some BASICs treat the first printing position as print position 0 rather than as print position 1.

Case Study 11: Sorting

One of the most common tasks performed by computers is **sorting**, the arranging of a list of data items into some meaningful order. Alphabetizing a list of names and placing a list of golf scores into increasing order are examples of sorting.

In upper-level computer science courses, much time is spent studying various sorting methods. Some run faster than others, some use less computer memory than others, and some are more effective for certain types of data than others. In this section we consider one of the simplest sorting methods, the **bubble sort**, which is easy to program and efficient enough for sorting small lists.

Suppose we are asked to sort the numbers 68, 85, 79, 74, and 65 into increasing order. The bubble sort compares the first and second numbers, 68 and 85, and determines that they are in order so it leaves them as they are. Now the sort compares the second and third numbers, 85 and 79. These numbers are out of order, so the sort swaps them and the list becomes 68, 79, 85, 74, 65. The sort then swaps the third and fourth numbers, 85 and 74, producing the list 68, 79, 74, 85, 65. Then the sort compares the fourth and fifth elements, 85 and 65, and swaps them producing the list 68, 79, 74, 65, 85. At this point, the sort has made one complete **pass** of the five numbers. The resulting list is not as yet sorted, but the order of the elements has been improved somewhat. In particular, the largest number, 85 has moved to the bottom of the list. (Why does the bubble sort guarantee that the largest number will move to the bottom of the list on the first pass?) Therefore, on the next pass we need only examine the first four elements, and we will be guaranteed that the largest of these will be in the fourth position after the pass. After the third pass the third largest element will be in the third position. After the fourth pass the fourth largest element will be in the second position—this automatically means that the fifth largest (that is, the smallest) element will be in the first position, so a fifth pass is unnecessary. Thus, to sort five elements with a bubble sort, we need to make at most four passes. In general, to sort n elements with a bubble sort we need to make at most $n-1$ passes.

Problem Statement:

Write a BASIC program that sorts a list of 12 golf scores to help rank the golfers at the end of the first round of a tournament.

Discussion:

The program and sample execution appear in Figure A-19. Some useful new features of BASIC are introduced.

Statement 180 states that array G has 12 elements. BASIC always provides 10 elements for an array if the user doesn't specify in a DIM (dimension) statement how large the array is.

Statements 190 through 210 read the 12 golf scores to be processed from DATA statement 350. The FOR-NEXT varies subscript I from 1 to 12. When I is 1, statement 200 reads the first golf score into G(1), when I is 2, statement 200 reads the next score into G(2), and so on.

The FOR-NEXT looping structure at statements 220 through 300 loops 11 times, once per pass of the bubble sort. For each pass, the inner FOR-NEXT at statements 230 through 290 compares the successive pairs of numbers and

```
LIST

100 REM   SORT 12 GOLF SCORES WITH BUBBLE SORT
110 REM   H + B DEITEL   JANUARY 11, 1985
120 REM
130 REM   VARIABLES:
140 REM      G: 12 ELEMENT GOLF SCORE ARRAY
150 REM      I: INDEX (SUBSCRIPT) FOR SEARCHING ARRAY
160 REM      T: TEMPORARY LOCATION FOR SWAPPING
170 REM      P: PASS NUMBER (1-11) OF BUBBLE SORT
175 REM
180 DIM G(12)
190 FOR I = 1 TO 12
200    READ G(I)
210 NEXT I
215 REM   MAKE 11 PASSES OF THE ARRAY
220 FOR P = 1 TO 11
225 REM   COMPARE 11 SUCCESSIVE PAIRS OF NUMBERS
230    FOR I = 1 TO 12 - P
240       IF G(I) > G(I + 1) THEN 260
250          GOTO 290
255          REM   SWAP ELEMENTS G(I) AND G(I + 1)
260          LET T = G(I)
270          LET G(I) = G(I + 1)
280          LET G(I + 1) = T
290    NEXT I
300 NEXT P
310 REM   PRINT THE SCORES
315 PRINT "THE GOLF SCORES FROM BEST TO WORST ARE:"
320 FOR I = 1 TO 12
330    PRINT G(I);
340 NEXT I
350 DATA 76,78,68,84,92,77,67,87,74,72,83,91
999 END

RUN

THE GOLF SCORES FROM BEST TO WORST ARE:
 67  68  72  74  76  77  78  83  84  87  91  92
```

Figure A-19 A bubble sort program and a sample execution.

makes swaps when necessary. Notice that the FOR statement at 230 varies the subscript I from 1 TO 12-P. Thus on the first pass, when P is 1, the inner loop will make 12−1, or 11, comparisons, on the second pass the inner loop will make 12−2, or 10, comparisons, and on the eleventh (or last) pass the inner loop will make 12−11, or only a single, comparison.

Statement 240 compares the first number in the pair, G(I), to the second number, G(I + 1), to see if a swap is necessary. If it is, the swap is performed at statements 260 through 280. Notice that the swap requires the use of one additional temporary location, T. (Why can't the swap be performed in only two statements without a temporary location?)

The NEXT I at statement 290 causes the next pair to be chosen within a pass. When NEXT I increases I past 12-P, then the NEXT P at statement 300 causes the next pass of the bubble sort to begin. When the NEXT P increases P to be higher than 11, the program continues with lines 315 through 340 that print the 12 scores in increasing order.

A new feature of the PRINT statement is introduced in line 330. Notice that the semicolon is used after G(I) but that no variable name appears to its right. This simply means that the next item the program prints will appear next to the value of G(I) printed by this statement. This feature is called a **dangling (or trailing) semicolon**. It is also possible to use a **dangling (or trailing) comma**, in which case the next item to be printed will appear at the start of the next print zone. The program ends at line 999.

Case Study 12: Double-Subscripted Arrays

We have seen how arrays make it convenient to store and reference groups of related data items. We have studied arrays with one subscript in which each item in the array is identified by its position (1, 2, 3, . . .) from the start of the array. A **double-subscripted array** is a convenient way to represent a table or grid of information. In some versions of BASIC, arrays may have many subscripts, but we will confine our attention to either single-subscripted arrays or double-subscripted arrays.

BASIC automatically assumes a double-subscripted array to be 10 by 10, that is, 10 rows by 10 columns, unless the programmer specifies otherwise in a DIM statement. The programmer would use a statement like

```
200 DIM B(15,20)
```

to reserve space for array B with 15 rows and 20 columns (or a total of 300 elements).

Figure A-20 is a double-subscripted array that shows sales volumes for last week by salesperson and product. The company has four salespeople and sells five products. Notice that the array has four rows, one per salesperson, and five columns, one per product. If we want information about salesperson 3, then we refer to row 3 of the table. If we want information about product 2, then we refer to column 2 of the table.

The table contains 20 entries (4 rows times 5 entries per row). Each entry shows the dollar amount of a particular product sold last week by a particular salesperson. For example, the entry in the top left of the table shows the sales of product 1 last week by salesperson 1 (in this case, $642.31); the entry in the bottom right of the table shows the sales of product 5 last week by salesperson 4 (in this case, $119.37).

		Product				
		1	2	3	4	5
Salesperson	1	642.31	714.83	382.75	963.74	817.42
	2	914.87	312.46	287.95	814.71	612.93
	3	421.15	541.86	799.12	847.75	300.00
	4	519.72	295.00	845.00	916.85	119.37

Figure A-20 A double-subscripted array of sales figures for last week by salesperson and by product.

Figure A-21 shows the same array S with the names of each of its 20 elements indicated in the array. Notice that all the elements in the first row have a first subscript of 1. All the elements in the third column have a second subscript of 3.

To total the elements of a given row, R, we may use the following segment of BASIC:

```
700     LET T = 0
710     FOR C = 1 TO 5
720        LET T = T + S(R,C)
730     NEXT C
740     PRINT "SALESPERSON"; R; "SALES"; T
```

To total the elements of a given column, C, we may use the following segment of BASIC:

```
800     LET T = 0
810     FOR R = 1 to 4
820        LET T = T + S(R,C)
830     NEXT R
840     PRINT "PRODUCT"; C; "SALES"; T
```

If we wish to find the total sales for the entire company for last week, we total all of the elements of the array. We choose to do this row by row. We

		Product				
		1	2	3	4	5
Salesperson	1	S(1,1)	S(1,2)	S(1,3)	S(1,4)	S(1,5)
	2	S(2,1)	S(2,2)	S(2,3)	S(2,4)	S(2,5)
	3	S(3,1)	S(3,2)	S(3,3)	S(3,4)	S(3,5)
	4	S(4,1)	S(4,2)	S(4,3)	S(4,4)	S(4,5)

Figure A-21 A double-subscripted array showing the names of each of its 20 elements.

use one FOR-NEXT loop to vary the row number from 1 to 4, and a second FOR-NEXT loop to total all of the elements in a particular row. The second FOR-NEXT loop is said to be **nested** within the first. Nested FOR-NEXT loops are commonly used for any manipulation of a double array in which we have to consider all of the elements of the array.

```
900    LET T = 0
910    REM   OUTER LOOP CHOOSES ROW
920    FOR R = 1 TO 4
930       REM   INNER LOOP CHOOSES COLUMN
940       FOR C = 1 TO 5
950          LET T = T + S(R,C)
960       NEXT C
970    NEXT R
980    PRINT "TOTAL SALES FOR LAST WEEK"; T
```

Case Study 13: Randomness

All the computer programs we have studied so far have one thing in common: Each time they run they perform in exactly the same way. A program that prints the numbers from 1 to 10 will faithfully repeat its outputs time and time again.

In this case study, we investigate how BASIC enables programmers to incorporate the element of chance into their programs. Once you master these techniques you'll be able to write programs that simulate coin tossing, dice rolling, and even card dealing. Even the operation of our economy has been simulated with these methods.

The key feature of BASIC for introducing randomness into BASIC programs is the **built-in function RND**. RND is a part of the BASIC language. Whenever it is used in a program, it generates a number at random between zero and one but never exactly one. We sometimes call these numbers the decimal fractions. Thus, one time when we use RND it might generate .04, another time it might generate .99997, another time it might generate .5, and so on. But RND would never generate −3.5, 1, 92, and so on.

Figure A-22 contains a program that generates 40 values of RND. Notice that we have used the form RND(0). Some versions of BASIC allow RND to be used directly without the need to supply a number or letter in parentheses.

Indeed, every one of the random numbers produced in the sample execution is a decimal fraction. Programmers rarely use the values in the form generated by RND. Instead, they often process these values in special ways to generate whole numbers (integers) like 1 or 2 to simulate the two faces of a coin, 1 through 6 to simulate the six sides of a die, or 1 through 52 to simulate the 52 cards in a deck.

The key to being able to do this is to multiply the value of RND by some meaningful integer and then to discard everything to the right of the decimal point, leaving a whole number result. Another BASIC built-in function, INT, is used for this purpose. INT takes only the integer part of a positive number, so

```
LIST

100 REM    GENERATE 40 RANDOM NUMBERS
110 FOR I = 1 TO 10
120     FOR J = 1 TO 4
130         PRINT RND(0),
140     NEXT J
150     PRINT
160 NEXT I
999 END
```

```
RUN

 .91959          .996966         .900457         .245936
 .736043         .768552         .306855         .284351
 .778323         .429066         .209496         .293205
 .850568         .128592         .196209         .941628
 .615313         .442022         .0647852        .56574
 .20287          .540925         .0573502        .215529
 .570696         .115424         .844742         .451724
 .612774         .0460758        .260883         .892673
 .0189835        .825738         .787158         .511216
 .884479         .731449         .786788         .681558
```

Figure A-22 A program (and sample execution) that generates 40 random numbers.

INT(4.5) gives the value 4, INT(2.71634) gives the value 2, and INT(0.513) gives the value 0. (Caution: INT works differently with negative numbers. See what your computer prints, for example, when you tell it to print the integer part of −3.5 using INT.) Figure A-23 summarizes BASIC's built-in functions. Many of these will be of interest to readers who use BASIC to solve mathematical problems.

Now let's see how RND and INT work together to simulate the flipping of a coin. The statement

```
100 PRINT 1 + INT(2 * RND)
```

will print 1 or 2 with equal likelihood. The statement

```
200 PRINT 1 + INT(6 * RND)
```

will print 1, 2, 3, 4, 5, or 6 with equal likelihood. The statement

```
300 PRINT 1 + INT(52 * RND)
```

will print 1, or 2, . . . , or 52 with equal likelihood. In general, the statement

```
400 PRINT X + INT(Y * RND)
```

Function	Explanation
ABS(X)	Absolute value of *x*
ATN(X)	Trigonometric arctangent of *x* (Returns the angle, in radians whose trigonometric tangent is *x*.)
COS(X)	Trigonometric cosine of *x* (*x* in radians)
EXP(X)	Exponential function e^x (*e* is 2.71828...)
INT(X)	Greatest integer that is less than or equal to *x*
LOG(X)	Natural logarithm of *x* (base *e*)
LOG10(X)	Common logarithm of *x* (base 10)
RND(X)	Random number between 0 and 1 (Never 1; the use of *x* varies between BASICs)
SGN(X)	Algebraic sign of *x* SGN(X) is 1 if *x* is positive SGN(X) is 0 if *x* is zero SGN(X) is −1 if *x* is negative
SIN(X)	Trigonometric sine of *x* (*x* in radians)
SQR(X)	Square root of *x* (positive root only)
TAN(X)	Trigonometric tangent of *x* (*x* in radians)

Figure A-23 BASIC's built-in functions. These may vary between versions of BASIC.

will print an integer selected from the range beginning with X and Y consecutive numbers wide. For example

```
500 PRINT 3 + INT(5 * RND)
```

will print 3, 4, 5, 6, or 7 with equal likelihood.

Problem Statement:

Many dice games require that two dice be rolled and that their face values be summed to produce a random number. Because each die has six faces numbered 1 through 6, the possible sums are 2 through 12. Write a BASIC program that simulates 600 rolls of two dice. Use a 12-element array of counters to record the number of times each possible sum appears. When the dice rolls are complete, print a table showing each possible sum and the number of times that it appeared. Study the table and determine which sum appeared most frequently. The mathematical probability of rolling a seven with two dice is 1/6, or one chance in six. Therefore, our program should produce approximately 100 sevens in 600 tries. Let's see if this is the case. The program and a sample execution are shown in Figure A-24. What can you say about the number of sevens that actually appeared?

Many versions of BASIC offer a second feature, the **RANDOMIZE** statement, for controlling randomness. In these versions, a program that does not contain the RANDOMIZE statement will produce the same sequence of "random" numbers each time it is run. This can be especially useful while debug-

```
LIST

100 REM   DICE ROLLING PROGRAM
110 REM   H + B DEITEL   JANUARY 11, 1985
120 REM
130 REM   VARIABLES:
140 REM      D1: FACE VALUE (1 THROUGH 6) OF FIRST DIE
150 REM      D2: FACE VALUE (1 THROUGH 6) OF SECOND DIE
160 REM      S: SUM OF TWO DICE (D1 + D2)
170 REM      C: 12 ELEMENT ARRAY OF COUNTERS
180 REM      R: ROLL COUNTER (1 TO 600)
190 REM
193 DIM C(12)
195 REM   ROLL DIE 600 TIMES AND TABULATE SUMS
200 FOR R = 1 TO 600
210    LET D1 = 1 + INT(6 * RND(0))
220    LET D2 = 1 + INT(6 * RND(0))
230    LET S = D1 + D2
240    LET C(S) = C(S) + 1
250 NEXT R
260 REM   PRINT TABLE OF RESULTS
270 PRINT "SUM", "ROLLS"
280 FOR S = 2 TO 12
290    PRINT S, C(S)
300 NEXT S
999 END
```

```
RUN

SUM          ROLLS
 2            24
 3            37
 4            54
 5            70
 6            72
 7            97
 8            81
 9            70
 10           45
 11           34
 12           16
```

Figure A-24 A program that illustrates the use of randomness to simulate 600 rolls of two dice.

ging a program that uses randomness. When a bug is supposedly fixed, the program can be rerun with the same sequence of random numbers to be sure that it is now working properly. When testing is completed, the RANDOMIZE statement is inserted so that the program will in fact generate different sequences each time it is run.

Self-Review Exercises 

Matching

Next to the term in column A, place the letter of the statement in column B that best describes it.

Column A

1. Pass
2. RND
3. Dangling semicolon
4. PRINT TAB
5. DIM(10,10)
6. RANDOMIZE
7. Nested FOR-NEXT loops
8. #
9. PRINT USING
10. Bubble sort

Column B

A. Varies random numbers produced on different runs
B. PRINT USING place holder
C. Can align a column of dollar amounts
D. Gradually improves order of the data
E. Used in double-subscripted array manipulations
F. BASIC assumes this for a double array if the programmer doesn't provide DIM
G. Allows printing to begin in any position
H. Generates a random number
I. Next item printed will be adjacent to last item printed
J. Bubble sort may make $n - 1$ of these

Fill-in-the-Blanks

Fill in the blanks in each of the following:

1. The variable name of the element in the third column and second row of array X is ______.

2. The arranging of a list of items into some meaningful order is called ______.

3. By using ______ at the end of a PRINT statement the programmer ensures that the next item printed will appear in the next print zone.

4. All of the elements in the seventh column of double-subscripted array M have a (first/second) ______ subscript of ______.

5. The key features of BASIC for introducing randomness into programs are the built-in function ______ and the ______ statement.

6. What should the values of A and B be in the following BASIC statement so that a random integer from 1 to 10 will print? ______

```
200 PRINT A + INT(B * RND)
```

7. Write a BASIC statement at line 400 that will print an asterisk in print position 70. ______

8. A bubble sort has been written to sort 100 numbers in array L. Besides the array itself, how many additional storage locations, if any, does the sort need to hold the data at any time during the sort. Why? ______

9. Unless the programmer specifies how large a single-subscripted array is in a ______ statement, BASIC automatically provides ______ locations.

10. Programmers may represent tables or grids as ______ in BASIC.

Answers to Self-Review Exercises

Matching: 1 J, 2 H, 3 I, 4 G, 5 F, 6 A, 7 E, 8 B, 9 C, 10 D

Fill-in-the-Blanks:

1. X(2,3)
2. sorting
3. dangling comma
4. second, 7
5. RND, RANDOMIZE
6. A should be 1 and B should be 10.
7. 400 PRINT TAB(70); "*"
8. one, for the temporary location used in swapping
9. DIM, 10
10. double-subscripted arrays

Problems

1. Modify the program developed in Case Study 9 to take advantage of the print formatting capabilities of the PRINT USING statement.

2. Show how to modify the bubble sort program so that it will execute in fewer than $n - 1$ passes if the data is sorted to begin with, or if it falls into sorted order on an early pass.

3. Write a section of a BASIC program that will calculate and print the sum of the elements of double-subscripted array P that has three rows and five columns.

4. For double-subscripted array Q with four rows and two columns, write a FOR-NEXT loop that will calculate and print the sum of the elements in the second column.

5. For double-subscripted array R with 7 rows and 13 columns, write a FOR-NEXT loop that will calculate and print the sum of the elements in the fifth row.

6. One important property of any random number generator is that it should produce random numbers with equal likelihood. Write a BASIC program that rolls a six-sided die 6000 times. Your program should use a six-element array of counters to keep track of how many times each of the faces appears. After rolling the die, print the values of the six counters. If indeed the random numbers are being produced with equal likelihood, each of the faces should appear about 1000 times. Comment on the results you get when you run your program.

Appendix B

Number Systems

After reading this appendix you will understand:

1. What number systems are
2. What the base of a number system is
3. The decimal, binary, octal, and hexadecimal number systems
4. How the octal and hexadecimal number systems allow the convenient abbreviation of binary numbers
5. How to convert numbers from one base to another

Outline

Most of us are comfortable with performing arithmetic operations in the decimal number system. We use the **digits** 0, 1, 2, 3, 4, 5, 6, 7, 8, and 9. We are familiar with the notion of **decimal places**. We know that multiplying a number by 10 moves the decimal point one place to the right and dividing a number by 10 moves the decimal point one place to the left; thus, 14.73 times 10 is 147.3 and 14.73 divided by 10 is 1.473.

We know that when we write a decimal number, the position to the left of the decimal point is the ones or units position. The next position left is the tens position, the next is the hundreds position, the next is the thousands position, and so on, with each position farther left denoting a quantity 10 times larger than in the previous position. The first position to the right of the decimal point is the tenths position, the next position right is the hundredths position, the next is the thousandths position, and so on.

When we are adding two decimal numbers, we add them column by column from right to left. If the two digits in one column add to more than 9, that is, if the sum is a two-digit number, we write the rightmost digit at the bottom of the column and the leftmost digit is used as a **carry** to the next position to the left.

So we are quite familiar with certain concepts as they apply to decimal numbers, numbers that are based upon the number 10. We say that the **base** or **radix** of the decimal number system is 10. Other popular number systems are based on numbers other than 10. In this appendix we consider the **binary number system**, also called the **base 2 number system**; the **octal number system**, also called the **base 8 number system**; and the **hexadecimal number system**, also called the **base 16 number system**. These number systems are useful because they help express number manipulations in a manner more closely related to the internal operation of computers than the decimal number system does. We will consider only whole-number (integer) arithmetic.

Digit Value and Positional Value

As we have seen, when we write a number using the decimal number system, each digit has a **digit value** from 0 to 9. Each digit also has a **positional value** determined by how many places to the left or right of the decimal point the digit is written. The positional values of the decimal number system are shown in Figure B-1. Digit values and positional values for each number system depend on that number system's base. The digit values vary from zero to one less than the base, that is, base eight digits are 0 through 8-1 or 0, 1, 2, 3, 4, 5, 6, and 7, for examples. Positional values are increasing powers of the base as we move left and decreasing powers of the base as we move right.

Let's consider how digit values and positional values are used to form a number's true value. For example, the real decimal value of 547 is obtained by realizing that the 5 means 5 one hundreds (500), the 4 means 4 tens (40), and the 7 means 7 ones. So the value of 547 is the sum of 500, 40, and 7. This is expressed mathematically by using the decimal positional values as in Figure B-2. Most of us take this meaning for granted because we are so used to working with decimal numbers. But as we'll soon see, this kind of interpretation is a big help in understanding what numbers in other number systems really mean.

... 10^4	10^3	10^2	10^1	10^0
... 5th position	4th position	3rd position	2nd position	1st position
... 10000	1000	100	10	1

Figure B-1 The positional values of the decimal number system.

$$547 = 5 \times 10^2 + 4 \times 10^1 + 7 \times 10^0$$
$$= 500 \quad + \quad 40 \quad + \quad 7$$

Figure B-2 Using digit values and positional values to represent a decimal number.

The Binary Number System

In the binary, or base 2, number system, there are only two digits, namely 0 and 1. In fact, in any number system there are as many digits as the name of the base: Base 10 has 10 digits, base 2 has 2, base 8 has 8, and base 16 has 16. In each number system, the lowest digit is 0 and the highest is one less than the base itself. Thus, in the decimal number system the highest digit is 9, in the binary number system the highest digit is 1, in the octal number system the highest digit is 7. The same is true for the hexadecimal number system, but we'll postpone discussing a highest "digit" of 15 for the moment.

In the binary number system, counting proceeds as follows: 0, then 1, then, because we've reached the highest digit of the base, we must carry a 1, so the next number is 10, then 11, then a carry to the third position yielding 100. The first 17 binary numbers are shown in Figure B-3.

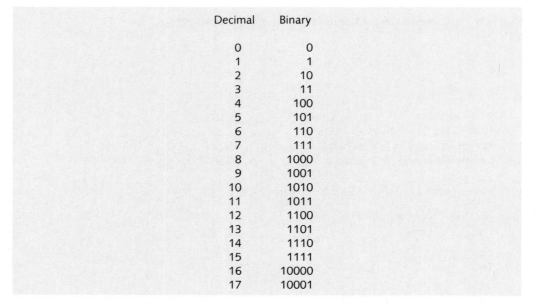

Decimal	Binary
0	0
1	1
2	10
3	11
4	100
5	101
6	110
7	111
8	1000
9	1001
10	1010
11	1011
12	1100
13	1101
14	1110
15	1111
16	10000
17	10001

Figure B-3 The first 17 binary numbers.

Now let's do some binary calculations.

```
  0        0        1        1
 +0       +1       +0       +1
 --       --       --       --
  0        1        1       10
```

The last answer requires two digits because 1 is the largest value that can be expressed in one digit in binary.

```
 101
+010
----
 111
```

That was straightforward because there were no carries.

```
 110
+011
----
1001
```

Here a carry was generated in the second column, and this forced a carry in the third column as well.

Subtraction without borrowing is straightforward:

```
 111
-101
----
 010
```

Subtraction of a larger digit from a smaller digit must, of course, involve 1 being subtracted from 0:

$$\begin{array}{r} 10 \\ -1 \\ \hline 1 \end{array}$$

In the first column, we attempt to subtract 1 from 0. This forces a borrow from the 1 in the second column. Since the second column in binary is the "two's column," we bring 2 to the first column, and subtract 1 from 2 to get the result of 1.

Let us convert 11011 (base 2) to decimal. We perform the decimal calculation

$$(1 \times 2^4) + (1 \times 2^3) + (0 \times 2^2) + (1 \times 2^1) + (1 \times 2^0)$$

$$\text{or } (1 \times 16) + (1 \times 8) + (0 \times 4) + (1 \times 2) + (1 \times 1)$$

which is 16 + 8 + 0 + 2 + 1 = 27 (base 10).

To convert from decimal to binary we make use of the binary positional values in Figure B-4.

2^7	2^6	2^5	2^4	2^3	2^2	2^1	2^0
8th position	7th position	6th position	5th position	4th position	3rd position	2nd position	1st position
128	64	32	16	8	4	2	1

Figure B-4 Positional values in the binary number system.

Let us convert 85 from decimal to binary. Because 85 is less than 128 and greater than 64, we see from Figure B-4 that the binary result will have seven digits. Dividing 64 into 85 yields 1 (the first digit of the result) and a remainder of 21; this simply says that 85 contains one 64. Because 32 does not divide evenly into 21, the second digit of the result is 0; this simply says that 21 contains no 32's. Dividing 16 into 21 yields 1 (the third digit of the result) and a remainder of 5. Because 8 doesn't divide into 5 evenly, the fourth digit of the result is 0. Dividing 4 into 5 yields 1 (the fifth digit of the result) and a remainder of 1. Because 2 doesn't divide into 1, the sixth digit of the result is zero. Finally, because 1 divides into 1, the seventh digit of the result is 1, and thus

$$85_{10} = 1010101_2$$

Converting from decimal to binary can be performed more mechanically by the technique of **remaindering.** We keep dividing the decimal number by 2, and we write a list of the remainders from right to left to form the binary number. Figure B-5 shows the conversion of 85 from decimal to binary using remaindering. (We leave it to the more mathematically inclined reader to determine why this technique works.)

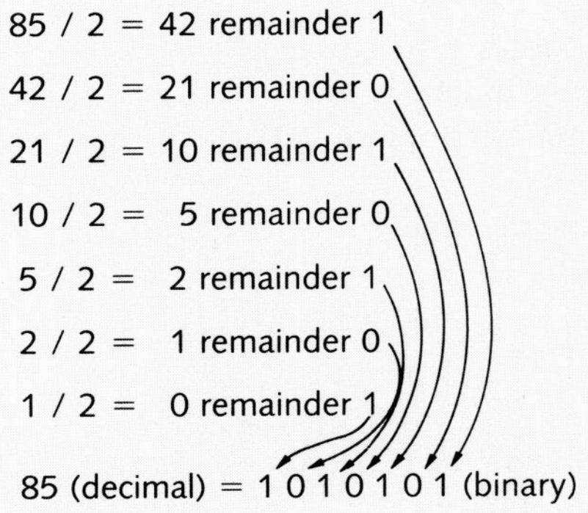

```
85 / 2 = 42 remainder 1
42 / 2 = 21 remainder 0
21 / 2 = 10 remainder 1
10 / 2 =  5 remainder 0
 5 / 2 =  2 remainder 1
 2 / 2 =  1 remainder 0
 1 / 2 =  0 remainder 1

85 (decimal) = 1 0 1 0 1 0 1 (binary)
```

Figure B-5 Decimal to binary conversion with the technique of remaindering.

The Octal Number System

In the octal, or base 8, number system there are eight digits, namely 0, 1, 2, 3, 4, 5, 6, and 7. When counting in octal, we keep adding one to a particular digit in a particular place until we get to 7. When we try to add one more to a 7, we then reset that position to 0 and carry a 1 to the next column to the left. The first 17 octal numbers are shown in Figure B-6.

Decimal	Octal
0	0
1	1
2	2
3	3
4	4
5	5
6	6
7	7
8	10
9	11
10	12
11	13
12	14
13	15
14	16
15	17
16	20
17	21

Figure B-6 A comparison of octal and decimal numbers.

The positional values of the octal number system are shown in Figure B-7.

...	8^4	8^3	8^2	8^1	8^0
...	5th position	4th position	3rd position	2nd position	1st position
...	4096	512	64	8	1

Figure B-7 The positional values of the octal number system.

Now let's do some octal calculations

```
  3  (octal)
 +7  (octal)
 --
 12  (octal)
```

For many people, the simplest way to view this is to handle the calculation in decimal: 7 + 3 is decimal 10, which is larger than the highest digit (7) allowed in an octal position. So we simply subtract the base (8) from the decimal sum (10), carry a 1 to the second column, and leave the difference, 2, in the first column. This gives the result octal 12. Because the positional value of the rightmost column is 1 and the positional value of the next column to the left is 8, we have (1 × 8) + (2 × 1), which is indeed decimal 10.

Now let's add some octal numbers that are each several digits long.

```
  234  (octal)
 +516  (octal)
 ----
  752  (octal)
```

Here we see that 4 + 6 is decimal 10, which is larger than the base eight. Subtract 8 from 10, leaving the difference of 2 in the first position, and carry a 1 to the second column. The second column now adds to 3 + 1 + the carry of 1 from the first column which equals 5. The third column is quite simply 5 + 2 = 7.

Subtraction in base 8 is similar to subtraction in base 10. Whenever we try to subtract a larger digit from a smaller digit, we must borrow from the column to the left. That reduces the column to the left by one and allows us to add 8 (the base) to the column in which we're doing the subtraction. Let's try some examples.

```
  7  (octal)
 -3  (octal)
 --
  4  (octal)
```

This calculation was straightforward because no borrowing was necessary. Let's try another.

```
  46  (octal)
 -23  (octal)
 ---
  23  (octal)
```

Here, too, no borrowing was necessary. Now try

```
  12  (octal)
 -6   (octal)
 ---
   4  (octal)
```

When we try to subtract 6 from 2 in the first column, we must borrow 1 from the second column and add 8 (the base) to the 2 in the first column. Therefore, we are really subtracting 6 from 10 to get the correct result of 4.

Now consider

```
 476  (octal)
-377  (octal)
----
  77  (octal)
```

In the first column, 7 is larger than 6, so we borrow 1 from the 7 in the second column and add 8 to the first column. The actual subtraction in the first column is now 14 − 7 or 7 (where the 14 is in decimal). In the second column we again must subtract 7 from 6. We borrow 1 from the 4 in the third column, and add 8 to the second column. So 14 − 7 in the second column is also 7 and the result is 77 (octal).

Now let's consider how to convert decimal numbers to octal numbers. In particular, we will convert 1647 (decimal) to base 8. We compare 1647 to the octal positional values for each column (Figure B-7). Because 1647 is smaller than 4096 and larger than 512, we know that it is equivalent to a four-digit octal number. We observe that 512 divides into 1647 three times with a remainder of 111, so the leftmost octal digit is a 3. Dividing 111 by 64 yields 1 (the next octal digit of the result) and a remainder of 47. Dividing 47 by 8 yields 5, the next octal digit of the result, and a remainder of 7. Finally, dividing 7 by 1 yields 7, the rightmost octal digit of the result. Thus we have the relationship

$$1647_{10} = 3157_8$$

To check this result we convert it back to decimal by performing the decimal calculation

$$(3 \times 8^3) + (1 \times 8^2) + (5 \times 8^1) + (7 \times 8^0)$$

$$\text{or } (3 \times 512) + (1 \times 64) + (5 \times 8) + (7 \times 1)$$

which is 1536 + 64 + 40 + 7 = 1647.

Converting from decimal to octal can also be performed by the technique of remaindering. We keep dividing the decimal number by 8, and we write a list of the remainders from right to left to form the octal number. Figure B-8 shows the conversion of 1647 from decimal to octal using remaindering.

1647 / 8 = 205 remainder 7
205 / 8 = 25 remainder 5
25 / 8 = 3 remainder 1
3 / 8 = 0 remainder 3

1647 (decimal) = 3 1 5 7 (octal)

Figure B-8 Decimal to octal conversion with the technique of remaindering.

The octal number system provides a convenient means for abbreviating binary numbers. To convert a number from binary to octal we begin at the right and take groups of three bits at a time assigning octal values as in Figure B-9.

Binary	Octal
000	0
001	1
010	2
011	3
100	4
101	5
110	6
111	7

Figure B-9 Octal equivalents of three-bit groups of binary digits.

For example, to convert the number 11010111101001100 to octal, we form the following groups of three bits each (the leftmost group is one bit short so we fill it with a leading 0)

011	010	111	101	001	100
3	2	7	5	1	4

Thus we have that

$$011010111101001100_2 = 327514_8$$

The reason for the ease of conversion back and forth between base 2 numbers and base 8 numbers is simply that 8 is a power of 2. Because 16 is also a power of 2, it is equally convenient to convert back and forth between binary numbers and hexadecimal numbers. Because of this ease of conversion, people who must deal with binary numbers will normally abbreviate them by writing their octal or hexadecimal equivalents. Hexadecimal is the more popular number system today because most computers now use 8-bit bytes; each byte can be abbreviated as two hexadecimal digits.

The Hexadecimal Number System

The hexadecimal, or base 16, number system is unique among the number systems we have considered in that it has 16 different digits, more than the decimal system has. Since we are familiar with the decimal system, it's hard to imagine digits other than 0 through 9. In fact, the hexadecimal system uses the letters A through F to represent the digits greater than 9 as in Figure B-10.

Decimal	Hexadecimal	Binary	Octal
0	0	0	0
1	1	1	1
2	2	10	2
3	3	11	3
4	4	100	4
5	5	101	5
6	6	110	6
7	7	111	7
8	8	1000	10
9	9	1001	11
10	A	1010	12
11	B	1011	13
12	C	1100	14
13	D	1101	15
14	E	1110	16
15	F	1111	17
16	10	10000	20
17	11	10001	21

Figure B-10 A comparison of the key number systems discussed in this appendix.

So, to "think hexadecimal," we must equate A with 10, B with 11, C with 12, D with 13, E with 14, and F with 15. This can be frustrating.

Let's consider some arithmetic in hexadecimal.

F − E is 1

D − 9 is 4

E − 1 is D

The key to simplifying these calculations is to think in decimal.

```
 EEFD
-DCBA
-----
 1243
```

That's interesting! We can subtract two quantities full of letters and get a quantity full of numbers! Many people find this rather awkward.

Addition without carries is straightforward:

$$\begin{array}{r} 3456 \\ +6789 \\ \hline 9BDF \end{array}$$

Addition with carries causes us to subtract the base and carry a 1:

$$\begin{array}{r} 6B9D \\ +32A5 \\ \hline 9E42 \end{array}$$

Now let us consider how to convert hexadecimal numbers to decimal. To convert 7B5A (base 16) to decimal, for example, we perform the decimal calculation

$$(7 \times 16^3) + (11 \times 16^2) + (5 \times 16^1) + (10 \times 16^0)$$

$$\text{or } (7 \times 4096) + (11 \times 256) + (5 \times 16) + (10 \times 1)$$

which is 28672 + 2816 + 80 + 10 = 31578. Therefore

$$7B5A_{16} = 31578_{10}$$

To convert from decimal to hexadecimal, we make use of the hexadecimal position values. Let us convert 5214 (base 10) to hexadecimal. The hexadecimal positional values are shown in Figure B-11.

16^4	16^3	16^2	16^1	16^0
1st position	2nd position	3rd position	4th position	5th position
65536	4096	256	16	1

Figure B-11 The positional values of the hexadecimal number system.

Because 5214 is smaller than 65536 and larger than 4096, we know that its hexadecimal equivalent has four digits. Since 4096 divides into 5214 once with a remainder of 1118, the first digit of the hexadecimal result is 1. Dividing 1118 by 256 yields a quotient of 4 (the second digit of the result) and a remainder of 94. Dividing 16 into 94 yields a quotient of 5 (the third digit of the result) and a remainder of 14. Of course, 14 divided by 1 is 14 with no remainder, so the last digit of the result is E, the hexadecimal equivalent of 14. Therefore

$$5214_{10} = 145E_{16}$$

To check this we convert 145E (base 16) back to decimal by performing the decimal calculation

$$(1 \times 16^3) + (4 \times 16^2) + (5 \times 16^1) + (14 \times 16^0)$$

$$\text{or } (1 \times 4096) + (4 \times 256) + (5 \times 16) + (14 \times 1)$$

which is 4096 + 1024 + 80 + 14 = 5214.

Converting from decimal to hexadecimal can be performed more mechanically by the technique of remaindering. We keep dividing the decimal number by 16, and we write a list of the remainders from right to left to form the hexadecimal number. Figure B-12 shows the conversion of 5214 from decimal to hexadecimal using remaindering.

```
5214 / 16 = 325 remainder 14 (hexadecimal E)
 325 / 16 =  20 remainder  5
  20 / 16 =   1 remainder  4
   1 / 16 =   0 remainder  1

5214 (decimal) = 1 4 5 E (hexadecimal)
```

Figure B-12 Decimal to hexadecimal conversion with the technique of remaindering.

Hexadecimal is also a useful means of abbreviating binary numbers. We group binary digits (from the right of the number) in fours and, if necessary, fill the leftmost group with leading zeros. Then each group of four binary digits is replaced with its hexadecimal equivalent. For example, to convert 101101011110100001 to hexadecimal, we separate the number into groups of four bits each as follows:

10 1101 0111 1010 0001

We then fill the leftmost group with leading zeros and convert as follows:

```
0010 1101 0111 1010 0001
  2    D    7    A    1
```

Thus

$$101101011110100001_2 = 2D7A1_{16}$$

To convert hexadecimal to binary we simply replace each hexadecimal digit with its corresponding four-bit binary equivalent as in

$$B3F_{16} = 101100111111_2$$

because B (hexadecimal) is 1011 (binary), 3 (hexadecimal) is 0011 (binary), and F (hexadecimal) is 1111 (binary).

Self-Review Exercises 

Matching

Next to the term in column A, place the letter of the statement in column B that best describes it.

Column A	Column B
1. Octal number system	A. Positional values in decimal number system
2. Hexadecimal number system	B. 16
3. Binary number system	C. Group bits in threes
4. Ones, tens, hundreds, thousands, and so on	D. 4
5. Number of digits in hexadecimal number system	E. Uses letters for certain digits
6. Highest digit in octal number system	F. Replace each digit with four bits
7. Key to simplifying conversions between binary and octal	G. 7
8. Number of digits in octal equivalent of 4095 (base 10)	H. Base 8
9. Number of digits in binary equivalent of 27 (base 10)	I. 5
10. Key to simplifying conversions from hexadecimal to binary	J. Highest digit is 1

Fill-in-the-Blanks

Fill in the blanks in each of the following:

1. The number 68470 is a valid number in the ______ and ______ number systems discussed in this appendix.

2. The equivalent of a given decimal number would have the most digits in the ______ number system.

3. The equivalent of a given decimal number would have the fewest digits in the ______ number system discussed in this appendix.

4. In the base 7 number system there are ______ different digits and the highest digit is ______.

5. The ______ and ______ number systems discussed in this appendix provide effective means of abbreviating binary numbers because their bases are ______.

6. (True/False) Two hexadecimal numbers containing only the digits 0 through 9 may, when added together, produce a result containing only the digits A through F.

7. When converting a decimal number to an octal number, how can we quickly determine the number of octal digits that will be in the result? ______.

8. The positional value of the sixth position to the left of the "binary point" in a binary number is ______.

9. The carry generated by 7 + 7 in the hexadecimal number system is ______.

10. In subtracting one octal number from another, when we borrow 1 from the column to the left of the column in which we are performing the subtraction, we add ______ to the number at the top of the column in which we are performing the subtraction.

Answers to Self-Review Exercises

Matching: 1 H, 2 E, 3 J, 4 A, 5 B, 6 G, 7 C, 8 D, 9 I, 10 F

Fill-in-the-Blanks:

1. decimal, hexadecimal
2. binary
3. hexadecimal
4. 7, 6
5. octal, hexadecimal, powers of 2
6. True
7. List the octal positional values in decimal. Compare the decimal number to these. Find the first octal positional value (from the right) larger than the number being converted. All positions to the right of this will be used. If the number being converted is equal to one of the octal positional values, this digit will be 1 and all the digits to its right will be zeros.
8. 2 to the 5th power, or 32
9. zero (there is no carry; 7 + 7 is simply E)
10. 8

Problems 

1. Draw a chart comparing the four number systems discussed in this appendix. For each number system show:

A. its base
B. its radix
C. its lowest digit
D. its highest digit
E. its number of digits
F. one key fact that best describes why that number system is important.

2. Distinguish between digit value and positional value.

3. $1101011_2 = ?_{10}$

4. $97_{10} = ?_2$

5. $47_8 + 54_8 = ?_8$

6. $164_8 - 135_8 = ?_8$

7. $432_{10} = ?_8$

8. $432_8 = ?_{10}$

9. $10111010101100_2 = ?_8$

10. $\mathrm{EFAB}_{16} - \mathrm{ABCD}_{16} = ?_{16}$

11. $\mathrm{CD52}_{16} = ?_{10}$

12. $4782_{10} = ?_{16}$

13. $10111010110111_2 = ?_{16}$

14. $\mathrm{EF2}_{16} = ?_2$

Appendix C

The Computing Profession

After reading this appendix you will understand:

1. What kinds of opportunities are open to people considering careers in computing
2. The educational requirements and opportunities for various careers in computing
3. The purposes and objectives of the major professional organizations in computing
4. The various certification programs available in computing to establish professional competence
5. Some of the key employers in the computing field

Outline

- Computing Careers
  - Computer Retailing
  - Computing as an Auxiliary Discipline
  - Computer Applications Specialists
- Education
- Professional Organizations
  - American Federation of Information Processing Societies (AFIPS)
  - Association for Computing Machinery (ACM)
  - Data Processing Management Association (DPMA)
  - IEEE Computer Society
- Professional Certification
- Professional Conferences and Trade Shows
- Seeking Employment
  - The Résumé and Cover Letter
  - The Electronic Sweat Shop
  - A Sampling of Employers
    - Computer Manufacturers
    - Software Developers
    - Computer Retailers
    - Management Consulting
    - Computer Services Organizations
    - Peripheral Equipment Manufacturers
    - Personal Computers
    - Artificial Intelligence and Expert Systems
    - Office Automation
    - Japanese Computer Companies
    - Chip Manufacturers
    - Data Communications
    - CAD/CAM
    - Major Banks and Insurance Companies
    - High-Tech Companies
    - Trade Publications

The computer field didn't exist in the early 1940s, yet incredibly, within a decade from now, more than 2 million people will be employed in the computer industry in the United States alone.

In this appendix we describe the computing profession, how to enter it, the kind of education that is needed for various computing careers, how to advance within the field, and so on. If you are looking for an exciting field with unlimited potential for growth and innovation, computing may be right for you.

Computing careers, however, are not without their difficulties. Many companies with bright prospects have seen their fortunes change for the worse almost overnight. The stress caused by deadline pressures and long hours in this highly competitive industry may account for the fact that computing people have one of the highest divorce rates among career professionals (second only to air traffic controllers, according to one study).

Admission to the field has become more competitive in recent years. There is tremendous interest in computing among people currently choosing their careers. University programs in computer science are often heavily oversubscribed, with many degree programs requiring a competitive admissions process even after the student has been admitted to the university. Professional organizations are pushing for demanding and challenging degree requirements. Professional certification programs are receiving increasing interest, especially from large companies that employ significant numbers of computing professionals.

Competition among companies for experienced computer people is fierce. One company recently offered $2000 in cash and a fully equipped personal computer to anyone who supplied the name of a computer professional who was eventually hired and completed three months' work. Another company advertised recently to potential hirees that "you will receive a bonus paid upon employment equal to ten percent of your starting salary if you are hired as a result of this advertisement."

Computing Careers

Throughout the text we have touched upon dozens of career opportunities in computing. Some of these require only informal on-the-job training. Others require two-year associate's degrees or four-year bachelor's degrees. For some of the ultra-high-tech jobs, master's degrees and even Ph.D.s are necessary.

Jobs for **keypunch operators** and **data entry clerks** in general are on the decline because of advances in source data automation and direct data entry.

The need for **computer operators** to run computer systems is expected to more than double over the next decade. In fact, the Bureau of Labor Statistics rates computer operations along with programming and systems analysis as three of the nation's fastest growing fields.

Word processing specialists are rapidly replacing typists. But one person working efficiently on a word processor can do the job of several typists, so there will be a net reduction in typing-related jobs, while the technical training required for such office clerical jobs will increase greatly.

Computer engineers who design computer systems generally have bachelor's or master's degrees in electrical engineering or computer engineering. These people are being aggressively recruited, and the prospects for such careers remain bright for years to come. Computer engineers are primarily hardware specialists, but they also take many software courses.

EDP managers control complete data processing installations. They generally have dual backgrounds with management degrees and concentrations or degrees in computing.

Database managers control their organizations' databases. Their responsibilities are substantial, and they are among the best paid computing professionals. They generally have bachelor's degrees in computer science and related fields.

Telecommunications specialists, also called **data communications specialists**, are concerned with the data communications networks of organizations. They need to be familiar with computer hardware and software, and communications hardware and software. A bachelor's degree in electrical engineering is a particularly appropriate credential for this field; a degree in computer science with some hardware courses is also appropriate.

Jobs for factory workers who assemble computer systems are expected to decline as the use of robotics and flexible automation increases. But at least one major study has estimated that robotics may generate twice as many jobs as it eliminates. Unfortunately, the workers whose jobs are eliminated are not likely to be the beneficiaries of the newly created jobs in designing, programming, and servicing industrial robots.

Sales and marketing specialists have traditionally been among the highest paid computing professionals by a very wide margin. But these statistics can be deceiving because they tend to measure the successes of the survivors; many people who set out on careers in this field often drop out quickly because of the incredibly competitive environment.

A large and growing market exists for **customer support specialists**. These people assist customers in learning and using hardware and software systems. This type of work can be very rewarding for computing professionals who are people-oriented and who are more concerned with the application of existing computer systems than with the development of new ones.

For the free-spirited person who doesn't want to be tied down to a large company, a career as an **independent computer consultant** may be ideal. Consultants usually have many years of valuable experience, and are essentially their own employers. They sell their expertise in a given area to companies that lack such expertise or have temporary surges in needs because of vacations, illness, or rapid growth. Most commonly, independent computer consultants serve as contract programmers. Some consultants prefer very flexible hours. Some like to work for many companies at once on different kinds of projects, while others prefer to work on one project full time until it is completed. Consultants often get very high hourly rates, but it is important to remember that they must pay for their own benefits, including vacation time, and that a significant portion of their time may be devoted to tracking down new business. When times are good consultants can do very well indeed, but when companies pull back, consultants may be the first people affected. If you want to be your own boss, consulting may be for you. Many consulting enterprises often turn into full-scale companies. Information about independent consulting careers may be obtained from:

Independent Computer Consultants Association
P.O. Box 27412
St. Louis, MO 63141

EDP auditors are concerned with certifying that computer systems are operating properly and without fraud. Their task is similar to that of auditors examining the financial records of a firm. In fact, the large accounting firms that specialize in financial auditing are among the leading firms in the field of EDP auditing as well. EDP auditors generally have dual backgrounds in which they have concentrated their efforts in computing as well as in business operations. A bachelor's degree in management, accounting, or business administration, with a concentration in computing, is an appropriate background for a starting EDP auditor.

There is a fine market for **data processing educators** and **computer science educators**, especially in the colleges and universities. Fewer than 300 Ph.D.s in computer science are being produced annually in the United States, and many of them are enticed into high-paying industry positions. In fact, one major research company is rumored to have a standing offer to hire any fresh computer science Ph.D.

Computer Retailing

Until the personal computer revolution caught on in the late 1970s, computers were simply too expensive to be sold in retail stores. Today thousands of retail stores sell modestly priced personal computers, software, books, magazines, supplies, service, and educational services. Tens of thousands of people are employed in this rapidly growing industry.

Working in a computer retail store is a marvelous way to enter the computer field. You'll spend a great deal of time familiarizing yourself with the latest computer hardware and software packages. You'll meet many interesting people with a wide variety of business computing needs. You'll become adept at configuring computer hardware and software for small businesses. You'll design communications solutions for these companies. And you'll become familiar with the complex problems of administering a business. You may eventually decide to open your own computer store.

Some computer stores are located in suburban shopping areas; these stores tend to have a clientele interested in home computers, game playing, and small business systems. Other computer chains have focused their efforts on selling substantial business systems for thousands of dollars; these stores are generally located in financial districts in major population centers.

Retailing is a hard business that requires long hours, many of which must be spent dealing with problems of customer dissatisfaction and irritation. It takes a special kind of person to be successful in this business, someone who particularly enjoys dealing with the general public.

If you think you are interested in computer retailing, then you should talk with people who are in the field and working at computer stores. If you want to own or operate a franchised store, you should contact some of the leading national chains such as ComputerLand, Businessland, and MicroAge Computer Stores.

The following publications are among those distributed free to qualified professionals in the field. Try to obtain several recent issues of these publications and read them to get a sense of what's going on in computer retailing:

Computer Retail News
CMP Publications, Inc.
111 East Shore Road
Manhasset, NY 11030

Micro Marketworld
Circulation Department
375 Cochituate Road
Box 875
Framingham, MA 01701

Many of the national computer chains advertise regularly in the business opportunities sections of Sunday newspapers. For more information about computer retailing, contact:

Computer Retailers Association
634 South Central Expressway
Richardson, TX 75080

Western Computer Dealers Association
2233 El Camino Real
Palo Alto, CA 94306

Computing as an Auxiliary Discipline

One really exciting aspect of the computer field is that computers are applicable to virtually every other field of endeavor. Thus, if you are already committed to a career in another field but you also have a strong interest in computing, you may be able to combine both your interests quite easily.

This is actually much easier than it may seem. The reason is that educational institutions have been encouraging the integration of computers into all aspects of their curricula. So, as a chemistry student you'll probably work with computer models, as a finance student you'll probably work with electronic spreadsheets, as a mechanical engineering student you'll probably work with CAD/CAM systems, and so on.

Computer Applications Specialists

There is a great need for people who are thoroughly familiar with a wide range of software packages and the hardware systems that may be used to solve business problems. These people are called **computer applications specialists.**

Education

Students may take bachelor's, master's, and even Ph.D. degrees in computer science, management information systems, and related fields at colleges and universities throughout the world. Two-year certificate programs are normally focused on programming, computer servicing, or other specialty areas. Adult education and continuing education courses are extremely popular. State-of-the-art professional development seminars are widely subscribed, with fees as high as $500 per day not uncommon.

The publishing industry has responded with a deluge of new books and dozens of magazines and newspapers in the last several years alone. Bookstores now devote major shelf space to computer titles. Newspapers and magazines run regular columns on computers. TV specials frequently discuss developments in the field. Public television networks have offered complete courses in computer literacy. Many publishers have developed interactive computer software to teach computer literacy.

Many people already employed in the field are reluctant to go back to

school. They feel that they simply can't afford the time commitment. For these people, educational institutions are now developing educational software based on the use of the laser videodisks with personal computers. Complete degree programs will soon be available for home study. These will offer tremendous opportunities to people who can't afford the time to go to a university, cannot commute because of some physical handicap, or are simply not located near a university offering appropriate programs. An additional benefit is that students will be more inclined to interact with teaching machines in a one-on-one environment in the privacy of their own homes. Interaction is severely limited by large class sizes in universities, and by fear of embarrassment if the student supplies a wrong answer or asks a silly question.

The computer field evolves so quickly that it is essential to have a firm foundation in the basics and to continue your education while working. Some companies have made arrangements with major universities to have complete part-time degree programs presented on-site for the convenience of their employees. The availability of programs like these is often an indication of a very high-quality employer. Many companies offer full or partial reimbursement of tuition expenses for taking job-related courses. Look for companies with established training programs. Remember that the computer field changes very quickly, so it is necessary for you to continue your education even after you complete your formal schooling.

There has been a proliferation of so-called data processing schools. These schools generally offer highly concentrated programs in programming, computer repair, and electronics. A list of such programs and some important facts about the schools that offer them may be obtained from:

The National Association of Trade and Technical Schools
2021 K Street, N.W.
Washington, DC 20006

Write to the professional associations discussed later in this chapter for a list of colleges offering bachelor's, master's, and Ph.D. programs in computer-related fields.

Write to the American Association of Colleges and Schools of Business (AACSB) for a list of business schools throughout the country that offer concentrations and majors in computer-related disciplines:

The American Association of Colleges and Schools of Business
605 Old Ballas Road
St. Louis, MO 63141

If you are interested in the relationship of computer technology to education, you might contact:

Association for Educational Data Systems
1201 16th Street, N.W.
Washington, DC 20036

At least one institution of higher learning has been spawned by the computer field. Dr. An Wang, the founder of Wang Laboratories, a leading computer company specializing in office automation systems, perceived the need for highly skilled software professionals. He created the Wang Institute in Massachusetts to offer a master's degree program in **software engineering**, a field concerned with the development of correct, reliable, and maintainable software systems. To date, the Wang Institute remains highly focused in its goal of producing a small number of carefully educated software specialists each year. A catalog of its programs and an application for admission may be obtained from:

The Wang Institute of Graduate Studies
Tyng Road
Tyngsboro, MA 01879

Professional Organizations

As the field has matured, a number of professional organizations have developed to help set standards of professional competence and ethics for the industry. Some of these organizations are oriented toward commercial endeavors, while others are more concerned with academic research. We have included addresses so that the reader may write to these groups and obtain more detailed information.

American Federation of Information Processing Societies (AFIPS)

AFIPS is a blanket organization to which various computer professional organizations subscribe. It supervises the annual convention activities in which the various organizations participate. Its stated goals are to represent U.S. information processing societies in international organizations, provide leadership and coordinate joint activities among AFIPS constituent societies, promote information exchange in the information processing field, conduct research and development activities in the information processing field, and provide the general public with reliable information on information processing and its progress.

The organizations that belong to AFIPS are:

American Society for Information Science
American Statistical Association
Association for Computational Linguistics
Association for Computing Machinery
Association for Educational Data Systems
Data Processing Management Association
Institute of Electrical and Electronics Engineers
Instrument Society of America

Society for Computer Simulation
Society for Industrial and Applied Mathematics
Society for Information Display

AFIPS may be reached at:

AFIPS Headquarters
1899 Preston White Drive
Reston, VA 22091

Ask for their latest publications catalog. For history buffs, AFIPS publishes the *Annals of the History of Computing.*

Association for Computing Machinery (ACM)

The ACM is one of the key academic societies whose main goal is to foster research in computer science. It is very involved in curriculum issues for the university programs in computer science. It publishes several research journals read widely by practicing professionals. The ACM sponsors an annual conference (fall) and its Computer Science Conference (winter). Its most widely read publication is *Communications of the ACM*, published monthly. ACM and several of the other professional societies we discuss here offer student memberships at discount rates. Contact the ACM at:

Association for Computing Machinery
11 West 42nd Street
New York, NY 10036

Data Processing Management Association (DPMA)

The DPMA is primarily oriented toward people who are concerned with the commercial applications of computing. It is very concerned with professional competence and has fostered the development of various certification programs (now administered by the Institute for the Certification of Computer Professionals) that we discuss later in this appendix. Its major publication is *Data Management* magazine. Contact the DPMA at:

Data Processing Management Association
505 Busse Highway
Park Ridge, IL 60068

IEEE Computer Society

The Institute of Electrical and Electronics Engineers created the **IEEE Computer Society** in recognition of the importance of electrical engineering to the development and continuing evolution of modern computers. It, too, is academic in its orientation and has a series of magazines and journals primarily of academic interest. It also offers economical student memberships. Its major publication, *Computer*, includes tutorial and survey papers covering hardware and software design and applications. Contact the IEEE at:

IEEE Computer Society
10662 Los Vaqueros Circle
Los Alamitos, CA 90720

Professional Certification

The DPMA has fostered the development of several certification programs in its efforts to help improve the image of the profession. Its efforts have resulted in several of the major computer societies cooperating in the formation of the Institute for the Certification of Computer Professionals to administer these certification programs. Two of the most popular certifications offered are the **Certificate in Data Processing** (CDP) and the **Certificate in Computer Programming** (CCP). Exams for each of these are administered on a regular basis at locations throughout the world. These certifications are of interest primarily to practicing computer professionals who work in commercial data processing environments, particularly in large companies such as banks and insurance companies.

The CDP exam contains five major sections including:

1. Hardware
2. Software
3. Systems analysis and design
4. Management
5. Quantitative methods

Texts like *Computers and Data Processing* are generally appropriate for preparing for the first three sections. The other two sections require preparation in management principles and mathematics.

The exam for the Certificate in Computer Programming is designed to measure knowledge in business, scientific, and applications programming.

To receive copies of the examination announcements and study guides for the CDP and CCP exams, write to:

Institute for the Certification of Computer Professionals
35 East Wacker Drive
Chicago, IL 60601

These brochures include applications; test site lists; exam outlines; suggested readings; and the codes of ethics, conduct, and good practice. Ask for an order form for the *CDP Instruction Manual* and the *CCP Instruction Manual.*

Professional Conferences and Trade Shows

The computer industry holds some of the largest professional conferences and trade shows in the United States each year. There are several notable conferences, including the **National Computer Conference** (NCC), held in late spring or early summer, and the **Office Automation Conference** (OAC), held in midwinter. There are also hundreds of smaller regional conferences and shows. Many computer professionals regularly attend related conferences such as the **Consumer Electronics Show** that feature many computer-controlled electronic devices and appliances.

To get an idea of the significance of these events, consider that the National Computer Conference held in Las Vegas in 1984 was the largest conference in the history of Las Vegas. To put this in perspective, Las Vegas is the second largest convention center in the United States (Chicago is the largest). At this Las Vegas NCC more than 700 companies exhibited in an exhibition space of more than 380,000 square feet! Information about the NCC and OAC conferences can be obtained from:

AFIPS Headquarters
1899 Preston White Drive
Reston, VA 22091

Seeking Employment

The prospects in the computer field are very bright for experienced people; the field is somewhat saturated at the entry level.

Many employment agencies specialize in high-tech jobs in general, and in computing jobs in particular. Their services are primarily oriented toward experienced people, but agencies are often delighted to mail their brochures to entry-level people in the hopes of establishing a relationship for the future. Write to each of these employment agencies (as well as others in your area), requesting their literature on computing careers:

Source EDP
P. O. Box 7100
Mountain View, CA 94039

Computer Assisted Recruitment International, Inc.
1501 Woodfield Road
Schaumberg, IL 60195

Career System
Corporate Service Division
1675 Palm Beach Lakes Boulevard
West Palm Beach, FL 33401

Job hunting in this high-tech field has itself gone high tech; many computerized database services are offered that enable employers and job seekers to list their requirements and capabilities on line for people to interrogate with personal computers. The subscriber pays a fixed rate per hour to search through the on-line information. Some people like this because it is much more private than walking into an employment agency and declaring that you are unhappy with your present job. Many small companies that can't afford the fees charged by professional employment agencies find that services like these may give them a chance to recruit top candidates at more modest costs.

Listing yourself with an on-line service may be done blind—you don't have to reveal your name. Instead you state your experience, education, work record and job qualifications, and the computer matches you with various job descriptions supplied by employers.

One of these on-line services is

Connexions
55 Wheeler Street
Cambridge, MA 02138

Connexions contains job listings by companies seeking experienced personnel. It allows the user to dial in and examine job listings anonymously. You can create your own resume on line by responding to a series of questions. You can restrict access to information about yourself to selected companies.

Many on-line services offer a brief free session to help you decide if you want to become a subscriber. But remember that most of these services and employment agencies are for experienced people. If you are looking for your first position out of school, you may be better off dealing directly with potential employers. Another of these on-line services is:

The Human Resources Selection Network, Inc.
20 Park Plaza
Boston, MA 02116

You may find other such services in your own vicinity.

Some companies arrange job fairs and open houses where you can meet with representatives of dozens of employers. One company specializing in this field is:

Multi-Corp Open Houses
A Lendman Company
374 Millburn Avenue
Millburn, NJ 07041

Watch the help-wanted sections and the financial pages of your newspapers for information on upcoming job fairs in your area.

The Résumé and Cover Letter

When you are ready to seek employment you should prepare two documents for distribution to potential employers. First, you must prepare a high-quality **résumé** listing some basic facts about yourself, including your educational background and work experience. Many professional résumé services are available to help you write your résumé and then perhaps even typeset it so it appears professionally printed. If you are just getting started in the field, a typeset résumé may be overkill; it may be better to prepare a neatly typed and informal resume. *Hint*: Put a fresh ribbon in your typewriter or computer printer and use high-quality rag bond paper.

You should also prepare a **cover letter** that introduces you to potential employers and states that your résumé is enclosed for their consideration. The cover letter should be brief and should express your enthusiasm for interviewing with the company. *Hint*: Provide phone numbers where you can be reached at various times. Personnel people are busy and may be flooded with résumés. If you provide this information, it will be easier for them to reach you; this just might help you get that return phone call. If you think this isn't important, then consider that several major computer manufacturers each get more than 10,000 résumés per month in the mail! And of course you want yours to percolate to the top of the pile!

We can't emphasize enough the importance of writing an effective résumé and keeping it up-to-date so that you can respond quickly to job opportunities. One excellent brochure on résumé preparation is:

Résumé Workbook & Career Planner
Scientific Placement, Inc.
14925 Memorial Drive
P.O. Box 19949
Houston, TX 77224

One problem you may face is that the computer field is drawing huge numbers of people who want to "get into computers." This has created a glut of so-called entry-level people, so breaking into the computer field may be harder than you have been led to believe. You may have to accept something less than your ideal job and salary in order to get started. But the market for experienced people is quite good and the prospects are for it to remain so for many years, so it may be worth your while to start modestly.

One problem this causes is that people tend to start with one company and leave as soon as they become experienced. Job hopping has always been a serious problem in the computer industry. Because of the continuing shortage of skilled personnel, it is not uncommon for people to change jobs every few years and receive substantial raises with each move. Keep in mind, however, that many employers will show little interest in people who tend to change jobs frequently.

The Electronic Sweat Shop

There are many virtues to work-at-home programs for handicapped people, parents raising children, moonlighters, and others. Many people work for one company full time and moonlight for others part time. But work at home has its problems. The unions feel that people who work at home don't have the opportunities to organize and bargain collectively with their employers for improved circumstances. One prominent sociologist has labeled these home work environments **electronic sweat shops**. Current indications, however, are that the vast majority of home workers are pleased with their job arrangements.

A Sampling of Employers

There are many thousands of places to seek interesting and exciting employment in the computer field. In this section we present the names and addresses of a small number of prominent companies and their respective fields of endeavor. We do this solely to help you connect with the field. The omission of a company from our limited list means nothing. You should write to and interview with other companies you read about as well as companies that are recommended to you by friends, relatives, and associates.

We have limited the list mostly to computer companies and computer-related enterprises. You should keep in mind that tens of thousands of companies outside the computer field also offer fine career opportunities in computing. These companies normally advertise in the help-wanted sections of Sunday newspapers.

If you are nearing the completion of your schooling and preparing to start searching for a job, you might send letters to a large number of companies in your area asking for general information about working for them. Many of these companies will send you interesting information that will help you refine your job search. When you are ready to apply to specific companies, you should send each one a cover letter and a résumé. For each of the companies mentioned in this section, you should direct all correspondence to the director of personnel.

We cannot guarantee the accuracy of the names, addresses, and phone numbers in this section. Nor can we guarantee that the companies will respond when you write or call. Our purpose is simply to provide you with information that will help you make contacts that may prove helpful. We hope you'll find this information useful.

Computer Manufacturers

AT&T Information Systems
1 Speedwell Avenue
Morristown, NJ 07960

Burroughs Corporation
Burroughs Place
Detroit, MI 48232

Control Data Corporation
8100 34th Avenue, South
Minneapolis, MN 55440

Cray Research, Inc.
608 Second Avenue, South
Minneapolis, MN 55402

Data General
4400 Computer Drive
Westboro, MA 01581

Datapoint Corporation
9725 Datapoint Drive
San Antonio, TX 78284

Digital Equipment Corporation
146 Main Street
Maynard, MA 01754

Honeywell Information Systems, Inc.
200 Smith Street
Waltham, MA 02154

International Business Machines Corporation
1133 Westchester Avenue
White Plains, NY 10601

NCR Corporation
1700 South Patterson Boulevard
Dayton, OH 45479

Nixdorf Computer Corporation
300 Third Avenue
Waltham, MA 02154

Prime Computer
Prime Park
Natick, MA 01760

Sperry Univac
Division of Sperry Corporation
P.O. Box 500
Blue Bell, PA 19424

Tandem Computers, Inc.
19333 Vallco Parkway
Cupertino, CA 95014

Software Developers

Applied Data Research, Inc.
Route 206 and Orchard Road
CN-8, Princeton, NJ 08540

Ashton-Tate
10150 West Jefferson Boulevard
Culver City, CA 90230

Cincom Systems, Inc.
2300 Montana Avenue
Cincinnati, OH 45211

Computer Sciences Corporation
System Sciences Division
4600 Powder Mill Road
Bettsville, MD 20705

Cullinet Software, Inc.
400 Blue Hill Drive
Westwood, MA 02090

Digital Research, Inc.
160 Central
Pacific Grove, CA 93950

Integrated Software Systems Corporation
10505 Sorrento Valley Boulevard
San Diego, CA 92121

Lotus Development Corporation
161 First Street
Cambridge, MA 02142

Management Science of America, Inc.
3445 Peachtree Road, N.E.
Atlanta, GA 30326

McCormack & Dodge
1225 Worcester Road
Natick, MA 01760

Microsoft
10700 Northup Way
Bellevue, WA 98004

Pansophic Systems, Inc.
709 Enterprise Drive
Oak Brook, IL 60521

Softech, Inc.
460 Totten Pond Road
Waltham, MA 02154

Software AG of North America, Inc.
11800 Sunrise Valley Drive
Reston, VA 22091

Software Arts, Inc.
27 Mica Lane
Wellesley, MA 02181

University Computing Company
UCCEL Tower
Exchange Park
Dallas, TX 75235

VisiCorp
2895 Zanker Road
San Jose, CA 95134

Computer Retailers

Businessland, Inc.
Center Development Team
Corporate Headquarters
3600 Stevens Creek Boulevard
San Jose, CA 95117
(800)228-BUSL

ComputerLand
(800)772-3545 (California)

MicroAge Computer Stores
1457 West Alameda
Tempe, AZ 85282

Programs Unlimited Computer Centers
125 South Service Road
Jericho, NY 11753

Management Consulting

Arthur Andersen & Company
Management Information Consulting Division
33 West Monroe Street
Chicago, IL 60603

Bolt Beranek and Newman, Inc.
10 Moulton Street
Cambridge, MA 02238

Coopers & Lybrand
Management Consulting Services
1251 Avenue of the Americas
New York, NY 10020

System Development Corporation
2500 Colorado Avenue
Santa Monica, CA 90406

Computer Services Organizations

Boeing Computer Services
7980 Gallows Court
Vienna, VA 22180

CompuServe
Network Services Division
5000 Arlington Centre Boulevard
Columbus, OH 43220

D & B Computing Services
Dun & Bradstreet Corporation
187 Danbury Road
Wilton, CT 06897

Electronic Data Systems Corporation
7171 Forrest Lane
Dallas, TX 75230

General Electric Information Services Company
1221 Avenue of the Americas
New York, NY 10020

McDonnell Douglas Automation Company
McDonnell Boulevard
St. Louis, MO 63166

Tymshare, Inc.
20705 Valley Green Drive
Cupertino, CA 95014

Xerox Computer Services
5310 Beethoven Street
Los Angeles, CA 90066

Peripheral Equipment Manufacturers

Anderson Jacobson, Inc.
521 Charcot Avenue
San Jose, CA 95131

Applied Digital Data Systems, Inc.
A Subsidiary of NCR Corporation
100 Marcus Boulevard
Hauppauge, NY 11788

Centronics Corporation
1 Wall Street
Hudson, NH 03051

Computer Identics
The Bar Code Company
5 Shawmut Road
Canton, MA 02021

Dataproducts Corporation
6200 Canoga Avenue
Woodland Hills, CA 91365

ITT Courier Terminal Systems
P.O. Box 29039
Phoenix, AZ 85038

Kurzweil Computer Products Corporation
185 Albany Street
Cambridge, MA 02139

Lear Siegler, Inc.
Data Products Division
901 East Ball Road
Anaheim, CA 92805

Mohawk Data Sciences Corporation
7 Century Drive
Parsippany, NJ 07054

Perkin-Elmer Corporation
Data Systems Group
2 Crescent Place
Oceanport, NJ 07757

Qume Corporation
A Subsidiary of ITT
2350 Qume Drive
San Jose, CA 95131

Storage Technology Corporation
2270 South 88th Street
Louisville, CO 80028

Telex Computer Products, Inc.
6422 East 41st Street
Tulsa, OK 75135

Personal Computers

Apple Computer Corporation
20525 Mariani Avenue
Cupertino, CA 95014

COMPAQ Computer Corporation
20333 FM149
Houston, TX 77070

Hewlett-Packard Company
3000 Hanover Street
Palo Alto, CA 94304

International Business Machines Corporation
1133 Westchester Avenue
White Plains, NY 10601

Kaypro Corporation
533 Stevens
Solana Beach, CA 92075

Radio Shack Division of Tandy Corporation
300 One Tandy Center
Fort Worth, TX 76102

Texas Instruments, Inc.
Data Systems Group
P.O. Box 809063
Dallas, TX 75240

Artificial Intelligence and Expert Systems

Symbolics
Four Cambridge Center
Cambridge, MA 02142

United Technologies Research Center
Silver Lane
East Hartford, CT 06108

Office Automation

Burroughs Corporation
4820 Adohr Lane
Camarillo, CA 93010

Compugraphic Corporation
200 Ballardvale Street
Wilmington, MA 01887

Exxon Office Systems Company
777 Long Ridge Road
Stamford, CT 06902

Lanier Business Products, Inc.
1700 Chantilly Drive
Atlanta, GA 30324

Motorola/Four-Phase
10700 North De Anza Boulevard
Cupertino, CA 95014

NBI, Inc.
3450 Mitchell Lane
Boulder, CO 80301

Rolm Corporation
4900 Old Ironsides Road
Santa Clara, CA 95050

Wang Laboratories, Inc.
One Industrial Avenue
Lowell, MA 01851

Xerox Corporation
Information Products Division
1341 West Mockingbird Lane
Dallas, TX 75247

Japanese Computer Companies

Epson America, Inc.
3415 Kashiwa Street
Torrance, CA 90505

Fujitsu America, Inc.
2945 Oakmead Village Court
Santa Clara, CA 95051

Mitsubishi Electronics America, Inc.
991 Knox Street
Torrance, CA 90502

NEC America, Inc.
532 Broad Hollow Road
Melville, NY 11747

Sony Corporation of America
Sony Drive
Park Ridge, NJ 07656

Toshiba America, Inc.
2441 Michelle Drive
Tustin, CA 92680

Chip Manufacturers

Fairchild Camera & Instrument Corporation
464 Ellis Street
Mountain View, CA 94042

Intel
3065 Bowers Avenue
Santa Clara, CA 95051

Mostek Corp.
1215 West Crosby Road
Carrollton, TX 75006

Motorola, Inc.
725 South Madison Drive
Tempe, AZ 85281

Data Communications

AT&T
1 Speedwell Avenue
Morristown, NJ 07960

Codex, Inc.
20 Cabot Boulevard
Mansfield, MA 02048

Digital Communications Associates, Inc.
303 Research Drive
Norcross, GA 30092

GTE Telenet Communications Corporation
8229 Boone Boulevard
Vienna, VA 22180

Harris Corporation
1025 West Nasa Boulevard
Melbourne, FL 32919

Hayes Microcomputer Products, Inc.
5923 Peachtree Industrial Boulevard
Norcross, GA 30092

MCI Telecommunications Corporation
1133 19th Street, N.W.
Washington, DC 20036

Network Systems Corporation
7600 Boone Avenue North
Minneapolis, MN 55428

Northern Telecom, Inc.
Greenway Plaza
2150 Lakeside Boulevard
Richardson, TX 75081

RCA Data Communications Products
New Holland Avenue
Lancaster, PA 17604

Ungermann-Bass, Inc.
2560 Mission College Boulevard
Santa Clara, CA 95050

CAD/CAM

Calma Company
Subsidiary of General Electric Company
5155 Old Ironsides Drive
Santa Clara, CA 95050

Computervision Corporation
14-3 Crosby Drive
Bedford, MA 01730

Lexidata Corporation
755 Middlesex Turnpike
Billerica, MA 01865

Computer Supplies

Dysan Corporation
5201 Patrick Henry Drive
Santa Clara, CA 95050

Maxell Corporation of America
60 Oxford Drive
Moonachie, NJ 07074

Memorex Corporation
1125 Memorex Drive
Santa Clara, CA 95052

Shugart Associates
475 Oakmead Parkway
Sunnyvale, CA 94086

Major Banks and Insurance Companies

Bank of America
555 California Street
San Francisco, CA 94104

Citibank NA
399 Park Avenue
New York, NY 10043

Manufacturers Hanover Trust
55 Water Street
New York, NY 10015

Aetna Life & Casualty
900 Asylum Avenue
Hartford, CT 06156

John Hancock Mutual Life Insurance Company
John Hancock Place
Boston, MA 02117

Metropolitan Life Insurance Company
One Madison Avenue
New York, NY 10010

High-Tech Companies

Litton Data Command Systems
Division of Litton Industries, Inc.
Agoura, CA 91301

Texas Instruments, Inc.
Software Staffing Coordinator
Equipment Group
P.O. Box 405, MS3426
Lewisville, TX 75067

TRW
One Space Park
Redondo Beach, CA 90278

United Technologies
Pratt & Whitney
P.O. Box 2691
West Palm Beach, FL 33402

Trade Publications

Computer Decisions
10 Mulholland Drive
Hasbrouck Heights, NJ 07604

Computers and Electronics Magazine
Ziff-Davis Publishing Company
One Park Avenue
New York, NY 10016

Computerworld
CW Communications, Inc.
375 Cochituate Road
Framingham, MA 01701

Data Communications Magazine
McGraw-Hill Publications Company
1221 Avenue of the Americas
New York, NY 10020

Data Sources
20 Brace Road
Cherry Hill, NJ 08034

Datamation
875 Third Avenue
New York, NY 10022

Datapro Research Corporation
1805 Underwood Boulevard
Delran, NJ 08075

Electronic News
7 East 12th Street
New York, NY 10003

Infosystems
Hitchcock Building
Wheaton, IL 60188

Modern Office Technology
111 Chester Avenue
Cleveland, OH 44114

National Technical Information Service
5285 Port Royal Road
Springfield, VA 22161

Popular Computing Magazine
McGraw-Hill Publications
70 Main Street
Petersborough, NH 03458

Software News
5 Kane Industrial Drive
Hudson, MA 01749

Other Names and Addresses of Interest

Women in Information Processing, Inc.
1000 Connecticut Avenue N.W.
Washington, DC 20036

National Association for Women in Computing
Suite 44
55 Sutter Street
San Francisco, CA 94104

Computer and Business Equipment Manufacturers Association
Suite 500
311 First Street N.W.
Washington, DC 20001

Association for Systems Management
24587 Bagley Road
Cleveland, OH 44138

For a subscription to *Computer Opportunities in New England* write to:

The UNICORN Publishing Group
P.O. Box K
Sudbury, MA 01776

Self-Review Exercises 

Matching

Next to the term in column A, place the letter of the statement in column B that best describes it.

Column A

1. Computer engineer
2. CDP
3. EDP manager
4. AFIPS
5. ACM
6. Telecommunications specialist
7. Computer store worker
8. Database manager
9. CCP
10. DPMA

Column B

A. Computing society devoted to fostering academic research
B. Responsible for controlling an organizations's information base
C. Programming certification
D. Deals with general public
E. Computing society concerned with the commercial applications of computing
F. Responsible for controlling an organization's information networks
G. Runs NCC and OAC
H. Hardware specialist
I. Controls a complete computer installation
J. Data processing certification

Fill-in-the-Blanks

Fill in the blanks in each of the following:

1. Jobs for keypunch operators and data entry clerks in general are on the decline because of advances in ________ and ________.

2. Jobs for factory workers who assemble computer systems are expected to decline as the use of ________ and ________ increases.

3. (True/False) Most people should not be concerned about losing their jobs to robots because robotics may generate twice as many jobs as it eliminates. ________.

4. Home work environments have been labeled ________ because home workers don't generally have union representation to bargain collectively with their employers for improved circumstances.

5. The widespread use of word processors will result in a net (increase/decrease) ________ in typing-related jobs while at the same time the amount of technical training required for these jobs will (increase/decrease) ________ greatly.

6. The high earnings for sales and marketing specialists are somewhat deceiving because ________.

7. Most commonly, independent computer consultants serve as ________.

8. An institution of higher learning that was spawned by the needs of the computer field is ________.

9. ________ are concerned with certifying that computer systems are operating properly and without fraud.

10. The ________ was formed in recognition of the importance of electrical engineering to the development and continuing evolution of modern computers.

Answers to Self-Review Exercises

Matching: 1 H, 2 J, 3 I, 4 G, 5 A, 6 F, 7 D, 8 B, 9 C, 10 E

Fill-in-the-Blanks:

1. source data automation, direct data entry
2. robotics, flexible automation
3. False
4. electronic sweat shops
5. decrease, increase
6. unsuccessful sales and marketing people tend to drop out quickly
7. contract programmers
8. the Wang Institute
9. EDP auditors
10. IEEE Computer Society

Projects 

1. Prepare a list of the major computer companies in your area. Write to each of these companies for information about working for them. Visit as many of these companies as possible. Speak with various employees as well as people in the personnel departments. Write a report summarizing career opportunities with computer companies in your area.

2. Prepare a list of the major employers in your area that are not computer-related companies. Write to these companies about computing career opportunities they may offer. Speak with various employees as well as people in the personnel departments. Write a report summarizing the computing career opportunities these companies offer.

3. Several of the professional organizations listed in this appendix encourage the formation of student chapters. Write to the ACM, the IEEE Computer Society, and the DPMA for information about starting a student chapter at your school if you don't already have one. Once you start your student chapter, arrange for interesting guest speakers and arrange trips to various computer companies and major computer installations in your area.

4. Here is a fine project for your student chapter of the ACM, IEEE Computer Society, or DPMA: Work with the administration of your school to arrange a computer job fair. Invite recruiters from several local employers to participate. Encourage students interested in computing careers to attend. Prepare a booklet of the résumés of these students (with each student's permission, of course) and distribute copies to the recruiters attending the job fair. Make an introductory welcoming speech, and then have several of the recruiters introduce themselves and their companies briefly. Then provide each of the recruiters with a table and chairs so that the students may circulate and ask questions. Serve light refreshments. Within a few days of the job fair, send a personal thank-you note to each of the recruiters who attended and to your school administrators who assisted your group. Be sure to ask for their comments and suggestions as well as whether they would be interested in making your group's job fair an annual event. *Hints*: Encourage the recruiters to bring lots of literature about their companies and prepare name tags for each of the attendees.

Glossary

Abacus. The world's oldest computing device; an instrument that uses beads on wires to represent numbers and facilitate calculations.
Abilityphone. A computerized telephone device for handicapped people; it can call for help, remind a person to take medication, speak out messages for the deaf, and so on.
Acceptance testing. A period of time during which users test a computer system in a production environment to determine if it fulfills their requirements.
Access code. A secret code that is used to gain access to a computer.
Accounts payable system. One of the key systems in a management information system; it enables suppliers to be paid on time to maintain good business relationships and takes advantage of discounts offered by suppliers for prompt payment.
Accounts receivable system. One of the key systems in a management information system; it handles collections and informs the credit and collection department of poor payers.
Accumulator. A register in the ALU; it holds numbers involved in calculations.
Ada. A high-level programming language named after Augusta Ada Byron, Countess of Lovelace; Ada was developed by the Department of Defense, which requires its use in military software systems.
Address. An identifier used by the computer to refer to a particular location in main storage.
Ad hoc inquiry and reporting. A capability of DSS systems that allows managers to request special purpose reports.
Airborne Electronic Terrain Map System. A computerized navigation system being developed by the Air Force; it will enable a pilot to fly a plane safely at night, in poor weather conditions, or over unfamiliar territory.
ALGOL. A high-level programming language originally developed and used in Europe in the early 1960s.
Alphageometric graphics. Graphics generated by following instructions to create certain common shapes and to position them on a display screen; used in certain videotex systems.
Alphamosaic graphics. A technique for generating graphics in videotex systems; the screen is divided into 24 lines, each containing 40 blocks; a block is either a single dot-matrix character or one of a variety of small graphics shapes; graphics produced appear somewhat boxy.
Ambiguity. Uncertainty of meaning; the key problem that prevents us from producing perfect natural language translation systems.
American National Standards Institute (ANSI). A government agency that sets uniform standards for various industries.
Ameslan. American sign language; a means of communication used by the deaf.
Angiography. A computerized technique for diagnosing heart and blood vessel problems.
Anthropomorphic robot. A robot that resembles a human.
APA (all-points-addressable) graphics. Any dot on a page can be set on or off; enables a dot matrix printer to produce pictures.
APL. A highly mathematical high-level programming language requiring the use of many special symbols; it has powerful grid manipulation capabilities and has a character set different from ASCII.
Apple Macintosh. An especially user-friendly personal computer introduced by Apple in 1984.
Applications programs. Programs that solve various users' computing needs.
Archival storage. Storage media for retaining older and less active documents for historical purposes; ordinarily, these documents do not need to be readily accessible.
Arithmetic and logic unit (ALU). Component of the CPU that performs arithmetic calculations and makes logical decisions.
Array. A table or list of related data entries.
Artificial body parts. Replacement body parts built from computerized electromechanical components and customized to an individual's needs.
Artificial intelligence (AI). The study of making computers exhibit intelligent behavior.
Artificial organs. Replacement body organs (such as hearts and lungs) built from computerized electromechanical components and customized to an individual's needs.

Artificial vision. An artificial sense of sight to enable a blind person to see. Microprocessors are essential components in artificial vision systems under development.
Asimov's Laws of Robotics. Three laws that robots must obey; proposed by Isaac Asimov in a work of fiction.
Assembler. A program that translates assembly language programs into machine language programs.
Assembly language. A machine-dependent programming language that allows a programmer to use Englishlike abbreviations for machine language instructions.
Assembly robot. A robot that works on an assembly line, assembling parts into larger components.
Asynchronous transmission. Each transmitted character's bit pattern is enclosed between a start bit and a stop bit to mark the beginning and end of transmission.
Audio-animatron. A computerized electromechanical device designed by Disney Imagineers to resemble a human or an animal and primarily used for entertainment.
Auditing around the computer. An auditor examines computer inputs and outputs to determine if the computer is processing data properly.
Auditing through the computer. A computer auditor or auditing program traces outputs back to inputs by examining the detailed processing of data inside the computer system.
Automated clearing house. A computer center where electronic funds transfers are handled; run by the Federal Reserve.
Automated teller machine (ATM). A computerized device that automatically performs many of the same services as human bank tellers.
Automatic callback. The feature of a computerized branch exchange (CBX) that rings a caller back when a busy party hangs up.
Automatic ticketing machine. A microprocessor-controlled device that can print out tickets for airline flights, sports events, theater performances, and so on.
Automatic Traffic Advisory and Resolution Service (ATARS). A computerized air traffic control system that works in conjuction with the DABS system to monitor planes' positions to avoid collisions.

Babbage's Analytical Engine. A computing device organized similarly to modern computers but proposed by Charles Babbage 100 years before computers appeared. Punched cards were to hold the sequence of instructions to be performed and the data to be entered into the machine. It consisted of four units: the store to hold the data and the results of calculations; the mill to perform mathematical operations; a system of gears and levers to transfer data back and forth between the store and the mill; the input/output unit to read data from outside the machine into its store and mill and display the results of its calculations. Babbage never completed the machine.
Babbage's Difference Engine. Proposed by Charles Babbage, a machine for automatically calculating and printing mathematical tables; Babbage eventually abandoned this project to work on the more ambitious Analytical Engine.
Backing up. Making copies of programs and data for security purposes.
Band printer. An impact printer in which characters and symbols are arranged on a continuous loop that spins at high speed; hammers strike the band against a ribbon at appropriate times to imprint the characters or symbols on paper.
Bar code reading. The optical reading of information stored as patterns of wide and narrow bars; the Universal Product Code (UPC) is the most widely known bar code.
Base two number system. A number system in which all numbers are expressed as combinations of ones and zeros; also called the binary number system.
BASIC. An easy to learn interactive high-level programming language developed by John Kemeny and Thomas Kurtz at Dartmouth College in the mid-1960s; the most popular programming language for personal computers.
Batch processing. A form of data processing in which data is collected, entered into the computer, and processed in groups called batches.
Beacon Collision Avoidance System (BCAS). A computerized air-based collision avoidance system that is capable of operating even when ground-based systems fail.
Binary digit. A digit that has the value zero or one.
Binary number system. A number system in which all numbers are expressed as combinations of ones and zeros; also called the base two number system.
Bin picking problem. The complex problem of having a robot reach into a bin containing many different parts mixed together and pick the correct one in order to assemble a product on an assembly line.
Biochip. A "living" computer made of proteins; biochips will be able to grow and reproduce; they may be the key to the development of replacement body parts.
Biomedical engineering. The application of computers, electronics, and other technologies to medicine.
Bionic body parts. Computerized replacement body parts designed and developed by biomedical engineers.
Bit. A unit of information that can have the value zero or the value one; an abbreviation for "binary digit."
Block. A group of logical records that are read from

or written to a secondary storage device such as tape or disk as a unit.
Boolean logic. The mathematics of variables with values that can only be "true" or "false"; it is especially useful in the design of computer circuits.
Bootstrap loader. A program in ROM that reads a fresh copy of the operating system from disk and starts executing it.
Boundary registers. Computer hardware devices that restrict a program to referencing a limited range of storage locations; prevent users from interfering with one another in multi-user computer systems.
Braille. Notation, consisting of raised dots embossed on paper, that allows the blind to read by using their sense of touch; computer printers are available that print their outputs in braille.
Braille, Louis. Developed the braille language for the blind in 1824. Today, various computerized devices such as braille terminals enable blind people to use computers effectively.
Braille computer terminal. A computer terminal that uses braille symbols; enables a blind person to work in a computer-related job.
Broadcast. To send an electronic mail message to many people simultaneously.
Bubble memory. A device that stores bits as the presence or absence of magnetic bubbles on a thin film of synthetic garnet.
Buffer. An area of primary storage that is set aside for communication between the processor and a channel.
Bug. A computerese term for an error.
Bus network. A single multidrop line shared by many nodes.
Byte. A unit of information that, on most current computer systems, consists of eight bits.

C. A structured high-level programming language resembling Pascal; C was developed at Bell Laboratories and used to program the UNIX operating system.
CADUCEUS. An expert computer system for performing medical diagnoses.
Call back queueing. A feature of a computerized branch exchange (CBX); if a particular telephone line is busy the CBX automatically calls that person back when the line becomes free.
Call forwarding. A feature of a computerized branch exchange (CBX) that automatically forwards calls to someone who has moved to another number.
Call notification. A feature of a computerized branch exchange (CBX) that notifies a person talking on the phone that someone else is trying to get through.
Card reader. An input device that reads punched cards into a computer.
Card verifier. A device that double checks data on punched cards to be sure it is correct before being entered into the computer.
Car pooling. Several commuters share a car to conserve fuel and reduce commuting costs; computers help match up commuters for car pools.
Cashless/checkless society. A society in which all financial transactions would be made electronically; it is more likely that we will have a less cash/less check society.
Cathode ray tube (**CRT**). A display screen output device that functions much like a TV set.
CAT scan. A noninvasive diagnostic device that combines x-ray technology and computer technology to produce pictures of "slices" of the human body.
CBX (**computerized branch exchange**). A computerized private branch exchange that can handle both voice and data communications under central network control; many organizations use CBXs as alternatives to special-purpose local area networks.
Central processing unit (**CPU**). The part of every digital computer system that guides the computer through the various steps it takes to solve problems; consists of the ALU, main storage, and the control unit.
Channel. (1) A section of tape on which a row of bits is recorded; also called a track. (2) A hardware device that transfers data between primary storage and peripheral devices; it can operate in parallel with the CPU.
Character. The smallest unit of data that people normally handle; also called a byte.
Character printer. A printer that prints one character at a time.
Chart of accounts. A listing of all the categories to which a general ledger system applies charges and payments.
Chief programmer team. An approach to developing computer software systems in which a chief programmer leads a team of members functioning in supporting roles; the team consists of a chief programmer, copilot, administrator, editor, two secretaries, a program clerk, toolsmith, tester, and a language lawyer.
Ciphertext. An encrypted (coded) message.
Clapp's Laws of Robotics. A set of guidelines for smoothing labor-management relations when installing robots; proposed by Neale Clapp.
Clicking. Pushing down the button on a mouse to inform the computer to perform an indicated operation.
Closed captioning. Text is presented on a TV screen so deaf people can read what is being said; the first widespread use of teletext.
Coaxial cable. A single wire cable with a very high capacity (large bandwidth); commonly used in local area networks.
COBOL (**Common Business Oriented Language**). A

high-level programming language developed for business data processing applications by CODASYL (the Conference on Data Systems Languages) in 1959.

Cohesion. A property of a software system composed of modules; functions placed within a single module should be as closely related to one another as possible.

Collision. When two values hash into the same location; also called a hash crash.

Collision avoidance system. The use of radar and computers to prevent moving vehicles from colliding with one another; a key application of computers in advanced transportation systems.

Collision concept. When two terminals in a local area network attempt to transmit at once, their transmissions collide; they both stop transmitting and wait a random amount of time before attempting to transmit again.

Common carrier. A company authorized by the government to provide communications services to the public.

Compiler. A program that translates high-level language programs into machine language programs.

CompuServe. An on-line database service that offers services similar to videotex but for people with personal computers.

Computer-assisted anesthesiology. The use of computer technology to monitor and control anesthetics that make a patient unconscious and immobile during surgery.

Computer-assisted image processing. Using a computer system to facilitate locating information maintained on microfilm.

Computer-assisted instruction (CAI). Using computers to facilitate the learning process.

Computer-assisted tomography (CAT). A noninvasive diagnostic technique that uses x-rays and computers to take pictures of the inside of the human body; also called computer-axial tomography.

Computer-based scanning systems. Any of a number of noninvasive diagnostic devices that combine computers and x-ray, gamma ray, and ultrasound devices to obtain information from inside the human body.

Computer Command Control. A microprocessor-controlled device that monitors various engine functions in General Motors cars.

Computer-controlled lasers. Computerized lasers typically used in such applications as eye surgery to kill tumors and fuse detached retinas.

Computerized Branch Exchange. *See* CBX.

Computerized diagnosis. The use of computerized expert systems to help doctors diagnose medical problems.

Computerized medical libraries. Databases of current medical information that may be accessed over communications networks.

Computerized patient monitoring. The use of computerized devices, generally in intensive care units of hospitals, to monitor a patient's vital signs, control drug flow, and adjust devices attached to the patient.

Computerized robot. A software-programmable robot.

Computerized sailing ships. A ship whose sails are controlled by a computer so that the ship can take advantage of wind energy and conserve fuel.

Computerized terrain map. A terrain map produced by a mapping computer and displayed on a terminal to help pilots fly at night, in bad weather, or over unfamiliar territory.

Computer output microfilm (COM). A form of computer output in which information is output directly onto various kinds of microfilm.

Computer program. A set of instructions a computer follows to solve a problem.

Computer programmer. A person who writes computer programs.

Concentrator. A device used in data communications systems; temporarily stores data on disk for later transmission when a busy transmission line again becomes available.

Control structures. Features of programming languages that enable programmers to specify the sequencing, selection, and repetition of operations; programmers use these structures as building blocks to construct neat, understandable, and debuggable programs.

Control unit. The unit of the CPU that coordinates the operations of the other units of the computer.

Conversion. The process of changing from one computer system to another, preferably with minimal disruption of an organization's operations.

Coupling. A property of software systems composed of modules; ideally, separate modules should have minimal coupling, that is, they should be as independent of one another as possible.

CP/M. A personal computer operating system developed by Gary Kildall in 1976; it is currently one of the most widely used operating systems in the world.

Credit and collection system. One of the key systems in a management information system; it maintains in-house records on all customers, uses credit information supplied by outside credit bureaus, and facilitates the collection of money from overdue accounts.

Credit authorization terminal. A terminal connected via communications lines to a computer system that maintains current information on credit card holders and check cashers; used for verifying a customer's credit quickly at the point of sale.

Cursor. A blip of light that appears on a display screen; it can be moved to any location on the screen to draw the user's attention.

Cut and paste. A feature of word processors that allows a user to remove text from one location in a document and reinsert it elsewhere in that or another document.
Cylinder. The stack of tracks traced out by each fixed position of the read/write heads on a disk drive.

Daisy-wheel printer. A character printer whose print element has each letter or symbol attached to a long finger connected to a circular carrier that spins at high speed; it produces letter-quality output.
Database. A collection of data stored on a secondary storage medium in a manner designed to facilitate rapid access by authorized users.
Database/data communications (DB/DC) system. A system for accessing a database of information over communications lines, for example, an airline reservations system.
Database integrity. A property of a database—the data that is supposed to be in the database is there, and the data that is not supposed to be there is not.
Database management system (DBMS). A computer system that creates a database, keeps it up-to-date, and provides ready access to the data for authorized users.
Data communications. The transmission of data between computer systems and terminals.
Data definition instructions. Programming language instructions that specify the data to be used by a program.
Data dictionary. A complete listing of all the components and data elements of a system as defined in the system's data flow diagram.
Data diddling. A computer crime technique in which a computer program is modified so that information either entering or leaving the system can be changed.
Data flow diagram. A graphical model showing how data flows through a system.
Data movement instructions. Programming language instructions that specify that data items are to be moved between locations and registers in a computer.
Data transfer time. The time it takes for a complete record on disk to pass under the read/write head.
Deadlock. A serious problem in multiuser systems; several users may be unable to proceed because each is waiting for others to release resources; ideally, systems should be carefully designed to avoid this possibility.
Deaf Communications Institute. An organization concerned with developing means of communications for the deaf.
Deafnet. Electronic mail service provided for the deaf by GTE Telenet.
Debit card. A plastic card resembling a credit card; when a debit card is used to make a purchase, it causes the immediate transfer of funds over the EFT networks from the card holder's account to the account of the company from which the purchase is being made.
Debugging. Removing errors from a program.
Decision support system (DSS). An interactive computer system that supports management decision-making activities.
Decision table. A systems analysis aid that graphically depicts in a table structure the decisions to be made and the actions to be taken.
Decision tree. A systems analysis aid that graphically depicts in a tree structure the decisions to be made and the actions to be taken.
Density. The number of characters per inch that can be recorded on a secondary storage medium such as tape or disk.
Destructive read-in. When a computer stores data in a location, it destroys the previous contents of that location.
Detail file. Contains all the transactions to be applied to the master file; for example, an accounts receivable detail file would contain payments and purchases to be applied to customer balances on an accounts receivable master file.
Direct access. Allows immediate access to a certain record on a disk without the need for a sequential search of every record before the desired one; also called random access.
Direct data entry. Information is captured at its source and entered directly into the computer without producing paper documents.
Direct deposit. An early form of EFT; employee pay is deposited electronically into employee bank accounts without printing paychecks.
Discrete Address Beacon System (DABS). A ground-based radar and computer system to track individual aircraft for collision avoidance.
Disk. A direct access secondary storage device that resembles a phonograph record; information is recorded as magnetized spots on the disk's surface.
Documentation. Information that describes a system to help other people understand it and to facilitate its modification.
Domain. A field in a relational database.
Domain expert. A human expert in a particular field; a knowledge engineer obtains the knowledge of that field from the domain expert for use in an expert system.
Dot-matrix printer. A character printer that forms character images as patterns of dots.
Double buffering. Two buffers are used to increase the rate of transmission over a channel; while the channel is transmitting from one buffer the CPU can fill the second buffer. Also called flip-flop buffering.
Dow Jones News/Retrieval Service. An on-line data-

base service that provides an abundance of business news and statistics.

Drug conflict warnings. Computers verify that a patient may indeed use several different medications without adverse side effects; warnings are issued to prevent the prescription of conflicting drugs.

Drum printer. A line printer with characters arranged in circles around a cylindrical drum; each circle of characters contains all the letters and symbols.

Dry-silver film processing. A convenient technique for producing computer output microfilm (COM) without the use of liquid chemicals.

Dynamic Spatial Reconstructor (DSR). A computerized scanning device that produces three-dimensional moving pictures of the insides of the human body.

Edit check. Ensures that digits are not entered where letters are required and vice versa.

Education Privacy Act of 1974. Applies to schools that receive federal funds; it ensures the privacy and security of academic and behavioral records and permits access to a student's records only by that student, the student's parents, or authorized school officials.

Egoless programming. Encourages all members of a programming project to share their techniques and to review one another's work.

Electrocardiogram (EKG). A graphical record of a person's heart activity.

Electronic calendar. Every person in an automated office can maintain a file that lists appointments and open times; when someone needs to schedule a meeting, the computer can check the attendees' calendars to determine a good time and date.

Electronic dictionary. A feature of word processing systems that automatically checks the spelling of each word in a document against a large number of words prestored in the computer.

Electronic funds transfer (EFT). The process by which money is transferred electronically by computers and data communications systems from one bank account to another.

Electronic Funds Transfer Act of 1978. Legislation that specifies how EFT systems are to be monitored and controlled.

Electronic mail. Correspondence sent electronically through computer networks rather than by the movement of paper.

Electronic mailbox. A file on disk to which a computer delivers an electronic mail message.

Electronic map. A terrain map produced by a computer to help airline pilots navigate at night or in bad weather when they can't see the ground below.

Electrostatic printer. A page printer that uses light beams to induce electric charges on paper or a metal drum. The charged areas attract toner chemical to form images.

Encryption/decryption. The coding and decoding of computerized data to render it useless to unauthorized users.

Ergonomics. The study of the relationship of people and machines; sometimes called human engineering.

Error trapping. Stopping an error before it can cause real damage, for example, when a running program tries to refer to a storage address outside the range specified in its boundary registers, the hardware stops the reference to prevent damage to someone else's programs and data.

Even parity. The coding scheme used in UPC coding; the representations of the digits have an even number of ones (or an even number of bars). If the UPC scanner detects an odd number of bars, it issues a warning to re-scan the package.

Execute a program. When a computer performs the instructions in a computer program.

Expert system. A computer system that can provide advice at the level of a human expert in a particular field.

Explanation system. The component of an expert system that details for the user precisely how each conclusion is reached in an expert system.

Externally programmable control device. An implanted device whose functions can be reprogrammed from outside the body.

Eye-tracking device. A computerized device that can determine what the eye is looking at, and can speak or perform some indicated action in behalf of its handicapped user.

Facilities management. One company hires another to create and run the client company's entire data processing operation.

Facsimile (FAX). A device that is essentially a long-distance copier; page images are transmitted at electronic speeds.

Fair Credit Reporting Act of 1970. Legislation that resulted from the increased collection of credit information made possible by computers; individuals have the right to determine what credit information is being collected about them and to force the correction of inaccurate information.

Family of computers. A series of related computers ranging from small data processing computers to large-scale supercomputers; the computers are normally upwards compatible, that is, programs that will run on one model will usually run on all larger models in the family without modification.

Feasibility study. A systems analyst examines a user's operations and how these relate to the rest of the organization to determine if a proposed new system is feasible.
Fiber optics. A communications technology in which laser light is transmitted over incredibly pure glass wires.
Field. A group of related characters.
File. A group of related records.
File and record definition instructions. Instructions that allow a programmer to specify which files of data will be processed by a program, which secondary storage devices contain those files, and the characteristics of the files.
File integrity. Ensures that the data in a file is correct and that all the data that is supposed to be in the file is, in fact, there.
Firmware. Between hardware and software; an example is a read-only memory (ROM) containing programs.
Fixed word-length machine. A computer that processes all information as fixed-size words.
Flexible automation. The ability to readjust an automated assembly line quickly to process different items in small groups or batches.
Flight simulator. A computerized device that helps pilots learn how to fly without leaving the ground.
Flip-flop. The device inside a computer that represents a single bit.
Flip-flop buffering. *See* double buffering.
Floppy disk. A small flexible magnetic disk used as secondary storage medium on personal computers.
Flowcharting. A graphical means for designing programs by using symbols indicating the operations to be performed and, flowlines (arrows) to show the order of operations.
Formatting. The recording of sector information on a floppy disk; also called initializing the disk.
Forth. An increasingly popular high-level programming language used with personal computers.
FORTRAN (FORmula TRANslator). The first widely used high-level programming language; it was developed by IBM in the 1950s for performing complex mathematical computations.
Fragmentation. A serious problem caused in segmentation systems; many small and unusable free-storage holes dot primary storage.
Freedom of Information Act of 1966. Legislation that gives individuals the right to know the operation and structure of federal agencies and which federal agencies keep records on them; it allows people to access their records and make sure they are correct.
Frequency-division multiplexing (**FDM**). A transmission mode in which different frequency ranges are assigned to different terminals so that several transmissions may occur simultaneously.
Fuel planning system. A computer system that determines how much fuel will be needed by a plane by analyzing weather conditions, number of passengers, cargo weight, and so on.
Full definition video image. A complete graphic prepared by a videotex computer and transmitted in its entirety to the user. This requires much greater bandwidths than today's videotex systems offer.
Full-duplex transmission. Data is transmitted in both directions simultaneously.

General ledger system. One of the key systems in a management information system; it keeps track of a company's financial records and produces reports summarizing the financial health of the company; the two key reports produced are the balance sheet and the profit and loss statement.
Generations of computers. Major periods in the evolution of computers; marked by significant advances in electronics over those periods.
Genetic engineering. The science of the structure of DNA. This field is receiving increased interest because of the evolution of biochips (living computers).
Global replace. A capability of a word processor; allows the user to change all occurrences of a word or phrase in a document to a new word or phrase.
Goal seeking. A capability of a decision support system; management states the financial goal to be achieved and the computer performs calculations to determine how to achieve that goal.
GOTO statement. A statement that causes a transfer of control to a designated place in a computer program; a goal in structured programming is to use control structures to minimize or even eliminate the use of GOTOs.
Gridlock. A devastating situation that occurs when traffic is so congested that intersections are blocked and impassable and all traffic comes to a halt.
GTE Telenet. The computer network system that operates the Deafnet electronic mail network.

Half-adder. One of the most common circuits used in today's computers, it adds two binary digits and produces a sum and a carry when appropriate.
Half-duplex transmission. Data is transmitted in both directions, but in only one direction at a time.
Hard copy. A paper document produced by a computer on an output device; distinguished from soft copy (a screen display).
Hardware. The actual computing equipment, includ-

ing the central processing unit, disks drives, tape drives, printers, card readers, and so on.
Hashing. A technique for facilitating direct access; the address where the record is to be placed on disk is determined by a calculation involving the record's key field.
Heuristic. A rule of good judgment or a rule of thumb based on experience or intuition that human experts may use to attempt to solve a difficult problem. Knowledge engineers attempt to determine heuristics by interviewing human experts; these heuristics are then incorporated into expert systems.
Hierarchical database. Data records are arranged in a strict parent/child or boss/employee relationship; each parent may have many children, but each child may have only one parent.
Hierarchical data structuring. A feature of the COBOL programming language that enables a programmer to specify the structure of data in increasing levels of detail.
High-level language. A programming language in which programmers write statements that appear similar to everyday English and use familiar mathemetical notations.
Holding pattern. Flight patterns that planes fly while waiting to land; computerized flight monitoring and control is helping to minimize the time planes spend in holding patterns.
Hologram. A three-dimensional picture produced by lasers. Computer-controlled lasers may eventually make three-dimensional television possible.

IBM Personal Computer. First introduced in 1981, it rapidly became the world's most popular personal computer.
Icon. A picture or graphic that describes an operation to be performed or an application being selected; Apple uses icons in the user interface for its user-friendly Macintosh personal computer.
If-then rules. Rules incorporated into expert systems to help them draw conclusions.
Impact printer. A printer that strikes a metal hammer against a ribbon to leave an impression on paper.
Implantable computerized device. A microprocessor-controlled device that is implanted in the body to function as a heart controller, insulin dispenser, and the like.
Implementation phase. The system development phase in which the implementation team programs the system, tests it to uncover any bugs, corrects the bugs, and retests the system until it is functioning properly.
Indefinite postponement. A serious problem in multiuser systems that occurs when a steady stream of high-priority users prevents a low-priority user from receiving any service for an indefinite period of time; systems should be carefully designed to avoid this possibility.
Index. The position number of a table entry relative to the beginning of the table; also called a subscript.
Indexed sequential organization. A file organization in which the records of a file may be accessed either sequentially or randomly (directly).
Industrial robot. A mechanical arm that is used in industry for jobs such as welding, spray painting, lifting, tending hot ovens, and manipulating nuclear fuel rods.
Inference engine. The component of an expert system that reasons from the information contained in the knowledge base.
Information amplification. A means of helping handicapped people work at a more normal speed; for example, a nonvocal handicapped person could press a single key to indicate, "I need more parts to continue assembling these devices."
Information providers. Commercial enterprises that distribute information electronically, for example, viewdata/videotex services, teletext services, and the on-line databases.
Information Revolution. A period of enormous social change brought about by the advent of computer technology and improvements in communications.
Initialize. To set a variable to an appropriate initial value; an example is to clear a total or a count to zero.
Input unit. A device such as a keyboard or a terminal used for entering information into a computer.
Integrated circuit. A device containing hundreds or even thousands of transistors on a small silicon chip; integrated circuit technology spawned the third generation of computers.
Intelligent computer. A computer that exhibits what appears to be intelligent behavior.
Intelligent control. The use of computers, especially microprocessors, to control the operation of various kinds of devices.
Intensive care unit (ICU). A specially equipped hospital facility in which patients are constantly monitored; today's ICUs make heavy use of computerized monitoring and control devices.
Interblock gap. A section of empty tape that a read/write head passes over while the tape drive accelerates and decelerates between blocks of recorded information.
Intermediate Capacity Transit System (ICTS). A completely computerized train system operating in Canada.
Interpreter. An alternative to a compiler; it is a translator program that actually runs a source program directly without first translating it into machine language.
Interrupt. A hardware signal that gains the attention of the processor.
Inventory control system. One of the key systems in a management information system; it monitors the

amount of goods on hand and makes sure that sufficient quantities are in stock to satisfy production needs and customer requests.

Irradiation device. A device that administers radiation to cancer patients; today's irradiation devices are precisely controlled by computers.

Jacquard loom. A device for controlling weaving looms; it used punched cards to program the loom to create a specific pattern; this device was a forerunner of the punched-card devices eventually used with computers.

Josephson junction. An incredibly fast computer switch designed to operate at temperatures near absolute zero where some metals become superconductive and offer no resistence to the flow of an electric current.

Key. A code that identifies a particular record in a file.

Keypunch. An input device that punches holes into computer cards.

Key-to-disk device. An input device with which information is keystroked directly onto magnetic disk.

Key-to-tape device. An input device with which information is keystroked directly onto magnetic tape.

Knowledge base. The component of an expert system that contains the factual knowledge and the rules of thumb of the given area of expertise.

Knowledge engineer. A highly skilled person who painstakingly interviews a human expert to extract that person's expertise for use in an expert system.

Knowledge structure. A structure used to store knowledge in expert systems; one common structure is a set of if-then rules.

Kurzweil Reading Machine. An optical character recognition, computer-controlled device that reads pages of text to the deaf.

Large Print Video Terminal. A computer terminal for the partially sighted; it displays text in very large letters.

Large-scale integrated circuitry (LSI). A circuit technology that enables hundreds of thousands of transistors to be etched onto the surface of a single silicon chip; this technology spawned the fourth generation of computing.

Laser. A device that creates an intense beam of monochromatic (one color) light. Laser technology is used in data communications and a wide variety of computer applications.

Laser printer. The fastest nonimpact printer, it uses the precise light of laser beams to guide crisp dots of light to exact locations on a page.

Latency time. The time it takes for the desired record to spin around to the read/write head of a disk; also called rotational delay.

Leased line. A dedicated line reserved for use by a particular party who is charged for the undivided attention of the line.

Least cost routing. The feature of a computerized branch exchange (CBX) that finds the most economical way to place a call.

Leibniz's Stepped Reckoner. A calculating machine developed by Gottfried Leibniz; it was capable of performing multiplication and division directly; it implemented multiplication as a series of additions, and division as a series of subtractions.

Light pen. A device used to enter data into the computer by "writing" on the display screen.

Linear induction motor (LIM). A motor that works on the principles of magnetic attraction and repulsion; LIMs are likely to be used in the computer-controlled transportation systems of the future.

Linear predictive coding. A mathematical approach for producing synthetic speech; a series of mathematical formulas is used to describe to a speech generator device the way human speech is produced.

Line printer. A printer that prints an entire line at once.

LISP (LISt Processor). A high-level programming language developed by John McCarthy at MIT in 1960; it was one of the first symbol manipulation languages and one of the first languages used for text processing; it has become the preferred language for implementing artificial intelligence applications.

Lisp machines. Powerful computers with very large memories and very fast CPUs specifically designed to run Lisp programs efficiently.

List processing. A feature of a word processor that allows a user to generate mass mailings.

Local replace. The feature of a word processor that enables the user to replace one occurrence of a word or phrase in a document with a new word or phrase.

Location. A place in main storage that may contain either a data item or an instruction; every location has an address and a value.

LOGO. A high-level programming language that contains powerful graphics manipulation capabilities called turtle graphics; originally designed for use by children.

Looping. A capability in programming languages; allows the computer to reuse certain instructions many times, thus reducing the number of instructions the programmer must write to accomplish a repetitive task.

Machine dependent. Machine languages and assembly languages are said to be machine dependent because they are closely related to the design of particular computers.
Machine language instruction. An operation that a computer can interpret and perform directly without the need for translation.
Macro instruction. One instruction (written in an assembly language program) that is translated into several machine language instructions.
Magnetic core memory. A type of computer storage developed in 1950 by Jay W. Forrester for use in the Whirlwind I computer; it is made up of tiny donut-shaped pieces of metal that can be magnetized in one of two directions to correspond to the binary 0 or 1.
Magnetic ink character recognition (MICR). An input technology in which information is entered into the computer using magnetized ink; used extensively by the banking industry for check processing.
Magnetic levitation (maglev). Used in transportation systems; using the principle that like magnetic poles repel, maglev trains actually float on air above a track.
Main storage. One of the three logical units that make up the CPU, it stores information arriving via the input unit so that the information is available to the ALU when calculations are performed; it holds executing programs and the data they reference.
Management information system (MIS). A computerized system that on a regular schedule provides managers with the information they need to perform their key tasks of planning, organizing, directing, and controlling.
Manufacturing resources planning system (MRP). A computerized system that helps with the complex planning, resource allocation, and progress reporting functions associated with the manufacturing of products.
Master file. A main file of information to which updates and transactions are applied.
Microcomputer. A complete computer on a silicon chip or on a few chips.
Microfiche. A 4-inch by 6-inch microfilm card; computer output microfilm (COM) systems can produce computer outputs directly onto microfiche (and other forms of microfilm) at very high speeds.
Microprocessor. A computer processor etched onto a thin sliver of silicon called a silicon chip; the microprocessor spawned the personal computer revolution.
Minicomputer. A small, powerful, low-priced third-generation computer made possible by the development of integrated-circuit technology.
Minspeak. A system for information amplification; uses a special keyboard containing numbers, letters, names, and words to enable nonvocal handicapped people to convey a wide variety of ideas by pressing a relatively small number of keys.
Modem (modulator/demodulator). Converts digital data from computers to analog data for transmission over communications lines and vice versa.
Modulated displacement system. Microprocessor-controlled device that at appropriate times automatically reduces the number of cylinders in operation in an automobile engine to conserve fuel.
Module. A program piece such as a subroutine; programs written as a collection of small, meaningfully defined modules are generally much easier to understand, debug, and maintain than large, one-piece programs.
Mouse. An input device that the user moves around on a flat surface to move a cursor around on a screen; the user clicks a button on the mouse to indicate that the application or operation pointed to on the screen is selected or is to be performed.
MS-DOS. The operating system developed by Microsoft for the IBM Personal Computer (IBM calls it "PC-DOS").
Multidrop line. A single transmission line shared by several terminals.
Multiplexor. A device that enables sharing of a high-speed communications line by dividing the line capacity to make the line appear to be several low-speed lines.
Multiprocessing. Processing performed by a computer that has more than one processor; a multiprocessor computer can truly execute several instructions simultaneously.
Multiprogramming. Allowing several user jobs to be in progress on a computer at once.
Multitasking. A special case of multiprogramming in which each user may have multiple activities in progress at once.

Napier's bones. Developed by John Napier; a computing device that facilitates the operations of multiplication and division by using sticks marked in a manner similar to the multiplication tables used today.
National Commission on Electronic Funds Transfers (NCEFT). A group created by Congress and given the responsibility of recommending legislation that would specify how EFT systems should be monitored and controlled.
Natural language processing. The field of computer research concerned with the problems of developing machines that understand natural languages such as English, French, and Spanish.
Nested structure. A control structure embedded within an outer control structure.
Network. A group of cooperating computers that share information over communications lines.

Network database. A method of organizing a database to facilitate answering a wide variety of questions without having to provide duplicate data or to reorganize the database; each parent may have many children and vice versa.
Nondestructive read-out. The process of reading data out of a storage location; the data is copied to another location and the original data is left intact.
Nonimpact printer. A printer that uses electronic or photographic techniques to produce reports at high speeds.
Noninvasive diagnostic techniques. Diagnostic techniques that enable doctors to get precise pictures of the inside of the human body without the need for exploratory surgery; computers are essential components in such noninvasive diagnostic devices as the CAT scan and the PET scan.
Nybble. The left half or the right half of a byte.

Obtaining medical histories. Using interactive computer systems to obtain detailed medical histories of patients; the patient communicates directly with the computer.
Office automation (OA). The use of computers and communications in automating information processing functions in offices.
Off-line. Not directly connected to a computer; for example, a keypunch machine is an off-line device.
Omnifont device. An optical character recognition device that can read most printed fonts. Omnifont devices generally have the capability to learn new fonts.
On-line. Directly connected to a computer; for example, a computer terminal is an on-line device.
On-line databases. Information providers that offer services similar to videotex but specifically to people with personal computers; CompuServe and The Source are two of the larger on-line databases.
Operating system. The software system that manages the computer's hardware and makes it more "friendly" and usable to authorized computer users; the set of systems programs on a computer.
Operation phase. The phase when a system has been implemented and accepted and goes into regular operation.
Optacon. A device that enables a blind person to read by vibrations.
Optical character recognition (OCR). An input technology in which handwritten or typewritten characters and symbols are read, using computerized photo-optical techniques, and converted into computer codes.
Optical disk. A secondary storage medium in which bits are burned into the surface of a disk with a pin-point laser beam and read by a less intense laser beam; today's optical disks have enormous storage capacities, but they are write-once devices.
Optical mark recognition (OMR). An input technology in which pencil marks placed in particular positions are read with photo-optical techniques; commonly used in exam grading and utility meter reading and billing applications.
Optimizing compiler. A translator program that produces highly efficient machine language programs that execute quickly and use a minimal amount of main storage.
Orator. A computer output device that allows a computer to speak its outputs; especially useful for blind computer users.
Order entry system. One of the key systems in a management information system; it accepts customer orders for merchandise and services and puts in motion the mechanisms to ensure that the orders are fulfilled.
Organ matching. Using computer systems and data communications to facilitate the matching of organ donors and recipients for transplant operations.
Output. The results that computers produce; outputs can be printed on paper, displayed on screens, spoken, exposed on microfilm, played as music, and so on.
Output unit. A device, such as a printer or video screen, on which a computer presents its output results.
Overlapped processing. Concurrent operations performed by a computer; computers can get more work done by performing several operations in parallel.

Pacemaker. An implantable, computer-controlled device that controls heart functions.
Packet switching. A means of ensuring highly accurate data transmission by providing error correction and detection capabilities through prefixed identifiers on blocks of data called packets.
Page printer. A printer that prints an entire page at one time.
Paging. A technique used in operating systems; programs and data are divided into equal-sized pieces called pages and only the most active pages of each user are kept in main storage, while less active pages remain on disk until they are needed.
Paperless office. A goal of many office automation systems; the complete elimination of paper copies as a means for storing and communicating information.
Parity bit. An extra bit transmitted with each byte of data to ensure correct transmission; parity may be odd or even; in odd parity systems the extra bit is chosen to make the total number of one bits in a byte odd.
Pascal. A high-level programming language developed by Nicklaus Wirth in 1971 and named for Blaise Pas-

cal; it is a structured language with powerful features for defining and manipulating complex data structures.

Pascal's arithmetic machine. A calculating device for performing addition and subtraction developed by Blaise Pascal; it used a series of cleverly connected wheels, each wheel contained the digits 0 through 9; operated in a similar fashion to today's automobile odometers.

Payroll system. One of the key systems in a management information system; it calculates each employee's gross pay, calculates all deductions to be withheld, prints paychecks, and maintains appropriate payroll records.

PBX (Private Branch Exchange). A device for controlling voice and data communications over standard telephone lines in an office environment.

People Mover System. A computer-controlled transportation system built by Westinghouse to move people between the main terminal and the concourses at the Atlanta Airport.

Peripheral device. An input, output, or secondary storage device separate from the processing unit and main storage of the computer; for example, a disk drive, tape drive, or printer.

Personal computer. A complete computer system that can fit on a desk top and is economical enough to be dedicated to the use of one person.

Personal identification number (PIN). A secret code that identifies a user to an automated teller machine so that person may use the machine for banking transactions.

PET scan. A computerized, noninvasive diagnostic device that monitors brain activity.

Phoneme. One of the set of common sounds in the English language from which all English words are formed.

Phoneme coding. A method of speech synthesis in which the computer speaks words by successively speaking the phoneme sounds that make up the words.

Pick-and-place robot. A dumb device that picks up an object from one place and puts it in another; the device assumes that the object will be properly positioned.

PL/1. Programming Language 1, developed by IBM for its System/360 series of computers; a large, structured programming language that incorporates the better features of FORTRAN, COBOL, and ALGOL.

Plaintext. An unencrypted (not coded) message.

Planetran. A train of the future that would operate on LIMs in tubes beneath the surface of the earth; computers would be essential to controlling the precise movement of the trains through the tubes.

Platter. One of the disks in a disk pack.

Plotter. An output device that draws dots, lines, and shapes on paper to create text and graphics.

Plug compatible mainframers (PCMs). Companies that produce hardware that is similar to the hardware produced by other mainframe computer makers, especially IBM, and can operate the software of these other manufacturers.

Point-of-sale (POS) terminal. A computer terminal that facilitates retail transactions in stores, supermarkets, and other places of business; it is connected to a central computer system containing price, sales, and inventory information that is kept up-to-the-minute.

Point-to-point line. Connects a computer directly to a computer terminal or another computer in a network; no other devices are on the line.

Polling. A communications controller successively tests each terminal on a multidrop line to see if that terminal is ready to transmit data to the central computer.

Portable computer. A computer that can be carried conveniently from place to place; portable computers are frequently used as portable terminals.

Portable terminal. A computer terminal that is small enough to be carried from place to place; it can be attached to a telephone with a modem for transmitting information to a central computer.

Positron emission tomography (PET). *See* PET scan.

Preauthorized computer-initiated payments. Automatic payment of an installment loan directly from a borrower's bank account; no checks are written.

Predefined process symbol. A rectangular flowcharting symbol with vertical bars near its left and right borders; used to indicate that a subroutine is to be called.

Print spooling. Allows users to run their programs even when the printer is not available; outputs are temporarily saved on disk until the printer becomes available.

Privacy Act of 1974. Legislation that prevents the federal government from keeping secret files on individuals.

Private Branch Exchange. *See* PBX.

Problem-oriented language. A special-purpose programming language designed to solve specific types of problems.

Procedure-oriented language. A general-purpose programming language that can be used to solve many different types of problems.

Process control computer. A computer used in the control of production lines, laboratories, refineries, and so on, to control various types of industrial processes.

Production environment. An environment in which a computer program or system is used on a regular schedule to handle a portion of a business's information processing needs.

Program development environment. An environment in which computer programs are developed and debugged.

Programmable robot. A robot that learns a new function by having a person lead the robot's arm manually through the series of movements and tasks to be performed.
Programming language. A language used by a person called a computer programmer to write computer programs that detail to a computer how it is to solve specific problems.
Pseudocode. Englishlike sentences that a programmer writes to explain how a program is supposed to operate; also called structured English; it is especially appropriate for developing programs using top-down, stepwise refinement.
Pull-down menu. A list of options available to the user; made popular on Apple's Macintosh personal computer released in 1984.
Punched card. A thick paper card used as computer input and output medium; letters, digits, and symbols are punched into the card as patterns of holes.
Punched-card control. Used in the Jacquard loom; the patterns to be woven into cloth were described as holes punched in cards.

"Quick-and-dirty" compiler. A fast-executing compiler that translates source programs quickly, but the machine language programs produced do not run as fast as possible and may use more primary storage than necessary; useful in program development environments, but optimizing compilers are preferred in production environments.

Random access. Allows immediate access to a certain record on disk without a sequential search of every record that precedes it in a file; also called direct access.
Range check. Ensures that a data item has a value that falls within a specific range, for example, a month number should fall between 1 and 12.
Read/write head. The hardware component that reads and writes information on tapes and disks.
Real-time system. A type of computer system in which the most important goal is responsiveness; an example is an air traffic control system, where avoiding a collision might require immediate action on the part of the computer system.
Reasonableness check. Ensures that a data item is reasonable; an example is checking an age to see if it is less than 125.
Record. A group of related fields.
Redundancy. When the same data appears in more than one file; redundancy can be wasteful, but it is an effective backup and security measure.
Reentrant program. A program that does not modify itself while executing; in a multiuser system one copy of a reentrant program may be executed simultaneously by several users.
Register. A temporary storage device in the ALU; sometimes called an accumulator.
Regulation E. Implements the provisions of the Electronic Funds Transfer Act and provides considerable protection to users of EFT systems.
Rehabilitation engineering. Applying technology to improve the lives of the handicapped.
Relational database. A user-friendly database organization in which the data is stored as tables called relations.
Relocatable program. A program that can run when placed anywhere in primary storage.
Repetition structure. Indicates that certain operations are to be repeated until some terminating condition is met.
Requirements definition phase. The systems development phase in which users list their new needs.
Requirements document. The list of needs produced by the users in the requirements definition phase.
Reservations and ticketing system. A computerized system that keeps track of airline flights (or some other means of transportation), times, available seating, special meals, handicapped people needing assistance, and so on.
Residual capabilities. Those senses and movements a handicapped person has that still function properly; many computerized systems for handicapped people require the use of residual capabilities to operate devices that compensate for lost capabilities.
Return statement. The last statement executed in any subroutine; causes the main program to continue executing at the first statement after the one that called the subroutine.
Right to Financial Privacy Act of 1978. Legislation that gives people the right to review the data about their personal finances maintained by financial institutions; individuals may also force the correction of incorrect data.
Ring network. A common communications network arrangement for local environments; various computers in the network are arranged around a ring, and each computer can communicate with any other.
Robot. (1) A machine that resembles a person and does routine tasks on command; (2) A reprogrammable multifunctional manipulator designed to move material, parts, tools or specialized devices.
Robotics. A term coined by Dr. Isaac Asimov, one of the world's foremost science fiction writers, to describe the study of robots.

RPG (Report Program Generator). A problem-oriented, high-level programming language developed by IBM; the programmer fills in specifications forms that tell the computer what is to be done, and the RPG translator then produces the program to accomplish the desired tasks.
RS-232 interface. Gives the computer the ability to pass one character at a time to a modem for transmission, or to receive one character at a time from a modem; other devices may also communicate with computers across RS-232 interfaces.

Salami method. A computer crime method in which a program is run that takes small amounts (slices) from many different accounts and places these amounts into the account of the thief.
Scavenging method. A computer crime method in which a person rummages through the trash for computer printouts and documentation or runs a memory dump to obtain copies of programs and data in the computer.
Secondary storage. A storage medium such as disk or tape used for the storage and retrieval of massive amounts of computer-accessible information.
Sector. A wedge-shaped storage area on a floppy disk.
Seek. The process of moving the read/write head between tracks on a disk.
Segmentation. Programs and data are divided into pieces of different sizes, and these pieces are placed into possibly widely separated free areas in main storage.
Selection structure. A control structure that designates that the operations to be performed in the future depend on whether a certain condition is currently true or false.
Sensory robot. A robot that has one or more artificial senses such as sight or touch.
Sentinel value. A special marker that indicates the end of data entry; also called a signal value, dummy value, or flag value.
Sequence structure. A control structure indicating that one operation is to be performed immediately after another in sequence.
Sequential access. The records of a file are placed in order one after the other; to reference a record located in the middle of a file, the records before it must be examined first.
Service bureau. A company that develops a centralized computer installation with hardware, software, and databases, and makes these available to users for a fee.
Shared-logic system. A multistation word processing system in which each workstation shares the central processor, storage, and peripheral devices.
Shared-resources system. A multistation word processing system in which each workstation has its own processor, but peripheral devices are shared.
Silicon chip. A tiny sliver of silicon into which electronic circuits are etched.
Simplex transmission. A data transmission method in which data travels in only one direction.
Simulator. A computerized device used for driver training, flight training, ship pilot training, train engineer training, and so on; the computer creates the illusion of a car driving, a plane landing, a ship entering a harbor, and so on.
Smart card. A credit-card-sized plastic card that contains computer memory chips or laser storage; smart cards can hold a patient's complete medical history or they can be used in other applications including electronic banking.
Smith-Kettlewell Institute of Visual Science. Develops various devices for the benefit of blind people.
Soft copy. Computer outputs presented on a display screen; no paper documents are produced.
Soft copy Braille output device. A computer output device for the blind; a microprocessor causes metal pins to move up and down on a flat surface to form braille letters; after one line is displayed, the pins are set to display the next line.
Software. The sets of instructions, also called computer programs, that describe to computers the operations they are to perform to solve specific problems.
Software package. A program or software system produced by an individual or company for sale to other individuals or companies.
Sonar sight. Sound waves bounce back off objects and are interpreted by a microprocessor that bleeps out various noises indicating the nature of and distance to nearby objects.
The Source. An on-line database service available to people with personal computers.
Source data automation. Describes input techniques such as optical character recognition (OCR) and optical mark recognition (OMR) that capture information automatically, thus avoiding the need for time-consuming and error-prone manual keystroking.
Space Shuttle. The most heavily computerized transportation system ever developed.
Specification. Restates the user's needs (originally specified in the requirements document) in terms that are meaningful to systems people, and describes the type of system that the systems analyst feels would be appropriate to satisfy those needs.
Speech recognition. The ability of a computer to understand spoken commands; speech recognition is believed to be one of the key technologies essential to the development of highly user-friendly systems.

Speech synthesis. Computerized speech generation as a form of computer output.
Stand-alone system. A complete single-user word processing system containing a processor, keyboard, screen, printer, and disk storage.
Star network. A data communications network organization in which a central computer communicates with various terminals and other computers over point-to-point lines; uses centralized control rather than distributed control.
Stat mux (statistical multiplexor). Gives unused line capacity to other terminals that are ready to transmit, instead of letting that capacity go to waste as with conventional multiplexors.
Steel collar worker. Just as people are described as white collar workers or blue collar workers, robots are described as "steel collar workers."
Storage protection. A feature of multi-user computer systems that prevents users from interfering with one another's programs; each user's programs and data are restricted to reside in and reference only that portion of main storage that has been allocated by the operating system to that user.
Stored program concept. Proposed by John von Neumann; the program as well as the data it operates on should be stored in the computer's memory.
Stored speech. Prerecorded human speech stored in a computer for playback; stored speech systems generally have a higher quality of speech than synthetic speech systems, but their vocabulary is severely limited.
Strategic planning. Long-term planning that is handled by upper-level management.
Structured English. Another name for pseudocode.
Structured programming. The use of control structures and program modules as building blocks to construct neat, understandable, debuggable, and maintainable programs.
Structured systems analysis. A systems analyst reviews a client's requirements and proposes a system to meet those requirements; the analyst produces the specification that describes the proposed system.
Structured systems design. The process of translating the logical model of what a system does into a physical model that describes how the system is to be built and how it is to operate.
Structured systems specification. A clear and precise description of what the proposed system is supposed to do; this is the end product of the systems analysis phase.
Structured walkthrough. A peer group review of an individual's work.
Sturdy disk. The 3 1/2-inch disk used with the Apple Macintosh personal computer.
Subroutine. A program piece also called a module; designing programs as sets of carefully chosen interacting subroutines is an effective technique for producing understandable, debuggable, and maintainable programs.
Subscript. The position number of an entry relative to the beginning of an array or table; also called an index.
Supercomputer. An enormously powerful computer used to perform the most complex mathematical and scientific calculations.
Super-zap method. A computer crime technique in which the perpetrator uses legitmate computer programs designed to override normal system controls and modify data.
Switched line. Communications lines available through the regular telephone switching network, as opposed to dedicated lines.
Synchronous transmission. Characters are transmitted as one continuous stream of bits.
Synthetic speech. Computer-generated speech; synthetic speech systems have an essentially unlimited vocabulary, but the quality of speech is not as good as in stored speech systems.
Systems analysis phase. Systems analysts act as intermediaries between users, management, and systems designers, helping each of these groups to understand the needs and problems of the others; the analyst translates the user's needs as stated in the requirements document into the more formal structured system specification, a document more meaningful to the systems designers who take over from there.
Systems design phase. Systems designers decide how to construct the system that is to perform the desired operations described in the structured system specification.
Systems life cycle. A series of phases through which a new system evolves as it is developed, placed into operation, and modified on an ongoing basis to meet changing needs.
Systems performance audit. A regularly performed audit to evaluate a system and determine if it is operating properly and efficiently.

Table searching. Searching an array of information to determine if a particular data item is stored in the array.
Tactical planning. Short-term planning that is handled by middle managers.
Telecommuting. The ability to work at home by using a personal computer, a modem, and data communications.
Teleconferencing. Incorporates audio, video, and computer conferencing techniques; instead of traveling, conferees sit in specially designed rooms with video

screens and computer terminals and use satellite transmission to hold a conference with participants located possibly throughout the world.

Teletext. A one-way transmission service that repeatedly broadcasts a certain common base of information to its subscribers, who receive it on their TV sets; teletext information is transmitted in the black bars between TV pictures (these are called vertical blanking intervals).

Terminal. A device used to input information into a computer (usually on a keyboard), and to receive outputs from a computer (usually on a screen or printer).

Testing. The process of demonstrating that a system operates according to its specifications.

Thermal printer. A dot-matrix printer that operates by driving heated pins against special heat-sensitive paper to "burn" the image onto the paper.

Thimble printer. A printer that uses a formed-character print element that resembles a thimble used in sewing.

Tickler message. A reminder sent to oneself on an electronic mail or voice mail system.

Time bomb. A computer crime technique in which instructions are planted in a program to destroy programs and data after a period of time.

Time-division multiplexing (TDM). A method of sharing a communications line; the line is dedicated to each terminal for brief periods of time so that only one terminal is transmitting at a time.

Timesharing. A method of sharing a computer in which tens or hundreds of users can access the central computer through terminals; the CPU is rapidly switched between users to create the illusion that all the users are running simultaneously.

Token passing. A strategy used in local networks to determine which node transmits next; a bit pattern called a token is passed from node to node, and possession of the token gives a node the right to transmit.

Tomography. The description of slices; the technique used in the CAT scan to form pictures of the insides of the human body without the need for diagnostic surgery.

Top-down stepwise refinement. The gradual process of developing increasingly detailed solutions to a problem using such aids as structured flowcharts and pseudocode.

Touch sensing. A computer input technology in which the user touches a symbol on a display screen or touch pad to select an operation to be performed or to indicate the data that is to be operated on.

Track. A circle of information on a disk; each position of a read/write head accesses a different track of information.

Tracking system. A computerized system that keeps track of the location and contents of vehicles.

Traffic control. Using a computerized system to monitor traffic conditions and minimize congestion, such as by controlling traffic lights.

Train Dynamics Analyzer (TDA). A computerized simulator that helps instruct new train engineers.

Transaction processing system. A computer system in which data items that are entered into the system are processed immediately rather than being gathered up in batches for processing in groups.

Transistor. An electronic circuit element developed by Bell Laboratories in 1948; it spawned the second generation of computers.

Translator program. A program that translates programs from one language, called the source language, to another language, called the object language; compilers and assemblers are translator programs.

Transponder. A device that sends a reply automatically when it receives a certain signal.

Trapdoor method. A computer crime method in which secret instructions are placed in target programs so the computer criminal can use these programs at will.

Trojan horse method. A computer crime method that involves placing special instructions into a computer program; the instructions perform secret functions while the program appears to be running normally.

TRS-80. A line of personal computers marketed by Tandy Corporation through its Radio Shack retail stores; one of the first widely marketed personal computers.

Tufts Interactive Communicator. A computerized device that helps nonvocal handicapped people communicate by forming words one letter at a time, usually by flipping a switch as the letter is scanned on a screen.

Tuple. A row of a relation in a relational database; also called a record.

Turing Test. A test proposed by Alan Turing to determine if a machine is exhibiting intelligent behavior.

Turnaround document. A computer-produced document on which additional information may be recorded or changes made; the document is then resubmitted to the computer for further processing.

Turnkey system. A complete computing system including hardware, software, documentation, and even training programs supplied by a single vendor.

Twisted-pair wire. A communications medium consisting of a pair of insulated copper wires twisted together.

Ultra-large-scale integration (ULSI). The placement of hundreds of thousands or even millions of transistors on a single silicon chip; this is the state-of-the-art in electronics technology research today.

Ultrasound. A noninvasive diagnostic technique in which sound waves are aimed at the body and analyzed by computer to "see" inside the body.
UNDO key. Allows a user to cancel the effects of the current activity and go back to the previous activity; an important capability in a user-friendly interface.
Unimation. One of the leading companies in the field of industrial robotics.
Uninterruptible power supply (UPS). A hardware device that supplies a computer installation with emergency power during a power failure.
Universal Product Code (UPC). The bar code scheme used to identify products sold in retail stores.
Universal programming language. A single programming language that would be all things to all people; it is unlikely that such a language will ever be developed.
UNIX. A popular operating system developed by Bell Laboratories; it is a multiuser, multitasking system originally used with 16-bit minicomputers; it is evolving into a possible standard operating system for personal computers.
Upwards compatible. Programs that can run on a small model of a family of related computers can run on the larger models also, but not necessarily vice versa.
User-friendly. Easy to use; an important goal is to make computer systems user-friendly so that the general public will be able to benefit by computers.

Vacuum tube. The key electrical component in first generation computers.
Variable word-length machine. A computer that allows fields to occupy as many bytes as needed (within certain limits).
Vertical blanking interval. The black band that appears when the vertical hold on a TV set goes out of control; it provides information-carrying capabilities for teletext systems.
Very-large-scale integration (VLSI). Placing hundreds of thousands of transistors on a single silicon chip; today's computers use VLSI circuits.
Videoconferencing. A teleconferencing technique specifically including the use of video signals.
Videotex. A two-way transmission service sent over the subscriber's telephone or two-way cable TV channel; videotex terminals are specially designed so that the general public may use them conveniently.
Viewdata. The name used in Europe to mean videotex.
Viewtron. A videotex service offered by Knight-Ridder Newspapers.
Virtual storage. A technique combining hardware features and operating system features to create the illusion of an enormously large memory, much larger in fact than main storage; this makes it much more convenient for users to develop programs because they may ignore main storage limitations.
VisiCalc. One of the most successful personal computer software packages of all time; an electronic worksheet.
Voice mail. A form of electronic mail in which messages are sent and stored as digitized human voice rather than as streams of text.
Voice response systems. Computer output systems in which the outputs are spoken rather than printed or displayed.
Voting scheme. When high reliability is needed, a group of computers is used with each computer performing the same calculations; a majority of the computers must agree on a course of action before it will be taken.

Wand reader. A hand-held device that reads OCR-coded information.
Waveform digitization. A technique for generating synthetic speech.
What-if planning. An interactive dialogue with a computer, used in decision support systems; the user queries "what if" certain changes are made, and the computer determines what would happen.
Winchester disk. A sealed disk drive and disk pack manufactured under clean room conditions.
Word processing. Using computers to facilitate the creation and manipulation of text.
Word wraparound. A feature of word processors; when a word breaks across the margin, the complete word is automatically moved to the next line.
Work-at-home program. Allows handicapped people, and others who have difficulty commuting, to work at home by using computer terminals connected to a company's central computers.
Workstation. A computer system or terminal at a worker's desk that the worker uses in the performance of duties.

XENIX. A licensed version of the UNIX system designed by Microsoft for use with personal computers.

Trademarks

IBM is a registered trademark of International Business Machines Corporation. Apple, the Apple logo, Lisa, MacWrite and MacPaint are trademarks of Apple Computer, Inc. Macintosh is a trademark licensed to Apple Computer, Inc. WordStar is a registered trademark of Micro Pro International Inc. Microsoft Word is a trademark of Microsoft, Inc. CP/M, MP/M, CP/NET, and CP/M-86 are registered trademarks of Digital Research, Inc. UNIX is a trademark of Bell Laboratories, Inc. XENIX is a trademark of Microsoft Corporation. VisiCalc is a registered trademark of VisiCorp. MS-DOS is a trademark of Microsoft Corporation. VAX is a trademark of Digital Equipment Corporation. TRS-80 is a trademark of the Radio Shack Division of Tandy Corporation. Ada is a registered trademark of the United States Government, Joint Program Office. VisiOn Calc is a trademark of VisiCorp. Atari is a registered trademark of Atari, Inc. PET is a registered trademark of Commodore Business Machines, Inc. CompuServe Information Service is a registered trademark of CompuServe Incorporated. DEC is a registered trademark of Digital Equipment Corporation. Mailgram is a registered trademark of Western Union Telegraph Company. Xerox is a registered trademark of Xerox Corporation. The Source is a service mark of Source Telecomputing Corporation, a subsidiary of The Reader's Digest Association, Inc. Sceptre is a trademark of AT&T. Apple II, Apple II Plus, Apple III, and Apple IIe are trademarks of Apple Computer, Inc. Viewtron is a registered service mark applicable only to the service provided by Viewdata Corporation of America, Inc., a wholly owned subsidiary of Knight-Ridder Newspapers, Microsoft and Multiplan are registered trademarks of Microsoft Corporation.

Illustration Credits

Chapter 1: pp. xx and 2: Copyright 1982 Ron Sherman, Courtesy of Sonat; p. 4: Fig. 1-1, Courtesy General Motors Corporation; p. 5: Cartoon, Copyright Luci Meighan, March 1980; Fig. 1-2, Courtesy AT&T Bell Laboratories; Fig. 1-3, Courtesy IBM Corporation; p. 7: Cartoon, Cartoons by Johns, Box 1300, Pebble Beach, CA 93953; Fig. 1-4, Courtesy International Power Machines (IPM); p. 8: Fig. 1-5, Copyright 1983 by Newsweek, Inc. All rights reserved. Reprinted by permission. Christoph Blumrich/NEWSWEEK; Cartoon, From the Wall Street Journal—Permission, Cartoon Features Syndicate; p. 9: Fig. 2, Courtesy IBM Corporation; Fig. 3, Photo courtesy of Hewlett-Packard Company; Fig. 4, Courtesy IBM Corporation; p. 10: Cartoon, Courtesy Ron Morgan and COMPUTERWORLD Magazine; Fig. 5, Storage Technology Corporation, copyright 1983; p. 11: Fig. 6, Courtesy Siemens; Fig. 7, Copyright Enrico Ferorelli/Dot; p. 12: Fig. 8, Courtesy VisiCorp; Fig. 9, Reprinted by permission of Canon U.S.A., Inc.; p. 13: Fig. 10, Courtesy NEC Home Electronics; Fig. 11, Photograph provided courtesy of Paradyne Corporation, Largo, Florida; p. 14: Cartoon, Cartoons by Johns, Box 1300, Pebble Beach, CA 93953; Fig. 12, First Interstate Bancorp; Fig. 13, Grand-Master™ is a registered trademark of Milton Bradley Company; p. 15: Fig. 14, Photo courtesy of RB Robot Corporation, Golden, Colorado; Fig. 15, Howard Sochurek, copyright 1981, DISCOVER Magazine, Time, Inc.; p. 16: Fig. 16, Carl Skalak, copyright 1983, DISCOVER Magazine, Time, Inc.; Fig. 17, Illustration by Lance R. Mayamoto, copyright 1983. First appeared in SCIENCE DIGEST, copyright 1983 by the Hearst Corporation. **Chapter 2:** pp. xx & p. 20: top, Photo courtesy of Sperry Corporation; bottom, Goodyear Aerospace Corporation; p. 23: Cartoon, Reprinted from INFOSYSTEMS, April 1979, Copyright Hitchcock Publishing Company; p. 24: Fig. 2-2, The Computer Museum, Marlboro, Mass.; Fig. 2-3, Copyright 1979. DATA MANAGEMENT Magazine. All rights reserved; Fig. 2-4, Copyright Tom Hill 1981. All rights reserved; p. 25: Fig. 2-5, Historical Pictures Service, Chicago; Fig. 2-6, Courtesy IBM Corporation; Fig. 2-7, Historical Pictures Service, Chicago; p. 26: Fig. 2-8, Historical Pictures Service, Chicago; Fig. 2-9, Historical Pictures Service, Chicago; p. 27: Fig. 2-10, Historical Pictures Service, Chicago; Fig. 2-11, Courtesy Intermetrics, artist Robin C. Camardo; p. 28: Fig. 2-12, Copyright Tom Hill 1981. All rights reserved; p. 29: Fig. 2-13, Courtesy IBM Corporation; p. 30: Box, Copyright 1937 New York News Inc. Reprinted by permission; p. 31: Box, Courtesy IBM Corporation; p. 32: Fig. 2-14, Photo courtesy Iowa State University; p. 33: Box, AP/Wide World Photos; p. 34: Fig. 2-15, Photo courtesy of Sperry Corporation; p. 35: Fig. 2-16, Roger Tully/Black Star; p. 36: Fig. 2-17, The Mitre Corporation Archives; Fig. 2-18, The Computer Museum, Marlboro, Massachusetts; Fig. 2-19, Courtesy AT&T Bell Laboratories; p. 37: Fig. 2-20, Courtesy Fairchild Semiconductor; Fig. 2-21, Courtesy IBM Corporation; p. 38: Fig. 2-22, Photo courtesy of Digital Equipment Corporation; Fig. 2-23, Photo courtesy of Digital Equipment Corporation; p. 39: Fig. 2-24, Courtesy Cray Research, Incorporated; p. 40: Box, Courtesy of Control Data Corporation. **Chapter 3:** pp. 44 & 46: First Interstate Bancorp; p. 48: Cartoon, Carlesekstra (CORK); p. 50: Fig. 3-3, Courtesy AT&T Bell Laboratories; p. 52: Fig. 1, Photo courtesy of Sperry Corporation; Fig. 2, Photo courtesy Storage Technology Corporation, copyright 1983; Fig. 3, Photo courtesy of Unitrode Corporation; Fig. 4, Courtesy Auto-trol Technology Corporation; p. 53: Fig. 5, Courtesy RCA; Fig. 6, Photo courtesy of NEC Corporation; p. 54: Fig. 7, Photo courtesy of Unitrode Corporation; Fig. 8, Photo courtesy of Sperry Corporation; Fig. 9, Jack Caspary/TIME Magazine; Fig. 10, Photo courtesy of Rockwell International; p. 55: Fig. 11, Photo courtesy of Sperry Corporation; Fig. 12, Courtesy Siemens; Fig. 13, Courtesy 3M; Fig. 14, Copyright Howard Sochurek 1983. All rights reserved; p. 56: Cartoon, Bill Shelly, first published in COMPUTERWORLD 1983; Fig. 15, Photo courtesy of Unitrode Corporation; Fig. 16, John Alderson/Atoz Images. All other rights are reserved; p. 57: Fig. 17, Photo courtesy of Storage Technology Corporation, copyright 1983; Fig. 18, Photo courtesy of Storage Technology Corporation, copyright 1983; Fig. 19, Robert Isaacs. Courtesy FORTUNE Magazine; p. 61: Cartoon, Reprinted from INFOSYSTEMS, October 1980, Copyright Hitchcock Publishing Company; p. 63: Cartoon, Drawing by Richter; Copyright 1983, The New Yorker Magazine, Inc.; p. 67: Fig. 3-11, Courtesy AT&T Bell Laboratories; p. 68: Cartoon, Copyright 1982 Sydney Harris. Created for DISCOVER. **Chapter 4:** pp. 44 and 72: Courtesy Xerox Computer Services; p. 74: Fig. 4-1, Courtesy IBM Corporation; p. 75: Fig. 4-2, Courtesy IBM Corporation; p. 76: Fig. 4-4, Courtesy IBM Corporation; Cartoon, Cartoon by Sandy Dean; p. 77: Fig. 4-5, Barbara P. Van Cleve/Atoz Images. All other rights are reserved; p. 78: Fig. 4-6, Courtesy Honeywell; Fig. 4-7, Mohawk Data Sciences Corp. (MDS); Cartoon, Reprinted by INFOSYSTEMS December, 1980. Copyright Hitchcock

Publishing Company; p. 79: Fig. 4-8, Courtesy of Xerox Corporation; p. 80: Fig. 4-9, Adapted courtesy of IEEE Computer; Fig. 4-10, Picture provided courtesy of Paradyne Corporation, Largo, Florida; p. 81: Fig. 4-11, Copyright 1982 by John Fluke Mfg. Co., Inc., material provided courtesy of the copyright owner; p. 82: Fig. 4-12, Courtesy of Houston Instrument, Division of Bausch & Lomb; Fig. 4-13, Courtesy Carroll Touch Technology Corp.; p. 83: Fig. 4-14, Courtesy Consolidated Freightways, Inc.; Fig. 4-15, Courtesy Summagraphics Corporation; Fig. 4-16, CASI, Computer Amusement Systems, Inc., New York, NY; Fig. 4-17, Courtesy RCA; Fig. 4-18, Polhemus Navigation Sciences Division, McDonnell Douglas Electronics Company, Box 560, Colchester, VT 05446; p. 84: Fig. 4-19, Courtesy Micropad, Inc.; Fig. 4-20, Radio Shack, A Division of Tandy Corporation; Fig. 4-21, Courtesy IBM Corporation; Fig. 4-22, Courtesy IBM Corporation; p. 85: Fig. 4-23, Courtesy IBM Corporation; Fig. 4-24, Courtesy IBM Corporation; p. 88: Fig. 4-29, Courtesy Dennison Manufacturing Company; p. 89: Fig. 1, Courtesy Kurzweil Computer Products; Fig. 2, Courtesy Kurzweil Computer Products; p. 90: Fig. 4-30, Published by permission of National Computer Systems, Inc., 4401 W. 76th Street, Minneapolis, MN 55435; Fig. 4-31, Published by permission of National Computer Systems, Inc., 4401 W. 76th Street, Minneapolis, MN 55435; p. 91: Fig. 4-32, Courtesy Intermec Corporation; Fig. 4-33, Courtesy Intermec Corporation; Fig. 4-34, Courtesy Intermec Corporation; Box, Courtesy IBM Corporation; p. 92: Fig. 1, Photo courtesy Peggy Barnett and Revlon; p. 93: Fig. 2, Courtesy Intermec Corporation; Fig. 3, Courtesy Intermec Corporation; Fig. 4, From MODERN MATERIALS HANDLING–1983 CASEBOOK/ DIRECTORY, page 42. Copyright 1983 Cahners Publishing Co., Inc. Division of Reed Holdings; p. 94: Fig. 4-34, Courtesy Intermec Corporation; Box, Courtesy IBM Corporation; Fig. 4-35, Courtesy Intermec Corporation; Fig. 4-36, Marion Trikosko, U.S. NEWS & WORLD REPORT; p. 95: Cartoon, Cartoon courtesy Stuart Leeds; Fig. 4-37, Reproduction of soup labels by permission of Campbell Soup Co., Camden, NJ 08101. **Chapter 5:** pp. 44 & 100: Photo courtesy of Digital Equipment Corporation; p. 103: Fig. 5-1, Courtesy McDonnell Douglas Automation Company (McAuto); Fig. 5-2, Courtesy Rose & Company; p. 104: Fig. 5-3, Courtesy of NEBS Computer Forms, 12 South Street, Townsend, MA 01469; Fig. 5-4, Discount Data Forms, Inc., Lombard, IL. Computer Forms and Supplies; p. 105: Fig. 5-5, Courtesy of DATAPOINT Corporation. All rights reserved; Fig. 5-6, Photo courtesy of Digital Equipment Corporation; Fig. 5-7, Courtesy IBM Corporation; p. 106: Fig. 5-8, Courtesy IBM Corporation; Fig. 5-9, Courtesy of Micro Peripherals, Inc.; Fig. 5-10, Courtesy Printonix, Inc.; p. 107: Fig. 5-11, Courtesy Printonix, Inc.; Fig. 5-12, Courtesy Printonix, Inc.; Fig. 5-13, Courtesy of Santec Corporation; Fig. 5-14, Courtesy Printonix, Inc.; p. 108: Fig. 5-15, Photo courtesy Xerox Corporation; Fig. 5-16, Courtesy of NEC Information Systems, Inc.; Fig. 5-17, Courtesy of Qume Corporation, A Subsidiary of ITT Corporation; p. 109: Fig. 5-18, Courtesy of Mannesmann Tally Corporation; Fig. 5-19, Dataproducts Corporation; Fig. 5-20, Courtesy Storage Technology Corporation, Copyright 1983; Fig. 5-21, Courtesy Storage Technology Corporation, copyright 1984; p. 110: Fig. 5-22, Dataproducts Corporation; Fig. 5-23, Courtesy RCA; p. 111: Fig. 5-24, Courtesy of Xerox Corporation; p. 112: Fig. 5-25, Radio Shack, A Division of Tandy Corporation; p. 113: Box, Courtesy IBM Corporation; p. 114: Fig. 5-26, I.E.E.E. Computer, copyright 1978; Cartoon, The Family Circus, Reprinted Courtesy The Register and Tribune Syndicate, Inc.; p. 115: Fig. 5-28, Courtesy of Hewlett-Packard Company; Cartoon, Anthony Cresci, first published in COMPUTERWORLD; p. 116: Fig. 5-29, Courtesy IBM Corporation; Fig. 5-30, Courtesy of Texas Instruments; Fig. 5-31, Courtesy Computer Transceiver Systems, Inc.; p. 117: Fig. 1, Courtesy of IMLAC Corporation, 150 A Street, Needham, MA 02194; Fig. 2, Photo courtesy of Hewlett-Packard Company; p. 118: Fig. 4, Courtesy of Advanced Color Technology, Inc.; Fig. 5, Radio Shack, A Division of Tandy Corporation; p. 119: Fig. 6, Courtesy Hewlett-Packard Company; Fig. 7, Courtesy of Motorola, Inc.; Fig. 8, Courtesy of California Computer Products, Inc.; p. 120: Fig. 9, Photo-MP 1000 MICRO-CADD™ Plotter Courtesy Western Graphtec, Inc. (Formerly Watanabe Instruments); Fig. 10, Courtesy of Hewlett-Packard Company; Fig. 11, Courtesy of Versatec, A Xerox Company; p. 121: Fig. 12, Courtesy Image Resource Corp.; Fig. 13, Courtesy Computervision Corporation; p. 122: Fig. 14, Courtesy Applicon; Fig. 15, Roger Rutman, Rutman Computer Services; Cartoon, Cartoons by Johns, Box 1300, Pebble Beach, CA 93953; p. 123: Fig. 16, American Buildings Company, Subsidiary of Cronus Industries, Inc.; Fig. 17, Courtesy of Control Data Corporation; Cartoon, Cartoon by Dave Harbaugh; p. 124: Fig. 5-32, Courtesy of Eastman Kodak Company; p. 125: Fig. 5-33, Courtesy of DuPont; p. 126: Fig. 5-34, Courtesy of Texas Instruments; p. 127: Fig. 5-35, Reprinted from POPULAR ELECTRONICS. Copyright 1982, Ziff-Davis Publishing Company; p. 128: Fig. 1, Vernon Miller/Brooks Institute, Copyright 1978; Fig. 2, Vernon Miller/ Brooks Institute, Copyright 1978. **Chapter 6:** pp. 44 & 132: Photo courtesy Storage Technology Corporation, Copyright 1983; p. 134: Fig. 6-1, Photo courtesy of Computervision Corporation, Bedford, MA; Fig. 6-2, Courtesy IBM Corporation; Fig. 6-3, Packaging and application photography provided by 3M/Data Recording Products; p. 135: Fig. 6-4, Courtesy NCR Corporation; Fig. 6-5, Photo courtesy Storage Technology Corporation, Copyright 1983; p. 136: Fig. 6-6, Photo courtesy Storage Technology Corporation, Copyright 1983; Cartoon, Cartoon by Schochet from SCIENCE '81; p. 138: Fig. 6-9, Photo courtesy Storage Technology Corporation, Copyright 1983; Cartoon, Cartoon by David Howell. Reprinted from CREATIVE COMPUTING Magazine, copyright 1983, AHL Computing Co.; p. 139: Fig. 6-11, Courtesy of Control Data Corporation; Fig. 6-12, Photo courtesy of Storage Technology Corporation, copyright 1983; p. 140: Fig. 6-13, Photo courtesy of Storage Technology Corporation, Copyright 1983; Fig. 6-15, Packaging and application photography provided by 3M/Data Recording Products; p. 141: Fig. 6-17, Packaging and application photography provided by 3M/Data Recording Products; Fig. 6-18, Packaging and application photography provided by 3M/Data Recording Products; p. 142: Fig. 6-21, Packaging and application photography provided by 3M/Data Recording Products; p. 143: Fig. 6-22, Packaging and application photography provided by 3M/Data Recording Products; Fig. 6-23, Courtesy Moore Business Forms, Inc.; Fig. 6-24, Packaging and application photography provided by 3M/Data Recording Products; p. 144: Fig. 6-25, Adapted courtesy of 3M/Data Recording Products; Fig. 6-26, Courtesy Tandon Corporation; p. 146: Fig. 6-29, Courtesy IBM Corporation; Fig. 6-30, Courtesy IBM Corporation; Fig. 6-31, Courtesy IBM Corporation; Fig. 6-32, Courtesy Braegen Corporation; p. 147: Fig. 6-33, Courtesy Braegen Corporation; Fig. 6-34, Courtesy Braegen Corporation; Fig. 6-35, Courtesy IBM Corporation; p. 148: Cartoon, Copyright 1982 Sydney Harris, Created for DISCOVER; p. 149: Fig. 6-36, Photo courtesy Storage Technology Corporation, copyright 1983; Fig. 6-37, Photo courtesy Optical Recording Project/3M. **Chapter 7:** pp. 44 & 154: Courtesy Siemens; p. 156: Fig. 7-1, From *The World Book Encyclopedia.* Copyright 1983 World Book, Inc.; p. 158: Fig. 7-3, Tom Campbell/FPG; p. 163: Fig. 7-13, Kim Steele/Black Star; Fig. 7-14, E. Nagele/FPG; p. 164: Fig. 7-15, Courtesy Raytheon Company; Fig. 7-16, Fred Ward/Black Star; Fig. 7-17, Courtesy Western Electric; p. 165: Fig. 7-19, James A. Sugar/Black Star; p. 166: Box, Courtesy AT&T Bell Laboratories; p. 172: Fig. 7-27, Courtesy of Xerox Corporation; Fig. 7-28, Drawing courtesy of Times Fiber Communications, Inc.; p. 173: Fig. 7-29, Photo courtesy of Times Fiber Communications, Inc.; p. 176: Fig. 7-33, Courtesy Raytheon Company. **Chapter 8:** pp. 182 and 184: Policy Management Systems Corporation/Photo by Coates Crewe; p. 189: Fig. 8-2, Photo by Carroll Morgan; Fig. 8-3, Photo by Carroll Morgan; p. 197: Cartoon, Copyright Luci Meighan, April, 1980. **Chapter 9:** p. 223: Fig. 9-3, Program courtesy of Ramtek Corporation; p. 226: Cartoon, Courtesy James D'Angelo. Reprinted from CREATIVE COMPUTING Magazine. Copyright 1980, AHL Computing Co.; p. 227: Cartoon, Cartoons by Johns, Box 1300, Pebble Beach, CA 93953; p. 229: Fig. 9-8, Copyright Eric H. Poggenpohl; p. 234: Fig. 9-14, Courtesy IBM Corporation; p. 235: Fig. 9-15, Photo courtesy of Digital Equipment Corporation; p. 236: Fig. 9-16, Program courtesy of Ramtek Corporation; p. 237: Fig. 9-18, Program courtesy of Western Digital, Irvine, CA; p. 239: Cartoon, Courtesy Martin Bucella. Reprinted from CREATIVE COMPUTING Magazine. Copyright AHL Computing Co. **Chapter 10:** pp. 182 and 244: Courtesy AGS Management Systems, Inc. Copyright 1983; p. 250: Fig. 10-3, Courtesy IBM Corporation; p. 254: Cartoon, Courtesy Julie M. Girden; p. 259: Cartoon, Courtesy Frans de boer (Ebbe). **Chapter 11:** pp. 182 and 272: Courtesy General Electric; p. 280: Fig. 11-5, Material provided courtesy of Cincom Systems, Inc.; p. 281: Cartoon, Courtesy Carlisekstra (CORK); p. 282: Fig. 11-6, Courtesy American Software; p. 283: Fig. 11-7, The application matrix is provided courtesy of Cullinet Software, Inc.; Fig. 11-8, From MANAGEMENT INFORMATION SYSTEMS: CONCEPTUAL FOUNDATIONS, STRUCTURES AND DEVELOPMENT by Gordon B. Davis, Copyright 1974 McGraw-Hill; p. 285: Fig. 2, Courtesy of Hewlett-Packard; p. 286: Fig. 3, Courtesy American Software; p. 287: Fig. 4, Courtesy RCA; Fig. 5, Reproduced courtesy of Data General Corporation; p. 288: Fig. 6, Reproduced courtesy of Data General Corporation; Fig. 7, Reproduced courtesy of Data General Corporation; p. 289: Fig. 8, Courtesy Discount Data Forms, Inc., Lombard, IL. Computer forms and supplies; p. 290: Fig. 9, Courtesy Discount Data Forms, Inc., Lombard, IL. Computer forms and supplies; p. 291: Fig. 11-11, Courtesy of American Management Systems, Inc.; p. 292: Fig. 11-12, Courtesy of American Management Systems, Inc.; p. 293: Fig. 11-13, Courtesy of NEBS Computer Forms; Fig. 11-14, Courtesy of NEBS Computer Forms; p. 295: Fig. 11-15, Courtesy NEC Home Electronics (U.S.A.) Inc.; Fig. 11-16, GRW Systems, Inc., Sunnyvale, CA/ p. 296: Fig. 11-9, Courtesy of Artificial Intelligence Corporation, 100 Fifth Avenue, Waltham, MA 02254; p. 297: Fig. 11-10, Courtesy Qantel; p. 302: Cartoon, From the Wall Street Journal-Permission, Cartoon Features Syndicate; Cartoon, Reprinted from INFOSYSTEMS, May, 1979. Copyright Hitchcock Publishing Company. **Chapter 12:** pp. 182 and 306: Used with permission from Monroe Systems for Business; p. 313: Cartoon, Cartoon by Mike Artell; p. 318: Cartoon, Courtesy Julie M. Girden; Fig. 12-10, Courtesy International Power Machines Corporation (IPM). **Chapter 13:** pp. 330 and 332: Opener, Courtesy IBM Corporation; p. 334: Cartoon, Drawing by R. Chast; copyright 1983 The New Yorker Magazine, Inc.; p. 335: Fig. 13-1, Copyright 1982 Time Inc. All rights reserved; p. 336: Fig. 13-2, Courtesy of Apple Computer, Inc.; Fig. 13-3, Courtesy of Radio Shack, A Division of Tandy Corporation; Fig. 1, Courtesy IBM Corporation; p. 338: Fig. 2, Courtesy IBM Corporation; Fig. 3, Courtesy IBM Corporation; p. 339: Fig. 4, Courtesy IBM Corporation; Fig. 5, Copyright 1983, Bruce Surber. Microsoft and Multiplan are registered trademarks of Microsoft Corporation; p. 340: Fig. 6, Courtesy IBM Corporation; Fig. 1, Macintosh is a trademark licensed to Apple Computer, Inc.; p. 341: Fig. 2, Reprinted by permission. Copyright 1984, Apple Computer, Inc.; Fig. 3, Reprinted by permission. Copyright 1984, Apple Computer, Inc.; p. 342: Fig. 4, Macintosh is a trademark licensed to Apple Computer, Inc.; Fig. 5, Reprinted by permission of MACWORLD from Premier (March/April) issue, 1984, published at 555 DeHaro Street, San Francisco, CA 94107; p. 343: Fig. 6, Copyright 1983, Bruce Surber. Microsoft and Multiplan are registered trademarks of Microsoft Corporation; p. 344: Fig. 7, Reprinted by permission. Copyright 1984, Apple

Computer, Inc.; p. 345: Fig. 8, Reprinted by permission. Copyright 1984, Apple Computer, Inc.; Fig. 9, Reprinted by permission. Copyright 1984, Apple Computer, Inc.; Fig. 10, Reprinted by permission. Copyright 1984, Apple Computer, Inc.; Fig. 11, Reprinted by permission. Copyright 1984, Apple Computer, Inc.; p. 346: Reprinted by permission. Copyright 1984, Apple Computer, Inc.; p. 347: Reprinted by permission. Copyright 1984, Apple Computer, Inc.; p. 348: Reprinted by permission. Copyright 1984, Apple Computer, Inc.; Fig. 12, Reprinted by permission. Copyright 1984, Apple Computer, Inc.; Fig. 13, Macintosh is a trademark licensed to Apple Computer, Inc.; p. 349: Fig. 14, Reprinted by permission. Copyright 1984, Apple Computer, Inc.; Fig. 13-4, Courtesy Osborne Computer Corporation; p. 350: Fig. 13-5, Photo courtesy of Epson America; Fig. 13-6, Reproduced with permission of Texas Instruments, Inc.; p. 351: Fig. 13-7, Courtesy of Radio Shack, A Division of Tandy Corporation; Fig. 13-8, Courtesy Gavilan Computer Corporation; Cartoon, Drawing by Ziegler; copyright 1983, The New Yorker Magazine, Inc.; p. 352: Fig. 13-9, Courtesy of Radio Shack, A Division of Tandy Corporation; Fig. 13-10, Courtesy of Yamaha International Corporation, Specialty Products Division; Fig. 13-11, Photography by Dick Zimmerman; p. 353: Cartoon, COMPUTERWORLD/Copyright Bob Glueckstein; Cartoon, Copyright 1983, Joel Pett in the Phi Delta Kappan; p. 354: Fig. 13-12, Reproduced with permission of Texas Instruments, Inc.; Fig. 13-13, Reproduced with permission of Texas Instruments, Inc.; Cartoon, Copyright 1982 GOOD HOUSEKEEPING, reprinted by permission of Orlando Busino; p. 355: Cartoon, COMPUTERWORLD/copyright Tom Niemann; Fig. 13-14, Reproduced with permission of Texas Instruments, Inc.; p. 356: Fig. 13-15, Reprinted from CREATIVE COMPUTING, September, 1979, Copyright 1979, AHL Computing, Inc.; Cartoon, Copyright 1982 by Sidney Harris, created for DISCOVER; p. 357: Cartoon, COMPUTERWORLD/Copyright Bob Glueckstein; p. 359: Fig. 1, Copyright Viewdata Corporation of America 1984; p. 360: Fig. 2, Copyright Viewdata Corporation of America 1984; Fig. 3, Copyright Viewdata Corporation of America 1984; Fig. 4, Copyright Viewdata Corporation of America 1984; p. 363: Fig. 5, Copyright Viewdata Corporation of America 1984; p. 364: Fig. 6, Copyright Viewdata Corporation of America 1984. **Chapter 14:** pp. 330 and 368: Courtesy Burroughs Corporation; p. 370: Cartoon, Drawing by Weber; copyright 1978. The New Yorker Magazine, Inc.; p. 371: Fig. 14-1, Courtesy IBM Corporation; Fig. 14-2, Photo courtesy of Haworth, Inc., Holland, MI; p. 372: Fig. 14-3, Photo courtesy of Xerox Corp.; Fig. 14-4, Courtesy of Xerox Corp.; p. 373: Fig. 14-5, Courtesy VisiCorp; Fig. 14-6, Arthur Grace/TIME Magazine; p. 374: Fig. 14-7, Lanier Business Products, Inc. A Harris Company; Fig. 14-8, Courtesy Cado Systems Corporation; p. 375: Fig. 14-9, Lanier Business Products, Inc., A Harris Company; p. 376: Fig. 14-10, Courtesy IBM Corporation; Inc., A Harris Company; p. 376: Fig. 14-10, Courtesy IBM Corporation; p. 384: Cartoon, Cartoons by Johns, Box 1300, Pebble Beach, CA 93953; p. 385: Fig. 14-11, Photo courtesy Xerox Corp.; p. 386: Fig. 14-12, Dan Dickas; p. 387: Fig. 14-13, Courtesy NEC America, Fairfax, VA; Cartoon, Copyright 1982 by Sidney Harris, Created for DISCOVER; p. 388: Fig. 14-14, Courtesy of AT&T Bell Laboratories; p. 389: Fig. 14-15, Compugraphic Corporation, Wilmington, MA; p. 390: Cartoon, Reprinted courtesy OMNI Magazine, Copyright 1983; Cartoon, Copyright DATAMATION Magazine. Reprinted with permission of David Harbaugh; p. 391: Cartoon, Copyrighted 1981 by Sidney Harris, Created for DISCOVER; p. 392: Fig. 14-16, Motorola, Inc., Communications Sector, Schaumburg, IL; Cartoon, Copyright DATAMATION Magazine. Reprinted with permission of Eli Stein. **Chapter 15:** pp. 396 and 339: Drawing by Stevenson; copyright 1983 The New Yorker Magazine, Inc.; p. 399: Fig. 15-1, Courtesy Honeywell; Fig. 15-2, Terry Qing/Freelance Photographers Guild; p. 400: Fig. 15-3, Enrico Ferorelli/Dot; Fig. 15-4, First Interstate Bancorp; p. 401: Cartoon, Reprinted by permission. Middlesex News; p. 403: Fig. 15-5, Model 9460, Courtesy Perry Data Systems, Inc.; Cartoon, Cartoon by Mike Artell; p. 404: Cartoon, COMPUTERWORLD/Copyright 1980, Martin J. Bucella; p. 409: Fig. 1, Courtesy of Fellowes Manufacturing Co.; p. 410: Cartoon, Reprinted by permission. Copyright 1981 NEA, Inc.; p. 411: Fig. 15-6, Flash Fleischer; p. 412: Cartoon, Rich Tennant; Fig. 15-7, Honeywell Commercial Division photo; Fig. 15-8, Honeywell Commercial Division photo; p. 413: Fig. 15-9, Courtesy Wright Line Computer Accessories, Division of Barry Wright Corp.; p. 414: Fig. 15-10, Reprinted from U.S. NEWS & WORLD REPORT issue of July 12, 1982. Copyright 1982, U.S. News & World Report, Inc.; p. 415; Cartoon, From the Wall Street Journal, Permission-Cartoons Feature Syndicate; Cartoon, Copyright 1984, University Press Syndicate. Reprinted by permission. All rights reserved. **Chapter 16:** pp. 420 and 422: The Bettmann Archive, Inc.; p. 425: Fig. 16-1, Copyright Lucasfilm Ltd. (LFL) 1977. All rights reserved. Courtesy of Lucasfilm Ltd.; Fig. 16-2, Photo courtesy of the National Broadcasting Company, Inc.; Fig. 16-3, Courtesy Cincinnati Milacron; p. 426: Fig. 16-4, Courtesy AT&T Bell Laboratories; Fig. 16-5, Courtesy NASA and U.S. Geological Survey; Fig. 16-6, Georg Fischer/VISUM, First published in GEO Magazine; Cartoon, Cartoon by Marcelo Rodriguez, Humaita 6976, 1408 Buenos Aires, Argentina. Used with permission; p. 427: Fig. 16-7, From the Westinghouse Historical Collection; Fig. 16-8, Georg Fischer/VISUM, First published in GEO Magazine; Fig. 16-9, Photo courtesy Storage Technology Corporation, Copyright 1983; p. 428: Fig. 16-10, Courtesy Cincinnati Milacron; p. 429: Fig. 16-11, General Motors Corporation; Fig. 16-12; p. 431: Fig. 16-13, Photos and caption data courtesy of Lockheed; p. 432: Fig. 16-14, Fred Ward, copyright 1981 DISCOVER Magazine, Time, Inc.; Fig. 16-15, Georg Fischer/VISUM, First published in GEO Magazine; Fig. 16-16, Courtesy Automatix; p. 433:

Fig. 16-17, Georg Fischer/VISUM, First published in GEO Magazine; Fig. 16-18, Georg Fischer/VISUM, First published in GEO Magazine; p. 434: Cartoon, Copyright 1982 by Frank Tabor. Reprinted by permission of INFOWORLD, Menlo Park, CA; p. 435: Box, Queens Devices, Long Island City; p. 436: Cartoon, Drawing by Chas. Addams; Copyright 1946, 1974, The New Yorker Magazine, Inc.; p. 437: Cartoon, Courtesy Gary L. Seekings. Reprinted from CREATIVE COMPUTING Magazine. Copyright 1981, AHL Computing Co.; Cartoon, Drawing by Chas. Addams; Copyright 1971. The New Yorker Magazine, Inc.; p. 438: Cartoon, COMPUTERWORLD/Copyright Tom Niemann; p. 439: Cartoon, Courtesy Joe E. Buresch. Reprinted from CREATIVE COMPUTING Magazine. Copyright AHL Computing Co.; p. 441: Cartoon, Reprinted from INFOSYSTEMS, December 1976. Copyright Hitchcock Publishing Company; p. 442: Cartoon, Reprinted by permission. Copyright 1984, NEA, Inc. **Chapter 17:** pp. 420 and 448: Toshiba Medical Systems; p. 450: Cartoon, Reprinted by permission of COMPUTERWORLD and Bo Brown; Cartoon, COMPUTERWORLD/Copyright 1980 Martin J. Bucella; p. 452: Fig. 17-1, Toshiba Medical Systems; Fig. 17-2, Howard Sochurek, Copyright 1981, DISCOVER Magazine, Time, Inc.; p. 454: Fig. 17-3, Copyright 1980, by Newsweek, Inc. All rights reserved. Reprinted by permission. Bernard Gotfryd/NEWSWEEK; p. 455: Fig. 17-4, Brookhaven National Laboratory and New York University Medical Center; Fig. 17-5, Howard Sochurek, Copyright 1981, DISCOVER Magazine, Time, Inc.; p. 456: Fig. 17-6, Courtesy Raytheon Company; p. 457: Cartoon, Lawrence Lariar/PARADE Magazine. Copyright 1979; p. 458: Fig. 17-7, Dan McCoy/TIME Magazine. **Chapter 18:** p. 468: Fig. 18-1, From The World Book Encyclopedia, Copyright 1983, World Book, Inc.; Fig. 18-2, Courtesy of United Way of Massachusetts Bay; p. 469: Fig. 18-3, ARTS Computer Products, Inc., 145 Tremont St., Suite 407, Boston, MA 02111; Fig. 18-4, Copyright 1981 by Newsweek, Inc. All Rights Reserved. Reprinted by permission. Jeff Lowenthal/NEWSWEEK; p. 470: Fig. 18-5, Copyright 1981. I.E.E.E. Computer. From "Braille Computer Terminals" by George F. Dalrymple, Massachusetts Institute of Technology; p. 471: Fig. 18-6, Georg Fischer/VISUM. First published in GEO Magazine; p. 472: Fig. 18-7, Reprinted with permission of the National Association of the Deaf, 814 Thayer Avenue, Silver Spring, MD 20910; Fig. 18-8, Courtesy IBM Corporation; Fig. 18-9, Copyright 1980 by NEWSWEEK, Inc. All Rights Reserved. Reprinted by permission; p. 473: Fig. 18-10, Courtesy AT&T Bell Laboratories; p. 474: Fig. 18-11, New England Medical Center (Boston, MA); p. 475: Fig. 18-13, New England Medical Center (Boston, MA); Fig. 18-14, New England Medical Center (Boston, MA); p. 477: Fig. 18-15, From "Minspeak" by Bruce Baker appearing in the September 1982 issue of BYTE Magazine. Copyright 1982 Byte Publications, Inc. Used with the permission of Byte Publications, Inc.; p. 478: Fig. 18-16, Copyright 1979, I.E.E.E. Computer. From "Microcomputer Aided Eating for the Severely Handicapped" by R. L. Ramey, J. H. Aylor, R. D. Williams, I.E.E.E. Computer; Fig. 18-17, Ray Ameijide, Copyright 1981, DISCOVER Magazine, Time, Inc.; p. 479: Fig. 18-18, Enrico Ferorelli, Copyright 1982, DISCOVER Magazine, Time, Inc.; Fig. 18-19, Enrico Ferorelli, Copyright 1982, DISCOVER Magazine, Time, Inc.; p. 480: Fig. 18-20, Courtesy IBM Corporation; p. 481: Fig. 18-21, Copyright 1982 by NEWSWEEK, Inc. All Rights Reserved. Reprinted by permission; p. 483: Fig. 18-22, Courtesy Selective Electronic, Inc., (Selcom), Box 250, Valdese, NC 28690; Fig. 18-23, Courtesy Selective Electronic, Inc., (Selcom), Box 250, Valdese, NC 28690. **Chapter 19:** pp. 420 and 488: NASA; p. 491: Fig. 19-1, Illustration courtesy of Delco Electronics Division, GMC; Fig. 19-2, Photo courtesy of Delco Electronics Division, GMC; p. 492: Cartoon, Copyright 1980 Sydney Harris. Created for DISCOVER; p. 493: Cartoon, Courtesy Otha J. Collins. Reprinted from CREATIVE COMPUTING Magazine. Copyright 1979 AHL Computing Co.; p. 494: Fig. 19-3, Courtesy Raytheon Company; p. 495: Fig. 19-4, Courtesy of I.E.E.E. Spectrum. From "Collision-Proof Airspace" by Thomas G. Lombardo, Copyright 1980; Fig. 19-5, U.S. Air Force; p. 496: Fig. 19-6, Courtesy Intel Corporation; p. 497: Fig. 19-7, FlightSafety International, photograph by Paul Bowen; Fig. 19-8, FlightSafety International, photograph by Paul Bowen; Fig. 19-9, FlightSafety International, photograph by Paul Bowen; p. 498: Fig. 19-10, Courtesy Southwest Airlines; Fig. 19-11, Reprinted from POPULAR SCIENCE with permission, Copyright 1980, Times Mirror Magazine, Inc.; p. 499: Fig. 19-12, Illustration by David Schleinkofer. First appeared in SCIENCE DIGEST, Copyright 1981 by The Hearst Corporation; p. 500: Fig. 19-13, Courtesy Japan National Railways; Fig. 19-14, Copyright CSX Corporation, 1983; p. 501: Fig. 19-15, Reprinted from POPULAR SCIENCE with permission, Copyright 1980, Times Mirror Magazines, Inc.; p. 502: Fig. 19-16, Reprinted from POPULAR SCIENCE with permission, Copyright 1980, Times Mirror Magazines, Inc.; Fig. 19-17, Courtesy Raytheon Company; Fig. 19-18, Courtesy Raytheon Company; p. 503: Fig. 19-19, FlightSafety International, photograph by Paul Bowen. **Appendix C:** p. 584, Copyright 1984, Universal Press Syndicate. Reprinted with permission. All rights reserved.

Index

A 5
B 6
C 7
D 8
E 9
F 0
G 1
H 2